THE SUPREME COURT
IN UNITED STATES HISTORY

VOLUME TWO

ROGER BROOKE TANEY
From the portrait by G. P. A. Healy.

THE SUPREME COURT

IN

UNITED STATES HISTORY

BY

CHARLES WARREN

FORMERLY ASSISTANT ATTORNEY-GENERAL OF THE UNITED STATES
AUTHOR OF "A HISTORY OF THE AMERICAN BAR"

REVISED EDITION

IN TWO VOLUMES

VOLUME TWO

1836-1918

LITTLE, BROWN, AND COMPANY

Boston   Toronto

PRINTED IN THE UNITED STATES OF AMERICA

CONTENTS

VOLUME TWO

CONTENTS

Volume Two

ILLUSTRATIONS

Volume Two

ABBREVIATIONS OF TITLES OF BOOKS FREQUENTLY CITED

[For the purpose of conciseness in the citation of books most frequently quoted, the following abbreviations have been used in the notes.]

J. Q. Adams, Memoirs of John Quincy Adams (1874–1877), edited by Charles Francis Adams, 12 vols.

J. Q. Adams' Writings, The Writings of John Quincy Adams (1913–1915), edited by Worthington Chauncey Ford, 7 vols.

Clay, The Works of Henry Clay (1904), edited by Calvin Colton, Federal edition, 10 vols.

Curtis, The Life and Writings of Benjamin Robbins Curtis, LL.D. (1879), edited by Benjamin R. Curtis, 2 vols.

Hamilton, The Works of Alexander Hamilton (1904), edited by Henry Cabot Lodge, 12 vols.

Hamilton (Lodge's ed.), The Works of Alexander Hamilton (1885–1886), edited by Henry Cabot Lodge, 9 vols.

Hamilton (J. C. Hamilton's ed.), The Works of Alexander Hamilton (1850–1851), edited by John Church Hamilton, 7 vols.

Iredell, Life and Correspondence of James Iredell (1858), edited by Griffith John McRee, 2 vols.

Jay, The Correspondence and Public Papers of John Jay (1890–1893), edited by Henry Phelps Johnston, 4 vols.

Jefferson, The Works of Thomas Jefferson (1904–1908), edited by Paul Leicester Ford, 12 vols.

Jefferson (A. C. Lipscomb ed.), The Writings of Thomas Jefferson (1903–1904), edited by Andrew C. Lipscomb, 20 vols.

Jefferson (H. A. Washington ed.), The Writings of Thomas Jefferson (1853–1854), edited by Henry Augustine Washington, 9 vols.

King, The Life and Correspondence of Rufus King (1894–1900), edited by Charles Ray King, 6 vols.

Madison, The Writings of James Madison (1906–1910), edited by Gaillard Hunt, 9 vols.

Madison (1865), Letters and Other Writings of James Madison (1865), published by order of Congress, 4 vols.

Marshall, Life of John Marshall (1916–1919), by Albert Jeremiah Beveridge, 4 vols.

Mason, Memoir and Correspondence of Jeremiah Mason (1873), edited by George S. Hillard.

Monroe, The Writings of James Monroe (1898–1903), edited by Stanislaus Murray Hamilton, 7 vols.

Story, Life and Letters of Joseph Story (1851), by William Waldo Story, 2 vols.

Sumner, Memoir and Letters of Charles Sumner (1877–1893), by Edward Lillie Pierce, 4 vols.

Taney, Memoir of Roger Brooke Taney (1872), by Samuel Tyler

Ticknor, Life, Letters and Journals of George Ticknor (1876), 2 vols.

Washington, Writings of George Washington (1834–1837), edited by Jared Sparks, 11 vols.

Washington (Ford's ed.), *Writings of George Washington* (1886–1893), edited by Worthington Chauncey Ford, 14 vols.

Webster, The Writings and Speeches of Daniel Webster (1903), 18 vols.

Wirt, Memoirs of the Life of William Wirt (1849), by John Pendleton Kennedy, 2 vols.

THE SUPREME COURT
IN UNITED STATES HISTORY

THE SUPREME COURT
IN UNITED STATES HISTORY

VOLUME TWO

CHAPTER TWENTY-ONE

CHIEF JUSTICE TANEY AND WHIG PESSIMISM

1835–1837

THE appointment of Marshall's successor was looked forward to with painful interest by the legal profession and by the country at large. The Democrats were hopeful of the appointment of a Chief Justice who would curb what they termed the policy of prostration of the States. "Nearly every State of the Union," said the *Democratic Review*, " had been brought up for sentence . . . passed through the Caudine Forks of a subjugation which has more than revived the suability of States. Beginning with Madison's case, there are near forty of these fulminations.[1] . . ." The Whigs gravely feared that President Jackson's choice would be a purely political one, and they were despondent of the future, "if the appointment be a party appointment — if the Chief Justiceship too is to be deemed one of the spoils which the ravenous clutches of party may seize and appropriate to its sordid purposes." "Well may the country look forward with absorbing interest to the choice of Judge Marshall's successor," said

[1] *Democratic Review* (Jan., 1838), I, 165

a prominent Whig paper, "for on it, we conscientiously believe depends the character, in a great degree, of its future destinies." Another Whig organ said : "The peculiar position of our public affairs and the crisis which is evidently approaching, involving the existence of our institutions, renders this one of the most important and most to be regretted deaths which has occurred since the decease of Washington. His identity with the Supreme Court of the United States, and the disreputable assaults now making upon that sheet-anchor of our Government, for party purposes, create a new era in affairs which may result most calamitously for the country." Another said: "In reference to the party principles of the man who should be elevated to the Supreme Bench, all that need be remarked is, that the instant the question is asked and acted upon in the selection of an individual for that station — 'will his decisions be on the Democratic or on the Federal or on any other side?' instead of — 'Is he honest, is he capable?' that instant the majesty and utility of that great tribunal are destroyed; that instant, instead of being a safeguard of our rights and liberties, it becomes a party engine which may be wielded with tremendous irresistible power for their subversion." [1]

John Quincy Adams wrote in his diary a characteristically pungent review of the situation of the Court: [2]

He has held this appointment thirty five years. It was the last act of my father's administration, and one of the most important services rendered by him to his country. All constitutional governments are flexible things; and as the Supreme Judicial Court is the tribunal of last resort for the construction of the Constitution and the laws, the

---

[1] *National Intelligencer*, July 16, 1835; *New York Courier*, July 8, 1835; *National Gazette*, July 13, 1835; *New York Daily Advertiser*, July 8, 25, 27, 1835.
[2] *J. Q. Adams*, IX, July 10, Aug. 10, 1835.

office of Chief Justice of that Court is a station of the highest trust, of the deepest responsibility, and of influence far more extensive than that of the President of the United States. The Associate Judges from the time of his appointment have generally been taken from the Democratic or Jeffersonian party. Not one of them, excepting Story, has been a man of great ability. Several of them have been men of strong prejudices, warm passions, and contracted minds; one of them, occasionally insane.[1] Marshall, by the ascendency of his genius, by the amenity of his deportment, and by the imperturbable command of his temper, has given a permanent and systematic character to the decisions of the Court, and settled many great constitutional questions favorably to the continuance of the Union. Marshall has cemented the Union which the crafty and quixotic democracy of Jefferson had a perpetual tendency to dissolve. Jefferson hated and dreaded him. . . . It is much to be feared that a successor will be appointed of a very different character. The President of the United States now in office, has already appointed three Judges of the Supreme Court; with the next appointment, he will have constituted the Chief Justice and a majority of the Court. He has not yet made one good appointment. His Chief Justice will be no better than the rest.

Some Whigs even went so far as to assert that the accession of a Democrat to the Chief Justiceship meant the destruction of the Constitution. "At no time," said a New York paper, "could such a melancholy event have been more unfortunate for this country, at a period when legal talent and acquirement are treated by the party in power with the utmost contempt, and ignorance not only considered a virtue, but a stepping to office and favour. The friends of constitutional liberty will look upon the decease of Judge Marshall as one of the greatest calamities that could

---

[1] Marshall wrote to Story, Dec. 25, 1832, referring to Baldwin's affliction; and Webster wrote, Dec. 27, that Baldwin had recently manifested an alienation of mind.

befall the Nation.   He was one of the last pillars of the
Constitution, which had withstood the ravages of the
Goths and Vandals; and the event will be hailed by
them secretly as a new triumph to their cause, while
it will be a source of deep sorrow to every true friend of
his country."   Another New York paper even doubted
the existence of any Democratic lawyer fit to succeed
Marshall: "The liberties of a great people are put in
peril by the departure of the most eminent of their conservators — the man who of all others was best calculated to fill the office, which, of all others, was most
important, in its power of giving perpetuity to institutions threatened with subversion by other departments of the Government.   We mourn not merely the
loss of a great and good man, but we tremble in the contemplation of the risque we run in his successor.   We
know that the prerogative of nomination, possibly
that of appointment, is in bad hands, and we have
everything to apprehend from its weak or wicked
exercise.   We do not say that it would be impossible
to find a successor capable of filling Judge Marshall's
place among his surviving country men; but no unprejudiced American citizen will disagree with us when
we say that it not only is not possible to find a suitable
successor to that great man and upright Judge among
those from which the present National Executive will
make the selection; but the liveliest alarm must be
felt lest the President shall so select as to endanger
the very existence of our liberties.   Heaven grant
that our well-grounded apprehension may be disappointed!" [1]   A Whig correspondent wrote from Washington: " The Executive and his Cabinet . . . consider
the late Chief Justice as the most formidable obstacle
which they were likely to encounter in the pursuit of

[1] *New York Daily Advertiser*, July 8, 27, 1835; *New York Courier*, July 9, 1835.

their great scheme of reform. . . . The conspirators now expect, from the reform to be worked in the Supreme Court, to carry on their future assaults on the Constitution under the cover of law. . . . Our Constitution is in imminent danger. It guarantees too securely the Legislative and Judicial checks on the Executive, to suit the temper and views of the present Administration."

Such apprehensions and such political bias were almost humorous; but the supercilious attitude toward the capacity of those lawyers who belonged to the Democratic Party was highly characteristic of the heated partisanship of the times. Fair or impartial consideration of anything which President Jackson might do was not to be expected. There had been nothing, however, in the record of Jackson's previous appointments to the Bench which warranted any such pessimistic apprehensions. McLean, Baldwin, Wayne and Barbour had all been men of high personal character and of eminent legal ability, and as jurists of standing they compared exceedingly favorably with the appointment of Associate Justices made by Washington or Adams. It was undoubtedly true that Jackson would consider only the appointment of a Democrat to fill the vacancy in the position of Chief Justice; and it was natural that he should desire a Democrat in sympathy with his constitutional views, just as President Adams had originally appointed Marshall as a strong Federalist. It by no means followed, as the Whigs seemed to assume, that no consideration should be given to the views of the appointee on the subject of politics, taking politics in its highest and philosophic sense as involving the theories of human rights and the principles of government. Political partisanship should of course be no qualification; but, as a leading paper in the South said:[1] "It would be indeed strange if, in selecting the members of so august a tribunal, no weight should be attached to the views entertained by its members of the Constitution, or their acquirements in the science of politics in its relations to the form of government under which we live. We can imagine the horror with which the annunciation would be received throughout the country of the elevation of a thorough Nullifier, however able and accomplished and learned, to the chief place in the interpretation of the Constitution. Yet the exclusion of a Nullifier would be the admission of a political, or it may in this sense be called, a party test, and it is one which the country will approve." The Democratic papers, in fact, demanded that a man should be selected "whose principles, profession and practice afford a sure guarantee that on all questions involving the power of the government, he will strictly adhere to the letter of the Constitution and faithfully abide by the stern dictates of popular opinion", — a man who would "keep pace with the steady progress of publick liberty and popular reform." They asserted that the Whig papers, in expressing a fear lest Marshall's successor should be "a party man", were indulging in "hypocritical cant." "There are none so base as to treat with disrespect the memory of the venerable Chief Justice; but when the Whigs, for party purposes, attempt to draw around his judicial decisions a sacredness not warranted, compare his acts with those of the administration of General Jackson, and represent him as frequently stepping between 'the bleeding Constitu-

[1] *Mobile Register*, quoted in *Washington Globe*, Aug. 13, 1835. The *New York Evening Post*, July 29, 1835, quoted the *Baltimore Republican* as saying that the Chief Justice was, throughout life, a party man, appointed as a Federalist by a Federalist: "Away then with the pretence that a man's belonging to a party, particularly when that party is in the majority, is a sound objection to his appointment to the Bench."

tion and usurpations of Jackson', mourn over his death because it will devolve upon General Jackson to nominate a successor, it becomes necessary that they should be met and their assertions canvassed." "The seat of Chief Justice ought to be filled by a man who has given evidence to the people of firmness and courage in the practice of Democratick principles." "We hope the President will justify the hopes of the country and give a sane jurist, an orthodox constitutional lawyer and an eminent citizen." "There is no doubt that as yet the Democratick tendencies of the Nation have never yet been fairly represented in that tribunal. It has been the stronghold of the antiquated, strong-government, Federal ideas, which, in every other branch of the Government, have been long since discarded." [1]

No one of the Judges on the Supreme Bench seemed to be a possible choice. Judge Story (whom most lawyers considered the logical successor of Marshall) would certainly be unacceptable to the President; and Story himself realized this, for he wrote to friends: "As to the Chief Justice's successor, I do not even venture to hazard an opinion, or even a conjecture. I shall await events. Whoever succeeds him will have a most painful and discouraging duty. He will follow a man who cannot be equalled, and all the public will see, or think they see, the difference. A situation which provokes a comparison so constant and so discouraging is not enviable. Let me only add, for your eye, lest there be some idle conjecture elsewhere, that I have never for a moment imagined that I should be thought of. So that I am equally beyond hope or anxiety.". . . "I take it for granted that all of us who are on the Bench

---

[1] See *Fayettesville Green Mountain Democrat; Columbus Centinel; Mobile Register; Baltimore Republican*, quoted in *New York Evening Post*, July, August, 1835, *passim*, Nov. 10, 1835.

are *hors du combat.*" [1] Judge McLean also, while originally appointed by Jackson, seemed to the Democrats
to share too largely in Marshall's views of the Constitution, though some papers strongly urged his appointment. The names of many distinguished lawyers were mentioned in the newspapers as possible
appointees: [2] Henry St. George Tucker (President of
the Court of Appeals of Virginia); Philip P. Barbour
of Virginia; William Gaston (Chief Justice of the Supreme Court of North Carolina); [3] Edward Livingston
and Benjamin F. Butler of New York; Horace Binney
of Pennsylvania; Thomas H. Benton of Missouri [4] and
Louis McLane of Delaware. [5] Many papers, not only
in the North but in the South, strongly advocated the

[1] *Story*, II, 200, 208, letter to Peters, July 24, 1835; to McLean, Oct. 12, 1835.
See also *Andrew Jackson and His Collision with Judges and Lawyers*, by Seymour
D. Thompson, *Amer. Law Rev.*, XXI. Judge Story was regarded with considerable
bitterness by Democratic Party leaders, and a newspaper at this time (*Fayettesville
Green Mountain Democrat*) termed him "the contemptible apostate, Story, arrogant
and supercilious."

[2] *Niles Register*, XLIX, Nov. 7, 1835; *New York Evening Post*, Aug. 15, 1835,
quoting the *Baltimore Republican* as copying from the *Mobile Register*, "what
we consider the very best article on Marshall's successor", and saying that
Livingston, McLane, Taney, Benton and Webster were suggested; see also
Washington Globe, Aug. 13, 1835.

[3] The *New York Courier*, July 22, 1835, said as to Gaston: "No possible chance
for the country under its present misrule to be blessed with such a man upon the
Supreme Bench. He is too pure a patriot and too good a man, and possesses too
much fitness for the station, to be thought of for a moment at the White House. . . .
He has never cursed his old acquaintances, and truckled to the caprices of the poor
old man who thinks he is President of the United States, but who is really the mere
puppet of Amos Kendall and Mr. Van Buren."

[4] The *Trenton True American* said, July 11, 1835: "Col. Benton having been
spoken of as the probable successor of the late Chief Justice, Marshall, the *Globe*
asserts positively that the Col. would not accept, should the office be tendered him.
The people cannot spare Benton from the Senate so long as the Bank is in the field,
but Livingston for Chief Justice would be highly acceptable"; and, July 18,
it said that the suggestion of Livingston "meets with general approbation from
Democratic Journals."

[5] See *Richmond Enquirer*, July 14, 1835, quoting various papers. An interesting story is told in James A. Hamilton's *Reminiscences* (1869), 130, to the
effect that in 1829 Jackson promised to appoint Louis McLane to any vacancy
caused by Duval's retirement; McLane was Minister to England in 1835,
and was aggrieved at Jackson's failure to appoint him Chief Justice. This is
fully substantiated in *Autobiography of Martin Van Buren, Amer. Hist. Ass. Rep.*
(1918), II.

appointment of Daniel Webster,[1] but the Democrats as a rule opposed Webster because of his ultra-Federal principles. "These are too much in unison with the decisions of the Supreme Court itself, to command the support of the Republican party," said the *Richmond Enquirer*. "The Court has done more to change the character of that instrument and to shape, as it were, a new Constitution for us, than all the other departments of the Government put together. The President will nominate a Democratic Chief Justice, and thus, we hope, give some opportunity for the good old State-Rights doctrines of Virginia of '98–'99 to be heard and weighed on the Federal Bench. The very profound and brilliant abilities, with which they have been hitherto opposed in the Supreme Court, have only contributed to make us more anxious to bring back the ship to the Republican tack. We believe that Taney is a strong State-Rights man."[2] While President Jackson gave no definite intimation as to his choice, it became very generally understood that

[1] See *Alexandria Gazette* (Va.); *Charleston Courier* (S. C.); *Georgia Journal* referred to in *Richmond Enquirer*, July 14, 24, 28, Aug. 14, 1835; *Nashville Banner* (Tenn.), referred to in *New York Evening Post*, Aug. 22, 1835.

[2] The *Richmond Enquirer*, July 28, 1835, commented on the fact that while some Whig editors opposed Taney as a Roman Catholic, other Whig editors favored William Gaston who was also a Roman Catholic.

In the diary of John Quincy Adams, Jan. 29, 1829, there is a curious entry as to a suggestion that he might have appointed Daniel Webster as Marshall's successor, if Marshall had resigned during Adams' term: "Mr. Burnet, Senator from the State of Ohio, said he came to me on an unpleasant subject. He had a letter from Charles Hammond stating that Mr. Doddridge of Virginia had written to me that he (Mr. Burnet) had said that the elder Adams, by the appointment of John Marshall as Chief Justice, had entailed a curse upon the country, and that if I should have the opportunity to appoint Daniel Webster as Marshall's successor, it would be a still greater curse. He said there were not two men in the world for whom he had a greater veneration than for Chief Justice Marshall and Mr. Webster. I said Mr. Hammond had been misinformed. Mr. Doddridge, whom I scarcely knew, had written to me that he had heard Mr. Burnet had expressed disapprobation of the decisions of the Supreme Court of the United States with reference to questions involving the State authorities. He had not named Mr. Webster. Mr. Burnet said he had expressed the opinion that perhaps the decisions of the Supreme Court had sometimes encroached upon the State-Rights."

Roger Brooke Taney of Maryland was to be appointed.[1] No official announcement was made until December 28, 1835, when Jackson sent in to the Senate the name of Taney for Chief Justice, and at the same time appointed Philip P. Barbour of Virginia to fill the vacancy among the Associate Judges caused by Duval's resignation.[2] The Taney appointment was received with gloom and pessimism by the Whigs. "Judge Story thinks the Supreme Court is *gone*, and I think so too," wrote Webster.[3] The attack upon

[1] As early as July 11, 13, 1835, Taney's name was announced in the *Norfolk Herald;* see *New York Evening Post,* July 14, 15, 16, 1835, and *National Intelligencer,* July 15, 1835. As early as Dec. 12, 1835, the *National Gazette* said that: "It is stated from Washington, that Mr. Taney will certainly be nominated as Chief Justice to the Senate and Judge Tucker, Judge Barbour or Mr. Daniel in place of Judge Duval." The *New York Daily Advertiser,* Dec. 15, 1835, published the following bitter invective from its Washington correspondent, writing Dec. 11:

"The rumor that the famous Roger Brooke Taney will be nominated to fill the chair of Chief Justice vacated by the death of the lamented Marshall, gains strength every hour. If it is the will of the President, and who of his, or the partisans of Van Buren, dare raise a finger against it — not one I am sure who are in power or dependent upon the party clan. No! not even that vandal horde who from the housetop at daybreak and at sunset proclaimed against the Federalism of Chief Justice Marshall. They can swallow Taney's Federalism, Jacksonism, Van Burenism, Johnsonism, and every ism which feeds them upon the loaves and fishes of office. The great and good Marshall was a Federalist, say they, and we could not support him. The notorious Taney is a Federalist, and this is recommendation to office — the purity of his past life, especially his political life, is the great lever which is to raise him to this exalted station — shame upon such inconsistency."

[2] As to the urgent demand in Virginia for Barbour's appointment, see letter of Dabney Carr to Martin Van Buren, Dec. 21, 1835. *Van Buren Papers MSS.*

[3] *Letters of Daniel Webster* (1902), ed. by C. H. Van Tyne; see other letters as follows: Dec. 23, 1835. ". . . No Chief Justice is yet nominated but it is expected Mr. Taney will be the man. The President has a party tomorrow eve — viz. card enclosed. . . . I have not been out — have invited no company — and occupy myself with common Congress matters or with some preparation for the Court — though in the Court, I have not a great deal to do this year and wish I had less." Dec. 28, 1835. "The President's party I forgot to mention. I was not present, but understand it was something quite new, and *went off* — as you New Yorkers say, very brilliantly. There was dancing in the East Room, a sumptuous supper in the dining room and so on." Jan. 10, 1836. "Judge Story arrived last evening in good health, but bad spirits. He thinks the Supreme Court is *gone* and I think so too; and almost everything is gone or seems rapidly going. We are in a state of some excitement about the French business. The President is warm and warlike. Mr. Van Buren more pacific. . . . Congress is not at all prepared for war, but no one knows what might be done if Gen'l. Jackson should sound a loud war note."

the appointment, however, was entirely political. The
Whigs in general, and the adherents of the Bank of the
United States in particular, could never forget or for-
give Taney's action when Secretary of the Treasury
in complying with Jackson's directions to remove the
Government deposits from the Bank; and in Whig
eyes anything which Jackson did was condemnable.[1]
Taney is "unworthy of public confidence, a supple,
cringing tool of power", said a New York paper.[2]
Taney owes his appointment "to his latitudinarian
doctrines as to the extent of the Executive power and
to his vindication of the President's pet measure",
said another New York paper, in a violent attack upon
the appointment.[3]   To these attacks, the Democrats
replied, with equal political bias, that "all the venom
of the Bank cabal, and the ambitious, electioneering
rancor and influence of Whig Senators and the vile
machinations" of the incongruous, Federal, Whig Party
would be impotent to defeat the appointment; that
the only objection which the Whigs could bring
against Taney was "his proud honesty and independence and his want of subserviency to the United
States Bank and other ' monied monsters '; but this
is, in fact, one of his principal recommendations.   Law-
learning and superior talents may also be found among
the prominent men of the Federal Whig party, but
where is there one who can be safely trusted to hold
the scales of Justice, when all the wealth of the country
concentrated in the United States Bank and the Whig

[1] The *Washington Globe* said, Dec. 9, 1835: "No man, we believe, ever had more
falsehoods invented and propagated against him in a short space of time, than
Mr. Taney has since he removed the deposits."

[2] *New York Courier*, Jan. 23, 1836; *New York American*, Jan. 14, 1836.

[3] To this, the *New York Evening Post*, July 16, 1835, said: "If Mr. Taney owes
his appointment to his manly and patriotick conduct in seconding the great measures of the Executive in relation to the United States Bank, he owes it to a cause
of which he may be justly proud."

party is placed on one scale and right and justice and the good of the country are its only opposing weight?" "He has shown by his firmness, independence, and disregard of his own personal benefit, by his sound judgment and pure patriotism, by his incorruptible integrity and purity of character, that he is eminently qualified, including his admitted great talents and legal knowledge, for the exalted station." "Mr. Taney is as sincere and thorough a Democrat as any in the country. He is not merely a Democrat according to party usages, he is not a loaf and fish Democrat, a *tutissimus ibis* Democrat; he is a sound, anti-monopoly Democrat. As a lawyer, even the *American* will hardly question his fitness for the office of Chief Justice, so far as legal talents and acquirements are concerned." [1]

In the calm light of history, it is now seen that the attacks upon Taney on political grounds had little reasonable basis; and as Judge Wayne said, after Taney's death, "the party contests of that day have passed away, with the admission of those who were engaged in them that his course was sincere and sustained with ability."

While a few Whig papers admitted that "as a lawyer, so far as regards his juridical abilities and acquirement, there could be no objection", and that he was "an able lawyer and profound civilian",[2] the Bar throughout the North, being largely Whig, entirely ignored Taney's eminent legal qualifications, and his brilliant legal career, during which he had shared with William Wirt the leadership of the Maryland Bar and had attained high rank at the Supreme Court Bar, both before and after his service as Attorney-General of the United States. "I believe it was

[1] *Boston Post*, Dec. 1, 15, 1835; *New York Evening Post*, July 16, 21, Aug. 12, 1835.
[2] *Columbian Centinel*, quoted in *Boston Post*, Dec. 1, 15, 1835.

then a general impression, in this part of the country, that he was neither a learned nor a profound lawyer," said ex-Judge Benjamin R. Curtis, at a meeting of the Boston Bar on Taney's death in 1864. "This was certainly a mistake. His mind was thoroughly imbued with the rules of the common law and of equity law; and when I first knew him, he was master of all that peculiar jurisprudence which it is the special province of the Courts of the United States to administer and apply. His skill in applying it was of the highest order. His power of subtle analysis exceeded that of any man I ever knew . . . in his case balanced and checked by excellent common sense and by great experience in practical business, both public and private. . . . It is certainly true, and I am happy to be able to bear direct testimony to it, that the surpassing ability of the Chief Justice, and all his great qualities of character and mind, were more fully and constantly exhibited in the consultation room, while presiding over and assisting the deliberation of his brethren, than the public knew or can ever justly estimate. There, his dignity, his love of order, his gentleness, his caution, his accuracy, his discrimination, were of incalculable importance. The real intrinsic character of the tribunal was greatly influenced by them, and always for the better."

For over two months and a half, the Senate struggled with the nomination, the Whig opposition being violently supported by the party organs.[1] "The nomination of Taney is made for the sole purpose of insulting and degrading the Senate," said a New York paper. "Should Mr. Taney now become Chief Justice 'by and with the advice of the Senate', the myrmidons of power will make the welkin ring with

---

[1] *New York Courier*, Jan. 21, 1836; *Boston Courier*, Jan. 4, 1836.

shouts of triumph that the President had now prostrated
at his feet that branch of the Government which represented the States as States, that the Senate was no
longer a refractory member of the Government, that
General Jackson's will and pleasure was weal and woe
to the individual or State that should dare to moot
that point with him." And a leading Boston Whig
paper said: "But if Mr. Barbour's appointment is
extremely objectionable, what can be said of the appointment of Mr. Taney? The ready and most obsequious
agent of the severest and most dangerous blow which has
been given to our Constitution and law; before, rejected
by the Senate for a trust far less critical and important,
on account of his partisan servility; now, nominated
as the Judicial High Priest of the nation! Will the
Senate bow to such an insult? If they do, *then* no one
can pity. But above all will they permit themselves
and the Supreme Court of the United States to be
prostrated at the same blow, in the depths of political pollution? To confirm this nomination would be,
and would be considered, the general signal for defeat,
dismay and despair. . . . If Mr. Taney be now confirmed, all will be lost."

It was stated on February 2, 1836, that the Senate
was divided into twenty-two Administration and twenty-
four Anti-Administration men, with two Senators
doubtful. Shortly after this, John Tyler of Virginia
resigned because of his unwillingness to support the
Administration's Expunging Resolution; and his place
was taken by William L. Rives who was favorable to
Jackson's policies.[1] Finally, on March 15, Taney

[1] *National Gazette*, Feb. 2, 1836; on March 14, it said: "In consequence of
Mr. Tyler's retiring, the Administration will probably be able to carry all its
measures. If Roger B. Taney should now be appointed Chief Justice of the
Supreme Court, who should be held responsible for the disgrace that would thereupon fall upon the Nation? Who, but John Tyler of Virginia? The man whc

was confirmed by a vote of twenty-nine to fifteen;
but Calhoun, and Clay, Crittenden, Ewing, Southard,
White and Webster [1] held out to the end against
Jackson's nominee. The fight had, in fact, been led
throughout by Webster and Clay. "There was hardly
an opprobrious epithet which, as he told me himself,
afterwards, Clay failed to use against the nomination,"
said Reverdy Johnson,[2] "and from a conviction that
the nominee was unfit and would prove to be unfit
for the discharge of the duties of the judicial station."
How deeply his political bias colored Clay's views
was interestingly shown by the fact that, within a
few years, he frankly admitted his regret for his action.
As described by Johnson: "After Taney had been
upon the Bench for some four or five years, and Mr.
Clay had been the witness, from having practiced before
him and read his decisions, of the manner in which
his duties had been discharged, he, as he told me himself,
after hearing an opinion delivered by the presiding
Judge, went to his quarters to see him, and found him
alone; he said he felt the embarrassment necessarily
incident to the object of his visit, and after exchanging
salutations suited to the occasion, and being about

meanly shrunk from the performance of his duty to gratify one of the most ridiculous and affected whims that ever disturbed the weak head of a weak and silly
politician."

[1] It appears that Webster was consistent in his action as it is said that he voted
against all previous nominees to the Supreme Court Bench; for George F. Hoar
in his *Autobiography* (1903), states that Judge Rockwood F. Hoar related the following incident of a visit to Washington in 1836: "Webster received him with
great kindness, showed him about the Capitol and took him to the Supreme Court
where he argued a case.   Mr. Webster began by alluding very impressively to the
great change which had taken place in that Tribunal since he first appeared as
counsel before them.   He said: 'No one of the Judges who were here then, remains.
It has been my duty to pass upon the confirmation of every member of the Bench;
and I may say that I treated your honors with entire impartiality, for I voted
against every one of you.' "   If Hoar was correct as to the date, Webster's remark
was not strictly true as to Judge Story or Judge Thompson who were appointed
on the Bench in 1811 and in 1823, before Webster became Senator in 1826.

[2] *38th Cong., 1st Sess.*, 1363, speech of Senator Reverdy Johnson, March
31, 1864.

to leave him, he took him by the hand and said:
'Mr. Chief Justice, there was no man in the land
who regretted your appointment to the place you
now hold more than I did; there was no member of
the Senate who opposed it more than I did; but I
have come to say to you, and I say it now in parting,
perhaps for the last time, — I have witnessed your
judicial career, and it is due to myself and due to you
that I should say what has been the result; that I
am satisfied now that no man in the United States
could have been selected, more abundantly able to
wear the ermine which Chief Justice Marshall honored.'
And with the tears trickling down the cheeks of both —
I speak the words of Henry Clay — they parted; and
that opinion he continued to hold, up to the last moment,
that his life was a blessing to the country."

The Whigs accepted the confirmation of Taney
with very bad grace.[1] "The pure ermine of the Supreme
Court is sullied by the appointment of that political
hack, Roger B. Taney," said one of their New York
papers. Another said: "Roger B. Taney of Maryland,
has been paid the price for removing the deposits. . . .
And today, we see a man elevated to the Chief Justiceship for violating the laws of the land "; and another
said: "General Jackson has at length succeeded in
his attempts to subdue the independent spirit of the
Senate and has brought that branch of the Government
under his feet. The consequence of this triumph
over public spirit and patriotism, over talents, integrity
and virtue, has been to place Roger B. Taney at the
head of the Judiciary. . . . The feelings of the new
Chief Justice, when he takes his place at the head of
the Court, will not be envied by any highminded and

---

[1] *New York American*, March 17, 1836; *Boston Courier*, March 22, 1836; *New
York Daily Advertiser*, March 21, 1836; *National Gazette*, March 19, 1836.

United States — and both changes effected by the force of public opinion in a free country." [1]

Within ten days after the opening of the Term, the Court heard the final rearguments in the three celebrated constitutional cases which had been pending, one for six years and the others for three years — awaiting the existence of a full Court. The first of these, *Charles River Bridge* v. *Warren Bridge*, 11 Pet. 420, had been argued at the 1831 Term (as Judge Story said) "with great learning, research, and ability, and renewed with equal learning, research and ability, at the present Term"; and it was now reargued on January 19, 21, 23, 24, 26, 1837, by Daniel Webster and Warren Dutton against Simon Greenleaf and John Davis (all of Massachusetts). The important question involved was, whether the obligation of contract contained in a charter to a corporation authorizing the construction of a toll bridge was impaired by a charter, subsequently granted to another corporation, authorizing the construction of a free bridge paralleling the toll bridge. In view of the economic conditions of the times and of the increasing construction of railroads paralleling previously chartered canals, the decision was likely to be of vast consequence to the development of the country; and the active interest shown in the case was illustrated by the vivid descriptions of the arguments of counsel which appeared in contemporary newspapers and letters.[2] A Washington press correspondent wrote, January 24:

Today the Supreme Court was the great scene of attraction at the Capitol. Mr. Webster was expected to speak, and at an early hour all the seats within and without the bar,

---

[1] *Richmond Enquirer*, March 9, 1837; *Washington Globe*, March 13, 1837; *Pennsylvanian*, Feb. 27, 1837.

[2] *Boston Daily Advertiser*, Jan. 30, 1837, quoting *New York Commercial Advertiser*; *History of the American Bar* (1911), by Charles Warren, 423, 424.

except those occupied by the counsel engaged in the cause, were filled with ladies, whose beauty and splendid attire and waving plumes gave to the Court-room an animated and brilliant appearance such as it seldom wears. By the bye, this chamber presents just now, in itself, a better look than it ever did before. A great deal of the furniture is new, the carpets are rich and beautiful; the desks and chairs of the Judges of a pattern unsurpassed for beauty and convenience, and the whole appointments of the room, in short, in excellent taste. The whole Court was present. . . . Mr. Davis made a very powerful argument in behalf of the defendants in error. Mr. Webster followed him in a speech which is generally spoken of as a most masterly effort of argument and ingenuity. I only heard a portion of it. He was describing the localities of the bridges. I never heard or read any description more clear or accurate. Painting could not have conveyed a better idea of the places to the mind of the spectator than his picturesque description did to the auditors. I envied the dashing young belles of the metropolis their privilege of hearing Mr. Webster throughout; though I doubt not their looks distracted the attention of many a man who went to listen to him.

On the same day, Simon Greenleaf wrote to Charles Sumner:

For a week, I have had scarcely a thought that was not upon Warren Bridge. The argument was begun Thursday by Mr. Dutton, who concluded Saturday morning. I spoke about two hours on Saturday and nearly three on Monday, and yet merely went straight over my brief, answering, by the way, a few objections on the other side. Mr. Davis followed me yesterday and concluded in three hours today, in a most cogent, close, clear and convincing argument. Peters, the Supreme Court Reporter, says the cause was not nearly as well argued before as now; and in proof of it says that his own opinion is changed by it and that he now goes for the Def'ts! Mr. Webster spoke about an hour this afternoon on general and miscellaneous topics in the cause, and will probably occupy all day tomorrow, as he said he should consume considerable time. He told us he should "tear our arguments to pieces", and abuse me. The former will puzzle him; the latter I doubt he will do, as he was observed to be very uneasy and moody during the whole defense. Both Mr. Davis and I avoided everything "peoplish" in our remarks, confining ourselves closely to legal views alone. But we expect a great effort from Mr. W. to-morrow.

Judge Story wrote to Sumner, January 25, 1837:

Every argument was very good, above and beyond expectation, and that is truly no slight praise, considering all circumstances. Our friend Greenleaf's argument was excellent — full of ability, point, learning, condensed thought, and strong illustration — delivered with great presence of mind, modestly, calmly and resolutely. It was every way worthy of him and the cause. It has given him a high character with the Bench and with the Bar. . . . At the same time, I do not say he will win the cause. That is uncertain yet, will not probably be decided under weeks to come. I say so the more resolutely, because on some points he did not convince me; but I felt the force of his argument. Governor Davis made a sound argument, exhibiting a great deal of acuteness and power of thinking. Dutton's argument was strong, clear, pointed, and replete with learning. Webster's closing reply was in his best manner,[1] but with a little too much of *fierté* here and there. He had manifestly studied it with great care and sobriety of spirit. On the whole, it was a glorious exhibition for old Massachusetts; four of her leading men brought out in the same cause, and none of them inferior to those who are accustomed to the lead here. The audience was very large, especially as the cause advanced; — a large circle of ladies, of the highest fashion, and taste, and intelligence, numerous lawyers, and gentlemen of both houses of Congress, and towards the close, the foreign ministers, or at least some two or three of them.

Within three weeks after the close of the argument, Chief Justice Taney delivered the opinion of the Court,

---

[1] Webster evidently expected to lose his case, his son, D. Fletcher Webster writing to him Feb. 24, 1837: "I regret that you will lose the Bridge case — perhaps you may be mistaken. I cannot but hope so, more especially as it may be, as you say, your last case." *Letters of Daniel Webster* (1902), ed. by C. H. Van Tyne; *Story*, II, 205.

upholding the validity of the statute, and establishing
the doctrine that in the absence of express words granting exclusive privileges in a corporate charter, no such
grant can be inferred as against the State. "No
opinion of the Court," said one of its Judges, fifteen
years later, "more fully satisfied the legal judgment
of the country, and consequently none has exerted
more influence upon its legislation." The rigid principle of the *Dartmouth College Case* which heretofore
"had acted like a band of iron on legislative action"
was modified by this decision in favor of the public
interests.[1]

Except among the irreconcilable opponents of Jackson, the case was very soon recognized as a bulwark
to the people in general, as well as to all business men
who contemplated investments of capital in new
corporate enterprises and who were relieved against
claims of monopoly concealed in ambiguous clauses of
old charters. Coming, as it did, just at the period when
the new systems of transportation by railroads and
canals were first developing, the decision was an
immense factor in their successful competition; for
as Taney pointed out, if contracts of monopoly were to
be implied by the mere grant of a charter for trans-

[1] See Campbell, J., dissenting in *Piqua Branch of the State Bank of Ohio* v. *Knoop*
(1854), 16 How. 409; and see Taney, C. J., in *Ohio Life Insurance Co.* v. *Debolt*
(1854), 16 How. 435: "Nor does the rule rest merely on the authority of adjudged
cases. It is founded in principles of justice, and necessary for the safety and well-
being of every State in the Union. For it is a matter of public history, which this
Court cannot refuse to notice, that almost every bill for the incorporation of banking companies, insurance and trust companies, railroad companies or other corporations, is drawn originally by the parties who are personally interested in
obtaining the charter; and that they are often passed by the Legislature in the
last days of its session when, from the nature of our political institutions, the
business is unavoidably transacted in a hurried manner, and it is impossible that
every member can deliberately examine every provision in every bill upon which
he is called on to act." See especially the principles of the *Charles River Bridge Case*
applied in an extreme case of competing railroads in *Richmond, Fredericksburg and
Potomac R. R.* v. *The Louisa R. R. Co.* (1851), 13 How. 71; see also *Legislative
Control over Railway Charters*, in *Amer. Law Rev.* (1867), I; *Private Turnpikes and
Bridges* by Clinton T. Evans, *ibid.* (1916), L.

portation facilities, "the millions of property which have been invested in railroads and canals, upon lines of travel which had been before occupied by turnpike corporations, will be put in jeopardy. We shall be thrown back to the improvements of the last century, and obliged to stand still, until the claims of the old turnpike corporations shall be satisfied, and they shall consent to permit these States to avail themselves of the lights of modern science, and to partake of the benefit of those improvements which are now adding to the wealth and prosperity, and the convenience and comfort, of every other part of the civilized world." Nevertheless, while a decision to the contrary would unquestionably have had a disastrous effect upon the development of the country, there were many men who took the view presented in Judge Story's dissenting opinion, saying: "I can conceive of no surer plan to arrest all public improvements founded on private capital and enterprise, than to make the outlay of that capital uncertain and questionable, both as to security and as to productiveness. . . . The very agitation of a question of this sort is sufficient to alarm every stockholder in every public enterprise of this sort throughout the whole country." The conservative lawyers and the corporate interests also regarded the decision as radical, revolutionary and calamitous.[1] "The vested-rights class cry out bloody murder, and your friend, John Davis, has had the credit of maintaining radical and revolutionary doctrines," wrote a Washington correspondent of a Boston paper.

On the day after the argument in the *Bridge Case*, the *Mayor of the City of New York* v. *Miln*, 11 Pet. 102,

---

[1] Story wrote to his wife, Feb. 14, 1837: "A case of grosser injustice or more oppressive legislation never existed." Webster wrote: "The decision of the Court will have completely overturned, in my judgment, a great provision of the Constitution." *Story*, II, 268; *Boston Courier*, Feb. 22, 1837.

was argued, January 27, 28, by D. B. Ogden and Blount against Walter Jones and Joseph M. White of Florida. The case involved a New York statute passed to protect the State from the influx of foreign paupers, requiring all masters of vessels arriving at the port of New York to report lists of passengers. It was argued for the State that this was no interference with the Federal power to regulate foreign commerce but a mere police regulation. "Such a condition," it was said, "produces no inconvenience, but, on the contrary, promotes a public good. It vests power where there is an inducement to exercise it. In Congress, there is no such inducement. The West seeks to encourage emigration, and it is but of little importance to them how many of the crowd are left as a burden upon the city of New York." Ogden referred to the dangers to the Constitution from an arousal of State feeling, saying: "To suffer State Legislatures to disregard the Constitution of the Union, which all their members are sworn to support, would soon leave the Constitution a dead letter, destroy the efficiency and put an end to every hope of benefit to be derived from it. On the other hand, to take from the Legislatures of the different States the powers legitimately vested in them, by a forced construction of the Constitution, would be equally fatal to it, by exciting State pride and State feelings against it; and thus driving it from that place in the good opinion, feelings and affection of the people without which it cannot long exist." The Court sustained the view that the statute was a mere exercise of police power to enforce the poor laws of the State, and that it was not a regulation of commerce, or at least not such an interference with the dominant power of Congress to regulate commerce as would come within the doctrine of *Gibbons* v. *Ogden*.

As soon as argument closed in the *Miln Case*, the third great long-pending constitutional case was begun, *Briscoe* v. *Bank of the Commonwealth of Kentucky*, 11 Pet. 257. It was argued by Joseph M. White and Samuel L. Southard against Henry Clay and Benjamin Hardin, January 28, February 1, 1837, and involved a Kentucky statute which authorized the issue of notes by a chartered bank, all of whose stock was owned by the State. Within ten days, on February 11, the Court reached a conclusion sustaining the State statute, and holding that these notes were not bills of credit, the issue of which by a State was prohibited by the Constitution.

In all three of these cases, Judge Story dissented, and stated that Marshall before his death concurred with his (Story's) views.

It has frequently been charged that in these three decisions the Court reversed the broad lines of construction on which Marshall and his Court had been proceeding. But this criticism can hardly be sustained in full. The *Miln Case* turned on a very narrow point, and the Court did not challenge in any way Marshall's opinion in *Gibbons* v. *Ogden*. In fact, it did not depart from Marshall's broad doctrines on interstate commerce as far as Marshall himself had gone in *Wilson* v. *Blackbird Creek Marsh Company*. Moreover, as Judge Baldwin explained (11 Pet., App. 2), the Court would have decided the case in the same way, even if Marshall had been alive. The *Briscoe Case* turned on an historical question of what constituted a bill of credit at the date of the Constitution. Marshall had only carried a bare majority of the Court with him in *Craig* v. *Missouri*, in 1830; and Baldwin now pointed out that, if the facts in the *Craig Case* had been similar to those in the *Briscoe Case*, Marshall would have been

in the minority.[1] In the *Bridge Case*, the Court did
not derogate from the doctrine of the *Dartmouth College Case* that a charter was a contract, but merely decided that such a contract was to be construed strictly
and in favor of the State, and that nothing was to
pass by implication; in this case, however, Marshall's
Court would have undoubtedly reached the opposite
conclusion, for Baldwin stated that at the first argument, in 1831, he stood alone.

That the decisions met with great disapproval in
many quarters at the time is evident. So great was
Judge Story's despondency that he wrote to Judge
McLean: "The opinion delivered by the Chief Justice
in the *Bridge Case* has not been deemed satisfactory;
and indeed, I think I may say that a great majority of
our ablest lawyers are against the decision of the Court;
and those who think otherwise are not content with the
views taken by the Chief Justice. . . . There will not,
I fear, ever in our day, be any case in which a law
of a State or of Congress will be declared unconstitutional; for the old constitutional doctrines are fast
fading away, and a change has come over the public
mind from which I augur little good." [2] Kent wrote

[1] A curious situation arose as to this Kentucky statute. A suit was brought in
Missouri and the Kentucky statute was held unconstitutional by the Missouri
State Court on the strength of *Craig* v. *Missouri*. Later on, in 1840, in view of
the *Briscoe Case* decision, an attempt was made to take the case to the United States
Supreme Court, but the latter Court held it had no jurisdiction under the 25th
Section of the Judiciary Act which only applied where decisions of State Courts
were in favor of constitutionality — *Commonwealth Bank of Kentucky* v. *Griffith*
(1840), 14 Pet. 56.

[2] *Story*, II, 272, 270, letter to McLean, May 10, 1837, letter of Kent, June 23, 1837;
Sumner wrote to Story, March 25, 1837: "As I read Taney's before I read yours,
I felt agreeably surprised by the clearness and distinctness with which he had
expressed himself, and the analysis by which he appeared to have been able to avoid
the consideration of many of the topics introduced into the argument. But on
reverting to his opinion again, after a thorough study of yours, it seemed meagre
indeed. Your richness of learning and argument was wanting. I thought of Wilkes'
exclamation on hearing the opinion of Lord Mansfield and his associates in his
famous case — that listening to the latter after the former, was taking hog-wash
after champagne." *Mass. Hist. Soc. Proc., 2d Series*, XV.

to Story: "I have re-perused the *Charles River Bridge Case*, and with increased disgust. It abandons, or over-throws, a great principle of constitutional morality, and I think goes to destroy the security and value of legislative franchises. It injures the moral sense of the community, and destroys the sanctity of contracts. If the Legislature can quibble away, or whittle away its contracts with impunity, the people will be sure to follow. *Quidquid delirant reges plectuntur Achivi.* I abhor the doctrine that the Legislature is not bound by everything that is necessarily implied in a contract in order to give it effect and value, and by nothing that is not expressed *in haec verba;* that one rule of inter-pretation is to be applied to their engagements, and another rule to the contracts of individuals. . . . But I had the consolation, in reading the case, to know that you have vindicated the principles and authority of the old settled law, with your accustomed learning, vigor, and warmth, and force. But the decision in *Briscoe* v. *The Bank of Kentucky* is quite as alarming and distressing. . . . It is in collision with the case of *Craig* v. *The State of Missouri.* . . . I have lost my confidence and hopes in the constitutional guardianship and protection of the Supreme Court." Other promi-nent Whigs expressed their apprehensions that the Legislatures of the States were hereafter to be free and unrestrained, "that they may pass ex post facto laws or such as impair the obligation of contracts, or issue bills of credit, without let or hindrance of the Supreme Court. A new era is begun and new lights have arisen. The provisions of the Constitution have been mis-understood by Judge Marshall and his Associates and new interpretations are to be given. Any clear mani-festation of the popular will, in opposition to the powers of the Constitution as hitherto expounded by the Court,

will be regarded with all due deference and embodied
in the new code. That same popular will will be
looked to as the leading star of the new dynasty and
as the only exponent of the Constitution. Those among
your friends who have already invested, or propose
to invest their property, upon the faith of charters will
do well to remember that this kind of property is no
longer under the protection of law, but is held at
the good pleasure of the Legislature." [1]   Equally
doleful prophecies were uttered by a writer in a prominent Whig review, who stated that it was undeniable
that "the tone and character of the decision chime in
with doctrines which tend or may be urged, deplorably,
to the subversion of the principles of law and property.
. . . Within a brief space, we have seen the highest
judicial corps of the Union wheel about in almost
solid column, and retread some of its most important
steps. It is quite obvious that old things are passing
away. The authority of former decisions, which had
long been set as landmarks in the law, is assailed and
overthrown, by a steady, destructive aim from the
summit of that stronghold, within which they had been
entrenched and established. It is very remarkable, also,
that all the principles yielded by these decisions, either
have relation to the sovereign powers of the Union,
or to the very essence of social obligation. . . . We
can hardly avoid the reluctant impression that it
(the Judiciary) has already capitulated to the spirit of
the old confederation; and that we are fast returning,

---

[1] See a letter from Washington to the *Boston Daily Advertiser*, Feb. 21, 1837;
it continued: "Those who are satisfied of the good faith, equity and justice of
that body will go on with the great work of internal improvement, but such as, from
past experience, have doubts may well be excused. It is not improbable that in the
downward course of things, this popular will, expressed in its accustomed forms, and
which is hereafter to dictate to all the departments of Government, may demand
a different tenure of judicial office; and I confess, for one, that I shall not be very
anxious to retain the form when the substance is gone. The Lord Chancellor
always goes out with the Minister."

among other things, to an old continental currency, and
to what were once denominated, moreover, anti-federal
doctrines. Under the progressive genius of this new
judicial administration, we can see the whole fair
system of the Constitution beginning to dissolve like the
baseless fabric of a vision." [1] Another leading Whig
magazine evinced even more solemn despair. After
lauding the Court as "the balance wheel in the machinery of the Constitution. The people of the United
States have confided to it the transcendent trust of
preserving the Constitution, unimpaired and vigorous
in all its parts, equally to be protected from the encroachments of the National departments, and from the
more popular and more dangerous assaults of the
State governments. It is looked up to as the last
asylum of persecuted justice. There is no other
tribunal on earth, so august in its functions, so vast
in influence and so fearful in its responsibilities";
it stated that "under the new dynasty", it perceived
"an altered tone and a narrower spirit, not only in
Chief Justice Taney, but even in some of the old Associates of Chief Justice Marshall, when they handle
constitutional questions. The change is so great and
ominous that a gathering gloom is cast over the future."
Commenting on the *Charles River Bridge Case*, it termed
"the most alarming and the most heretical" part of
the opinion, "the new fangled doctrine that the contracts of the State are to be construed strictly as against
the grantee, and that nothing can be raised by implication. . . . Such a cold-blooded commentary on
the contract, such a desolating doctrine coming from
the head of the highest tribunal of the Nation . . .
merits the severest animadversion that wounded justice and indignant patriotism can bestow." The

[1] *North Amer. Rev.* (1838), LVI, 153; *New York Rev.* (1838), II, 372–404.

Miln Case it called: "a fatal breach made in the
Constitution. . . . The Court has yielded up the
exclusive nature of the grant, and let loose upon us
the old Confederation claim of the States to interfere,
and perplex, and burden and alter the Congressional
regulation of commerce with foreign nations, under
pretexts (never wanting) that they were exercising
only police authority for their own local interest and
convenience." And it concluded with gloomy predictions as to the future of the Republic, because of
the "revolution in opinion, in policy and in numbers
that has recently changed the character of the Supreme
Court. . . . The asylum of the Nation's safety from
the violence of faction and the horrors of disunion was
fondly confided to the firm tenure and powers and all
pervading influence of the Supreme Court, and to the
noble and elevated virtues which such confidence
ought to inspire. And if the Constitution be destined
prematurely to perish, and the last refuge of justice,
and the last hopes of temperate and civilized freedom
be destroyed, the expiring struggle will be witnessed
in the decisions of that Court. Is it not possible to
bring intelligent and enlightened public opinion to
bear upon the Supreme Court and to endeavor to inspire it with a larger infusion of the spirit of moderation
and forbearance?"

To this Whig pessimism, the *Democratic Review*
replied that "the most ultra radical in this country
never wrote a severer article against the Supreme
Court"; but since at the date of the article, "the whole
country was under furious excitement, we ought
perhaps to make allowance for the influence of such a
state of feeling." It added that while it revered
Marshall's name, it was "sickened by the attempt
to connect his name with a particular party of the

present day, and make it the representative of all the ultra notions of those who, for a splendid government, would reason away the Constitution and all its checks and balances; who would, with one breath, make corporations override all individual and public interests, hold in check the power of the States, and defy that of the General Government — and at another moment would prostrate them all, to gratify some new whim or in advocating some new extreme of policy." [1]

All of these Whig forebodings were unjustified; and equally unfulfilled were the Democratic hopes that Taney's appointment would mean a reversal of the Court's constitutional doctrines. "His republican notions, together with those of his democratick associates, will produce a revolution in some important particulars in the doctrines heretofore advanced by the tribunal, over which he is called to preside, highly favorable to the independence of the States, and the substantial freedom of the people" had been the sentiment expressed by his strongest newspaper advocates.[2]   There was, however, no real relaxation in the determination of the Court to uphold the National dignity and sovereignty, in any case where it was really attacked; and in fact, in the succeeding years, Chief Justice Taney went even further than Marshall had been willing to go in extending the jurisdiction of the Federal Courts in admiralty and corporation cases and in many other directions.   If any real change in the course of the Court in cases affecting the National powers can be detected, between the thirty years after 1836 and the years prior, it may be said to amount only to this : that in doubtful cases, the Court possibly tended to give the benefit of the doubt to the State

---

[1] *Democratic Review* (June, 1840), VII, 497–515.
[2] *New York Evening Post,* March 17, 1836.

more than in Marshall's time, and even this statement cannot be made without qualification. But Taney differed from Marshall in one respect very fundamentally, and this difference was clearly shown in the decisions of the Court. Marshall's interests were largely in the constitutional aspects of the cases before him; Taney's were largely economic and social. Marshall was, as his latest biographer has said, "the Supreme Conservative;" Taney was a Democrat in the broadest sense, in his beliefs and sympathies. Under Marshall, "the leading doctrine of constitutional law during the first generation of our National history was the doctrine of vested rights." Like his contemporary in England, Sir Robert Peel, he believed that "the whole duty of government is to prevent crime and to preserve contracts." Under Taney, however, there took place a rapid development of the doctrine of the police power, "the right of the State Legislature to take such action as it saw fit, in the furtherance of the security, morality and general welfare of the community, save only as it was prevented from exercising its discretion by very specific restrictions in the written Constitution." [1] "The object and end of all government," Taney had said with great emphasis in the *Charles River Bridge Case*, "is to promote the happiness and prosperity of the community by which it is established, and it can never be assumed that the Government intended to diminish the power of accomplishing the end for which it was created. . . . We cannot deal thus with the rights reserved to the States, and by legal intendments and mere technical reasoning take away from them any portion of that power over their own internal police and improvement, which is so necessary to their well being

[1] *National Supremacy* (1913), by Edward S. Corwin, 113–115; see also Andrew C. McLaughlin's review of Beveridge's *Marshall*, in *Amer. Bar Ass. Journ.* (1921), VII, 231–233.

and prosperity." It was this change of emphasis from vested, individual property rights to the personal rights and welfare of the general community which characterized Chief Justice Taney's Court. And this change was but a recognition of the general change in the social and economic conditions and in the political atmosphere of that period, brought about by the adoption of universal manhood suffrage, by the revolution in methods of business and industry and in means of transportation, and by the expansion of the Nation and its activities. The period from 1830 to 1860 was an era of liberal legislation — the emancipation of married women, the abolition of imprisonment for debt, the treatment of bankruptcy as a misfortune and not a crime, prison reform, homestead laws, abolition of property and religious qualifications for the electorate, recognition of labor unions, liberalizing of rules of evidence and criminal penalties. It was but natural that the Courts amid such progressive conditions should acquire a new outlook responsive thereto. As has been well said, at the very moment when the election of Jackson meant the supremacy of the doctrine of strict construction, there arrived an era in the National life "when the demand went forth for a large governmental programme; for the public construction of canals and railroads, for free schools, for laws regulating the professions, for anti-liquor legislation, for universal suffrage." Taney came to the Bench with the view that the States must possess the sovereign and complete power to carry out this programme and to enact useful legislation for their respective populations. To Taney, the paramountcy of National power within the sphere of its competence was of equal but no greater importance than complete maintenance of the reserved sovereignty of the

States. Neither must be unduly favored or promoted.[1]   The difference between the point of Marshall and that of Taney can be best understood by a
study of the long series of letters of warm personal
friendship which Taney sent to Jackson, between 1836
and 1844; for in them the former's sympathies with
the broad rights of the people, as opposed to the individual rights of any monied or privileged class, are
strongly set forth.   Marshall's services to the Nation
as a political organism can never be overvalued; but
his whole temperament would have made it impossible
for him to write as Taney wrote to Jackson, in 1838:[2]
"In large commercial cities, the money power is, I fear
irresistible.   It is not by open corruption that it always,
or even most generally operates.   But when men, who
have families to support who depend for bread on their
exertions, are aware that on the one side they will be
employed and enriched by those who have the power to
distribute wealth, and that, if they take the other,
they must struggle with many difficulties that can be
thrown in their way, they are very apt to persuade
themselves that that path is the best one in which they
meet fewest difficulties and most favour, and surrender
the lasting blessings of freedom and manly independence for temporary pecuniary advantages.   They

[1] *Doctrine of Due Process of Law before the Civil War*, by Edward S. Corwin,
Harv. Law Rev. (1911), XXIV.
   "It is his (Taney's) glory that, with a sane mind, untroubled by the criticism
of partisans, sincere and otherwise, he so interpreted the Constitution, or lent
the weight of his influence to its interpretation, as to preserve unimpaired to the
States the rights reserved to them, and at the same time, to give full effect to all
the powers granted by the States to the Federal Government." *Roger Brooke
Taney*, by William E. Mikell, *Great American Lawyers* (1908), IV, 128.
[2] See *Jackson Papers MSS*, letter of Sept. 12, 1838, letter of Oct. 15, 1836, in
which Taney wrote that the freemen of the States "will never barter their liberties
for money, nor shrink before the frowns of the money aristocracy.   The same spirit
will, I doubt not, be found to prevail in the great majority of the people of the
United States."   See also *ibid.*, letters of Aug. 31, 1839, April 24, 1841, Sept. 30,
1841, Oct. 24, 1842, Oct. 18, 1843.

forget the grinding oppression that awaits them from
the power they are contributing to establish, as soon as
it is firmly seated in the saddle and no longer needs
their support.   These attempts to destroy the spirit
of freedom and manly independence in the working
classes of society are new in this country.   Ten years
ago, such an attempt would have destroyed any party
that countenanced such a principle.   It is not so now.
It appears to be daily more and more openly announced
and acted upon; and it has been successful too, to a
great extent.   How far it will be able to go, it is difficult
to foresee.   I trust there is a saving spirit yet in the
people of this country which will induce the honest of
all parties, before long, to frown upon it and put it
down.   But one thing is clear, that if the effort to
render the laboring classes of this country servile and
corrupt and to destroy their independent spirit and
self-respect shall be successful, that class of society
who are striving to produce it, will be the first and most
terrible victims of their own policy.   The lessons of
history upon this point are too plain to mislead us.
But I confidently believe that, before long, public
sentiment will put down these attempts to debase the
character of our own people, and that honest men of
all parties will refuse to purchase temporary success by
inflicting a lasting and irreparable injury upon their
own country."
    Again, he wrote in 1843 to Jackson: "I remember
your unshaken confidence in the virtue and intelligence
of the people, and I trust they will yet, in due time,
bring matters right   Nevertheless, I cannot conceal
from myself that paper money and its necessary consequences — that is, speculation and the desire of
growing rich suddenly and without labor, have made
fearful inroads upon the patriotism and public spirit

of what are called the higher classes; and if, in our divisions, they get that root of all evil, another Bank, it is not easy to foresee how far its powers of corruption may extend." Holding views like these, it is evident that Taney would approach a case from the human rather than the juristic standpoint, and that he would regard, as of the higher importance, the State power, which touched the individual and the community more closely than the National power.

NOTE. For a description of Taney, see *Southern Literary Messenger* (June, 1838), IV, quoted in *Life of Roger Brooke Taney* (1922), by Bernard C. Steiner: "His manner was strikingly impressive, when his slow and solemn form was seen rising in Court. . . . So soft and amiable was his deportment, that, even amidst the heat and turmoil of *nisi prius* litigation, he was never known to offend the feelings of any of his brethren; his conversation was never roughened by austerity of pedantry; and when his gallant bearing extorted from all the most unfeigned praise, he would almost hide himself from public admiration with the unaffected modesty of his native character. . . . In his person, he is full six feet high, spare, yet so dignified in deportment that you are at once impressed with an instinctive reverence and awe. . . . He sheds around him, in whatever circle he may move, a moral influence of the highest order." Reverdy Johnson said of Taney, in his speech, March 31, 1864: "Often his associate, and often his opponent, I had constant opportunities of judging of his legal learning, of his ability in its use, and the fair and elevated ground upon which he ever acted. In neither relation is it possible to exaggerate his excellence."

As to the reasons for the doctrine of the *Charles River Bridge Case*, see esp. *Blair* v. *Chicago* (1906), 201 U. S. 400, 472; *Russell* v. *Sebastian* (1914), 233 U. S. 195, 205. George W. Biddle in *Constitutional History of the United States as seen in the Development of American Law* (1889) said: "Unless the luxuriant growth, the result of the decision in 4 Wheaton (*i.e.*, the *Dartmouth College Case*), had been lopped and cut away by the somewhat trenchant reasoning of the Chief Justice, the whole field of legislation would have been choked and rendered useless, in time to come, for the production of any law that would have met the needs of the increasing and highly developed energies of a steadily advancing community."

CHAPTER TWENTY-TWO

CORPORATIONS AND SLAVERY

1838-1841

WHEN the Court met for the 1838 Term, two new
and additional Judges sat upon the Bench, as a result
of legislation which had been enacted on the last day
of President Jackson's term of office — the Act of
March 3, 1837. With the passage of this statute increasing the number of Associate Judges of the Supreme
Court from six to eight, establishing two new Circuits
in the West and Southwest, and abolishing Circuit
Court jurisdiction of the District Courts, the long contest which had been waged for twenty years came to
an end.[1] Hitherto (as has been described in previous
chapters) propositions to increase the number of Judges
and of Circuits, though recommended at various times
by Presidents Madison, Monroe, Adams and Jackson,
had failed to receive the approval of Congress, owing
to its unwillingness to allow the new appointments to
be made by the existing President.[2] Meanwhile, the

---

[1] Jackson, in his first Annual Message to Congress, Dec. 8, 1829, had said that
the benefit of the judicial system should be given to all the States equally. In his
Message, Dec. 6, 1831, he pointed out that one quarter of the States of the Union
did not participate in the benefit of Circuit Courts, and that all should be on the
same footing. "I trust that Congress will not adjourn, leaving this anomaly in
our system." In his Message, Dec. 4, 1832, he hoped that "this duty will be neg-
lected no longer." In his Messages of Dec. 6, 1834, and Dec. 7, 1835, he spoke of
the "great injustice" of the present system of Circuits. The bill passed the Senate
Jan. 6, 1836, and the House, March 3, 1837. *24th Cong., 2d Sess.* By an Act of
Feb. 19, 1831, partial relief had been given by extending Circuit Court jurisdiction
to certain District Courts in New York, Pennsylvania, Indiana, Illinois, Missouri,
Mississippi and Alabama.

[2] See *National Intelligencer*, March 9, 1837.

crowded conditions of the inferior Federal Courts in the States of the West and the Southwest had become such as to make relief absolutely necessary, and its refusal a scandalous denial of justice to those parts of the country.

Jackson filled the new positions on March 3, 1837, before he went out of office, by appointing John Catron of Tennessee and William Smith of Alabama. Catron, fifty-one years old, was Chief Justice of the Supreme Court of Tennessee; he also had the further qualification of being a master of the law of real property, a subject as to which there was much litigation in the Federal Courts. As a Southerner who had been a vigorous Union man throughout the Nullification movement and a warm supporter of Jackson's policy of maintenance of Federal supremacy, he was a valuable addition to the strength of the Court.[1] Smith, who had been a United States Senator from South Carolina, and who was also an active Jackson supporter though a more radical State-Rights man than Catron, declined the position and issued a public statement of refreshing frankness. "It has become a matter of considerable inquiry, as well as of some speculation, why I would decline a very dignified office of light labors, and a permanent salary of $5000 a year," he wrote, and he explained that it was not due to bodily infirmity or "to any doubt of my legal learning" nor "to cold indifference to the honor", but rather to his desire to retain his freedom to take part in political discussion in support of Jackson's policies. For, he continued, "although I have always believed a Judge was not bound by any moral principle to abstain from the polit-

[1] See interesting letter from Catron to Jackson, Jan. 2, 1833, setting forth his views as to energetic form of action which should be employed to put down Nullification in South Carolina. *Jackson Papers MSS.* The nominations were confirmed, March 8, 1837.

ical discussions that so much agitate our country, I have, nevertheless, believed him under the strongest prudential motives to do so; as he might, with perfect innocence, in discussing a political subject elsewhere, express an opinion which might afterwards cross his judicial path whilst on the Bench, place him in a delicate situation, and in public estimation cast a blot upon the sacred ermine." [1] In place of Smith, President Van Buren appointed, April 22, 1837, John McKinley of Alabama, a former United States Senator, then fifty-seven years of age.[2] The Bar in general considered the appointments to be entirely adequate; but the Whig politicians harshly criticized the choice of Southern men and of Democrats, in spite of the fact that, since the new Circuits were in the Southwest, it had been necessary to appoint lawyers from that region, and the further fact that there were then but two Judges on the Court (Wayne and McLean) from west of the Alleghanies or south of Virginia. The Whig fear that, since all the Judges (with the exception of Story and Thompson) had been appointed by Jackson and Van Buren, the decisions of the Court would respond to its politics seems to have been equally the Democratic hope; for the *Democratic Review*, newly established in Washington, said in February, 1838: "The late renovation in the constitution of this august body, by the creation of seven of the nine members under the auspices of the present Democratic ascendancy, may be regarded as the closing of an old and the

[1] *Niles Register*, LII, May 20, 1837. Chief Justice Taney wrote to Jackson, Sept. 12, 1838, that the more he saw of Catron the more he had been impressed "with the strength of his judgment, legal knowledge and high integrity of character. He is a most valuable acquisition . . . and will, I am confident, continue to rise in public estimation, as he was a stranger at the time of his appointment." *Jackson Papers MSS.* Henry Clay, on the other hand, remarked sarcastically in a letter of March 7, 1837: "And what Judges they will make!" *Clay*, IV.

[2] McKinley's nomination was sent to the Senate, Sept. 18, 1837, and was confirmed, Sept. 25.

opening of a new era in its history." [1] But, as in
every other instance in the history of the Court when
it has been either feared or hoped that it would divide
on party lines, the expectations of the politicians were
unfulfilled. The Court continued to decide its cases
without regard to party, and pursued its calm and
majestic course, protecting the National sovereignty,
the rights of the States, the rights of individuals and
the rights of property, uncontrolled by the political
views of its members or by the desires of officials at
whose hands the individual Judges had received their
appointments.

That the enlargement of the Court in numbers did
not have the effect of adding to its efficiency may be
inferred from a letter by Judge Story, at the end of the
1838 Term: "You may ask how the Judges got along
together? We made very slow progress, and did less
in the same time than I ever knew. The addition to
our number has most sensibly affected our facility as
well as rapidity of doing business. 'Many men of many
minds' require a great deal of discussion to compel
them to come to definite results; and we found ourselves often involved in long and very tedious debates.
I verily believe, if there were twelve Judges, we should
do no business at all, or at least very little." [2]

At this 1838 Term, two cases of historic importance
were presented. In *Rhode Island* v. *Massachusetts*,
12 Pet. 657, the Court was called upon for the first
time to decide whether it possessed jurisdiction under
the Constitution to decide a conflict between two

[1] To this remark, the *National Gazette* replied, Jan. 25, 1838 : "That is, the Supreme
Court has been renovated, since seven party men, including the apostate Federalist, Judge Taney gained access to it. Such opinions may suit an electioneering
official like the *Globe*, but they ill befit anything pretending to the dignity of a review." See also bitter Whig attack on the *Democratic Review* and its articles on
the Supreme Court, in *Amer. Monthly Mag.* (March, 1838), XI.
[2] *Story*, II, 296, letter of March 15, 1838.

States of the Union, involving a disputed boundary line and the sovereignty over disputed territory. On a motion to dismiss, argued by Daniel Webster and James T. Austin, Attorney-General of Massachusetts, the Court (Chief Justice Taney strongly dissenting) held that it had jurisdiction. That adherence to the doctrine of State-Rights was not peculiar to the Southern States was interestingly shown in this case by the argument of Austin, who questioned the Court's power to execute its judgment against the State. To this, Daniel Hazard, counsel for Rhode Island, very properly answered: "I could not help feeling great surprise when I heard the Attorney-General of Massachusetts so solemnly and portentously warning this Court of consequences, and expressing his anxious hopes that if it should decide against Massachusetts it will, for the honor of the Court and for the honor of the country, be sure to find some way to execute its decree. What! Does Massachusetts threaten? Is Massachusetts ready to become a nullifying State, and to set up her own will in defiance of the decrees of this Court and of the Constitution itself?" And the Court, through Judge Baldwin, took occasion to notice Austin's unfortunate argument, by saying at the conclusion of its opinion: "In the case of Olmstead, this Court expressed its opinion that if State Legislatures may annul the judgments of the Courts of the United States, and the rights thereby acquired, the Constitution becomes a solemn mockery, and the Nation is deprived of the means of enforcing its laws, by its own tribunal. So fatal a result must be deprecated by all; and the people of every State must feel a deep interest in resisting principles so destructive of the Union, and in averting consequences so fatal to themselves."

In *Kendall* v. *United States*, 12 Pet. 524, the Court

settled a serious controversy between the Executive
and the Judiciary, and established the power of the
Circuit Court of the District of Columbia to issue writ
of mandamus to Government officers — a power previously held not to be possessed by the Circuit Courts
of the United States.[1] The case had given rise to much
political feeling, which was plainly shown in the argument by Richard S. Coxe and Reverdy Johnson
against Francis Scott Key and Attorney-General Butler. Kendall, Jackson's Postmaster-General, had revoked the settlement of certain claims of postal con-
tractors made by his predecessors; thereupon, Congress had referred the claims to be adjusted and settled
by the Solicitor of the Treasury; the latter official
having allowed them, Kendall still refused to recognize
the claims (by President Jackson's order, so it was
said); whereupon, the Circuit Court of the District
issued a mandamus to the Postmaster-General. The
case took on the aspect of a struggle between the Court
and the President. It was argued by Key that this
was an attempt by the Court to control the Executive, or one of his officials, in the performance of an
Executive duty. Coxe retorted that the mandate of
the Judiciary had been disregarded in language "highly
menacing in its character" by an "insubordinate inferior who still hangs out the flag of defiance." Butler replied, deprecating the "very brilliant vituperative eloquence" of opposing counsel, and said that the
hall of the Supreme Court had hitherto "been regarded
as holy ground . . . one spot where questions of constitutional law could be discussed with calmness of
mind and liberality of temper . . . where it was usually deemed repugnant to good taste to offer as argument the outpourings of excited feeling or the creations

---

[1] *McIntyre* v. *Wood*, 7 Cranch, 504; *McClung* v. *Silliman*, 6 Wheat. 598.

of an inflamed imagination, and where vehement invective and passionate appeals, even though facts
existed which in some other forum might justify their
use, were regarded as sounds unmeet for the judicial
ear." The Court, through Judge Thompson, stated in
a striking and dignified opinion that it did not think
that the proceedings in the case interfered "in any
respect whatever with the rights or duties of the Executive, or that it involves any conflict of powers between the Executive and Judicial departments of the
Government." It held that the mandamus was properly issued to the Postmaster-General "to enforce the
performance of a mere ministerial act, which neither
he nor the President had any authority to deny or control"; that while "there are certain political duties
imposed upon many officers in the Executive department, the discharge of which is under the direction of
the President . . . it would be an alarming doctrine
that Congress cannot impose upon any Executive officer any duty they may think proper, which is not repugnant to any rights secured and protected by the
Constitution; and in such cases the duty and responsibility grow out of and are subject to the control of
the law, and not to the direction of the President."
The *National Intelligencer*, in reviewing this decision,
congratulated its readers "upon the spirit of independence and of resistance to the insidious encroachments of despotism which are embodied in it. . . .
This opinion confirms and fixes our respect for the
character of the Supreme Court and our reverence for
the principle of judicial independence, so intimately
blended in our mind with those of judicial integrity
and consistency. It will stand as a beacon to mark to
demagogues in office, for all future time, the point at
which their presumption and tyrannous disposition

will be rebuked and effectively stayed." [1] One episode connected with the opinion in this case does not appear in the official report, but is of striking interest, in view of the general belief among the Whigs that President Jackson considered that the Executive was not bound by the decisions of the Court and that he was an independent and coördinate branch of the Government, with a right to execute the laws and Constitution as he understood them. From a newspaper article which appeared years afterward,[2] it seems that the Court in the case of *Kendall* v. *Stokes* originally intended to controvert this doctrine of Jackson's, and that Judge Thompson had inserted in his opinion a very strong paragraph, which was read when the opinion was delivered in open Court, but which does not appear in the printed report except as follows:

It was urged at the bar that the Postmaster-General was alone subject to the direction and control of the President with respect to the execution of the duties imposed upon him by this law; and the right of the President is claimed as growing out of the obligation imposed upon him by the Constitution to take care that the laws be faithfully executed. This is a doctrine that cannot receive the sanction of this Court. It would be vesting in the President a dispensing power which has no countenance for its support in any part of the Constitution, and is asserting a principle which, if carried out in its results to all cases falling within it, would be clothing the President with a power entirely to control the legislation of Congress and paralyze the administration of justice.

When the opinion containing the above paragraph was read, Attorney-General Butler rose, and said that: "in that opinion, it had been stated that the obligation imposed on the President to see the laws faith-

---

[1] *National Intelligencer*, March 13, 1838.
[2] *National Intelligencer*, Oct. 14, 1854. See also *Public Men and Events* (1875), by Nathan Sargent.

fully executed implied a power to forbid their execution. For himself, he disclaimed such a doctrine . . . but he felt it to be a duty he owed to himself and the station he occupied to repudiate such a doctrine as contrary to his long-established opinions, and he hoped that the Court would either expunge that part of the opinion or so modify it as to exonerate him from the imputation of having asserted such a principle." Judge Thompson said he had "endeavored faithfully and impartially to state the arguments of counsel, but if he had fallen into error, in this respect, he was always willing to rectify it. In this case, the opinion as delivered had been submitted to all the Judges in conference, and no one had intimated that the argument had been misapprehended." Judges Baldwin, McKinley and Wayne stated that they had also understood counsel to make the assertion, now controverted; and Judge Wayne said that: "There was neither mistake nor misapprehension in the matter. He had heard the doctrine, as stated in the opinion, advanced by counsel, with equal astonishment and indignation. He had not supposed there was any intelligent man in the country so ignorant of the principles of our Government and institutions as to entertain such a principle; much less could he have anticipated that it would ever be advanced before that tribunal by distinguished professional gentlemen. He was, however, in favor of granting the application to modify the opinion of the Court in the matter adverted to; but he wished to be distinctly understood that it was upon one ground, and but one; which was, that no memorial should go down to posterity which would state that such a dangerous and unfounded doctrine had ever been addressed to and heard by the Supreme Court." Though the opinion was modified in conformity with Mr. Butler's request, it was stated by the *National Intelli-gencer*, in 1854, that the original opinion, as read, would be found in the handwriting of Mr. Justice Thompson, among the archives of the Court, and that it still showed how it stood before the alteration. "Thus," said the editor, "in the Tribunal of the highest resort under the Constitution were the prerogative claims and arbitrary constructions of his own power by Pres-ident Jackson stamped with the seal of condemnation, decisively, irreversibly, now and forever." [1]

Both the majority and the dissenting opinions be-came the subject of political attack.[2] President Van Buren took the very unusual step of criticizing the decision in his Annual Message to Congress, December 3, 1838, — a "decision which has resulted," he said, "in the judgment of money out of the National Treas-ury, for the first time since the establishment of the Government, by judicial compulsion exercised by the common law writ of mandamus . . . a decision founded upon a process of reasoning which, in my judgment, renders further legislative provision indispensable to the public interest and the equal administration of justice." The extraordinary result of the decision was, as he pointed out, that "the officers of the United States stationed in different parts of the United States are, in respect to the performance of their official duties, subject to different laws and to a different supervision. . . . In the District, their official conduct is subject to a judicial control from which in the States they are exempt, and a very different one. . . . Disparaging discrepancies in the law and in the administration of

<hr/>

[1] *National Intelligencer*, Oct. 14, 1854, which states that "the circumstances which we shall now relate have never before, that we know of, found their way into print, but which can be corroborated by the testimony of all who were present to witness them."

[2] *Taney*, 306, 317, letter to Richard Peters, March 27, 1838, declining to reply to attacks.

justice ought not to be permitted to continue." Congress
paid no attention to this recommendation, and the power
to issue writs of mandamus directed to Federal officials
still rests in the Court of the District of Columbia.[1]

At this Term, a curious episode occurred, in the refusal of the Judges (with the exception of Baldwin)
to attend the funeral of Congressman Jonathan Cilley
of Maine, to which, in accordance with the usual
custom, the Court had been invited. Cilley had been
killed in a duel with Congressman William J. Graves
of Kentucky — "the natural fruit of the ferocious
spirit manifested in Congressional debates during the
past few years", said the *National Gazette*.[2] The
Judges, in declining, passed a resolution which they
ordered recorded on the minutes of the Court, that
"with every desire to manifest their respect for the
House of Representatives and the Committee of the
House by whom they have been invited, the Justices
of the Supreme Court cannot, consistently with the
duties they owe to the public, attend in their official
character the funeral of one who has fallen in a duel."
"Whether they will be sustained by public opinion in
taking this stand," wrote Story, "is more than I can
pretend to conjecture. But we shall in any event be
satisfied with having done our duty, and our appropriate duty." [3]

[1] A bill to repeal the power of the Courts of the District of Columbia to issue
writs of mandamus passed the Senate in 1839.   That neither the Chief Justice, nor
the Court, however, were inclined to interfere with Executive officials unless the
official duty as to which mandamus was asked was clearly ministerial was made
perfectly plain when, two years later, it unanimously refused to grant a mandamus
against Van Buren's Secretary of the Navy, in *Decatur* v. *Paulding*, 14 Pet. 497,
on the ground that the duty involved was executive and not ministerial.   "The
interference of the Courts with the performance of the ordinary duties of the Executive departments of the government," said Taney, "would be productive of nothing but mischief; and we are quite satisfied that such a power was never intended
to be given to them." See also *Federal Judges and Quasi Judges*, by Edward B.
Whitridge, *Yale Law Journ.* (1896), VI.

[2] *National Gazette*, March 1, 3, 1838.   [3] *Story*, II, 289, letter of March 5, 1838.

At the 1839 Term, the Court was confronted with a question of immense consequence to the commercial development of the country — the power of a corporation to make a contract outside of the State in which it was chartered. It was presented in three cases argued together — *Bank of Augusta* v. *Earle, Bank of the United States* v. *Primrose* and *New Orleans and Carrollton R. R.* v. *Earle,* 13 Pet. 519. The three plaintiff banking corporations, one chartered in Georgia, one in Pennsylvania and one in Louisiana, having through agents in Alabama purchased or discounted bills of exchange in that State, the makers of the bills refused to pay them on the ground of want of power in the banking corporations to do any business in Alabama and outside their home States. This contention had been upheld by Judge McKinley, in the United States Circuit Court in Alabama, by a decision which produced surprise and consternation throughout the business world, and which was graphically commented upon by Judge Story in a letter to Charles Sumner. "My brother, McKinley, has recently made a most sweeping decision in the Circuit Court in Alabama which has frightened half the lawyers and all the corporations of the country out of their proprieties. He has held that a corporation created in one State has no power to contract (or, it would seem, even to act) in any other State, either directly or by an agent. So banks, insurance companies, manufacturing companies, etc., have no capacity to take or discount notes in another State, or to underwrite policies or to buy or sell goods. The cases in which he has made these decisions have gone to the Supreme Court. What say you to all this? So we go!" [1] As the Bank of the United

---

[1] *Sumner Papers MSS,* letter of June 17, 1838. A dispatch from Mobile in the *National Intelligencer,* April 28, 1838, said: "The decision produced great excite-

States (which, on the expiration of its Federal charter in 1836, had been incorporated by the State of Pennsylvania) and other moneyed corporations had, for many years, been in the habit of discounting bills in States throughout the country, the decision opened the door to widespread repudiation of their obligations by debtors. They at once took advantage of the defense thus offered to them. Manufacturing and trading corporations hesitated to continue to do business in outside States. Fire and life insurance companies, which were just beginning their development in the country, curtailed the writing of policies. General commercial confusion ensued; and the result of the decision was likely to be the more disastrous because of the fact that it came at a time when the effects of the great financial panic of 1837 were still being severely felt. The opinion of the Bar was almost unanimous against the decision, ex-Chancellor Kent giving a very strong adverse opinion.[1] On the other hand, the decision was hailed with enthusiasm by large sections of the Democratic, or Locofoco, Party who were anti-corporation men, and especially by the radical Jackson and Van Buren antagonists of the Bank of the United States who felt the decision to be "an aftermath of Jackson's mortal combat with the Bank."[2]

ment here and is the subject of general conversations and alarm. Its ruinous consequences, if it be sustained, can scarcely be imagined." The *Mobile Commercial Register* on the other hand, May 8, 1838, spoke of the decision on the rights of foreign corporations and said as to Judge McKinley: "The new Judge by his promptness, ability and urbanity has received an abiding popularity with the Bar and the suitors in the Court."

[1] See opinion of Kent in *Law Reporter* (July, 1838), I, 57; see also *Remarks on Chancellor Kent's Opinion*, by J. R., *ibid.*, 185.

[2] See *The Position of Foreign Corporations in American Constitutional Law* (1918), by Gerard C. Henderson, 42 *et seq.* The Bank's newspaper organ, the *National Gazette* in Philadelphia, even went so far as to intimate that the decision was intended as an attack on the Bank, and said, May 2, 1835: "The importance of this case does not appear to be duly estimated. . . . If this is a covert attack on the dead monster, we suspect that it proceeds from that infusion of Democracy into the Judiciary of which Mr. Dallas boasted."

The supporters of State banks also welcomed the chance that the lucrative business of the Bank of the United States might now be monopolized by them, as a result of the decision.

The case was argued in the Supreme Court on January 30, 31, February 1, 2, 9, 1839, by David B. Ogden, John Sergeant and Daniel Webster for the banks, against Charles J. Ingersoll, William H. Crawford of Georgia and Van de Gruff of Alabama. "We consider it," said a leading Whig paper, "one of the most important questions to the Union of the States, affecting the commercial intercourse which binds them together, that can arise." [1] Another Whig paper, in New York, describing the argument, said that the Court-room was "thronged to overflowing with as brilliant and intelligent an audience as ever met within the walls of a single room. A case of immense importance, not to the parties concerned, but to the whole country, was to be argued. . . . The importance attached to this decision is that upon it rests the business of a large class of commercial men and the practice of numerous corporations. . . . Mr. Webster has gone to the foundation of the question and discussed it constitutionally, legally and socially. The most interesting and eloquent part of his argument, the peroration excepted which was singularly striking and effective with the Court, was a statement of the constitutional and social relationship of the States and the Union one to another. . . . There were also some fine passages of eloquence conceived and spoken in the peculiar vein of this great-minded pleader." And the *National Intelligencer* said : "When we say that the argument which we have heard was profoundly learned,

[1] *Madisonian* (Wash., D. C.), Feb. 2, 1839; *New York Express,* Feb. 15, 1839; *National Intelligencer,* Feb. 11, 1839.

as well as original and luminously illustrated, we express no more than everyone has a right to expect from the great New England jurist and legislator." The arguments took a very wide range over the financial, economic and social conditions of the United States. "A learned gentleman on the other side said, the other day, that he thought he might regard himself in this cause as having the country for his client," said Webster. "I agree with the learned gentleman, and I go indeed far beyond him, in my estimate of the importance of this case to the country. . . . For myself, I see neither limit nor end to the calamitous consequences of such a decision. I do not know where it would not reach, what interests it would not disturb, or how any part of the commercial system of the country would be free from its influences, direct or remote. . . . The decision, now under revision by this Court is, in its principle, anti-commercial and anti-social, new and unheard of in our system, and calculated to break up the harmony which has so long prevailed among the States and people of this Union. . . . But it is for you, Mr. Chief Justice and Judges, on this, as on other occasions of high importance, to speak and to decide for the country. The guardianship of her commercial interests; the preservation of the harmonious intercourse of all her citizens; the fulfilling, in this respect, of the great object of the Constitution, are in your hands; and I am not in doubt that the trust will be so performed as to sustain at once the high National objects and the character of this tribunal." And Ogden portrayed in his argument the commercial complications which would ensue. "The proposition in the Circuit Court," he said, "is that a corporation of one State can do no commercial business, can make no contract and can do nothing in any State of the Union

but in that in which by the law of the State it has been
created. This proposition is the more injurious, as
in the United States associated capital is essentially
necessary to the operations of commerce and the creation and improvement of the facilities of intercourse,
which can only be accomplished by large means. . . .
One of the most important objects and interests for the
preservation of the Union is the establishment of railroads. Cannot the railroad corporations of New York,
Pennsylvania or Maryland make a contract out of the
State for materials for the construction of a railroad?
Cannot these companies procure machinery to use on
their railroads, in another State?'' On the other side,
Charles J. Ingersoll delivered a vigorous anti-corporation argument, pointing out the danger of increasing
the power of corporations in this country, and insist-
ing that a State ought not to be forced, by any doctrine
of comity or otherwise, to allow a corporation of another
State to do business within its borders: ''It is confidently submitted to this Court that it will best fulfill its duties by holding the States united by sovereign
ties; by the State remaining sovereign and the corporations subject; not by sovereign corporations and
subject States. . . . If Courts are bound by common
law to restrict corporations to the specific purposes of
their creation, they are bound by the same common
law to prevent their wandering out of place, as much
as out of purpose. . . . As to the ruinous consequences denounced . . . such have always been au-
gured, and always will be, of measures offensive to
certain political prejudices. They are abundantly
disproved by the improvement and prosperity of the
country. The Court, instead of being alarmed from
its duty, by such appeals, should feel encouraged to
support the laws of State sovereignty, which, well

understood, were the broad foundations of the general welfare. Neither man nor State can stand erect without these self-preserving rights, against which the pleas of comity and cries of politics are equally futile and unavailing in this Court as now constituted."

A vivid picture of the political aspect of the case from the Democratic standpoint was given by the *Washington Globe*, which stated that after Judge McKinley's "strikingly just and proper" decision in the lower Court, "the Bank press forthwith opened its batteries of abuse, not only against the judgment, but the character and purity of the Judge who gave it. Wall Street was conspicuous in these calumnies, stimulated by which, a great corporation had the audacity to procure and publish the opinion of an old Federal lawyer of New York, of course condemning Judge McKinley's opinion out and out, in order to forestall that of the Supreme Court here." After describing Ingersoll's argument in the Court demolishing Ogden's "tissue of arrogant technicality", it stated that "Judge McKinley fortunately arrived and took his seat on the Bench, just in time to hear a complete vindication of his position, and a conclusive argument against the right of these money-mongering monsters to stray from their spheres and invade the quiet regions of distant States, there to ravage, monopolize and *destroy*. Messrs. Clay, Webster and Sergeant were all in attendance, the two latter busily taking notes of Mr. Ingersoll's thorough exposition of legal, political and economical principles, which, if we are not mistaken, have inflicted the *coup de grace* on, at any rate, *wandering* corporations. Vagabond banks are in a fair way to be chained up, to bite and bark only at their own houses. The Court-room was crowded with a brilliant audience of both sexes and from all parts, many of whose countenances seemed to respond to Mr. Ingersoll's argument, of many hours' duration, in favor of a recurrence to first principles, and upholding them against the speculations of upstart combinations and their advocates. What a blessing it would be if the Judiciary should interpose to administer law upon the wrongdoers whose rapacity has so deeply encroached on the best interests and institutions of the country !"

This highly improper animadversion on the Court was noticed by Webster in his argument; and the *National Intelligencer* stated that: "With the solemnity which well became the magnitude of the questions at issue, Mr. Webster alluded in an impressive manner to the indignity offered to the Court by a publication in a newspaper of this city, since the opening of the argument in this very case; and repelled with a proper indignation the attempt from that quarter to dictate to the Court, and almost to command what judgment it should render in the premises." [1]

Within two weeks, Chief Justice Taney rendered an opinion, in which it was held that while no corporation could make a contract in a State outside of its home State, without the sanction express or implied of the outside State, nevertheless, under the law of comity among nations which prevailed among the several sovereignties of the Union, power to make such contract was to be presumed in the absence of any prohibition by the outside State. In other words, while recognizing the right of a State to exclude foreign corporations, the Court would not assume that such right had been exercised, unless its exercise were clearly shown. A singular misunderstanding as to the exact

[1] *Washington Globe*, Feb. 1, 1839; *Ohio Statesman*, Feb. 8, 1839; *National Intelligencer*, Feb. 11, 1839; the *National Gazette*, April 6, 1839, referred to the "terms of vilest insolence" in the *Globe's* article, which, it stated, emanated from Postmaster-General Amos Kendall.

scope of the opinion of the Court prevailed for some time in the press. The Whig newspapers hailed it as a just rebuke to Democratic doctrines and to Democratic politicians, and were delighted that it had been rendered by a Court composed of appointees of two Democratic Presidents.[1] Thus, the *National Gazette* said: "The result of this decision by the Supreme Court, which so utterly disregarded the Kitchen's decree, shows that its revolutionary doctrines are repudiated in that high place, and that patriotism may still find a tribunal high above the destructive and depraving influence of party." The *National Intelligencer* considered that the anti-corporation feeling in the country was merely a symbol of Locofocoism, which it defined as "the levelling or pulling down principle" — "the enmity to the established order of things", "the disposition to set the poor against the rich, the idle against the industrious, the unruly against the law-abiding and finally the State government against the government of the Union." Misinterpreting the decision of the Court to mean that a State could not exclude a foreign corporation, it hailed the decision as a check and a signal rebuke to Locofocoism "in its most towering and ambitious flight", and "in its first attempt to wrest the judicial authority to its aid"; and it exulted "that there is in our political system a barrier, which power cannot break down nor party undermine. This decision, following that in the mandamus case at the preceding Term of the Court, has given increased confidence to our glorious institutions, and doubled the security of the tenure by which every individual in the community holds his life, his liberty and his property. . . . It has shown to us, by one bright example more, the inappreciable

[1] *National Gazette*, April 6, 1839; *New York Express*, March 12, 1839.

value of an independent Judiciary." A New York
Whig paper said: "The reversal is one of the happiest
and best omens of the signs of the times. Important
as is every election, and of the gravest importance as
are sometimes the appeals to the Ballot Box, yet they
all dwindle into comparative insignificance, when contrasted with some great principle now and then brought
before that High Tribunal, the Supreme Court, upon
a proper and just settlement of which hang both the
Constitution and the Union of the States. Such a
principle was this, in substance, whether a corporation
of a State can maintain a suit or a contract, or collect
a debt, in the Courts of another State or in the Courts
of the United States. If such debts and contracts
were not binding, it is certain the Union would be of
little value for any of the purposes of commerce; and
if an individual could thus nullify a contract, the States
would hardly be as well off, the one to the other, as any
State and a foreign Government." And this prominent
Whig representative actually admitted that Taney
was not to be as greatly feared as the Whigs had apprehended: "The progress of Locofocoism, as it took its
strides from the Palace to the Capitol, we feared had
reached the Supreme Court. Mr. Justice McKinley,
the country saw, was infected by it. The course of
Mr. Taney as Secretary of the Treasury naturally
created a great deal of apprehension as to the course
of Mr. Chief Justice Taney; and it was feared, and
greatly feared, that the fabric of constitutional law
which the great Marshall had so long been rearing
would be demolished at once by a new impression of
Locofocoism upon the Supreme Bench. In the words
of Mr. Webster then, 'we breathe freer and deeper'
upon the discovery that such is not the fact. The
Supreme Court is yet sound; and much as we cherish

Whig victories, yet we cherish this Conservative victory much more; it is the triumph of the Constitution and the Union again." "We are rejoiced that the march of agrarianism which had reached the ermine, has been stayed by the Supreme Court," said another Whig paper, "in the reversals, by that tribunal, of Judge McKinley, who is of the *Globe* and C. J. Ingersoll School, in his hostility to banks. The decisions of Judge McKinley struck at the root of all commercial intercourse between the States, and if they had not been reversed must have utterly annihilated it." "The decision will give great satisfaction to the business community at large. It will increase the confidence of the people in the purity and independence of the Court. The insolent organ of the Executive has found its attempts at dictation in this instance repelled," said a leading commercial paper.[1] "Your opinion in the corporation cases," wrote Judge Story to Taney, "has given very general satisfaction to the public, and I hope you will allow me to say that I think it does great honor to yourself, as well as to the Court."[2] "It is a most consolatory reflection," wrote Joseph R. Ingersoll to Charles Sumner, "that while the Executive Department is likely to be imbued with too popular a hue, the fears of Judicial radicalism have not been realized. Your professional feelings will be gratified at the combined judgment in the Ala-

---

[1] *National Gazette*, April 16, 1839; *Madisonian*, March 13, 1839; *Boston Daily Advertiser*, March 13, 1839, quoting *New York Commercial Advertiser;* see also *New York Courier*, March 12, 1839: "The opinion read by Chief Justice Taney is as far from Loco-Foco doctrine as Alexander Hamilton himself could have desired." The *Mobile Commercial Register*, March 19, 1839, pointed out that the report of the decision in the *National Intelligencer* was not to be trusted, inasmuch as all Whig political papers were inclined to color their reports. "Anything which aims a blow at the sovereignty of the States, or goes to justify Mr. Jefferson's apprehensions of the Supreme Court that it tended to federal consolidation, chimes with their wishes and accords with the public lives of its editors."

[2] *Taney*, 288, letter from Story, April 19, 1839.

bama case. If the Judiciary remain strong in principle and conduct, and no recall shall take place of the
reign of Jacksonism, the necessity for *dent operam
consules* will not arise." [1]

On the other hand, the Democratic, or Locofoco,
papers equally misconceiving the scope of the decision,
attacked the Court for the "deadly blow to the rights
of the States" in the sanction given "by this august
tribunal, of the vandal overrunning by these paper
corporations of the policy and laws and Constitutions
of the sovereign States." An Alabama paper said
that it was unwilling to believe that the Court had
announced a doctrine "subversive of the dearest rights
of the States" and that it was confident that the
Court would "protect States-rights and personal rights
from being swallowed up by the encroachments of
chartered companies." A radical Pennsylvania paper
stated that : "We are not prepared to submit to this doctrine. We are prepared to take our stand, now and
forever, against it. We are ready to battle for the
rights, the inalienable rights of the People; and the
first blow that we strike is against the *Life Judiciary
of the United States* — the judicial noblemen of America." Little support was given through the country
to such revolutionary talk; and it was well said, in
reply, in the *National Intelligencer* that "this is war
against the Constitution", and that without the safeguard of an independent Judiciary "all the reservations to the States and to the People contained in the
Constitution, would be no more worth than the strip
of parchment on which they are engrossed, and our
Government would become one vast, illimitable and
unfathomable despotism." [2] It is interesting to note

---

[1] *Sumner Papers MSS*, letter of April 22, 1839.

[2] *Mobile Commercial Register*, March 11, 19, 1839; on May 14, it said that it
was "agreeably disappointed" and that the decision "leaves us in the enjoyment

that this Democratic diatribe, leveled against a Democratic Court and a Chief Justice appointed by Jackson, is of almost exactly the same tenor as that previously made against a Federalist Court and Chief Justice appointed by Adams. The incident affords again a striking proof that contentment with the Court's decisions did not depend upon the political composition of the Court.

The fact is that the decision did not wholly satisfy the extremists of either party.[1] On the one hand, the Chief Justice denied Webster's contention that a corporation of one State was entitled to the constitutional rights and privileges of a citizen of another State; on the other hand, he refused to adopt the defendant's contention that a foreign corporation had no power whatever to do business outside of its own State. By his rejection of the extreme Nationalistic views, he saved to the States the vital right to say what corporations should do business within their boundaries, and on what terms.[2] In emphatically proclaiming the power of a State by express action to repudiate the principle of comity and to refuse recognition to a foreign corporation, he gave sanction to the immense mass of State legislation regulating foreign corporations which followed in later years. The views held by the Court, however, as to the status of a corporation outside the boundaries of its home State produced con-

of much of our constitutional right which we had been led to apprehend had been entirely swept away." *National Intelligencer*, April 18, 1839, quoting a *Harrisburg Reporter* editorial, which, it said, was "in the true Locofoco spirit, upon the decision of the Supreme Court, showing the exasperation of that party at being foiled by the firmness of the Judges of the Supreme Court in their attempt to obtain its sanction to their levelling and demoralizing doctrines."

[1] Bitter criticisms of the opinion were made by the leading anti-bank counsel, Charles J. Ingersoll, to which, however, a prominent Pennsylvania colleague at the Bar, Henry D. Gilpin, retorted that "he should not be worried at his inability to defeat a corporation, when the whole country had to bear them, as Sinbad had his burden." *Life of Charles J. Ingersoll* (1897), by William M. Meigs.

[2] *Roger B. Taney*, by William W. Mikell, *Great American Lawyers* (1908), IV.

siderable confusion in the law, and the invention of
legal fictions as to implied consent to extraterritorial
service in case of suits against foreign corporations
actually doing business in outside States.[1]

Two other cases connected with the commercial
development of the country may be briefly noted. In
Stokes v. *Saltonstall*, 13 Pet. 181, there appeared for
the first time a subject which has later filled the reports — negligence of a common carrier (in this case,
a stage-coach owner).[2] In *Smith* v. *Richards*, 13 Pet.
26, there occurred the first case connected with mining,
and involving alleged fraud in the sale of a Virginia
gold mine. The arguments on January 23, 24, by Webster and John J. Crittenden (the Senator from Kentucky), were interestingly described in the press as
follows: "The Supreme Court has been the scene of
attraction today. . . . Mr. Crittenden is a volume of
pungent satyre, and whether the Senator or the Lawyer, he wields his satyrical weapons in a manner the
most effective. He has eloquence, too, of a high order;
he is as well read in law as politics, and always looks
'quite through the deeds of men.' Mr. Webster drew
a great crowd to hear him and will fill the Supreme
Court-room tomorrow. He is more of a giant at the
bar than in the forum, and never appears so well as
when discussing great principles of law and equity.
No one becomes tired of hearing him, and the dull-
est plodder listens to him with interest and attention.
. . . Webster concluded his argument. He was Dan-

---

[1] See *The Position of Foreign Corporations in American Constitutional Law* (1918),
by Gerard C. Henderson; see also *State Control of Foreign Corporations*, by G. W.
Wickersham, in *Kentucky State Bar Ass. Report* (1909). See also for résumé of
the effect of the decision, *Runyon* v. *Coster* (1840), 14 Pet. 122. It is to be noted
that the decision had no practical effect in behalf of foreign corporations in Alabama, for that State immediately passed a statute forbidding transaction of business by agents of foreign banks.

[2] The first case on the docket of the Court in which a railroad was a party was a
patent case in 1840 — *Philadelphia & Trenton R. R.* v. *Stimpson*, 14 Pet. 448.

iel Webster to the last, clear, logical, powerful, with all the simplicity of a child and backed by the strength of a giant. The Court-room was thronged to hear him." [1]

In *Ex Parte Hennen*, 13 Pet. 230, a topic on which much political controversy has raged in this country was involved — the power of removal from office. The Court, having been asked to issue a mandamus to the District Court to restore the Clerk of the Court to office, held that in the absence of constitutional or statutory regulation, "it would seem to be a sound and necessary rule to consider the power of removal as incident to the power of appointment" and that "it was very early adopted as the practical construction of the Constitution that the power was vested in the President alone" with reference to all Presidential appointees. It refused the mandamus, saying that "if the Judge is chargeable with any abuse of his power, this is not the tribunal to which he is amenable." [2]

The 1840 Term, in the closing years of Van Buren's Administration, was not marked by notable cases, but there were two which exercised an important influence on the country's history.[3]

[1] *New York Express*, Jan. 25, 28, 1839. In his dissenting opinion (concurred in by Judges McLean and Baldwin) Judge Story used the following picturesque language: "In my opinion the appellant stands acquitted of fraud, the victim, if you please, of a heated and deluded imagination, indulging in golden dreams; but in this respect, he is in the same predicament with the appellee."

[2] Two matters relating to the practice of the Court may be noted. For the first time, by Rule 46, all motions were required to be reduced to writing and to contain a brief statement of the facts and objects of the motion. Theretofore it had been one of the duties of the Associate Justice for the Fourth Circuit to attend in Washington on the first Monday of August annually "to make orders respecting the business of the Supreme Court." This duty was now abolished by the Act of Feb. 28, 1839, c. 36. "For many years past, the business of the Court had been entirely *pro forma* requiring neither attendance of counsel nor decision by the Court, and the attendance of the Judge has not always been deemed necessary." *Niles Register*, LIV, Aug. 4, 1838.

[3] *Story*, II, 327–328, Judge Story wrote, Feb. 6, 9, 1840: "We are going on steadily in the Supreme Court with our business. None of it is of very great public interest, but there have been a few questions of a commercial nature of considerable

In *United States* v. *Gratiot*, 14 Pet. 526, the plenary power of the United States over its public lands, even when situated in the States, was firmly upheld, and the power of Congress to lease lead mines on public lands in the State of Illinois (and the Territory of Wisconsin) and formerly in the Territory of Indiana was sustained. Thomas H. Benton had contended that the original States would never have ceded to the United States the lands in this territory, "if Congress were to have the power to establish a tenantry to the United States upon them. The State-Rights principles would have resisted this: no lands would have been ceded." Under the Constitution, he said, the lands are "to be disposed of" by Congress, not "held by the United States." The Court held that "there can be no apprehensions of any encroachments upon State-Rights by the creation of a numerous tenantry within their borders, as has been so strenuously urged in the argument"; and that the right to dispose of the lands meant disposal at the discretion of Congress and included a lease as well as a sale. The importance of this decision upon the future control and conservation of public lands is evident.

Following this case upholding the power of the Federal Government came another of importance, *Holmes* v. *Jennison*, 14 Pet. 540. In this, though the suit was dismissed for want of jurisdiction, a superbly able opinion was given by Chief Justice Taney (concurred in by Judges Story, McLean and Wayne), asserting

importance. . . . The nomination of Harrison runs like wild-fire on the prairies. It astonishes all persons, friends and foes. The general impression here is that he will certainly be chosen President. Mr. Webster told me last evening that there was not the slightest doubt of it. The Administration party are evidently in great alarm, and some are preparing to leap overboard before the ship sinks. In the meantime, the farmers of the West are beginning to feel the public pressure most severely. All their produce is at a very low price, money is exceedingly scarce and business at a dead stand. . . . What I most anxiously desire is, to see a President who shall act as President of the country, and not as a mere puppet of party."

the exclusive authority of the Federal Government to control the foreign relations of the United States, and denying the power of a State to surrender to a foreign nation a fugitive criminal found within the State. The case involved the right of the Governor of Vermont to order the delivery to the Canadian authorities of a Canadian murderer, no extradition treaty with Great Britain being then in existence, and the Vermont State Court having sustained the Governor in his order to send the fugitive back to Canada.[1] "This involves an inquiry into the relative powers of the Federal and State governments, upon a subject which is sometimes one of great delicacy," said Taney, the principle to be decided in which "in times of war and of great public excitement may reach cases where great public interests are concerned and where the surrender may materially affect the peace of the Union. . . . It was one of the main objects of the Constitution to make us, so far as regarded our foreign relations, one people and one nation; and to cut off all communications between foreign governments and the several State Governments." In using this prophetic language, Taney undoubtedly had in mind the somewhat strained relations already existing between the United States and Canada and Great Britain; for, two years before, an expedition from Canada had invaded New York in December, 1837, and had burned the steamer *Caroline*, and killed an American citizen. There had been vigorous diplomatic negotiations over the episode. Within one year after the decision in the *Holmes Case*, the

[1] The *Pennsylvanian*, March 14, 1839, quoted the *Burlington Sentinel* (Vt.): "We understand that the President (Van Buren) has declined acting upon the application for surrender of Dr. Holmes and referred the subject to Gov. Jennison. We understand the position taken at Washington to be that, inasmuch as neither the Constitution nor the laws of Congress provide for the case at all, it must rest on the ground of mere comity between the British provinces and the adjoining States, and therefore the decision should be left to the State authorities."

indictment and trial in New York of McLeod for murder in connection with this expedition, and the refusal
of the State of New York to yield her rights even at
the request of the United States Government, had
brought the United States and Great Britain to the
verge of war. The most striking feature, however, of
Taney's notable opinion was the fact that it sustained
the supremacy of the powers of the Federal Government, with a breadth and completeness which had been
excelled by no one of Marshall's opinions. While,
therefore, it was naturally received with enthusiasm
by men like Judge Story, who wrote that it "is a masterly one and does his sound judgment and discrimination very great credit. . . . I entirely concurred
in that opinion with all my heart; and was surprised
that it was not unanimously adopted", the opinion
was criticized by Democrats. And James Buchanan
stated in the Senate that he had " always entertained
the highest respect for the present Chief Justice of the
United States; but I must say, and I am sorry in my
very heart to say it, that some portions of his opinion
in the case are latitudinous and centralizing beyond anything I have ever read in any other judicial opinion." [1]

The next Term, beginning in January, 1841, was
held at an exciting period in American history. The
twelve years of the Democratic Administrations of
Jackson and Van Buren, with their long contests
against banking and corporate monopolies, had come
to an end. New problems and new conditions appeared likely to confront the country under the leadership of the Whig President, Harrison; and control of
Congress by the Whigs rendered it probable that the

---

[1] *Taney*, 290, letter of Story to Richard Peters, May, 1840; *27th Cong., 2d Sess.,
App.*, speeches in the Senate of Buchanan, May 9, 1842, Robert J. Walker of Mississippi, June 21, 1842.

virulent attacks on Jacksonian policies would moderate. It is interesting to note, however, that so fully had Jackson's appointees on the Court satisfied the country, that political criticism of its decisions had already almost entirely disappeared. It was, therefore, with expectations on all sides of a period of comparative political calm in all branches of the Government that the Court convened. "I hope that the Court will have a harmonious session," wrote Story, "and I am sure that the Chief Justice and a majority of my brethren will do all that is proper to accomplish the purpose. The change in the Administration will produce no change in my own conduct. I mean to stand by the Court, and do all I can to sustain its dignity and the public confidence in it. Indeed, I should think myself utterly inexcusable, if I could be brought to act otherwise." [1] The most important case decided at this Term, however, brought the Court into contact with a dangerous political issue, when, in *Groves* v. *Slaughter*, 15 Pet. 449, for the first time opinions were elicited from the Judges on the subject of the respective powers of the States and of the Federal Government over the introduction of slaves within State borders. Though it was this case on which, after the Mexican War, the slavery men in Congress rested their arguments in behalf of Squatter Sovereignty and Territorial and State control of slavery, the actual decision of the Court, nevertheless, was rendered on a point distinct from the slavery issue. [2] The Constitution of

[1] *Story*, II, 341, letter to Richard Peters, Jr., Dec. 4, 1840.

[2] For interesting citations and discussions of *Groves* v. *Slaughter* in Congress, see *29th Cong., 2d Sess.*, speeches of Burt of South Carolina, Jan. 14, 1847, and Bowdon of Alabama, Jan. 16, 1847; *30th Cong., 1st Sess.*, speech of Bayly of Virginia, Aug. 3, 1848, saying: "In that case was discussed the extent of the power of Congress over what is familiarly called the internal slavetrade . . . it went to the Supreme Court; it was there decided; and the decision has tended greatly to put an end to the agitation growing out of it." See also speeches of Hunter and Clay, in the House, Aug. 23, 1850. *31st Cong., 1st Sess.*

Mississippi of 1832 had declared that "the introduction of slaves into this State as merchandise or for sale shall be prohibited from and after the first day of May, 1833."[1] The question before the Court was whether a note given for the purchase of such slaves after that date was void, and, if so, whether the State Constitution itself was invalid, as conflicting with the power of Congress over interstate commerce. The presence of the latter question in the case was the cause of the splendid array of counsel — United States Attorney-General Henry D. Gilpin and Robert J. Walker of Mississippi appearing for the State against Henry Clay and Daniel Webster "the Ajax and Achilles of the Bar" (as their associate counsel, Walter Jones, termed them). The argument was elaborate, lasting for seven days, from February 12 to 19, 1841. "Very many of the distinguished counsellors of the country were present and scores of men eminent in other professions; the ladies occupied all the vacant seats of the Court-room and crowded everyone but the Judges and counsel out of the bar," said a newspaper account. "Mr. Clay spoke for some three hours, and with a patient audience to the end. With a jury, he would be irresistible. With grave Judges to address, of course he is less successful; but many who heard him today pronounced his argument to be a very able one. Mr. Webster followed. The Senate Chamber has

[1] It may be noted, as a curious sidelight upon this Mississippi case, that the State prohibition of the introduction of slaves for sale was a financial rather than a slavery measure. Owing to the great financial difficulties into which that State had been plunged, its Governor had recommended such prohibition in order to check the drain of capital away from the State, through withdrawal to other States of the purchase price of slaves so introduced. The decision of *Groves* v. *Slaughter* in the lower Court, declaring that the note was void, it was said by a Natchez paper, "will have an important bearing on Northern negro debts to the amount of at least $2,000,000." See *Law Reporter* (Feb., 1840), II; and see *Washington Globe*, May 16, 1838, March 28, 1839; also see *History of the People of the United States*, by John Bach McMaster, VI, 398, for vivid pictures of the conditions of financial distress, bankruptcy and repudiation in Mississippi.

presented a beggarly account of empty boxes through
this week thus far, in consequence of the interesting
trial going on in the Court-room. . . . Many come
to mark the contrast between Mr. Clay's and Mr. Webster's mode of address. . . . As usual, Mr. Webster
wasted not a word. He spoke about two hours, with
a closeness of logic no other man in the country can
equal. There was not the least attempt at display,
and a child of ten years could have kept the run of the
whole case. It is a curious case under our complex
Government. Mr. Clay says that two or three million
dollars depend on it. Among the auditors was John
Quincy Adams, intent throughout, who, for a wonder,
deserted the Representative wing of the Capitol in
business hours, for once." [1] Many contemporaries
believed that Walter Jones, who appeared as the associate of Clay and Webster, was fully their equal in legal ability. "A small, spare man of insignificant appearance, with plain features, except his eyes, which
for piercing intelligence and shrewdness of expression
I have never seen surpassed, his mental activity spoke
in them. His voice was a thin, high pitched one, and
he was without any pretension to grace of manner.
Few men who occupied prominent places in the pro-

[1] *New York Express*, Feb. 19, 23, 1841. The *Southern Patriot* (Charleston, S. C.),
March 4, 1841, said that the Court-room was crowded "in consequence of the
great display of argument and eloquence. Mr. Clay made a splendid argument.
He connected it a little with the popular topic of abolition, intimating that his
view of the question was the anti-abolition view." Adams wrote in his diary,
Feb. 19, 1841: "I left the House, and went into the Supreme Court, and heard the
argument of Mr. Webster on the second Mississippi Slavery case, and the closing
argument of Mr. Walker, the Senator from Mississippi, in reply. The question is
whether a State of this Union can constitutionally prohibit the importation within
her borders of slaves as merchandise. Mr. Walker threatened tremendous consequences if this right should be denied to the State — all of which consequences
sounded to me like argument for the constitutional authority to prohibit it in all
the States, and for the exercise of it." Senator Westcott of Florida, July 25, 1848,
described Robert J. Walker's argument as "in my judgment never excelled by any
made in that Court for masterly ability, profound learning and accomplished eloquence." *30th Cong., 1st Sess.*

fession were ever listened to with more interest than
Mr. Jones," wrote a fellow member of the Federal Bar.
"His fluency was only equalled by the choiceness of
his language. He was so deliberate, so quiet that perhaps fluency does not accurately describe his oratory.
He was one of the closest reasoners. He never spoke
at random. His style was simplicity itself." [1]

The case appeared to present questions of a most
explosive nature, and to require the Court to decide
whether, if negro slaves were articles of commerce, the
State Constitution was repugnant to the Commerce
Clause of the Federal Constitution; or, if slaves were
persons, whether they were citizens of the United States
whose constitutional rights had been infringed by the
State Constitution. A decision on the latter question
would have caused the Court to confront, in 1841, the
same mighty problem which was to come before it,
fifteen years later, in the *Dred Scott Case.* When,
however, on March 10, 1841, three weeks after the argument, the Court gave its decision, it found itself
fortunately able to avoid the slavery issue, since a ma-

---

[1] *Life and Times of John H. B. Latrobe* (1917), by John E. Semmes; see also,
for a picturesque description of Walter Jones, *The Black Book or a Continuation of
Travels in the United States* (1828), by Mrs. Anne Royall, 127. A correspondent
of the *Boston Post,* Jan. 30, 1839, wrote: "He is a great lawyer, as eccentric in his
dress as John Randolph. The other day he appeared in Court in gray, and a
stranger would sooner have taken him for a Georgia cracker than the eminently
great lawyer." A correspondent of the *New York Tribune* wrote, Feb. 4, 1850, of
him: "The rival of Pinkney and Wirt and Webster and other leading counsel in past
days. As a common law counsellor, he excelled them all in depth and variety of
learning. He has received enormous fees in former times, and has had several
large legacies; but is now without fortune, and still engaged in practice, though
he must be more than seventy years old. He speaks slowly and in a low tone, but
with great purity of diction and clearness of thought. There is, however, a great
want of force in his manner, and few listen to him. Some years ago, a citizen of
Ohio, after being in Court during an argument of General Jones, said to one of his
acquaintances that he had witnessed that day the greatest curiosity which had
ever met his observation; he had heard a man talk for two hours in his sleep! The
appearance and dress of this distinguished and worthy gentleman are most peculiar, and it would be hardly fair to describe them. He is universally respected, and,
by those who know him, warmly beloved." See also *Gen. Walter Jones,* by Joseph
Packard, *Virg. Law Reg.* (1901), VII.

jority of the Judges, Thompson, Taney, Baldwin and
Wayne (two Northern and two Southern men), agreed
in holding that, on a proper construction of the language of the State Constitution, statutory legislation
was contemplated and necessary before it could take
effect, and that hence, as no such legislation had been
enacted, the decision of the Circuit Court in favor of
the validity of the notes in question was correct. Judge
Thompson in delivering the opinion stated that as the
Court had reached the above conclusion, it became
unnecessary to inquire if the State Constitution was
repugnant to the Federal Constitution.[1] Judge Mc-
Lean, an ardent anti-slavery man, however, felt that
it was his duty to express his views on the slavery question. "As one view of this case," he said, "involves
the construction of the Constitution of the United
States in a most important part, and in regard to its
bearing upon a momentous and most delicate subject,
I will state in a few words my own views on that branch
of the case . . . and although the question I am to
consider is not necessary to a decision of the case, yet
it is so intimately connected with it, and has been so
elaborately argued, that under existing circumstances,
I deem it fit and proper to express my opinion upon
it."[2] He, thereupon, entered into a defense of the

[1] Judge Catron was ill and did not sit; Judge Barbour was present at the argument, but died before the decision. Baldwin, alone of all the Judges, was of opinion that the power to regulate introduction of slaves was vested solely in Congress.
Judge Story and Judge McKinley dissented, holding the notes void, but were of
the opinion that the Federal Constitution did not interfere with the provisions of
the State Constitution.

[2] From the diary entry by John Quincy Adams in his *Memoirs*, X, March 10,
1841, the decisions were rendered in a different way from that in which they are
reported in 15 Peters, and it would appear that Taney (instead of Thompson) read
the opinion of the Court. Adams' account is as follows: "The Chief Justice read
an opinion upon the Mississippi Slavery Case, whereupon Judge McLean took from
his pocket and read a counter-opinion, unexpectedly to the other Judges, to which
the Judges, Thompson, Baldwin, and McKinley severally replied, each differing
from all the others. About one, the Court adjourned without delay."

right of his native State of Ohio to exclude slaves, saying that : "Each State has a right to protect itself against
the avarice and intrusion of the slave dealer; to guard
its citizens against the inconveniences and dangers
of a slave population. The right to exercise this
power by a State is higher and deeper than the Constitution. The evil involves the prosperity and may
endanger the existence of a State. Its power to guard
against, or to remedy the evil, rests upon the law of
self-preservation; a law vital to every community,
and especially to a sovereign State." These were
the plainest and boldest words on the slavery question which had yet been uttered by a Judge of the
Court, and while gratifying the anti-slavery men of the
North as an indorsement of their efforts to prevent the
spread of slavery, Judge McLean's dictum was equally
satisfactory to the slavery party and to the South, who
regarded it as a confirmation of their contention that
they had exclusive power to regulate all questions affecting slavery within their borders. "All the abolitionists who respect the unanimous opinion of the
Supreme Court will now abandon so much of their petitions as call on Congress to regulate or prohibit transportation of slaves," said a Mississippi paper. "One
point of the abolition controversy (and that the most
important) is solemnly settled in favor of the South." [1]
McLean's dictum, furthermore, was regarded as as-
suring the validity of the laws of South Carolina, Georgia and Louisiana, forbidding the entrance of free negroes. While these laws had produced much friction
with these States of the North, who considered such
free negroes to be citizens, the South had long argued
that the quarantine principle justified all laws which
provided for the safety of the people in relation to their

[1] *Columbus Democrat* (Miss.), May 8, 1841.

slaves, and that such laws were an absolute necessity, "when in the very bosom of the Northern States, the fell abolitionists are to be found whose fanaticism would provoke every species of excess against our laws and institutions." [1]

On the day after the argument of this great case closed, the Court entered upon another involving the slavery issue, *United States* v. *Schooner Amistad*, 15 Pet. 518. It was of interest, not only in its singular facts, but owing to the appearance at the Bar, for the first time in thirty-two years, of Ex-President John Quincy Adams, then seventy-four years of age. With Adams, there appeared Roger S. Baldwin of Connecticut and against him the Attorney-General, Henry D. Gilpin, and eight days were devoted to the arguments.[2] The question presented was the right to freedom of certain negroes who, while being brought to this country illegally by slave traders, had gained mastery of the vessel and murdered the officers. On being carried here by a United States war vessel, they were claimed as slaves by their alleged Spanish owners. As Baldwin said in opening his argument, the case "involves considerations deeply affecting our National character in the eyes of the whole civilized world, as well as questions of power on the part of the Government of the United States, which are regarded with anxiety and alarm by a large portion of our citizens. It presents, for the first time, the question whether that Government . . . can, consistently with the genius of our in-

[1] *Georgia Journal*, Jan. 26, 1841.

[2] "The *Amistad Case* will create much feeling for itself, and for the reason that Mr. Adams will take the prominent part as counsel for the prisoners." *New York Express*, Feb. 25, 1841; the *National Intelligencer* said that the "Supreme Court was yesterday the theater of great interest and attracted a crowded audience, the occasion being the argument of Ex-President Adams as an attorney at the Bar of that Court." The last previous professional appearance by John Quincy Adams was in 1809, in *Hope Insurance Co.* v. *Boardman*, 5 Cranch, 56.

stitutions, become a party to proceedings for the enslavement of human beings cast upon our shores, and found in the condition of freemen within the territorial limits of a free and sovereign State." Much political feeling had been aroused by the case; and as Adams was then the most vigorous of all the anti-slavery advocates in Congress, and consequently, of all statesmen, the most obnoxious to the South, his argument was awaited with great interest by the public. Of its preparation and delivery Adams himself has written a vivid depiction : [1]

February 22. I walked to the Capitol with a thoroughly bewildered mind — so bewildered as to leave me nothing but fervent prayer that presence of mind may not utterly fail me at the trial I am about to go through. At the opening of the Court, Judge Thompson read a decision of the Court on a certain case. . . . The Attorney-General Henry D. Gilpin then delivered his argument in the case of the Amistad Captives. It occupied two hours. . . . Mr. Baldwin followed, in a sound and eloquent but exceedingly mild and moderate argument in behalf of the captives, till half past three, when the Court adjourned.

February 23. With increasing agitation of mind, now little short of agony, I rode in a hack to the Capitol. . . . The very skeleton of my argument is not yet put together. When the Court met, Judge Wayne and Judge Story read in succession two decisions of the Court, and Mr. Baldwin occupied the remainder of the day, four hours, in closing

[1] *J. Q. Adams*, X. Of his retainer, he wrote, Nov. 27, 1839: "Mr. Ellis Gray Loring of Boston and Mr. Lewis Tappan of New York, called on me this morning, and earnestly entreated of me to assume, as assistant counsel to Mr. Baldwin of Connecticut, the defence of the Africans before the Supreme Court of the United States, at their next January Term. I endeavored to excuse myself, upon the plea of my age and inefficiency, of the oppressive burdens of my duties as a member of the House of Representatives, and of my inexperience, after a lapse of more than thirty years, in the forms and technicals of argument before judicial tribunals, — but they urged me so much, and represented the case of those unfortunate men as so critical, it being a case of life and death, that I yielded."

The *Madisonian*, Feb. 16, 1842, said that Mr. Adams was responsible for much of the disorder in Congress on the slavery question, and that it had no desire "to shield that venomous old man from public reprobation."

his argument. . . . The point upon which he dwelt with most emphatic earnestness was the motion to dismiss the appeal of the United States on the contest of their right to appear as parties in the cause, they having no interest therein. His reasoning therein was powerful and perhaps conclusive. But I am apprehensive there are precedents and an Executive influence operating upon the Court which will turn the balance against us on that point. . . . He closed at half past three and left the day open for me to-morrow.

February 24. . . . The Court-room was full but not crowded and there were not many ladies. I had been deeply distressed and agitated till the moment when I rose; and then my spirit did not sink within me. With grateful heart for aid from above, though in humiliation for the weakness incident to the limits of my powers, I spoke four hours and a half, with sufficient method and order to witness little flagging of attention by the Judges or the auditory — till half past three o'clock. . . . The structure of my argument, so far as I have yet proceeded, is perfectly simple and comprehensive, needing no artificial division into distinct points but admitting the steady and undeviating pursuit of one fundamental principle — the ministration of *justice*. I then assigned my reason for inviting *justice* specially, aware that this was *always* the duty of the Court, but because an immense array of power — the Executive Administration, instigated by the Ministers of a foreign nation — has been brought to bear, in this case, on the side of injustice. . . . I did not, I could not, answer public expectation; but I have not yet utterly failed. God speed me to the end!

February 25. The agitation of mind under which I have been laboring for weeks had yesterday gradually subsided, in a continuous extemporaneous discourse of four hours and a half, through which I was enabled to pass, but the exhaustion consequent upon the effort, and the remnant of mental solicitude still heavily weighing upon my spirits, I had an uneasy, restless night, and short, not undisturbed repose. I rose however, with much encouraged and cheerful feeling. . . .

March 1. I went to the Supreme Court and concluded my argument. . . . I spoke about four hours and then

closed somewhat abruptly. . . . I was unwilling to encroach
upon the time of the Court for half of a third day . . . and
finished with a very short personal address to the Court.

March 2. The Attorney-General then closed the argument on the part of the United States in about three hours,
reviewing with great moderation of manner chiefly Mr.
Baldwin's argument and very slightly noticing mine.

Judge Story, writing to his wife, February 28, 1841,
described the old man as full of accustomed virility
and belligerency and spoke of the "extraordinary"
argument made by him. "Extraordinary, I say, for
its power and its bitter sarcasm, and its dealing with
topics far beyond the record and points of discussion." [1]
Within one week after the close of the argument, the
Court, on March 9, through Judge Story decided the case,
holding that the negroes should be freed and sent back to
Africa, and thus adjudging in favor of Adams' clients.[2]

On the day after this decision, the Court, through
Chief Justice Taney, took a further step in the great
case which had been long pending between the two
sovereign States — *Rhode Island* v. *Massachusetts*,
15 Pet. 233, — by overruling the demurrer of the latter State and ordering her to file an answer.[3] That the

---

[1] *Story*, II, 348.

[2] Adams, writing to Richard Peters, Jr., May 19, 1841, with reference to the report of his argument in *Peters Reports* said (*Peters Papers MSS*): "If you leave
out my flagellation of the later Secretary of State and of the man of Kinderhook
for his *lettre de cachet*, because the Court took no notice of them — no more than
of the bright intellect of the South, or of the *Globe* of 7 Jan., 1841 — you may put
in what you please for my speech. The best epigram upon the *lettre de cachet* was
the decree of the Court pronouncing the negroes *free*. The rest is 'leather and prunella.' "

Writing in his diary, a year later, Feb. 17, 1842, Adams referred to his victory,
with striking modesty for an old man of seventy-six: "I went into the room where
the Supreme Court of the United States were in session. This room I re-entered
with a silent thrill of delight, for the first time since I was there at this time last
year, under such a heavy pressure of responsibility and with so glorious a result. I
dare not trust myself with the exultation of my own heart on this occasion, so fearful am I of incurring the guilt of presumptuous vanity, for the feeling of deep humility." *J. Q. Adams*, X.

[3] It is interesting to note that Daniel Webster argued this case for Massachusetts,
March 8, 1841, after his appointment as Secretary of State under President Harrison.

members of the Court, though appointed by Democratic Presidents, were obtaining the confidence even of the Whig Bar of the North is seen from a comment on this case which appeared in a highly conservative magazine edited by Boston Whigs: "Although we are certainly disappointed with the reasoning of the Court on the demurrer, still we have entire confidence in the intelligence and fidelity of that dignified tribunal. There is, we are sorry to perceive, a disposition sometimes apparent to undervalue its high and commanding character. Because its decisions on some questions are not in unison with our general opinions, and because some principles are adopted which are not in harmony with the doctrines of our schools, and possibly because a majority of the members are of a political party in opposition to the one to which we belong, we are in danger of losing our respect for its learning, its authority and its power. But the members of this high Court have, as a body, no superiors in all the great qualities of mind and heart, in honor, integrity, ability and learning, which are the ornaments of the Bench and the security of its people. We should encourage this belief." [1]

It is to be noted that there was a break in the argument of the *Amistad Case*, from February 25 to March 1. This was due to the death of Judge Barbour, which occurred with great suddenness on February 25.[2] He "had been daily with us in the hall, listening to the animated and earnest discussions which the great subjects in controversy here naturally produce," said Taney at the meeting of the Court held in his memory,

---

[1] *Law Reporter* (May, 1841), IV.
[2] Adams wrote in his diary: "At eleven o'clock the surviving Judges came in. Excepting Judge McKinley, all in their robes, and in procession. They took their seats and Chief Justice Taney said: 'One of the Judges of the Court — Brother Barbour — is dead. The Court will adjourn till Monday.'"

"and he had been with us also in the calmer scenes of the conference room, taking a full share in the deliberations of the Court, and always listened to with the most respectful attention. It was from one of these meetings, which had been protracted to a late hour of the night, that we all parted from him apparently in the usual health; and in the morning we found that the Associate whom we so highly respected and the friend we so greatly esteemed had been called away from us." In view of the Whig criticisms which had been leveled against President Jackson for the appointment of Barbour, it is interesting to note that Judge Story now wrote of him: "He was a man of great integrity, of a very solid and acute understanding, of considerable legal attainments (in which he was daily improving) and altogether a very conscientious, upright and laborious Judge, whom we respected for his talents and virtues, and his high sense of duty." [1]

This death occasioned a contest in Congress over a bill to reorganize the judicial Circuits which had been long needed. While there were then six Circuits for the Eastern and Southern States, the whole West and Southwest had only three Circuits, in which the traveling distances for the Judges were immense, and the amount of litigation, due to complicated land titles, the deranged state of the currency and the rage for speculation, was unbearably heavy. It was proposed to abolish the present Fourth Circuit (consisting of Virginia and North Carolina), and to throw Virginia into the Circuit with Maryland, and North Carolina into the Circuit with South Carolina and Georgia, thus eliminating one Eastern Circuit and giving it to the Southwest. As Barbour had come from Virginia, it

---

[1] Judge Story wrote, Feb. 28, 1841: "He dined heartily, and remained with the Judges in conference until after ten o'clock in the evening, and then in a most cheerful humor." *Story*, II, 348–350.

was felt that it was a peculiarly fortunate time to make
the change, there now being no Supreme Court Judge
from the Fourth Circuit. The proposition, however,
touching Virginia's State pride, was bitterly resented
by her Senators, and the bill after passing the Senate
was finally lost in the House, on its adjournment.[1] It
may be noted that Senator Benton of Missouri opposed
the bill, on the ground that the real remedy for the increase of business in the West was the increase of the
number of Judges on the Supreme Court to twelve,
since "to determine these weighty matters, there should
be an ample number and they should be brought from
every great section of the country." Senator Buchanan
of Pennsylvania, on the other hand, thought that "the
present number of Judges was already greater than
he could have desired. Nine was too large a number
if it could have been avoided." As soon as it was
seen that the Circuits were not to be altered, President
Van Buren, in the last moments of his Administration,
on February 26, nominated to fill the vacancy Peter
V. Daniel of Virginia. Daniel was fifty-six years old
and was serving as United States District Judge in
Virginia, having succeeded Barbour in that position;
he had also been tendered the position of Attorney-
General on Taney's resignation of that post, but had
declined. Of the new Judge, a leading Democratic
paper said: "With talent, both natural and acquired,
equal to all the duties of the office, he combines the

---

[1] *26th Cong., 2d Sess.*, Feb. 27, 1841. The bill proposed to make three Circuits
in the Southwest — Alabama and Louisiana in one; Mississippi and Tennessee in
another; and Arkansas, Missouri and Kentucky in the third. One object sought to
be accomplished was, to eliminate Judge McKinley from the Mississippi Circuit;
for owing to the fact that he had been bodily assaulted in the street in Jackson,
Miss., by a deputy marshal, he had declined to hold a Circuit Court in that State
in 1840 and 1841, and for this action he had been the subject of severe criticism in
a debate in Congress, on a proposal to deduct $500 from the salary of any Judge
who failed to hold his Circuit Court. *27th Cong., 2d Sess.*, April 6, 1842.

moral qualifications, that are not only valuable in themselves but indispensable to our security; a steadiness
and firmness which no strategies can overcome, which
all the arts of sophistry and the seduction of power and
acumen cannot overreach or deceive"; and another
said that "the selection has afforded general satisfaction; he is one of the strict construction, State-Rights
school." [1] The Whig Senators, however, were indignant at this appointment, made so soon before the inauguration of the new President, Harrison. They
denounced Daniel as a political partisan, though admitting his purity of character and legal ability; and,
with the exception of Smith of Indiana, they all left
the Senate Chamber before the final vote was taken
on confirmation. The appointment was confirmed, on
March 2, by a vote of twenty-two to five — less than
a majority of the Senators. The action was criticized
with true party acridity by the Whig papers, one of
which gave the following vivid description of this episode of another "Midnight Judge." "It appears
that the Senate, by an unexampled majority, had passed
a bill abolishing the Circuit which the late Justice Barbour was attached to, and whilst that bill was pending
before the House of Representatives, a majority of
the Senate took up the nomination of Mr. Daniel as
a Judge of the Supreme Court of the United States, on
Tuesday night. It was in vain that the Whigs protested against filling an office, which had been suspended so far as the Senate could act; it was in vain
that they plead for time, by laying the nomination
on the table or referring it until it was known whether
the House would reject or agree to the bill of the Senate. All postponement was refused, and about 12

[1] *Richmond Enquirer*, March 5, 1841; *Charleston Courier*, Feb. 27, 1841; *Daily
Georgian*, March 6, 1841.

o'clock at night, after all the Whigs but one had retired, the nomination of Mr. Daniel was confirmed by a small majority, several of his own political friends voting against him. The nomination of Mr. J. Y. Mason to the office of District Judge of Virginia which had been filled by Mr. Daniel was also confirmed. The public cannot fail to contrast the conduct of the party, fortunately now no longer dominant, when Mr. Adams was going out of power, with what it is when Mr. Van Buren is retiring. Then, the nomination of Mr. Crittenden, whose great merits are now so generally recognized for a seat on the bench of the Supreme Court, was laid on the table. Now, that of Mr. Daniel is refused to be laid on the table, taken up in the very Senate which had passed a bill dispensing with it, and the nomination confirmed, whilst that bill is actually pending before the House of Representatives. True to the spoils principles in these last moments of their expiring power, a gentleman who had signalized himself as a partisan in an inferior judicial station is elevated to the exalted office of a Judge of the Supreme Court of the United States."

Other Whig papers denounced the President's action as "another flagitious act. The breath was hardly out of Judge Barbour's body before Van Buren hurries a successor into the Senate Chamber; and an approval of him is insisted upon, and carried at midnight by dragging Senators out of their bed. It is not an easy thing, one would think, to find a Judge fit for the Supreme Bench in 24 hours, but Mr. Van Buren found no difficulty in it. . . . Thus, in shame, and dishonor, injustice and disgrace ends the career of Mr. Van Buren."[1] In thus assailing a Democratic President,

---

[1] *National Intelligencer*, March 4, 5, 1841; *New York Express*, March 9, 1841; *Richmond Enquirer*, March 9, 11, 1841.

however, the Whigs conveniently forgot that he was but following the precedent set by President Adams, a Federalist, in appointing John Marshall during the closing days of his Administration; and in view of the extremely harsh and violent campaign of invective waged by Harrison and Tyler against Van Buren in the preceding fall, the expectation that he would defer to his successor in the matter of appointments was hardly reasonable.[1]

[1] It is interesting to note that another Whig opportunity to make an appointment on the Court during this year was lost when Judge McLean declined to resign from the Bench to take a position in the Cabinet. The expectation, never fulfilled, had been that John J. Crittenden of Kentucky would receive the appointment; but again, as in 1829, Crittenden's chance to go upon the Bench escaped him. *Crittenden Papers MSS*, letter of Reverdy Johnson to Crittenden, Sept. 5, 1841.

NOTE. As to *Kendall* v. *Stokes* (p. 44, *supra*), William Smith of Virginia wrote to Kendall, July 6, 1837: "The ground taken by the Court would not only destroy that beautiful trinity into which all power, to be controlled, must divide, but, if maintained, would indeed make the Judiciary the despotic branch." *Autobiography of Amos Kendall* (1872), p. 365. Judge Catron, dissenting in *Decatur* v. *Paulding* (1840), 14 Peters, 497, said: "Between the Circuit Court of this District and the Executive Administration of the United States there is an open contest for power. . . . The conflict between the Executive and Judiciary Department could not well be more direct, nor more dangerous. . . . For nearly forty years, this fearful claim to power has neither been exerted nor was it supposed to exist; but now that it is assumed, we are struck with the peculiar impropriety of the Circuit Court of this District becoming the brunt of opposition to the Executive Administration."

It is interesting to note that a case involving slavery coming from the United States District Court in Alabama, *Hagan* v. *Forson* (1836), 10 Peters, 160, was dismissed for want of jurisdiction, the record not showing that $2000 was involved, and Judge Story saying that: "Here the whole matter in controversy is the ownership of one negro woman and two children who are slaves, and it is not supposed that their value can be equal to $2000." See also *Bennett* v. *Butterworth* (1850), 11 How. 669, for question of jurisdiction in a suit to try title to slaves.

CHAPTER TWENTY-THREE

FEDERAL POWERS, TYLER, AND THE GIRARD WILL CASE

1842–1844

Two phases of the delicate issue of slavery having been passed upon at its session in the first year of the new Whig Administration of Harrison and Tyler, still another phase of this question was presented at the 1842 Term. Now for the first time in its history the Court's attitude in this connection became the subject of attack, after its decision in *Prigg* v. *Pennsylvania*, 16 Pet. 539, in which the constitutionality of the Pennsylvania statute relative to fugitive slaves was involved.[1] The increasing tension in the community over the issue of the respective powers of the States and of Congress as to such slaves was clearly shown at the argument. A denial of the right of the State to legislate on this subject, said the Attorney-General of Pennsylvania, will "arouse a spirit of discord and resistance that will neither shrink nor slumber till the obligation itself be cancelled or the Union which creates it be dissolved"; and another of the State's counsel said that of all solemn questions ever argued before this

[1] Owing to the illness of the Chief Justice, Judge Story presided during most of the 1842 Term. His situation, Story amusingly described in a talk with one of his classes at the Harvard Law School, as follows: " Was Tyler President or Acting President at the demise of Gen. Harrison? A nice question, gentlemen, and hard to solve. The question was debated in cabinet meeting, and on Mr. Webster's opinion, Tyler was addressed as President. On one occasion, when Chief Justice Taney was ill, I took his place as Chief Justice and was thus addressed. At first, I felt nervous, but soon becoming used to it, found it, like public money to new members of Congress, '*not bad to take.*' And this was probably the feeling with Mr. Tyler." *Western Law Journ.* (1846), II, 432; *Story*, II, 506.

Court "no one has arisen of more commanding import, or wider scope in its influence, or on which hung mightier results for good or ill to the Nation"; and he stated that it involved "a subject which is even now heaving the political tides of the country, which has caused enthusiasm to throw her lighted torch into the temples of religion, and the halls of science and learning, while the forum of justice, and the village barroom have equally resounded with the discussion. . . . Whilst it has become 'sore as gangrene' in one region, it is the football of the enthusiast in another." That the Court itself fully realized the seriousness of the situation was shown in the opening words of its opinion, delivered by Judge Story: "Few questions which have ever come before this Court involve more delicate and important considerations, and few upon which the public at large may be presumed to feel a more profound and pervading interest." Fortunately, the Court found itself able to deliver a unanimous opinion, holding that the power of Congress over the subject of fugitive slaves was exclusive, and that the State statute, being in conflict with the Federal Fugitive Slave Law, was consequently unconstitutional. But while all agreed that a State statute could not interfere with the provisions of the Federal law, there was a sharp dissent by Chief Justice Taney and Judges Thompson and Daniel from the further proposition laid down by Judge Story (and concurred in by the majority of the Court, including the Southern Judge, Wayne) to the effect that the power of Congress was so exclusive as to render invalid every State statute on the subject, whether in aid of, or in conflict with, the Federal law. The decision was equally unsatisfactory to both pro-slavery and anti-slavery men. The former regarded it as a severe blow to State-

Rights, even though it sustained their views on the slavery question.[1] Among the latter, the decision was regarded as a complete surrender to the South. John Quincy Adams wrote in his diary, March 10, that he had spent much of the day in reading the various opinions delivered by the seven Judges, " everyone of them dissenting from the reasoning of all the rest, and everyone of them coming to the same conclusion, the transcendent omnipotence of slavery in these United States, riveted by a clause in the Constitution." For his part in the "ignoble compliance with the slaveholders' will", Judge Story was hotly assailed at the North; but such criticism could not perturb a Judge who had penned to a friend the following noble words: "I shall never hesitate to do my duty as a Judge under the Constitution and laws of the United States, be the consequences what they may. That Constitution I have sworn to support, and I cannot forget or repudiate my solemn obligations at pleasure. You know full well that I have ever been opposed to slavery. But I take my standard of duty as a Judge from the Constitution." [2] To the State of New York, the *Prigg Case* decision gave particular offense; for it completely nullified a law of that State which, by granting jury trials in case of the arrest of fugitive slaves, had heretofore resulted in rendering utterly nugatory the provisions of the Federal Fugitive Slave Law, and which had very naturally caused great friction between New York and Southern States. "Thus ends the controversy between New York and Virginia, and between New York

---

[1] In a strongly adverse review of Judge Story's life in the *New York Evening Post*, Jan. 27, 1852, it was said: "The Supreme Court has never struck a more decisive and fatal blow at State-Rights than in this decision, and there is no one of Judge Story's honors of which he has less reason to be proud than that of being selected to deliver the opinion of the Bench."

[2] *Story*, II, 430, letter of Story to E. Bacon, relating to the case of *La Belle Eugénie*.

and Georgia," said a leading New York paper. "The conclusion to which the Court have arrived involves consequences which can by no means be satisfactory to this part of the country. A freeman now may be arrested and carried into slavery, after but a slight investigation before a magistrate and without the intervention of a jury. The (Federal) Law of 1793, the practice under which New York and Pennsylvania endeavored to correct, is now pronounced to be supreme law." [1]

Since, however, public attention, at this date was absorbed in the bitter contests over the Sub-Treasury, the Banks, the Texas and the Oregon questions and the struggle between President Tyler and the Whigs, the slavery issue, for the time being, became subordinate; the excitement over the *Prigg Case* died away; and the *North American Review*, the very next year, in speaking of "the beneficial action of the Judiciary in quieting public contests and maintaining unruffled the majesty of the law", referred to the effect of the *Prigg Case* as follows: "At this majestic bar, the matter was argued with as much dignity and calmness as if it has never set the country in a flame; and the judgment was received by the public with the quiet submission which they usually manifest when ordinary judicial decisions are announced. Some murmurs were heard from both parties about the insufficiency or hardship of certain provisions in the Constitution. We hardly heard a whisper against the fidelity and even-handed justice with which that judgment had been expounded by the Court." [2]

[1] *New York Daily Express*, March 8, 1842.

[2] *The Independence of the Judiciary*, in North Amer. Rev. (Oct. 1843), LVII; and see Crawford, J., *In re Booth* (1859), 3 Wisc. 79, for the view taken of the *Prigg Case* by contemporaneous opinion; see also article in *New York American*, quoted in *New York Express*, March 5, 1842. The case was discussed on many occasions in Congress during the next seven years. See especially *30th Cong., 1st Sess.*, speeches of Ashmun of Massachusetts, April 10, 1848, Bayly of Virginia and McLane

Undoubtedly, the chief reason for the equanimity with which the decision was finally accepted was the rapid realization by the Northern States of the effective weapon which had been placed in their hands. Those portions of Judge Story's opinion which declared that the States were prohibited not only from passing laws in violation of the fugitive slave provision of the Constitution, but from enacting legislation in furtherance of it, and that the States were not bound and could not be obliged to enforce this provision of the Constitution through State officers, were seized upon by anti-slavery States as a justification for legislative measures refusing the assistance of their officials to enforce the Federal Fugitive Slave Law.[1] Relying on this theory, Massachusetts, as early as 1843, passed a statute which made it a penal offense for any State officer or constable to aid in any way in carrying the Federal Law into effect. Other States soon followed with similar legislation;[2] and the difficulty of reclaiming a fugitive slave became so great as to force Congress to enact new and more stringent Federal legislation, in 1850, and thus to precipitate the great conflict between State and Federal authority which finally led to war.[3]

of Maryland, April 11, 1848; *30th Cong., 2d Sess.*, speech of Baldwin of Connecticut, Jan. 22, 1849, Crisfield of Maryland, Feb. 17, 1849.

[1] Story himself believed that "a great point had been gained for liberty — so great a point, indeed, that on his return from Washington," wrote his son: "He repeatedly and earnestly spoke of it to his family and his intimate friends as being 'a triumph of freedom.'" *Story*, II, 392, 394.

[2] Personal Liberty Laws (so called) similar to that of Massachusetts, were enacted in Vermont in 1843, Connecticut in 1844, New Hampshire in 1846, Pennsylvania in 1847, Rhode Island in 1848, Wisconsin in 1857. On the other hand, South Carolina, Mississippi and Missouri passed laws prohibiting free negroes from entering their boundaries. For one of the best summaries of the Personal Liberty Laws, see *National Intelligencer*, Dec. 11, 12, 1860.

[3] Slavery was further involved at this 1842 Term in a singular case, *Gordon* v. *Longest*, 16 Pet. 97. In this suit, argued by John J. Crittenden against Thomas H. Benton, and involving a Kentucky statute forbidding steamboats to take on board slaves from the Ohio shore, Judge McLean in his opinion said: "This is the first instance known to us in which a State Court has refused to a party a right to remove his cause to the Circuit Court of the United States."

While the Court, composed of a majority of State-Rights Democrats, had thus upheld the exclusiveness of Federal power in relation to the limited subject of fugitive slaves, it took an even greater step at this Term in expanding the domain of Federal power with relation to a great variety of subjects. For in *Swift* v. *Tyson*, 16 Pet. 1, it announced for the first time that the Federal Courts had the authority to lay down principles of general law, without regard to the decision of State Courts, even where no question of the Federal Constitution or laws was involved. Marshall himself had never asserted such power for the Court; and theretofore it had been commonly assumed (and there had been loose expressions of the Court to the effect) that the Thirty-Fourth Section of the Judiciary Act which provided "that the laws of the several States . . . shall be regarded as rules of decision in trials at common law" in the Federal Courts, included within the scope of the meaning of the word "laws", the decisions of the local State Courts as well as statutory laws.[1] Now, in 1842, in this case of *Swift* v. *Tyson* the question arose whether the Court would hold itself bound to follow the doctrine laid down by the Courts of New York relative to the law of bills of exchange. The case had been previously argued, in 1840, by Daniel Webster against Richard H. Dana of Massachusetts, and was now submitted on briefs by William P. Fessenden of Maine and by Dana. Judge Story held (without noticing any expression to the contrary in previous decisions of the Court) that this Section of the Judiciary Act did not apply to "questions of a more general nature not at all dependent upon local statutes or usages of a fixed and per-

---

[1] In *Bank of Kentucky* v. *Wister*, 2 Pet. 318, 324, however, as late as 1829, the Court had said that it was "unnecessary at this time to enter into the inquiry how far its decisions and those of other States upon a question of a general, not a local case or character, are to be controlled by those of any particular State."

manent operation"; that as to such questions, the
Federal Courts were not to be bound by the law of the
States as laid down by the State Courts; that the interpretation and effect of contracts and other instruments of a commercial nature, were to be sought "in
the general principles and doctrines of commercial
jurisprudence"; and that in this case, the Court would
not follow the law as to negotiable instruments laid
down by the New York Courts, but would ascertain
the law for itself.   This decision, which, as the newspapers said, "settled an important commercial question which ought to be soon and generally known",
introduced a novel and original doctrine into Federal
law — that there existed in the United States a general
commercial law independent of the decisions of a
State.[1] Probably no decision of the Court has ever
given rise to more uncertainty as to legal rights; and
though doubtless intended to promote uniformity in
the operation of business transactions, its chief effect
has been to render it difficult for business men to know
in advance to what particular topic the Court would
apply the doctrine; and the adverse criticisms by
Judges and jurists, which have continued to the present day, have had much justification.[2]   In another
famous case at this Term, *Martin* v. *Waddell's Lessee*,

---

[1] In the *Western Law Journ.* (April, 1844), the editor expressed a hope that
Judge Story would prepare a bill "founded on the power of Congress to regulate
commerce, which might have the effect of rendering the law of commerce as well
as of navigation uniform throughout this country. Think, for example, of the
evils arising from the conflicting doctrines as held in different States on the subject
of negotiable paper and insurance."   See also review in *Law Reporter* (1842), V.

[2] *Is there a General Commercial Law*, by Robert G. Street, *Amer. Law Reg.*
(1873), XXI; *Federal Common Law*, by Hunsdon Cary, *Virg. Law Reg.* (1904), X;
Common Law Jurisdiction of the United States, by Alton B. Parker, *Yale Law Journ.*
(1904), XVII; *The Non-Federal Law Administered in Federal Courts*, by W.
Trickett, *Amer. Law Rev.* (1906), XLI.   See also comments on Judge Story and his
decision in this case by John C. Gray in *The Nature and Sources of the Law* (1909);
see also especially Field, J., in *Baltimore & Ohio R. R.* v. *Baugh* (1892), 149 U. S.
368. 401.

16 Pet. 367, the Court still further limited its obligation to follow the law of the State under the Thirty-Fourth Section of the Judiciary Act. This case involved the right of the State of New Jersey to grant exclusive oyster-bed rights in flats under its tide-waters, a question which had "created much ill-blood in the past twenty years." The Court was called upon to construe certain royal charters and deeds of surrender by the Colonial Proprietors, which had already been construed and the legal question presented by which had been decided by the New Jersey Supreme Court, as early as 1818. While deciding in favor of the State, the Court, through Judge Taney, held that as the question did not depend "upon the meaning of instruments framed by the people of New Jersey or by their authority", the State Court ruling did not bind the Federal Court, though it was "unquestionably entitled to great weight." "The very learned and lucid opinion of Taney will give as much satisfaction to the lovers of law as the decision gives to the people of New Jersey," said a New York paper. "It will increase the general confidence in the uprightness and legal capability of this truly august tribunal." [1] One other instance of the scrupulous zeal with which this Democratic Court adhered to its determination to protect the functions of the Federal Government against encroachment by the States was seen in *Dobbins* v. *Erie County*, 16 Pet. 435. In this case, a statute of Pennsylvania imposing a tax on the income of a Federal revenue officer was held unconstitutional as an "interference with the constitutional means which have been legislated by the government of the United States to carry into effect its powers to lay and collect taxes, duties, imports, etc., and to regulate commerce", and as diminishing the recompense

---

[1] *New York Journal of Commerce*, quoted in *Boston Daily Advertiser*, Feb. 14, 1842.

secured to the Federal officer by Federal laws. The decision, rendered through a Southern Judge, Wayne, reaffirming and applying the doctrines of *McCulloch* v. *Maryland*, met with criticism from State-Rights Democrats. "This appears to be a carrying of the doctrine of National Sovereignty very far," said the *Pennsylvanian*. "When the tax is laid on all persons indiscriminately who receive official salaries, on State officers as well as National, there appears no danger of the action of the National Government being impeded by the tax. . . . It is a natural weakness of the human mind for the officers of every government and every branch of government to be prone to stretch the powers of their own government or department and to abridge those of others. Hence, there has been generally a disposition in the Courts of the United States to encroach somewhat on the rights of the States as understood by the Democratic party. We do not undertake to pronounce that the decision is erroneous, but we should have been well pleased, had the Constitution been framed or the Judges so construed it, that no such decision should have been made."[1]

The stand taken by the Court, composed chiefly of Democratic Judges, in support of the powers of the Federal Government was the more marked, by reason of the fact that during the past two years, 1841 and 1842, the Democratic Party in Congress and throughout the country had been peculiarly violent in assailing the extension of Federal power contained in the Whig legislation of these years. The Whig Congress, as soon as it convened after the death of President Harrison and the accession of John Tyler to the Presidency, had passed a series of statutes, each of which had been charged by the Democrats to be violative of the sovereignty

---

[1] *Pennsylvanian*, April 21, 1842.

of the States—the Fiscal Bank Acts, the National Bankruptcy Act, the Habeas Corpus Act and the Congressional District Election Act.   As the debates on these
measures produced the first criticisms which had been
made upon the Court and its functions since the year
1833, and as the discussion of the effect of the Court's
position in constitutional Government was conducted
with masterful ability, these debates deserve the attention of all students of American legal history.

As to the Fiscal Bank Acts, the discussion naturally
centered about the power of Congress to charter a
National Bank ; and this much-argued question, which
had been the source of party conflict since 1789 and which
had been supposed to have been settled by the decisions
of the Court in *McCulloch* v. *Maryland* and *Osborn* v.
Bank of the United States, twenty-two and seventeen
years before, was now reargued with increased fervor.
The views which Jefferson, Jackson and Calhoun
had advanced, as to the non-binding force of Court
decisions upon the President or the Congress, when
acting in Executive or Legislative capacity, were now
reasserted by the Democrats with great vigor.   "A
Senator must exercise his own judgment as a legislator
on the question of the constitutional power of Congress
to charter a Bank," said James Buchanan of Pennsylvania :   "I respect judicial decisions within their
appropriate sphere, as much as any Senator.   They
put at rest forever the controversy immediately before
the Court ; and as a general rule they govern all future
cases of the same character ; but even these decisions,
like all other human things, are modified and changed
by the experience of time and the lights of knowledge.
The law is not now what it was fifty years ago, nor what
it will be fifty years hereafter. . . .   But even if the
Judiciary had settled the question, I should never hold

myself bound by their decision, whilst acting in a legislative character. . . . I cannot agree that 'its judicial expositions are of equal authority with the text of the Constitution.' This is an infallibility which was never before claimed for any human tribunal. . . . No man holds in higher estimation than I do the memory of Chief Justice Marshall; but I should never have consented to make even him the final arbiter between the Government and people of this country on questions of constitutional liberty. . . . It is notorious that the Court, during the whole period which he presided over it, embracing so many years of its existence, has inclined towards the highest assertion of Federal power. That this has been done honestly and conscientiously I entertain not a doubt." [1] Similar views were expressed in the House by John T. Mason of Maryland, who, though the youngest Congressman, voiced the old fears of Federalism: "The Court is not authorized to interfere with the free exercise by Congress of its constitutional functions. While I have the highest veneration for the ability and purity of the late Chief Justice, yet I would be unwilling that upon this question his opinions should govern my judgment, for the plain reason that his prejudices, his partialities, his interests and his education, all contributed to the formation of an opinion which should be entirely free from the bias of either."

On the other hand, the binding force of the decision of the Court in *McCulloch* v. *Maryland*, even upon Congress, was supported by many strong lawyers, both Democratic and Whig — such as Senator John M.

---

[1] *27th Cong., 1st Sess.*, and *App.*, 161, 298, speeches of Buchanan, July 7, 1841, Israel Smith of Connecticut, July 20, 1841, Levi Woodbury of New Hampshire, July 10, 1841; speeches in the House, of John T. Mason of Maryland, Aug. 3, 1841, Ezra Dean of Ohio, Aug. 5, 1841, John Hastings of Ohio, Aug. 9, 1841, Henry A. Wise of Virginia, Aug. 5, 1841.

Berrien of Georgia (who had been Attorney-General under President Jackson), and Henry Clay of Kentucky, Jabez W. Huntington of Connecticut and James Simmons of Rhode Island. "The Supreme Court have repeatedly and unanimously decided that Congress have the constitutional power to establish a National Bank and this is the only constitutional mode of determining the question," said Simmons. "The decisions have been uniform, always recognized and submitted to by every State Court, by every State Government, and by the whole people. If after this, men will contend that it is an open question, a doubtful question, they by it insist that no question can be settled under our Constitution."[1] And Berrien eloquently protested against "that political heresy of the most alarming character . . . that the interpretation of the Constitution by its own appointed arbiter is not obligatory on any man who is called, in the discharge of his official duty, to interpret that instrument, but that he is at liberty to follow out implicitly the dictates of his own understanding uncontrolled by that decision. . . . To the judicial power belongs, by the express provisions of the Constitution itself, in all cases properly brought before it, the right to interpret that instrument, to decide what it permits and what it forbids : in fine, to determine what it is. Each judicial decision, so made under the authority of the Constitution, becomes incorporated in, and is part and parcel of, the instrument itself, enlarging, restraining or modifying the original text, according to the legal import and effect of such decision. He who disregards it, whether he be legislator or executive officer, disregards

[1] *27th Cong., 1st Sess.*, and *App.*, 358, speeches of Berrien, Sept. 1, 1841, Archer of Virginia, Sept. 2, Huntington, July 3; speeches in the House of Clay, July 1, Simmons, July 2; *27th Cong., 2d Sess.*, speech of Berrien, Jan. 26, 1842; see, however, vigorous denial of Berrien's doctrine by Israel Smith of Connecticut, Jan. 23, 1842.

the Constitution itself, of which it is a part and confessedly of higher authority than the original text, since
in all cases of supposed conflict it controls that text." [1]
While thus maintaining that in their legislative capacity,
they were not bound by Court decisions, the Democratic
Senators advanced further a view of the effect of the
decision in the *McCulloch Case*, which was more ten-
able, and consideration of which has been sometimes
lost sight of by Judges and jurists. " That decision,"
said Buchanan, " amounted only to this, that the Court
would not rejudge the discretion of Congress, but it
necessarily referred the constitutional question back
to the conscience of each member about to vote for or
against a new Bank, untrammelled by any judicial exposition." [2] All that the Court decided was that
Congress, in 1816, in determining that a National Bank
was a necessary and proper means of executing certain
express powers of the Constitution, was acting then within its powers ; but the question whether a Bank was such
a necessary and proper means was for the exclusive
determination of Congress in the first instance ; hence,
each successive Congress had full and untrammeled
power so to determine.   And as Senator Levi Woodbury
of New Hampshire said : " The decision of the Supreme

---

[1] Berrien also urged further an interesting argument to the effect that the State-
Rights advocates ought not to reject this principle for they were insistent that the
Supreme Court, in adhering to its doctrine of following the laws of the States,
should follow that law as construed by the State Courts. "It is upon the very
principle for which I am contending that our State laws receive the interpretation,
which those who framed them designed they should have, that the intention of our
State Legislatures is carried out when these laws are brought into controversy in the
Federal tribunals. The decisions of State Judges are considered in these tribunals
as part and parcel of the laws which they are called to interpret, the principle which
I maintained being equally applicable to acts of ordinary legislation and to the
fundamental law. When a question arises there upon the construction of a State
law, the Judges of these tribunals do not undertake to interpret it according to
their own understanding. The immediate inquiry is, what construction has been
given to this law by the State Judiciary ; and that construction is the rule of interpretation in the Federal tribunal."

[2] *27th Cong., 1st Sess.*, and *App.*, 161, 341, 180, 201, speeches of Buchanan, July
7, Sept. 2, Woodbury, July 10, Benton, July 27, 1841.

Court that a National Bank is constitutional, however
much urged on the other side as binding and final, has
been merely a decision contingent on certain facts. It
is, that any existing institution, first agreed by Congress
to be necessary and proper, is by them [the Court] considered in that event constitutional, but not so in any
other event. . . . Such a judicial opinion covers the legality of only that special charter granted under those
special facts, and decides nothing as to any other period
or any other proposed charter."   And, as Benton said :
"It decides that the constitutionality of the institution
depends upon its necessity to the Government, and that
of this necessity Congress is the sole judge."

This debate on the Fiscal Bank bill also produced
severe criticisms of the Court's decision in the *Dartmouth College Case*.   " I think it is not law and could
not be recognized as law, were the question again
brought before that Court," said Benjamin Tappan of
Ohio.   " It is, in truth, an instance of judicial Con-
stitution-making, not very uncommon formerly with the
Court who gave the decision . . . an ægis manufactured by judicial charlatans for preservation of bank
charters."   Denying that a charter was a contract, or
ever intended to be included within the term "impairment of obligation of contract," he continued : "Nothing proves more clearly the great influence of corporations in a society than the prevailing opinion that it
would be unsafe to trust Legislatures with the power
of repealing charters. Why unsafe? . . . Even if
your Legislative Assembly is composed of the most intelligent, pure and upright men, they cannot foresee the
effect of their legislation in all cases. They may incor-
porate companies which to their judgment can only be
used beneficially for the public, and yet they may be mistaken ; the chartered powers which they have conferred

may prove to be powers of mischief and destruction, instead of being used to promote the public interest and welfare; guided by a private cupidity, they may be used to corrupt the morals of the people and sap the foundations of our government, and yet upon this theory of vested rights, there is no remedy—the enslaved people must submit." [1]

The second extension of Federal power denounced by the Democrats was the enactment of the Whig National Bankruptcy Act of August 12, 1841. This measure, which extended the privilege of voluntary bankruptcy to all classes of persons, had been passed as a result of earnest pressure from debtors ruined by the banking and currency troubles and the land speculations of the past decade. The fact that imprisonment for debt still existed in many of the States rendered the condition of many debtors utterly desperate. The number of insolvents was estimated by some as high as five hundred thousand. At the South, the situation was particularly distressing.[2] In spite of the economic pressure for this legislation, however, there was a vigorous political opposition to the Act from the Democrats, based chiefly on two grounds: first, its unconstitutionality, as being in fact an insolvency law and not a bankruptcy law within the meaning of the Constitution;

[1] *27th Cong., 1st Sess.*, and *App.*, 195, speeches in the Senate of Benjamin Tappan of Ohio, July 14, Thomas H. Benton of Missouri, July 27, 1841.

[2] John J. Crittenden wrote Dec. 9, 1842, as to the Bankruptcy Act: "It was one of a series of measures urgently sought for by the Whigs of New York, Louisiana, etc. and rather conceded to them than desired by those of the Kentucky Whigs who supported it. It has to a great extent accomplished its object, and though there may have been abuses, it has relieved from imprisonment (for in many of the States that remedy is continued) and a hopeless mass of debt, many an honest man whose fortunes had been wrecked in the disastrous times through which we have passed." *Life of John J. Crittenden* (1871), by Ann M. B. Coleman, I.

It should be noted that the need of national bankruptcy legislation had been recently emphasized by the decision of the Court in 1840 in *Suydam* v. *Broadnax*, 14 Pet. 67, reaffirming the doctrine that a State insolvent law could not operate to bar contracts made in another State.

second, its invasion of the sovereignty of the States. "It is much more glaringly unconstitutional, much more immoral than the Alien and Sedition Laws," said Senator Benton. "The most daring attack on the State laws and the rights of property and on public morals which the history of Europe or America has exhibited. . . . It broke down the line between the jurisdiction of the Federal Courts and the State Courts in the whole department of debtors and creditors . . . bringing all local debts and dealings into the Federal Courts at the will of the debtors." [1] Senator Woodbury said that it brought the States "into the whirlpool of the Federal Courts, and is an alarming encroachment on State-Rights, because such an act, coupled with a like usurping power . . . to transfer from the States the trial of all burnings and murders like those of McLeod to the same Federal Courts, . . . tends most rapidly to prostrate all State independence, as well as to build up a frightful, monopolizing, overshadowing despotism at the centre, which neither our fathers contemplated, nor we should tolerate." A leading Democratic paper, after describing the bill as "working a regular process of encroachment on State jurisdiction," said that : "The whole latitudinarian school will go for it, because it invades State jurisdiction, extends Federal power, destroys contracts and brings the persons and property of the people under the sceptre of the Federal Judges." [2]

The third extension of Federal power was the Act of August 29, 1842, conferring upon the Federal Courts authority to issue writs of habeas corpus in certain cases of persons confined by the States. This legislation had

[1] *Thirty Years' View* (1856), by Thomas H. Benton, II, 464, 233; *27th Cong., 3d Sess.*, speech of Woodbury, Feb. 25, 1843.

[2] *Washington Globe*, March 8, 1842; see *ibid.*, May 5, 1842; and for description of the political factors in bankruptcy legislation see *New York Evening Post*, Feb. 26, 1840; *Story*, II, 404, 405, letters to Berrien, April 29, July 23, 1842; *J. Q. Adams*, X, 529.

originated in the dangerous complications which had
arisen out of the trial in the New York State Court of
Alexander McLeod, a British citizen, indicted for murder, in connection with the steamer *Caroline* episode in
1838. Though McLeod's defense was founded on international law, and though Great Britain denied the
right of the State of New York to insist on trial under
the international circumstances, the Federal Government had been powerless to prevent the trial. To ob-
viate such a condition and to enable the Federal Courts
to take jurisdiction, a bill was introduced providing for
the issue of a writ of habeas corpus by such Courts, in
case a foreign citizen should be imprisoned by any State
for "any act done or committed under any alleged right,
title, authority, privilege, protection or exemption set
up or claimed under the commission, order or sanction
of any foreign state or sovereignty, the validity and
effect whereof depend upon the law of nations or under
color thereof." This measure, favored by Webster and
the Whigs generally, encountered heated opposition from
the Democrats. "It is one of the most high-handed,
daring invasions of State-Rights which Federalism
has ever yet attempted," said the *Washington Globe*.
"Truly between the bankrupt law, which invades and
captures nearly all the civil jurisdiction of the State
Courts, and this habeas corpus against the States, which
may oust them of all their criminal jurisdiction, the poor
States stand a good chance to be stripped of nearly all
their judicial authority." [1] Senator Buchanan termed
it "a dangerous and untried experiment, calculated to
bring the sovereign States into collision with the Fed-

---

[1] *Washington Globe*, April 27, 1842, further said: "The friends of the reserved
rights of the States will not be frightened into a surrender of their rights upon any
cry, real or sham, of war with an arrogant power which seized the present brief
period when Federalism is in power to bear down upon us. This bill is a British
bill and is properly brought forward now."

eral Government, and thus to endanger the peace and
harmony of the Union . . . an extension of the jurisdiction of the Federal Courts over criminal cases arising in the sovereign States under their own laws, which,
from its very nature, cannot fail to wound their sensibility and arouse their jealousy." "It will produce
dangerous collision between the Federal and State authorities," he said,"and you will have to enforce the mandates of the District Judge by the armed power of the
Executive. There are cases in which the States will
not patiently submit to be stripped of their inherent
jurisdiction over criminals." [1] This bill is "one of
those silent encroachments in the march to power, not
likely to attract the attention of the great body
of the people;" said Arthur P. Bagby of Alabama,
but "the idea of State sovereignty is lost, if this
colossal power can be exercised constitutionally by the
Government." Senator Benton termed it "the
infamous act . . . polluting our code of law." [2]

The bill requiring the States to elect their Congressmen by districts was the last of the extensions of Federal control, and was equally attacked as unconstitutional and unjustifiable. [3] "All the dangerous collisions
which have ever existed between the State and Federal
authorities have arisen from the exercise of doubtful

[1] *27th Cong., 2d Sess.*, and *App.*, 382, 355, speeches in the Senate, of Buchanan,
May 9, Arthur P. Bagby of Virginia and Calhoun, July 8, Robert J. Walker of
Mississippi, June 21, Aug. 3, 1842; speeches in the House of John G. Floyd of New
York, Samuel Gordon of New York, William Smith of Virginia, Aug. 15, 1842. See
also especially speeches in Senate of Berrien of Georgia, April 26, Huntington of
Connecticut, May 10, 11, Choate of Massachusetts, July 8, 1842, supporting the
bill. The bill passed by a strict party vote, and see speech of John McKean of
New York in the House, Jan. 12, 1843. *27th Cong., 3d Sess.*

[2] *Thirty Years' View* (1856), by Thomas H. Benton, II, 276–304, 437.

[3] *27th Cong., 2d Sess.*, speeches of Buchanan and Woodbury, June 2, 4, 1842. It
was stated in the House, April 6, 1846, that New Hampshire, Mississippi and Missouri had failed to comply with the Congressional Districting Act, and were electing
their members by general ticket. "This is rank, practical Nullification." *29th
Cong., 1st Sess.*

and dangerous powers by Congress," said Buchanan. "This is an attempt to interfere with what immediately concerns the dearest domestic institutions of the States, their discretion as to the mode in which they will elect their Representatives to Congress." Senator Woodbury said that there had been more alarming encroachment by the General Government on the sacred rights of the States in the last twelve months than in the previous half century — "the bankrupt law, in a form voluntary, novel, unconstitutional, and absorbing within the vortex of the General Government the jurisdiction over almost the whole system of contracts as well as liens and of the action of the State Courts over them — the distribution bill by which all the States were to come and feed from the public crib of the General Government and be subjected, in return for it, to unconstitutional taxation. . . . Next, close at the heels of the others, was the attempt to strip the States of all criminal jurisdiction for burnings and murders committed within their limits, if defenses were set up like those of McLeod. . . . Last of all, a bill unprecedented in our annals, a bill dictating to the States as to their system of elections, and no less encroaching in its principle and overshadowing in its influence on State independence than the numerous other measures that have, in such rapid succession, characterized the policy, so fatal towards the States, of those now in power in the General Government."

That these reiterated attacks by the Democrats in Congress upon the alleged encroachments on the sovereignty of the States met with little response in the Court was interestingly shown at its next session, in 1843, when, in the only decision of historic importance rendered by it, the doctrine of the *Dartmouth College Case* was applied with great strictness, and a State statute seriously affecting commercial relations in the States was held unconstitutional. The case of *Bronson* v. *Kinzie*, 1 How. 311, in which this decision was rendered, had involved a recent statute of Illinois providing that a mortgagor's equity should not be lost for twelve months after foreclosure sale and that no sale should occur unless two thirds of the appraised value should be bid for the property. This was one of the many statutes which had been the outcome of the frightful state of business and finance then prevalent. The country had just passed through the panic of 1837; it was in the midst of the era of State bank failures and of State debt repudiations; scarcity of hard money had destroyed the inflated value of property; men who had debts to pay were forced to dispose of their property at ruinous prices to the few who had money to buy. As a consequence of these conditions, State after State had enacted statutes for the relief of debtors, stay-laws postponing collection of debts, relief-laws modifying remedies on contracts, laws granting exemption from execution and postponing sales on execution and foreclosure of mortgages.[1] So far as these statutes applied to contracts made prior to their enactment, they were everywhere attacked by creditors as mere attempts to enable debtors to escape payment of their just debts. And newspapers in the commercial centers, criticizing "the unconstitutionality as well as the impolicy of the dishonest and knavish legislation which, more than all the defalcations of individual swindlers though multiplied a thousand-fold, attests the almost hopeless depravity and corruption of the age", expressed the confident hope that the Court would "determine the paramount law of the land to

---

[1] See laws of Pennsylvania, Virginia, Ohio, Indiana, Illinois, Michigan, Mississippi, New York, Georgia, Kentucky, Tennessee, Michigan, Missouri. *History of the People of the United States*, by John Bach McMaster, VII, 44–48.

be in strict accordance with the immutable principles of honesty and justice. Meanwhile, we congratulate the whole business community that the vexed question will soon be put at rest, and in a way, we trust, that will command their hearty acquiescence." [1] The hope so expressed was made a reality by the Court; for in its decision, speedily rendered, it held that statutes of this nature, changing the mortgage laws of the State, affected the rights, and not merely the remedies, of a mortgagee, and were, therefore, in violation of the clause of the Constitution forbidding the impairment of obligation of a contract. "It would be unjust to the memory of the distinguished men who framed the Constitution," said Taney, " to suppose that it was designed to protect a mere barren and abstract right, without any practical operation upon the business of life. It was undoubtedly adopted as a part of the Constitution for a great and useful purpose. It was to maintain the integrity of contracts and to secure their faithful execution throughout this Union by placing them under the protection of the Constitution." [2] Those who, in 1837, had feared that in his decision in the *Charles River Bridge Case* Taney had departed from Marshall's doctrines, now witnessed him announcing a decision which carried Marshall's view of obligation of contract even further than Marshall had himself. "I read the opinion," wrote Story to Taney, "with the highest satisfaction, and entirely concur in it. I think your opinion is drawn up with great ability, and in my judgment is entirely conclusive," and after regretting Judge

[1] *New York Journal of Commerce*, Feb. 8, 1843.

[2] In view of the widespread and important interests involved, it was singular that the case was not argued orally; and as Taney said in delivering the opinion: " On the part of the complainant, a printed argument has been filed (by Isaac N. Arold), but none has been offered on behalf of the defendant. As the case involves a constitutional question of great importance, we should have preferred a full argument at the bar."

McLean's dissent, Story added: "There are times in which the Court is called upon to support every sound constitutional doctrine in support of the rights of property and of creditors." [1]

Unquestionably, the country owes much of its prosperity to the unflinching courage with which, in the face of attack, the Court has maintained its firm stand in behalf of high standards of business morale, requiring honest payment of debts and strict performance of contracts; and its rigid construction of the Constitution to this end has been one of the glories of the Judiciary. That its decisions should, at times, have met with disfavor among the debtor class was, however, entirely natural; and while, ultimately, these debtor-relief-laws have always proved to be injurious to the very class they were designed to relieve and to increase the financial distress, fraud and extortion, temporarily, debtors have always believed such laws to be their salvation and have resented judicial decisions holding them invalid. Consequently, this opinion of the Court in the *Bronson Case* aroused great antagonism in the Western States. In Illinois, a mass meeting was held which resolved that the decision ought not to be heeded, called on Illinois officials to withstand the findings of the Court or resign and declared that they would resist peaceably or forcibly as might be necessary.[2] Judge McLean (who had warmly dissented) stated, in holding Circuit Court in Illinois, that he should hold the law invalid in that Court, not because he believed it so, but only because of the controlling power of the Supreme tribunal; but he refused to hold invalid a stay-law relative to sales on execution, although containing similar provisions to the mortgage

[1] *Taney*, 289, letter of Story, March 25, 1843.
[2] See *Sangamon Journal* (Springfield, Ill.), March 16, 1843; *Missouri Republican*, March 6, 1843; *Niles Register*, LXIV, June 17, 1843.

law.[1]   An Ohio law magazine termed the Bronson decision "a wide departure," and spoke of the "uncertainties in title to real estate already produced in Indiana and Illinois, and the consequent sacrifice of prosperity." [2]   Later, deference to the antagonism aroused
against the Court by this decision was made when the
Senator from Illinois, James Semple, introduced in the
Senate in 1846, a joint resolution proposing a Constitutional Amendment to prohibit the Supreme Court from
declaring void "any Act of Congress or any State regulation on the ground that it is contrary to the Constitution of the United States or contrary to the Constitution
of any particular State." [3]   The effect of the Bronson
decision upon the financial conditions of the country
was rendered the more severe by reason of the fact
that, almost coincident with that decision, came the
repeal of the National Bankruptcy Act by Congress, on
March 3, 1843 ; and thus, at the same moment, relief was
denied to debtors under both State and Federal laws.

At the end of this 1843 Term, it became evident that
a considerable change in the membership of the Court
was impending.   The death of Judge Baldwin, whose
mental powers had been impaired, was expected at any
moment ; Judge Thompson was seriously ill ; and Judge
Story was considering his resignation, for his relations
with his Associates had been unpleasantly affected by
an episode occurring during the Term — the appoint-

[1] A similar stay-law of Illinois as to executions was held invalid in 1844, in
McCracken v. *Hayward*, 2 How. 608 ; and a similar law in Indiana in 1845, *Gantly*
v. *Ewing*, 3 How. 707 ; see also *Law Reporter* (1843), VI, 46.

[2] *Western Law Journ.* (1846–47), IV, 254 ; V, 173 ; "Who can foresee the amount
of litigation, who can foretell the evils to flow from this unhappy confusion of obligation, and remedy, of contract and judgment ? "   Chief Justice Gibson in *Chad-
wick* v. *Moore* (1844), 8 Watts & Serg. 49, refused to follow the decisions of the Supreme Court of the United States as to this form of statute.

[3] *29th Cong., 2d Sess.*   John M. Berrien, Senator from Georgia, introduced a bill
to regulate the appellate jurisdiction of the Court, on Jan. 19, 1847.   Both of these
measures died, however, in the Committee on the Judiciary.

ment of Gen. Benjamin C. Howard of Maryland as Reporter of the Court in place of Richard Peters. Though Peters had served since 1828, personal friction had long existed between him and Judges Baldwin and Catron; there had been complaint also as to delays in publication of his reports;[1] and the newspaper press had resented difficulties put in its way by the Reporter relative to the furnishing of copies of opinions.[2] His removal, while possibly justifiable, had been made in so extraordinarily summary a manner as to arouse considerable sympathy; for no advance intimation of such a step had been given by members of the Court, and it was taken at a time when neither Judge Story nor Judge McKinley had reached Washington and when the vote of the other Judges was divided — Baldwin, Wayne, Catron and Daniel favoring Howard, and Chief Justice Taney and Judges McLean and Thompson voting for Peters.[3] Of this action, Judge Story wrote to McLean that he had "seldom been more pained", and that the removal was wholly unexpected and beyond anything

[1] See *Sumner Papers MSS*, letter of Peters to Sumner, Aug. 23, 1843, as to "a most unexpected and unmerited attack by the publication of what he (Catron) calls *Errata* spread out into three pages in the volume of Mr. Howard." See also *McLean Papers MSS*, letter of Peters to McLean, Jan. 23, 1843 (five days before Peters' removal), explaining that delays were frequently due to withholding of opinions from the Reporter by the Judges, and stating that publication of Vol. 16 of *Peters Reports* "was delayed five weeks for want of your own opinion in the *Prigg Case*."

[2] *National Intelligencer*, March 3, 1842; March 12, 1844. The *National Intelligencer*, March 17, 1835, published a correspondence between Richard S. Coxe, Richard Peters and Chief Justice Marshall relative to publication to Supreme Court opinions by Duff Green, the editor of the *United States Telegraph*, as interfering with the official reports. To Peters, Marshall had written, March 14, 1835: "Your gentlemanly deportment and the accuracy and fidelity with which your official duties have been performed, have secured the lasting esteem of, dear Sir, your obedient servant, J. M."

[3] The appointment of Howard was made under the recent Act of Aug. 26, 1842; see also comments on this appointment in *United States Gazette*, Jan. 29, Feb. 1, 1843; *National Intelligencer*, Jan. 30, 1843; *Western Law Journ.*, I, 83. Peters himself wrote an indignant letter to Charles Sumner, Feb. 11, denouncing the "coarse, rude, and ungentlemanly mode" in which the removal was made without any intimation of it to him in advance, and attributed it largely to the "malignant hostility" of Judge Baldwin, *Sumner Papers MSS*.

he could have dreamed of; that Peters had always been most courteous and deferential to the Court and "ought not to have been subjected to the mortification of an ejection from office without notice and without enquiry." He also wrote that he felt personally "the full force of this neglect and want of courtesy", of the other Judges in making the appointment in his absence, "an occurrence which never before took place during the absence of a Judge, accidental or otherwise, since I have belonged to the Court, in matters that equally concerned all of them. But let it pass, I no longer ever expect to see revived the kind and frank courtesy of the old Court, and I am content to take things as they are." [1]

On December 18, 1843, Judge Smith Thompson died, after twenty years of service on the Bench. "He was not only their honored and respected Associate in the discharge of their official duties, but he was beloved as their friend and endeared to everyone by his frankness, his kindness and his unstained honor," said the Court in response to the resolutions of the Bar. The vacancy caused by his death (which left Judge Story the only survivor of the old Marshall Court) gave rise to a prolonged contest between the Executive and Senate. The bitter political feud between President Tyler and the Whigs was now at its height. Tyler had determined to become a candidate for the Democratic nomination for President; and any nomination for the Bench which he might make was certain to be subjected to searching scrutiny by the Senate. No one, however, anticipated the extraordinary move which Tyler now made. Mar-

[1] *McLean Papers MSS*, letter of Story to McLean, Feb. 9, 1843. Charles Sumner wrote to McLean, Feb. 2, 1843, *ibid.*: "I think that nothing has occurred at Washington which has affected his (Story's) spirits so deeply. His sleep was destroyed the night after he received your letter." (Incidentally, Sumner added that if Peters had resigned, he himself would have liked to be a candidate for the position, as suggested by Story and McLean.)

tin Van Buren, seemingly at the height of his popularity, was the leading candidate of the Democracy for the Presidency; and it was to this political opponent and rival that Tyler ingenuously made the offer of the vacant position on the Court. The episode was described by Silas Wright, Senator from New York and leader of the Van Buren Democracy (then becoming known as the Locofocos), in an extraordinary, vivid letter to Van Buren, as follows : [1]

Our day yesterday was beautiful and the consequence was a very great press at the President's house. I was there about one o'clock and never saw more people, and never so few whom I knew. It is said that very few of the prominent Whig members or their families presented themselves. Still, I doubt not that the Captain is delighted this morning, and is now more than ever satisfied that the *masses* are clearly for him, and that he is even more personally popular with them than even Gen. Jackson was. The fact that the Clay-Whigs staid away will increase his confidence and his joy. Is it not happy to be so constituted? . . . I never knew the city so entirely destitute of strangers at this season of the year or the hotels appearing so desolate. You will ask where our crowd have come from? I suppose mostly from the City, and from Georgetown, Alexandria and Baltimore. I never saw so few carriages at the levee by quite the half, and yet I doubt whether there were ever more people. So that you will see I shall agree with the Capt. that it was a *democratic* turnout. Indeed I never knew half so many of the dignitaries and their ladies walk.

But enough of this, as you have a more direct interest now discussing here, of which it is my object to speak and not of the proceedings at Court, on New Year's Day. You have been made a candidate for the vacancy upon the bench of the Supreme Court, for a week past, and for a portion of this time your prospects have been said to be decidedly promising — better even than those of our friend Spencer. You

[1] *Van Buren Papers MSS;* letter of Wright to Van Buren, Jan. 2, 1844; see *History of the People of the United States*, by John Bach McMaster, VII, 345, quoting part of this letter.

must not suppose me as attempting to hoax you or to play off a joke upon you. I am telling you the mere truth, and for the last week and a half, I expected your nomination to us as an Associate Justice of the S. C. of the U. S. The first intimation of this sort which came to me was from General Mason of Michigan, the father of the late Gov. Mason, whom you doubtless know very well. He called upon me very diplomatically and broke the subject to me in the most solemn and formal manner. I can usually keep my face when I try hard to do so and have any warning that the effort will be required, but this took me too much by surprise and I did not succeed at all, but met the suggestion by a most immediate fit of laughter. Seeing that this annoyed the General more than I could suppose it ought, the idea at once occurred to me that he had been sent to me from a high quarter. I at once changed my manner and left him at liberty to talk on — I discovered too that he had a carriage at the door, and apologized for detaining him and leaving his driver exposed to the storm, for I think he had sat an hour and it rained and blew most violently. He said that was of no consequence and remained, I think, for full another hour. I told him very gravely that I was sure you would not seek, or accept, the place, if your name had not been and was not to be connected with the Presidential election at all, and so believing I must suppose you would be compelled respectfully to decline the offer, if made, situated as you was, but really treated the matter decorously. This seemed to please him, and he talked very freely, professed to be strongly your friend, but was perfectly convinced you could not be elected President, if nominated; and what was more sagacious, entertained quite as deep a conviction that the consequence of your appointment as Judge would be *my* nomination for President with the certainty of an election. I asked him very gravely if Mr. Tyler thought as he did upon that point, and then he said he had not seen, or conversed, with Mr. Tyler upon either subject, but he *knew* that your name had been presented to him, as a proper one to be used in his nomination of Judge, and that too by some of your best friends.

In the course of the conversation, he often asked me if I thought either you, or your friends, could look upon your nomination by the President as an act of hostility to you or as an attempt to degrade you, and whether, if you were nominated, your friends in the Senate and even I *could* vote against you, and he seemed anxious to have my answers upon those points.   I finally told him that to propose a man for a place upon that elevated Bench, and thus proclaim to the country his fitness and that by a political opponent, could not be tortured into an act of hostility; that no man in this Country was so high as to be authorized to feel himself degraded by the offer of such a position, and that I certainly could not vote to *reject* your nomination for such an office. These replies seemed to delight him, and his answer was quick and triumphant with deep laughter: "You are right, you are right, you *can't* vote against him."   At length, rising to go, he asked me what, upon the whole, I thought of the proposition.   I replied, very steadily looking him in the face: "Tell Mr. Tyler from me that if he desires to give the whole country a broader, deeper, heartier laugh than it ever had, and at his own expense, he can effect it by making that nomination." This did not seem to please him, and he left at once.   I laughed myself almost sick, not entertaining a doubt, as I do not now, that the Capt. had sent him to me.   Still, I kept the communication wholly to myself, only getting my wife to help me keep it and to help me laugh, and did not hear another word upon the subject for two or three days, when all at once the matter became one of public notoriety, and conversation and laugh; and since that time I have it from Davies, who gets his news from Parmelee, that the President has been, upon various occasions, determined to send your name, and has considered the movement one of the most happy which ever occurred to a statesman, and that his friends had had great trouble to keep him from doing it. My information of yesterday, however, is that your prospects are at an end and that Spencer's name will be given to us tomorrow.

Wright's discouragement of Tyler's project to appoint Van Buren had its effect; and on January 8, 1844, the President sent to the Senate the name of John C. Spencer of New York, a lawyer of great talent, but a man whose varying course in politics had brought upon him the violent enmity of a portion of the Whig Party. Though an ardent Whig in politics, a strong former opponent of Tyler, his opposition to Henry Clay as a Presidential candidate had led him to accept from President Tyler appointments, first as Secretary of War, and next as Secretary of the Treasury. He had administered the latter office "with an ability, assiduity, integrity and faithfulness seldom equalled since the days of Hamilton", wrote a contemporary, "a man of great abilities, industry and endurance, curt manners and irascible temper." [1] The appointment was highly obnoxious to the Clay Whigs.[2] "I have no confidence in the political integrity of Mr. Spencer," wrote Erastus Root of New York to Senator John J. Crittenden. "He was always first to foist himself into any political party which could give him hopes of preferment. . . . There is but one consideration in this instance to recommend him to Whig favor; that is, to place him in a situation where he can inflict but little political injury." Henry Clay wrote to Crittenden that "if Spencer be confirmed he will have run a short career of more profligate conduct and good luck than any man I recollect." Francis Granger of New York wrote that Spencer's recreant course at Washington had "developed a character that should not be approved by an appointment to one of the most dignified positions in the world"; that ninety out of one hundred Whigs in New York were opposed to

[1] *Public Men and Events* (1875), by Nathan Sargent. "Before being tendered a position in Mr. Tyler's Cabinet, he had written an address upon his (Tyler's) treachery to the Whig party, more severe than anything that appeared from any other quarter. He fairly flayed the President, lashing him as with a whip of scorpions."

[2] *John J. Crittenden Papers MSS*, letters of Erastus Root, Jan. 1, 1844, Henry Clay, Jan. 24, 1844, Francis Granger, Feb. 3, 1844. Stephen Van Rensselaer wrote to Crittenden from Albany, Jan. 20, 1844, that it would be a great injury to the Whig cause to confirm "one who has been and always will be bitterly opposed to the elevation of Mr. Clay to the Presidency", and that in politics "he is the most finished scoundrel I know." The *New York Herald*, Feb. 9, 14, 1844, stated that the opposition to Spencer was headed by Webster.

Spencer's confirmation, that the universal sentiment
was: "Well, if such treachery is to be rewarded by the
votes of those who have been betrayed, we do not see
any necessity for political integrity." In view of the
nominee's unpopularity, and of the Whig bitterness
towards him, it became evident that he could not be
confirmed, although, wrote a Washington correspondent,
"all acknowledge his legal ability to fill with honor the
office." [1] On January 31, 1844, the Senate rejected
the nomination by a vote of twenty-one to twenty-
six. "Spencer has terrible but just punishment," wrote
Thurlow Weed. "But it was hard, killing him. He
made a tremendous struggle for confirmation." "The
Senators felt," said the *New York Herald*, " that our Supreme Court is our last bulwark, our fortress, our rock
and tower of defence when all else fails and the vacancy
must be filled with a man of diamond purity, and ada-
mantine integrity." "I consider the rejection of Spencer as one of the very best acts of the Senate," wrote Senator Crittenden to Granger. "His confirmation would
have been a plain violation of all public political morality and would have been to make the Supreme Court an
asylum for broken down, disgraced and guilty politicians. As far as I can hear, the people everywhere approve his rejection." [2] While the rejection was thus

[1] *New York Herald*, Jan. 6, Feb. 2, 1844. On Jan. 16, 1844, the correspondent
wrote that there was considerable feeling in Washington that the appointment
ought to be confirmed, out of justice to the President and respect to the Supreme
Court, in order that the Bench might be filled before the argument of so great cases
as those of the *Girard Will* and of *Myra Gaines* then pending.

[2] *Francis Granger–Thurlow Weed Papers MSS;* letter of Weed to Granger, March
11, 1844, letter of Crittenden to Granger, Feb. 10, 1844. Crittenden continued in
this letter: "I congratulate you on the bright and heightening prospects of the
Whigs. Unless all human reasonings and appearances are vain, there can be no
doubt of the success of their cause, and the election of Clay to the Presidency."
Eliphalet Nott wrote to Chesselden Ellis (Congressman from New York), Feb.
4, 1844: "I perceive that the die is cast and that our friend Spencer is rejected.
So be it, I only hope that a worse man may not be forced, through party animosity,
upon the country." *Mass. Hist. Soc. Proc.*, LIII. The *Madisonian*, the Tyler
Administration paper in Washington, hotly criticized "the sanguinary proceedings

JOHN SERGEANT

HORACE BINNEY

REVERDY JOHNSON

JOHN J. CRITTENDEN

placed upon high moral grounds, the fact was that it was due solely to Whig politics.

After this rejection of an eminently qualified lawyer from New York in the Second Circuit, President Tyler next made the unusual move of offering the position to two of the great leaders of the Supreme Court Bar, coming from another Circuit (the Third) — John Sergeant and Horace Binney of Philadelphia. These two lawyers were then engaged in arguing the *Girard Will Case* before the Court, and their ability had strongly impressed the President. The curious manner in which the offers of appointment were received has been told by Henry A. Wise of Virginia, through whom they were made, as follows: [1] "The evening after Mr. Binney had concluded his great argument . . . Mr. Sergeant was visited by us, at his hotel, to deliver the message of Mr. Tyler. Mr. Binney was in the next room. Mr. Sergeant received the compliment with graciousness and evident pleasure; but he hesitated not to decline the tender of a place upon the Supreme Bench. Before he assigned his reason, he enjoined secrecy during his life, and especially it was not to be disclosed to Mr. Binney. It was that he was past sixty years of age, and that he ought not to accept, but he regarded Mr. Binney as being much more robust than himself, considered that Mr. Binney might accept, and did not wish him to know that he had declined because he considered himself too old, and requested that the President would make the tender of the place to him. It was tendered to Mr. Binney at once, and, behold, he declined it for the same

of the Senate", "the private pique and party considerations" which had led to Spencer's rejection, and stated that it was principally due to Senator Thomas H. Benton; see issues of Jan. 24, 31, Feb. 10, 12, 13, 1844.

[1] *Seven Decades of the Union* (1876), by Henry A. Wise. In the *Life of Horace Binney* (1903), by Charles C. Binney, a doubt is intimated as to the accuracy of the details given by Wise, but, in the main, Wise's account seems to be accurate.

reason, but begged that Mr. Sergeant should not be informed of his reason, and that the place might be tendered to him.   Neither, we believe, ever knew the reason of the other for declining." Failing to secure the acceptance of either of these Philadelphia lawyers, the President again turned to the Second Circuit; and several lawyers of distinction were considered for the position.   At one time, the newspapers stated that the nomination of Henry Wheaton of New York, the former distinguished Reporter of the Court and recently Minister to Prussia, had been absolutely determined upon.   William L. Marcy, Governor of New York, who had resigned from Tyler's Cabinet, had strong friends "who knew and appreciated his worth and peculiar fitness", and his chances for appointment were considered favorable.[1] Hiram Ketchum of New York was said to be backed by Tyler's Secretary of State, Daniel Webster; and Ralph J. Ingersoll of Connecticut, and Cornelius Peter Van Ness of New York were considered as possibilities.   In March, Tyler twice offered the position to the Democratic leader of the Senate, Silas Wright who, though urged by Judge Daniel to accept, twice declined the position, probably wisely, as his

[1] *New York Journal of Commerce*, Feb. 17, 21, March 9, 1844; *Boston Post*, Feb. 19, 1844; *New York Tribune*, Feb. 13, 17, 1844. Marcy's chances of appointment apparently disappeared when his warm supporter, Thomas W. Gilmer of Virginia, Secretary of the Navy, was killed Feb. 28, 1844, in the shocking explosion on the gunboat *Princeton*, on the Potomac River below Mt. Vernon, of which Silas Wright wrote to Van Buren, March 1, 1844 (*Van Buren Papers MSS*): "We are at this moment as much in the dark about the Judgeship as you can be. Two weeks ago, I thought the Chancellor had some prospect, and one week ago, I supposed the same thing of Marcy, but the delay has induced me to suppose that neither nomination is now probable. I relied upon Gov. Gilmer for Marcy's prospect and the awful calamity which we have witnessed here has deprived us of his support further. I cannot write of that shocking affair. The papers will tell you all I know and it is too horrible to think of. It was rumored, a few days since, that the Whigs were making another effort at conciliation, so as to secure the Judge, and I think the fact was so; and you can see, if it was so then, and for that single office, how much more likely such an attempt will be now vigorously made when the two Cabinet places fall in to be struggled for."

confirmation by the Senate would have been doubtful.[1] " No one can conjecture what we shall have as a
Judge for the Second Circuit. What the President will
do, we cannot determine," wrote Judge Story. "I
have my own wishes on the subject, strong and warm,
but I have no hope that they will be gratified. I want
an associate of the highest integrity, with youth and
ambition enough to make him become a deep student
in all the law, and with a spirit of love for the Constitution, and an independence to proclaim it, which shall
make him superior to all popular clamors — and these
to be united with courtesy of manners and kindness of
heart. These, I admit, are high qualities; but I think
I could find them, and so could you, if either of us had
the appointment." [2]

Finally, on March 13, 1844, Tyler sent to the Senate
the name of Reuben H. Walworth, then Chancellor of
the State of New York. The new appointee, though
unquestionably of the highest legal ability, was not only
personally unpopular but politically disliked by the
Whigs; and Thurlow Weed of New York wrote at once
to Senator Crittenden: [3] " He is recommended by
many distinguished Members of the Bar of the State
*merely because they are anxious to get rid of a querulous,
disagreeable, unpopular Chancellor.* Indeed so odious
is he that our Senate, when a majority of his own political friends were members, voted to abolish the office
of Chancellor. Those who recommended him admit
and avow that they did so to get him out of his present

[1] *New York Tribune*, Feb. 16, 1844; *New York Journal of Commerce*, March 9, 14, 1844; *Life and Times of Silas Wright* (1874), by Ransom H. Gillet.

[2] *Story*, II, 480, letter to Kent, March 2, 1844; and on April 25, he wrote to Kent: "O! that I had your excellent son (William Kent) as my colleague on the Bench; then should I feel ready to depart in peace. I have even thought that he and Mr. (Daniel) Lord were the only candidates that, as to age, qualifications and character, a President ought to select for the office."

[3] *John J. Crittenden Papers MSS*, letter of Weed to Crittenden, March 17, 1844.

office.   Should this nomination be confirmed, we shall
have a Loco Foco appointed to the office of Chancellor.
If suffered to remain 'unfinished business', we may expect to see the Nation profit by the appointment of a
better Judge of the Supreme Court, and when Walworth reaches the age of sixty, we may *hope* to get a
better Chancellor."

While this nomination was pending, Judge Baldwin
died, April 21, 1844, after serving thirteen years on the
Court.   "Poor Baldwin is gone.   Another vacancy
on the Bench.   How nobly it might be filled !   But we
are doomed to disappointment," wrote Judge Story to
Ex-Chancellor Kent.   "What can we hope from such a
head of an Administration as we now have but a total
disregard of all elevated principles and objects ?   I dare
not trust my pen to speak of him as I think.   Do you
know (for I was so informed at Washington) that Tyler
said he never would appoint a Judge 'of the school of
Kent' ?" [1]   To fill this second vacancy, President Tyler
first tendered the position to James Buchanan who declined ; [2] he then nominated Judge Edward King, a
distinguished lawyer of Philadelphia, June 5, 1844.

The heated contest which had long prevailed between
the President and the Whig Senate made it unlikely
that his appointments would be confirmed.   Moreover,
Congress was again considering a rearrangement of the
Circuits ; and the Presidential election was approaching.
And furthermore, John J. Crittenden, who had failed of
confirmation in 1829 in the closing days of the Adams
Administration, still had his eye on the Supreme Court ;
for, should Henry Clay, the Whig candidate for the
President against James K. Polk, be elected, Crittenden
no doubt would receive the appointment, if the filling

[1] Letter of Story to Kent, April 25, 1844, *Mass. Hist. Soc. Proc., 2d Series,* XIV
[2] *New York Journal of Commerce,* June 20, 1844; *National Intelligencer,* June 19,
1844.

of the vacancy could be delayed until after the election.[1]
Although influenced solely by personal prejudice, the
Senate was sustained by the Whig newspapers, one
of their leaders saying that it deprecated the evils of an
incompetent, complying or corrupt Judiciary, and that
it looked with entire confidence to the Senate. "Better
the Bench should be vacant for a year, than filled for
half a century by corrupt or feeble men, or partisans
committed in advance to particular beliefs."[2] This
statement, entirely unwarranted by the facts or by the
character of the eminent lawyers nominated, illustrated
the bitterness of the hostility to the President. Accordingly, on June 15, on the last day of the session, the
Senate ordered the nominations to lie on the table —
an act which brought upon the Whigs the bitter condemnation of the Democrats.[3] Five months later, Whig
hopes were crushed by the election of Polk as President;
and there was no longer the slightest excuse for a failure
to confirm Tyler's appointees. A striking view of the
situation was given in a letter from the former Reporter
of the Court, Richard Peters, himself a Whig, to Judge
McLean:[4]

I look forward with growing apprehension to the condition
of the Supreme Court within the next four years. May
heaven in its tenderest mercy preserve the life of our good
Chief Justice. Catron will succeed him, if he should, while
Polk is President, be called to a better world. . . . The
nominations of Judge King and Chancellor Walworth, now

---

[1] *New York Journal of Commerce*, March 19, 1844.

[2] *National Intelligencer*, April 26, 1844.

[3] See editorial of the *New York Evening Post*, quoted in the *Washington Post Globe*,
June 27, 1844, speaking of the "pitiful, canting defense of the Whig Senators."
See also *National Intelligencer*, June 17, 1844, and *ibid.*, June 18, which describes a
curious maneuver of Tyler's, who withdrew the nomination of Walworth and
substituted Spencer's name; objection being made to its consideration, he withdrew Spencer's name and again reinstated the Walworth nomination. The vote on
June 15 to lay on the table the nomination of Walworth was 27 to 20; as to King,
29 to 18.

[4] *John McLean Papers MSS*, letter of Peters to McLean, Dec. 6, 1844.

before the Senate, present an opportunity, by the confirmation of the first, to put on the Bench a man of sound opinions on all the great questions which have come before that Court. I was not the advocate of the confirmation of Judge King, when hopes were entertained that we should elect Mr. Clay. The question is now presented in very different aspects, and I most earnestly desire that he shall be confirmed. He is a man of very strong mind, with extraordinary judicial faculties. His opinions are all that you can desire. (See *Ashmead's Reports*.) For yourself, Judge Story, and such of the Court with whom you agree and associate, he has the highest respect. Altho' he has not the manner in private intercourse as polished as you justly appreciate, yet he has a strong sense of decorum and propriety. He and I have never belonged to the same political school, but I have always regarded him as possessed of perfect probity of character, and his judicial duties have always been performed with perfect impartiality. . . . If King is rejected the next nominee will be John M. Read, as suited for a Judge as I am for an admiral.

And a view of the King nomination from the opposite political standpoint is found in a letter written by John C. Calhoun to Francis Wharton, of Philadelphia, after the election of Polk, in November:[1]

I must say that your letter places his character in a light, which I have not heretofore regarded it. I had taken the impression, that although a man of talents, his political association connected him with a set of politicians of a very objectionable character which subjected his to doubt. Under this impression, I was disinclined to his nomination, without, however, taking any part against it while before the Senate. It is due to the occasion to say that the impression made on my mind, has, I am inclined to think, been made on that of many others; so much so, that his nomination will be in great danger, unless it should be well sustained from the respectable portion of your Bar and the City, especially if your two Senators should be opposed to him. I take it, that the wing of the party, usually opposed to the nomi-

[1] *Amer. Hist. Ass. Rep.* (1899), II, letter of Calhoun to Wharton, Nov. 20, 1844.

nations of the President, will be against him, which would
certainly cause his defeat, unless he should receive the support of the better portion of the Whig party.   If, however,
your two Senators will support him, I should think his prospects would be fair. . . .   I regard the defeat of Clay and
the election of Polk, under all circumstances as a great political revolution.   Great events may grow out of it, if the
victory be used with prudence and moderation.   There is
much to be done to bring things right, and save the Government; but in order to be successfully done, it must be done
gradually and systematically.   I say, save the Government;
for to my mind it is clear, that it cannot go on much longer
as it has for the last 15 or 20 years, and especially the last 8.

In the closing days of his Administration, Tyler made
a last attempt to fill the two vacancies on the Bench by
withdrawing King's nomination[1] and sending in the
name of John Meredith Read of Philadelphia, a former
United States District Attorney, and by withdrawing
Walworth's name and nominating Samuel Nelson of New
York.   Nelson was a lawyer of conspicuous ability, fifty-
two years old, a Judge of the Supreme Court of New
York for fourteen years and for seven years its Chief
Justice.   The choice was so preëminently a wise one
that the Senate at once confirmed it, February 14, 1845,
and on March 5, 1845, Nelson took his seat on the Bench,
where he served for twenty-seven years.   As to Tyler's
other appointment, there was more difference of opinion.   Richard Peters wrote to Judge McLean that Read
was "as suited for a Judge as I am for an admiral."
On the other hand, an equally strong Philadelphia Whig
wrote to W. P. Mangum, the Whig Senator from North
Carolina, that Read was "one of the very best appointments Mr. Tyler ever made"; that "a more correct
gentlemanly man I never knew" and that the Whigs

[1] Tyler renominated King, Dec. 4, 1844, and withdrew the nomination, Feb. 7,
1845.   Nelson was nominated, Feb. 4, and Read, Feb. 7.

wanted his confirmation rather than risk an appointment by President Polk. The Democratic papers
stated him to be "a sound and able lawyer and a firm,
true man", and they rejoiced that the Senate must
either confirm him or leave the appointment to Polk;
"and in either case the Democracy of the country now
have a reasonable assurance that this fearful tribunal,
the Federal Court, will be more in harmony than heretofore with the Democratic principles and doctrines of
the apostle of republicanism." And James Buchanan
wrote of Read that "there are few lawyers, if any, in
Philadelphia his superior, a man of firmness, energy,
and industry. . . . He holds a ready and powerful political pen and is a gentleman of the strictest honour and
integrity." [1] The Senate, however, adjourned without
acting on Read's nomination.

By a decision rendered at this 1844 Term, the future
business of the Federal Courts was enormously aug-
mented and the growth of corporations in the country
was undoubtedly stimulated when the Court decided, in
Louisville etc. R. R. v. *Letson*, 2 How. 497, that for the
purposes of a suit in a Federal Court brought on the
ground of diverse citizenship, a corporation was presumed
to be a citizen of the State in which it was chartered. For
over thirty-five years, the Federal Courts had held that
they had no jurisdiction, on the ground of diverse citizenship, in a case in which a corporation was a party, unless
all the individual stockholders were citizens of a State
other than the State of the opposing party to the suit.[2]

---

[1] *John McLean Papers MSS; Willie P. Mangum Papers MSS*, letter of William
G. Cochran to Mangum, Feb. 8, 1845; *New York Herald*, Feb. 8, 1845; *Boston
Post*, Feb. 15, 1845; *Works of James Buchanan*, VI, letter to Gov. Shunk, Dec. 18,
1844. A letter to Judge McLean from B. W. Richards of Philadelphia, Feb. 10,
1845, termed Read a man of "great energy, very considerable talents, and irreproachable habits — a man of political zeal ", who held Jacksonian beliefs but
" whose political aspirations would terminate when he took a seat on the Bench."

[2] See *Strawbridge* v. *Curtiss*, 3 Cranch, 267, *Hope Ins. Co.* v. *Boardman*, 5 Cranch,
57, and *Bank of the United States* v. *Deveaux*, 5 Cranch, 61.

There had been strong protests made and good reasons advanced against this doctrine. Thus, John Quincy Adams, arguing in 1809, had well said that : "The reason of giving jurisdiction to the Courts of the United States in cases between citizens of different States, applies with the greatest force to the case of a powerful moneyed corporation erected within and under the laws of a particular State. If there was a probability that an individual citizen of a State could influence State Courts in his favor, how much stronger is the probability that they could be influenced in favor of a powerful moneyed institution which might be composed of the most influential characters in the State. What chance for justice could a plaintiff have against such a powerful association in the Courts of a small State whose Judges perhaps were annually elected, or held their office at the will of the Legislature ?" And Robert G. Harper had argued at the same time : "One great object in allowing citizens of different States to sue in the Federal Court was to obtain a uniformity of decision in cases of a commercial nature. The most numerous and important class of those cases, and the class in which it is most important to have uniform rules and principles, is that of insurance cases. They are almost wholly confined to corporations, though most frequently, in fact, between citizens of different States." Judge Wayne now, in deciding the *Letson Case*, said that the old cases had "never been satisfactory to the Bar" nor "entirely satisfactory to the Court that made them"; and he practically overruled them. Of this decision, Story wrote to Kent that he rejoiced that the Supreme Court "has at last come to the conclusion that a corporation is a citizen, an artificial citizen, I agree, but still a citizen. It gets rid of a great anomaly in our jurisprudence. This was always Judge Washington's opinion. I have held

the same opinion for very many years, and Mr. Chief
Justice Marshall had, before his death, arrived at the
conclusion, that our early decisions were wrong." [1]
Though several later decisions of the Court firmly established this jurisdiction of the Federal Courts in corporation cases, there were strong dissenting opinions
which met the approval of many persons who feared the
establishment of any doctrine favorable to the corporations of the day, so rapidly growing in power and corrupt influence.   This fear was expressed later by Judge
Campbell: "Nor can we tell when the mischief will
end.   It may be safely assumed that no offering could
be made to the wealthy, powerful and ambitious corporations of the populous and commercial States of the
Union so valuable, and none which would so serve to
enlarge the influence of those States, as the adoption, to
its full import, of the conclusion, 'that to all intents and
purposes, for the objects of their incorporation, these
artificial persons are capable of being treated as a citizen
as much as a natural person.' . . . The litigation before this Court, during this Term, suffices to disclose the
complication, difficulty and danger of the controversies
that must arise. . . . I am not willing to strengthen or
to enlarge the connections between the Courts of the
United States and these litigants." [2]   On the other
hand, as Judge Catron later pointed out: "If the
United States Courts could be ousted of jurisdiction,
and citizens of other States and subjects of foreign countries be forced into the State Courts, without the power
of election, they would often be deprived, in great cases,
of all benefit contemplated by the Constitution; and in

---

[1] *Story*, II, 469, letter of Aug. 31, 1844.
[2] Campbell, J., diss. in *Marshall* v. *B. & O. R. R.* (1853), 16 How. 314, 353; see
also Daniel, J., diss. in *Rundle* v. *Delaware & Raritan Canal Co.* (1852), 14 How. 80,
95, and in *Northern Indiana R. R.* v. *Michigan Central R. R.* (1853), 15 How. 233,
249, and in *Marshall* v. *B. & O. R. R.* (1853), 16 How. 314, 339.

many cases, be compelled to submit their rights to Judges and juries who are inhabitants of the cities where the suit must be tried, and to contend with powerful corporations in local Courts, where the chances of impartial justice would be greatly against them, and where no prudent man would engage with such an antagonist, if he could help it." [1]

Fifty years after the *Letson Case*, Judge Taft (now Chief Justice of the Court) warmly defended the decision, on the ground that "the ruling was directly in the interest of the new States, who were thirsting for foreign capital, because it removed one of the hindrances to its coming. . . . While the provision of the Constitution was of course intended to avoid actual injustice from local prejudice, its more especial purpose was to allay the fears of such injustice in the minds of those whose material aid was necessary in developing the commercial intercourse between the States, and thus to induce such intercourse and the investment of capital owned in one State in another." [2]   An opponent of the doctrine, on the other hand, pointed out that the decision was rendered at the beginning of the era of railroad building, "when public opinion ran strongly in favor of railroad enterprise", and that at that time, as most corporations were chartered by special acts, and as there was no such thing as a "tramp corporation", the evil possibilities in the doctrine were obscured.   In view of the vast amount of litigation in modern times which would have been eliminated from the Federal Courts, and in view of the popular hostility towards them which has risen from the extensive resort to these Courts by cor-

[1] *Rundle* v. *Delaware & Raritan Canal Co.* (1852), 14 How. 80, 95; Taney, C. J., in *Covington Drawbridge Co.* v. *Shephard* (1857), 20 How. 227.
[2] *Criticism of the Federal Judiciary*, by William H. Taft, *Amer. Law Rev.* (1895), XXIX; *Federal Jurisdiction in Case of Corporations*, by Seymour D. Thompson, *ibid.;* see also *John Archibald Campbell* (1920), by Henry G. Connor, 30.

porations challenging the validity of State legislation, it
may well be doubted whether the Court would not have
acted more wisely, if it had adopted Judge Campbell's
views.[1]

A second case at this 1844 Term, *Vidal et al.* v.
Philadelphia, 2 How. 127, had an important connection
with the history of the country and of the Court; for
its argument by one of the counsel, Daniel Webster,
was utilized as a factor in his campaign for the Presidency; the arguments of two of the other counsel, Horace Binney and John Sergeant, resulted in the offer to
them by President Tyler of appointment on the Court;
and owing to the very peculiar facts of the case, and to
the extraordinarily vivid and picturesque description
of the arguments by contemporary newspapers, few
cases ever more keenly interested the general public or
brought it more closely in contact with the Court.
Under the will of Stephen Girard, a bequest of several
million dollars had been left to the City of Philadelphia
to found a College for the benefit of poor white orphans,
but subject to the unusual condition that all ecclesiastics, missionaries and ministers of any sort were to be
excluded from holding or exercising any station or duty
in the College or even visiting the same.   Three questions were presented in the case: whether a city was
capable of acting as trustee of such a trust; whether the
trust was too indefinite to be enforced in a Court of
Chancery; and whether the trust by reason of its ex-

[1] Simeon E. Baldwin in *A Legal Fiction with its Wings Clipped, Amer. Law Rev.*
(1907), XLI, said that legal fictions are of service "because they make bridges between several epochs, useful while travel goes that way, easily burned or shifted
to new positions when it may be forwarded to some new goal."   See also *Abrogation of Federal Jurisdiction Over State Corporations*, by Alfred W. Russell, *Harv.
Law Rev.* (1893), VII, in which it was said "the welfare of the Federal Courts demands the non-existence of jurisdiction over State corporations."   The first legislative recognition of Federal jurisdiction over corporations in suits based on diverse citizenship was in the Judiciary Act of March 3, 1887, which, for the first
time, used the word "corporation."

clusion of ecclesiastics was contrary to public policy, as being opposed to the Christian religion.   The case was argued for ten days; by Walter Jones on February 2, 3, 5, 1844; by Horace Binney, February 5, 6, 7, 8; by John Sergeant, February 8, 9; and by Daniel Webster (who had just resigned as Secretary of State under Tyler), February 10, 12, 13, — Jones and Webster undertaking the task of breaking down the will.[1]   Of the opening arguments by Jones, an interesting description has been given by a prominent Member of Congress, who was present in the Court-room, Henry A. Wise of Virginia:[2]

In his quaint insinuating, lisping tones, he said: "Mr. Girard had devised more nourishment for the mind, without care of moral instruction, and the trustees had expended an immense sum in erecting a temple to the 'unknown God.' The testator had not meant to make the College religiously free, but to make it free of all religion.   The orphans needed a fish, but they were given a serpent; bread, and they had gotten a stone!"   All this was taken to be personal to Mr. Sergeant who was one of the chief counsellors of the city of Philadelphia in administering the charity; and the point of Mr. Jones was a poniard to him — the more so, because he had always admired and respected Mr. Jones as one of the first forensic men of his day.   Jones did not seem to be conscious of where or whom his point touched, but whilst he was speaking in front of the Judge's seat, Mr. Sergeant was boiling with indignation and wrath in the Court lobby, and the moment Mr. Jones was done, he took him to the lobby and called him to severe account.   Jones was astonished, disclaimed all personality, and calmly remonstrated against

[1] The *National Intelligencer*, Feb. 13, 1844, said: "The interest excited by the nature and magnitude of the great suit growing out of the will of the late Stephen Girard and the fame of the eminent counsel engaged in the cause — Messrs. Jones, Sergeant, Binney and Webster — have for some days past made the hall of the Supreme Court, the centre of attraction.   On Saturday, and yesterday especially, the multitudes of both sexes which crowded into the hall and filled every nook of it, even with the sanction of the Bench itself, exceeded anything which we have for a long time seen in the way of packing a room."

[2] *Seven Decades of the Union* (1876), by Henry A. Wise; see also *Public Men and Events* (1875), by Nathan Sargent; *Life of Horace Binney* (1903), by Charles C. Binney, 215 *et seq.*

Mr. Sergeant's wrath; but the latter was not appeased, and it was feared that some one would have to interpose to prevent serious collision between these two, giants of intellect and champions of argument, but both small in stature. They were finally reconciled, however, though the one was sore under the figure of speech, and the other was sore from the scolding he got for it. . . . Again there was another scene — When Mr. Binney rose to deliver his argument, Mr. Webster having the conclusion, was obliged, by rule, to furnish him with all his points and all his authorities. This he did with great urbanity, just as Mr. Binney was about to open his address to the Court. . . . Mr. Binney had taken a moment to retire to the anteroom of the Court to adjust his personal attire and presence. He was particular about that, and came into the Court refreshed by water and smooth from the comb and brush. He was always very serene in his aspect, and without a forward look, expressed a composed self-reliance. He had just begun, when Mr. Webster rose and apologized for not having obeyed the rule before, and then cited his points and references. Mr. Binney paused to hear him, with his arms folded, and when he was done, smiled a sweet smile of indifference, and gently said, with a slight wave of his hand, that he "fully excused his brother for his delay of citation, for he would have no occasion to touch a single point or anything cited by him"; . . . Mr. Webster was taken back and staggered. Mr. Binney was no better lawyer than Mr. Sergeant, but was a far better speaker, and his style was as rich and pure as that of any other orator or writer of English in his days. . . . His forte was lucid order, perfectly expressed by the clearest logic and the richest but most chaste figure. Mr. Sergeant's forte was solid terseness, direct to the truth, but didactically dry. Neither was superior to Mr. Jones as a forensic debater.

The personalities, by-plays and clashes of counsel were most picturesquely described from day to day by the correspondents of the *New York Herald:* [1]

February 5: The highest judicial officers of the Nation, each robed in a black silk gown, and sitting in a large arm-

[1] *New York Herald*, Feb. 7, 8, 10, 12, 13, 14, 1844.

chair, before his separate table, Justice Story presiding, as Chief Justice Taney is confined to his room by sickness. In front, and some distance off, are four mahogany tables; seated at one of these is a small old gentleman, that is the celebrated Gen. Walter Jones; next is Daniel Webster with beetled brow and dark eyes, poring over the papers, books or printed statements of facts in the case; behind him sits John Calwalader, Esq., of Philadelphia and, in this cause, the principal grubber after facts and documents. He is Horace Binney's son-in-law. At the table parallel to Mr. Webster you behold Horace Binney, white hair, a large head and frame, wearing spectacles, and with strongly marked features. Next to him is John Sergeant. . . . Mr. Jones' argument, probably owing to his ill health, was a rather dull affair, and he spoke so low and with so much hesitancy as to keep the Court on nettles all the time. Mr. Binney appears to have a very ample brief, and to have every link in his chain of argument in its place. The best evidence of this is the fact that Webster and the Judges are kept busy with their pens, noting his points and positions. The argument is very close, searching and logical; and every now and then Webster stops, takes a long breath and goes at his pen again. Daniel evidently has woke up, he is not taking up notes for nothing. . . . It is going to be a tall fight and no mistake, and as the clear voice of the speaker sounds through the arches, you can see the people stretching their necks round the pillars and over the screens, wondering at the transition from Gen. Jones' soporifics. Tomorrow the grand fight begins, and I have no doubt the cars will bring a fresh stock of lawyers.

February 6: The Court-room was densely crowded this morning with ladies and gentlemen at a very early hour. Distinguished members of the legal profession were in diligent and earnest attendance from every part of the United States, intently eager to hear the arguments of these mighty and gigantic intellects. . . . Mr. Webster evidently enjoys his opponent's argument very much, although now and then I think Mr. Binney took the Court and the rest of the counsel into deeper waters than they commonly swim in. . . . Mr. Binney is a pleasant speaker, with a good voice, and evidently a belles lettres scholar. . . . Today in quoting from one of Mr. Webster's own arguments in 13 Peters, he begged him to answer his own authorities. Webster answered: "That was a *bad* case and I had to make my arguments to suit my case." This raised quite a laugh. Throughout the Court-room there is a great silence, save now and then when a bevy of ladies come in. In fact, it looks more like a ballroom sometimes; and if old Lord Eldon and the defunct Judges of Westminster would walk in from their graves, each particular whalebone in their wigs would stand on end at this mixture of men and women, law and politeness, ogling and flirtation, bowing and curtesying, going on in the highest tribunal in America.

February 7: Mr. Binney is still evolving his mighty argument; Mr. Webster looks on with undisguised dismay. It seems he has hitherto regarded the moderate sized octavo brief, which Mr. Binney has been using, as the mighty engine with which he had to contend. But the direful fact has been revealed today that it is but one of seven thunders, and that there are six more yet to come. The Court was astounded at the discovery. There is but one opinion among all those who have listened to this masterly argument; that it has been like a huge screw, slowly turning round on its threads. . . . It has pulverized Mr. Jones' argument. . . . It remains to be seen what Mr. Webster will do; that he will be more powerful as a speaker and more effective with his audience is very probable; but that he can pull Mr. Binney's argument to pieces and build up a better one in its place may well be doubted.

February 10: Daniel Webster is speaking. . . . There is a tremendous squeeze, you can scarcely get a case knife in edgeways. . . . Hundreds and hundreds went away, unable to obtain admittance. There never were so many persons in the Court-room since it was built. Over 200 ladies were there; crowded, squeezed and almost jammed in that little room; in front of the Judges and behind the Judges; in front of Mr. Webster and behind him and on each side of him were rows and rows of beautiful women dressed "to the highest." Senators, Members of the House, Whigs and Locos, foreign Ministers, Cabinet officers, old and young — all kinds of people were there. Both the President's sons, with a cluster of handsome girls, were present. John Quincy Adams sat through the whole of it, listening attentively to every word. Mr. Crittenden sat on Webster's left side, and Horace Binney on his right. The body of the room, the sides, the aisles, the entrances, all were blocked up with people. And it was curious to see on the bench a row of beautiful women, seated and filling up the spaces between the chairs of the Judges, so as to look like a second and a female Bench of beautiful Judges.[1]

February 13: All of the seats of the members of the Bar and half the area behind the Judges were occupied. The audience trespassed hard upon the Judge once. But few persons of the great multitude who desired to be present could get within hearing distance. The opening of the argument was remarkable for all the impressiveness of manner, clearness of expression and power of analysis for which Mr. Webster is so distinguished. The closing part of his address for the day produced a thrilling effect upon those who heard him, and many at times were shedding tears, from his eloquent defence of the power and influences of the Christian religion. The Court adjourned at three o'clock. Mr. Webster finished his argument nobly. Some evil minded persons, as I have no doubt they might be proved to be, have delicately insinuated that Mr. Webster made rather a failure. If it were a failure, they say it must have been either because he was on the wrong side of the case, or else because he had not allowed himself sufficient time to prepare his brief. Others think that Mr. Binney's arguments were so double-and-twisted and tied-up together that Mr. Webster was somewhat bothered to disentangle and tear them to pieces.

" The curious part of the case is that the whole discussion has assumed a semi-theological character," wrote Judge Story to his wife. "Mr. Girard excluded ministers of all sects from being admitted into his college as instructors or visitors; but he required the scholars to be taught the love of truth, morality, and benevolence

[1] Judge Story wrote to his wife, Feb. 10: "The Court room was crowded to suffocation, with ladies and gentlemen to hear him. Even the space behind the Judges, close home to their chairs . . . all presented a dense mass of listeners." *Story*, II, 467.

to their fellow-men. Mr. Jones and Mr. Webster contended that these restrictions were anti-Christian, and illegal, Mr. Binney and Mr. Sergeant contended that they were valid, and Christian, founded upon the great difficulty of making ministers cease to be controversialists, and forbearing to teach the doctrines of their sect. I was not a little amused with the manner in which, on each side, the language of the Scriptures and the doctrines of Christianity were brought in to point the argument; and to find the Court engaged in hearing homilies of faith and exposition of Christianity, with almost the formality of lectures from the pulpit." "To escape an hour or two of soporifics," wrote Adams in his diary, "left the Hall (of Representatives) and went into that where the Supreme Court were in session to see what had become of Stephen Girard's will, and the scramble of lawyers and collaterals for the fragments of his colossal and misshapen endowment of an infidel charity school for orphan boys. Webster had just before closed his argument, for which, it is said, if he succeeds, he is to have fifty thousand dollars for his share of the plunder." [1] And another Member of Congress, John Wentworth of Illinois, wrote regarding the remarkable effect of Webster's argument upon his auditors: "One day, a member came into the House and exclaimed that 'Preaching was played out. There was no use for ministers now. Daniel Webster is down in the Supreme Court-room, eclipsing them all by a defense of the Christian religion. Hereafter we are to have the Gospel according to Webster.' . . . As I entered the Court-room, here are his first words: 'And these words which I command thee this day, shall be in thy heart.'. . . Then again: 'Suffer little *children* to come unto me',

---

[1] *J. Q. Adams*, XI, entries of Feb. 9, 10, 13, 1844; *Congressional Reminiscences* (1882), by John Wentworth, 36.

accenting the word, children.   He repeated it, accenting
the word, little.   Then rolling his eyes heavenward and
extending his arm, he repeated it thus : 'Suffer little
children to come unto *Me*, unto *Me*, unto *Me*, suffer
little children to come.'   So he went on for three days.
And it was the only three days' meeting that I ever attended where one man did all the preaching, and there
was neither praying nor singing.   I have heard such
stalwarts in the American pulpit as Lyman Beecher,
Robert J. Breckinridge, Hosea Ballou, William Ellery
Channing, and Alexander Campbell, but Webster overshadowed them all in his commendation of doctrines
which they held in common.   One could best be re-
minded of Paul at Mars Hill. . . .   There was the
closest attention and the most profound silence except
when, assuming an air of indignation with all the force
with which he was capable, he exclaimed : 'To even
argue upon the merits of such a will is an insult to the
understanding of every man.   It opposes all that is in
heaven and all on earth that is worth being on earth.'
Here the audience, with one accord, broke out in the
most enthusiastic applause.   This is the only time that
I ever heard applause in the Supreme Court-room.
The first day, I easily obtained a seat.   With difficulty,
the next.   But on the third, I scarcely found standing
room."   How widespread was the interest of the public
in Webster's argument was illustrated by an editorial
remark of the *New York Herald*, which was opposed to
Webster, but stated that the demand for its paper,
"yesterday among all the religious circles of the city
was truly extraordinary.   Parsons, clergymen, saints,
the elect of all sects, including sinners, seemed to make
a general rush for the only paper that contained the
wonderful argument of that wonderful man."   That
Webster, in making his eloquent plea in behalf of the

Christian religion, was influenced by the thought of its possible effect on his position as a Presidential candidate seems to have been generally believed, and one of his friends apparently had this in mind in writing to him : "It is a noble argument, and I think unanswerable ; if you are not the man for the clergy and all the clergy of the country, I greatly err in judgment." [1]   With a view to minimizing this political effect of the argument, the Washington correspondents of the Democratic papers evinced a disposition to ridicule it.   One wrote that: "Mr. Webster's sermon has created no small amuse-ment here among the members of the Bar.   It is not known when he will 'take orders.'"   Another wrote of the Court-room "crowded almost to suffocation to witness the greatest novelty of the season — Mr. Web-ster as the peculiar advocate of religion, . . . working himself up into such a fervor of piety as to shed tears while contemplating the malign influence which the bequest would exercise upon the destinies of the rising generation."   And another wrote : "The prevailing expectation is that the Supreme Court will sustain Girard's will.   Binney's rather lengthy *argument* was a most powerful position of professional cannons. Webster's reply today was only a *speech*, at which ladies wept, and reporters cried Amen, but only a speech after all. . . . *His* eulogium of religion ! *His* descrip-tion of the blessings of a holy Sabbath ! Mercy upon us ! What will this world come to ?   But the ladies were delighted, the reporters much edified and most of all who crammed the Court to surfeit thought it very fine indeed." [2]

Two weeks after the close of the arguments, the Court,

[1] *Webster Papers MSS, Van Tyne copies*, letter of Ketchum to Webster, Feb. 21, 1844 ; see also *Works of Daniel Webster* (1866), VI, 133.

[2] *Pennsylvanian*, Feb. 14, 1844 ; *Boston Post*, Feb. 16, 1844 ; *New York Herald*, Feb. 15, 18, 1844.

through Judge Story, on February 27, 1844, decided in
favor of the will, sustaining the trusts created by it and
rejecting Webster's contentions as to its invalidity.
"The great *Girard Case* has been decided against the
argument of Mr. Webster, by the unanimous opinion
of all the Judges; a circumstance somewhat unexpected,
as upon the former argument there was a considerable
diversity of opinion among the Judges," wrote Judge
Story to his wife; and to Kent, he wrote of the opinion
delivered by him: "Not a single sentence was altered
by my brothers as I originally drew it. . . . Mr. Webster did his best for the other side, but it seemed to me,
altogether, an address to the prejudices of the clergy." [1]
The loss of this famous case by Webster was followed
only four months later, by the loss of the Presidential
nomination, when, in May, Henry Clay was chosen as
the Whig candidate for President.

---

[1] *Story*, II, 473, 469, letters of March 3, Aug. 31, 1844. It is interesting to note
that in order to sustain the will, the Court was obliged practically to overrule a
decision of Chief Justice Marshall made in 1819; it was, however, aided in so doing
by the great development of information as to the old common law which had
taken place in England in the twenty-five years since that date, for Binney in his
brief had gleaned from the Calendars of the Proceedings in Chancery in the reign
of Elizabeth and prior reigns (published first in 1827), more than fifty instances of
an exercise of a chancery jurisdiction of which Marshall had stated there was no
trace whatever.

NOTE. As to *Bronson* v. *Kinzie* (p. 102, *supra*) and submission on brief of
cases involving constitutional questions, see views of Judge Wayne in Appendix to
December Term, 1849, 7 Howard, 615. See also criticism of this case by Judge
McLean in *Rire* v. *Decker* (1845), 2 McLean, 575, and *Mathewson* v. *Crawford* (1849),
4 McLean, 540.

On the death of Judge Thompson, the *Law Reporter* (Boston, Jan. 1844), VI,
said that he added lustre to the Bench "by his wisdom, his learning and thorough
moral purity of character . . . and with what an even hand and elevated purpose
he has for twenty years poised the scales of justice in the Nation's Capital, the
whole Bar of the country will testify."

CHAPTER TWENTY–FOUR

STATE POWERS, COMMERCE AND BOUNDARIES

1845–1848

WITH the year 1845 and the beginning of the Administration of President Polk, the country had entered upon a period of commercial and economic development in the trend of which the decisions of the Court were destined to play a considerable part. Hitherto, questions of law arising under the Commerce Clause of the Constitution had been few, and (with the exception of that in *Gibbons* v. *Ogden*) had aroused little general attention. Now, however, the interest of the country in a Nationalistic interpretation of that Clause was becoming increasingly evident. The new methods of interstate and foreign communication were rapidly expanding; in 1831, the first railroads were successfully operated by steam; in 1834, the first through railroad between New York and Philadelphia was opened; in 1846, a bill was reported in Congress to set aside public land for the construction of a railroad from Lake Michigan to Oregon on the Pacific Ocean;[1] by 1848, monopolistic conditions with reference to rail-

---

[1] *29th Cong., 1st Sess.*, see debate in the Senate, July 31, 1846. Senator Sidney Breese of Illinois said that the proposition though novel was "a subject of great importance to the whole Nation and to the world. If the work accomplished by this bill should be accomplished it must revolutionize the commerce of the world." Senator William Woodbridge of Michigan said that it was of consequence to tie the remote States together, to furnish facilities for commercial intercourse. Senator Benton of Missouri said in opposition that "the idea of granting 90,000,000 acres of land to individuals, for the purpose of constructing a road three or four thousand miles through a wilderness and over a range of mountains double the height of the Alleghenies, was one of the most absurd that could be presented to Congress." See also *30th Cong., 1st Sess.*, July 29, 1848.

roads in New Jersey had become so great a grievance to New York merchants as to result in petitions for Congressional action;[1] by 1851, Chicago had been connected with the East by rail, and by 1854, the railroad first reached the Mississippi from the East. The effect of this development upon the Union of the States was marked; and as early as 1830, a South Carolina railroad in asking the Senate for Federal aid had pointed out that: "It will, under the fostering care of the Government, be made to constitute a link of Union with the rising States of the West, attaching them more strongly, through the powerful influences of interest, to their Atlantic brethren." The first law book on railroads, *Angell on Carriers*, in 1849, spoke of their instrumental effect "in cementing in this connection and dependence sections of the country far removed from each other." Foreign commerce was also rapidly developing, since the arrival of the first ocean steamship in 1838. The express business originated in 1838, and the telegraph in 1844.[2] A cheaper postage law

[1] *30th Cong., 1st Sess.*, June 10, 1848, see petition of merchants of New York, presented by Tallmadge of New York in the House, asking for Federal relief against the monopolies granted by New Jersey to the Camden & Amboy R. R. and the Delaware and Raritan Canal Co.

[2] The electro-magnetic telegraph patent was first upheld in 1854 in *O'Reilly* v. *Morse*, 15 How. 62. The first public Morse telegraph instrument was located in a room adjoining the Supreme Court-room in the Capitol, and it was from that room in May, 1844, that the famous dispatches from the Democratic convention in Baltimore announcing the nomination of Polk were read to the large crowd assembled around the window outside, who received them with "speechless amazement." *National Intelligencer*, May 22, 28, 30, 1844; *Samuel F. B. Morse, His Letters and Journals* (1914), II, 221. Senator Willie P. Mangum, the Whig Senator from North Carolina, wrote, May 29, 1844: "The telegraph is in a room in the north end of the Capitol and under my room. Every new turn at Baltimore comes here in less than a twentieth part of a second — absolutely a miraculous triumph of science. Yesterday evening from 4 to 7 o'clock, more than a thousand people were in attendance at the window, at which placards in large letters were exhibited upon the receipt of each item of news. Today, from 700 to 900 were attending when the news came that Polk was unanimously nominated. I was out of my seat at a window above, observing and ready to enquire. Some one cried out 'Three Cheers for Clay.' The air resounded with the outpourings of 500 pairs of strong lungs in three hearty cheers. A call was made for three cheers for Polk, and the feeblest wail of some 20 or 30 voices were heard in modest, subdued and conquered

was enacted in 1846, and postage stamps were pro: vided for in 1847.[1] In 1842, the tide of immigration rose above the 100,000 mark, and from Great Britain and Germany there began to arrive that large influx of new population which became such a factor in the development of the cities and of the new West. The first broad general business corporation laws were enacted in 1848 and 1849, in New York and Pennsylvania. Gold was discovered in California in 1848. All these factors contributed to the importance of the interpretation which the Court should give to the Commerce Clause of the Constitution; and the potency of this Clause in its relation to the respective powers of the Federal and State Governments was recognized with apprehension by the advocates of State-Rights. These fears were interestingly expressed, as early as 1847, in a debate over a seemingly harmless proposition made in Congress to separate the House Committee on Commerce into two committees, one on interstate and one on foreign commerce — desirable, as Samuel F. Vinton of Ohio explained, because of the "vast extent of the Union, the great amount of its commerce and the growing importance of our commercial relations not only between the several States of the Union but with foreign nations." The change was vigorously opposed by Southern Congressmen;

strains, and they were in literal truth, a majority of them, boys who had with equal zeal joined for Clay." *Willie P. Mangum Papers MSS.*

The *National Intelligencer* of June 19, 1844, said that: "The Magnetic Telegraph continues to work wonders. Among the reports of its marvels in the *Patriot* of June 17, is that at 12 o'clock, Chief Justice Taney being at the Electric Register in Baltimore sent his respects to the President (then at the Capitol) with the hope that he was well. The President (Tyler) returned his compliments immediately, stating that he enjoyed good health, and *felt much better since Congress had finally adjourned.*"

[1] In 1846, the rate of postage was fixed at 3 cents up to 300 miles and 10 cents over 300 miles; in 1851, the rate was 3 cents up to 3000 miles and 10 cents over 3000 miles. Adhesive postage stamps were first authorized by the Act of March 3, 1847, and made compulsory by the Act of June 1, 1856.

Robert B. Rhett of South Carolina and Henry Bedinger of Virginia, who said that "the covert" and "the
greatest danger to the institutions and freedom of this
country is to be apprehended from the constant encroachments, or efforts at encroachment, of the confed-
erated Government upon the rights and sovereignty of
the individual States"; and that they feared "the
black cloud on the horizon", and the possibility that
the proposed Committee might interfere with the subject of slavery.[1] Similarly, a proposition for a new
Department of the Interior, or "Home Department",
was opposed as a measure to increase the power of the
Federal Government over the internal commerce and
internal improvements of the States, "to bring the
industrial pursuits of our people within the vortex of
Federal action", "to overshadow by the influence of
this great Federal power the interests of the States",
"another of the pernicious experiments which have
been made with a view to bring the people of the country
under the supervision of the Federal power." "There
is something ominous in the expression 'The Secretary
of the Interior'," said Senator Calhoun. "This Government was made to take charge of the exterior relations of the States. . . . This monstrous bill will
turn over the whole interior affairs of the country to
this Department, and it is one of the greatest steps that
ever has been made in my time to absorb all the remaining power of the States." To all these fears, and
to this "strange confusion of ideas which identified
creation of a new Department with extension of Fed-

[1] *30th Cong., 1st Sess.*, speeches in the House of Vinton and Rhett, Dec. 9, 1847,
of Rhett and Bedinger, Dec. 15, 1847; *30th Cong., 2d Sess.*, debate in the Senate
on the Home Department Act of March 3, 1849, speeches of Robert H. T. Hunter
of Virginia, James M. Mason of Virginia, John M. Niles of Connecticut, John C.
Calhoun of South Carolina opposing, and Daniel Webster of Massachusetts, George
E. Badger of North Carolina favoring, March 3.

eral powers", Webster made a remarkably sane and
patriotic reply, declaring : "I always feel respect for a
voice which is raised against encroachment of the
Federal Government, and always feel ready to co-
operate with those who declare a purpose to restrain
it to its constitutional limits.   But to restrain, is not to
cripple or to destroy.   Within their sphere, the powers
of the General Government are supreme, entitled to the
respect and support of all, and to be maintained and
defended with the same zeal with which encroachments
upon the reserved rights of a State should be resisted."

It was at this striking period in the country's economic development that the Court entered upon its
1845 Term.   Owing to the fact of the two vacancies
on the Court caused by the deaths of Judges Thompson and Baldwin and the refusal of the Senate to confirm Tyler's appointees, few cases of moment were decided.   The question as to the extent of the power of
the States over interstate commerce, in the absence of
Congressional legislation, arose in *Thurlow* v. *Massachusetts*, involving the temperance laws of several of
the Eastern States; but after an able argument by
Rufus Choate against Daniel Webster, a reargument
was ordered and decision was postponed, awaiting
completion of the full Court.[1]   A decision in *Searight*
v. *Stokes*, 3 How. 151, involving two subjects rapidly
becoming obsolete — turnpikes and mail coaches —
marked the growing tendency of the Court to sustain
the powers of the Federal Government, as it held in-

[1] Webster's appearance "drew a crowded audience of both sexes to hear him
speak; the first overflow of the Court-room that has occurred during the present
Term."   *National Intelligencer*, Feb. 1, 1845.   The Washington correspondent of
the *Boston Post*, Jan. 30, 1845, wrote : "Mr. Attorney Huntington arrived here and
took his lodgings with all the big wigs at Coleman's National Hotel.   The case
under the license laws of your State, involving their constitutionality, will be argued about the first of next month, and will be regarded as a great moral phenome-
non in the Capital, where if a man does not get absolutely drunk, he is considered
pretty temperate."

valid an attempt on the part of the State of Pennsylvania to tax vehicles carrying the United States mail on the old Cumberland Road.[1]

At the end of this Term, Judge Story finally decided to resign from the Bench, and to devote his entire time to his law professorship at the Harvard Law School. For some few years past, he had become greatly depressed over the trend of the Court and its decisions, as well as over the political conditions of the times.[2] The fact is that, though not an old man, he was prematurely worn by his long term of judicial service and by his labors on his great Commentaries on the law. Moreover, he was by nature and by association a conservative, to whom the progressive views of Taney and of other recent members of the Court did not appeal. "Although my personal position and intercourse with my brethren on the Bench has always been pleasant," he wrote to his long-time friend, Ezekiel Bacon, "yet I have been long convinced that the doctrines and opinions of the 'Old Court' were daily losing ground, and especially those on great constitutional questions. New men and new opinions have succeeded. The doctrines of the Constitution, so vital to the country, which in former times received the support of the whole Court, no longer maintain their ascendency. I am the last member now living of the old Court, and I cannot

---

[1] See also *Neil, Moore & Co.* v. *Ohio* (1845), 3 How. 720; and *Achison* v. *Huddleson* (1851), 12 How. 293, on this same subject.

[2] Story had written to Judge McLean, Aug. 16, 1844: "My heart sickens at the profligacy of public men, the low state of public morals, and the utter indifference of the people to all elevated virtue and even self respect. They are not only the willing victims but the devotees of Demagogues. I had a letter a few days ago from Chancellor Kent, in which he utters language of entire despondency. Is not the *theory* of our Government a total failure?" So again he wrote to Judge McLean, Nov. 23, 1844, after the election of Polk: "You will know that I have for a long time desponded as to the future fate of our country. I now believe that we are too corrupt, imbecile and slavish, in our dependence upon and under the auspices of Demagogues, to maintain any free Constitution, and we shall sink lower and lower in National degradation." *John McLean Papers MSS.*

consent to remain where I can no longer hope to see those doctrines recognized and enforced. For the future, I must be in a dead minority of the Court, with the painful alternative of either expressing an open dissent from the opinions of the Court, or by my silence, seeming to acquiesce in them. . . . I am persuaded that by remaining on the Bench, I could accomplish no good, either for myself or for my country." [1] This was but a repetition of a sentiment which he had voiced in almost each year since Chief Justice Marshall's death. "I am the last of the Judges who were on the Bench when I first took my seat there," he wrote to Richard Peters in 1836; and the next year: "I am the last of the old race of Judges. I stand their solitary representative with a pained heart and a subdued confidence;" and in 1838: "To me an attendance here is but a melancholy renewal of the memory of departed days and pleasures never to return."

Nothing is more strikingly illustrative of the extreme and bitter partisanship of the politics of the times than the manner in which the news of Story's proposed resignation was received by the Whigs. Loud in their lamentations, they professed the belief that no Judge of any fitness was left on the Bench, since most of the remaining Judges had been appointed by non-Whig Presidents. "I am not surprised at his (Story's) disgust with his service and the bench of the Supreme Court. Among the causes of regret on account of our recent defeat scarcely any is greater than that which arises out of the consequence that the Whigs cannot fill the two vacancies on the Supreme Court," wrote Clay to Crittenden. [2] "The Supreme Court has 'fallen

---

[1] *Story*, II, 527, 226, 275, 296, letter of April 12, 1845; and see letters of Feb. 8, 1836, April 7, 1837, March 15, 1838.

[2] *Life of John J. Crittenden* (1871), by Ann M. B. Coleman, I, 225, letter to Crittenden, Jan. 9, 1845.

from its high estate.' It will never rise again," said
Richard Peters, and again he wrote: "The Bench is
no longer fit for him. The glory of the Supreme Court
as *he* now leaves it will be for *history*. His retrospects
of his judicial life will be most gratifying. His days
in that tribunal were those of Marshall, Livingston,
Washington, Todd, and Trimble. McLean alone remains of that school — what a contrast! Taney is
an eminent and a good man, but he will never cease to
feel the influence of Jacksonism. . . . The presence
of Judge Story was very important, but I did not desire he should sacrifice himself to stay the progress of
evil. He could but have delayed it. The Court is
now composed of third-rate men, the Chief Justice and
McLean excepted. I suppose we shall have as small
a successor to Baldwin as any of the *Puny* Judges." [1]
Ex-Chancellor Kent (who died two years later) wrote
to Story one of his characteristically pessimistic and
conservative letters: "I have for some time from various reports and observations anticipated the sad event
of your retirement from the Bench. The loss will be
immense and altogether, and in any genial times, wholly
irreparable. But you have done your duty most successfully and most nobly, and your decisions and writings will 'delight and instruct the most distant posterity.' What a succession of great and estimable men
have you witnessed as Associates since you ascended
the Bench. Now what a 'melancholy mass' it presents!
I would not sit on that Bench for all the world! I do
not regard their decisions (yours always excepted) with
much reverence; and for a number of the Associates
I feel habitual scorn and contempt. I can never think
well of a man who consented to do what his predeces-

---

[1] *Sumner Papers MSS;* letters of Peters to Charles Sumner, Jan. 23, Sept. 11,
1845.

sor thought dishonest to do, that is, to remove the U. S. Bank deposits to gratify the malignant persecutions of a savage despot, and in palpable violation of contract. Indeed, the prospect of the country appears to me to be deplorable. I am very apprehensive our weak and wicked Administration of unprincipled demagogues will involve us in war, misery, disgrace. Considering such characters as Tyler and Polk, the idea of a great people electing their chief magistrate by popular vote, and with discretion, judgment and honesty, appears to me to be a complete humbug." [1]

On September 10, 1845, Judge Story died. His death came as a great blow to the Bar and to the public and as a genuine grief to the members of the Court. There was a general and universal mourning throughout the country, regardless of party or section. "What a loss the Court has sustained," wrote Chief Justice Taney. "It is irreparable, utterly irreparable in this generation; for there is nobody equal to him," [2] and in his reply to the address of the Supreme Court Bar, in December, he uttered these noble words: "It is here on this Bench that his real worth was best understood, and it is here that his loss is most severely and painfully felt. For we have not only known him as a learned and able Associate in the labors of the Court, but he was also endeared to us, as a man, by his kindness of heart, his frankness and high and pure integrity." But though the affection and esteem felt for the personal character of the deceased Judge were widespread, for some years there had been a feeling, especially among the Democrats, that his exaggerated conservatism was to be deplored; and a few of the more radical

---

[1] *Mass. Hist. Soc. Proc., 2d Sess.*, XIV, letter of June 17, 1845.
[2] *Taney*, 290, letter to Richard Peters, Nov., 1845.

papers now indulged in criticisms, which, while not
generally indorsed, were nevertheless symptomatic of
an increasing desire for a more modern attitude towards
the laws in those who sat upon the Bench. "While
we would pay the profoundest tribute of respect to his
memory as a great lawyer, and to his preëminent social virtues as a man," said the *Boston Post*, "we are
not among those who regard his action as a Judge or
his authority as a commentator, on the whole favorable to our institutions, or his decisions in questions
between general right and exclusive privilege, as sufficiently republican to form the code of laws by which
the highest constitutional tribunal should hereafter
be governed." It stated that the tendencies of the
Court had always been "to a high toned conservatism,"
and "to sustain privilege and monopoly," which must
be counteracted "by placing on the Bench, American Judges instead of British lawyers or learned civilians — men so thoroughly imbued with the spirit of
our democratic institution that they cannot be swerved
from the right, by the possession of uncontrolled power,
or the precedents of English Judges, however profound,
but which are drawn from and go to sustain monarchical and privileged institutions, and whose utmost merit
is that they protect the strictly legal rights of the poor
man, but take care never to extend those rights by construction, while they always favor vested privileges of
exclusive classes, even beyond the letter and spirit of
the written law." This paper rejoiced that President
Polk now had a chance to make an appointment of a
Judge who should have moral courage, as well as learning, and who should look to the American people,
rather than to British precedents, "for the sanction
and approval of the doctrines of popular rights and
constitutional construction that ought to govern the

decision of this tribunal." [1]   Such form of criticism
had of course been prevalent from the earliest days,
since the Judges of the Court were oftentimes required
to oppose themselves, in excited periods of financial or
economic stress, to temporary popular demands for
legislation which would overthrow the cardinal principles of honesty and good faith in the observance of
contracts. The charge, however, that Story lacked
anything of Americanism in his principles was of course
ridiculous, and arose only from ignorance on the part
of his critics. Nevertheless, since law writers have
usually indulged in indiscriminate praise of Story's
judicial career, it is important, in considering the relations of the Court to the development of the country
and the effect of its decisions upon contemporary
thought and action, to bear in mind the fact that the
views and decisions of both Story and Marshall were
disliked and distrusted by a considerable section of
the American people, in many cases affecting the social
and political conditions. Yet, in spite of these temporary adverse comments, Story well earned the place
of honor in American legal history to which he was assigned by the Bar; and his decisions will always be
one of the great glories of the American Judiciary. [2]

   To succeed Judge Story, the names of three strong

[1] *Boston Post*, Sept. 13, 1845. Seven years after Story's death, a writer in the
New York Evening Post, Jan. 29, Feb. 4, 1852, which was violently opposed to his
political and economic views, sharply criticized his judicial decisions: "The truth
is Judge Story had an insatiable appetite for admiration; for he was never contented with any position in which that appetite was not indulged, and he preferred
lecturing awe-stricken boys at Cambridge, where everybody sneezed when he
took snuff, to sitting upon the bench of the Supreme Court at Washington by the
side of men of more influence and the objects of more public attention than himself. . . . The fame which he left behind him as a Judge, we think, will not last
long. He has been author of a great deal of bad law, some of which he himself
lived long enough to regret. His opinions are unnecessarily lengthy and display
a vast amount of unprofitable learning which contributes neither to his clearness
as a writer nor to the education of his readers."

[2] See *Judge Story in the Making of American Law*, by Roscoe Pound, *Amer. Law
Rev.* (1914), XLVIII.

Democratic Judges were urged upon President Polk,
— Ether Shepley, Chief Justice of the Supreme Court
of Maine; Marcus Morton, former Governor, and
Judge of the Supreme Court of Massachusetts; and
Levi Woodbury of New Hampshire. On September
20, 1845, Polk finally appointed the latter during the
recess of the Senate (recommissioning him on January
3, 1846). Woodbury was fifty-six years of age; he
had been a Judge of the State Supreme Court, Governor and Senator of his State, Secretary of the Navy
under Jackson, Secretary of the Treasury under
Van Buren, and, when appointed on the Court, was again
serving in the Senate. "A thorough American statesman and jurist, and a sagacious, sound, and always
republican expounder of the Constitution," said a leading Democratic paper, "possessing also every personal quality, urbanity, courtesy, dignity, and every
moral requisite of firmness, fidelity and discretion
which would render him an ornament to the Bench, and
above all a faithful and fearless guardian there of the
constitutional rights of the States and the people.
Taking the whole Union, no man can be named who
would carry to the Bench higher qualifications." [1]
Woodbury's term of judicial service unfortunately
was a short five years, as he died in 1851.

Polk had still one vacancy to fill, that caused by
Judge Baldwin's death in 1844, for which his predecessor, Tyler, had in vain sent in several nominations.
The situation was difficult and complicated, owing
to the rivalries of Pennsylvania politics. He would
have been glad to appoint his Secretary of State, James
Buchanan; but the latter, after announcing in Septem-

---

[1] *Boston Post*, Sept. 13, 1845. It appears from a letter of John Fairfield, of Saco,
Maine, to Martin Van Buren, May 16, 1845, that the Woodbury appointment was
not approved in Maine, the Bar of which wished the appointment of Shepley.
Van Buren Papers MSS.

ber his desire for the position, decided in November to remain in the Cabinet, and indorsed Tyler's appointee, John Meredith Read of Pennsylvania.[1] The claims of Peter D. Vroom, Governor of New Jersey, and of Charles J. Ingersoll and Robert C. Grier of Pennsylvania were also urged upon the President with much pertinacity.[2] Finally, on the recommendation of George M. Dallas, his Secretary of the Treasury, Polk nominated, December 23, 1845, George W. Woodward, a Judge of a Pennsylvania inferior Court.[3]

[1] See *Diary of James K. Polk* (1910), pub. by the *Chicago Hist. Soc.*, entries of Sept. 23, Sept. 29, Nov. 19, Dec. 24, 1845. Buchanan wrote to Louis McLane, Feb. 26, 1846: "I have for years been anxious to obtain a seat on the bench of the Supreme Court. This has been several times within my power, but circumstances have always prevented me from accepting the offered boon. I cannot desert the President, at the present moment, against his protestation. If the Oregon question should not be speedily settled, the vacancy must be filled; and then farewell to my wishes." *Works of James Buchanan* (1908–1911), VII.

George Bancroft wrote to Louis McLane, June 23, 1846: "He (Buchanan) goes upon the Bench, to fill the vacancy in the Pennsylvania and New Jersey Circuit. But of this, the public is as yet uninformed." *Life and Letters of George Bancroft* (1908), by Mark A. E. W. Howe.

[2] *New York Herald*, March 8, 1845.

[3] Thomas Corwin wrote, Jan. 14, 1846: "The Cabinet is perfectly mosaic in its lines. Buchanan is treated as no gentleman would treat a sensible hireling. For instance, Woodward from Pa. is nominated by the President for the vacant seat on the Bench of the Supreme Court, and Buch. does not know of this till a friend drops him a note (in pencil) saying 'it has been done yesterday.' Thus Dallas and Walker prevail over Pennsylvania's favorite son, yet the ass bears his burden and still shakes his ears and is Secy. of State!!" *Quart. Pub. of Hist. and Phil. Soc. of Ohio* (1918).

Richard Peters wrote to Judge McLean, Dec. 25, 1845: "You have a nomination for a Judge for this Circuit. The gentleman who is before the Senate has high talents and much private worth. In both of these respects, he is certainly superior to either of those who have been presented to Mr. Polk. He was a member of the Convention which altered the Constitution of Pennsylvania and there manifested very considerable ability. But he was *radical* in all his views. In favor of a limited term of the judicial office — of the election of Justices of the Peace, and of all such errors. No doubt, when made a Judge of the Supreme Court, he will think a *life tenure* of his office *most* safe and *most* proper. King would have made a better Judge, and he was *sound* on all constitutional questions. Those who prevented his appointment last winter have now their reward! We hear that the Secretary of State was not advised of the nomination of Woodward until after it was sent to the Senate! Modern politicians are like spaniels; the more they are beaten, the more they love their masters." *John McLean Papers MSS.*

The *New York Herald*, Jan. 3, 9, 15, 18, 26, 1846, gave an entertaining account of the opposition to Woodward by the Irish-Americans, whom he had offended by certain "Native American" expressions contained in a speech by him; and it

Woodward was a man of high talents and sterling ability, but without any extended reputation and somewhat radical in his views. He had become obnoxious, however, to certain elements of the party owing to alleged "native American sentiments"; and for this reason and owing to the opposition of Senator Cameron of Pennsylvania, the Senate rejected the nomination, January 22, 1846, by a vote of twenty to twenty-nine. Polk then again turned to Buchanan, who, it was generally understood, would now accept. "The country would unquestionably hail with universal approval the acquisition of the learning and ability of James Buchanan to the highest judicial tribunal in the land," said the *Boston Post*. In June, Polk informed Buchanan that he had again decided to nominate him, and Buchanan accepted, but in August changed his mind for a second time and favored William Bradford Reed, a former Attorney-General of Pennsylvania. Thereupon, the President nominated Robert Cooper Grier, of Pennsylvania who was confirmed, August 4, 1846.[1] Grier was fifty-two years of age, and had been Judge of the District Court of Allegheny County for eight years. He served on the Bench twenty-four years, resigning in 1870.

The Supreme Court met in December, 1845, for the first time under the recent statute lengthening its Term and providing for its convening on the second Monday

stated that in the Senate every Whig voted against him and that he had only nineteen Democratic votes and these were given to him out of compliment to the President; it also stated that the Virginia Democrats opposed Woodward as "scene shifters in this interesting drama of decapitation, to get Buchanan into the Court and Stevenson of Virginia into the Cabinet"; see also *Boston Post*, Sept. 13, 1846. In *The Forum* (1856), by David Paul Brown, II, 734, there is an interesting sketch of Judge Woodward.

[1] As early as Jan. 29, 1846, the *New York Herald* stated that Grier would be appointed, though George M. Dallas was also a strong candidate. See also as to Grier, *The Forum; Green Bag* (1904), XVI. Hampton L. Carson in his *History of the Supreme Court of the United States*, 343, states erroneously that Grier was commissioned by President Tyler, Aug. 4, 1844.

of December in each year.[1] The most important case
decided at this Term was that involving the great conflict between two sovereign States, *Rhode Island* v.
Massachusetts, 4 How. 591, a bill in equity brought
by Rhode Island alleging a mistake in the original location of the boundary line between the two States,
and demanding its establishment by judgment of the
Court and the restoration and confirmation of Rhode
Island in the sovereignty and jurisdiction over the disputed territory. The case had been pending in the
Court for ten years, pursuing the long road of an ordinary equity suit, although it involved the sovereign
rights over territory claimed by two States. Counsel
of the highest ability had presented every point of
which legal skill and strategy were capable, and rulings had been made at successive Terms on many
points of pleading, in all of which Massachusetts had
been heretofore defeated.[2] In 1838, Webster had argued
against Benjamin Hazard that the Court had no jurisdiction in such a controversy. The Court, however,
settled this question of supreme importance, by holding that it possessed jurisdiction in cases involving
disputes as to boundary lines between States (Taney
dissenting on the ground that Rhode Island was suing
for merely political rights). In February, 1844, Rufus
Choate, one of the counsel for Massachusetts, wrote
to Charles Sumner, in the following lively fashion, as
to the enforced continuance of the case due to the two
vacancies on the Bench: "The cause is assigned for
the 20th, and being, as Mr. Justice Catron expressly

[1] Act of June 17, 1844. By this statute, the Judges of the Supreme Court were
relieved of holding more than one Term of the Circuit Court within any District
of such Circuit, in any one year. The result of this provision was to enable the
Court to sit later each Spring in Washington; and in alternate years thereafter
it made a practice of sitting through March, adjourning through April, and sitting
again in May.

[2] See 12 Pet. 657, 755; 13 Pet. 23; 14 Pet. 210; 15 Pet. 233.

declared, a case of 'Sovereign States' it has, before this tribunal of strict constructionists, a terrified and implicit precedence. Great swelling words of prescription ought to be spoken. For the rest, I see no great fertility or heights in it." And on February 17, he wrote: "To my horror and annoyance, the Court has continued our cause to the next Term! The counsel of Rhode Island moved it yesterday, assigning for cause that the Court was not full; that the Chief Justice could not sit, by reason of ill-health; Mr. Justice Story did not sit; and there was a vacancy on the Bench. The Court was, therefore, reduced to six Judges. We opposed the motion. Today Judge McLean said, that on interchanging views they found that three of the six who would try it have formally, on the argument or the plea, come to an opinion in favor of Massachusetts, and that therefore they thought it not proper to proceed. If Rhode Island should fail, he suggested, she might have cause of dissatisfaction. I regret this result, on all accounts, and especially that the constant preparatory labors of a month are, for the present, wholly lost. I had actually withdrawn from the Senate Chamber to make up this argument, which may now never be of any use to anybody." The case was finally argued on the merits, in February, 1846, by Richard K. Randolph and John Whipple against Webster and Choate; and Massachusetts won a complete and signal victory, in an opinion in her favor. The brilliancy and power of Rufus Choate's oratory made a strong impression on the Court; and it is said that Judge Catron was so charmed by it that at future sessions of the Court it became a standing inquiry with him whether Choate was coming on to argue any case.[1]

---

[1] *Life of Rufus Choate* (1878) by Samuel G. Brown, 103. The *New York Express*, Feb. 7, 1846, said that Choate's argument was "adorned with all that was

"I have heard the most eminent advocates," he said, "but he surpasses them all." Of Webster's argument, a newspaper correspondent wrote that "it was of solid masonry and apparently impregnable" and that "Mr. Choate, with his remarkable diction, with his clear and searching analysis and his subtle logic, went far utterly to destroy the work of the preceding three days. Everyone who heard that argument must have felt that there was something new under the sun, and that such a man as Mr. Choate had never been heard in that Court before."

This case set a precedent of most solemn and serious import in the subsequent relations of the States of the Union, and was of high consequence in inspiring a respect for the position of the Court as an arbitrator between sovereignties. Its immediate effect was seen, the next year, in the filing of a similar bill to settle a boundary dispute between two States in the West which had almost led to armed conflict. On December 10, 1847, an original bill was filed in the Court by Missouri against Iowa to determine the rights to a valuable strip of territory, two thousand square miles on the northern and southern boundaries respectively of the two States. The controversy had been in existence for ten years (during which time Iowa had been a Territory). At one time, fifteen thousand troops had been called for by the Governor of Missouri and fifteen hundred had marched to the line to protect the State's alleged rights, while the Governor of Iowa had called out eleven hundred men under arms to retain possession.[1] Missouri had finally abandoned forcible action and appealed to the Court, where the case

able in logic and beautiful in imagery. The Court-room was crowded and all hearers must have been delighted with its power and brilliancy."

[1] See *National Politics and the Admission of Iowa into the Union*, in *Amer. Hist. Ass. Ann. Report* (1897); *The Southern Boundary of Iowa*, by Charles Negus, in *Annals of Iowa — State Hist. Soc.* (Oct., 1866–Jan., 1867); *Iowa Journ. of Hist. and Econ.*, IX, 245 (1909).

was finally decided against her and in favor of Iowa.[1]
The long line of boundary disputes between the States
which have been determined by the Court since 1846,
and with complete acquiescence on the part of the
States in the results, is evidence of the success of the
exercise of its jurisdiction in this class of cases; and
no more eloquent tribute to the influence of such jurisdiction has ever been paid than that which was uttered
by Lewis Cass in the Senate, in 1855.[2] "It is an impressive spectacle, almost a sublime one, to see nine
men, all of them of mature age and some of them in the
extremity of human life, sitting here in the Supreme
Court, establishing great principles, essential to private and to public prosperity, and to the duration of
the Government, whose influence is felt through the
whole Union and whose decrees are implicity obeyed.
It is the triumph of moral force. It is not the influence
of the sword. . . . I repeat, it is a great moral spectacle to see the decrees of the Judges of our Supreme
Court on the most vital questions obeyed in such a
country as this. They determine questions of boundaries between independent States, proud of their character and position, and tenacious of their rights, but
who yet submit. They have stopped armed men in
our country. Iowa and Missouri had almost got to
arms about their boundary line, but they were stopped
by the intervention of the Court. In Europe, armies
run lines, and they run them with bayonets and cannon. They are marked with ruin and devastation.
In our country they are run by an order of the Court.
They are run by an unarmed surveyor with his chain and
his compass, and the monuments which he puts down are
not monuments of devastation but peaceable ones."

[1] *Missouri* v. *Iowa* (1849), 7 How. 660.
[2] *33d Cong., 2d Sess.*, Jan. 17, 1855, 298.

Though the Term beginning in December, 1846, was held in the midst of the War with Mexico, no question connected with the War came before the Court, but the Term was notable for the number of cases in which the question of State-Rights was involved and decided from many different angles.

The problem of the extent to which the States might go in regulating commerce was once more involved in the *License Cases, Thurlow* v. *Massachusetts,* 5 How. 504. In these cases, the Northern States were urging upon the Court the strictest possible construction of the Constitution, in defense of their State laws, and were adopting the extreme Southern State-Rights point of view. "The fact is," said a Democratic Boston newspaper, "Massachusetts by her narrow legislation has sought to nullify the laws of Congress in liquors, while she denounced South Carolina for doing the like in woolens and cottons. She has undertaken in the same way to defraud a constitutional power of the General Government. She dare not pass a law to prohibit commerce direct in this article, but she has evasively empowered her agents, the county commissioners, to do what she had no power to do herself. . . . It is now in a way to be exploded by a tribunal that will not suffer a plain power in the Constitution to be annulled for one purpose, under pretence of arriving at another purpose." [1] At the first hearing of the case, in 1845, the Court had paid great attention to the arguments of Daniel Webster and Rufus Choate attacking the validity of the statutes. "Mr. Choate as usual held his audience during his whole speech which was very able, ingenious and beautiful," wrote a Washington correspondent. "He took the ground that a law of Congress authorizing importation on payment of

[1] *Boston Post,* Feb. 15, 1845.

duties was a license to the importer to enjoy the *consuming ability* of the country, and that any law breaking any link in the chain of traffic from the importer to the final consumer was unconstitutional. The grave consideration the Court gave to the argument against the validity of these laws, which was pressed with the highest vigor by Mr. Webster, should have shamed the Courts, lawyers and juries of Massachusetts who have treated it so flippantly. . . . The impression here is very strong that the Court will decide against their validity." Owing to the two vacancies on the Bench in 1845, the Court had reached no decision, but had ordered a reargument.[1] In 1846, the case was again continued owing to illness of two Judges; but it was finally argued in 1847 (with two cases from New Hampshire and Rhode Island) by the following array of counsel — Daniel Webster against John Davis of Massachusetts, Samuel Ames and John Whipple against Richard W. Greene of Rhode Island, and John P. Hale against Edmund Burke of New Hampshire. "One would have wished to have been today, as Mrs. Malaprop would say, 'like Cerberus', three gentlemen at once," wrote a newspaper correspondent, "that he might have heard Webster in the Supreme Court, Calhoun in the Senate, and the debate on the Wilmot Proviso in the House. Mr. Webster made in the Supreme Court an argument with his usual ability."[2] Of these arguments, those of Webster, Davis and Hale were of particular weight; and it is interesting to note that Hale, who only five years later, as one of the leading abolitionist Senators in Congress, devoted most of his time to attacking the Court and its authority, now, as counsel, concluded his arguments

---

[1] *Boston Post*, Feb. 15, 1845, March 6, 1846.
[2] *New York Tribune*, Feb. 11, 1847.

with this eloquent tribute to the Court: "My clients rely with confidence upon that protection to commerce which this Court on divers occasions have extended, though in so doing they have been under the necessity of pronouncing the legislation of more than one State invalid and unconstitutional. It was to protect commerce that this Union was established. Take away that power from the General Government, and the Union cannot long last. . . . I leave this case, in the confidence that my clients, in common with all the other citizens of this whole country, will ever find (as they ever have in times past) in this Court, a full and ample protection for their constitutional rights, against which the waves of fanaticism, as well as of faction, may beat harmlessly." The Court rendered a decision, upholding the State statute in each case, but differing greatly among themselves as to the grounds of decision — six Judges rendering separate opinions upon the much vexed points as to the exclusiveness of the power of Congress to regulate commerce, and as to the definition of the word "regulate." That partisan politics did not enter into the result may be seen, however, from the fact that the newspapers of both parties praised the decision.[1] The *New York Tribune* said editorially: "The decision is so manifestly right that we never for a moment dreamed or feared that any other could be given. Overwhelming as is the power of the leading counsel on the beaten side, it was morally impossible that he should prevail in this case, without subverting the powers of the State to regulate the sale of poisons or gunpowder and all dangerous substances whatever. Regarding this decision as in-

[1] *New York Tribune,* March 13, 1847; *Boston Post,* March 10, 1847. The *Western Law Journ.* (1847), IV, 525, said that since the decision of the *License Cases,* "there seems to be increased excitement upon that subject. This is especially the case in Massachusetts."

evitable from the outset, we have regretted the delay in pronouncing it, only as giving a sort of countenance to a state of anarchy and pernicious license which could not fail to prove injurious to public morals and that salutary reverence for law which should be cherished in every community." The *Boston Post* said that the decision "will happily put the question of power at rest and settle beyond successful legal controversy the power of the States over the retail trade in ardent spirits." While the decision was naturally of intense interest to the supporters of the Temperance Movement, it was unsatisfactory to the Bar, because of the diversity of reasoning by which the Judges reached their conclusions; and it was not until five years later, when the case of *Cooley* v. *Port Wardens* was decided in 1852, that a lawyer could advise a client with any degree of safety as to the validity of a State law having any connection with commerce between the States.

The relation of the States to the slavery question was presented again in *Jones* v. *Van Zandt*, 5 How. 215, a case argued by William H. Seward of New York and Salmon P. Chase of Ohio against Senator James T. Morehead, and involving the constitutionality of the Federal Fugitive Slave Law of 1793.[1] The Court, through Judge Woodbury, once more upheld the full power of the Nation over this subject, asserting that: "While the compromises of the Constitution exist, it is impossible to do justice to their requirement, or ful-

---

[1] *Western Law Journ.* (1846–47), IV, 286, said as to Chase's argument: "We do not know where, within the same compass, can be found so complete and yet so dispassionate a view of the bearing of the great question of slavery upon the relations of the States, so far as fugitives are concerned." See for account of this case *Life of William H. Seward* (1900), by Frederick Bancroft; *Life and Public Services of Salmon P. Chase* (1849), by J. W. Shuckers; see also the other fugitive slave cases of *Norris* v. *Crocker* (1851), 13 How. 429, and *Moore* v. *Illinois* (1852), 14 How. 13; and the *First Fugitive Slave Case of Record in Ohio, Amer. Hist. Ass. Rep.* (1893).

fill the duty incumbent on us towards all the members of the Union, under its provisions, without sustaining such enactments as those of the statute of 1793." To the argument urging the Court to disregard the Constitution and the Act of Congress, on account of the supposed inexpediency and invalidity of all laws recognizing slavery or any right of property in man, Judge Woodbury very properly replied: "That is a political question, settled by each State for itself; and the Federal power over it is limited and regulated by the people of the States in the Constitution itself, as one of its sacred compromises, and which we possess no authority as a judicial body to modify or overrule. Whatever may be the theoretical opinions of any as to the expediency of some of those compromises, or of the right of property in persons which they recognize, this Court has no alternative, while they exist, but to stand by the Constitution and laws with fidelity to their duties and their oaths. Their path is a straight and narrow one, to go where the Constitution and laws lead, and not to break both, by travelling without or beyond them." The utterance of such views, and the fact that Judges like Story and Woodbury, though strongly opposed to slavery, should have given the opinion of the Court in the *Prigg Case* and the *Van Zandt Case*, ought, it would seem, to have preserved the Court from attack by the abolitionists. But the latter now began an incessant war on the Court, charging it with prejudice, partisanship and even corrupt control by the slavery interest. So extreme were their views that Judge McLean himself, the strongest anti-slavery man on the Court, felt called upon now to address a public letter to one of the abolitionist editors, deploring such accusations and saying:[1]

[1] *John McLean Papers MSS*, undated letter to a Mr. Mathews in 1847.

It is an easy matter to denounce the action of any Court who may differ from our own views, and thereby endeavor to lessen the public confidence in such Court. But denunciation is not argument, and however well it may be calculated to create prejudice and mislead ignorant minds and thereby promote party purposes, it is not the best mode of attaining a high and honorable object. Had you examined the facts of the cases referred to, I am quite sure you would have been restrained from saying, in effect, that the Court was corrupt and that its decisions were always in favor of slavery. . . . Mr. Justice Story wrote the opinion of the Court in the case of *Prigg* which you also refer to. That great Judge has gone to his account, and he has not left behind him in the country or in England a lawyer or Judge of greater learning or purity. All who knew him knew well how strongly he was opposed to slavery. No man had a deeper conviction of its impolicy and injustice than he had. But this could not influence his judgment when he was called upon, under the highest sanctions, to give construction to the Constitution. . . . Differences of opinion may exist as to this judgment of the Court, but no man acquainted with Judge Story could suppose that any motive except that of a conscientious discharge of duty could have influenced his judgment. His reputation is safe. It is above reproach. In Europe and America, he is considered as an honor to his country. I speak of him, as he wrote the opinion. A charge of corruption against such a man, and against Judges Thompson and Baldwin who have also gone to their account, and who were opposed to slavery, to say nothing of the Judges who still live and who agreed with Judge Story, should not be lightly made. . . . It is known to every one that Judges are sworn to support the Constitution and laws. They cannot consider slavery in the abstract. If they disregard what they conscientiously believe to be the written law in any case, they act corruptly and are traitors to their country. The Constitution and Act of Congress give to the master of a slave a right to reclaim him in a free State. So plain are the provisions on this subject that no one can mistake them. How is it expected or desired that a Judge shall substitute his own notions for positive law? While this shall become the rule of judicial action, there will be no security for character, property or life.

In one other case at this Term, the Court showed its freedom from sectional or partisan bias in relation to the slavery issue, and its determination not to adopt the extreme State-Rights point of view in its decisions. In *Rowan* v. *Runnels*, 5 How. 134, it was argued that the decision in *Groves* v. *Slaughter*, relating to contracts for the sale of slaves in Mississippi, should be reversed, because of the fact that since that case the Mississippi Court had adopted a contrary view. Chief Justice Taney held, however, that although the Court would always feel bound to respect State Court decisions, yet, since the State Court had not given any opinion before *Groves* v. *Slaughter*, this Court was not required now to reverse itself; and he stated that if the comity due to State decisions were "pushed to this extent, it is evident that the provision in the Constitution of the United States which secures to the citizens of another State the right to sue in the Courts of the United States might become utterly useless and nugatory." [1]   This decision met with severe criticism in Mississippi where it was regarded as an extreme attack upon the dignity of the State, the importance of which could not be exaggerated.   It was even charged that the Judiciary department of the government was "silently absorbing the rights of the States, and destroying those of the people, without attracting that attention which the magnitude of the interests require. . . . What, in this state of things it becomes the State of Mississippi to do, in order to vindicate its sovereign dignity and protect the rights of its citizens, is a subject for the profoundest reflection of her wisest men.   Tamely to ac-

[1] See an article on *Constitutional Law* severely criticizing this case, in *Western Law Journ.* (1847–48), V.

quiesce is voluntarily to assume a position subordinate
to that of every other State in the Union," and it was
urged that Mississippi should call to the attention of
the other States "the invidious discrimination, which
in an unguarded hour, has been made against her institutions and people by the Supreme Court." [1]

But while it jealously guarded its right to construe
State laws for itself, in the absence of previous decisions by the State Courts, the Court made it plain in
several cases that it was not inclined to press unduly
the Federal authority in this respect.   Thus in *Commercial Bank of Cincinnati* v. *Buckingham's Exors.*, 5 How.
317, it held that no question was presented under the
Judiciary Act, inasmuch as "it was the peculiar province and privilege of the State Courts to construe
their own statutes and it is no part of the functions
of this Court to review their decisions or assume jurisdiction over them on the pretense that their judgments
have impaired the obligation of contracts.   The power
delegated to us is for the restraint of unconstitutional
legislation by the States, and not for the correction of
alleged errors committed by their Judiciary."   And
in *Walker* v. *Tailor*, 5 How. 64, it stated that the power
of reviewing State Court decisions "has been, in some
instances, looked upon with jealousy.   Our decisions
may fail to command respect, unless we carefully confine ourselves within the bounds prescribed for us by
the Constitution and laws." [2]

Three decisions at the Term beginning in Decem-

[1] See *Mississippian* (Jackson, Miss.), March 5, 1847;   March 30, 1849.

[2] In this connection, the case of *Scott* v. *Jones*, 5 How. 343, is especially interesting.   The dry facts in the report of the case do not reveal the historic episode out
of which it arose — "the Toledo War", in which the States of Ohio and Michigan
had been arrayed in arms against each other in 1836, prior to the admission of
Michigan to the Union.   See especially   *Ohio-Michigan Boundary Line Dispute*,
by Todd B. Galloway, *Ohio State Archaeological and Historical Society Reports*, IV;
History of the People of the United States, by John Bach McMaster, VI, 243, 249, 303,
307; *History of Ohio* (1912), by Emilius O. Randall and Daniel J. Ryan, II, 438, 446.

ber, 1847, profoundly affected the commercial development of the country. The first of these was rendered in *New Jersey Steam Navigation Company* v. *Merchants' Bank*, 6 How. 344, arising out of the loss of the steamer *Lexington* with most of her passengers, crew and freight, through fire caused by gross negligence. Suit had been brought by the Bank for loss of specie shipped on board through an expressman, the latter having contracted with the steamboat company that goods shipped were to be at his risk. Because of the alarming increase in steamboat explosions and conflagrations during the past five years, and in view of the rapid development of the express business and that of other common carriers, a decision by the Court as to a carrier's right by contract to restrict his liability for loss was of utmost consequence to the business community. The case had been argued at the previous Term, and was now reargued by Samuel Ames and John Whipple of Rhode Island, against Webster and Richard W. Greene of Rhode Island. "We have the same Judges here as last year, and no more," wrote Webster. "The second argument, therefore, appears to me a very useless labor. Yet it is ordered, and must be had; and if the case is to be again argued at all, it must be thoroughly argued. I shall be obliged to listen to other counsel, and take notes for five days at least, before time for closing the argument will arrive. Mr. Greene thinks that the opinions of the Judges last session in a collision case on the Mississippi, or some of them, give him new hopes of success in the *Lexington Case*, on the question of jurisdiction. I hope it may be so; but I look for much division and diversity. The Court wants a strong and leading mind." [1] Ten days later,

---

[1] The case referred to was *Waring* v. *Clarke*, 5 How. 441; *Correspondence of Daniel Webster* (1857), letters to Franklin Haven, Dec. 28, 1847, Jan. 8, 1848; see also letter of March 18, 1848.

Webster wrote: "We finished the argument of the *Lexington* about the middle of this week, after a discussion of some eight days. I am glad the cause was re-argued; I think we gained by it; and now begin to feel a good deal of hope about the result. I think it now probable, that the Court, by a majority, greater or less, will decide that it is a case of Admiralty jurisdiction; that the owners of the Boat are common carriers, and so answerable, at all events, for the loss, without going into any proof of actual negligence; that the Bank has a right to call on the owners of the Boat, directly; and cannot be turned over to Harnden, by virtue of his notice, etc. These three great propositions of course give us the case; and at this moment I have confidence they will all be sustained. I wish you, however, to keep this communication to yourself, or regard it as confidential for the present. Mr. Greene is going home, but I shall keep all necessary look out." Webster's predictions as to the final decision were exceedingly accurate. The Court sustained the jurisdiction of the lower Court in Admiralty over maritime freight contracts, and made the important finding of substantive law that a common carrier could not by contract relieve itself from liability for want of care, and that, even if it could restrict its liability for gross negligence or absolute insurance, it could only do so by express agreement, brought home to the shipper.[1]

The second decision of importance to the business interests of the country was that in *Planters' Bank of Mississippi* v. *Sharp*, 6 How. 301, a case which had

---

[1] In *Morewood* v. *Enequist* (1860), 23 How. 491. Judge Grier said that the Court would not review the *Lexington Case* as "the whole subject was most thoroughly investigated by counsel and the Court," and "everything which the industry, learning and research of most able counsel could discover was brought to our attention."

been very elaborately argued by Francis Wharton and
John Sergeant of Philadelphia, against Daniel Webster, and Henry D. Gilpin, January 31 and February
1, 2, 3, 4, 1848. It presented the following facts: the
State of Mississippi, after chartering the plaintiff bank
with power to discount bills and notes and to grant
and dispose of property, subsequently enacted statutes
making it unlawful for a bank to transfer any bill or
note; this was designed to enforce another statute
requiring banks to receive their own bank-notes in
payment of debts due to them, for, because of the fact of
the bank-notes being below par, it had been found that
the banks, to evade this statutory form of payment
of bills and notes held by them, would transfer such
bills and notes to a third person. The statute involved
was illustrative of the unsettled conditions of State
banking and of the extreme hostility felt at this time
towards banking corporations —"giant monsters in
a mad career of speculation and fraud", "long and iniquitous violators of every line and letter of their charters, as well as of the general laws of the land" (as they
were termed by a Mississippi paper).[1] The Court
held that the statute impaired the obligation both of
the contract contained in the bank's charter, and of
the contract between the maker of the note and the
bank.[2] At the same time, the Court, through Judge

[1] *Mississippian* (Jackson, Miss.), March 19, 25, 1846; see also *Mississippi Free
Trader* (Natchez, Miss.), Feb. 23, 1848, speaking of the "utter disregard to the
rights of the people always exhibited by bank corporations."

[2] A similar case arising out of the disorganization of State banking was *Woodruff* v. *Trapnall* (1851), 10 How. 190, in which an Arkansas statute repealing a provision in a State bank charter that the notes of the bank should be received in payment of debts due to the State was held to be an impairment of the obligation of
the contract made by the State with the holder of the bank's notes. "A State can
no more impair, by legislation, the obligation of its own contracts," said Judge
McLean, "than it can impair the obligation of contracts of individuals. We naturally look to the action of a sovereign State, to be characterized by a more scrupu-
ous regard to justice, and a higher morality, than belong to the ordinary transactions of individuals."

Woodbury, again expressed its views that the most favorable and least hypercritical construction must be given to acts of State Legislatures in passing upon their validity. "Those public bodies must be presumed to act from public consideration, being in a high public trust; and when their measures relate to matters of general interest, and can be vindicated under express or justly implied powers, and more especially when they appear intended for improvements, made in the true spirit of the age, or for statutory reforms in abuses, the disposition in the Judiciary should be strong to uphold them." The decision was an example of the influence which the Judiciary exerted upon the financial conditions of the country by its insistence upon the rigid observance of contracts.[1]

That the Court, however, was not inclined to allow the doctrine of impairment of the obligations of contracts to limit the State police power or its power of eminent domain was seen by its decision in *West River Bridge Company* v. *Dix*, 6 How. 507. This case was argued by Webster and Jacob Collamer against Samuel S. Phelps of Vermont on January 5, 6, 7, 1848, and presented the question of the constitutional validity of a State law passed under the exercise of the right of eminent domain and condemning a toll bridge operated under a previous State charter. Webster in his argument stated that: " This power, the eminent domain, which only within a few years was first recognized and naturalized in this country, is unknown to our Constitution or that of the States. It has been adopted from writers on other and arbitrary governments. . . . But being now recognized in Court, our only security is to be found in this tribunal, to keep it within some safe

[1] The decision caused some consternation in Mississippi. See *Mississippi Free Trader* (Natchez, Miss.), March 21, 1848.

and well-defined limits, or our State Governments will
be but unlimited despotisms over the private citizens."
"If the Legislature," he said, "or their agents are to
be the sole judges of what is to be taken, and to what
public use it is to be appropriated, the most levelling
ultraisms of Anti-rentism or Agrarianism or Abolition-
ism may be successfully advanced." [1] It is notable
that as late as 1848, the doctrine of eminent domain
(now so axiomatic in our law) should have been regarded as novel. That fears should have been expressed as to its employment to further radical doctrines was less singular. The Court held the statute
constitutional, saying that all contracts are made in
subordination to certain conditions "superinduced by
the pre-existing and higher authority of the laws of
nature, of nations, or of the community to which the
parties belong . . . conditions inherent and paramount,
wherever a necessity for their execution shall occur."
It is difficult to conceive how disastrously a decision
to the contrary would have affected the development
of the country and of its commerce, the improvement
of means of communication by railroad, and the abolition of toll-roads and bridges; and the decision was
hailed with enthusiasm by the many who regarded the
Courts as having hitherto gone to an extreme to protect corporate rights. "It is one of the most important decisions ever given," said the *Boston Post*.
"Thus has a new era appeared upon the power of monopolies by a broad decision in favor of popular rights,
in the high tribunal which, under the guidance of Judge
Story, seems to have been constituted for no purpose
but to secure exclusive privileges to corporations and
monopolies. It is a great blow at monopoly, and will

[1] "Mr. Webster argued this as a new case and as one of much importance, and
it is unquestionably one of great importance as a precedent." *Boston Post*, Jan.
10, 1848.

hold up a wholesome rod over the railroad corporations. . . . Under this decision, any State has the
power to check the assumption of these corporations,
while, at the same time, all the necessary privileges
of corporations are as well secured as ever, and their
real value and utility enhanced by thus harmonizing
them with popular sentiment. The Supreme Court
has done a great act, and posterity will honor and
thank them for it. The motto now is in corporations,
as in civil institutions: 'The present is not the slave
of the past.'" [1]   One Southern paper commended the
decision "to the particular notice of those who consider corporations too sacred to be made amenable to
the laws"; while another termed it "a very important decision which reverses some of the humbuggery
which has hereto been considered law. . . . In its
decision, the Court has triumphantly sustained the
republican doctrine that a corporation can have no
more rights than individuals, and has declared that the
franchise of a corporation is as much property as the
materials it owns, and, as such, may be appropriated
for public use, on reasonable compensation, by the
power of eminent domain in the State. This is a great
triumph of progress over the absurd and venerable
dogmas that have hitherto made charters too holy to
be repealed or legislated on." [2]

This Term was made further notable by reason of
an argument from two veterans of the Bar, who now,
in 1848, opposed each other practically for the last time
before the Court — Henry Clay and John Sergeant.
Though the case, *Houston* v. *City Bank of New Orleans*,
6 How. 486, presented an uninteresting question arising under the defunct Bankrupt Law, nevertheless, as

[1] *Boston Post*, Feb. 4, 1848.
[2] *Mississippi Free Trader*, Feb. 27, 1848; *Mississippian*, Feb. 25, 1848.

was usual whenever Clay appeared in Washington, public interest was intense. "At an early hour, the avenues leading to the Capitol were thronged with crowds of the aged and young, the beautiful and gay, all anxious to hear, perhaps for the last time, the voice of the sage of Ashland," wrote a newspaper correspondent. "On no former occasion was the Supreme Court so densely packed — every inch of space was occupied, even to the lobbies leading to the Senate. Mr. Clay rose a few minutes after eleven o'clock, the hour at which the Court is organized. It has been often said, and truly, that he never was and never could be, reported successfully. His magic manner, the captivating tones of his voice, and a natural grace, singular in its influence, and peculiarly his own, can never be transferred to paper." [1]   Another correspondent wrote: "The Supreme Court this morning was at an early hour, inundated by ladies. They not only filled all and every seat appropriated for the usual audience, but got within the bar and crowded the Judges in their seats — almost pushed them from their stools. The *liberty of the press* never carried to a more dangerous extent. Mr. Clay has always been a great favorite with the ladies. Justly so. The gallantry of his bearing, the dignity of his gestures, the warmth of his manners, his sonorous voice, and the many graces with which he is ideally associated in the general imagination make him the proper favorite of the more discriminating portion of Creation. It is a barren case in which he is interested. It carries no general interest save as it is connected with the constitutionality of

[1] *Works of Henry Clay* (1897), III, 79; *New York Tribune*, Feb. 12, 15, 1848; *Philadelphia North American*, Feb, 14, 1848; *Baltimore Republican*, Feb. 9, 1848; the *National Intelligencer* stated, Feb. 12, 1848: "The Supreme Court-room was, as we had anticipated, crowded almost to suffocation yesterday to see and hear Mr. Clay. . .   Very many were unable to get into the room."

the Bankrupt Law. . . . It mattered not to the audience, however, how dry or intrinsically uninteresting the subject. It was Mr. Clay they wished to hear. . . . They hung upon his words as if each was an inspiration. He looks well. Three score years and ten have passed over him without diminishing the brilliancy of his eye or his towering form. He is every inch a man." Another correspondent wrote that, by the common consent of the Court and the Bar, "Mr. Clay exhibited as much vigor of intellect, clearness of elucidation, power of logic and legal analysis, as he ever did in his palmiest day." In opening his argument, Clay recalled to the Judges that not a face was on that Bench which was seen when he first had the honor of appearing there; [1] and he stated that "it was a grateful reflection that amidst all the political shocks to which the country had been subject, the Court had maintained its elevated name, its dignity and its purity, untouched and unsuspected"; he alluded to "his high gratification at the manifestations of respect he had now met with from old friends of the Bar and Members of Congress, as well as from private citizens, on his reluctant return to scenes of former action; it was usual, he said, for the Court to extend peculiar leniency to young practitioners, and though not of that class, he might have need of indulgence with those not having familiarity with the practice of the Bar." [2]

[1] Clay was seventy-one years old; he had first appeared before the Court in 1807 in *Marshall* v. *Currie*, 4 Cranch, 172. An interesting contemporary account of his early days in Washington is given in the diary of William Plumer.

[2] *New York Times*, Feb. 12, 1848. While Clay remained in Washington to await the decision of the case (which he finally won) his former friend, the aged Ex-President, John Quincy Adams, was stricken ill, while in his seat in the hall of the House of Representatives, and died two days later, February 23, 1848; and in the Supreme Court, the next day in the midst of an argument by Thomas Ewing, of Ohio, the Chief Justice said: "Gentlemen of the Bar, in consequence of the death of Mr. Adams, the Court will not proceed with the case under argument. From the long public service of Mr. Adams, and the distinguished station he has held in the Government, the Court thinks it their duty to show their respect to his memory by

The Term beginning in December, 1848, was marked by the elaborate argument and opinions rendered in the long pending *Passenger Cases, Smith* v. *Turner* and *Norris* v. *Boston*, 7 How. 283. For ten years, the increasing tide of immigration, particularly of paupers and petty criminals from Great Britain, had alarmed the seaboard States; legislation had been enacted to guard against this evil by the imposition of taxes upon alien passengers, and by the requirement of bonds from masters of vessels carrying immigrants; and it was laws of this nature in the States of Massachusetts and of New York whose constitutionality was now challenged, on the ground that Congress had exclusive power over this form of commerce. But while the validity of these laws was the ostensible issue, there was, in reality, a far greater interest at stake, since it was believed by the South that much of its slavery legislation depended on the position which the Court should finally take relative to the scope of the Commerce Clause. Once more it was clearly shown that the opposition of Southern statesmen to the expansion of the power of Congress over commerce was based but slightly on abstract political doctrines relative to strict or broad constructions of the Constitution, and very greatly on the concrete fear as to its effect on the power of the Southern States over slavery.

The relation of the slavery issue to the question of interstate commerce had arisen first in connection with the refusal of two Northern States to extradite persons charged with kidnaping slaves in the South. In 1837 and again in 1838, the Governor of Maine had declined to surrender such persons indicted for violation of criminal statutes of Georgia; and in 1839,

adjourning today without transacting any business." *National Intelligencer*, Feb. 28, 1848.

Governor Seward of New York took a similar action with regard to persons indicted in Virginia. These acts had aroused great indignation in the Southern States, which was further enhanced by the passage of a law in New York granting jury trial in fugitive slave cases.[1] As a retaliation for what they termed "the incendiary dogmas and unconstitutional legislation of New York", the States of South Carolina and Virginia passed laws, in 1840 and 1841, directed against the departure of slaves on vessels and specifically restricting New York-owned vessels; and their newspapers said that "it will not be long before every State in the South . . . will array itself under the example of Virginia against the encroachments of New York on the Constitution and the dangers of these encroachments." [2] That these retaliatory laws were unquestionably in violation of the Commerce Clause and other provisions of the Constitution cannot now be doubted. And that they would be so held, if brought before the Court, was anticipated as early as 1841, when a leading Southern newspaper thus voiced its alarm: "There have hitherto been said to be two 'sweeping clauses' in the Constitution, threatening to sweep off the rights of the States and the People; first the 'necessary and proper' clause; second the 'general welfare' clause. But a third sweeping clause has been

[1] *The Rise and Fall of the Slave Power in America* (1874), by Henry Wilson, I, 474–475; *Law Reporter* (Jan., 1846); *American Jurist* (July, 1840); *26th Cong., 1st Sess.*, speech of John H. Lumpkin of Georgia, in the Senate, March 11, 1840; *30th Cong., 2d Sess.*, speech of Joseph Mullin of New York in the House, Feb. 26, 1849. In *Van Zandt* v. *Jones*, 2 McLean, 596, 671, laws of Kentucky punishing kidnaping of slaves, etc., were upheld at a trial in 1840, and later in *Jones* v. *Van Zandt*, 5 How. 215, in 1846.

[2] *Washington Globe*, Feb. 17, 1842. The statute passed by South Carolina in 1841 provided that any vessel owned or commanded or navigated by a citizen or resident of New York or owned by any citizen other than of South Carolina and departing from any port in New York should not sail with any slaves on board, and if arriving and owned as above by citizens of New York, the vessel should be held and bond for $1000 given to pay all judgments for runaway slaves.

sprung, which threatens to do us as much mischief
as its two predecessors. This is the power over commerce." After speaking of the "dangerous excesses
to which the Federalists are prepared to carry this
power", it said: "In the name of Heaven, what power
would the States have of protecting the lives and property of their own citizens, if this sweeping power of
Commerce were admitted? What becomes of our
quarantine laws, inspection laws, pilot laws — laws
which would prevent the seeds of yellow fever from
being imported from New Orleans? What becomes
of the power to keep the citizens of New York from
stealing our property and refusing to give it up or
those who stole it, if we cannot pass such a bill as may
authorize us to search their vessels, or to demand bond
and security for the indemnity of masters, whose
slaves may be stolen, by every kidnapper?" [1] In opposition to this extreme assertion of State supremacy,
the *National Intelligencer* expressed the view taken by
the more conservative men in all sections of the country that: "If every State may take the laws into its
own hands, in regard to questions involving the regulation of commerce among the several States, and if
the States are to be allowed to do what Congress cannot do, that is, to give preference by regulation of
commerce to the vessels of one State over those of
another, or to vessels of all other States over those of
any one State — then has the Constitution failed in
one among the most important of the purposes for
which it was established. These attempts of the
State to usurp authority belonging to the Government of the United States are becoming more and
more frequent. The success of such an attempt in
New York lately brought us to the verge of a war with

[1] *Richmond Enquirer*, March 4, 1841; *National Intelligencer*, Feb. 17, 1842.

a foreign power, as the attempt itself on the part of another State did with the same power, three years ago; and now two or three States are about having a war of commercial interdicts among themselves, which, unless ended by judicial interposition, may be attended with consequences ever to be lamented."

Owing to the decision of the Court in the *Prigg Case* in 1842, and a decision of the New York Supreme Court based upon it, holding the New York jury trial law invalid, the dangerous question as to the scope of the Commerce Clause of the Constitution and its effect upon these retaliatory laws of South Carolina and Virginia was not presented to the Court. Between 1842 and 1848, however, the question arose in connection with other slavery legislation. For many years, South Carolina had been enforcing its statute against the entry of free negroes into its ports, disregarding entirely the fact that it had been held unconstitutional by Judge Johnson in the United States Circuit Court, in 1823. Louisiana had enacted similar legislation, in 1842; and the Territory of Florida, seeking admission as a State, in 1845, had embodied in its Constitution express power to its Legislature to pass laws for the exclusion of free negroes. The constitutionality of such laws had been the subject of frequent debate in Congress, the anti-slavery men of the North contending that they were in clear violation of the Commerce Clause and of Section Two of Article Four of the Constitution guaranteeing the privileges and immunities of citizens of the several States. The Southerners, on the other hand, claimed that the laws were a valid exercise of the State police power, and like quarantine laws, necessary as a "protection against what is infinitely more dangerous than physical contagion — the introduction of free persons of color into a community where slavery exists, with the means of practicing upon the ignorance of these people, of deluding them into insurrection and of placing in jeopardy the lives of the people of the States." "On the very same principle by which a State may prevent the introduction of infected persons or goods and articles dangerous to the person and property of its citizens, it may exclude paupers, incendiaries, vicious, dishonest and corrupt persons such as may endanger the morals, health or property of the people. The whole subject is necessarily connected with the internal police of a State, no item of which has to any extent been delegated to Congress," argued Senator Lumpkin of Georgia in 1840.[1] In the debate in 1845, on the admission of Florida as a State, the question was discussed with much warmth, on a motion by George Evans of Maine for a proviso withholding from Florida the power to prevent the entrance of free negroes. The proposal was attacked by Robert J. Walker of Mississippi, and by John M. Berrien of Georgia who said: "Each State has the power to protect

---

[1] See *supra*, II, 83–87; and see *26th Cong., 1st Sess.*, speech of Lumpkin in the Senate, March 11, 1840, on a bill to require the United States District Judge to require the surrender of persons found in any State charged with crime committed in another State; *28th Cong., 1st Sess.*, speeches of John Quincy Adams in the House, Dec. 22, 1843, pointing out that South Carolina had officially declared that she preferred both dissolution of the Union and war with Great Britain to repeal of her laws against the introduction of free negroes; *28th Cong., 2d Sess.*, speeches of George Evans of Maine, Robert J. Walker of Mississippi, John M. Berrien of Georgia, Rufus Choate of Massachusetts, William S. Archer of Virginia, in the Senate, March 1, 1845; *30th Cong., 1st Sess.*, speeches of Thomas H. Bayly of Virginia, and George Ashmun of Massachusetts, in the House, April 10, 11, 1848; *30th Cong., 2d Sess.*, speeches of Charles Hudson of Massachusetts, Robert B. Rhett of South Carolina, Isaac E. Holmes of South Carolina, George Ashmun of Massachusetts, in the House, Jan. 31, 1849; *31st Cong., 1st Sess.*, speeches of Jefferson Davis of Mississippi and Berrien, and *passim* in the debate on the Fugitive Slave Law, in the Senate (pp. 1581–1630), Aug. 19–23, 1850, speech of Roger S. Baldwin of Connecticut in the Senate, March 28, 1850. See also *The Rise and Fall of the Slave Power in America* (1874), by Henry Wilson, I, 576–586, II, 1–6; and see *New York Evening Post*, Jan. 24, 31, Feb. 7, 25, 1851, on the official correspondence with England as to these South Carolina statutes in their effect on English subjects.

itself — a power which never would be surrendered. It is, therefore, useless for the other States to attempt to deprive any one of them of the right . . . to suppress a moral pestilence within her borders. I shall rejoice to see this question carried to the Supreme Court for its decision. I have not the slightest doubt that the power of the States to pass police laws for their own protection will be recognized." Rufus Choate of Massachusetts replied that his State would also welcome a decision of the Court; and he pointed out that Massachusetts had, in 1844, appointed an agent, Samuel Hoar, to go to South Carolina to protect the rights of her free colored citizens, and that South Carolina had by statute penalized any attempt by Hoar to litigate the question.[1] William S. Archer of Virginia replied that: "Though Massachusetts is the most enlightened State in the Union, this position has not restrained her from being the instrument of throwing distraction into the Federal councils of the Union by her action on this slavery subject. . . . If we believe that the vessels of New England and Maine are about to bring firebrands to cast into the midst of our cities, we will take precautions to keep off and keep out such an element of mischief. . . . We cannot allow shiploads of persons calling themselves sailors from Massachusetts to come into these ports . . . for the purpose of stirring up the latent embers of the worst forms of civil combustion. . . . Are we going to let the fire break out and conflagrate our cities and towns, in deference to what they call their constitutional rights?"

Under such circumstances, and with so inflammable a political question involved, it is not surprising that

[1] See long article in *Boston Post*, Feb. 12, 1845, on South Carolina and Massachusetts and the Hoar mission, written from the Democratic standpoint.

the Judges of the Court should have made every effort to confine their decisions relating to the scope of
the Commerce Clause of the Constitution to the particular statute presented in each case, rather than to
enounce any broad interpretation or definition of the
language of the Clause.   Since 1845, however, there
had been pending on the docket cases involving the
validity of the New York and of the Massachusetts
immigrant laws, the decision of which apparently
would require a consideration of the questions presented by the free-negro legislation of the South, for
the Massachusetts laws appeared to be similarly repugnant to the Constitution. "Everything may be
said of them," wrote Daniel Webster, "that Massachusetts says against South Carolina"; and one of
the Democratic Party organs also remarked: "Massachusetts is getting a terribly bad reputation abroad
for her ultraism, mock-morals, false philanthropy
and illiberal laws infringing trade and commercial
intercourse." [1]   These laws, however, were warmly
defended by the Whigs of the North, who, equally
with the Democrats of the South, sought to uphold
a strict construction of the Constitution, whenever
legislation which touched their particular social or
economic interest was involved. Owing to the importance of the issue, and to the fact that for three
Terms there had been vacancies on the Bench, the
Court had reached no final decision before the December Term of 1848. The case involving the New York
immigrant law had been the first to be argued, Decem-

---

[1] *Boston Post*, Feb. 10, 12, 1847. "The passenger law is a barbaric law in its
operation. . . .   Add this illiberality in her laws to her constant assaults upon
the Union through her extreme anti-slavery doctrines . . . and you may well
suppose that in the broad theatre of the country the conduct of the Whig Legislature of Massachusetts is giving in the nostrils of the people the very opposite
savor to anything like National odor."

ber 10, 11, 15, 1845, by David B. Ogden and Daniel Webster against John Van Buren (then Attorney-General of New York), and Willis Hall (ex-Attorney-General of New York); the Massachusetts case was first argued by Webster and Rufus Choate against John Davis of Massachusetts, February 5, 8, 9, 1847; both cases were reargued in December, 1847, and again in December, 1848. Of Webster's argument in 1847, a Washington correspondent wrote: "The Court-room was crowded, the ladies occupying most of the seats assigned to the audience. The argument was eminently Websterian, close, compact, powerful. I know not when I have heard Mr. Webster with more pleasure of instruction. His reply to Mr. Van Buren was distinguished for point, force and great playfulness, particularly in answering the argument that it was New York which poured of her abundance into the lap of the National Treasury. . . . Mr. Webster spoke powerfully of the sanctity of the decisions of the Supreme Court, in reply to a remark of the opposite counsel that people were beginning to forget the life-tenure of the Judges, in consequence of the infusion of popular sentiment into the decisions of the Court. He considered this as a very left-handed compliment at best, and it was one he certainly should not pay the Court. The early decisions of the Court were, in some measure inherent to the Constitution itself. They were, indeed, a part of the Constitution, and he could not be so disrespectful to the memory of Jay, Ellsworth, Marshall, Thompson, Baldwin, Iredell, and others, as to reflect upon decisions made by them and interwoven as they were with the Constitution of the Government. Mr. Webster early came to the argument of the case, and spoke with a power and force which cannot be surpassed, if equalled

by any counsel or jurist in the land." [1] A lively description of Webster's young and able opponent from
New York, John Van Buren, was given by another
newspaper correspondent, who termed him "one of
the ablest, most logical and graceful debaters of the
day" in whom "the old constitutional expounder
finds a competitor that taxes severely his great powers
of mind and acknowledged legal acumen. It was
amusing to see with what attention and apparent
eagerness Webster listened to the young debater";
and Van Buren's noted wit was illustrated by the
request to the Court with which he closed, urging upon
it the importance of an early decision as desirable in
every point of view, "but especially in reference to the
poor devils who are now at Quarantine. The cholera
is raging among them with fearful mortality, and it
would be a consolation to their friends to know that
they are dying constitutionally." [2] Webster's own views
of the case and a singularly accurate prophecy as to
the final outcome were vividly presented in a series of
letters written by him to his son, Fletcher Webster,
and to his friend, Peter Harvey. [3] Writing, February 7, 1847, after the first argument of the Massachusetts case, he said:

The Massachusetts law laying a tax on passengers is
now under discussion in the Supreme Court. It is strange
to me how any Legislature of Massachusetts could pass
such a law. In the days of Marshall and Story, it could
not have stood one moment. The present Judges, I fear,
are quite too much inclined to find apologies for irregular

[1] *Baltimore American*, Dec. 24, 1847. The *National Intelligencer*, Dec. 27, 1848,
described Webster's argument as "a surpassing example of the highest power of
reasoning and eloquence."

[2] Letter to *Cleveland Plain Dealer*, quoted in *Mississippi Free Trader*, Jan.
20, 1848; *Savannah Republican*, March 7, 1849.

[3] *Webster*, XVI, XVIII; *Letters of Daniel Webster*, edited by C. H. Van Tyne
(1902); see also *Life of Daniel Webster* (1870), by George T. Curtis, II, 374;
also *Law Reporter*, XI, 478.

and dangerous acts of State Legislatures; but whether the law of Massachusetts can stand, even with the advantages of all these predispositions, is doubtful. There is just about an even chance, I think, that it will be pronounced unconstitutional. Mr. Choate examined the subject, on Friday, in an argument of great strength and clearness. Mr. Davis is on the other side, and I shall reply.

Nobody can tell what will be done with the License Law, so great is the difference of opinion on all these subjects on the Bench. My own opinion is that the License Law will be sustained; that the Passenger Law of Massachusetts will not be sustained. This, however, is opinion merely.

After the second argument, he wrote, December 29, 1847: "At present I am engaged in those old causes now on second argument. I am tired of these constitutional questions. This is no Court for them." After the third argument, he wrote, December 26, 1848:

Saving and excepting a stiff back, I am quite well. I suppose I took cold in the Court room on Friday; when I finished, the heat was suffocating, the thermometer being at 90. The Court immediately adjourned — all the doors and windows were opened, and the damp air rushed in. I did all I could to protect myself. It was just such an exposure which caused Mr. Pinkney's death. He had been arguing against me, the cause arising on Gov. Dudley's will, the first case in 10 or 11 Wheaton. He came into Court the next morning, pale as a ghost; spoke to me, went to his lodgings at Brown's, and never again went out alive. I argued my cause well enough, and if I were not always unlucky nowadays in such cases, I should think I saw a glimmering of success. But tho' we shall get 4 Judges, I fear we may not a 5th.

Just before the final decision, he wrote, February 3, 1849:

There is a great interest here to hear the opinions of the Judges on Tuesday. . . . Several opinions will be read, drawn with the best abilities of the writers. In my poor judgment, the decision will be more important to the country than any decision since that in the steamboat cause. That was one of my earliest arguments of a constitutional question. This will probably be — and I am content it should be — my last. I am willing to confess to the vanity of thinking that my efforts in these two cases have done something towards explaining and upholding the just powers of the government of the United States on the great subject of Commerce. The last, though by far the most laborious and persevering, has been made under great discouragements and evil auspices. Whatever I may think of the ability of my argument — and I do think highly of it — I yet feel pleasure in reflecting that I have held on and held out to the end. But no more of self-praise.

The decision holding the laws of both States unconstitutional was rendered on February 7, 1849, each of the Judges reading an opinion, so that seven hours were thus occupied.[1] Judges McLean, Wayne, Catron, McKinley and Grier held that the laws were a regulation of commerce and conflicted with Congressional legislation, the first two Judges (one from the North and the other from the South) viewing the Federal power over commerce as exclusive, the other three ruling that it was unnecessary to decide the point. Chief Justice Taney, and Judges Nelson, Daniel and Woodbury, dissented, either on the ground that regulation of passengers was not regulation of commerce, or that the tax did not conflict with any Federal statute. As illustrating the freedom from political bias in the decision of this case, it was stated by one of the Washington correspondents that the deciding vote against the State laws was given by the most ardent State-Rights Judge, Judge McKinley.[2]

[1] *Boston Courier*, Feb. 13, 1849.

[2] The Washington correspondent of the *New York Commercial Advertiser*, quoted in the *Boston Post*, Jan. 25, 1849, wrote: "The New York case was once about to be decided on the opinion of four to three. It was then concluded to postpone judgment, until after another argument before a full Bench. Since then, the

The diversity, however, of the views of the Judges, as expressed in their various separate opinions, was so great that the Reporter himself, in perplexity, very frankly declared that there was no opinion of the Court as a Court. Equally perplexed were the members of the Bar and the newspapers. A Baltimore paper said: "Sailors say, in a very hard blow, point no point is the only one you can safely make. In the present gale of judicial wind, that is about the only point discernible. Seriously, the excess of words on the Bench is a great grievance. These seven or eight long opinions will greatly obscure the points really decided, and impair the force of the decision." [1] A New York paper stated that the Judges "have put the whole question of the constitutionality of such laws in doubt and mist. A slight change in the composition of the Court of nine Judges will upset the decision"; and it wisely said: "These separate opinions are to be deprecated as a great nuisance. It is of more consequence to society that the law should be settled, than that it should be wise. We can alter a bad law — we can even change the Constitution — but uncertain law is tyranny." Another New York paper stated that the questions raised "were the highest which ever have been or can be raised in Court", and that the decision "may be regarded as perhaps the most important which has ever received the sanction of this highest Court"; but it deplored the fact that "the Court have, by a meager majority of one, reversed the laws of so many States.

Judges have stood four to four, and upon the arrival of Judge McKinley, it was found that his opinion was adverse to the claims of the States." The *Washington Union*, Feb. 14, 1849, said that few cases were of more importance, and it termed the opinion of Chief Justice Taney "one of the ablest which ever emanated from that distinguished Bench."

[1] *Baltimore Sun*, Feb. 10, 1849; *New York Journal of Commerce*, Feb. 12, 1849; *Boston Daily Advertiser*, Feb. 12, 1849, quoting the *New York Express*.

At one fell swoop the taxing powers of many of the States, New York, Massachusetts, Maryland, Louisiana, go by the board — and one branch of the New York law, that imposing a tax upon passengers from the States of the Union, the Court unanimously condemn. This domestic question has not, however, been before the Court, but being a part of the law of New York, and apprehensive that silence might be deemed acquiescence, the Chief Justice spoke of it as unconstitutional. . . . In listening to the opinions of the eminent men who were heard in Court today, it was impossible not to be more impressed with what are sometimes called 'the glorious uncertainties of the law' than with the stability of the wisest of human judgments. The Chief Justice remarked more than once, and I thought conclusively proved, that the opinion of today was practically a reversion of the previous judgment of the Court."

The decision of the Court, overturning the State laws, was regarded as a disastrous judgment by the dissenting Judges who held strict State-Rights views. Judge Daniel termed it a "trampling on some of the strongest defences of the safety and independence of the States of the Confederacy. . . . I am unable to suppress my alarm at the approach of power claimed to be uncontrollable and unlimited"; and Judge Woodbury said that: "A course of prohibitions and nullifications as to their domestic policies in doubtful cases, and this by mere implied power is a violation of sound principle and will alienate and justly offend, and tend ultimately, no less than disastrously, to dissolve the bands of that Union so useful and glorious to all concerned." These expressions of apprehension were undoubtedly due to the fact that the Judges feared the application of the doctrines of the majority to the slavery legislation of the South. At the argument of the case, warning of this had been explicitly given by counsel for the States. Davis, for Massachusetts had asked, if Massachusetts cannot exclude immigrants likely to be paupers, "on what principle can the laws expelling or forbidding the introduction of free negroes be sustained?" Van Buren, for New York, cited laws forbidding or regulating the admission of free persons of color in fifteen States, non-slaveholding as well as slaveholding. Taney, in dissenting, stated that it must "rest with the State to determine whether any particular class or description of persons are likely to produce discontent or insurrection in its territory or to taint the morals of its citizens, or to bring among them contagious diseases, or the evils and burdens of a numerous pauper population . . . and to remove from among their people and to prevent from entering the State, any person or class or description of persons, whom it may deem dangerous or injurious to the interests and welfare of its citizens." Judge Woodbury in his dissent expressed the same view, and Judge Wayne, of the majority of the Court, stated that "the States where slaves are have a constitutional right to exclude all such as are, from a common ancestry and country, of the same class of men;" [1] the other four Judges of the majority, while failing to rule specifically on this phase of the question, announced views affecting it, which Taney evidently believed to be opposed to his own. The result of the decision was to give great alarm to the South.[2] Thus, the *Charleston Mercury*

---

[1] 7 Howard, 467, 543–544, 426.

[2] *Richmond Enquirer*, March 4, 1841. Thomas J. Turner of Ohio said in the House, Feb. 22, 1849: "The Supreme Court in the celebrated case which has lately been adjudicated within the Capitol says, in effect, that the law of South Carolina is unconstitutional." *30th Cong., 2d Sess.*

said of it : "The intellectual, as well as judicial, weight of the Court is clearly against the decision, but numbers prevailed. If we correctly understand the points decided, they sweep away our inspection laws enacted to prevent the abduction of our slaves in Northern vessels. They sweep away also all our laws enacted to prevent free colored persons — citizens of Massachusetts — or whatever abolition region, from entering our ports and cities. Thus it seems as if the Union is to be so administered as to strip the South of all power of self-protection and to make submission to its rule equivalent to ruin and degradation." [1] A leading Southern Quarterly stated with truculence that: "We have little doubt that the decision will be repudiated by the sober judgment of public opinion, as so many other decisions of the Supreme Court on constitutional questions have been before, and that, if ever the Court should be again filled with such men as formerly occupied its seats, this and other crudities of the present majority of little men would be swept away like chaff before the wind. In the meantime, we hope that the States of New York and Massachusetts will continue to collect their taxes, notwithstanding the adverse decision of the Supreme Court. There are some States in the confederacy, which, if we are not mistaken, would exercise their sovereign rights, in spite of Mr. Justice Wayne and his Associates."

That the dogma of State-Rights was not confined to the South, was strikingly illustrated by the case of *Peck* v. *Jenness*, 7 How. 612, the decision in which at this Term ended a seven years' controversy between the State of New Hampshire and the inferior

---

[1] *Charleston Mercury*, Feb. 14, 1849, quoted in *Boston Courier*, Feb. 21, 1849, and in *Richmond Enquirer*, Feb. 22, 1849; *Southern Quart. Rev.* (Charleston, S. C., Jan., 1850), XVI, 444.

Federal Courts. In 1842, Judge Story in the Circuit Court had held that the clause of the Federal Bankruptcy Act of 1841 preserving "all liens, mortgages or other securities on property, real or personal, which may be valid by the laws of the States respectively", did not apply to attachments on mesne process, and that property so attached in the State Courts should be turned over to the Federal assignee in bankruptcy, and that the Federal Courts had the power to restrain the State Courts by injunction from giving effect to such attachments.[1] This decision was immediately regarded by the Democrats as a confirmation of their fears of the National Bankruptcy Act, and of their claim that the Act was but a step in a general "process of encroachment on State jurisdiction." [2] In January, 1844, in another case, arising in the Supreme Court of New Hampshire, the Chief Justice of that State, Joel Parker, strenuously denied the correctness of Story's doctrine; but in July, 1844, Story reaffirmed his decision, saying that it would be his duty to enjoin a creditor or the State sheriff from proceeding to levy on property of a bankrupt attached in the State Court and that the laws and Courts of the United States were paramount to those of the State. To this, Judge Parker retorted, in another case in 1844, that Story's opinion "may well astonish, if it does not alarm us. . . . There is no principle, or pretence of a principle, of which we are aware, in which we can admit the right of the Circuit or District Court in any manner to interfere and stop the execution of the final process of the Courts of this State. It is an assumption of power that cannot be tolerated for a

---

[1] See *Ex parte Foster*, 2 Story, 131; *Kittredge* v. *Warren*, 14 N. H. 509; *Bellows* v. *Peck*, 3 Story, 428; *Kittredge* v. *Emerson*, 15 N. H. 227; *Peck* v. *Jenness*, 16 N. H. 516. See also *Amer. Law Rev.* (1876), X, 235.

[2] *Washington Globe*, May 5, 1842.

single instant," and he added that a resort to "coercive measures" by the Federal officers "might possibly not be entirely safe." [1] In June, 1844, the Governor of New Hampshire called the attention of the Legislature to the controversy, and to the perils that must flow from it; and that body passed a joint resolution sustaining "the firm and decided stand of the Court" in opposition to "the unwarrantable and dangerous assumption of the Circuit Court of the United States." In taking this stand, the State of New Hampshire used almost precisely the same arguments in behalf of State Sovereignty which South Carolina and other Southern States had so long been maintaining. On December 31, 1844, Judge Story, in an opinion in *Ex parte Christy*, 3 How. 292, attempted to settle the question; [2] but as the case did not call for the decision of the point (the Court holding that it had no jurisdiction), Judge Parker, in a case arising in the State Court, the next year (1845), absolutely disregarded Story's opinion. It was this latter case, *Jenness* v. *Peck*, which now came before the Court for final decision. Jenness had attached goods of Peck; later Peck had gone into bankruptcy, and the United States District Court had decreed that the attachment was not a lien, and had ordered the State sheriff to deliver

[1] The *New York Evening Post*, Dec. 10, 1856, said editorially: "This remarkable controversy between the Federal and State jurisdiction produced a deep excitement in New Hampshire. Judge Story, who with all his blandness and bonhommie, was inclined to an arbitrary exercise of his prerogatives, did not brook pleasantly the resistance of a Judge who, though his superior in ability, was, as he thought, subordinate in judicial rank. Judge Parker, however, as Chief Justice of a Sovereign State, was equally indisposed to submit, and quite electrified his opponent by the declaration from the bench, that he should enforce the judgment of his Court against Federal usurpation with all the power the State would put at his command — an exploit reminding one of the threat of Ethan Allen, of retiring to the Green Mountains and waging war against human nature at large. The Chief Justice had fairly got his back up, and would doubtless have been sustained by the Legislature of his State, even to the point of armed collision with the General Government."

[2] See letter of Story, Jan. 1, 1845, *Story*, II. 509.

the property to the bankruptcy assignee. The case was argued by Charles B. Goodrich for the creditor against Webster. The Court, in its decision, sustained fully the contention of the State, disregarded Judge Story's *dictum*, and held, through Judge Grier, that the District Court had no authority to restrain proceedings in the State Court, or "much less to take property out of its custody or possession with a strong hand." It stated that: "An attempt to enforce the decree would probably have met with resistance, and resulted in a collision of jurisdictions much to be deprecated. . . . We can find no precedent for the proceeding, . . . and no grant of power to make such decree, or to execute it, either in direct terms or by necessary implication, from any provisions of the Bankrupt Act; and we are not at liberty to interpolate it on any supposed ground of policy or expediency." That the Court, however, was not blindly adhering to any extreme view of State powers was to be seen from *United States* v. *City of Chicago*, 7 How. 185, in which it held that the city had no right to open streets through property belonging to the United States. "Though this Court," said Judge Woodbury, "possesses a strong disposition to sustain the right of the States, and local authorities claiming under them, when clearly not ceded, or when clearly reserved, yet it is equally our duty to support the General Government in the exercise of all which is plainly granted to it and is necessary for the efficient discharge of the great powers entrusted to it by the people and the States."

Of all the cases decided at this December, 1848, Term, none had aroused so great an interest politically as that which involved the legality of the new and liberal People's Government and Constitution in

Rhode Island, out of which had grown the so-called Dorr's Rebellion, in 1841–1842. By its decision in this case, *Luther* v. *Borden*, 7 How. 1, which had been pending for five years, and which was now decided in January, 1849, the Court completely disproved the dark forebodings and the mischievously false predictions as to its partisan bias, made by Clay, Kent, Peters and other Whigs, upon the retirement of Judge Story. No case had ever come before it in which the possibility of division on political lines was greater; and yet the Court rendered an opinion (with but one dissenting voice), in opposition to the views of the political party from whose ranks most of the Judges had been appointed. Thomas W. Dorr, the head of the alleged State Government, the valid existence of which was questioned in the case, represented the popular cause — the right of the people to change, in its own way, its form of government. He had secured the support of a considerable portion of the Locofoco, or Democratic, Party in States outside of Rhode Island; and after the failure of his movement to establish his Government, and upon his conviction in 1844 and imprisonment for treason, he had received the sympathy of the Democratic press.[1] His cause, therefore, became distinctly a party issue. In 1845, he had tried to elicit the Court's opinion on the legality of his contentions, by means of an original petition for a writ of habeas corpus; but in *Ex parte Dorr*, 3 How. 103, the Court had unanimously held that it had no jurisdiction to issue an original writ for any prisoner held in custody under the sentence or execution of a State Court.[2] The legality of the

[1] See *Tammany Hall and the Dorr Rebellion*, by Arthur May Mowry, *Amer. Hist. Rev.* (1898), III.

[2] See especially *Niles Register*, LXVII, 242, 257, 289, Dec. 21, 1844. Richard Peters wrote to Judge McLean, Dec. 6, 1844, a prediction that if President Tyler's

Dorr Government, however, came before the Court in another case in 1845, *Luther* v. *Borden*, a suit in trespass brought against members of the Rhode Island militia, acting under martial law declared by the State Legislature, the plaintiff claiming that the act of the Legislature was void, inasmuch as the Dorr Government was the legal authority of the State elected by the people.[1] "This cause," said a leading Democratic paper, "will command the profound deliberation of this high Court, and the people look to the result with the deepest interest. It is, so far as this Court goes, to settle or overthrow the whole doctrines of the Declaration of Independence;" and again it stated that the decision of the case "will determine whether the American doctrine proclaimed in the Declaration of Independence or the doctrine of the divine right of rulers avowed in the manifests of the holy allies of Europe is the real theory of our institutions. A vast responsibility to the country and to all times rests upon the Supreme Court in this weighty cause." Since there were then pending two vacancies in the Supreme Court to be filled, either by President Tyler or President Polk, the *Boston Post* stated its belief that under this aspect "Governor Dorr's cause thus brightens"; and it predicted "that the day of triumph will come, when the great doctrine of popular sovereignty now pending before this high tribunal, and for which he is suffering in the accursed dungeons of reprobate Rhode Island will be reaffirmed

appointees, Walworth and Read, should be confirmed, a majority of the Court, Walworth, Catron, Daniel and Read and Taney would issue a writ of habeas corpus for Dorr and discharge him. The falseness of the prediction is seen from the fact that when the petition was actually presented, within a month, Catron, Daniel and Taney concurred in McLean's decision adverse to the writ. *John McLean Papers MSS.*

[1] See *Life and Times of Thomas W. Dorr* (1859), by D. King; *History of the Dorr War* (1901), by Arthur May Mowry.

as the supreme law of the land." The counsel for the plaintiff, Robert J. Walker of Mississippi and Benjamin F. Hallett of Massachusetts, representing the Dorr faction, and John Whipple of Rhode Island for the defendant, were prepared to argue the case in the spring of each of the years, 1845, 1846 and 1847; but owing to still pending vacancies and illness of Judges, the Court postponed the argument, being unwilling, without full numbers, to decide a case involving so critical issues and as to which so great political excitement had been aroused.[1] It was not until January 22, 1848, therefore, that it was finally argued, at a time when the Mexican War, the Wilmot Proviso and President Polk's policies were causing the sharpest of political divisions throughout the country. Hallett and Nathan Clifford appeared in behalf of the Dorr party, and Webster and Whipple in opposition. The warmth of partisan feeling developed by the argument (which lasted six days) may be seen in a comparison of the accounts by the Washington correspondents of the Whig and Democratic newspapers. One of the former wrote that Hallett had occupied three days, and that: "Mr. Webster's speech on Dorrism will be worth hearing. The Attorney-General of the United States (Nathan Clifford) will close the case in favor of the Dorr movement. Pretty work for the law adviser of the President!" Two days later, it said: "Mr. Webster demolished what was left of Dorrism. His argument was alike brilliant and profound. . . . The report of his speech will be read with eagerness, as it is, perhaps, the best exposition of constitutional liberty ever made. It is a subject that interests everyone. . . . He used up the last remnant of Dorrism. The Court-room was crowded

[1] *Boston Post*, Feb. 5, 15, 1845, Jan. 16, 1846, Feb. 12, 17, 26, 1847.

with ladies and distinguished gentlemen to listen to
the great effort." And on the next day: "Mr. Attorney-General Clifford undertook to defend Dorrism.
If he was no more successful in making the Court
understand it than he seemed to comprehend it himself, the defence must have recoiled upon its author." [1]
This paper rejoiced that, " as Locofocoism made some
capital out of this question in the contest of 1844, . . .
our tribunal of highest resort, which is about to settle
the law of the matter authoritatively, is almost entirely Loco-Foco, the only Whig on the Bench being
John McLean of Ohio, and he a very moderate partisan. The case comes up as an appeal of the Dorr-
ites from the District Court, and the first of their
seven points is as follows: 1. 'That the sovereignty
of the People is supreme and may act in forming a
government without the assent of the existing Government. . . . We can't believe they really think their
case has a leg to stand upon. At all events, we rejoice that the decision rests with Judges of their own
party, appointed by Presidents of their own choice;
and we trust these Judges will meet it manfully, deciding the question on its merits, and not evading it
by a decision based on some incident or technicality.
Let us have Dorrism fairly weighed and measured in
the Supreme Court of the Union." After Webster's
argument, another leading Whig paper wrote that:
"If anything was left of Dorrism and all its abominable Jacobin doctrines, it has, this day, been swept
from the face of existence. . . . In the whole range
of political controversy, there was no one subject better calculated to call forth all the powers of that giant
intellect than this, involving as it did an investiga-

[1] *New York Tribune*, Jan. 25, 26, 27, 28, 29, 31, Feb. 23, March 2, 1848; see also
National Intelligencer, Jan. 26, 1848.

tion of the whole character of the Constitution, the
relations between the Federal and State Governments, and a philosophical analysis of what really
constituted government at all. The occasion and the
man were worthy of each other. The argument was
one mass of lucid reasoning and conviction, that left
not a vestige of the miserable pretexts and dema-
gogism which had been piled up by the opposite
counsel.''[1] The Democratic press, on the other hand,
regarded the case as involving a fundamental principle — the right of the people to change its form of
government; and they hotly assailed Webster's argument that a new Constitution could be adopted by
the people of the States only in the manner prescribed
by statute or previous practice. The *Boston Post*
wrote of it as ''worthy of a monarchist and a despiser
of everything democratic or republican. It is in the
very face and eyes of the institutions of this country. . . . If it was made in consideration of a fee,
it reflects discredit and dishonor on the man who can
be hired to embrace and enforce dogmas that are only
calculated to oppress, debase and enslave a free people.
If it embraces the real opinion of the man, they
are entitled, with their author, to popular execration.
The sentiments breathed in that comment are infamous.'' Another paper spoke of the case as the
greatest ever before the Court, involving ''a question
of the greatest moment to the people of any that ever
will or can be passed upon by any power on earth.
It is the question; are the people or are their rulers
or servants, the sovereign power?''   Of Clifford's

[1] *Philadelphia North American*, Jan. 29, 1848; the *New York Courier* said that
Webster's argument was the ''event of the day, one of his finest and most admirable efforts''; and that the whole argument ''had a degree of public importance from its connection with great questions of government not often possessed
by argument on legal points before our Courts.'' See also *Savannah Daily Republican*, Feb. 3, 1848.

argument, which the Whig papers derided, the *Boston Post* said that it had been termed "by lawyers of the highest eminence who were present, to have been one of the most powerful efforts ever made at that forum upon any great constitutional question. The broad platform on which Mr. Clifford stood . . . was that the right of the people to remodel their Constitution is an absolute, unqualified right, inherent in themselves, and may be exercised independently of the existing government, or without any request or recommendation of the same. . . . The triumphant manner in which Mr. Clifford maintained the proposition met with a hearty response from the large audience who listened to his arguments, and frequently could be seen the interchange of approving smiles, when the Federal doctrines of Mr. Webster and the Federalist *himself* received from the speaker the severe lesson of stern and sometimes indignant rebuke. Mr. Webster remained but a short time in the Court-room during Mr. Clifford's argument. . . . It was natural for the opposer of such doctrines to place himself beyond the sound of the eloquent and impressive censure which followed the enumeration of those antirepublican principles which had just before been the theme of his logic and praise. At the close of Mr. Clifford's speech, many learned members of the Supreme Court Bar stepped forward to congratulate him. Amongst the number was Henry Clay, who expressed himself warmly upon the eloquent and able manner in which the cause had been concluded and submitted to the Court." [1] Another representative

---

[1] It is interesting to note that the rivalry between Henry Clay and Webster at this time for the Presidential nomination was so keen as to lead to a coolness between them, and several newspapers commented on the fact that Clay should so pointedly compliment Webster's opponents in this case. *Baltimore Sun*, Jan. 31, 1848; *Boston Post*, Feb. 10, 1848.

Democratic paper rejoiced "that such a discussion as this has been commenced, under the solemn auspices of a contest before the Supreme Court of our great Nation; and we are content that Mr. Webster should be the exponent of the conservatives or Federalists in avowing the doctrines contained in his speech before that grave body. He is a profound lawyer and has a great name as a statesman. He is, moreover, the very embodiment of Federalism in this country. . . . The question shortly to be decided by the Supreme Court is one that lies at the very foundation of our free institutions . . . and that is so clearly an attribute of popular governments as to be the very breath of their nostrils. It is the question whether the people in this country have the right in themselves to alter or abolish the governments under which they exist. It is this which Mr. Webster has undertaken to disprove and to deny! It is this which the Supreme Court will be called upon to decide. . . . We need not repeat that the whole country will await the decision of the question with intense anxiety."[1]

Three weeks later, after the argument in February, 1848, it was reported in Washington that the Court had decided against Dorr, and the *Tribune* correspondent wrote: "The Dorr case, it is said, is decided in favor of Law and Order. . . . There will probably be some delay in the delivery of the decision,

[1] The *Pennsylvanian* (Phil.), Feb. 1, 3, 1848, quoted the *New York Evening Post* as follows: "It is nothing unusual that Mr. Webster and the Whigs generally should undertake to convince the public that the institutions of government, with all their offices and honors and emoluments and the distinction that attaches to its ministers, is far above and supreme over the plain, simple and humble mass of the people. . . . Are the people sovereign?" The *Boston Post*, Feb. 2, 1848, said: "The bringing up of these causes has been highly useful, whatever may be the result, in making the true issue of the Rhode Island question understood; and since the argument in the Supreme Court, and the deep attention given to them by the learned Judges, no man who respects himself will be found to speak lightly of the issues involved."

but Dorrism has been pronounced a 'miserable stain' by the Supreme Court of the United States, composed of eight Loco-Foco and only one Whig. Judge Taney, the friend and disciple of Jackson, is to be, it is said, its Executor. What *will* Loco-Focoism say to that? It is said that sometime since three of the Judges — Grier, Catron and Woodbury — were in favor of sustaining Dorrism. I wonder whether they will dissent." [1] Owing to the illness of the Chief Justice, no decision in the case was announced until the next Term, when in January, 1849, Taney delivered a magnificent opinion in which the firm position was taken that the question involved in the case, viz., which of the two opposing Governments in Rhode Island was the legitimate one, was purely a question of political power; that the political department of the State had determined it and the State Courts had recognized and acted upon this determination; and that this Court must, consequently, decline to pass upon the question. By this decision, the Court removed itself from the realm of purely political subjects, and proved its determination to withstand appeals to any partisan views which it might be supposed to hold. The fact that both political parties professed to be satisfied with the decision was a singular feature in this disposition of the case. A Whig paper in New York said: "Dorrism has at length received its quietus and in a form from which it can never hope to recover." Another said editorially: "The decision is unanimous against Dorrism. That this humbug should die out we all know; but that the last breath should be knocked out of it by the Chief Justice who was appointed by the great idol of Loco-Focoism was 'the unkindest cut of all.' If there

[1] *New York Tribune*, Feb. 23, 1848.

were any principles which B. F. Hallett & Co. loved, they were Cass and Dorr; and both are defunct. 'Green be the turf above them.' " Another said that the Court had "driven the last nail in the coffin of Dorrism." On the other hand, the Washington correspondent of the leading Democratic paper in Boston wrote that the decision recognized "Dorrism and Dorrism alone to be the fundamental principle of the political institutions of the country", and it continued this curiously erroneous view, by stating that the Court had sustained the right of the majority of the people "to modify or change their constitutional form, without the concurrence or consent of the existing holders of political power." The Administration paper in Washington, however, while recognizing that the Court had not decided in favor of "Dorrism", correctly stated that the Whig papers were wrong in contending that the Court "had denounced Dorrism and overruled all its principles and claims." And the leading Democratic paper in Pennsylvania also correctly said that, while the Court fully sanctioned the right of a majority to determine upon a Constitution, "they regard it to be a cardinal political principle which does not belong to the jurisdiction of the Judiciary. . . . No judicial tribunal can prescribe the rules under which the sense of the majority is to be ascertained. . . . It is therefore, purely a political question, and must be determined by such public agents as are clothed with political authority." [1] La-

---

[1] *New York Courier*, Jan. 4, 1849; *New York Tribune*, Feb. 5, 1849; the *Philadelphia North American*, Jan. 5, 1849; *Washington Union*, Jan. 12, 1849; *Boston Post*, Jan. 5, 1849; *Pennsylvanian*, Jan. 27, 1849.

It is interesting to note that Judge Woodbury, who dissented on a subordinate question as to the right of a State to declare martial law, agreed with his Democratic colleague, the Chief Justice, on the ruling that the case presented a political and not a judicial question; the three other Democratic Judges, Catron, Daniel and McKinley, owing to illness and other causes, did not sit.

ter, however, it was generally regarded by the Bar
and the public that the failure of the Court to sustain
the Dorr Government by an explicit ruling constituted a defeat for the Democracy; and the decision
did much to establish confidence in the minds of the
American people in the integrity and freedom from
partisan bias of the Court as then established.[1] In
the excited debates which ensued in Congress, a few
years later, in 1856, 1858 and 1859, over the admission of Kansas as a State and over the validity of the
Lecompton and Topeka Constitutions adopted respectively by the pro-slavery and anti-slavery factions in that State, *Luther* v. *Borden* was frequently
cited with approval, on both sides, as showing that
the question as to which Constitution was the legal
one was not for the Court but for Congress to decide.[2]

One further case decided at this Term should be
mentioned — *Lewis* v. *Lewis*, 7 How. 776 — not because of any important point involved, but because
it was the first case argued before the Court by Abraham Lincoln (then a member of Congress from Illinois). It was decided against him, March 7, 1849.

As the number of cases on its docket continued to
increase in number and importance, the Court now
found itself unable to give proper attention to its Circuit duties, and a bill was introduced in the House
in February, 1848, to relieve the Judges of all such
duties for one year.[3] This project was hotly opposed,

---

[1] "The fundamental doctrines thus so lucidly and cogently announced . . .
have never been doubted or questioned since, and have afforded the light, guid-
ing the orderly development of our constitutional system from the day of the de-
liverance of that decision up to the present time." White, C. J., in *Pacific States
Tel. & Tel. Co.* v. *Oregon* (1912), 223 U. S. 118, 148.

[2] See speeches in the House of Henry W. Davis of Maryland, March 12, 1856,
34th Cong., 1st Sess.

[3] *30th Cong., 1st Sess.*, and *App.*, Feb. 29, March 6, April 7, 17, 18, 1848. On
Jan. 29, 1846, *29th Cong., 1st Sess.*, Senator Johnson had introduced a resolution
to modify the Judiciary system, relieve the Judges of Circuit duty, and to form a

as it was felt to be the opening wedge for the permanent abolition of Circuit Court duty; and accordingly the old battle of 1825–26 was refought.   James B. Bowlin of Missouri argued in the House: "Make your Supreme Court a fixture here, with no associations but the corrupt and the corrupting influences of the metropolis; make them the drones of the great hive of American industry and American enterprise, and you will destroy (what is as essential in a Judge as legal learning) good old-fashioned common sense. . . . Let gentlemen of the distant States look to it, before they bind themselves to the car of centralism and consolidation. . . .   Alienate the Judges from the States, consolidate the Court in the metropolis, and the day is not far distant, when the sovereign rights of the free States of this Confederacy will be swallowed up in this mighty vortex of power."   He feared the effect upon the character of judicial appointments and that "the Supreme Court would be the place for the retirement of antiquated politicians, who might desire to spend the remnant of their days at the metropolis."   In the Senate, William Allen of North Carolina voiced the curious fear that the Supreme Court permanently established in Washington would absorb the whole Government; would connect itself with the Executive and would have a large influence over the deliberation of Congress.   George E. Badger, Senator from North Carolina, said: "We shall have these gentlemen as Judges of the Supreme Court of appeals, not mingling with the ordinary transactions of busi-

new Circuit of Louisiana and Texas. He stated that at the end of the last Term in 1845, there were 109 cases on the docket left undecided; that two new Circuits were necessary, one of Louisiana and Texas, and another of Iowa and Wisconsin; that the Court ought not to be enlarged to eleven by the addition of two new members but that it should be reduced to seven, the vacancy then existing (by the death of Judge Baldwin) should not be filled, and the Court should be relieved of Circuit duty.

ness, not accustomed to the 'forensic *strepitus*' in the Courts below, not seeing the rules of evidence practically applied to the cases before them, not enlightened upon the laws of the several States, which they have finally to administer here, by the discussion of able and learned counsel in the Courts below, not seen by the people of the United States, not known and recognized by them, not touching them, as it were, in the administration of their high office, not felt, and understood, and realized as part and parcel of this great popular Government; but sitting here alone, becoming philosophical and speculative in their inquiries as to law, becoming necessarily more and more dim as to the nature of the law of the various States from want of familiar and daily connection with them, unseen, final arbiters of justice, issuing their decrees as it were from a secret chamber, moving invisibly amongst us as far as the whole community is concerned; and, in my judgment, losing in fact the ability to discharge their duties as well as that responsive confidence of the people which adds so essentially to the sanction of all the acts of the officers of Government."

The bill passed the House, but was defeated in the Senate, April 18, 1848. A new bill to abolish Circuit Court duty for the next two Terms and to compel the Court to sit in Washington until the first Monday in July passed the Senate, but was rejected in the House, August 8, 1848. Out of the debate on this bill, however, there grew a Rule of Court which substantially relieved the pressure on the Court by imposing for the first time a limitation on the length of counsel's argument. In the debate, Congressman Bowlin objected to the argument being made a form of spectacle: he objected to the public being invited by the press to attend, and particularly to the at-

tendance of ladies "to witness the displays of elocution; and that too, in a case which, if rightly argued
upon the plain, stern principles of the law, could afford no kind of amusement — no kind of interest to
the idle spectator." Senators Crittenden, Allen and
Badger also objected to the latitude of talk allowed
by the Court and the length of arguments, the latter
saying: "Has the Court been careful to prevent
discussion of questions which might be regarded as
axiomatic in this country—dissertations or scholastic
essays, like those delivered to young men prosecuting their studies in a lawyer's office, in the expectation of obtaining a license? It is quite familiar to
us all, that in a case which attracted some attention,
one of the learned counsel occupied an entire day for
the purpose of demonstrating this very difficult proposition in America, that the people are sovereign;
and then pursued his argument on the second day by
endeavoring to make out the extremely difficult conclusion from the first proposition, that being sovereign they had a right to frame their own constitution! Well, now, if the Court sit quietly while
gentlemen, from whatever motive, either to gain distinction from an exhibition of their polemical powers,
capacity for didactic discussion, or any other reason,
occupy the attention of the Court with such discussions, what hope, what expectation can be entertained, that this bill will supply any remedy for the
evil of a surcharged docket?" Senator Reverdy
Johnson of Maryland, while agreeing that the arguments were often too long, said that it was dangerous
to suppress them; and that the people would term
such an attempt an interference with freedom of
speech: "There was a case in the Supreme Court at
the last Term, which involved the constitutionality

of the famous Dorr government in Rhode Island. I heard pamphlet after pamphlet, Fourth of July speech after Fourth of July speech, written and delivered years ago, read before that tribunal, to prove that a free people have the right to establish that form of government they think best. Sir, I imagine that if the Chief Justice, speaking for himself and his Associates, had said that no such authority should be cited, the press of the country would have run mad, particularly if the result had been, as in all probability it will be, that on the unanimous judgment of that tribunal, the Dorr revolution was nothing but naked and inexcusable rebellion. Besides, sir, as to stopping counsel in their argument, which of the Judges is to take it upon himself to do so? Is it to be left to any one of them, to the Chief Justice, to say what point is to be argued, and what not? Is he to arrest counsel? My life for it, before such a rule is practised for one Term, the Chief Justice would be told by some one of his Associates, on either side of him, that it was a point on which he wished to be enlightened." Johnson also described the daily work of the Judges, saying that they met at eleven in the morning, heard arguments until four (sometimes five), dined at five, went into consultation almost every day at seven and sat until nine, ten, eleven, or twelve at night. This was labor, he said, which could not be added to. "They are all, and should be all, comparatively old men. I do not wish to see young men placed upon the bench of such a tribunal. There is many a crude thought in the mind of a young man which the reflection of riper years enables him to see the folly of. They ought to have arrived at the period when man is found to possess the greatest vigor of mind and a matured experience."

That the Court itself evidently paid attention to this criticism of its laxness towards counsel may be gathered from the fact that on March 12, 1849, it adopted a new Rule of Court to the effect that no counsel would be permitted to argue more than two hours, without special leave granted before the argument began.[1]

Of the appearance of the Court-room and of the personal characteristics of the Judges at this era, interesting accounts were written in the journals.[2] "Let us to that scene repair, if we can, amid the winding corridors of the basement of the Capitol, succeed in finding it," wrote one correspondent. "Beyond the railing are the Judges' seats, upon pretty nearly

[1] On February 1, 1844, Judge Story (in the absence of the Chief Justice who was ill) had issued a formal address to the Bar, asking them to submit on brief, and to condense their argument, saying: "He was directed by the Court to call the attention of the Bar to the present state of the docket and in the spirit, not of complaint, but of the most entire courtesy and kindness, to make some few suggestions for their consideration. It must be apparent to all persons connected with the Court that the present docket was so large (arising from the great increase of the business of the country and the magnitude and importance of the interests involved in it) that the Court could accomplish little of themselves without the cordial coöperation of the Bar in the endeavor to dispose of the causes before it. The Court felt a deep anxiety, in which there could be no doubt that the Bar equally participated, to make a sensible impression upon the docket, and thus to give repose to suitors and satisfaction to their fellow citizens at large. Indeed, upon such a subject, it was obvious that the Court and Bar had a common interest with the public; and it had occurred to the Court that the suggestions which he was about to make might, therefore, be favorably received. In the first place, under the rule of the Court, the parties were entitled, if they chose, to lay before the Court printed arguments on both sides when a speedy decision was desired; and in such cases, the Court would have ample opportunity to come to a final decision by devoting the intervals of their leisure, not occupied in hearing arguments in Court, to that purpose. In the next place, although the Court was aware that, in many cases of great importance and difficulty, prolonged arguments must necessarily occur, in order to present their full merits, yet the condensation of these arguments, as far as it could be made by the Bar, consistently with their duty to their clients, would be of great utility and aid to the Court. And in the next place, where there were two counsel, one of whom was immediately to follow the other in argument, much time would be saved in cases embracing different points, if the counsel would divide those points, and each should argue when practicable the points not occupied by the other." See *National Intelligencer*, Feb. 2, 1844.

[2] *The Supreme Court of the United States in 1853–54*, by George N. Searle, *Amer. Law Reg.* (1854), II; *New York Tribune*, Feb. 4, 1850.

a level with the floor of the room, not elevated. . . .
By the side of the railing are nine neat desks, and behind them as many comfortable, high-backed chairs
for the use of the Judges. . . . In an alcove back
of the seat of the Chief Justice and nearly up to the
ceiling is a small portrait of Chief Justice Marshall —
the only ornament . . . except a representation of
the scales of justice, worked in marble, on the opposite
side of the room." Another correspondent wrote:
"The Court-room is in the northern wing of the Capitol on the ground floor. It is broken by pillars and
arched walls, and is badly lighted. It is handsomely
furnished with rich Wilton carpets, silken drapery,
etc. The light is admitted from the rear windows
alone, and the Judges sit with their backs to the light;
the counsel who address them can scarcely see their
faces. At 11 o'clock they enter deliberately, all
dressed in black and with gowns. After they are
seated, the crier proclaims 'Oyez, oyez, oyez! The
Supreme Court of the United States is now in session; all persons having business therein are admon-
ished to draw near and give their attendance (sic).
God save the United States and these honorable
Judges!'" The Chief Justice, he described as "tall,
sallow, thin, hard-featured, and careless in dress. . . .
His opinions are terse, pointed and luminous, not
incumbered with unnecessary learning, but exceedingly logical and convincing. He has great tenacity
of purpose and strength of will, and I may add stubborn prejudices. The sincerity of his convictions
no one doubts. There is about him an unmistak-
able air of intellect and authority, and he is a not unworthy successor of John Marshall. He is a devout
Roman Catholic, and rigid in his observance of religious forms and duties." On the right hand of the

Chief Justice sat McLean. "He is a well-dressed, dignified person, about six feet in height, exceedingly well-formed, with fine teeth, a clear gray eye, lofty brow and forehead, thin hair but not gray, and in the general outline of his features the breadth of the lower part of his face, and the general carriage of his head, exceedingly like the statue of Washington by Houdon in the Capitol at Richmond. He is an upright and sensible man, with unquestionable, administrative talents, but not an accurate or profound lawyer. It is believed by some that he is not satisfied with his present position but is desirous of obtaining a higher position. He is a member of the Methodist Church, and is in high favor with that denomination." Next to McLean was Catron — "a stout, healthy man, respectable and solid in appearance, with a face and head more indicative of urbanity and benevolence than of intellect; with good sense, moderate learning, great benevolence of feeling, and kindness of demeanor, he is universally regarded as a useful, unpretending, respectable Judge." Next sat Daniel — "tall, bony, angular, with high cheek bones and dark complexion, and looks as if he had some Indian blood in his veins. His mind is narrow in its conceptions, and limited in its investigations, and his style is crude and confused; but his learning is accurate and his deductions sound and clear. He often dissents from the majority of the Court, and not unfrequently in favor of State-Rights. His amiability and honesty are universally conceded." Next to Daniel was Woodbury — "nearly six feet in height, of round and compact form, well-moulded features, a prominent and bright eye that at a distance appears dark but in nearer view is seen to be a blueish gray. He is strictly temperate in his habits, drinks nothing but cold water and a great deal of that, and works with surpassing rapidity and earnestness. He has great talent for research, and his opinions are crowded with its results. As a reasoner, he is cogent and accurate but not concise, and is apt to spend too much labor in proving what ought to be assumed as settled. His decisions would be the better for pruning and thinning, but the growth is deep-rooted and vigorous." On the Chief Justice's left was Wayne — "an exceedingly handsome man, about 5 feet 10 inches high, of stout but graceful figure, ruddy complexion, fine teeth and clustering wavy hair now mingled with gray; very courteous in manner and with a tone of refinement in his elocution and address that are very pleasing. He has cultivated the graces and has aimed (it is said not without success) to be in favor with ladies. He has an ingenious, copious mind, is fluent and rapid in expression, but lacks conciseness, lucid arrangement and vigor. He is, however, by no means deficient in learning, even of a technical character." Next to Wayne sat Nelson (McKinley being absent) — "a man of handsome features, bland and gentleman-like in expression, very courteous in manner, and dignified yet easy in deportment. He possesses much good sense, and is an excellent lawyer. His apprehension is not rapid, but he thinks clearly and reasons strongly. He is probably the best commercial lawyer on the Bench, thanks to his New York education. Since his elevation to his present place, he has shown an unusual degree of energy and industry, and is evidently working for a reputation. He is not suspected of ulterior political views, and his integrity and independence are not doubted." Next sat Grier — "He has a large, broad form, an expansive angular brow, blue eyes and looks like a strong minded, sagacious

German — such, I believe, is his descent (more probably Scotch — Ed. *Tribune*). His voice is very curious; he reads in a low, rapid, monotonous tone for
some seconds, and then he will catch on a word, to
spin round it as on a pivot, and start off to renew the
same course. His opinions are unpretending and
sensible, well expressed, and concise. His position
as a Judge is hardly yet defined." [1] The manner of
the deliberations of the Court at this period, in conference, "their most responsible and arduous duty"
was interestingly described later by Judge Campbell: [2] "The Chief Justice presided, the deliberations were usually frank and candid.   It was a rare

[1] The *American Law Register* (Oct., 1854), II, gave the following personal description of some of these Judges: "Mr. Justice Daniel, an older man in his prim
wig and spectacles; next to him is Mr. Justice Wayne with his cheerful and ruddy
face and hair slightly gray, decidedly the best looking man upon the Bench. By
his side is the Chief Justice, Taney, broken in health and unattractive in personal
appearance, but unquestionably the strongest man upon the Bench. Next is Mr.
Justice McLean of Ohio, a large noble-looking man, bold and fearless, looking
the personation of the upright Judge. By him is Judge Nelson of New York,
short and slender built, looking kindly upon all."

"The two strong men are Chief Justice Taney and Judge McLean," wrote
Oliver H. Smith, Senator from Indiana, about this time. "Nature so declared.
Their powers of mind were stamped upon their faces, and their high judicial character distinctly marked upon the whole external man. . . . The Chief Justice
was tall and slender, considerably bent with years, his face deeply furrowed, his
hair hanging carelessly over his high forehead, which he frequently wiped away.
His arms and fingers were long and bony and hairy, not unlike those of John Randolph. His countenance was marked by the study of many years. His dress,
plain black. He sat, pen in hand, attentively listening to Mr. Cushing addressing the Court, frequently taking notes, as the arguments progressed." *Early
Indiana Trials and Sketches* (1858), by Oliver H. Smith.

[2] See Meeting of the Bar on the death of Benjamin R. Curtis, October 12, 1874,
20 Wallace, ix. The *Boston Post's* Washington correspondent, March 18, 1847,
wrote of the "remarkable degree of decorum and propriety" in the Court proceedings, and of the fact that "the feelings of the practitioner are never wounded or
his pride offended by harsh and unkind treatment." He wrote again, Jan. 27,
1848: "The Supreme Court, with the dignity and uniform suavity that marks
that elevated tribunal, are trying the elaborate causes before them. Their intercourse with the Bar is of the most agreeable character, becoming to them, and
most grateful to those who have business before them." See also *How the Judges
of the United States Supreme Court Consult*, *Amer. Law Rev.* (1896), XXX, 903;
Working of the United States Supreme Court, *ibid.* (1900), XXXIV, 77; *Three
Courts*, by Seymour D. Thompson, *ibid.* (1900), XXXIV; *How a Justice is Installed*, *ibid.* (1888), XXII, 276; *A Day in the United States Supreme Court*, by
Fred Harper, *Virg. Law Reg.* (1901), VII, 239.

incident in the whole of this period, the slightest disturbance from irritation, excitement, passion or impatience. There was habitually courtesy, good breeding, self-control, mutual deference — in Judge Curtis, invariably so. There was nothing of cabal, combination or exorbitant desire to carry questions or cases. . . . The venerable age of the Chief Justice, his gentleness, refinement, and feminine sense of propriety, were felt and realized in the privacy and confidence of these consultations. . . . The Chief Justice usually called the case. He stated the pleadings and facts that they presented, the arguments and his conclusions in regard to them, and invited discussion. The discussion was free and open among the Justices till all were satisfied. The question was put, whether the judgment or decree should be reversed, and each Justice according to his precedence, commencing with the junior Judge, was required to give his judgment and his reasons for his conclusion. The concurring opinions of the majority decided the cause and signified the matter of the opinion to be given. The Chief Justice designated the Judge to prepare it."

NOTE. For an extreme example of the reluctance of the Court to pass on constitutional questions, see *Nelson* v. *Carland* (1843), 1 How. 265, in which the validity of the Federal Bankruptcy Act was attempted to be tested, but without success; see Catron, J. in *Ex parte Christy* (1845), 3 How. 323.

It was a singular fact that no case involving the constitutionality of laws of the Southern States restrictive of entry of free negroes ever reached the Supreme Court. A South Carolina law of 1835 was upheld in 1853 in *Roberts* v. *Yates* in the United States Circuit Court; and it was stated in *Law Reporter* (May, 1853), XVI, that it was to be appealed to the Supreme Court. See also *Charleston Courier*, April 22, 1853; *Federal Cases* No. 11919.

It is interesting to note that the motion to dismiss on ground of lack of jurisdiction, in the great case of *Rhode Island* v. *Massachusetts* (1838), 12 Peters, 657, 687, was made by Webster as an oral motion; and that Hazard, arguing for Rhode Island, complained that it should have been presented in writing and have contained the specific grounds on which it was based.

CHAPTER TWENTY-FIVE

SLAVERY AND STATE DEFIANCE

1848–1855

In the years 1848–49, the Court may be said to have reached its height in the confidence of the people of the country. While there were extremists and radicals in both parties, in the North as in the South, who inveighed against it and its decisions, yet the general mass of the public and the Bar had faith in its impartiality and its ability. The old partisan bitterness towards Chief Justice Taney had largely passed away, and even an ardent anti-slavery Senator, like William H. Seward, wrote to Taney of "the high regard which, in common with the whole American people, I entertain for you as the head of the Judicial Department." [1] Congressional attacks upon the Court had almost entirely ceased, and the serious attempts to destroy its most vital jurisdiction, which had been made during the last twenty years of Marshall's Chief Justiceship, seemed now to be forgotten and abandoned.

Only one subject — slavery — seemed likely to involve the Court once more in partisan controversy. Thus far, no serious complications had arisen in connection with this subject; and Martin Van Buren, writing his autobiography about this time, said, with keen perception, that since the Bank of the United States had "happily ceased to exist, we have not only been exempted from any such overwhelming convulsions as

[1] *Taney*, 317, letter of June 30, 1851; see eulogy of Taney by Reverdy Johnson, *30th Cong., 1st Sess., App.*, 588, April 18, 1848.

THE SENATE CHAMBER IN 1850

those caused by it, but the Supreme Court has occupied itself with its legitimate duties — the administration of justice between man and man — without being, as formerly, constantly assailed by applications for latitudinarian construction of the Constitution, in support of enormous corporate pretensions. We might, perhaps, have expected that in such a calm, even Mr. Jefferson's alarm, if he had lived to see, would, at least in some degree, have subsided; but this state of things can only be expected to last until a similar or equally strong interest is brought under discussion, of a character to excite the whole country and to enlist the sympathies of a majority of the Court, and requiring the intervention of that high tribunal to sustain its unconstitutional assumptions, by unauthorized and unrestrained construction. Whether the institution of domestic slavery is destined to be such an interest, remains to be seen."[1] The question thus presented by Van Buren was soon answered. For in the summer of 1848, the Court was thrown into the midst of the seething political issue, when a Whig Senator, John M. Clayton of Delaware, conceived the idea that the question of the power of Congress over slavery in the Territories and in the States annexed from Mexico might properly be settled by the Court. By the introduction of a bill for this purpose, he set in motion a train of circumstances which led directly to the crash of the Court's reputation, nine years later, in the Dred Scott decision. For many years after the Missouri Compromise in 1820, the question of Congressional authority over slavery in the Territories had lapsed as a serious issue in politics, or as a cause of serious division among statesmen. With the close of the Mexican War, however, the status of slavery in the newly acquired territory became a flaming

[1] See *Amer. Hist. Ass. Rep.* (1918), II, 184.

question; and on February 19, 1847, Calhoun introduced in the Senate a resolution announcing the dogma
that Congress had no power to prohibit slavery in the
Territories. The next year, when the bill to admit
Oregon as a State was debated, he advanced the further
contention that the Constitution itself, upon its extension to the Territories, carried with it the institution of slavery — "the doctrine of the self-extension
of slavery into all the Territories by the self-expan-
sion of the Constitution over them." [1]   But while
this issue was not acute in relation to Oregon, which
lay north of the Missouri Compromise line, it had
become exceedingly grave in connection with the
bills which were proposed for the admission of California as a State and of New Mexico as a Territory
(New Mexico then embracing the present States of Arizona, Utah, Nevada and parts of Colorado, Wyoming
and the present New Mexico).   Hot debate ensued over
the question of the respective rights of Congress and
of the Territorial and State Legislatures to establish
or prohibit slavery.   In the summer of 1848, Senator
Clayton brought forward his unfortunate proposal for
a compromise, in a bill providing: first, for the admission of Oregon with its existing laws against slavery so
far as not incompatible with the Constitution; second,
for the admission of California and New Mexico, with
a prohibition against the passage of laws by their Territorial Legislatures either establishing or prohibiting
slavery; third, for the right of an appeal to the Supreme
Court of the United States from the Territorial Courts.
By this plan, Clayton argued, the whole question as to
the power of Congress over slavery in the Territories
would be referred to the Supreme Court for its decision.

[1] See *Thirty Years' View* (1856), by Thomas H. Benton, II, 696, 713, 729; see also
30th Cong., 1st Sess., June 1, July 8, 10, 1848, speeches of Calhoun, Berrien, Reverdy Johnson in the Senate.

"The bill leaves the entire question in dispute to the Judiciary," he said. "Any man who desires discord will oppose the bill. But he who does not desire to distract the country by a question merely political, will be able, by voting for this bill, to refer the whole matter to the Judiciary. In any case, in which it may be deemed important, any lawyer can carry the question to the Supreme Court. . . . The people being law-abiding, will submit to the decision of that Court which occupies the highest place in their confidence. . . . In this dark and gloomy hour, that is the dial-plate which glitters through and which will, I trust, guide us to a safe and harmonious result."[1] Opinions varied greatly in the Senate, however, as to the wisdom of implicating the Court in so delicate and so explosive a question.[2] Democrats from the South and Free-soil Whigs from the North, alike, opposed the measure. Southerners argued that the Court, as then composed, was certain to decide against slavery. Northerners were equally confident that it would decide in favor of slavery — a difference of view which constituted a marked tribute to the freedom from sectional bias of the prior decisions of the Court. John P. Hale of New Hampshire, the most violent abolitionist in the Senate, attacked the Court with vigor, stating that he had no confidence in that tribunal as then constituted and was unwilling that it should decide the question. Thomas Corwin of Ohio, a Whig, asserted his belief that the Senators from the South would not vote for the bill unless they believed the decision of the Court would be in their favor. Henry S. Foote of Mississippi, an ardent pro-slavery Democrat, on the other hand, stated that he feared that the decision of the Court, as then con-

[1] 30th Cong., 1st Sess., 988, 1031, App., 1140, July 22, Aug. 3, 1848.
[2] 30th Cong., 1st Sess., July 22, 24, 25, 26, 1848, and App., 993, 1000, 1145, 1155, 1170.

stituted, would be against the South. George E.
Badger of North Carolina, a Whig, thought the bill
surrendered all the rights of the South. On the other
hand, Samuel S. Phelps of Vermont, a Whig, said that
he was "greatly surprised to find Whigs of the North
disowning or distrusting the constitutional authority
of the Supreme Court. I have yet to learn, either from
political friends or political opponents, that that Court
has in any degree forfeited the confidence of the country.
In the integrity and capacity of that Court, I have equal
confidence. Who doubts the integrity or the learning of
the distinguished Chief Justice? And who is prepared
to say that that Court has become so degenerate and
is filled with such unworthy men, that it is not to be
trusted with the power conferred upon it by the Constitution? I can preach no such heresy, and I am perfectly willing to leave this constitutional question to
that Court. If the Court decide against me, I will
submit. If we cannot trust the power there, where, in
Heaven's name, shall we repose it?" Reverdy Johnson of Maryland, a Democrat, said that the appeal to
the Court was "the only amicable mode of adjusting a
question which threatened the honor and integrity of
the South. . . . From the character of the Supreme
Court, I am sure the compromise in this particular,
will be acquiesced in by the country. . . . The members
of the Supreme Court are not politicians. They are
born in a different atmosphere, and address themselves
to different hearers. . . . It ought not to be expected
that the South shall surrender all that is dear to her and
do the bidding of the North. They are willing to adopt
the appeal to the Supreme Court, and if the decision of
that Court be against them, they will be satisfied. . . .
The question whether a slave owner is entitled to carry
his slaves into the Territory will be decided on the first

appeal, and that will decide the matter in every future case which can arise." Hannibal Hamlin of Maine, a Democrat, assailed; "this shuffling off, this skulking from, shrinking behind a political question which it is our duty to meet, and throwing it upon the Supreme Court to decide"; and he asserted that, since appeals to the Supreme Court under existing law could only be taken in cases involving a certain money value, the question of the rights and liberties of a slave could not be the subject of an appeal. Answering this latter objection, Sidney Breese of Illinois made a suggestion which was of singular interest, inasmuch as it set forth the exact method by which the famous *Dred Scott Case* was taken up to the Supreme Court, six years later. "Could not the question of servitude," he asked, "be brought before the Supreme Court very readily, by an action by the slave of assault and battery and false imprisonment? The master pleads that, true it is he holds the plaintiff in his custody, as he has a right to do, for he is his slave; the slave replies, setting forth the fact that California, on its cession to the United States, was free, that slavery did not exist there, and that it is not recognized by the Constitution, or any Act of Congress, and that by virtue of that Constitution he is free; the defendant demurs; and the question of law arising thereon is decided by the Court."

To meet this objection as to lack of remedy, Clayton amended his bill, and for the first time in the history of the country introduced the question of slavery into Federal judicial process and procedure, by providing specifically, that in all cases involving title to slaves writs of error or appeals should be allowed, without regard to the value of the matter in controversy, and that an appeal should be allowed to the Supreme Court from the decision of Territorial Courts and Judges

upon any writ of habeas corpus "involving the question of personal freedom"—both provisions being new
to Federal law. With such an amendment the compromise measure passed the Senate, July 26, 1848, by
a vote of thirty-three to twenty-two, Democrats and
Whigs, both of the South and North, voting on each
side of the question.

When the bill was debated in the House of Representatives, both Southern and Northern Congressmen, with
few exceptions, opposed it, showing clearer comprehension, than had the Senators, of the evils of dragging the Court into the dangerous whirlpool of politics.[1]
The Whigs strongly attacked the proposition, one of
them, George P. Marsh of Vermont, portraying in vivid
colors the inevitable effect upon the Court as follows:

Is that Court a fit tribunal for the determination of a great
political question like this? I am far from desiring to dis-
parage the impartiality or the ability of a tribunal, distinguished for the possession of every judicial excellence, and
which I hold in the highest reverence as the great bulwark of
our constitutional liberties. Its pre-eminent ability is recognized by the universal voice of the legal profession; and
its stern impartiality has been attested by decisions in the
great cases of the *Amistad* negroes and *Prigg* v. *Pennsylvania*.
But it is precisely because of my reverence for that Court,
and my exalted estimate of its value as a conservative element in our system that I would not impose upon it the painful and dangerous obligation . . . of determining so weighty
and so delicate a question as this. We should hazard not its
impartiality and its high moral influence only, but its constitution and even its existence. During the long period of
the pendency of this question, it would be incessantly exposed to every adverse influence. Local sympathies, long-
cherished prejudices, the predilections of party, the known
wishes of the Administration and of the National Legislature,
would all conspire to bias the decision; intervening vacancies

[1] *30th Cong., 1st Sess.*, July 29, 31, Aug. 3, 7, 8, 1848, and *App.*, 1072–1076.

would be filled with reference to the supposed, perhaps even pledged, opinion of the candidate upon this one question, and when, finally, the decision should be promulgated, the Court itself would become, with the defeated party, the object of a hostility, as deep-rooted, as persevering, as widely diffused, and as rancorous as are at this moment the feelings and prejudices of the parties now arrayed against each other upon this great issue. Could a tribunal which relies for its support upon moral force and public opinion alone, awes not by lictor and fasces, enforces its decrees by no armed satellites, dispenses no patronage, and is sustained by no Executive power, long withstand the malignant influence which would thus be brought to bear?

Every word of this was prophetic of the storm of odium which the Court brought upon its own head when it attempted, in the *Dred Scott Case*, nine years later, to make a decision of the very question which the statute now under debate sought to obtain from it. A Democratic Congressman from North Carolina, John R. T. Daniell, took the same view, saying that if the bill should pass, a political struggle would inevitably result, and "the moral influence of the Court must be forever destroyed in one section or the other of the Union." Another Democrat from Tennessee, John H. Crozier, said — once more prophetically: "If the decision should be against the North, the North would not abide by it. They would agitate the country a great deal more than they do now on the subject. They would insist that the decision had been made by a Court, a majority of whose members were from the South and slaveholders; that their decision was either corrupt, or their judgment had been warped by prejudice and interest." This was, in fact, the precise attitude which was adopted by the North nine years later when it refused to accept the decision in the *Dred Scott Case*.

While the Whigs were absolutely right in their disapproval of dragging the Court into a political contest, the fact that many of them expressed a distrust of the Court, and even a refusal to abide by any judicial decision, showed how far they had drifted from their old position as the staunch defenders of the Judiciary, against Democratic attack; and for this change, they were taunted (with much reason) by many of the Southern Democrats. "It is a new position with the Whig party," said Thomas H. Bayly of Virginia, "that the Supreme Court is an unfit tribunal to decide such a question as this. In the memorable contest which preceded the political revolution of 1800, their predecessors, the old Federalists, maintained that even in contests as to the reserved rights of the States, the Federal Judiciary was the ultimate arbiter. Even in a controversy between the States and the General Government about State-Rights, the Federalists insisted that one of the departments of the latter was the exclusive judge, and again in the days of Nullification, the Whig party took the same ground," yet now in a question, not of a State, but simply of the right of an individual citizen slaveholder, the Whigs are unwilling to trust to the Court. And an eloquent expression of the public confidence in the Court was voiced by Franklin W. Bowdon of Alabama (who, though he believed the Court would decide against the South, was willing to accept its opinion as impartial). "The Supreme Court is elevated above the influence of popular clamor," he said. "That high tribunal is responsible to no local constituency, and would be swayed in the discharge of its great duties by none of the sectional prejudices which here prevail, or the political interests which exert upon our deliberations so baleful an influence. A decision from this elevated source would exercise a commanding influence upon public opinion, and go very far to restore harmony to the country. Should the decision of the much-mooted question be in accordance with either Southern or Northern opinion, it would command both respect and acquiescence. . . . The Supreme Court would act under a high sense of duty, free from any immediate influences to give direction to their action; its members come from the East, the West, the North, and the South; they have the confidence of the country; they have no party schemes to subserve, and their settlement of this question of constitutional law would appeal with irresistible force to the great body of the people, North and South." In spite of this optimistic view of the situation, the bill was defeated in the House; and the project to solve the slavery issue by a Court decision was temporarily abandoned.[1] The whole tenor of the debate had shown, however, the dangers which might threaten the Court's position in the confidence of the people, should the duty of attempting such a solution be imposed upon it. On the other hand, the conservative wing of the Whig Party continued to believe in this form of settlement. "Your project for settling the slavery question strikes me very favorably," wrote Crittenden to Clayton, "and seems to be quite practicable. You cannot render a greater service than by endeavoring to keep all our friends, and especially our tropical friends of the South, cool and temperate on that subject. They must see that numbers are against them, and that they must be beaten on the question of the extension of slavery. To be beaten in the least offensive and injurious form is the best that I can anticipate for them. And the very necessity of the case ought to teach them to look at it with com-

---

[1] See interesting letter from Alexander H. Stephens of Georgia, to the editor of the *Federal Union* (Milledgeville, Ga.), Aug. 30, 1848, explaining why he, as a Southern Democrat, opposed the compromise bill in the House. *Amer. Hist. Ass. Rep.* (1911), I, 120.

posure. The right to carry slaves to New Mexico or California is no very great matter, whether granted or denied. And the more especially when it seems to be agreed that no sensible man would carry his slaves there if he could. For the North or the South to talk about dissolving the Union for such a question, decided the one way or the other, sounds to my ears like nonsense, or something worse." [1]

At the session of Congress in 1849, it became increasingly evident that the Free-soilers were preparing to enter upon a deliberate campaign to undermine popular confidence in the Court, and in its impartiality of decision in any case involving even remotely the slavery issue. On the other hand, the Democrats, both of the North and South, reaffirmed on every occasion their belief in the Court's freedom from bias. "If the Constitution does not guarantee our rights as we contend, the Court would certainly so decide," said Senator Herschell V. Johnson of Georgia. "The Supreme Court has been established for the very purpose of giving it authoritative interpretation, and as a lover of the Union, I am willing to abide its solemn decision." [2] Richard W. Thompson of Indiana said in the House: "Nothing can be more dangerous to our peace and prosperity as a Nation than these repeated attempts to appeal from the decision of our highest Courts to the tribunal of party and of faction. . . . We have seen, more than once in the last ten years, both the Constitution and the law trodden under the feet of party. We have seen Dorrism, and other isms not less odious, ready to spring up upon their shattered fragments. . . . I hold that man to be an enemy to the public welfare and the public peace, who, for political party purposes,

---

[1] *John M. Clayton Papers MSS*, letters of Crittenden to Clayton, Dec. 19, 1848, Feb. 2, 1849.

[2] *30th Cong., 2d Sess.*, Feb. 27, 28, 1849, *App.*, 187, Jan. 25, 1849.

seeks to array popular prejudice against that Constitution and law, thus settled and fixed." Samuel F. Vinton of Ohio proposed to settle the dangerous dispute as to the boundary between Texas and New Mexico (which involved the possible extension of slave territory) by leaving it to be decided by a suit in the Supreme Court where "it would receive the solemn, serious, calm consideration which belonged to such a tribunal." All propositions of this kind were hotly opposed by the Free-soilers, who, realizing that the decision of the Court in favor of the claim of Texas would carry slavery into a territory much larger than the whole of New England, were unwilling to commit such a question to that tribunal. Some of the Free-soilers could not refrain from attacking the Court, even on a measure utterly disconnected with slavery, such as a bill to authorize the appointment of a clerk to relieve the Judges of the labor of transcribing their own opinions; and their sneers elicited warm defense of the Court. "The people of this great Union," said Thomas Ewing of Ohio, in the House, "revere it as one of the institutions of our forefathers, illustrated and adorned by the genius and erudition of a Marshall and a Story, and even now upheld and sustained by men scarcely inferior to those mighty masters of their profession. I shall, in the darkest hour of our Republic, look to the Supreme Court as the palladium of our institutions and as one of the brightest and purest ornaments of our system." [1]

With the cloud of slavery thus hanging over its head, and during the years when the fateful Compromise Acts of 1850 were debated and enacted by Congress, the Court held two Terms, at neither of which were many cases of signal consequence decided. Its most important decision was rendered in the first case which

[1] *31st Cong., 1st Sess.*, Feb. 13, 14, 1850.

had arisen out of the War with Mexico, and which involved the legality of the collection of tariff duties on goods imported into Philadelphia from Tampico, during March and April, 1847, *Fleming* v. *Page*, 9 How. 603. The case presented for the first time the question of the status under the Constitution of territory conquered and held in possession by the United States. The Mexican War had begun in May, 1846; the battles of Palo Alto and Monterey had been fought in May and September; Tampico had been occupied in December; President Polk had suggested to Mexico negotiations for peace in January, 1847; Buena Vista was fought in February; Nicholas P. Trist, the President's Peace Commissioner, had arrived in Mexico in May, and had discussed peace terms until October; in November he had been recalled, but had finally signed a treaty, February 3, 1848. During all this period, from December, 1846, to February, 1848, the legal status of the occupied territory had been as unsettled as the peace negotiations. "What a state our Mexican affairs are in!" wrote Francis Lieber, in October, 1847. "Verily 'the next dreadful thing to a defeat is a victory', as Wellington is reported to have said. We conquer, beat and occupy; and peace, like a shadow, recedes. The fact is, I believe Mr. Polk cannot make a peace." [1] This *Tampico Duties Case* was elaborately argued by Daniel Webster and Peter McCall against the Attorney-General, Reverdy Johnson. Its decision, rendered by the Court on May 31, 1850, established a most important doctrine in American law and history, and one which was to constitute a potent factor in the great *Insular Cases*, fifty-one years later, that conquered territory remained foreign for the purpose of collection of duties until Congress should take action. "The genius and

[1] *Francis Lieber Papers MSS*, letter to Samuel B. Ruggles, Oct. 23, 1847.

character of our institutions," said Taney, "are peaceful, and the power to declare war was not conferred upon Congress for the purposes of aggression or aggrandizement, but to enable the General Government to vindicate by arms, if it should become necessary, its own rights and the rights of its citizens. A war, therefore, declared by Congress, can never be presumed to be waged for the purpose of conquest or the acquisition of territory. . . . The United States, it is true, may extend its boundaries by conquest or treaty. . . . But this can be done only by the treaty-making power or the legislative authority." [1] Three cases, in 1850, arising from the then recently admitted State of Texas had a certain historical interest. In *League* v. *Texas*, 11 How. 185, it was held that a statute of Texas, enacted before its admission into the Union in 1845, "however unjust or tyrannical," could not be interfered with by the Court under its Judiciary Act jurisdiction. In *Randon* v. *Toby*, 11 How. 493, and in *Bennett* v. *Butterworth*, 11 How. 669, the confused condition of legal procedure in the new

[1] On the other hand, the Court at this Term decided that a treaty is binding from the date of its execution, so that the nation ceding territory thereby may not exercise the power of making grants in such territory after that date. See *United States* v. *Reynes*, 9 How. 127. The same point was involved in *Davis* v. *Police Jury of the Parish of Concordia*, 9 How. 280, in which the opinion by Judge Wayne is of great historical interest, giving, as it does, a very lively account of the influences which led Napoleon to agree to the Louisiana Treaty of 1803. The Mexican War gave rise to very few cases in the Court; but the following may be noted as of interest: in *United States* v. *Guillem*, 11 How. 47, argued in 1850 by Attorney-General Crittenden against Pierre Soulé, it was held that a French citizen residing in Mexico was entitled to leave with his property to return to France, even though the French vessel on which he embarked was forfeited for breach of the blockade of Vera Cruz; in *Mitchell* v. *Harmony*, 13 How. 115, argued in 1852 by Attorney-General Crittenden against Cutting and Vinton, it was decided that a military officer sued for trespass for seizure of goods in Mexico was liable, unless his act of seizure was in a case of "immediate and impending danger" or "urgent necessity not admitting of delay"; in *Jecker* v. *Montgomery*, 13 How. 498, a question of prize law was involved for the first time since the long series of such cases between 1800 and 1825; *Cross* v. *Harrison*, 16 How. 164, decided in 1853, involved the question of the legality of the imposition of duties in California between the date of its military conquest in 1846 and the date when the Collector of Customs appointed under Act of Congress assumed his position, Nov. 13, 1849, the treaty of peace having been proclaimed, July 4, 1848, and notice having reached California, Aug. 7, 1848.

State was severely commented upon. One other earlier Texas case may be mentioned in this connection
because of its curious facts — *Brashear* v. *Mason*, 6
How. 92, argued by George M. Bibb and Walter Jones
against Attorney-General Clifford; the Joint Resolution
of 1845, annexing Texas and admitting it as a State, provided that Texas should cede to the United States her
navy; the plaintiff, who was commander-in-chief of the
Texas Navy consisting of four vessels, claimed that he
was a part of the navy ceded and therefore passed into
the Naval Service of the United States and became
entitled to pay as an officer of the Navy; the Court
held that the word "navy" did not comprise persons, and also that even if the plaintiff were entitled to
pay, a mandamus would not lie to the Secretary of the
Navy to enforce payment.

During these Terms of the Court of December, 1849,
and December, 1850, the rancor of the radical Free-
soilers became increasingly violent, in the course of the
long debate over the Compromise Acts proposed by
Henry Clay for the settlement of all pending slavery
questions.[1] They foresaw that the Court would inevitably be called upon to decide the question of the
existence and extent of the power of Congress over
slavery in the Territories; for these Compromise Acts
expressly remitted this issue to the Court, writs of error
or appeals from the Territorial Courts being allowed,
without any monetary limitation, in all cases involving
slavery, and also in all habeas corpus cases involving
questions of personal freedom. One of the bills also
proposed to settle the Texas-New Mexico boundary by

[1] These Compromise Acts provided for the admission of California as a State
with its existing laws against slavery; the amendment of the Fugitive Slave Law;
the organization of the Territory of New Mexico, without any condition as to slavery; and for the organization of the Territory of Utah, with a condition that when
admitted as a State it should be received into the Union, with or without slavery,
as its Constitution should then prescribe.

a suit in the Supreme Court; but this disposition was defeated.[1] In all the debates over these measures, lasting from January to September, 1850, Clay himself and the Southerners were, as a rule, willing to trust the Court as "the proper arbiter of this agitated and perplexed question between the two sections of the Union." Several Senators and Congressmen from the North, however, expressed vigorously their lack of confidence, chief among whom were Senator Salmon P. Chase of Ohio, John P. Hale of New Hampshire and Roger S. Baldwin of Connecticut. While, said Chase, no one would more cordially and respectfully acknowledge the probity, learning and ability of the distinguished Judges, yet "eminent and upright as they are, they are not more than other men, exempt from the bias of education, sympathy and interests," and the slaveholders have taken care to see that a majority of their number were placed on the Bench. Chase further assailed the decision of the Court in *Prigg* v. *Pennsylvania;* and, adopting the exact language of Jefferson and Jackson in their views of the power of the Court to construe the Constitution, denied that Congress was bound in any way to accept the Court's decision.[2] Hale charged that the opinions of the Court were "tinted and colored by geographical position", that its decisions had tended all in one direction, and that he had no doubt that it would decide in favor of slavery any case brought under the proposed bills. For this accusation, he was called to order by Henry S. Foote of Mississippi, who said that

[1] The right of the United States to sue a State for the determination of the boundary line between a Territory and a State was not determined until 1892, in *United States* v. *Texas*, 143 U. S. 621 ; see also *The State as Defendant under the Federal Constitution*, by William C. Coleman, *Harv. Law Rev.* (1917), XXXI.

[2] See *31st Cong., 1st Sess., App.*, speeches in the Senate of Yulee of Florida (p. 95), Phelps of Vermont (p. 96), Clay of Kentucky (p. 916), Butler of South Carolina (p. 926), Davis of Mississippi (p. 154), Turney of Tennessee (p. 297), Hunter of Virginia (p. 379), — all in favor of a Court decision; *ibid., App.*, 473 *et seq.*, 447 *et seq.* March 26, 1850.

Hale's language implied a charge of corruption on one of the coördinate branches of the Government. William L. Dayton of New Jersey also repelled Hale's charges with indignation, and said that however the Court was constituted, it had his unbounded confidence. "I look on them," he said, "as the sole and safe arbiter, and upon them I am willing to trust everything I have, and everything I feel, of interest in this country and its Constitution." It was important, he continued, that the Senate should sustain the Court "in the high confidence that it has heretofore held in the minds of the American people." Andrew P. Butler of South Carolina uttered a protest against the thought that Judges, "sworn to observe the Constitution, men who have the landmarks of precedent and law, and who have public opinion, the opinion of the whole Bar and of the world, to guide and control, could disregard those influences, would yield to the miserable and low suggestion of geographical lines." Thomas Ewing of Ohio said that he had practiced long before the Court, and that he had never known a case in which he thought he " had any right to impeach the motives, feelings or bias of a single Judge. . . . I look upon that Bench as above all political influence, above influence of every kind except the main object — right, justice and truth." Augustus C. Dodge of Iowa protested against Hale's general bill of indictment against the Court and cited, as a conclusive proof of the lack of sectional feeling, the Court's decision only a year previous, in 1849, in the boundary dispute between Missouri and his own State of Iowa — a case where feeling had run so high that troops of each State had been called out to enforce the State's contention. "If Iowa gained the suit, 2616 square miles became free territory; if Missouri gained, slavery would be extended over an area nearly twice the extent of Rhode Island. The Supreme Court, with whatever geographical bias the Senator from New Hampshire may ascribe to it, decided the long pending and angry dispute, and decided in favor of the free State of Iowa and against the slave State of Missouri." To all this, Hale retorted that he had nothing to retract, and that while " it is considered here as a sort of patriotic effort to express great confidence in the Supreme Court," he had no confidence in it, since the course of the Court on slavery questions had not been such "as to commend it to the friends of National freedom."

At the next session of Congress, in 1851, Hale returned to the attack with even more vituperative force.[1] " There is a tribunal which sits beneath this Senate Chamber which is the very citadel of American slavery. . . . Upon its decision rest the final hopes of slavery," he charged. For this, he was called to order by the President of the Senate, and Senators, Whigs and Democrats alike scored his language. Robert F. Stockton of New Jersey, Joseph R. Underwood of Kentucky, Lewis Cass of Michigan, and Butler of South Carolina challenged Hale to cite any decision where division of the Court had been on purely geographical lines. They noted that in the *Prigg Case*, settling the rights of the States and of Congress over fugitive slaves, "one of the most unfortunate decisions in its effect upon the South of any that has ever been made by that Bench ", Judge Wayne of Georgia had concurred with Judge Story of Massachusetts. Stephen A. Douglas of Illinois said that the Court had protected equally the rights of the North and the South, and that, while there

---

[1] *32d Cong., 1st Sess.*, Dec. 15, 17, 1851. The matter under debate was a resolution introduced into the Senate that "the Compromise Acts are, in the judgment of this body, entitled to be recognized as a definitive adjustment and settlement of the distracting questions growing out of the system of domestic slavery, and, as such, that said measures should be acquiesced in and faithfully observed by all good citizens."

had been much diversity of opinion on the Bench, both Southern and Northern Judges had divided amongst themselves. "If you examine the decisions on this question, you will see an entire absence of this supposed bias or impression on the minds of the Judges, growing out of locality of interest, or association, or both. . . . I believe the Court is above all such impression." The abolitionists were determined, however, to refuse to recognize the decisions of the Court on slavery; and at this same session, in 1852, Charles Sumner renewed Hale's attack, and in a debate on the repeal of the Fugitive Slave Law he stated that while he had respect for the Court, he declined to acknowledge its authority as binding on Congress. "It cannot control our duty as to legislation," he said, "and here I adopt the language of President Jackson in his memorable veto in 1832." The spectacle of a Massachusetts Free-soiler indorsing Jackson's view as to the Court's powers was a sign of the marked change towards that tribunal which was being effected in the North.[1]

Meanwhile, in the year 1851, the Court had become involved with the fugitive slave issue in three ways: first, through one of its decisions; second, through the filling of a vacancy upon the Bench; and third, through decisions of the Judges sitting on Circuit. In *Strader v. Graham*, 10 How. 82, which arose on a writ of error to the Kentucky Court of Appeals, the question was presented whether slaves, owned by a citizen of Kentucky, who had been allowed to go into Ohio to work, retained their status as slaves on their return to Kentucky, or whether by virtue of the laws of Ohio or of the Northwest Ordinance, they had acquired the status of freemen. The Court held unanimously that the ques-

---

[1] *32d Cong., 1st Sess., App.*, 1102 *et seq.*, Aug. 26, 1852. *The Constitutionality of the Fugitive Slave Acts*, by Allen Johnson, *Yale Law Journ.* (1921), **XXXI**

tion of their status depended entirely on the laws of Kentucky, and that "it was exclusively in the power of Kentucky to determine for itself whether their employment in another State should not make them free on their return"; hence, the Court decided that it had no jurisdiction over the case, since it presented no Federal question but only a matter of State law, already determined by the State Court. Had the Court adhered to its wise decision in this case, when the *Dred Scott Case* involving almost identical facts arose, six years later, the whole history of the country might have been changed. It is "a very clear, concise, and able opinion and will probably give general satisfaction to the Bar and the country," said the Democratic newspapers. "It settles the law on two very important questions, and *maugre* the grumbling of the abolitionists, will meet the general approbation of the country."[1] To the anti-slavery faction, this decision, so eminently reasonable and supported by well settled doctrines of the Court, was as objectionable as the *Prigg Case* had been; and the *New York Evening Post* said: "This has an important bearing on the Fugitive Slave Law. It shows that this Court will hold all men of color in slave States to be slaves, and will not look with favor upon their manumission. This serves to show what security a person transported from a free State on the charge of being a fugitive has for obtaining a trial by jury in the place to which he is conveyed. Looking at this decision in the view of common sense, it must be pronounced, in the language of Mr. Webster, 'not a respectable decision.' The Court needs reorganizing; instead of the four members allotted to the free States they should have six. . . . The history of this particular case illustrates the stupidity and danger of leaving to

[1] *Washington Union*, Jan. 7, 9, 12, 1851.

this tribunal the arbitration of issues that belong to the legislature or to the forum of popular discussion." [1] Such language might well have warned the Court that decisions on this subject of fugitive slaves must be rendered with extreme care. Further warning of its delicate position was given by the criticism which arose on the appointment of a successor to Judge Levi Woodbury, who died on September 4, 1851, after a brief but distinguished service on the Bench of only six years. [2] Within a week after his death, President Fillmore wrote to Webster, stating that he desired to "obtain as long a lease, and as much moral and judicial power as possible, from the new appointment" to be made by him, and that he "would therefore like to combine a vigorous constitution with high moral and intellectual qualifications, a good judicial mind, and such age as gives prospect of long service"; he added that he had formed a very high opinion of Benjamin Robbins Curtis of Boston, and he asked: "Does he fill the measure of my wishes?" This letter crossed in the mail a letter written by Webster to the President, in which Webster stated that the place should properly be offered to the famous Rufus Choate, a lawyer more extensively known and distinguished in public life; but that, as it was supposed

---

[1] New York Evening Post, Jan. 13, 1857.

[2] The Boston Post said, Feb. 3, 1846, in a letter from its Washington correspondent: "Judge Woodbury is taking a commanding position on the Bench which he dignifies and adorns, and the duties and details of which seem as familiar to him as if he had devoted his whole life to them. He has delivered several opinions, this Term, distinguished for ability, clearness and sound law which have elicited warm commendations from all quarters. In Judge Woodbury, I have great confidence that the country will find, what it rarely meets with, a Judge on the Bench, unchanged by his elevated position of irresponsibility to the people, and holding fast to the integrity of his original principles. It is hard to find a Judge who does not bury the fundamental rights of the people and the groundwork of democracy beneath his ermine, the moment he puts it on. But if ever the people had good cause to hope to find a true man in that position, Mr. Woodbury is the man." The Washington Union said of Woodbury, Jan. 12, 1851: "No man is more thoroughly known to the country as the firm and unwavering supporter of the Union, the Constitution and the laws." See ibid., July 25, Sept. 6, 8, 13, 1851.

that Choate would not accept, he believed the general, perhaps the universal, sentiment, was that the place should be filled by the appointment of Curtis — a man "of very suitable age, forty-one, good health, excellent habits, sufficient industry and love of labor, and in point of legal attainment and general character in every way fit." [1] Choate, as was expected, stated that he did not desire the place; [2] and accordingly the President appointed Curtis, September 22, 1851, giving him the place in preference to two able and experienced Judges of the United States District Court, who had been strongly urged for the vacancy, Judge Peleg Sprague of Massachusetts, and Judge John Pitman of Rhode Island. Of the appointment, a friend of Curtis wrote that President Fillmore, on his visit to Boston in the summer of 1851, had "assured himself that his intention of appointing a young man, provided he was the best man, could be best carried out by the appointment of Mr. B. R. Curtis; and he offered him the vacant seat solely because he thought it his duty to do so. . . . If there ever was a magistrate guided in every action by a stern sense of duty, that magistrate was Millard Fillmore. And I have reason to know that there was no act of his Administration in which he felt more pride and satisfaction than in this single appointment." [3] The Administration organ in Washington said that, though Curtis was a young man, "such is his profes-

[1] *Curtis*, I, 154 *et seq.*

[2] *Reminiscences of Rufus Choate* (1860), by Edward G. Parker, 299: "I wanted to know if he contemplated going on to the United States Supreme Court bench. He said he had received an intimation that he could have it, and had no doubt he could have the post, if he desired it; but that he would not on any account, spend a minute in Washington, absorbed as he should have to be in his evenings in labors and consultations, and in his days in court. 'Here,' said he, 'I can do just as I please; I can earn in three months as much as their whole salary; and I can work, more or less, as I please.' These views, expressed in 1857, were also held in 1851."

[3] *Curtis*, I, 166, 170, letter of March 22, 1879, from John O. Sargent to G. T. Curtis, remarks of Causten Browne.

sional reputation that there can be but one opinion
among the members of the Bar as to the propriety of
his selection. He has taken no very active part in
political affairs, but has been always a decided and consistent Whig." While the appointment was generally
commended by Democrats and Whigs alike, it was denounced by the radical anti-slavery men of the North,
who charged that Curtis was a tool of Webster, a supporter of the doctrine of Webster's Seventh of March
speech, and a believer in the constitutionality of the
Fugitive Slave Law.[1] Over this statute and the cases
arising out of it, a storm of partisan rage was now sweeping in the Northern States; and the anti-slavery men saw
their worst fears realized, when the new Judge, before
his confirmation by the Senate, proceeded to rule upon
the constitutionality of the obnoxious statute and to
sustain it, in *United States* v. *Robert Morris*, 1 Curtis
C. C. 23. This noted case in the United States Circuit
Court in Boston, involving the indictment of a young
colored lawyer and his associates for the rescue of the
fugitive slave Shadrach from the hands of the United
States marshal, had been argued by the abolitionist
lawyer and Senator, John P. Hale of New Hampshire,
who had contended that the jury were the rightful
judges of the law as well as the facts, and that if they
conscientiously believed the law to be unconstitutional,
they were bound by their oaths to disregard any instruction the Court might give. Among the extreme
anti-slavery men of the North this was a legal doctrine
which was finding high favor; and its controversion by
the new Judge, whose personal friends and associates
were largely imbued with this idea, was an act requiring

[1] *The Republic,* Sept. 23, 1851. The *New York Tribune* said, Jan. 29, 1856, that
Curtis had been given his position on the Bench, as a reward for a "heartless and
unscrupulous piece of sophistry" — an opinion in favor of the constitutionality of
the Fugitive Slave Law.

firmness of character of a high order. Judge Curtis, however, met the test without flinching and held:

This power and corresponding duty of the Court authoritatively to declare the law is one of the highest safeguards of the citizen. The sole end of Courts of justice is to enforce the laws uniformly and impartially, without respect of persons or times, or the opinions of men. To enforce popular laws is easy. But when an unpopular cause is a just cause, when a law, unpopular in some locality, is to be enforced there, then comes the strain upon the administration of justice; and few unprejudiced men would hesitate as to where that strain would be most firmly borne. . . . Finding that no Judge of any Court of the United States had in any published opinion examined it upon such grounds that I could feel I had a right to repose on his decision without more, I knew not how to avoid the duty which was then thrown upon me. My firm conviction is that under the Constitution of the United States, juries in criminal trials have not the right to decide any question of law; and that if they render a general verdict, their duty and their oath require them to apply to the facts, as they may find them, the law given to them by the Court.

Similar charges supporting the constitutionality of the Fugitive Slave Law, made by Judges Nelson, Woodbury and Grier, enhanced the growing feeling of hostility at the North towards the Judges of the United States Courts. The anti-slavery sentiment was still more aroused by the action of President Fillmore and of the Federal law officers and Courts, in connection with an alarming riot and murder which occurred at Christiana, Pennsylvania, arising out of the rescue of a fugitive slave and which resulted from inflammatory speeches counseling disobedience to the Fugitive Slave Law. The Administration, forced to the conclusion that stringent measures must be taken to suppress the increasing disloyalty of the abolitionists, resolved on indictments for

treason.[1] "An example should be made of some of
these pestilent agitators who excite the ignorant and
restless to treasonable violence," said the Whig organ
in Washington. Whig papers in New York and elsewhere said that "those who counsel resistance to law
should be regarded in their true light. They are virtually rebels, and practically public enemies;" and
another said that "an alarming tendency to anarchy"
was manifested in the North, and that "treason which
has been long preached from pulpits and the press begins to manifest itself in overt acts." Accordingly,
indictments for treason were pressed in the District
Court for the Eastern District of Pennsylvania, and the
law of treason was stated on very broad lines by District Judge Kane in a charge to the grand jury and later
confirmed by Judge Grier in a charge made at the trial
of the indicted men. In these charges, forcible resistance to a Federal law was held to be treasonable if
"with intent to overthrow the Government or to nullify
some law of the United States and totally to hinder its
execution or to compel its repeal." [2] Though the trial
resulted in an acquittal owing to insufficient evidence,
the action of the Federal Judges in sustaining the
application of the law of treason to cases of resistance to
the Fugitive Slave Law evoked bitter criticism from the
anti-slavery press. The *New York Evening Post* de-

[1] For full accounts of the Christiana riot and trials, see the Administration organ,
The Republic, Sept. 15, 19, 20, 24, 1851, quoting also *New York Courier*, *Albany
State Register* and *New York Times;* and the Democratic organ, the *Washington
Union*, Sept. 14, 16, 17, 18, 19, 21, Dec. 3, 10, 16, 17, 1851.

[2] Federal Cases No. 18276, 2 Wall. Jr. 134, charge of Judge Kane to grand jury,
Sept. 12, 1851; *United States* v. *Hanway*, Federal Cases No. 15299, 2 Wall. Jr. 139,
charge of Judge Grier, Oct. Term, 1854; see also charges of Judge Sprague and Judge
Curtis as to treason in the Shadrach rescue cases, Federal Cases No. 18263, March,
1851; Federal Cases No. 18269, 2 Curtis, 630, Oct. 15, 1851; and charge of Judge
Curtis as to obstruction of Federal process in the *Anthony Burns Case*, *United States*
v. *Stowell*, Federal Cases No. 16409, Oct. Term, 1854, 2 Curtis, 153; Federal Cases
No. 18250, June 7, 1854. See also *Law of Treason*, by Simon Greenleaf, *Law Reporter* (1851), XIV.

nounced "this monstrous doctrine", saying: "This strained doctrine of treason has slept till now, when it is revived by Mr. Fillmore and Mr. Webster." Again it said: "It is the constitutional duty, no less than the true policy of our Courts, as seldom as possible to recognize the existence of that disaffection to the Government which the crime of treason implies; and we are also clear that, if the law of treason had been defined by a bench of Democratic Judges, it would now be their recorded judgment that there has never been more than one case of treason proper, prosecuted in this country since the constitution was established." After the acquittal of the Pennsylvania rioters on the treason charge, this newspaper said: "Great pains were taken to prepare the people to accept this doctrine. Not only was the support of the Fugitive Slave Law to be made a test of political orthodoxy, but it was a law so sacred in its character that the violation of it was a higher crime than the violation of any other. . . . The Whig journals did their best to persuade their readers that treason had been committed. . . . Everybody seemed persuaded, but the people; and the question was, whether the people were ready to accept the view of the law taken by Fillmore and Webster. The trial was had, the prisoners were acquitted of treason, and the Administration sustained another mortifying defeat." [1]

It was at a time of such hostility to the enforcement of the law, that the Court met on December 1, 1851, the

[1] *New York Evening Post*, Oct. 25, Dec. 26, 1851, Oct. 11, 1853. The same paper noted Oct. 15, 16, 1853, that five hundred men had been engaged in rescuing a slave at Syracuse, N. Y., and said that the Administration journals were "clamorous for condemnation for treason."

The *Washington Union*, Dec. 16, 1851, said that the result of the treason trial was such as every one expected. "It is conclusive of one thing only, not that treason was not committed, but that it is and will be a very difficult thing to convict anyone of treason for resisting the Fugitive Slave Law, unless more vigilance and activity are exercised on the part of both Federal and State authorities."

new Judge Curtis taking his seat on the Bench, though his appointment was not sent in to the Senate until December 11, nor confirmed until December 20. Of his first impressions of Washington and of this December, 1851, Term, Curtis wrote: "I have now been here four weeks, — long enough to be settled both in my abode and occupations. I live at Brown's new hotel, where I have a comfortable and pleasant, though small room, and there are some pleasant people in the house. Judge and Mrs. McLean, and Judge and Mrs. Catron, live here, and probably Judge Wayne will come here on his return from New York, where he now is. The Bench is full, with the exception of Judge McKinley, and we have made uncommon good progress in our work. But it is already so great as to be beyond the ability of the Court to despatch it; and when the Texas and California land-titles get here, Congress will probably see that the judicial system of the country, fitted for fourteen States, with no Circuit Court west of the mountains, is not adequate to do the business of the United States now, when there are thirty-one States, and about four times as many people, and more than five times the wealth. In the days when Chief Justice Marshall used to deliver those great opinions, the calendar had about thirty causes on it; now it has two hundred and sixteen. I think there can be no question that, when the next Administration comes in, the Judges of the Supreme Court will be relieved from all duty out of that Court, and two sessions a year will be held; in which event, I shall live and keep house here a part of the year. I find rent, and all the necessary expenses of living, are less than in Boston, — I said to Mr. Appleton about twenty per cent less. . . . I do not hear much of politics, for there is a real and true separation of the Bench from politicians here, with perhaps one exception, — and

I do not know that there is any exception. But I think, from all I see and hear, Mr. Webster's chance for a nomination is very small. If the Democratic Party should nominate General Cass, or some other civilian from the North, the Whig party may possibly nominate Mr. Webster; but I doubt if the nomination would be of any value, for I think the Democrats will surely carry the next election. My brethren here have received me very kindly, and there are some pleasant gentlemen among them. I find my duties require constant labor; but there is no more than a fair day's work to be done in each day, and I have really more leisure than I have known for ten years. The great difference between my professional labors at the Bar and on the Bench consists in the entire freedom of the latter from anxiety and burdensome responsibility, and the certainty when I rise in the morning that no one can force me to do anything which I am not equal to; and, accordingly, my health has been better during the last month than any time for a year past. We have, argued and now under advisement, the case of the Wheeling Bridge, built across the Ohio under the authority of the State of Virginia. This is the first case since I have been here which involved constitutional questions on which the Court are likely to divide, though I have been obliged in one case to dissent from the majority. In general, we have thus far been very harmonious in our opinions."
Of the impression made upon Washington by Judge Curtis, a friend wrote in his diary, January 29, 1852:
"Judge Curtis impresses everybody most favorably by his modest demeanour and his agreeable conversation. He changes but little — he is of the same well-knit frame, with fine, expressive eyes, and white teeth, which you notice when he smiles, — not handsome, but his face lights up wonderfully. Crittenden who does not

like or dislike by halves is perfectly charmed with him."[1]

At this Term, the ever present conflict between State sovereignty and Congressional power over commerce came to the front again in a new aspect, in *Pennsylvania v. Wheeling and Belmont Bridge Co.*, 13 How. 518, in which Pennsylvania, charging that a bridge over the Ohio River, construction of which had been authorized by a statute of Virginia, was a nuisance and an obstruction to interstate commerce on a navigable river, sought to have it enjoined. This case, which had been before the Court twice before, and was now eloquently argued, December 18, 22, 1851, by Edwin M. Stanton against Reverdy Johnson, was unique, inasmuch as the State sued, not in the exercise of its sovereignty, but by virtue of ownership of property seeking protection.[2] For many years past, Pennsylvania had been engaged in making extensive improvements by canals, railroads and turnpikes for the facilitation of the transportation of goods and passengers; and it was claimed that any obstruction of the Ohio River to the free passage of steamboats to Pittsburg would injuriously affect and divert this transportation, diminish the trade and lessen the revenue of the States, and occasion an injury to the State as the principal proprietor of the lines of transpor-

[1] *Curtis*, I, 163, 167, letter of Dec. 27, 1851; diary entry of Jan. 29, 1852, by John O. Sargent.

An article in the *American Law Register* (1854), II, by George N. Searle of Boston, describing the Judges, said of Curtis' appointment: "The professional judgment of New England turned to but one man for the place, and the doubt was not, whether he would have the offer, but whether he would accept it. The promotion was doubly flattering to him, as it was a tribute solely to his professional ability, he having rendered little of mere political service. The good opinion, thus formed of him, has been more than fulfilled. We speak from report, but have reason to believe we speak truly, when we say that, during the first Term after his appointment, he took rank with the first of the Bench for sureness of judgment, keenness of analysis and accuracy of legal research."

[2] See 9 Howard, 647; 11 Howard, 528; see also *Life of Reverdy Johnson* (1914), by Bernard C. Steiner; *Life and Public Services of Edwin M. Stanton* (1899), by George C. Gorham.

tation. Fundamentally, the case presented one phase
of the great contest between the railroads and the steamboats in their struggle for supremacy and the development of modern means of transportation. "Few cases
have ever excited greater interest or seemed to affect
more extensively the internal commerce of the country
than this celebrated controversy," said the *Western
Law Journal.*[1] The Court held, February 6, 1852, that
the State was entitled to maintain its bill in equity on
the ground of nuisance, and that, inasmuch as Congress
had power to regulate navigation on the Ohio River and
had exercised its power in various statutes, interference
with such Congressional exercise of authority by the
State of Virginia was void. The Court, accordingly,
ordered an abatement of the nuisance, through a modification in the construction of the bridge. Chief Justice Taney and Judge Daniel vigorously dissented —
the latter saying that there never had been, " there perhaps never can be brought before the tribunal, for its
decision, a case of higher importance or of deeper interest than the present." While the decision caused
much excitement at the time, it had little practical effect
upon the law; for later cases very greatly narrowed its
compass.[2] Even the operation of the decree upon the
particular bridge involved was nullified by Congress,
which within six months passed a statute declaring the

[1] *Western Law Journ.*, IX (Sept., 1852). "The stupendous structure that spans the
Ohio at Wheeling connecting the State of Virginia and Ohio strikes the eye of the
traveller passing beneath it, as it looms above him in the darkness, as one of the
great architectural wonders of the age. To many, the controversy for a time seemed
to owe its origin to a spirit of contemptible rivalry between Pittsburg and Wheeling,
and to have no other aim than the selfish obstruction of a great national enterprise.
A long, careful, deliberate, conscientious, judicial investigation has shown it to be a
question deeply interesting to the people of the United States, in its actual and
immediate bearing on a trade embracing the transportation annually, of merchandise of over $40,000,000 and 80,000 passengers; and in the principles which it in-
volved, affecting more than one half of the whole trade of the nation."
[2] *Gilman* v. *Philadelphia* (1866), 3 Wall. 713; *Willamette Iron Bridge Co.* v. *Hatch*
(1888), 125 U. S. 1, 15.

bridge to be a lawful structure and not an obstruction to navigation.[1] This statute came before the Court, in 1856, and was upheld as constitutionally within the power of Congress to regulate the navigation of the river. "This was the first instance in the whole history of the Government," said the *New York Tribune*, "where Congress ever interposed or attempted to arrest a decree of the Supreme Court. The precedent may lead hereafter to serious embarrassments between the judicial and legislative departments; for if the law settled by the highest judicial tribunal be not accepted law of the land, and is liable to review by demagogues in Congress of their own motion, or by the usurpation of worse ones out of doors, the Court of last resort becomes but a mockery — *stat nominis umbra*." [2] Later, however, it admitted that the question had been properly settled "in conformity with the progressive spirit of the times. . . . The invention of railroads has quite changed the state of facts. . . . There are very few navigable rivers that, all things considered, can, as a medium of communication, taking passengers as well as goods into account, stand an advantageous comparison with a well built and well equipped railroad. . . . Under this new state of facts, it is evident that the old common law doctrine as to navigable waters must undergo a certain modification. . . . The public convenience will require that the uninterrupted freedom of passing up and down a river should give way, in cases of conflict, to facilities for crossing it."

Three days after the decision of this *Wheeling Bridge*

[1] See especially the debate over this measure, *32d Cong., 1st Sess., App.,* Aug. 13, 14, 16, 17, 18, 1852; see 18 How. 421.
[2] *New York Tribune,* Feb. 19, 1856, April 23, 1856. It is interesting to note that only one year from the above criticism, the *Tribune* itself was clamoring to have Congress set aside the decision of the Court in the *Dred Scott Case.* In *The Clinton Bridge* (1871), 10 Wall. 454, Congress again legalized a bridge, while a suit was pending.

Case in 1852, the Court heard an argument, February 9, 10, 11, by Job Tyson and Phineas Morris against James Campbell and George M. Dallas (all of Pennsylvania) in the important case of *Cooley* v. *Board of Wardens of the Port of Philadelphia*, 12 How. 299.   The validity of the State pilotage fee statute was involved, and again the Court was called upon to consider the question how far the power of Congress under the Commerce Clause of the Constitution was exclusive.   For years, the Judges had given hopelessly differing opinions on this subject.   The law now received considerable clarification and fixity, through an opinion of the Court rendered by the new Judge, Curtis.   Writing to George Ticknor, Curtis said: "I expect my opinion will excite surprise, because it is adverse to the exclusive authority of Congress, and not in accordance with the opinions of McLean and Wayne, who are the most high-toned Federalists on the Bench.   But it rests on grounds perfectly satisfactory to myself, and it has received the assent of five Judges out of eight, although for twenty years no majority has ever rested their decision on either view of this question, nor was it ever directly decided before." [1]   The doctrine thus finally adopted by the Court was evidently in the nature of a compromise between the previously conflicting views of the Judges; but it carried the Federal power to a greater height than it had hitherto attained.   It pointed out that : "The power to regulate commerce embraces a vast field, containing not only many, but exceedingly various subjects, quite unlike in their nature; some imperatively demanding a single uniform rule, operating equally on the commerce of the United States in every port; and some, like the subject now in question, imperatively demanding that diversity which alone can meet the local necessities of

[1] *Curtis*, I, letter of Feb. 29, 1852.

navigation. Either absolutely to affirm, or deny, that the nature of this power requires exclusive legislation by Congress, is to lose sight of the nature of the subjects of this power, and to assert, concerning all of them, what is really applicable but to a part. Whatever subjects of this power are in their nature National, or admit only of one uniform system, or plan of regulation, may justly be said to be of such a nature as to require exclusive legislation by Congress." But it held that the pilotage law in question did not come within this class of subjects, and hence was a constitutional exercise of power by the State. The doctrine, so laid down for the control of commerce was really the adoption of a rule first stated by a strong Democrat, Judge Woodbury, in the *Passenger Cases*.[1] Even this compromise was not satisfactory to three of the Court, Judges McLean and Wayne still considering the power of Congress to be exclusive,[2] and Judge Daniel taking the extreme view that enactment of pilotage laws was an original and inherent power of the States not possessed by the Federal Government.

While this *Pilot Case* presented a distinct advance by the Court towards a broader view of Federal powers than had hitherto prevailed, another case decided at

[1] Woodbury stated that; "So far as reasons exist to make the exercise of the commercial power exclusive, as on the matters of exterior, general, and uniform cognizance, the construction may be proper to render it exclusive, but no further, as the exclusiveness depends, in this case wholly on the reasons, and not on any express prohibition, and hence cannot extend beyond the reasons themselves. Where they disappear, the exclusiveness should halt," 7 How. 559; and see *Cases on Constitutional Law*, by James B. Thayer, 219. The rule, in the broadened form given to it in *State Freight Tax Cases* (1873), 15 Wall. 232, 280, is the law today.

[2] Judge McLean in dissenting said (p. 325): "From this race of legislation between Congress and the States, and between the States, if this principle be maintained, will arise a conflict similar to that which existed before the adoption of the Constitution." To this prediction, Judge Wayne made answer in *Gilman* v. *Philadelphia* (1866), 3 Wall. 713, fourteen years later: "In the Pilot case, the dissenting Judge drew an alarming picture of the evils to rush in at the break made, as he alleged, in the Constitution. None have appeared. The stream of events has since flowed on without a ripple due to the influence of that adjudication."

this Term marked an even greater enlargement of the domain of power of the Federal Government. In fact, few decisions had ever produced so revolutionary a change in Federal jurisdiction as that of *The Propeller Genesee Chief* v. *Fitzhugh*, 12 How. 443, in which the Court, in a remarkable opinion by Chief Justice Taney, held for the first time that the admiralty Courts of the United States had jurisdiction over the public navigable lakes and rive s of the country, regardless of the question of tidewater. The question decided arose as follows: By an Act of February 26, 1845, Congress had extended the jurisdiction of the Federal District Courts to certain cases upon the Great Lakes and inland navigation connecting them. Previous cases decided by Marshall and Story had held that the admiralty powers of the Constitution only extended over navigable water within the ebb and flow of the tide. During the last few years, a change of view on the part of the Court had been foreshadowed in *dicta* of various Judges in two cases, the facts of which, however, did not necessitate a ruling on the precise question.[1] "The conviction that this definition of admiralty powers was narrower than the Constitution contemplated," now said Chief Justice Taney, "has been growing stronger every day with the growing commerce on the lakes and navigable rivers of the Western States." Taney met the problem boldly. "There is certainly nothing in the ebb and flow of the tide that makes the waters peculiarly suitable for admiralty jurisdiction, nor anything in the absence of the tide that renders it unfit. If it is a public navigable water, on which commerce is carried on between different States or nations, the reason for the jurisdiction is

[1] *Waring* v. *Clarke* (1847), 5 How. 441, argued by Reverdy Johnson against John J. Crittenden; *New Jersey Steam Navigation Co.* v. *Merchants' Bank* (1848), 6 How. 544.

precisely the same," he said. He then, in a masterly exposition, pointed out that in England the measure of admiralty jurisdiction by the extent of tide and water was sound and reasonable, because there was in that country no navigable stream beyond the ebb and flow of the tide, and therefore in England "tidewater and navigable water are synonymous terms", and "they took the ebb and flow of the tide as the test, because it was a convenient one and more easily determined the character of the river. . . . The description of a public navigable river was substituted in the place of the thing intended to be described." It was natural, he pointed out, for the Courts of the United States in early times to adopt the restricted English definition of admiralty jurisdiction as limited by the tide, inasmuch as in the early days in this country "every public river was tidewater to the head of navigation"; and indeed "until the discovery of steamboats there could be nothing like foreign commerce upon waters with an unchanging current resisting the upward passage"; and he further pointed out that when the decision was made in a former case, *The Steamboat Thomas Jefferson*, 10 Wheat. 28, in 1825, "the commerce on the rivers of the West and on the lakes was in its infancy and of little importance, and but little regarded compared with that of the present day." Since there could be no reason for admiralty power over a public tidewater which did not apply with equal force to any other public water used for commercial purposes and foreign trade, Taney reached the conclusion, and the Court so held, that admiralty jurisdiction must extend to all such navigable waters. Judge Daniel, in a vigorous dissenting opinion, said that the Court had construed the Constitution by geographical considerations, and that though his opinion might be regarded as "contracted and antiquated, unsuited to the day in which we live", he had "the consolation of the support of Marshall, Kent and Story." While this decision established the jurisdiction of the admiralty Courts over the Great Lakes, the principle was extended in *Steamboat New World* v. *King*, 16 How. 469, to a river beyond the tidal flow, in the case of a libel by a passenger for injury due to negligence on a boat on the Sacramento River.[1]

Before the opening of the Term in December, 1852, Judge McKinley died on July 19, after fifteen years of service, during much of which he had been prevented by illness from sitting on the Bench.[2] The session of the Court which was held on December 8, 1852, to receive the resolutions of the Bar as to the Judge's death was memorable by reason of the fact that the Court mourned the loss, not only of its deceased Associate, but also of the three great leaders of the Federal Bar — Henry Clay, Daniel Webster and John Sergeant, all of whom had died since the end of the last Term.[3] "In a few short

[1] Judge Daniel in his dissenting opinion presenting a somewhat humorous hypothetical case, reminding one that in those days a stream called the Tiber flowed through Washington across Pennsylvania Avenue: "In the small estuary which traverses the avenue leading to this Court-room, the tides of the Potomac regularly ebb and flow. Although upon the receding of the tide this watercourse can be stepped over, upon the return of the tide, there may be seen on this water numerous boys battling or angling or passing in canoes. Should a conflict arise amongst these urchins, originating either in collision of canoes or an entanglement of fishing lines or from any similar cause, this would present a case of admiralty jurisdiction fully as legitimate as that which is made by the libel in the case before us."

[2] On April 14, 1852, a fire occurred at two A.M. in the Clerk's office. "We are happy, however, to be able to state," said the *National Intelligencer*, "that the valuable archives of the Court were very little if any defaced or injured." Regarding another fire, Judge Curtis wrote, Dec. 27, 1851: "The Court was not disturbed by the fire and sat as usual while the building was burning. We were not aware that we were showing any peculiar coolness by doing so; for having made all necessary arrangements to have the records, etc., removed in case of need, we saw no reason why the business of the day should not proceed. But I understand people thought it was like the Senate sitting when the Gauls came." *Curtis*, I, 165; *National Intelligencer*, April 15, 1852; *New York Tribune*, April 16, 1852.

[3] Clay died, June 29, 1852; Webster, Oct. 23; Sergeant, Nov. 23. It may be noted that while the Bar resolved to wear the usual badge of mourning, this action was not taken by the Court, the custom of former years in that respect apparently having fallen into disuse. See articles in *Amer. Law Reg.* (1853), I, 58, 193, on the deaths of Webster and Sergeant.

months, the Bar has been bereaved of its brightest and greatest monuments," said Attorney-General Critten-den in presenting the Bar Resolutions to McKinley. "Clay, Webster and Sergeant have gone to their immortal rest in quick succession. . . . Like bright stars they have sunk below the horizon and have left the land in widespread gloom. . . . This hall itself seems as though it were sensible of its loss, and even these marble pillars seem to sympathize, as they stand around us like so many majestic mourners." To this, Chief Justice Taney made response, speaking of the "deep sense which the Court entertained of the loss sustained at the Bar as well as on the Bench."

To succeed McKinley, President Fillmore nominated on August 16, 1852, Edward A. Bradford, a leading lawyer of Louisiana, but the Senate failed to act affirmatively upon the nomination before its adjournment.[1] Fillmore then turned his attention to candidates living outside of McKinley's Circuit. His personal preference was for the appointment of John J. Crittenden of Kentucky, but Senatorial complications seemed likely to render confirmation impossible. Humphrey Marshall of Kentucky and Thomas Ruffin, Chief Justice of North Carolina, had many supporters.[2] The choice finally fell upon George E. Badger of North Carolina, whose name Fillmore sent in to the Senate, January 10, 1853. Badger, a man of fifty-eight years of age, had been Secretary of the Navy under Presidents Harrison and Tyler, and United States Senator since 1846; he was an able and eloquent lawyer, well fitted

---

[1] A Washington dispatch to the *New York Tribune*, Aug. 27, 1852, stated that Bradford's nomination was certain to be rejected.

[2] *New York Tribune*, Dec. 30, 1852; *Washington Union*, Jan. 28, 1853; *Thomas Ruffin Papers*, letter of Edward Stanley to David Outlaw, Jan. 26, 1853, stating that the President had said that he would not appoint Ruffin, since if he should go out of the Circuit at all, he must nominate either Crittenden or Badger.

for the position, and a strongly conservative Whig.
Though it had been expected that the appointment of
one of its members would commend itself to the Senate
(then composed of thirty-six Democrats, twenty Whigs
and two Free-soilers), it soon became evident that there
was little chance of Badger's confirmation. The Democrats felt that Badger was too strong a partisan to
warrant his confirmation, on the very eve of the retirement of a Whig and the accession of a Democratic
President. The Democratic papers of the South were
particularly vigorous in opposition. One said that "old
Timothy Pickering himself was not a more thorough
and incorrigible Federalist" and that his extreme
Federalism would "lead him always to interpret the
Constitution so as to derogate from the rights of the
States and to augment the power of the General Government"; another termed him "a green-gilled Federalist." Another stated that: "It is no time to appoint
men whose principles lead them to strengthen the
powers of the Federal Government at the expense of the
reserved rights of the States. On the question of
slavery, Mr. Badger is worse than a Northern Abolitionist because, though a Southern Senator, he held
that the accursed Wilmot Proviso was a constitutional
measure." [1] The South also severely criticized the
appointment of any man residing outside the Circuit
in which the vacancy occurred; and the Free-soilers
opposed Badger as too favorable to the slavery cause.
Even the Northern Whigs were unenthusiastic in their
support. The *New York Tribune*, while expressing the
hope that Badger's nomination would be confirmed, and

[1] *Washington Union*, Jan. 28, Feb. 1, 2, 3, 1853, and *Petersburg Democrat, Mississippian, Mobile Register, Raleigh Standard, New Orleans Delta*, quoted in *ibid.* The
Mobile newspapers and Bar protested the appointment as "a corrupt effort to se-
duce the independence of the Senate by the kindly sentiments that exist in that
body for one of its members." *New York Times*, Jan. 14, 1853.

saying that he was "a lawyer of surpassing abilities" whom Judge McLean had once termed " the ablest lawyer practicing before the Court", had at the same time characterized Badger as "an iron-heeled old fogy . . . a genuine and spotless example of the breed-hunker", "wrongheaded, crabbed, intolerant, dogmatical, inveterate in his prejudices, dictatorial and unmannerly in his deportment . . . reserved, aristocratic and exclusive", and it had stated that "as a statesman, he is of no account, and as a politician detestable. He lacks breadth and comprehensiveness of view and a catholic roundabout sense essential to a man of affairs. . . . His nature is gnarled and stubbed and refuses to bend to new forms; it lacks flexibility. . . . Mr. Badger is by no means a great man. . . . Mr. Badger's qualifications are a tough, hard, wiry, mental organization, great clearness and distinctness of perception, method, exactness and strong grasp of mind. . . . He is a trained polemic, and plunges into a controversy with as good a will as a Newfoundland dog plunges into the water." [1] On February 11, the Senate by a vote of twenty-six to twenty-five postponed consideration of the nomination until March 4. "This is one of those purely party operations which the country will not sustain," said the *New York Times.* "There was no possible objection . . . except that he is a Whig. No man dared utter a word against his private character; no breath of suspicion has tarnished his fame as a jurist; and there are none to be found to dispute that he would have carried to the position . . . distinguished abilities, great caution, brilliant intellect, profound attainments, and true, most scrupulous regard for the blind goddess. . . . But the deed is done. All

[1] *New York Tribune*, Jan. 8, 1853; *The Republic* in Washington was Badger's chief active Whig supporter, Jan. 27, 1853.

JOHN McLEAN

BENJAMIN R. CURTIS

JOHN A. CAMPBELL

Photo. The F. Gutekunst Co., Phila.

JEREMIAH S. BLACK

considerations of justice and the public good have been sacrificed to partisan zeal." [1] President Fillmore, rightly regarding the action of the Senate as a rejection of Badger, decided to make one more attempt. Taking cognizance now of the sentiment demanding a candidate resident in the Circuit, but being unwilling to appoint either George Eustis of Louisiana or Solomon W. Downs, the Senator from that State, both of whom, as Unionist Whigs, had received strong indorsement, he offered the position to Judah P. Benjamin, and on the latter's declination owing to his recent election as Senator from Louisiana, he nominated Benjamin's law partner, William C. Micou, on February 24, 1853. [2] The Democratic Senate, however, was determined not to confirm any Whig appointee, at so late a date in the session. Accordingly, when the new President, Franklin Pierce, was inaugurated, he found the vacancy still existing, and, on March 21, he nominated John Archibald Campbell, the leading lawyer of Alabama, who was confirmed by the Senate, four days later. The new Judge was but forty-one years of age; he had had no former judicial experience, but his reputation as a lawyer was of the highest, and his appointment had been urged upon Pierce by the Judges of the Court, acting through Catron and Curtis. [3] Even the Whig papers admitted his

---

[1] *New York Times*, Feb. 16, 1853. Thomas Ruffin wrote to J. B. G. Roulhac, Feb. 7, 1853: "I have been blaming the Senate for rejecting, or attempting to reject, the President's nomination to the Judiciary, on party grounds. It is not a fit ground for refusing a proper man, one who would make a Judge. But I am sorry to find that the President also wishes a partisan Court and refuses to listen to representations of persons not of 'his party.' Now a nomination made on that principle, and for that reason, may reasonably be rejected. A party nomination may be justly met by party opposition, and the Senate it seems understood the President better than I did."

[2] See *New York Times*, Feb. 12, 14, 1853; *Judah P. Benjamin*, in *Great American Lawyers* (1908), VI.

[3] See 20 Wall. viii; *John Archibald Campbell* (1920), by Henry G. Connor. The Court had had an opportunity to observe Campbell, for he had argued in six cases at the December, 1851, Term, including the famous *Gaines* v. *Relf*, 12 How. 472.

full qualifications.[1] "His professional learning is said to be vast, and his industry very great. Outside his profession he is most liberally cultivated, and in this respect ranks beside Story. . . . His mind is singularly analytical. Added to all and crowning all, his perfect character is of the best stamp, modest, amiable, gentle, strictly temperate and inflexibly just," said one paper in New York, and even a strong anti-slavery paper like the *New York Tribune* termed Campbell "about the ablest man connected with the ultra State-Rights organization anywhere. That is, he is chock full of talent, genius, industry, and energy. . . . For the last ten years, he has been deservedly at the head of the Alabama Bar . . . exceedingly popular, and as a jurist and a man commands the respect and confidence of everyone." While the well-known fact that Campbell was extremely radical in his pro-Southern views alarmed some Northern papers, nevertheless, as the *New York Times* very truly pointed out, though "he is said to be a 'fire-eater', meaning thereby an extremist on the sectional question of North and South, or in other words a nullifier, there is reason to suppose that his fame on this score is more the result of warm personal and party devotion to the fortunes of Mr. Calhoun . . . than to his own settled convictions on the right of secession. He will, doubtless, in his new

[1] *New York Times*, March 22, 23, 1853. A correspondent in the *New York Tribune*, March 24, 1853, wrote that Campbell was "a gentleman of shining and profound talents, vast legal attainments and withal is irreproachable in character; but he is a fire-eater of the blazing school. He is a secessionist *per sole*, while two of his competitors, Senator Downs and Judge Eustis of Louisiana, are strong National Union or Compromise men, and pronounce the doctrine of secession a vile heresy." The *American Law Register* (Oct., 1854), II, said that Campbell was "an exceedingly able man of whom the largest expectation will not be disappointed." The *New York Tribune*, May 4, 1856, termed Judge Campbell "a man who, though pure and unexceptionable in private life, is filled with all the dogmas and mad metaphysics of Mr. Calhoun, and whose best conception of the Constitution is that it is the *aegis* of slavery." The *Washington Union* said that "as a statesman and jurist his elevation is justly an occasion of congratulation to the country." *New York Evening Post*, March 25, 1853.

estate, prove true to the Constitution and to the Union of States established by it . . . Past experience has shown that, once in this exalted post and for life, the professions of the partisan soon give place to the convictions and sense of high responsibilities of the jurist. . . . It was so with the present Chief Justice, and so with Justices Catron and Daniel, both, the nominees of President Jackson on the score of warm party service or devotion. . . . The highest-toned Federalists on the Bench have been taken from the Democratic ranks, and it will be strange if the views of a gentleman of first-rate legal talent, like Mr. Campbell should prove less conservative." [1] The conservative Whig sentiment as to the appointment was generously and favorably expressed by the unsuccessful candidate for Campbell's position, George E. Badger, who, in a Senate debate, two years later, speaking in advocacy of an increase of salary for the Judges, praised "the two Juniors of the Court, from the extreme points of the Union, North and South, men of the highest character for learning, for integrity, for talent, for judicial propriety and decorum: men who have been placed upon the Bench with the prospect of having a long career of usefulness to their country, and of honor for themselves, men led by a natural and honorable ambition, by a just professional pride, elevating them above sordid consideration to accept a position, the compensation of which does not exceed the fourth of what their profession would have produced and would have continued for many years to have produced for them."

At this December, 1852, Term of the Court, two cases

---

[1] Compare this with Henry Adams' comment on judicial appointments at an earlier period: "Jefferson and his party raised one Republican lawyer after another to the Bench, only to find that, when their professions of political opinion were tested in legal form, the Republican Judges rivalled Marshall in the Federalist and English tendencies of his law." *History of the United States* (1898), II, 195.

may be noted as of historic interest. Negligence of a
railroad — that topic in the law which later became so
productive of litigation — was involved for the first
time, in *Philadelphia and Reading R. R. Co.* v. *Derby*,
14 How. 468, in which case the Court spoke of the
"powerful but dangerous agency of steam" and held
that carriers must be held to the greatest possible care
and diligence even in the transportation of gratuitous
passengers, whose personal safety "should not be left
to the sport of chance or the negligence of careless
agents." Neutrality Laws were involved in *Kennett* v.
Chambers, 14 How. 38, — a case of particular significance, owing to the fact that during this decade illegal
military expeditions organized in this country in aid of
revolutionary movements in Cuba and Nicaragua had
frequently engaged the Government's attention. The
Court held that a contract, made in 1836 after the independence of Texas but before it had been recognized
by the United States, to furnish money to a Texas General for a military expedition from the United States,
was invalid and unenforceable. When the contract was
made, said Taney, "the constituted authorities were
endeavoring to maintain untarnished the honor of the
country, and to place it above the suspicion of taking any
part in the conflict. . . . It was made in direct opposition to the policy of the government, to which it was the
duty of every citizen to conform. . . . Every citizen . . .
is bound to commit no act of hostility against a nation
with which the government is in amity and friendship.
This principle is universally acknowledged by the law of
nations. It lies at the foundation of all government, as
there could be no order or peaceful relations between
the citizens of different countries without it." [1]

[1] Of this decision, the *National Intelligencer* said, Jan. 17, 1853: "Not to
speak of its immediate effect upon existing contracts, bonds, and obligations which
have been made, sold and bought in the prosecution of enterprises of the character,

The third case of note at the December, 1852, Term brought the Court again into contact with the dangerous question of the Fugitive Slave Law. The general defiance of this Law at the North during the past year, the refusal of State officials and others to aid in its enforcement, the State legislative impediments, the rescue of slaves from the lawful custody of Federal officials, had rightly and naturally alarmed and enraged the Southern States, and had resulted in many indictments under their laws punishing the harboring or secretion of fugitive slaves. In *Moore* v. *Illinois*, 14 How. 13, the validity of one of these laws was now upheld by the Court. Though this decision added to the anger of the antislavery forces, sanely thinking men could not deny that conditions justified, and even required, such legislation. "Experience has shown," said Judge Grier in his opinion, "that the results of such conduct as that prohibited by the statute in question are not only to demoralize their citizens who live in daily and open disregard of the duties imposed upon them by the Constitution and laws, but to destroy the harmony and kind feelings which should exist between citizens of this Union, to create border feuds and bitter animosities, and to cause breaches of the peace, violent assaults, riots and murder. No one can deny or doubt the right of a State to defend itself against evils of such magnitude, and punish those who perversely persist in conduct which promotes them."

At the next Term, in the spring of 1854, the Court

justly reprobated by this decision, it is easy to foresee how extensive will be its influence in the future, not only upon the action of individuals, but upon the habits of thinking of no inconsiderable portion of our fellow citizens, in regard to the duties of individuals to respect and obey the neutral obligations of their country." See also charges of Judge Campbell to the grand jury in the Circuit Court in Louisiana in 1854, *John Archibald Campbell* (1920), by Henry G. Connor; *Philadelphia North American*, Feb. 11, 1860; see also charges to the Grand Jury in the Circuit Court in Indiana, May 1851, Federal Cases No. 18266, 5 McLean, 249; in Ohio, Oct. 1858, Federal Cases No. 8267, 5 McLean, 306; in 1859, Federal Cases No. 18268.

was confronted with another delicate political issue — the anti-corporation movement — in several cases involving the right of banking corporations to exemption from taxation. It was an unfortunate chance that this question now arose in Ohio — a State in which the anti-slavery sentiment was the strongest, and in which hostility to the Federal Courts on that issue was already most pronounced; for a decision rendered against the State in reference to these corporations was certain to be met with enhanced opposition. Privileges granted to banks, railroads and other corporations had long been a point of attack by the Democratic Party. The numerous exemptions from taxation granted in corporate charters by State Legislatures during the past fifteen years had been a source of complaint and scandal. The right of a Legislature so to bind its successor had been hotly denied. A case brought to test this right, *Piqua Branch of the State Bank of Ohio* v. *Knoop*, 16 How. 369, was now argued on April 19–21, 1854, by Henry Stanbery against Rufus P. Spalding and George E. Pugh. The Bank, holding a charter containing a provision for exemption from certain taxation, claimed that a later statute, which imposed a tax, was an impairment of the obligation of the State's contract. The State claimed that no Legislature had the power, by a tax exemption, to relinquish part of the sovereign authority of the State. Immense financial interests all over the country depended on the decision of the Court. On May 24, 1854, the Court, through Judge McLean, rendered its decision declaring the law unconstitutional and holding that: "A State, in granting privileges to a bank with a view of affording a sound currency, or of advancing any policy connected with a public interest, exercises its sovereignty, and for a public purpose, of which it is exclusive judge;" and that those privileges, proffered by the State, accepted by the stockholders and in consideration of which funds were invested in the Bank, constituted a contract, " founded upon considerations of policy required by the general interests of the community" and which must be protected. In closing, Judge McLean stated that he would not discuss general theories of Government, which were "an unsafe rule for judicial action. Our prosperity, individually and Nationally, depends upon a close adherence to the settled rules of law and especially to the great fundamental law of the Union." The four Democratic Judges, the Chief Justice, Catron, Daniel and Campbell, filed a strong dissenting opinion, largely directed at the dangers of protecting the growth of corporate power; they held that the Courts of Ohio had already decided that the statute granting the charter did not constitute a contract for the tax exemption claimed by the Bank, and that no Legislature could legally place a portion of the sovereign political power beyond the reach of subsequent Legislatures, unless so authorized by the State Constitution. Judge Campbell further pointed out that : " The discussions before this Court in the Indiana Railroad and the Baltimore Railroad cases exposed to us the sly and stealthy arts to which State Legislatures are exposed, and the greedy appetites of adventurers for monopolies and immunities from the State right of Government. We cannot close our eyes to their insidious efforts to ignore the fundamental laws and institutions of the States, and to subject the highest popular interests to their central boards of control and directors' management." [1]

---

[1] At the December, 1853, Term, the growth of the lobby evil in the country had been strikingly shown in *Marshall* v. *Baltimore & Ohio R. R.*, 16 How. 314, in which the Court refused its aid to enforce a contract for a railroad agent's services before a Virginia Legislature. Judge Grier, after adverting to logrolling and other lobby methods, said that "legislators should act with a single eye to the true interest of

The decision upholding the corporate exemption from taxation produced a great sensation, not only in Ohio, but in many States whose Legislature had granted similar exemptions to State banks. "An important and extraordinary decision," said the *Cincinnati Enquirer*. "The Supreme Court has always leaned strongly to the Federal idea of a strong National Government, and has been very conservative in maintaining and carrying out the old English common law principle of the sacredness o. corporations and their immunity from legislation." In a later issue, it referred to "this outrageous decision by the truly Federal Court. The sober mind may begin to wonder how this unrighteousness can possibly be imposed upon a community in a democratic or, if you please, in a republican form of Government." It attacked the Court as a "silk-gowned fogydom, a goodly portion of it imbecile with age, a portion anti-republican in notions, a portion wedded to the antiquated doctrine of established precedents, no matter whether truth or fallacy." It contended, against the decision, that a Legis'ature could not give or barter away the sovereignty of the people; and it exclaimed: "People of Ohio, you see where you stand! . . . A crisis is here now, if it had not already been reached, and as this is the 'year of storms', look out for the greatest one yet to come." Again it said that the decision was clearly "an invasion of State sovereignty and a great outrage upon State-Rights —

the whole people, and Courts of Justice can give no countenance to the use of means which may subject them to be misled by the pertinacious importunity and indirect influences of interested and unscrupulous agents of solicitors. . . . The use of such means and such agents will have the effect to subject the State Governments to the combined capital of wealthy corporations and produce universal corruption, commencing with the representative and ending with the elector;" and the *New York Evening Post* referring to the decision said, Jan. 11, 1855, that it was "a melancholy thing to observe to what an extent the practice of corrupting and cajoling legislative bodies is carried on in this country by men who still preserve what is regarded as a respectable standing in society."

yet how is it to be met? It is the Court of last resort, and a large class of people have reluctance to being placed in any position that would cause any resistance to its judgment." [1] That the Court itself, however, realized the strength of the anti-corporation sentiment then prevailing in the country, as well as the grounds for its existence, and that it was not inclined to uphold corporate privilege in any case where such privilege was not clearly shown to be guaranteed by a State contract was shown in another Ohio bank case decided at this Term, *Ohio Life Insurance Company* v. *Debolt*, 16 How. 416. In this case, it held that the charter, properly construed, contained no such contract of tax exemption, and it pointed out in great detail many of the corporate evils of that day. Chief Justice Taney, referring to the doctrine that a charter carried nothing by implication, sagely said that the rule was "founded in principles of justice, and necessary for the safety and well-being of every State in the Union. For it is a matter of public history which this Court cannot refuse to notice, that almost every bill for the incorporation of banking companies, insurance and trust companies, railroad companies and other corporations, is drawn originally by the parties who are personally interested in obtaining the charter; and that they are often passed by the Legislature in the last days of its session, when, from the nature of our political institutions, the business is unavoidably transacted in a hurried manner, and it is impossible that every member can deliberately examine every provision in every bill upon which he is called to act. On the other hand, those who accept the charter have abundant time to examine and consider its provisions, before they invest their money. If they mean to claim under it any peculiar privileges, or any ex-

[1] *Cincinnati Enquirer*, May 26, 30, June 2, 1854.

emption from the burden of taxation, it is their duty to see that the right or exemption they intend to claim is granted in clear and unambiguous language." Judge Catron also spoke of " the unparalleled increase of corporations throughout the Union within the last few years; the ease with which charters containing exclusive privileges and exemptions are obtained; the vast amount of property, power and exclusive benefits, prejudicial to other classes of society, that are vested in and held by these bodies of associated wealth."

Two years later, however, the antagonism of the people of Ohio towards the Court was still further excited by a decision which carried the doctrine of the *Piqua Branch Case* to an even greater extreme; for in *Dodge* v. *Woolsey*, 18 How. 331, in 1856, the Court was confronted with the question whether a State Constitution containing a repeal of a prior statutory tax exemption was valid. After the Piqua Branch suit had been brought, involving the validity of a statute repealing a tax exemption, the people of Ohio amended their Constitution and inserted in it such a repeal clause. Suit to test this action had been instituted in a Federal Circuit Court by a stockholder, alleging that the directors of his bank were about to pay the tax, in spite of their belief in its invalidity. Thus confronted for the first time with the solemn question of its power to hold a Constitution of a sovereign State to be invalid, the Court did not flinch in its determination to hold a State to strict compliance with honesty in contracts; and accordingly it rendered its decision that the people of a State could no more impair the obligation of contracts by means of a Constitution than by a statute, and that the tax was consequently still invalid. "The moral obligations never die," it said. "If broken by States and Nations, though the terms of reproach are not the same

with which we are accustomed to designate the faith-
lessness of individuals, the violation of justice is not the
less." [1] A strong dissent was again filed by Judges
Campbell, Catron and Daniel, the former denouncing
"these extraordinary pretensions of corporations. . . .
They display a love of power, a preference for corporate
interests to moral or political principles or public duties,
and an antagonism to individual freedom, which have
marked them as objects of jealousy in every epoch of their
history." And he said that the consequence of establishing this "caste" would be "a new element of alienation and discord between the different classes of society,
and the introduction of a fresh cause of disturbance in
our distracted political and social system. In the end,
the doctrine of this decision may lead to a violent overturn of the whole system of corporate combinations."
The Ohio newspapers followed the dissenting Judges, in
prophesying future trouble from corporate wealth and
combination, and deplored the alleged tendency of the
Court to decide against the State, when "corporate
pretensions come in conflict with the sovereignty of the
people." "Whatever may be the excellencies of the
Supreme Court, and we are not disposed to deny that
they are many," said a leading paper, "a disposition
to curtail and limit corporation privileges, and to regard them with a jealous eye in their judicial action,
was never among them." And this paper earnestly
advised the banks, "having vanquished the State, to
waive voluntarily their obnoxious privilege. . . . We
are confident that it would be for their interest so to do,
as it would allay a well-founded public disgust at an

---

[1] The *New York Tribune*, April 9, 1856, said of the decision: "The case involved
the whole power of taxation and therefore was treated as one of the most important
ever considered." In *Sandusky City Bank* v. *Weber*, 7 Ohio State Rep. 48, the Ohio
Court held that the decision in *Dodge* v. *Woolsey* was not binding upon it, since
that case arose in the Federal Circuit Court.

odious distinction that cannot be sustained upon any principle of justice or equality." [1]

The gravity of the situation which was produced in Ohio by these decisions is seen from the fact that, for over two years from the date of the Piqua Branch decision, the Supreme Court of Ohio refused to enter the mandate of the Supreme Court of the United States. Finally, late in 1856, three Judges of the State Supreme Court decided to conform to the mandate which had been issued to it, stating that they were "not prepared to adopt the theory" on which a denial of the jurisdiction of the Supreme Court under the Judiciary Act was based. The State Chief Justice, dissenting, however, said that the doctrine of the decision in its "enormities and alarming import . . . wholly prostrates the municipal sovereignty of the people with the State." [2] Meanwhile, the same Chief Justice, sitting in the State District Court, in another case,[3] rendered a decision wholly denying the validity of the appellate jurisdiction of the United States Supreme Court under the Twenty-Fifth Section of the Judiciary Act, and overruling a motion to perfect the record of the State Court, so that the case might be taken up on writ of error.

While this serious attempt to derogate from the power

[1] *Cincinnati Daily Enquirer*, April 11, 1856. See also *Ohio Statesman*, Jan. 16, 1857.

[2] See for the Ohio decisions, *Ohio v. Commercial Bank*, 7 Ohio, Part I, 125; *Bank v. Knoop*, 1 Ohio State, 603; 6 Ohio State, 343; and *The Supreme Court and State Repudiation*, by John N. Pomeroy, *Amer. Law Rev.* (1883), XVII.

The seriousness of the situation may be seen from a description of Ohio conditions given in a California case, a few years later, *Warner v. Steamship Uncle Sam* (1858), 9 Calif. 697: "That State, for several years past, has been arrayed in hostility to the General Government; that this hostility has exhibited itself in the Legislative, the Judicial and the Executive departments of that State; that actual resistance to Federal authority on the part of the people is of common occurrence and is sanctioned and encouraged by legislative enactment. and justified by judicial decision — a part of a general system of resistance to the Constitution and laws of the United States, which has already led to the verge of civil war."

[3] *Stunt v. The Ohio* (1855), 3 Ohio Decisions Reprints. 362.

of the Court was taking place in the Central West, an
actual judicial decision denying the Court's jurisdiction
was made in the new and distant State of California.
In 1854, the Supreme Court of that State in *Johnson* v.
Gordon, 4 Calif. 368, refused to allow a writ of error to
the Supreme Court of the United States to a party
desiring to appeal from the decision of the State Court.
It held that acquiescence by other States in the exercise by that Court of jurisdiction over State Court
decisions did not constitute a sufficient reason for "the
surrender of a power which belongs to the sovereignty
we represent, involving an assumption of that power by
another jurisdiction in derogation of that sovereignty.
We think, too, that the acquiescence in this usurpation of the Federal Tribunal, under an Act of Congress
not warranted by the Constitution, is not so much owing
to a conviction of its propriety, as it is to the high character of the Court, and the general correctness of its
decisions." This hostile attitude towards the Court in
California was probably due to the peculiar isolated
situation of litigation in that State, at that period, when
there was absence of railroad communication, and little
contact with the rest of the Union ; and the inhabitants
felt, as counsel argued in the *Johnson Case*, that the
jurisdiction of the State Courts over these matters was
particularly important : " The delays and expense of
the Federal Courts, especially where great monopolies
are concerned, able to carry cases to the Supreme Court,
make litigation in these forums almost a denial of justice." Such an attack upon the supremacy of the
United States Supreme Court, however, was not long
tolerated in California ; for, the next year, on April 9,
1855, the Legislature, by a nearly unanimous vote of
both branches, passed a law to enforce compliance with
the sections of the Federal Judiciary Act by Judges and

Clerks of Courts; and in 1858, the Supreme Court of California reversed its ruling — Judges Joseph V. Baldwin and Stephen J. Field (later a Judge of the United States Supreme Court) recognizing the validity of the Twenty-Fifth Section of the Judiciary Act,[1] and stating that : " A long course of adjudication by Courts of the highest authority, State and National, commencing almost from the foundation of the Government, and the acquiescence of nearly all the State Governments in all of their departments, have given to this doctrine a recognition so strong and authentic that we feel no disposition to deny it at this late day, even if the reasons for such denial were more cogent than they seem to us to be." [2]

While Ohio and California, in 1854, were thus placed by their Courts in open opposition to the Supreme Court of the United States, they were joined by the State of Wisconsin. The case which led to this unfortunate condition arose out of the rescue of a fugitive slave from Missouri by an abolitionist editor named Booth and

[1] *Ferris* v. *Coover* (1858), 11 Calif. 175 ; see also *Warner* v. *Steamship Uncle Sam* (1858), 9 Calif. 697.

[2] The opposite view, however, was maintained by the Chief Justice of the Court — David S. Terry, who used the following quite unjustifiable language : "It has never been admitted in Virginia, has always been repudiated by Georgia, and has lately been questioned in several other States. The decisions of the United States Supreme Court on this question embody the political principles of a party which has passed away. . . . The force and authority of the opinions of the Supreme Court of the United States upon the question of jurisdiction, as well as all others of a political nature, is much weakened, by the consideration that the political sentiments of the Judges in such cases necessarily gave direction to the decisions of the Courts. The Legislative and Executive power of the Government had passed, or was rapidly passing into the hands of men entertaining opposite principles. Regarding the Judicial as the conservative department; believing the possession by the General Government of greater powers than those expressly granted by the Constitution to be absolutely necessary to its stability, they sought, by a latitudinarian construction of its provisions, to remedy the defects in that instrument, and by a course of judicial decisions to give direction to the future policy of the Union. Hoary usurpations of power and jurisdiction on the part of the Federal Judiciary, or time-honored encroachments on the reserved rights of the sovereign States, are entitled to no additional respect on account of their antiquity, and should be as little regarded by the State tribunals as if they were but things of yesterday."

various other citizens of Wisconsin.[1] Booth, having been arrested on a warrant issued by a United States Commissioner for violation of the Federal Fugitive Slave Law, and having been taken into custody by a United States marshal, had been discharged on a writ of habeas corpus issued by a Judge of the Wisconsin Supreme Court, on the ground that the Federal statute was unconstitutional. This extraordinary interference of a State Judge with a Federal marshal's custody having been sustained by the full bench of the State Supreme Court, the marshal, Ableman, at once sued out a writ of error to the United States Supreme Court, returnable in December, 1854, and the record was duly certified by State Court Clerk. In January, 1855, Booth was indicted, tried, convicted and sentenced in the United States District Court for violation of the Fugitive Slave Law; but he was at once released, on another writ of habeas corpus issued by the State Supreme Court. And this Court proceeded to hold that the Federal Court had been without jurisdiction, the Law being invalid.[2] This direct collision between State and Federal authority raised once more the old issue of Nullification. The doctrines formerly advocated by South Carolina were now maintained by the anti-slavery party in the North, and its newspapers now openly counseled disobedience to the Federal Courts and to the Federal laws.[3] "The

[1] The *New York Evening Post*, April 8, 1854, said that Booth, when arrested and brought before the magistrate, stated that "rather than have the great constitutional rights and safeguards of the people, the writ of habeas corpus and the right of trial by jury stricken down by the Fugitive law, I would prefer to see every Federal officer in Wisconsin hanged on a gallows fifty cubits higher than Haman."

[2] *In re Booth*, 3 Wisc. 1, 49, the case was ably argued by Byron Paine for Booth against Edward G. Ryan for Ableman (both Paine and Ryan becoming later Judges of the Wisconsin Supreme Court); see *A Historic Judicial Controversy*, by Stephen S. Gregory, *Michigan Law Rev.* (1913), I; *Story of a Great Court* (1912), by J. B. Winslow; *The Fugitive Slave Law in Wisconsin*, by Vroman Mason, *State Hist. Soc. Proc.* (1895); and see also authorities cited in *State Documents on Federal Relations* (1911), by Herman V. Ames, 304.

[3] *New York Tribune*, Feb. 2, 7, 8, 26, Aug. 1, 10, 1855. Charles Sumner wrote,

North is just now taking lessons in Southern jurisprudence," said the *New York Tribune*. "South Carolina, Georgia and little Florida have, at one time and another, displayed a glorious independence of Federal legislation, whenever it suited their purposes. We trust that, under the influence of such illustrious examples, the States of the North may be excused for an occasional assertion of their notion of their own rights. We doubt not that it is the opinion of a large majority of the people of the free States that the existing Fugitive Slave Law is unconstitutional, and their present aim is to make their State Court so declare it and adhere to the declaration. We are a law abiding people. But we purpose to have laws fit to abide by, and Courts fit to be obeyed. The difficulty has always been, and now is, that our Northern Courts derive their inspirations from a Federal slavery-upholding Court. Our local Judiciary has been poisoned by the virus of a National Bench, whereon sits a majority in the interest of the peculiar institution. But happily a most refreshing example of the independence of this influence is to be seen in the late action of the Supreme Court of Wisconsin. The Judges of that State have won a lasting title to regard and admiration by their late decision in the case of Booth and Ryecroft, and this Congress will have to legislate fast and long in order to deprive them of it. The example which Wisconsin has set will be as rapidly followed as circumstances admit. By another year, we expect to see Ohio holding the same noble course. After that, we anticipate a race among the other Free States in the same direction, till all have reached the goal of

Aug. 5, 1854, to Byron Paine: "God grant that Wisconsin may not fail to protect her own right and the rights of her citizens in the emergency now before it. To her belongs the lead which Massachusetts should have taken." See *New York Evening Post*, May 10, 1854, for conflict between Federal and State authorities in a habeas corpus case in Pennsylvania involving fugitive slaves; *U. S. ex rel. Crossman v. Allen; ibid.*, April 9, 1855, as to a similar conflict in Ohio.

State independence. By that time, we expect to see the United States Court so constituted that all pre-existing conflicts will have been ended. Improper decisions will have been reserved, and truth and justice commence their sway. . . . Let the North but maintain its high purpose, its unflinching resolve that it will not submit to slave-driving dictation, whether coming through Courts pledged to the support of that institution, or in whatever way it may show itself; and the usurpations enacted by Congress will be torn to ribbons and its impudently unconstitutional laws defied. All that is wanting to this end is independent State Courts, fearless Legislatures, Governors with backbones and a determined people behind them." Again, in urging that active measures be taken " against the usurpation of the slave power", it preached still more boldly a policy of Nullification, saying: "The North must learn to act as well as talk. . . . Wisconsin has taken one step in the true path. . . . It has always been the doctrine of the State-Rights or old Democratic party that the States had the right to judge of infraction of the Constitution, and in a case of importance to decide upon the mode and measure of redress. . . . The Free States may rightfully retaliate . . . by the overthrow and destruction of slavery itself. They are rightfully entitled to exercise this power under the Constitution, as expounded by its great authors." And again it said that " the Republican Party naturally stand on the State-Rights doctrine of Jefferson."[1]

Similar attempts by State Courts and State officials to interfere with the operation of the Federal Courts in Ohio and in Pennsylvania, about this time, were defeated by the firm action of the Federal Judges.

[1] See also editorial in *New York Tribune*, Jan. 29, 1856, entitled "A Star in the West."

In the former State, Judge McLean himself was called upon to sustain the supremacy of the Fugitive Slave Law over State action. In *Ex parte Robinson*, 6 McLean, 355, in April, 1855, a United States marshal had been imprisoned by a State Court, for re-arresting a fugitive slave whom the State Court, by a writ of habeas corpus, had taken from the marshal's lawful custody; the marshal sued out a writ of habeas corpus in the United States Circuit Court, under a Federal statute enacted in 1833 giving to the Federal Court the power to issue such a writ in cases of persons confined by State officials for an act done under authority of Federal law. Judge McLean, in spite of his anti-slavery views, granted the writ, and ordered the marshal's release by the State Court. The statute authorizing the writ, he said "was enacted to meet the Nullification doctrines proclaimed by South Carolina, but which in this respect, it is believed, were never acted upon by that State. Little was it supposed that the principle could ever have a necessary application to the Northern or Western States, whose Members of Congress advocated and voted for the law." Interference by a State Court with a case in a Federal Court before it was terminated was, he said, "unprecedented in judicial proceedings;" and he continued with this warning to the States: "There need be no apprehensions of the public peace being disturbed for any want of respect by the Federal authorities to the State Courts. State-Rights are invoked by the counsel. If these Rights are construed to mean a subversion of the Federal authorities, they may be somewhat in danger." [1]

Another case of assertion of Federal supremacy, which

[1] See denunciatory editorial in *New York Tribune*, April 18, 1855, entitled "Judge McLean's Jail Delivery."

arose in Pennsylvania in the summer of 1855 and which caused intense excitement, presented the following singular facts. While John H. Wheeler, the United States Minister to Nicaragua, was proceeding with his slaves from Washington to New York in order to embark for his post, certain abolitionists headed by Passmore Williamson deliberately took the slaves from his possession; Wheeler sued out a writ of habeas corpus against Williamson whom he alleged to be in control, of the rescued slaves. Williamson, denying having such control, declined to comply with the writ; and for this action he was sentenced to imprisonment for contempt of Court by United States District Judge Kane. Application was made by Williamson to the Supreme Court of Pennsylvania for a writ of habeas corpus to release him from the Federal sentence. Insistent demands were made by the abolitionist press that the State Court should assert its authority. That Court, however, declined thus to interfere with the Federal Judiciary. In a powerful opinion by Judge Jeremiah S. Black, it said that the District Court had power and jurisdiction to decide what actions constituted a contempt against it, and that:

Such conviction for contempt must be final, otherwise Courts totally unconnected with each other would be coming in constant collision. . . . There may be cases in which we ought to check usurpation of power by the Federal Courts. . . . But what we would not permit them to do against us, we will not do against them. We must maintain the rights of the State and its Courts, for to them alone can the people look for a competent administration of their domestic concerns; but we will do nothing to impair the constitutional vigour of the General Government, which is the "sheet-anchor of our peace at home and our safety abroad."

Judge Lowry also delivered an opinion in the case saying: "In the name of the order which we repre-

sent and entorce, I decline any and every usurpation
of power or control over the United States, it being a
system collateral to ours, as complete and efficient in
its organization, and as legitimate and final authority
as any other." [1]

The decisions of Judge Kane and of Judge Black
were bitterly assailed by the *New York Tribune* and
other similar papers, and the impeachment of Kane was
insistently demanded. "A system of insolent and alarming usurpation" must be terminated, it was said: "It
is high time that the insolence and tyranny of our
Federal Judges should be rebuked and punished."

With such views prevalent in many of the Northern
States, it now became evident that, if the supremacy of
the Federal Government and of its officials was to be
preserved, additional legislation was necessary for the
enforcement of this supremacy. Accordingly, early in
1855, Senator Toucey of Connecticut introduced a bill
in Congress to provide for the removal into the Federal
Courts of any suit against a Federal officer, instituted
in a State Court, for any act done under a Federal law
or authority or color thereof. Although, twenty years
later, this precise law was enacted by the Republican
Party when it desired to enforce against the South the
unpopular Reconstruction Acts, nevertheless, in 1855
it was denounced by Republican statesmen, as an instrument designed to enforce the monstrous Fugitive
Slave Law. In opposition to its passage, the Virginia
and Kentucky Resolutions of 1798–1799 were cited with
approval, and all the State-Rights doctrines, against
which the Whig Party had fought from 1800 to 1840,
were now adopted by the anti-slavery men with ardor.

[1] See *United States* v. *Williamson*, Federal Cases Nos. 16725, 16726, July 27,
Oct. 15, 1855; *Passmore Williamson's Case* (1855), 26 Penn. State, 9; *New
York Tribune*, July 28, Aug. 28, 29, Nov. 5, 1855, and *passim* through July, August
and September, 1855.

The bill was termed "a dangerous and preposterous usurpation of authority" by the Federal Government, an attempt "to abrogate the functions and jurisdiction of the State tribunals not for a moment to be tolerated", a bill to "bring the Judiciary of every State bound in chains to the foot of Federal power, and which ought to be spurned by the most vigorous assertion of the reserved powers of the States." [1]   Salmon P. Chase of Ohio called it "a bill to establish a great, central, consolidated Federal Government. It is a step — a stride rather — towards despotism"; and William H. Seward of New York, William P. Fessenden of Maine and Charles Sumner of Massachusetts argued similarly against the usurpation of the Federal Government and its Judiciary. "It will promote collisions between Federal and State jurisdiction — conflicts in which the States will never yield," said Benjamin F. Wade of Ohio. "Wisconsin has taught you a lesson, and it is only an incipient step. . . . State after State will fall in the wake of noble Wisconsin. . . . This is a most unfortunate time further to irritate a people, almost driven to desperation by what they consider your Federal usurpations. . . . I am no advocate for Nullification," he continued, "but in the nature of things, according to the true interpretation of our institutions, a State, in the last resort, crowded to the wall by the General Government seeking by the strong arm of its power to take away the rights of the State, is to judge of whether she shall stand on her reserved rights. . . . Wisconsin has availed herself of those great principles that Virginia asserted in times of danger."

Such sentiments were, of course, those of Nullifica-

---

[1] *33d Cong., 2d Sess., App.,* 210 *et seq.,* Feb. 23, 1855. *Philadelphia North American,* Feb. 26, 1855. The *New York Tribune,* Feb. 19, 27, 1855, termed the bill "The New Outrage", and a bill "under a very innocent title . . . for the better protection of negro-hunters."

tion, pure and simple. "The Senator from Ohio has raised in the Senate Chamber the standard of rebellion again against the Court," said Stephen A. Douglas of Illinois; and Judah P. Benjamin of Louisiana asked: "Who would ever have expected, a few years ago, to have heard it said in the Senate of the United States by Senators from the North, that State tribunals were vested with jurisdiction in the last resort to determine upon the constitutionality of laws enacted by the Congress of the United States, that their decisions were of greater weight and entitled to higher respect than the decision of the Supreme Court of the United States?" The bill passed the Senate, but was not acted upon in the House.

Antagonism to the Court cropped out at this session of Congress, in 1855, in connection with two other measures. A bill to increase the Judges' salaries was defeated, as Senator Badger said, simply because the Judges of the Supreme Court on Circuit "had done their duty in enforcing a law obnoxious to public opinion", — the Fugitive Slave Law.[1] The subject of slavery was also responsible for the defeat of a renewed attempt (similar to those made in 1826, in 1835 and in 1844) to reform the Judiciary system by establishing additional Circuits. The urgent need of this reform, owing to the great expansion in territory and the enormous increase of the Court's business, had become so clear that President Pierce, in his messages to Congress in 1853 and 1854, had urged immediate legislation. While the bill,

---

[1] *33d Cong., 2d Sess.*, Jan. 11, 1855. In showing the need for increase of salary, Senator Badger pointed out the fact that, in the six years beginning in 1809 and ending in 1815, the Court sat 206 days and decided 235 cases — an average of 30 days and 39 cases a year; in the six years between 1822 and 1827, the Court sat 263 days and decided 194 cases, an average of 44 days and 32 cases a year; but in the six years from 1848 to 1853 the Court had sat 664 days and decided 448 cases — an average of 110 days and 74 cases a year. See also *National Intelligencer*, Dec. 20, 1854.

so advocated, establishing eleven (instead of nine) Circuits, and relieving the Judges of Circuit Court duty, met with opposition based on the old argument that "if you shut the Judges up here, they become a centralized metropolitan Court, almost as shut out from public view as the Veiled Prophet was," and that the Judges should mingle with the local Bars and not remain in Washington to become "mere paper Judges, losing weight of authority and knowledge of local legislation and practice", nevertheless, in spite of these oft-repeated arguments, the bill would probably have passed, had it not now encountered another element of opposition — the fear of the anti-slavery men lest President Pierce should make the two new appointments in the interests of slavery.[1] It is interesting to note, however, that an opening wedge for the abolition of Circuit duty by the Supreme Court Judges was effected by the passage of a singular Act at this session of Congress, establishing a Circuit Court of the United States for California and Oregon with a separate Circuit Judge who should not be a member of the Supreme Court. This anomaly in the Federal Judicial system was made necessary by the fact that, as there was then no railroad communication between the Pacific Coast and the East, no Supreme Court Judge sitting in the Circuit could perform his duties in Washington.[2]

At the next sessions of Congress during the spring and winter of 1856, the abolitionist campaign against

[1] *33d Cong., 2d Sess.*, Jan. 5, 17, 18, 1855. The *New York Evening Post*, Jan. 12, 1855, said that the relief of the Supreme Court Judges from Circuit duty and their reduction in number from nine to six was generally favored. "There are, however, a few Senators who oppose any change in the present system until a more thorough reform can be effected — to secure, for instance, the substitution of a term of years for that of good behavior. They think that decisions infringing the inherent personal and political rights of the people would not come from a Bench, liable to a rejection every eight years."

[2] *33d Cong., 2d Sess.*, Feb. 6, 7, 12, 1855.

the Court was continued with increasing fervor throughout the debate on the admission of Kansas as a State.[1] Again and again, Hale used his favorite characterization of it as "the citadel of slavery"; Seward in the Senate and Bennett in the House reiterated the charge that the majority of the Judges were appointed in the slavery interests; Giddings asserted the doctrine of the right, both of Congressmen and of individuals, to refrain from executing, and to disregard and disobey, a law deemed unconstitutional. On the other side, the Democrats reaffirmed their entire willingness to leave the question of the power of Congress over slavery in the Territories to the Court, and to abide by its decision, and stated that it was the duty of Congress not to forestall by legislation a judicial decision, and "not to coerce and dragoon that Court in the decision of a constitutional question which is purely judicial."[2] Hale's diatribes were warmly refuted. "For purity, integrity, virtue, honor, and all that ennobles and dignifies, it stands unimpeached and unimpeachable," said James C. Jones of Tennessee. "The Judges are the sentinels and defenders of the Constitution; they do not decide by the 'higher law' of discretion and prejudice," said Andrew P. Butler of South Carolina, Chairman of the Senate Judiciary Committee. "I have never known a body of men more honestly disposed to do their duty. . . . I would rather regard that high tribunal as one which could look abroad upon the vast and beautiful horizon of truth and justice. I should not wish to see them governed by that popular agitation which is threatening

[1] *34th Cong., 1st Sess.*, and *App.*; *34th Cong., 3d Sess.*, and *App.*; see speeches in 1856 of Hale, Feb. 26, May 2, Dec. 11, Seward, May 2, Trumbull, Dec. 2, Wade, Dec. 4, in the Senate; Henry Bennett of New York, June 30, J. A. Bingham of Ohio, Jan. 13, 15, and many others in the House.

[2] See speeches of Benjamin, May 2, Douglas, June 9, Geyer, April 7, Cass, May 12, Dec. 11, Jones, Feb. 25, Butler, March 5, Rusk, Dec. 4, Jones, Dec. 18, in the Senate; David Ritchie, April 24, in the House.

to undermine the institutions of the country. . . . I wish it to stand firm, at least, as the type of the duration of the institutions of this country, and as an emblem of eternal justice." The falseness of the charge that the Court was controlled by the slavery interests was palpable. For, since the year 1840, when the slavery question first became a heated issue, the only appointments to the Bench had been those of Judges Grier, Nelson, Curtis and Campbell, of whom only one — Campbell — was from the South or of pro-slavery views, and that one simply succeeded Judge McKinley, who held like opinions on the subject. All the other Judges had been appointed to the Bench before the slavery question had become a vivid political and sectional issue. Moreover, the Judges had on numerous occasions proved their impartiality and lack of sectional bias in cases involving slavery decided by them since 1840 — the *Prigg Case*, a decision held by both South and North to be opposed to the respective interests of each — *Groves* v. *Slaughter* upholding the exclusive right of each State to deal with slavery within its borders, the *Passenger Cases* affecting laws both of the South and North, the *Missouri-Iowa Boundary Line Cases*. So far as the charge that Judges were appointed or were acting for political reasons was concerned, the South had more just reason to complain than the North; for the only Judge who had taken an active part in politics, or who had openly expressed his views on crucial political questions was a Northern Judge — John McLean of Ohio. In practically every campaign since his appointment to the Bench, Judge McLean had been, either actively or passively, a candidate for the Presidency; his name had been balloted for at several conventions; and he entertained and publicly expressed positive, though somewhat unusual, views as to the entire propriety of a Judge being a candidate for that office.[1] Moreover, Judge McLean had not hesitated to write for publication in the newspapers his views on burning political questions of the day. Such a letter written in 1847, containing an attack upon the Mexican War, had given rise to a criticism of the bitterest kind from men and newspapers of both political parties, who deprecated activities of this nature on the part of a member of the Judiciary.[2] In 1848, McLean had committed a more serious breach of judicial propriety, by writing a letter, which was published, expressing his views as to the power of Congress over slavery in the territories — a question which the Clayton Compromise Bill, in that very year, proposed should be submitted to the Court

[1] See letter of McLean to Gen. Duff Green, Sept. 16, 1829 (*John McLean Papers MSS*): "I did not suppose that you or any other person who had reflected upon the subject could entertain the least apprehension of any improper influence being used by a Judge who comes before the people in a popular election, and especially that it could lend to corrupt the Bench. This has not been realized in the election of Judges to the offices of Governor and Senator in Congress. . . . By what process of reasoning you could come to such a result, I cannot imagine. Sure I am that facts cannot aid you, however much might be gained by popular prejudice. So far from a Judge occupying a position which gives him a commanding influence in a popular election, it is without exception the most unfavorable post a candidate can occupy. He has no patronage to dispense. In every decision he gives, he disappoints one party and his counsel, who, though restrained in their expressions of resentment against him as Judge, would gladly in the exercise of their right of suffrage show their disapprobation. And if the Judge can be supposed to be influenced in any decision by popular consideration, his popularity is at once destroyed. A Judge can do nothing to advance his prospects which will not certainly destroy him. For the reasons stated he would be the last person to unite the Bar in his support. In the event of his being before the people, he would necessarily act with the utmost circumspection and not only avoid the least ground for an unfavorable imputation, but even the appearance of impropriety."

[2] See McLean's letter to the *National Intelligencer*, Dec. 28, 1847, quoted in speech of Dickinson, Aug. 1, 1848; *30th Cong., 1st Sess.* See among numerous criticisms, the *National Intelligencer*, Jan. 31, 1848, which said that the Judge was "dragging the ermine in the mire of politics"; the *Pennsylvanian*, Feb. 1, said that the letter was entitled to "indignant censure"; the *Mississippian*, Feb. 18, said it was written by a man "bereft of patriotism . . . unfit for the exalted station he holds"; the *Mississippi Free Trader*, Feb. 8, said he had "stained his ermine with the bitter waters of party"; the *Boston Post*, Feb. 7, said it was a "most melancholy exhibition of a partisan Judge . . . a display of party violence on the bench"; the *Washington Union*, Feb. 3, said: "He deserves impeachment at the bar of public opinion"; the *Trenton True American*, Feb. 4, termed him "a judicial politician."

for decision. For this action, the Judge was justly, though savagely, attacked in Congress by Senator Foote of Mississippi, as having been "guilty of high offense against public decency"; [1] and while the Judge was defended by Senator Corwin and Senator Reverdy Johnson, the latter was forced to say that: "The judgment of the public, in its almost universal censure of the step, will effectually guard against its repetition. A Judge should be separated, not only while he is upon the Bench, but forever, from all the agitating political topics of the day. Once a Judge, he should ever be a Judge. The ermine should never be polluted, not suspected of pollution; it should be the very type of Justice herself — pure, spotless, faultless." And a representative of a Democratic paper in Philadelphia said that: "The good sense of the whole country condemns this offensive intermingling in politics . . . and the moral sense of the country revolts at the solemn prejudgment of questions, which, in all probability, must at last be decided by the Supreme Court of which he is a member. They justly respect the high responsibilities of their position and the notorious feelings of the people, by keeping themselves aloof from the altercations and animosities, the differences and the difficulties of party strife. Justice McLean is an exception." Unfortunately, McLean did not take warning by these merited censures; and a public expression of his views on the slavery issue in 1856 again elicited strong Congressional disapprobation for "an extrajudicial opinion which has excited much surprise and

[1] *30th Cong., 2d Sess.*, Jan. 17, 23, 1849. The *Philadelphia North American*, a Whig paper and an ardent admirer of Judge McLean, referred, Jan. 19, 25, 1849, to Senator Foote's attack as "wanton and gross"; "a wanton and libellous assault, as destitute of truth as it was vile in expression", and stated that it called out "a general expression of derision from the chamber." Other papers, however, greatly deplored Judge McLean's action; see *National Intelligencer*, Jan. 22, 23, 1849; *Pennsylvanian*, Jan. 20, 22, 25, 1849.

regret." "In exciting times like these," it was said, "when all earthly tribunals, in order to command respect, must be firm, unswerving, and above raving, popular clamor; when, too, the merits of the question were much involved in a case to come before him as one of the Judges of the last resort — to have made a parade of his opinion, thus intermingling with the partisan debates of a passing hour — cannot certainly commend him to the approval of an intelligent public." [1]

While it thus appears that the South had more cause than the North to complain of political bias shown by a Judge of the Court, the charge that the Court was constituted for the sole purpose of upholding slavery continued to be reiterated by the abolitionists, not only in the Senate but in their newspapers. "The people had been changing the Senate on the slavery issue," they said, but the slavery men had "quietly and without any excitement, with no word of remonstrance on the part of the North, in a strictly constitutional way, obtained the nomination and approval of a majority of Southerners upon the bench of the Supreme Court." [2] Violent personal attacks upon the Judges themselves became frequent in the press. Of Curtis, the *New York Tribune* wrote: "He is not a Massachusetts Judge. He is a slave-catching Judge, appointed to office as a reward for his professional support given to the Fugitive Slave bill. . . . Having had so many exhibitions of the ingenuity and adroitness of Mr.

---

[1] *34th Cong., 1st Sess., App.*, 982 *et seq.*, speech of James A. Stewart of Maryland, in the House, July 23, 1856.

[2] *Independent*, Jan. 1, March 12, 1857; see also *New York Tribune*, May 14, 1856; *New York Courier*, Dec. 23, 1856.

As an example of the extreme language used by the Abolitionists, the *Washington Union*, Jan. 14, 1851, quoted from an article in the *Boston Chronotype*, twenty thousand copies of which were circulated among the lawyers of the country, in which Judge Story and other Judges of the Court were spoken of "as if they were a set of ignorant and corrupt knaves, wilfully perverting the Constitution, disregarding its mandates and pandering to the prejudices and interests of the South."

Curtis on the side of tyranny and injustice, they would like, for once at least, and just for a change, if nothing else, to see him employ his abilities on behalf of justice and freedom." Judge Grier was attacked by the same paper in a diatribe against the Judges from Pennsylvania: "What other member of the Federal Union has, in its most violent fermentation, ever thrown to the surface such a judicial trio as Baldwin, Grier, and (District Judge) Kane?" Judge Nelson was equally obnoxious; and even Judge McLean was referred to as having given "frequent instance of his ready subserviency to the slaveholders." [1] Of Chief Justice Taney, at this time, much milder views were expressed by the abolitionist press than of some of the other Judges; and in view of the onslaught on Taney, only two years later, the following letter from the *Tribune's* Washington correspondent, in December, 1855 is of singular interest: [2]

As the Court is now constituted, consisting of nine Judges, he has held and exercised a moral balance of power of vast advantage in the interpretation of large constitutional questions, while it served as an effective check upon the latitudinarian dogmas of some of his colleagues. The importance of this restraint may not be sufficiently estimated by the country at large. . . . But the value of such service is appreciated by the Bar, as it must be by members of the Court who sympathize and aid in the effort to protect the Court from the invasion of wild theories and nullifying notions wholly inconsistent with its spirit and letter. The loss of Judge Taney at any time would be a public calamity; but it would be peculiarly so now, when political considerations are pressed with so much pertinacity as almost to deprive the Executive of the exercise of that

[1] *New York Tribune*, April 9, 1855, referring to the indictment of Theodore Parker and Wendell Phillips, in the United States Circuit Court in Massachusetts, before Judge Curtis; *id.*, April 18, Oct. 16, 1855. See also *ibid.*, April 20, May 24, 1855, for editorials on "Judicial Infallibility" and "Judge Worshippers."

[2] *New York Tribune*, Dec. 18, 1855, letter from "Index" of Dec. 16.

discretion which he might otherwise be inclined to apply.
If a vacancy should occur now, reasons enough would be
trumped up for conferring that honor upon some faithful
adherent, whose party claims would be allowed to overshadow the merit and integrity of the man upon whom the
eye of the country would naturally rest.

While the anti-slavery men of the North thus expressed their distrust of the Court, there was also a
section of the Southern Democrats — the secessionists
or "fire-eaters" — led by William L. Yancey of Alabama, who contended that the Court had no power to
pass on the rights of the States over slavery,[1] and in
a radical speech directed against the Know-Nothing
platform, in 1855, Yancey said that the proposition to
submit the difficulty to the Court "is a monstrous
doctrine, simply a revival of the federalism of John
Adams' day. It was assailed by Jefferson in the revolution of 1798 and was successfully put down, and has
never found a party at the South to urge it, until it
was taken up by the Know-Nothings. There is no
warrant for it in the Constitution. In the Constitution,
a Judiciary is provided for to determine questions
of property arising under the granted powers. Yet
Know-Nothingism proposes to refer to the Supreme
Court questions involving the reserved rights of the
States, proposes to place the existence or non-existence
of State sovereignty in the opinion of that Court.
When or where, in what clause of the Constitution, did
the Sovereign States who framed this government
propose that any other but their own judgment should
determine whether their reserved rights had been in-

---

[1] *Life and Times of William Lowndes Yancey* (1892), by John W. DuBose, 295,
307. Yancey wrote to William H. Northington, June 23, 1855: "I must think the
revival of this long-repudiated and dangerous doctrine (that in all doubtful and disputed points of Federal law, the Constitution may be legally ascertained and expounded only by the judicial power of the United States) by so vigorous a party as
that of the Know-Nothings portends evil to the country."

vaded and the mode and manner of redress for the
grievance? . . . Imagine the great question of the
right of a State to secede to be brought before such a
Court for adjudication and the rendering of a decision
adverse to the right. What then?"

With such a campaign maintained by the anti-slavery
men in the Senate and in the press for the express purpose of undermining popular confidence in the Judges,
and with such radical views as to judicial power expressed by many in the South, it was small wonder that
the status of the Court was seriously weakened. Its
members themselves felt their position keenly, and
Judge Curtis wrote: "It cannot be doubted that the
position of the Judges of the Supreme Court, at this
time, is in a high degree onerous; and that while it
exposes them to attack, such as no honest Judiciary,
in any country within my knowledge have been subject to, they have not the consideration and support
to which they are entitled. Their salaries are so poor
that not one Judge on the bench can live upon what the
Government pays him, and the legislative branch of
the Government are not friendly to them. The people,
though retaining some of the respect which, in the formation of the government, made the judicial element
predominant over everything but the reserved power of
the people, yet are ready to listen without indignation
to the grossest charges against those who administer
the judicial power." [1] The attacks upon the Court in
Ohio, California and Wisconsin for the exercise of its
jurisdiction with reference to the State Courts also
gravely impaired its supremacy; and the country was,
with much reason, earnestly called upon by a leading
law magazine to rally to the defense of the Judiciary.[2]

[1] *Curtis*, I, 174, letter of Dec. 20, 1854.
[2] *Appellate Jurisdiction of the Federal over the States Courts*, *Amer. Law Reg.*
(Jan., 1856), IV, 129.

"Every disorganizing agency in the country appears to be at work. . . . There are those, we know, in some portions of the country, who profess to deride systematically all warnings of danger to the Union. This is the security of ignorance. Those who stand, as it were, upon the line which divides the sections, now so unhappily at variance, and can survey without prejudice the movements on either side see and know too well the imminence of the peril. There is such exasperation on one side and determination on the other, as was never known before; and it will need the greatest caution and good sense, to prevent an explosion which would rend the Union into fragments. . . . In such a crisis, it is the duty of all honest, thinking men to join in an endeavor to remove all those causes of controversy which are rankling and festering in the heart of the Nation, by submitting them to the peaceful arbitration of the Supreme Court. . . . To leave them, in the present temper of local politics, in the hands of State Courts could only tend to organize passion by giving it the sanction of law, and to convert party quarrels into the conflicts of States. Admit that the Federal Judiciary may in its time have been guilty of errors, that it has occasionally sought to wield more power than was safe, that it is as fallible as every other human institution. Yet it has been and is a vast agency for good; it has averted many a storm which threatened our peace, and has lent its powerful aid in uniting us together in the bonds of law and justice. Its very existence has proved a beacon of safety. And now, when the black cloud is again on the horizon, when the trembling of the earth and the stillness of the air are prophetic to our fears, and we turn to it instinctively for protection, — let us ask ourselves, with all its imagined faults, what is there that can replace it? Strip it of its power, and what shall we get in exchange?

Discord and confusion, statutes without obedience, Courts without authority, an anarchy of principles, and a chaos of decisions, till all law at last shall be extinguished by an appeal to arms."

These words came from the North. A leading Southern journal voiced the feeling of that section also towards the Court, expressing gratitude for its independence, and rejoicing that the then prevalent move towards popular election of Judges could not reach the Federal Judiciary. "The issue between the North and South," it said, "on the subject of slavery affords an illustration of the necessity for a perfectly independent Judiciary, and shows how difficult it is for a Judge, responsible to the people of a particular section, to decide with impartiality, where the conflicting claims of two sections are involved. The Federal Judiciary, in its freedom from bias, has been the great trust of the South for the preservation of those rights which only need for their support a just interpretation of the Constitution and an unprejudiced judgment on the principles of law. Men whose whole political life has been marked by an undeviating opposition to domestic slavery, have, in elaborate decisions from the bench of Federal justice, declared the constitutionality of the Fugitive Slave Law. Relieved from all fear of the consequences of their judgments, reason and right allowed them to form no other opinion. . . . If, however, a Federal Judge, sitting on a Northern Circuit, had held his place by the suffrages of the people of that section where his judgment was delivered, every motive of interest . . . would have placed in the way of such determination obstacles, to override which the highest moral courage and the most unselfish heart would have been required. . . . The tempest of popular feeling against Southern institutions seems to have overwhelmed in the North every political barrier against the invading flood of aggression. To the swelling tide, nothing seems to be opposed but the barrier of judicial independence which the great architects of the Constitution have set up. Gloomy will that day be for the cause of Constitutional order and State's Rights, when the mighty structure is levelled before the rolling waves of that angry ocean." [1]

[1] *Southern Quarterly Review* (Charleston, So. Car., 1855), XXVII, 359, 362. Referring to Taney, this review said: "The judgments of Chief Justice Taney are models of judicial style, and so clear and cogent in their logical power, that those even who hesitate at the conclusion can scarcely see where to detect the error. Those who have been so fortunate as to hear Judge Taney from the bench are well acquainted with that inimitable manner, that patient, never varying attention, that instant appreciation of an idea or an argument, that combination of admirable qualities which unite to make him pre-eminently distinguished as a presiding Judge."

NOTE. By 1850, Taney stood high in the estimation of men of both parties, Gen. Zachary Taylor wrote asking him to administer the Presidential oath, not only in compliance with custom but also to "give expression to the high respect I entertain for the Supreme Bench and its august presiding officer." Webster, in an address at the Pilgrim's Festival in New York, in 1850, said that "we are Protestants, but a Roman Catholic is Chief Justice and no man imagines that the administration of public justice is less respectable or less secure." In 1855, at the Maryland Institute in Baltimore, Ex-President Tyler said that he had voted against Taney's confirmation as Secretary of the Treasury, but "had I known him, as I have since, in his exalted office of Chief Justice of the United States, maugre any discrepancy of opinion which might have existed between us, there was no office, however exalted, either in the gift of the Executive or the people, for which I would not promptly have sustained him." *Life of Roger Brooke Taney* (1922), by Bernard C. Steiner, 316–318.

As early as Jan. 19, 1839, Judge Story wrote to Harriet Martineau: "The question of slavery is becoming more and more an absorbing one, and will, if it continues to extend its influence, lead to a dissolution of the Union. At least, there are many of our soundest statemen who look to this as a highly probable event."

As to Judge Curtis, Senator Henry S. Foote in his *A Casket of Reminiscences* (1874), p. 275, said: "I recollect that his elevation to a position to which he was so admirably adapted gave very general satisfaction to the country. . . . Not knowing the newly created Judge myself, I inquired of Mr. Webster what sort of a man precisely Mr. Curtis was, when he answered me in substance thus: 'Mr. Curtis I have known long most intimately. He is a man of sterling integrity; his mind is one of great vigor and activity; he had not a particle of sectional prejudice; he is unswervingly devoted to the cause of the Union; and is, in my judgment, the best common law lawyer now in Massachusetts.' "

See esp. *Constitutionality of the Fugitive Slave Acts*, by Allen Johnson, *Yale Law Journ.* (1921), XXXI. In the reports of McLean, Curtis and Wallace, Jr., nearly twenty fugitive slave cases are reported between 1842 and 1855; see also cases in *Law Reporter* (1851), XIV; *ibid.* (1853), XVI.

CHAPTER TWENTY-SIX

THE DRED SCOTT CASE

1856–1857

AT this critical juncture, when at the North the faith of the general public in the Court's impartiality had been seriously weakened by the undeserved attacks of the anti-slavery press and politicians, the famous case of *Dred Scott* v. *Sandford*, 19 How. 393, came on for argument in the spring of 1856. In attributing wholly to Chief Justice Taney's opinion in this case the passionate hostility towards the Court which followed its decision in 1857, historians have too largely overlooked the fact that the undermining campaign directed against the Court, preparatory to this overturn in the hearts of the people, had been carried on for nine years. The *Dred Scott Case* had been first docketed in the Court in December, 1854, at the same time when the appeals in the *Booth Cases* from Wisconsin were filed. While the former case has received more attention from jurists and historians, it was the latter which aroused the greatest attention and excitement at the time when they were pending. Of the *Dred Scott Case* little was generally known until shortly before it came on for argument in February, 1856. Although charges were made later that the case had been "fabricated" by the slavery party in order to secure a decision by the Court, the absurdity and falsity of the suggestion was apparent, when all the facts as to its history became known.[1]

[1] These charges were made and reiterated in the spring and winter of 1856; see the *New York Tribune* and the *New York Courier*, Dec. 18, 19, 1856, March 16.

In the autumn of 1846, and hence before the power of Congress over slavery in the Territories had become a vital issue, a negro, Dred Scott, began a suit against the widow of his former master, in the State Circuit Court in St. Louis, based on the ground that his former master, Dr. Emerson, had taken him into Illinois, and thence into the Louisiana Territory (now Minnesota), and that thereby, under the Northwest Territory Ordinance of 1787 and under the Missouri Compromise Act, he had become a free man, which status still affected him, when later his master took him back into the slave State of Missouri. In January, 1850, he obtained a verdict; but on appeal, the State Supreme Court held, in 1852, that under the laws of Missouri he resumed his character of slave on his return, irrespective of his status while out of the State. In November, 1853, noted anti-slavery lawyers in St. Louis instituted in the United States Circuit Court, on his behalf, a suit for trespass; and in order to vest jurisdiction in this Federal

1857; *Independent*, Jan. 1, 1857; *Ohio Statesman*, April 3, 1857; and counter-charges that the case was instituted and appealed by the anti-slavery party. Reverdy Johnson said, March 16, 1858: "The Senator's insinuation that the case was made by the master for the purpose of obtaining a decision by the Supreme Court is so far from being true, that the suspicion, at the time, was that the political friends of the Senator — the abolitionists — had had it instituted and brought here with that exclusive end. But that was equally unfounded, as was stated by Mr. Blair in open Court." *35th Cong., 1st Sess.* Dred Scott's counsel, Roswell M. Field of St. Louis, wrote to Montgomery Blair in Washington, that he believed that it would be better for the country to have the vexed question of slavery restriction decided contrary to his wishes, and in favor of the slaveholder, than not at all. And again he wrote, December 24, 1854: "A year ago, I was employed to bring suit for Scott. The question involved is the much vexed one, whether the removal by the master of his slave to Illinois or Wisconsin, works an absolute emancipation. . . . If you, or any other gentleman at Washington, should feel interest enough in the case as to bring it to a hearing and decision by the Court, the cause of humanity may perhaps be subserved, and at all events, a much disputed question would be settled by the highest Court of the Nation." *Life of Roger Brooke Taney* (1922), by Bernard C. Steiner, 331.

Prof. John W. Burgess in *The Middle Period* (1898), 449 *et seq.*, gives a detailed account of the origin of the case, obtained from A. C. Crane of St. Louis, a clerk in the office of Dred Scott's counsel, Roswell M. Field, and says: "There is certainly not the slightest evidence in the history of the case that the case was anything but a genuine proceeding, from beginning to end conducted by anti-slavery men."

Court on the ground of diverse citizenship, a fictitious sale of Scott was arranged by Mrs. Emerson (who had then become the wife of a strong abolitionist member of Congress from Massachusetts, Dr. C. C. Chaffee) to her brother, John F. A. Sandford of New York (a son-in-law of Pierre Chouteau of St. Louis).[1] In this suit, a verdict was found against Scott, on May 15, 1854, on rulings of law, and on writ of error the case was taken to the United States Supreme Court. At this stage, it seemed probable that its decision might call for an expression of opinion by the Court as to the hotly debated question of the power of Congress to exclude slavery from the Territories. Before the case was docketed, however, Congress had passed the Kansas-Nebraska Act, on May 30, 1854, repealing the Missouri Compromise Act by specifically enacting that it was "inoperative and void", and declaring that it was the true intent and meaning of the present Act, "not to legislate slavery into any Territory or State nor to exclude it therefrom." By this legislation, the power of Congress over the subject was denied, and the long-continued efforts of the Free-soilers to exclude slavery from the Territories by Congressional enactment seemed permanently defeated. Had the slavery party been responsible for the institution of the *Dred Scott Case*, it is clear that it had little to gain by risking a ruling from the Court on a point which Congress had already effectually decided, for itself. The anti-slavery party, on the other hand, had an interest in prosecuting the appeal; for an adverse judicial decision would not make their position any worse than it was under the Kansas-Nebraska Act, and a favorable decision might give

[1] Sandford became insane before the case was decided; and it was said that the appeal was fought in the United States Supreme Court contrary to his wish; see *New York Courier*, Dec. 18, 1856, March 16, 1857. The Court costs were paid by Taylor Blow of St. Louis, son of the man who sold Scott to Dr. Emerson.

their cause an effective moral impetus. The case came on for argument on Monday, February 11, 1856. "It involves questions of much political interest," said the newspapers. "They are first, whether a free black man is a citizen of the United States, so as to be competent to sue in the Courts of the United States; second, whether a slave carried voluntarily by his master into a free State and returning voluntarily with his master to his home, is a free man by virtue of such temporary residence; thirdly, whether the eighth Section of the Missouri Act of 1820, prohibiting slavery north of latitude 36′ 30″, is constitutional or not." Arguments were made for the negro by Montgomery Blair of St. Louis (who had been retained by the local Missouri counsel, Roswell M. Field)[1], and for the alleged owner,

[1] An interesting account by Blair of the manner in which he happened to argue the case appeared in the *National Intelligencer*, Dec. 24, 1856: "From an imperfect knowledge of the circumstances attending the suit for freedom before the Supreme Court, prosecuted by Dred Scott (a negro) several correspondents of the New York press have made suggestions tending to mislead public opinion. One intimates that the suit was a contrived case to operate on the late Presidential election by bringing under the review and judgment of the Supreme Court the questions which have so stirred the public mind since the repeal of the Missouri Compromise. Another surmises that selfish motives influenced certain distinguished members of the Bar in declining the request to lend me their assistance in behalf of my client's cause; and a third seems to suspect my own in conducting it alone. As the peculiar attitude of political affairs at this moment gives much interest to the case, I will be pardoned for giving a brief narrative of it. . . . As I perceived that the cause involved important issues which might possibly be engulphed in the great political controversy then just emerging in relation to the power of Congress over the territory of the United States, I felt it my duty to seek assistance, especially as when I found arrayed against me the Senator from Missouri, and the late Attorney-General, among the first men of the profession of the East and the West. I sought to obtain the support of one of the ablest men at the Bar in the South, and he had almost consented to yield it. His inclination was surrendered, not, I well know, from the selfish motive given in the press. I then applied to leading members of the profession in the North, and with the same result. The mercenary motive imputed for the reluctance shown to engage in it is equally unjust to all. The truth is, while some gave it up because their previous engagements interrupted, and others because the late application did not give time to make preparation, all perceived that, from the nature of the case, it must assume an aspect more or less affecting the party struggles impending, and were unwilling on all accounts to add to this embarrassment of the cause or that of the party with which they stood connected, by implicating either themselves or it by their action in the result. While I do myself deprecate the state of things which brings a political and

Sandford, by Henry S. Geyer (then Senator from Missouri) and Reverdy Johnson. On February 18, the Washington correspondent of the *New York Tribune*, James S. Pike, stated that a judgment was expected within a fortnight, and that though nothing could be positively known as to its character, "there is a speculation abroad which almost amounts to conviction that the decision of the Circuit Court will be affirmed, and principally upon the pretext that Scott voluntarily returned to the State of Missouri, by which act the authority of the owner was restored and the condition of slavery was resumed." [1] On February 28, Pike wrote that there were "some indications that a direct issue may be evaded, on the ground that Scott, being a colored man, is not a citizen of Missouri in the legal point of view, and therefore cannot bring an action properly. This judgment would deny the jurisdiction of the Supreme Court, and possibly prevent the expression of dissenting opinions on the constitutionality of the Missouri Compromise; an effort will be made to get a positive decree of some sort, and in that event, there is some hope of aid from the Southern members of the Court." These mere surmises as to the Court's probable action were surprisingly in accord with the facts. The Court, after adjourning during the month of March, reconvened on April 1; and Pike writing to the *Tribune*, April 7, stated that the Court had held two consultations on the case, that McLean, Curtis and Grier would probably concur in favor of the slave, that Nelson's attitude was uncertain, that sectional sentiment would unite the other five Judges from the South and that there was "a mani-

a partisan influence to act upon the public mind in connection with this case, and while willing to avoid it as much as possible, I yet felt it was my duty to call to its support all the aid I could command. When I first opened the case, therefore, I announced to the Court the regret I felt in not having prevailed in getting an associate in the cause."

[1] *New York Tribune*, Feb. 18, 20, 26, 29, April 9, 10, 11, 12, 1856.

fest disposition to avoid the real issue by the introduction of a question affecting the jurisdiction of the
Court." The next day, he wrote that four of the
Judges had already united in admitting the jurisdiction;
that there was hope that the decree might be made upon
the merits; and that the final consultation would be
held on the next (Wednesday) night. On Thursday, a
correspondent wrote that it was understood that a
majority had declared in favor of jurisdiction — Mc-
Lean, Curtis, Grier, Campbell and Catron against
Taney, Wayne, Nelson and Daniel; but that Catron
and Campbell would join with the minority in denying
freedom to the slave on the merits of the case; and that
McLean and Curtis, with Grier concurring, would give
dissenting opinions sustaining the constitutionality of
the Missouri Compromise; "the decree will be delivered next week and the opinion will make a sensation." [1] That this was merely a guess upon the part
of the newspapers is seen from the fact that at this very
time, Judge Curtis wrote to his uncle in Boston, George
Ticknor, in strict confidence, April 8, that "the Court
will not decide the question of the Missouri Compromise
line — a majority of the Judges being of opinion that it
is not necessary to do so." [2] And the incorrectness

[1] Another correspondent, writing Thursday, April 10, 1856, said: "The majority
of the Court will decide against him. But there is such a thing as a minority left
on the Bench notwithstanding the Court has been denounced as the Citadel of
Slavery; and unless all impressions are erroneous, Judge McLean will fortify their
position with an opinion that cannot fail to confound those who are prepared to
repudiate the judgments of Southern Courts and the practice of Southern States.
Judge Curtis it is believed will also contribute a powerful exposition of the case and
of all the incidental questions connected with it, and Judge Grier will concur with
both. Of course, the South will go in a body and probably carry Judge Nelson
with them."

[2] *Curtis*, I, 180. Curtis continued: "The one engrossing subject in both Houses
of Congress, and with all the members, is the Presidency; and upon this everything
done and omitted, except the most ordinary necessities of the country, depends.
Judge McLean hopes, I think, to be a candidate for office. He would be a good
President, but I am not willing to have a Judge in that most trying position of being
a candidate for this great office."

of the newspaper's statement as to the line-up of the
Judges was later proved by Judge Campbell's account.
It appears that the Court was divided on the question
as to whether the jurisdictional point as to citizenship
was properly before them — Taney, Wayne, Daniel,
Nelson and Curtis considering it to be so, but McLean,
Catron, Campbell and Grier taking the contrary view.
Nelson, however, entertaining doubts asked for a reargument, which was ordered, May 12, 1856.[1] As
the Presidential campaign was to occur in the fall of
1856, the sentiment very generally prevailed that the
Court had acted wisely in not giving a decision on this
delicate question prior to the election. And as the
New York Courier said, in praise of the Court's action:
"The great tribunal to which the country has been
taught for nearly three quarters of a century to look up
for the dispensation of justice upon the principles of
law, is not prepared to rush into the political arena, and
ruffle its ermine in the strife of politicians and the
squabbles of demagogues." The Court, however, was
assailed by the *New York Tribune*, which said that " the
black gowns have come to be artful dodgers."

For six months, while the Presidential campaign was
being fought, little notice of the case appeared in the
press or elsewhere. Its existence on the Court's docket
had hardly been known to the public, prior to its first
argument. In all the exhaustive debates in Congress
on the slavery issue throughout the years 1855 and 1856,
the case was not even adverted to. But by the time
when it was reached for its second argument, in December, 1856, the immense effect which a Court decision
upon the power of Congress might have, in connection
with future legislation as to slavery in the Territories,

[1] See Campbell's statement at the meeting of the Supreme Court Bar on the
death of Benjamin R. Curtis, Oct. 13, 1874, 20 Wall, x, xi.

was thoroughly realized. "Taking into consideration the state of the country . . . it may well be regarded as the most important that has ever been brought before that tribunal," said the *New York Courier*. "Never has the Supreme Court had a case before it so deeply affecting its own standing before the Nation. . . . The issue is of vast importance in itself, but there is another problem connected with it of far greater consequence. It is, whether the Supreme Court is a political Court made up of political judges. . . . While yet reeking with the passions of the political arena, this question is transferred to that tribunal, which of all others is supposed to be clearest of passion—a tribunal which has, in time past, challenged the deference of the country for its lofty impartiality and serene independence. How will the Judges abide the test now before them? . . . The Court, in trying this case, is itself on trial — a trial as vitally involving its character before the American people, as a confidence in its impartiality is vital to its authority. . . . The Court has thus far disappointed the hopes of the agitators, and vindicated its own high and conservative character. It refused to throw any opinion into the political arena, last summer." [1]

The second argument was made before the Court on December 15, 16, 17 and 18, 1856, by Blair, Geyer, Johnson and by George Ticknor Curtis of Massachusetts (who had been retained by Blair, after the case was

[1] *New York Courier*, Dec. 18, 23, 1856; *New York Tribune*, Dec. 19, 1856; Alexander H. Stephens of Georgia, Dec. 15, 1856 (the date on which the second argument began) wrote: "I have been urging all the influences I could bring to bear upon the Supreme Court to get them to postpone no longer the case on the Missouri Restriction before them, but to decide it. They take it up today. If they decide, as I have reason to believe they will, that the restriction was unconstitutional, that Congress had no power to pass it, then the question — the political question — as I think, will be ended as to the power of the people in their Territorial Legislatures. It will be in effect a re-adjudication." *Life of Alexander H. Stephens* (1883), by Richard M. Johnson and William H. Browne.

begun, to argue the constitutional point involved). Of the arguments, a Washington correspondent wrote: "Mr. Blair is a close, logical reasoner, a man of diligent and careful research, strong power of thought, but a very poor pleader. His manner is awkward, his gesticulation particularly painful, and his utterance slow and with the appearance of being obstructed. But his argument would read well. Reverdy Johnson, Esq., is an old stager in the elocutionary list, and drew a crowded chamber to listen to his plea. . . . The learned barrister entered into his argument, with all the fervor and power of appeal that has characterized the most ultra-Congressional and stump speeches for slavery to which it had been my misfortune to listen. The passions of his audience, the prejudices of the Judges were appealed to, until I came to the realization of the fact that our Supreme Court is composed of men, mere men after all, with the like passions and prejudices of the masses. . . . The closing argument of Mr. Curtis of Boston was able, clear and, to me, conclusive. It lacked in one feature — it was too brief. . . . This, however, was not the fault of the learned counsellor, but that of the Court, which limited him to one hour and a quarter." [1] Of Curtis' argument, his brother, Judge Curtis, wrote that it was made "in a manner exceedingly creditable to himself and to the Bar of New England. Judge Catron told me it was the best argument on a question of constitutional law, he had heard in the Court — and he has been here since General Jackson's time"; and the *New York Tribune* said that it "commanded marked attention from the Court, and attracted the largest audience from Congress that has yet assembled, as well as a number of the most distin-

[1] *Independent*, Jan. 1, 1857; see also *Boston Post* and *New York Tribune*, Dec. 16, 17, 18, 19, 1856, for full descriptions of the arguments of all the counsel.

guished jurists"; that it was "happily conceived in style
and manner. The admission was general and frank
on all sides that Mr. Curtis acquitted himself with eminent ability. . . . He was congratulated warmly and
by several Southern Senators." [1]   Of Johnson's argument, the *New York Courier* said that it would rank
with the finest efforts made at the Bar; that since
Webster's death Johnson had no superior; but that his
argument against the constitutionality of the Missouri
Compromise was not convincing.   The *New York
Times* said that while "well considered and compact,
it was about as remarkable for what it did not contain
as for what it did"; the *Tribune* said that it "partook
more of the character of a stump speech than that of a
jurist. It was brilliant, eloquent and witty, of course;
but in dealing with the grave question of human
freedom or slavery and the status of slavery under the
Constitution, the learned gentleman substituted sarcasm and ridicule of opposing views for the logic, which
alone can convince a mind, seeking to know the truth." [2]

At the close of the argument, the grave effect of the
coming decision upon political conditions was again reflected by Pike in the *Tribune*, saying: "The Court may
think it wise, under the existing circumstances of excitement on the topic throughout the country, to place
a decision of the case upon a subordinate issue. Yet
the urgency of the slave-power is great — the temper
of the slave holders within the Bar and without
the Bar, to say nothing of the Bench, is raised to
crush the rebellious spirit of the North; and a decision
of the Supreme Court is eagerly desired which shall
promote this end.   Prudence may, however, prevail,

[1] The *National Intelligencer*, Jan. 1, 1857, published the "confessedly very able
argument" of Curtis.
[2] *New York Courier*, Dec. 18, 19, 1856; *New York Times*, Dec. 20, 1856; *New
York Tribune*, Dec. 17, 18, 19, 20, 22, 24. 1856.

and the Court refrain from enunciating a decision which would neither enhance its reputation nor strengthen its influence." No one, he further said, could "have failed to observe, in the growth and development of the ideas which underlie the case now under adjudication, that our judicial decisions upon constitutional questions touching the subject of slavery are rapidly coming to be the enunciation of mere party dogmas; that the country is dividing geographically upon questions of constitutional law; and that, in the process of time, if we continue a united people, what the law of the country and the Courts is, will depend upon the political ascendancy for the time being of the doctrines of freedom or slavery."[1]

The pendency of the *Dred Scott Case* first became the subject of attention in Congress, when, on January 12, 1857, Benjamin Stanton of Ohio introduced a resolution in the House for legislation to reorganize the Court "so as to equalize the population and business of the several Circuits and districts and give to all sections of the Confederacy their equal and just representation on the Supreme Court."[2] In an elaborate speech, he pointed out the disproportionate representation of the South, and contended that unless this should be changed, the Court's decision "can have no moral power and cannot command the confidence of the people" and he added:

[1] *New York Tribune*, Dec. 20, 1856. For a reply to attacks of this nature, see *Boston Post*, Dec. 27, 1856.

[2] *34th Cong., 3d Sess.*, Jan. 12, 1857. The white population in the Circuits was:

1st (Maine, N. H., Mass., R. I.)	2,028,594
2d (N. Y., Conn., Vt.)	3,724,826
3d (Pa., N. J.)	2,723,669
4th (Del., Md., Va.)	1,383,912
5th (Ala., La.)	682,005
6th (No. Car., So. Car., Ga.)	1,394,163
7th (Ohio, Ind., Ill., Mich.)	4,173,309
8th (Ky., Tenn., Mo.)	2,110,253
9th (Miss., Ark.)	457,907

If the Supreme Court is to be called in to aid in the settlement of the great political questions which agitate the country, its organization becomes a matter of paramount importance. If the South choose to preserve its present partial and sectional organization, for the purpose of securing its aid in the political contests of the day, they will find they may destroy the Court, without aiding the party or section in whose favor it decides. . . . It is my deliberate conviction that nothing could do so much to weaken the bonds of this Confederacy, and destroy the confidence of the people in the Federal Government and the value of the Union, as a decision of that Court that Congress has no sovereign power over the Territories, and that it cannot legislate for them, either for the exclusion of slavery, or upon any other rightful subject of legislation.

He concluded his speech by contending for the right of a State, as proclaimed by the Virginia-Kentucky Resolutions of 1798–1799, to refuse obedience to any law which it deemed to be "a plain, palpable and deliberate violation of the Constitution", and to disregard a decision of the Court sustaining such a law. These sentiments from an Ohio Whig were controverted by a Virginia Democrat; and an anti-slavery paper noted that "the domineering sectionalists of the country already begin to see the value of Union, and nullifying South Carolina already denounces the move as 'an assault upon the integrity of the Supreme Court.' " [1]

The Court did not meet for conference as to its decision in the *Dred Scott Case*, until late in February; for, as Judge Curtis wrote to his brother: "Our aged Chief Justice, who will be eighty years old in a few days, and who grows more feeble in body, but retains his alacrity and force of mind wonderfully, is not able to write much. Judge Wayne has been ill much of the

---

[1] *New York Evening Post*, Jan. 13, 1857.

winter. Poor Judge Daniel has been prostrated for months by what was a sufficient cause; for his young and interesting wife was burned to death by her clothes accidentally taking fire, almost in his presence. So the rest of us have been kept at the oar, as Judge Story used to say 'double tides.'"[1] But in spite of the fact that there had been no conference, the newspaper correspondents in Washington filled the columns of their papers with detailed rumors as to the alleged decision which the Court had reached; and all agreed that the decision would be adverse to the plaintiff, though they differed as to the probable grounds on which it would be based.[2] The *Tribune* correspondent wrote on January 5, 1857: "The rumor that the Supreme Court has decided against the constitutionality of the power of Congress to restrict slavery in the Territories has been commented upon in the most unreserved manner at this metropolis. It is very generally considered that the moral weight of such a decision would be about equal to that of a political stump speech of a slaveholder or a doughface. Many have expressed the opinion that the question would not be met by the Court, and numbers are still of that way of thinking. It makes but little difference to slavery whether it gets a decision in its favor now or after the public mind shall have had time to cool. . . But it would be best for anti-slavery that the decision should come now, while the popular heart is in a fused condition. The impression it would thus make would be deeper and more distinct, and the whole

[1] *Curtis*, I, 192, letter of Feb., 1857.

[2] *New York Tribune*, Jan. 4, 5, 7, 8, 9, 1857; *New York Courier*, Jan. 7, 1857; *Independent*, Jan. 8, 1857. As early as January 2, 1857, the *Tribune's* Washington correspondent wrote that there was a rumor in Washington that the Court, with two dissenting, had reached a decision adverse to the constitutionality of the Missouri Compromise, and said that there was no truth in the statement, but that "whenever judgment shall be rendered it will be found, if the real merits of the case are considered, that the tribunal will be nearly divided, unless extraneous influences should prevail."

series of pro-slavery aggressions and triumphs would then be burned into it together. The Congress, the Court, and the Executive would then take their proper position of joint association, in the mind of the people, as confederates in the work of extending the intolerable nuisance of slavery. It is, therefore, to be preferred that the judicial department shall now put itself actively upon the side of the slaveholders, while the mind of the country is warm and burning, rather than wait and do it by and by, when apathy shall have again overspread it. . . . Judicial tyranny is hard enough to resist under any circumstances, for it comes in the guise of impartiality and with the prestige of fairness. If the Court is to take a political bias, and to give a political decision, then let us, by all means, have it distinctly, and now. The public mind is in a condition to receive it with the contempt it merits."

It is evident that the views entertained by the Court were very generally discussed around Washington. Alexander H. Stephens wrote to a friend, January 1, 1857, a summary which, though purporting to contain information obtained "*sub rosa*", was, at that date, an inaccurate statement of the decision then arrived at by the Court: "Today I send you the speech of Curtis on the *Dred Scott Case* before the Supreme Court. The speech I think chaste, elegant, forensic; but I do not think it convincing. The case is yet undecided. It is the great case before the Court, and involves the greatest questions, politically, of the day. I mean that the questions involved, let them be decided as they may, will have a greater political effect and bearing than any others of the day. The decision will be a marked epoch in our history. I feel a deep solicitude as to how it will be. From what I hear, *sub rosa*, it will be according to my own opinions on every point, as abstract

political questions. The restriction of 1820 will be
held to be unconstitutional. The Judges are all writing
out their opinions, I believe, *seriatim*. The Chief
Justice will give an elaborate one. Should this opinion
be as I suppose it will, 'Squatter Sovereignty speeches'
will be upon a par with 'Liberty speeches' at the North
in the last canvass." Montgomery Blair wrote to Van
Buren, February 5, that: "It seems to be the impression
that the opinion of the Court will be adverse to my
client and to the power of Congress over the Territories, but I am assured that the Court has not yet held
a conference on the case." [1]

It was not until February 15, that the Judges first
met in conference. An agreement was then reached
that the Court should give no opinion upon the constitutionality of the Missouri Compromise Act, but
should decide the case upon the point that, whatever
effect the negro's residence in Illinois and in the Northwest Territory had upon his status there, his status in
Missouri, after his return to that State, must depend
upon the law of Missouri; and that Missouri, by its
law as laid down by its Supreme Court, regarded him as
a slave, and hence incapable of maintaining suit in the
Federal Circuit Court. To Judge Nelson was assigned
the duty of writing the opinion of the Court. Within a
few days, however, it was found that the two dissenting
Judges — McLean and Curtis, intended to write opinions discussing at length and sustaining the constitutionality of the Compromise Act. This action forced
the majority of the Judges to reconsider the necessity
of discussing that point as well, themselves. Judge
Wayne (as he himself said in conversation, and as

[1] *Life of Alexander H. Stephens* (1883), by Richard M. Johnson and William H.
Browne, 318; *Van Buren Papers MSS*, letter of Blair to Van Buren, Feb. 5,
1857.

Judge Curtis stated later) "became convinced that it was practicable for the Court to quiet all agitation on the question of slavery in the Territories by affirming that Congress had no constitutional power to prohibit its introduction. With the best intentions, with entirely patriotic motives, and believing thoroughly that such was the law on this constitutional question, he regarded it as eminently expedient that it should be so determined by the Court."[1] Accordingly, Wayne succeeded in persuading Taney, Campbell, Daniel and Catron that the assignment of the opinion to Judge Nelson should be withdrawn, and that the Chief Justice should write the opinion of the Court, covering all the points involved. It appeared, however, that Judge Grier was still averse to expressing an opinion on the constitutional question; and consequently Judge Catron took the unusual course of writing a confidential letter to Buchanan, the President-elect, February 19, in which he informed Buchanan that the constitutional question would be decided by the Court (though he gave no statement as to the way in which it would be decided), and in which he asked Buchanan to "drop Grier a line, saying how necessary it is, and how good the opportunity is, to settle the agitation by an affirmative decision of the Supreme Court, the one way or the other. . . . He has no doubt about the question on the main contest, but has been persuaded to take the

---

[1] *Curtis*, I, 206, 234, 235, 236. G. T. Curtis stated: "I never heard Judge Curtis . . . impute to Judge Wayne or the Chief Justice any motive, but the mistaken supposition that the public excitement in regard to slavery in the Territories could be quieted by a judicial decision adverse to the power of Congress to prohibit its introduction. I think that he regarded this as Judge Wayne's motive, and with good reason; and that he was satisfied that Judge Wayne imparted this conviction to the Chief Justice. But I do not think that he ever, for an instant, imputed to Judge Wayne that he was influenced by Mr. Buchanan to do what he did, nor do I myself believe that such was the fact. Indeed, I do not imagine that Mr. Buchanan was a man who would tamper with the administration of justice, and I am sure that the Chief Justice and Judge Wayne would never have brooked such an attempt." See also *Taney*, 373–392.

smooth handle for the sake of repose." [1] Buchanan
apparently complied with Catron's request, and wrote
to Grier, who replied, February 23, in an interesting
letter, giving to Buchanan, in strict confidence, a full
statement of the manner in which the Judges had decided to treat the case. Such a letter would not at the
present time be regarded as one of strict propriety;
but at the time it was written, it was not an infrequent
occurrence for the Judges to impart, in confidence, to an
intimate friend or relative the probable outcome of a
pending case. Judge Curtis had so written to his uncle,
as to this very case, during the previous year; Judge
Story frequently indulged in the habit; and it seems to
have been regarded as a proper practice, provided the
seal of secrecy was imposed.[2] Grier's letter was as
follows:

Your letter came to hand this morning. I have taken the
liberty to show it, in confidence, to our mutual friends,
Judge Wayne and the Chief Justice.

[1] *Works of James Buchanan* (1908–1911), X, 106. The letter was as follows:
"The Dred Scott case has been before the Judges several times since last Saturday, and I think you may safely say in your Inaugural: 'That the question involving the constitutionality of the Missouri Compromise line is presented to the
appropriate tribunal to decide: to wit, to the Supreme Court of the United States.
It is due to its high and independent character to suppose that it will decide and
settle a controversy which has so long and seriously agitated the country, and
which *must* ultimately be decided by the Supreme Court. And until the case now
before it (on two arguments) presenting the direct question, is disposed of, I would
deem it improper to express any opinion on the subject.' A majority of my brethren will be forced up to this point by two dissentients. Will you drop Grier a line,
saying how necessary it is, and how good the opportunity is, to settle the agitation
by an affirmative decision of the Supreme Court, the one way or the other. He
ought not to occupy so doubtful a ground as the outside issue — that admitting the
constitutionality of the Missouri Compromise Law of 1820, still, as no domicile was
acquired by the negro at Fort Snelling, and he returned to Missouri, he was not
free. He has no doubt about the question on the main contest, but has been persuaded to take the smooth handle for the sake of repose."

[2] It is evident that Judge Campbell was ignorant of this correspondence, for he
wrote to Samuel Tyler (Taney's biographer), Nov. 24, 1870: "I have not the slightest information of any connection between Mr. Buchanan or any other person, with
the discussions in the Court or the conference, or with the preparation of any opinion of either of the Judges, save the Judges themselves."

We fully appreciate and concur in your views as to the desirableness at this time of having an expression of the opinion of the Court on this troublesome question. With their concurrence, I will give you in confidence the history of the case before us, with the probable result. Owing to the sickness and absence of a member of the Court, the case was not taken up in conference till lately. The first question which presented itself was the right of a negro to sue in the Courts of the United States. A majority of the Court were of the opinion that the question did not arise on the pleadings and that we were compelled to give an opinion on the merits. After much discussion it was finally agreed that the merits of the case might be satisfactorily decided without giving an opinion on the question of the Missouri Compromise; and the case was committed to Judge Nelson to write the opinion of the Court affirming the judgment of the Court below, but leaving these difficult questions untouched. But it appeared that our brothers who dissented from the majority, especially Justice McLean, were determined to come out with a long and labored dissent, including their opinions and arguments on both the troublesome points, although not necessary to a decision of the case. In our opinion both the points are *in* the case and may be legitimately considered. Those who hold a different opinion from Messrs. McLean and Curtis on the power of Congress and the validity of the Compromise Act feel compelled to express their opinions on the subject. Nelson and myself refusing to commit ourselves. A majority including all the Judges south of Mason and Dixon's line agreeing in the result, but not in their reasons, — as the question will be thus forced upon us, I am anxious that it should not appear that the line of latitude should mark the line of division in the Court. I feel also that the opinion of the majority will fail of much of its effect if founded on clashing and inconsistent arguments. On conversation with the Chief Justice, I have agreed to concur with him. Brother Wayne and myself will also use our endeavors to get brothers Daniel and Campbell and Catron to do the same. So that if the question must be met, there will be an opinion of the Court upon it, if possible, without the contradictory views which would weaken its force. But I fear some rather extreme views may be thrown out by some of our southern brethren. There will therefore be six, if not seven (perhaps Nelson will remain neutral) who will decide the Compromise law of 1820 to be of *non-effect*. But the opinions will not be delivered before Friday the 6th of March. We will not let any others of our brethren know anything about *the cause of our anxiety* to produce this result, and though contrary to our usual practice, we have thought it due to you to state to you in candor and confidence the real state of the matter.

As has been well said, these letters of Catron and Grier were "obviously inconsistent with, and tacitly refute, the charge that the *Dred Scott Case* was the result of a 'conspiracy' in which the Kansas-Nebraska bill was the first step. As the facts are narrated by Mr. Justice Grier, the action eventually taken in the case seems to have been brought about by the activity of the minority, rather than of the majority of the Court."[1] So far from being anxious to decide the constitutional question involved, the majority of the Judges appear to have tried to avoid committing themselves upon the point, until forced to do so by the insistence of the minority in expressing their views upon it.

On March 4, 1857, the new President, James Buchanan, came into office, and in his Inaugural Address, after reciting the fact that Congress had applied "to the settlement of the question of domestic slavery in the Territories . . . this simple rule that the will of the majority shall govern", and after saying that "a difference of opinion has arisen in regard to the point of time when the people of a Territory shall decide this question for themselves", he proceeded to state: "This is happily a matter of but little practical importance. Besides, it is a judicial question which legitimately belongs to the Supreme Court of the United States before whom it is now pending, and will, it is understood, be

[1] *Works of James Buchanan* (1910), X, 106–108, note.

speedily and finally settled. To their decision, in common with all good citizens, I shall cheerfully submit, whatever this may be, though it has ever been my individual opinion that, under the Kansas-Nebraska Act, the appropriate period will be when the number of actual residents in the Territory shall justify the formation of a Constitution with a view to its admission as a State into the Union." [1]

On the same day, Attorney-General Cushing addressed the Court for the last time in his official capacity, the new President having appointed Jeremiah S. Black as Attorney-General; and in his valedictory, Cushing paid the following eloquent tribute to the Court and to the confidence reposed in it by the country. "In the complex institutions of our country," he said, "you are the pivot point, upon which the rights and liberties of all, Government and people alike, turn; or rather, you are the central light of constitutional wisdom around which they perpetually revolve. Long may this Court retain the confidence of our country as the great conservators, not of the private peace only, but of the sanctity and integrity of the Constitution. . . . To you and your venerable Chief, venerable not more in years than in accumulated wisdom of a long life of high duties, to you, I say, worthy successors of the judicial Fathers of the Republic, our country looks with undoubting confidence, as the interpreters and guardians of the organic laws of the Union." [2] How little Cushing foresaw the storm which was to break upon the Court's head, within three days after his remarks, and how little the anti-slavery party was inclined to accept Buchanan's statement that the

[1] It is interesting to compare this with the statement suggested by Catron to be included in the Inaugural Address, in Catron's letter to Buchanan, *supra*.
[2] *National Intelligencer*, March 5, 1857.

question of slavery in the Territories was about to be "finally settled", by a decision of the Court, may be seen from the editorial comment of the *New York Tribune,* on the day after the Inauguration. "You may 'cheerfully submit', of course, you will," it said, addressing itself to Buchanan, "to whatever the five slaveholders and two or three doughfaces on the bench of the Supreme Court may be ready to utter on this subject. But not one man who really desires the triumph of Freedom over Slavery in the Territories will do so. We may be constrained to obey, as law, whatever that tribunal shall put forth; but happily this is a country in which the People make both laws and Judges, and they will try their strength on the issue here presented." Surmises as to the nature of the forthcoming decision were made in a letter from the *Tribune's* Washington correspondent, written March 5 (but not published until March 9), in which he stated that the Court had held a final consultation that morning, and would reach its opinion the next day. "No doubt now exists as to the character of the decree. A large majority will hold that the recent decisions of the Supreme Court of Missouri . . . determine the case . . . Judges McLean, Curtis and Grier will deliver dissenting opinions. . . The expectation is entertained that this decree will satisfy the country, and Mr. Buchanan referred to it with confidence in his inaugural, yesterday, founded upon a knowledge of the foreshadowed purpose." [1] This letter has often been cited as evidence that there was a "leak" as to the Court's decision; but the letter itself proves the contrary, for its statement of the ground on which the Court would rest its decree was erroneous, and similarly inaccurate was the statement as to Judge Grier's dissent.

[1] *New York Tribune,* March 5, 9, 1857.

Owing to the illness of the Chief Justice, due to exposure at the Inauguration ceremonies, the decision was not rendered until Friday, March 6. On that day, Chief Justice Taney read the opinion of the Court, *Dred Scott* v. *Sandford*, 19 How. 393, and Judge Nelson and Judge Catron read separate opinions. " The delivery of Taney's opinion," said the *National Intelligencer*, "occupied about two hours, and was listened to with profound attention by a crowded Court-room; and whether as a decision of the Supreme Court, or for the constitutional arguments on which it stands, will work a powerful influence throughout the United States." On Saturday, March 7, Judges McLean and Curtis delivered their elaborate dissenting opinions, and separate opinions were read by Judges Daniel, Grier, Campbell and Wayne — "these opinions were listened to with eager interest and profound respect by the Court and Bar and a larger number than usual of attentive auditors." [1]

While pamphlet after pamphlet, article after article, by lawyers and laymen alike, poured forth from the press, at the time, regarding the legal points involved in the opinion of the Court and of the various Judges, at the present date the technicalities of the case are of no particular interest; and the interminable discussion as to whether the Court was justified in deciding on the merits of the case, after holding that the Circuit Court had no jurisdiction, is now of very slight interest. It will suffice to say that six of the Judges — Taney,

[1] *National Intelligencer*, March 7, 9, 1857; *New York Tribune*, March 7, 1857; for able discussions of the law, see *Legal Review of the Dred Scott Case*, by John Lowell and Horace Gray, *Law Reporter* (June, 1857), XX; *The Dred Scott Case*, by Timothy Farrar, *North Amer. Rev.* (Oct., 1857), LXXXV; for excellent descriptions of this case, see *Political History of Secession*, by Daniel W. Howe (1914); *Legal and Historical Status of the Dred Scott Case* (1909), by Elbert W. H. Ewing; see also *Note on the Dred Scott Case*, by Hampton L. Carson, *Amer. Law. Rev.* (1902), XXXVI; *Decisive Battles of the Law* (1907), by Frederick T. Hill.

Wayne, Catron, Daniel, Grier and Campbell — concurred in holding, not only that a negro could not be a citizen of the United States, but also that Congress had no power to exclude slavery from the Territories; Nelson confined himself to the opinion which he had prepared to be read as the opinion of the Court (before his Associates had decided to pass upon all the questions involved in the case), and decided only that the Court was bound to follow the law as laid down by the Missouri Supreme Court, with reference to the appellant's status as a slave; McLean and Curtis, in dissenting, delivered very long and elaborate opinions taking the contrary position on all three points involved.[1]

---

[1] The final outcome of the case so far as the appellant himself was concerned is curious. During the argument of the case, the fact became public (theretofore not generally known) that the negro was actually still owned by Mrs. Emerson, who had become the wife of Calvin C. Chaffee, an abolitionist Congressman from Massachusetts (see *New Hampshire Patriot*, June 3, 1857, stating that the *Springfield* (Ill.) *Argus* "first exposed this fact to the world"). The *New York Courier*, Dec. 19, 1856, stated that Sandford, the reputed owner of the negro, intended to liberate him, whatever might be the result of the suit. The *New York Tribune*, March 17, 1857, published a letter from Dr. Chaffee denying that he had any control over the negro or over the course of the suit. On April 23, 1857, the *Washington Union* said: "Dred Scott — This doughty gentleman of color has become the hero of the day, if not of the age. He has thrown Anthony Burns, Bully Bowlegs, Uncle Tom and Fred Douglass into temporary, if not everlasting oblivion, annihilated the Missouri Compromise and almost healed the wounds of bleeding Kansas." About the same time, a St. Louis paper described the negro as follows (see *Washington Union*, April 11, 1857): "The distinguished colored individual, who has made such a noise in the world in connexion with the celebrated case of *Scott* v. *Sandford* and who has become tangled up with the Missouri Compromise and other great subjects — Dred Scott — is a resident, not a citizen of St. Louis. He is well known to many of our citizens and may frequently be seen passing along Third Street. He is an old inhabitant, having come to this city thirty years ago. Dred Scott was born in Virginia where he belonged to Capt. Peter Blow, the father of Henry T. Blow and Taylor Blow of this city. . . . Dred was at Corpus Christi at the breaking out of the Mexican War, as the servant of Captain Bainbridge. On his return from Mexico, he applied to his mistress, Mrs. Emerson, then living near St. Louis, for the purchase of himself and family, offering to pay part of the money down and give an eminent citizen of St. Louis, an officer in the Army, as security for the payment of the remainder. His mistress refused his proposition. . . . The suit was commenced about ten years ago, and has cost Dred $500 in cash, besides labor to a nearly equal amount. It has given him a 'heap o' trouble', he says, and if he had known that 'it was gwine to last so long', he would not have brought it. . . . Dred does not appear to be at all discouraged by the issue of the celebrated case, although it dooms him to slavery. He talks about the affair with the ease of a

It is evident that the Judges did not realize, in the slightest degree, the effect which their decision was to have, or foresee the course which the public at the North would pursue towards it. "On the principles of the Dred Scott decision," wrote Alexander H. Stephens, five months later, "depended, in all probability the destiny of this country;" but he, like the Judges, supposed that the Court's decision would be accepted by the country. Other Democrats seemed to have a fatuous confidence in the Court's power thus to settle the slavery issue, expressed by Judge Wayne in his opinion as follows: "The case involves private rights and constitutional principles of the highest importance, about which there had become such a difference of opinion that the peace and harmony of the country required the settlement of them by judicial decision." No one on the Court comprehended the fact that the intensity of feeling at the North on the subject of slavery was such that it would not tolerate the settlement of the issue "by judicial decision"; and that such an attempt at settlement would only serve to enflame rather than to extinguish. The effect of the decision upon the country, and especially upon the North has been so frequently and fully described by historians that it would be a work of supererogation to detail it here.[1] The whirlwind of abuse which swept upon

veteran litigant, though not exactly in technical language and is hugely tickled at the idea of finding himself a personage of such importance. He does not take on airs, however, but laughs heartily when talking of 'de fuss dey made dar in Washington 'bout de ole nigger.' He is about fifty-five years old, we should think, though he does not know his own age." See also *Frank Leslie's Weekly*, IV, June 27, 1857, for detailed account of Dred Scott, with pictures of him and his wife and children.

In May, 1857, Dred Scott was conveyed by Dr. Chaffee and Mrs. Emerson to Taylor Blow of St. Louis for the purpose of emancipation, and he was set free in Missouri, within three months after the Court denied him to possess any rights as a free man.

[1] The views of the anti-slavery men in general, and the effect of the decision upon Northern sentiment, are well illustrated in the letters received by Judge McLean, highly praising his opinion. *John McLean Papers MSS;* letters of

the Court, the loss of confidence theretofore entertained in it, and the ensuing damage to its reputation, were, however, in reality, due more largely to misunderstandings of the decision, and to falsehoods spread relative to Taney's opinion, than to the actual decision itself. While the Court was bitterly assailed for rendering any decision upon the constitutional point, after holding that the Circuit Court had no jurisdiction, the correctness of its action in so doing was, after all, a purely legal question.[1] The most serious attacks upon the Court arose from a gross and willful perversion of a sentence in the Chief Justice's opinion, which certain violent anti-slavery papers of New York spread throughout the country, — the charge, reiterated again and again, that Taney had stated in his opinion that the "negro has no rights which the white man was bound to respect." These newspapers never printed the corrections of this false charge, immediately and persistently made by supporters of the Court, who pointed out that Taney had never stated this sentiment as expressing his own view, but had merely recited it historically as the view held by men in general, in the eighteenth century.[2] By the brazen propagation of this lie the country was long deceived; and the prejudices and passions aroused against the Court and its decision were due far more to Taney's alleged statement than to the point of law decided by him. It was not until the

J. H. Martindale of New York, March 21, John Allison of Ohio, March 21, Oliver H. Browning of Illinois, March 23, Jacob Collamer of Vermont, April 1, C. C. Bradley of Vermont, April 20, 1857.

[1] The Washington correspondent of the *New York Courier* wrote, March 12, 1857 (see issue of March 16): "I discover that lawyers are disposed to take a very practical and professional view. . . . They say there was but one point decided, namely that of the citizenship of the colored man. Beyond that, all is 'leather and prunella.' . . . The stump speech of the Chief Justice was entirely gratuitous, without one particle of authority."

[2] See example of correction of this falsehood, *Ohio Statesman*, May 13, 1857. "Republican Lie No. 1."

year 1886 that the *Independent*, of New York, which
had been the chief offender in spreading the falsehood,
recanted and said : "It is but just to the memory of
Chief Justice Taney, as well as to the Supreme Court, to
note the fact that the whole language, including these
words, is simply that of historical narration. . . .
Chief Justice Taney did not say it in 1857, and the
Supreme Court did not say it. What Chief Justice
Taney said was by way of narrative, relating to a period
prior to the adoption of the Constitution." [1]

The manner in which the sentiment of the country
was aroused by the Northern press may be gathered
from a few fairly illustrative extracts from the most
influential anti-slavery papers. Immediately after the
decision, the *New York Tribune* commenced an onslaught, which it continued practically every day for a
month.[2] On March 6, its Washington correspondent
wrote that : "The whole slavery agitation was reopened
by the proceedings in the Supreme Court today, and
that tribunal voluntarily introduced itself into the
political arena. . . . Much feeling is excited by this
decree, and the opinion is freely expressed that a new
element of sectional strife has been wantonly imposed
upon the country." The next day, he wrote that its
character as an impartial judicial body had gone. "If
the action of the Court in this case has been atrocious,
the manner of it has been no better. The Court has
rushed into politics, voluntarily and without other
purpose than to subserve the cause of slavery. They
were not called upon, in the discharge of their duties,
to say a word about the subject. . . . The vote
stood seven to two — the five slaveholders and two

[1] *Independent*, April 3, 1886.
[2] See *New York Tribune*, especially March 7, 9, 10, 11, 12, 16, 17, 19, 20, 21, 25, 1857.

doughfaces making up the seven. Their cunning chief
had led the van, and plank by plank laid down a platform of historical falsehood and gross assumption, and
thereon they all stood exultingly, thinking, or feigning
to think, that their work would stand during the remainder of their lives at least." Another correspondent wrote that the decision "has been heard and commented upon here with mingled derision and contempt.
If epithets and denunciation could sink a judicial body,
the Supreme Court of the United States would never
be heard of again. Chief Justice Taney's opinion was
long, elaborate, able and Jesuitical. His arguments
were based on gross historical falsehoods and bold
assumptions and went the whole length of the Southern
doctrine." Editorially, the *Tribune* said that: "The
long trumpeted decision . . . having been held over
from last year in order not too flagrantly to alarm and
exasperate the Free States on the eve of an important
Presidential election, . . . is entitled to just so much
moral weight as would be the judgment of a majority
of those congregated in any Washington bar-room. It is
a *dictum* prescribed by the stump to the Bench." Three
days later, it said: "No wonder that the Chief Justice
should have sunk his voice to a whisper, conscious, as
he must have been, that the decision which he promulgated had been arrived at on grounds totally different
from those indicated in the opinion — that opinion
being but a mere collation of false statements and
shallow sophistries, got together to sustain a foregone
conclusion, — knowing that he was engaged in a pitiful
attempt to impose upon the public. However feeble
his voice might have been, what he had to say was still
feebler." The next day, it said: "Until that remote
period when different Judges sitting in this same Court
shall reverse this wicked and false judgment, the Con-

stitution of the United States is nothing better than the bulwark of inhumanity and oppression." Equal with the *Tribune* in its influence on the anti-slavery sentiment of the North was the *New York Independent*, which reached the great Congregationalist community, and whose columns were filled with invective against the Court.[1] On the day after the decision, its Washington correspondent wrote: "If there be not aroused a spirit of resistance and indignation, which shall wipe out this decision and all its results, as the lightning wipes out the object it falls upon, then indeed are the days of our Republic numbered, and the patriot shall see light only beyond the storms of revolution and blood. . . . The Missouri Compromise was a defeat of freedom. The Compromise of 1850 was a yet more humiliating surrender; but it was left to the Supreme Court to complete the utter subjugation and extermination of all that remained of the protesting voice of liberty. . . . In all this, I counsel no revolutions. . . . I invoke only in the name of Truth, which yet lives, that force of public sentiment which makes and unmakes Courts and decisions, as easily as it makes and unmakes Presidents and Legislatures. . . ." Editorially, it inveighed against Taney's "stump speech spoken for political effect" and the wickedness of the decision — the attempt "to foist this new and atrocious doctrine into the Constitution"; "this vain attempt to change the law by the power of Judges who have achieved only their own infamy." It said that: "The reverence for the Supreme Court, which has been so widely cherished, is a reverence for law. It is a reverence which assumes that the Judges of a tribunal, so far removed from the shifting winds of popular excitement, and so carefully guarded against the intrusion of

[1] *Independent*, March 12, 19, 26, Dec. 17, 1857.

factions and political influences, will be under no violent temptation to betray their trust"; and that the Judges now having debased themselves, the question had arisen as to whether Judges ought not to be chosen by popular election. Later, in an editorial headed, "The Decision of the Supreme Court is the Moral Assassination of a Race and Cannot be Obeyed", it said: "The moment the Supreme Judicial Court becomes a Court of injustice, a Court to carry schemes of oppression against classes of men, by forced constructions of the Constitution, that moment its claim to obedience ceases. The moment it becomes the Court of a political party, and not of the United States, and promulgates falsehoods, that moment its decisions cease to be binding, and impeachment, not obedience, belongs to it. . . . The decision is a deliberate iniquity. It is not a mistake . . . but it is a deliberate, willful perversion, for a particular purpose, and that purpose, the sanction and perpetuity of human slavery. If the people obey this decision, they disobey God." The *New York Evening Post* said that the consequences of the decision "are beyond the reach of human calculation", and that "the moral authority and consequent usefulness of that tribunal, under the present organization, is seriously impaired, if not destroyed. . . . A majority of its members have consented to become parties to a combination with the Administration to transfer the political control of the government to the hands of the slave oligarchy." [1] The *New York Courier* published a series of attacks, but of a less extreme character.[2] On the day after the decision, its owner, General Webb, wrote from Washington of the "sectional mummeries of

[1] *New York Evening Post*, March 7, 10, 11, 12, 13, 14, 26, 1857.
[2] *New York Courier*, see editorials and letters from Washington by its owner, Gen. James Watson Webb, and by "Inspector", March 7, 9, 10, 11, 12, 13, 16, 17, 19, 1857.

a Court which had become a mere party machine", and said that while all good citizens would submit to the decision, yet Congress and the people must prevail.   Later, he wrote that the Court, which had been hitherto "considered the mainstay of order and conservatism in the country, has been seized by an unreasoning and desperate fanaticism on one subject, which renders it blind to precedents, to the well-established principles of law, to justice and humanity"; and that henceforward it could never be spoken of "with that veneration and respect which the Nation has delighted to accord it." On March 11, the *Courier* said that the South would find no benefit from the decision which would only multiply agitation on the slavery question.   "The volunteered, sectional and partisan opinions . . . are in all respects unfortunate — unfortunate for the reputation and authority of the Court — unfortunate for the harmonious relations of the Free and Slave States — and unfortunate for the character of the country . . . fraught with immense mischief."   On March 12, it expressed a fear lest the Free States should assert their sovereignty to the extremest limit, and said that if this injured the Slave States, the latter "will only have slavery-devoted and innovating Judges to thank for it."   On March 13, it urged that the composition of the Court and the Circuits be remodeled. After pointing out the great preponderance of white persons in the four Free-soil Circuits as compared with the five Slavery Circuits, it said: "In its present sectional form, it is necessarily the object of suspicion.   To believe implicitly in its perfect candor and impartiality of judgment upon questions of a sectional bearing requires an effort, which, however the heart in its charity might allow, the understanding, with its appreciation of human nature as it is, utterly refuses.   Among a free people, the authority of a tribunal of law resides more in its moral power than in the civil force which stands at its back, and the very first requisite to the possession of this moral power is complete confidence in its impartiality."

The anti-slavery press throughout the North and Central West followed the example of these leading New York papers and indulged in even greater scurrility and abuse.

In most histories of the period, the effect of the Dred Scott decision has been portrayed in a somewhat disproportionate and exaggerated manner by omitting reference to the large body of newspapers which supported or defended the decision. Moreover, some papers like the *Times, Herald, Commercial Advertiser* and *Journal of Commerce*, in New York, took a conservative stand; and while impressed with the seriousness of the issue thrust upon the country by the Court's decision, they deplored the violence of the *Tribune* and its imitators.[1] The *Times* said, March 8, that while all looked with respect and some degree of reverence on the Court, "the circumstances attending the present decision have done much to divest it of moral influence and to impair the confidence of the country. . . . Among jurists, it is not considered to settle anything more than the denial of jurisdiction. . . . But it exhibited the eagerness of the majority of that tribunal to force an opinion upon the country and to thrust itself into the political contests." The next day, it said that while there would be no forcible opposition, the doctrines of the decision would germinate "the seeds of discontent and contest and disaster hereafter. . . . It has laid the only solid foundation which has ever yet

[1] *New York Times*, March 8, 9, 1857; *New York Herald*, March 7, 8, 12, 13, 14, 15, 17, 1857; *New York Journal of Commerce*, March 11, 12, 1857.

existed for an Abolition Party, and it will do more to stimulate the growth of such a party than has been done by any other event." The *Herald* said, March 7, that the decision would be accepted as the law, but "it will profoundly affect the public mind in regard to the general question of slavery." The next day, it termed the decision a "bombshell from the Supreme Court", which, "of vital importance . . . at a single blow shivers the anti-slavery platform of the late great Northern Republican party into atoms. . . . The supreme law is expounded by the supreme authority, and disobedience is rebellion, treason and revolution." Later, it said that some of the anti-slavery journals, "stunned by these late tremendous blows from the Supreme Court, are counseling an organized resistance. But that is folly, treason and rebellion." And it stated that one of the inevitable party issues, on which every Presidential contest would turn, would henceforward be — the reformation of the Supreme Court, so as to reverse the majority. The *New York Commercial Advertiser* very candidly said that, while it dissented from the opinion, "no one had a right to impugn the motives of the Court, and to do so is alike unjust and unwise. Least of all is it patriotic to endeavor to bring the highest tribunal of the republic into contempt, because it pronounced decisions at variance with our views or wishes. Such a course, though it may be congenial with our temper at the moment, is sadly perilous to the common weal, the interest of freedom and free government being always best upheld by maintaining respect for the officers of the government, especially those of the Judiciary." The *New York Journal of Commerce*, a strong Democratic paper, attacked the "indecent and contemptible calumnies" of the abolition press, and deplored the impugning of the "honesty and purity of the great constitutional lawyers" on the Bench. It stated that "outside the limited circle of disappointed factionists, whose vocation it is to foment strife and discord to subserve individual and selfish ends", the decision would be respected, honored and obeyed; and that this "authoritative and final settlement of the grievous sectional issues" would be hailed with satisfaction by all, "except the demagogues who wish to kindle flames of discord and fanaticism."

Other Democratic papers in the North were vigorous in support of the decision, and deplored the virulence of the "Black Republican press, brimful of elements of sedition, treason and insurrection." [1] "The *Tribune* may rave, and fanaticism make earth hideous with its howlings, but all in vain," said the *Pennsylvanian*. "There are certain points which are settled and beyond the reach of the fanatics of the Nation. . . . The decision is a closing and clinching confirmation of the settlement of the issue. . . . Whoever now seeks to revive sectionalism arrays himself against the Constitution, and consequently against the Union." A leading New Hampshire paper said: "The black press and pulpit unite in reviling the Court and denouncing this decision. . . . The Black Republicans' creed and purposes are at war with the Constitution, are treasonable, and contemplate the overthrow of the Union. . . . Let the patriotic of all parties think of the immense consequence of this Court to our National peace and harmony, and put the seal of reprobation on those who would destroy it or lessen its authority. The reflecting will be astonished at the language of the

---

[1] See, for example, *Pennsylvanian*, March 10, 11, 12, 1857; *New Hampshire Patriot*, March 18, 25, June 3, 1857; *Milwaukee Daily News* (Wisc.); *Rock Island Argus* (Ill.); *Springfield State Register* (Ill.); *Detroit Free Press* (Mich.); *Portland Eastern Argus* (Me.); *Missouri Republican*, quoted in *Washington Union*, April 7, 14, 16, May 1, 1857; *Ohio Statesman*, March 19, 23, May 13, 14, 15, 1857.

press as to the tribunal which has performed such priceless service, and given so much stability to law and strength to our National politics." "Pernicious and anarchical as have hitherto been the 'higher law' heresies," said the *Boston Post*, "we hazard nothing in saying that none have been more pernicious or full of anarchy than those which a few days have elicited as to the Supreme Court." A prominent Illinois paper said that: "No decision for a generation has created a deeper sensation. . . . This inquisition, blind and mad as it is, which has foisted itself into the pulpit and the forum, may be soon expected to sit with veiled face, in mocking of common sense and common decency, upon the last relic of constitutional liberty. A blow aimed at the third great branch of the government — the Judiciary — is tantamount to a blow struck at the heart of all law and order." A leading Ohio paper denounced the Republican papers for their attack on Taney, "this venerable father in the law, strong in mind but weak in body, tottering on the brink of an honored grave, with no fame to expect but that which erudition and judicial ability have already obtained for him", and for their attempt to destroy confidence in the Court. "This bulwark of self-imposed law is in the hearts of the people. To teach the people to laugh it to scorn is to weaken the bastions and mine the fortress."

The strongest defense of the Court appeared in a long series of editorials, during April and May, in the Administration paper, the *Daily Union*, of Washington. On the day after the decision, it said that it would "exert the most powerful and salutary influence throughout the United States"; on March 11, it said: "If the sectional question be not now settled, then we may despair of the Republic. We believe it is settled, and that henceforth sectionalism will cease to be a dangerous element in our political contests. . . . **Of** course, it is to be expected that fanaticism will rave and clamor against the decision of the Supreme Court. But fanaticism ceases to be a formidable enemy, when it seeks to measure strength with the Union-loving spirit of the people, sustained or confirmed by the great arbiter of constitutional questions." The next day, it said that it was confident that Taney's opinion "will be regarded with soberness and not with passion; and that it will thereby exert a mighty influence in diffusing sound opinions and restoring harmony and fraternal concord throughout the country." It deplored the "unbridled license of the press, and the vilification by Northern papers, and reciprocation by radical Southern papers." "There must be toleration, there must be forbearance," it concluded. Neither toleration nor forbearance, however, seemed possible, in the existing bitterness of the political situation — and the *Union's* later editorials gave increasing evidence of this.[1] On March 18, it spoke of the "ribald vituperations against the Court which made infamous some of the Republican journals." On March 26, in an editorial entitled the "Black Republican Crusade", it pointed out the necessity of retaining respect for, and confidence in, the Court — a doctrine which it said, had long been preached heretofore in the North; and it asked: "Is the whole structure of our government to be subverted, because a negro is determined by the highest judicial authority of the land not to be a citizen within the meaning of the Constitution?" On April 11, in an editorial entitled "The Higher Law Against the Con-

[1] See *Daily Union*, March 14, 17, 1857, saying that the "Black Republican press literally howl with rage . . . the vile epithets, reproaches in the treasonable calumnious papers of the North"; March 21, 1857, defending the Judges from the charges of acting politically; March 28, editorial on "the Supreme Court and the *New York Tribune*"; April 2, editorial on "What Courts Decide"; May 1, editorial on "The Supremacy of the Law."

stitution", it stated that there was now but one alternative — "obedience to the Constitution, or resistance to the supreme law of the land." A few papers expressed more calm and patriotic views. The *National Intelligencer* said, on May 29: "That the Supreme Court should have been called at all to pronounce upon questions involved in political controversy must be a matter of regret to all who would desire to preserve that high tribunal, not only from the influence of partisan bias in pronouncing its decisions, but from even the suspicion of it, on the part of any considerable portion of the community. . . . Whatever its decision might have been, it became inevitable, under these circumstances, that one political party or another, according to the views or prejudices of its members, was destined to be dissatisfied with the result; but the duty of acquiescing in that result, whether equally acknowledged by both parties or not, was equally imperative on both, and must remain so, as long as the forms of law receive that respect to which they are entitled." And *Harper's Weekly* said with great sanity: "The idea that any decision of the Supreme Court can reëstablish slavery in the Free States is a bugbear — an absurdity. The only result, therefore, that we can arrive at is, that, however repugnant the Dred Scott decision may be to the feelings of a portion of the Northern States, it can have no practical effects injurious to our tranquillity or to our institutions. The subject of slavery will be left to be decided, as it ultimately must be, by the laws which govern labor and production. It is, indeed, most devoutly to be desired that this great question should be left to be determined exclusively by those laws, free from the interference of the hotheads of the press and of the pulpit. If we would but permit Nature to have her own way for only a few short years!

. . . When political agitation shall have ceased, and the fires of religious fanaticism are burned out, these are the points on which this matter must ultimately be determined. . . . We have no doubt how it will finally be decided; nor have we any doubt how it would have been decided, years ago, if every agency that human wit can devise had not been systematically employed, at once to excite the passions, and blind the judgment of those to whom alone the disposition of the question rightfully belongs." [1]

Had the country been influenced by editorials like these, rather than by the hysterical, virulent and false outpourings of the *Tribune* and the *Independent*, the Court's action would have had less effect upon history, but it was otherwise destined. The surprise with which the attitude of the Republican press was greeted by the Democrats shows conclusively how little they realized the insidious effect upon public sentiment at the North produced by the undermining campaign against the Court which had been conducted by the anti-slavery leaders in Congress for the past seven years. And how little Chief Justice Taney himself realized the extent of the passions aroused by his opinion was seen in a letter written to Ex-President Pierce, August 29, 1857: [2]

You see I am passing through conflict, much like the one which followed the removal of the deposits, and the war is waged upon me in the same spirit and by many of the same men who distinguished themselves on that occasion by the unscrupulous means to which they resorted. At my time of life when my end must be near, I should have rejoiced to find that the irritating strifes of this world were over, and that I was about to depart in peace with all men and all men in peace with me. Yet perhaps it is best as it is. The mind

[1] *National Intelligencer*, May 29, 1857; *Harper's Weekly*, March 28, 1857.
[2] See *Amer. Hist. Rev.* (1904), X.

is less apt to feel the torpor of age when it is thus forced into action by public duties. And I have an abiding confidence that this act of my judicial life will stand the test of time and the sober judgment of the country, as well as the political act of which I have spoken. Your successor has, I think, a difficult time before him. Symptoms of discord are already appearing.

While, with the lapse of time, the opinion expressed by many earlier historians and statesmen that the Dred Scott decision was the most potent factor in bringing on the Civil War has been rejected, and the inevitability of that conflict has been realized, the really serious effect of this fatal decision by the Court was that which was foretold by a writer in the *North American Review*, as early as October, 1857 : "The country will feel the consequences of the decision more deeply and more permanently, in the loss of confidence in the sound judicial integrity and strictly legal character of their tribunals, than in anything beside; and this, perhaps, may well be accounted the greatest political calamity which this country, under our forms of government, could sustain." [1]

And this view of the case, which will be the probable final judgment of history, has been recently well expressed by a thoughtful jurist as follows : "The Dred Scott decision cannot be, with accuracy, written down as a usurpation, but it can and must be written down as a gross abuse of trust by the body which rendered it. The results from that abuse of trust were, moreover, momentous. During neither the Civil War nor the period of Reconstruction did the Supreme Court play anything like its due rôle of supervision, with the result

[1] *The Dred Scott Case*, by Timothy Farrar, *North Amer. Rev.* (1857), LXXXV; see also *Parties and Slavery* (1903), by Theodore Clarke Smith, 208 : "The only results of the *Dred Scott Case* were to damage the prestige of the Court in the North, and to stimulate a sectional hostility which threatened to recoil upon the Judges themselves."

that during the one period the military powers of the President underwent undue expansion, and during the other the legislative powers of Congress. The Court itself was conscious of its weakness, yet notwithstanding its prudent disposition to remain in the background, at no time since Jefferson's first Administration has its independence been in greater jeopardy than in the decade between 1860 and 1870. So slow and laborious was its task of recuperating its shattered reputation." [1]

It must be again emphasized, however, that the loss of confidence in the Court was due not merely to the Court's decision but to the false and malignant criticisms and portrayals of the Court which were spread widely through the North by influential newspapers, and of which no better illustration can be given than to quote in full the clever, but venomous, description of the members of the Court sent out by the *Tribune's* correspondent, ten days after the decision. [2]

"Mr. Wayne is an intelligent, prompt, good looking Georgian. He is radical on the slavery question, and would dispute the right of any Northern man to have an opinion on slavery or its relations, anyway. He entered with alacrity and vim into Judge Taney's views, and would stand by them, and either argue for them or fight for them, according to the necessities of the case. He is one of the Chivalry, and before he got old, the ladies used to be enamored of his flowing locks and general beauty of appearance, to which he was himself not wholly insensible. He was very much exercised in mind, during the delivery of Judge Curtis'

---

[1] *The Dred Scott Decision in the Light of Contemporary Legal Doctrine*, by Edward S. Corwin, *Amer. Hist. Rev.* (1911), XVII; *The Doctrine of Judicial Review* (1914), by Edward S. Corwin; *Note on the Dred Scott Case*, by Hampton L. Carson, *Amer. Law Rev.* (1902), XXXVI; *The Dred Scott Case in the Light of Later Events*, by Morris M. Cohn, *ibid.* (1912), XLVI; *Did the Decision in the Dred Scott Case Lead to the Civil War?* by Henry A. Forster, *ibid.* (1918), LII.

[2] *New York Tribune*, March 17, 1857.

opinion, and could not restrain the exhibition of his feelings. . . . He commented audibly, both to the Chief Justice, and to Judge Daniel who sat on either side of him. In fact, both he and the veteran Daniel seemed as uneasy, while Judge Curtis was reading, as though they were listening to an Abolition harangue.

"Judge Daniel of Virginia is old, and long, and lean, and sharp in the visage, and simply wears the aspect of a tremulous and fidgety old gentleman in glasses. His politics are those of a Virginia slaveholder and abstractionist, who swears by the resolutions of '98. Of course, he goes to the hilt on any point where the demands of the Oligarchy are concerned.

"Judge Catron of Tennessee is a robust, unintellectual man, advanced in years, whose judgments would be inevitably swayed by his political associations, but whose erroneous opinions would, as a general rule, more often result from obtuseness than from original sin. . . . He listened with a good deal of respectful surprise to Judge Curtis' exposition of the fallacy of his deductions. . . .

"Of Judge Campbell of Alabama, there is nothing to be said, except that on the subject in question he is more fanatical than the fanatics, more Southern than the extreme South from which he comes. A judicial . . . decision from him, where slavery is concerned, is of no more value than the cawing of a raven. He is a middle-aged, middle-sized man, bald, and possessed of middling talents.

"Grier of Pennsylvania followed his instincts and not his convictions, if a man may be said to have convictions who has not moral stamina enough to distinctly avow his real opinions. Grier is a man somewhat misunderstood. He is not what we fancy he is generally considered to be, a perverse, iron-sided, hard-shelled, soulless, pro-slavery, old curmudgeon. If anyone entertains this uncharitable opinion of Grier, we must beg to undeceive him. He is no such man. In the first place, the Judge is a blonde, of rotund figure. This alone intimates a denial of the character suggested, and the Judge's real characteristics closely conform to his external, physiological delineations. He is of a soft and rosy nature. He is facile and easy of suggestion. He succumbs under touch, and returns into shape on its removal. He is ardent and impressible. He is fickle and uncertain. . . . He is impulsive and precipitate. Let Grier associate with none but honest men, and be placed in no difficult or constraining circumstances, and he would not disgrace himself or his position. We concede to Mr. Grier another merit. If he belonged to a Black Republican Court, he would side with the majority.

". . . Of Nelson, it is needless to say more than that he is a New York Democrat of the perishing school. He hesitated to go with the Southern Judges in their revolutionary opinions, yet he had not sufficient virtue to boldly stand up against their heresies.

". . . Of Taney's opinion, it will be found to exhibit all the characteristics that have marked his career. It is subtle, ingenious, sophistical and false. It is the plea of a tricky lawyer and not the decree of an upright Judge. It is a singular, but not wonderful fact in nature, that the body to some extent intimates the character of the soul that inhabits it. This is the case with Judge Taney. He walks with inverted and hesitating steps. His forehead is contracted, his eye sunken and his visage has a sinister expression."

Such ridicule and abuse, published and republished and quoted by other newspapers throughout the Northern States, could not fail to weaken the Court's status with the people.

CHAPTER TWENTY-SEVEN

THE BOOTH CASE, AND CONGRESSIONAL ATTACKS

1858–1860

SHORTLY after the delivery of the Dred Scott decision and the adjournment of the Court on March 7, 1857, Judge Curtis determined to resign. While reaching this conclusion primarily because of the inadequacy of the salary, he was also influenced by his belief, regretfully held, that he could no longer expect to see the Court act on constitutional questions, with freedom from political considerations.[1] When this

---

[1] *Curtis*, I, 245, letter from G. T. Curtis, July 3, 1857. Considerable friction had arisen between the members of the Court, over the fact that Judges Curtis and McLean had filed with the Clerk, on March 9, their full opinions, which had been printed and widely circulated throughout the North, before Taney had filed the opinion of the Court, and before the other Judges had filed their separate opinions. An acrimonious correspondence on the subject ensued between Taney and Curtis; see *Curtis*, I, 211–230; on April 2, 1857, the *National Intelligencer* reprinted a letter from the Washington correspondent of the *New York Journal of Commerce*, dated March 28: "I called at the Clerk's office of the Supreme Court just now and ascertained that there is no mode of procuring official copies or any copies of the opinions of the Court in the Dred Scott case, until the Reporter of the Court, Mr. Howard, shall have them printed in his series of reports. The volume which is to contain them is nearly ready, and is only delayed until he can obtain the revised copies of the opinion. The opinion of the Court, as read by the Chief Justice, is not yet on file; but he expected to be ready to file it today. There will be no delay, or very little, about the others. The opinions of Justices McLean and Curtis were filed on the 9th. . . . These have been published at the North. The abstracts published of Chief Justice Taney's and Justice Nelson's opinions were taken in shorthand, and of course are imperfect." From an interesting, confidential letter written by a friend, James E. Harvey, to Judge McLean, April 3, it appears that various Judges modified the form of their opinions after their oral delivery. Harvey wrote: "There are strong surmises about the manipulations to which the majority opinions have been subjected. As the Appletons wrote to me to get them all for publication, I took some pains to inform myself about their status — if you allow that word, when not applied to slavery. Last week, they had not been filed and were inaccessible. Taney's had been twice copied for revision, and an application from the *Intelligencer* to publish was refused, owing to non-completion. That clause in Catron's, rebuking the discussion of the

resignation was presented on September 1, 1857, the news was received by the Bar of the North with the deepest regret.[1] Ex-President Fillmore wrote to him that his appointment was one "to which I and my friends could always point with proud satisfaction", and that he regarded the resignation as "a calamity" which he feared would "not only impair the confidence of all good and intelligent men in the stability of our institutions, but that the appointment of a successor may be most unfortunate. . . . You may know who will probably be selected, but I confess, I fear the worst." All of Curtis' Associates on the Bench (with the exception of Judge Daniel) sent letters of deep regret, though that of the Chief Justice was somewhat perfunctory. Judge McLean wrote despondingly that the loss was irreparable, and that while, in 1830 when he took his seat, the "Court commanded the respect and veneration of the country, it can never hope to regain so elevated a position in the future", and that he had "lost the interest and pride I once felt in the tribunal." Some old-line Whigs felt that Curtis should have sacrificed his personal feeling and remained on the Bench, rather than create a vacancy at this time. "How could so wise a man as our friend B. R. Curtis do so deplorable a thing as to resign . . . at this untimely moment?" wrote Robert C. Winthrop of Massachusetts, the former Speaker of the House of Representatives. "I may over-estimate the impor-

merits of the case after the denial of jurisdiction, has been expurgated. But a single copy was printed for his own use. Campbell's has been printed privately, but not for circulation. He forbade the printer from showing it to anybody." *John McLean Papers MSS.* The opinions were not officially published until the end of May, the *National Intelligencer* printing them first, on May 29.

[1] Curtis' opinion entirely revolutionized the former adverse views held regarding him by the anti-slavery men. An interesting example of their attitude is seen in a letter from Henry L. Higginson, in May, 1857: "Judge Taney's decision is infamous to the last degree. Ben Curtis for once has been honest." *Life and Letters of Henry Lee Higginson* (1921), by Bliss Perry, 110.

tance of his course, and I certainly esteem and respect him, but I have never known a resignation which has so much the air of desertion. Buchanan will have a chance to make the Court still less acceptable to this part of the country." [1]

The intensity of bitterness aroused against the Court in the North was well illustrated by the savage, unjust and untrue attacks which were made upon the man whom Buchanan now chose to fill the vacancy caused by the resignation of Judge Curtis. The President had at first been inclined to appoint Isaac Toucey of Connecticut, formerly United States Attorney-General; he had also even considered going outside the Circuit and appointing a Southerner, William L. Yancey of Alabama. Rufus Choate of Massachusetts had strong supporters; John J. Gilchrist of New Hampshire, who had formerly been Chief Justice of that State and was now Chief Justice of the new United States Court of Claims, was recommended by Choate himself, and by Reverdy Johnson and Charles O'Conor.[2] Buchanan finally determined on Nathan Clifford of Maine, and submitted his name to the Senate on December 9, 1857. Clifford was fifty-four years of age, and had served as Attorney-General, both of his State, and of the United States (under Polk). As his later career showed, he was amply qualified as a lawyer of great learning and powers of research. The moment, however, the nomination reached the Senate, it was subjected to the most venomous criticism by the radical anti-slavery men, particularly by John P. Hale,

[1] *Memoir of Robert C. Winthrop* (1897), by Robert C. Winthrop, Jr.

[2] See letter of Howell Cobb to Alexander H. Stephens, Sept. 22, 1857, *Amer. Hist. Ass. Rep.* (1911), I, 422; letters of J. J. Gilchrist to Pierce, Sept. 16, 1857, Cushing to Pierce, Oct. 2, 1857, *Franklin Pierce Papers MSS;* Richard K. Crallé wrote to R. M. T. Hunter, Oct. 24, 1857, that "I suppose the rumored transfer of Yancey to the Supreme Court Bench is to deprive you of all Cabinet connections." *Correspondence of R. M. T. Hunter, Amer. Hist. Ass. Rep.* (1916), II.

Senator from New Hampshire. The *New York Tribune's* Washington correspondent wrote that: "The President has determined to break down all exclusive privileges and monopolies, as anti-Democratic; and therefore, as New England has had Story and Curtis, upon which they have grown rather presumptuous, he has determined to bring them down to the level of the other Circuits and appoint Clifford. However, Clifford will be confirmed under party drill, although it is well known that the entire Bar of New England has protested against it as an outrage. Thus the process of deterioration goes on, and the Supreme Court is gradually becoming a mere party machine, to do the bidding of the dominant faction and to supply places to reward party hacks." [1] This statement that the entire Bar of New England had protested had no foundation; but it is true that there was considerable opposition, based largely on personal grounds. On January 12, 1858, nevertheless, the Senate confirmed the appointment by the close vote of twenty-six to twenty-three.[2] "Mr. Clifford owes this appointment exclusively to his party associations, unsupported by the wishes or recommendation of the Bar of his Circuit. His sympathies coincide entirely with those which the Court have manifested, and bring the strength of his vote to the sectional action of the Court, without any independence or great legal ability," said the *New York Evening Post*. "There is perhaps some satisfaction in the belief, which this appointment strengthens, that the weakness and evident character

---

[1] See *New York Tribune*, Dec. 18, 29, 1857, Jan. 13, 14, 16, 1858.

[2] The *New York Evening Post*, Jan. 14, 15, 1858, said that the defeat of Clifford's nomination had been thought certain, but that by reason of the absence of two of his opponents, Senators Charles Sumner and Simon Cameron, and the change of mind of Senator Allen of Rhode Island, he was confirmed. "The result is sufficiently to be regretted, but the negligence through which it was achieved is deplorable, and occasions great mortification, not unmixed with vexation."

of the Court, together with the inequality of its composition, will produce an entire remodelling of it;" and the *New York Tribune* also continued its attack: "On the principle which seems to have governed the selection of Mr. Clifford, that the proper business of the Northern minority on the Bench is merely to fall in with and say yes to any extravagances which the Southern majority may choose to promulgate, Mr. Clifford is admirably fitted for the place in which he has been put. We may be quite sure that he will never be driven, by his knowledge of the law and history or his logical perception of things, into playing the marplot, as Judge Curtis did in the *Dred Scott Case*, tumbling down the decision of the Court about its ears, and exposing that grave tribunal to popular derision and even contempt." To these partisan diatribes, Judge Clifford's distinguished judicial service of twenty-three years, until his death in 1881, afforded a complete refutal.

When the Court met for its December Term at the end of the year 1857, the newly elected Congress was being confronted with the slavery question in its most inflamed condition. The wrongs of "bleeding Kansas", the question of the admission of that Territory as a State, the question of the legality of its two Constitutions — one framed by slavery men at Lecompton, the other by anti-slavery men at Topeka — were all the subject of long and violent debates, which lasted through the sessions of 1858, 1859 and 1860. In addition, in 1859, the John Brown-Harper's Ferry episode elicited passionate speeches on this unescapable question. In all these debates, covering hundreds of pages of the *Congressional Globe*, the opinions of the Court in the *Dred Scott Case*, and the action of Chief Justice Taney and the other Judges formed a constant staple for assault and defense. Interminable discussions arose, also, as to the legal points involved in the case, and as to the applicability of the decision to the point at issue in Kansas — the right of a Territory to legislate on the subject of slavery. Few of these details are of interest now, but in the three years prior to the Civil War they formed the chief, almost the only, subject of concern in Congress; and the debates, centering as they did around the Court, had a most demoralizing effect upon the attitude of the general public towards the Judiciary. Illustrative of the general Republican attitude in the Senate were the speeches of Hale of New Hampshire, Trumbull of Illinois, Fessenden of Maine, Doolittle of Wisconsin, Collamer of Vermont, Seward of New York, Hamlin of Maine, and Wade of Ohio.[1] A few of their sentiments were as follows. Hale said that he had practically lost all respect for the Court since they had "come down from their place and thrown themselves into the political arena", and "when the excitement has passed away, the record of this decision will stand, not a monument to the wisdom or to the integrity of the Court, but it will stand as one of those unfortunate decisions which Courts have frequently made, when they have undertaken to mold eternal principles of justice and law to suit the purposes of power. . . . I denounce that opinion on every occasion. I invoke the public indignation upon it." Trumbull said that, by trying by *dicta* to settle points not before it, the

[1] *35th Cong., 1st Sess.* and *App.*, speeches in 1858, of Hale, Jan. 18, 20, Trumbull, Feb. 2, March 17, Fessenden, Feb. 8, Collamer, March 2, Wade, March 13, Hamlin, March 9, Seward, March 3; in 1859, of Hale, Feb. 23, Pugh, Jan. 3, Feb. 23, Chandler, Feb. 17; in 1860, of Doolittle, Jan. 3; see also in the House in 1858, speeches of Washburn, Jan. 7, Giddings, Jan. 18, Foster, March 10, Abbott, March 23, Olin, March 29, Tappan, March 31, Walton, March 31, Bliss, May 6; in 1859, speeches of Davies, Feb. 11, Bingham, Feb. 11, Granger, Feb. 17, Brown, Feb. 17; in 1860, speeches of Foster, Jan. 12, Gooch, May 3, Washburn, May 19.

Court "was a set of usurpers." Fessenden cited with approval a recent case in the Supreme Court of Georgia,[1] in which that Court had stated that it was not bound by decisions of the United States Supreme Court, especially partisan opinions — a doctrine which, be it noted, the Northern Whigs of former days had vigorously denounced. The most violent assaults, however, were made by Seward, Hamlin and Wade. Seward, in an elaborate and picturesque but venomous speech, made the direct charge that the *Dred Scott Case* was a dummy suit, manufactured by Buchanan and the slavery interests for their own purposes, that the argument was a "mock debate", that Buchanan and the Chief Justice had acted in collusion to cheat the country, and that the decision was the result of a political bargain between the Court and the President, who "alike forgot that judicial usurpation is more odious and intolerable, than any other among the manifold practices of tyranny."

It is evident that not one of these slanderous assertions was true; they were made, as Senator Judah P. Benjamin said in his eloquent reply, "without proof of a solitary fact, without the assertion even of a fact, on which to base the foul charge."[2] And the actual history of the case, its date of origin, the par-

[1] *Padelford* v. *Savannah* (1854,) 14 Ga. 438.

[2] Tyler, in his *Memoir of Roger Brooke Taney* (1872), 380–390, discussed at length Seward's attack and said: "This bungling sketch of an historical scene, by unskilful literary ambition is an unmitigated calumny from beginning to end"; and he published letters to him from Judge Campbell, Judge Nelson and Reverdy Johnson to disprove Seward's statements.

For Seward's charge, see *35th Cong., 1st Sess.*, 943. Prof. John W. Burgess in *The Middle Period* (1897), 457, said: "It is almost certain that the charge was an unfounded suspicion. The prevalence of the suspicion was, however, an ominous sign of the danger impending over the land. . . . Both Mr. Buchanan and Mr. Taney were men of the highest personal and official integrity and possessed the most delicate sense of the requirements and proprieties of the great stations which they occupied."

ties concerned in appealing it, and the manner in which the Judges arrived at the final disposition conclusively disprove Seward's statements. Nevertheless, similar charges were made by Hamlin, in a slashing speech in which he said that the slavery interests had secured control of the Legislative, the Executive and the Judiciary, and that the foreshadowing of the decision in the *Dred Scott Case* by Buchanan in his Inaugural Address was evidence of "political collusion and complicity" with the Court, whose "object was to rob the people and the States of the rights that belong to them." Wade also assailed the "late nefarious decision." "I wish I could entertain a good opinion of the Judges of that Court," he said. "I wish I could believe they were patriotic, unswerved by political considerations, or uninfluenced by anything but their duty. . . . I fear that the Court, swayed by political reasons, forgot the rights of Dred Scott, and plunged into this political whirlpool in order to control its currents." Like so many of their Republican associates at this time, both Wade and Hamlin entirely discarded the doctrines of John Marshall, and embraced with ardor the views of Jefferson relating to the functions of the Court. "I deny the doctrine that Judges have any right to decide the law of the land for every department of this Government," protested Wade. "You would have the most concentrated, irresponsible despotism on God's earth, if you give such an interpretation to the decisions of that or any other Court." "This is a purely political question, in regard to which Thomas Jefferson so early and so ably warned us against judicial interference," said Hamlin. "They had no more authority to decide a political question for us than we had to decide a judicial question for them."

Nor were the Republican speeches entirely confined to invective. Many Senators openly proclaimed the intention of their party to strive for a complete reformation or reorganization of the Court. Though the early accomplishment of this event did not seem, in 1858, very probable, since it would require the control of Congress and the Presidency by the Republican Party, nevertheless, Seward proclaimed with great earnestness: "Whether the Court recedes or not, we shall reorganize the Court, and thus reform its political sentiments and practices, and bring them into harmony with the Constitution and the laws of nature. In doing so, we shall not only reassume our own just authority, but we shall restore that high tribunal itself to the position it ought to maintain, since so many invaluable rights of citizens, and even of States themselves, depend upon its impartiality and its wisdom." And Zachariah Chandler of Michigan, stating that the present organization of the Court was "monstrous", since three fourths of the business was in the North with four Judges, and one quarter in the South with five Judges, said that the Republican Party meant "to annul the Dred Scott decision, the stump speech of Taney, the mere fanfaronade which is not a decision at all", by an entire reorganization of the Court. To these Republican extravagances of utterance, James F. Simmons of Rhode Island made a sane reply, saying: "I do not think there needs to be any reconstruction of the Court. . . . These decisions are not like the laws of the Medes and Persians. The decision of this Court in the *Dartmouth College Case* was thought to settle a principle, which induced our banks to refuse to pay the tax imposed upon them by the State, and the prevailing opinion at the Bar in Rhode Island was that the banks would be sustained by the Court. The

State brought the question here, and the Court decided in favor of the power of the State to tax corporations. . . . No such decision of this Court will stand, unless it has sound reason and sound law to rest upon. This question was decided when the public mind was in a feverish state, and the Court may have unwittingly been affected by the excitement. . . . We must wait until it subsides, and trust that then the errors it has occasioned will be corrected." [1]

On the Democratic side, lengthy and heated arguments were delivered in defense of the Court by Jefferson Davis of Mississippi, Stephen A. Douglas of Illinois, James A. Stewart of Maryland, Joseph Lane of Oregon and Judah P. Benjamin of Louisiana: and the latter made a full, eloquent and powerful answer to Seward's charges of corrupt bargaining between the President and the Court. George E. Pugh of Ohio, while not agreeing with the decision, stated that whenever the Court has decided the question as to the limits of territorial authority over slavery, "whatever may be my opinion as an individual, both as a Senator and a citizen, the judgment of the Court must be carried into effect. We cannot live an hour under any other doctrine. It is more important to the community, more important to the cause of good government, that a judgment, once pronounced by the appropriate tribunal, should go into effect, than that it should be decided rightly — far more." [2]

No discussion of the *Dred Scott Case*, either in Congress or elsewhere, had so potent an influence with the people as that which took place during the famous

---

[1] Speeches of Seward, March 3, 1858; Chandler, Feb. 17, 1859; Simmons, March 20, 1858.

[2] See especially speeches in 1858, of Davis, Feb. 8, Douglas, Feb. 8, 21, Stewart, March 24, Benjamin, March 11; in 1859, of Douglas, Feb. 23, Pugh, Dec. 19, in 1860, of Douglas, Jan. 12, Pugh, Jan. 12, Lane, Feb. 15; see also speeches in the House of Cox, Dec. 8, 1859, Noell, Dec. 12, 1859, Jan. 20, 1860.

series of joint debates between Abraham Lincoln and Stephen A. Douglas, in their Senatorial campaign in Illinois in the summer of 1858. Two years before, Lincoln had publicly expressed himself as willing to leave to the Supreme Court, the constitutionality of the Acts of Congress dealing with slavery in the Territories, and to submit to its decision.[1] In 1858, however, he stated that he declined to abide by the decision when rendered; and his views had a powerful effect upon the country. It is important, nevertheless, to note that Lincoln's position has, in later days, been greatly misrepresented by opponents of the Court, who cite him as authority for denying the Court's right to pass upon an Act of Congress. Such a doctrine was never asserted by him, and his attitude was summed up at Springfield, June 26, as follows: "Judicial decisions have two uses: first, to absolutely determine the case decided, and secondly, to indicate to the public how other similar cases will be decided when they arise. For the latter use, they are called 'precedents' and 'authorities.' We believe as much as Judge Douglas (perhaps more) in obedience to, and respect for, the judicial department of government. We think its decisions on constitutional questions, when fully settled, should control not only the particular cases decided, but the general policy of the country, subject to be disturbed only by Amendments of the Constitution, as provided in that instrument itself. More than this would be revolution. But we think

[1] See Lincoln's speech at Galena, Ill., Aug. 1, 1856, when he said: "I grant you that an unconstitutional act is not law; but I do not ask and will not take your construction of the Constitution. The Supreme Court of the United States is the tribunal to decide such a question, and we will submit to its decisions; and if you do also, there will be an end of the matter. Will you? If not, who are the disunionists, — you, or we?" *Works of Abraham Lincoln* (Federal Ed., 1905), II; see *ibid.*, III, Lincoln's speeches at Springfield, Ill., June 17, 1858, and at Chicago, July 10, 1858.

the Dred Scott decision is erroneous. We know the Court that made it has often overruled its own decisions, and we shall do what we can to have it overrule this. We offer no resistance to it." This was precisely the language which would be appropriately used by a lawyer and a statesman who held the Courts and orderly legal procedure in due respect; but it in no way justified any attempt to disregard or disobey the decision of the Court. And again in his Inaugural Address in 1861, Lincoln pointed out that while a Court decision on a constitutional question did not control the political policy which the country would pursue, nevertheless, it must be held binding upon parties in any suit involving such questions. "I do not forget the position, assumed by some, that constitutional questions are to be decided by the Supreme Court," he said, "nor do I deny that such decisions must be binding in any case, upon the parties to a suit, as to the object of that suit, while they are also entitled to very high respect and consideration in all parallel cases by all other departments of the Government. And while it is obviously possible that such decision may be erroneous in any given case, still the evil effect following it, being limited to that particular case, with the chance that it may be overruled and never become a precedent for other cases, can better be borne than could the evils of a different practice. At the same time, the candid citizen must confess that if the policy of the Government, upon vital questions affecting the whole people, is to be irrevocably fixed by decisions of the Supreme Court, the instant they are made in ordinary litigation between parties in personal actions, the people will have ceased to be their own rulers, having to that extent practically resigned their Government into the hands of that eminent tribunal. Nor is there in this view any assault upon the Court or the Judges. It is a duty from which they may not shrink to decide cases properly brought before them, and it is no fault of theirs if others seek to turn their decisions to political purposes."

While the Republican press and Republican leaders in Congress were thus continuing to arouse the sentiment of the country against the Court, the Supreme Court of Wisconsin had put itself in a position of open rebellion towards it. As has been already described, after the conviction of Booth in the United States District Court the Wisconsin Supreme Court ordered his release on habeas corpus, on the ground that the Fugitive Slave Law under which he had been convicted was unconstitutional.[1] A writ of error had been issued by the United States Supreme Court on motion of Attorney-General Caleb Cushing, returnable in December, 1855; but though this writ was duly served on its Clerk, the State Supreme Court directed him to make no return and to enter no order concerning the same on his journals or records. The Clerk, however, had already given a certified copy of the record to the United States District Attorney in March, 1855, before receiving any direction from the State Court. Accordingly, Attorney-General Cushing moved in the United States Supreme Court in May, 1856, to be allowed to file this copy. Before granting the motion

[1] One reason for the readiness of the State Courts to issue writs of habeas corpus for prisoners convicted in the inferior Federal Courts was the absence of any right of appeal to the Supreme Court of the United States for any person so convicted. At that period, no Federal statute provided any appeal in a criminal case. Repeated attempts to enact such a law failed in Congress. In August, and again in December, 1855, Senator Pugh, of Ohio, introduced a bill for writs of error in all such cases prosecuted by indictment in the Federal Courts, but Congress took no action. In January, 1859, a bill having been reported by the Committee on the Judiciary, a motion by Senator Bayard of Delaware to take it up was defeated. *35th Cong., 2d Sess.*, Jan. 13, 1859. In February, 1860, Pugh again introduced the bill. *36th Cong., 1st Sess.*, Feb. 18, 1860.

the Court decided to issue a special order to the State Court Clerk to make return, but the latter still refusing to comply, and there being thus a complete deadlock, the Court, on March 6, 1857 (the very day of its opinion in the *Dred Scott Case*), allowed the motion of the Attorney-General to file copy of the record, "to have the same effect and legal operation, as if filed by the Clerk with the writ of error." The case was not reached for final argument, until January 19, 1859. Meanwhile, however, a renewed effort was made in the abolitionist press and in Congress to weaken the authority of the Court, by a move to repeal the Twenty-Fifth Section of the Judiciary Act and to abolish the Court's jurisdiction on writs of error to State Courts; and bills for this purpose (originating in Ohio) were introduced in both the Senate and the House, in the spring of 1858.[1] While these measures failed of enactment by Congress, their introduction now by Northern statesmen marked a radical reversal in attitude towards the Court; for when similar repeals had been advocated in the past, in 1825–1826 and 1830–1833, their supporters were found almost entirely in the ranks of the Southern Democrats. "Twenty years ago, South Carolina denied the paramount authority of the Supreme Court of the United States and flew to arms to resist it," said the *New York Times*, "while Mas-

---

[1] *35th Cong., 1st Sess.;* see bill introduced by Senator George E. Pugh of Ohio, April 30, 1858, reported adversely by the Committee of the Judiciary, May 24, Dec. 16, 1858; Philemon Bliss of Ohio introduced a similar bill in the House. The only other Congressional attacks upon the constitution of the Court, which had taken place, in the twenty-seven years since the serious attack in 1831, were as follows: Senator Benjamin Tappan of Ohio had three times (1840, 1842, 1844) introduced a bill proposing a Constitutional Amendment to limit the term of office of Judges of the Supreme Court and of inferior Federal Courts; and in 1843, though defeated by a vote of eleven to twenty-four, such prominent Senators as James Buchanan, Thomas H. Benton and Levi Woodbury had voted for it; a similar bill had been introduced, in 1847, by Senator Sidney Breese of Illinois; see *26th Cong., 2d Sess.,* July 8, 9, Dec. 15, 1840; *27th Cong., 3d Sess.,* Dec. 12, 1842, Jan. 16, 1843; *28th Cong., 1st Sess.,* Feb. 20, 1844; *29th Cong., 2d Sess.,* Feb. 17, 1847.

sachusetts took the lead in asserting the absolute, un-qualified duty of every citizen and every State to yield implicit obedience to its decisions upon all questions of constitutional law. Today, the position of these two States and of the sections which they represent is likely to be reversed, . . . and this change of position illustrates the fact, to which it is due, that interest and not reason rules over and regulates the action of States, as well as of individuals." [1]   History had made plain that the North and South were equally willing to resort to an attack upon the jurisdiction of the Court, and that theories or principles of State-Rights or National Supremacy were adopted, or discarded, by the one or the other, according to the particular interests which were likely to be involved in the instant case. The change was well illustrated by a savage editorial in the *New York Tribune* at this time, in 1858, which said that it repudiated utterly "the abominable notion that a handful of political subalterns of the Federal Executive, his creatures and tools, appointed on partisan grounds and for political reasons, are to be permitted to sit in judgment on the political rights of great States, where those rights come in conflict with the exercise of that same Federal authority. If the Supreme Court behaves well enough to warrant a general confidence in it as a safe depository of private rights, so be it. But a safe depository of the political rights of the States, it never can be. . . . We rejoice in the hope that the doctrine of State Rights is at last to be reared above the mists of Virginia abstractionism and planted upon clear, solid ground. The theories of ancient Federalism in regard to the rights and powers of the States, though the offspring of wise heads and honest hearts, must give

[1] *New York Times*, March 9, 1857; *New York Tribune*, Feb. 18, 1858.

way before the advancing footsteps of a radical and clear-sighted democratic sentiment." And the bitterness of feeling towards the Court was expressed in the speech of Philemon Bliss, an ardent abolitionist Republican Congressman from Ohio : [1]

The spectacle of a gowned conclave, gravely setting aside statutes and Constitutions of States; enforcing powers not granted in the compact, and against the express reservations of the States; with eager zeal reversing the whole current of authority and law, to make universal a local and exceptional despotism; prompting its ministers to mayhem and murder, sure of their illegal shield, never darkened our fathers' vision. Had a tithe of what we stupidly suffer been anticipated by them, the Federation would have been an impossibility; at least the Court would have been but a Hamilton's dream of a life Executive and Senate. . . . There never was a more serious mistake. . . . In reading over the 25th Section of the Judiciary Act of 1789, I have often wondered at the tameness of the States, thus at once made vassals. . . . When from yon mysterious vault, the enrobed nine send forth their tomes, befogging by their diffuseness, even when announcing the plainest principles . . . when essaying some new constitutional construction, as they call their attacks upon the rights of the States and their citizens, we are taught to bow without question, as the faithful to the decrees of the Grand Lama.

And Bliss further said, in advocating, not only the repeal of the Twenty-Fifth Section of the Judiciary Act, but also the repeal of Section seven of the Act of March 2, 1833, a bill which had been passed at the instance of President Jackson to aid in the suppression of the Nullification movement in South Carolina and which authorized Federal Courts to grant writs of habeas corpus where a prisoner was confined for acts

[1] *35th Cong., 2d Sess., App.*, 72, Feb. 7, 1859. Bliss later became a Federal Judge, himself; he was appointed Chief Justice of Dakota by President Lincoln in 1861, and served on the Supreme Court of Missouri from 1868 to 1873; he became Dean of the Law Department of the State University of Missouri in 1873.

done or omitted in pursuance of the laws of the United States: "It is a clear usurpation of Federal authority. The States have a right to execute their criminal laws. . . . The people are becoming roused to the true nature and alarming encroachments of the Federation. They look upon the Judiciary as the right arm of these encroachments. They will never yield their liberty; and if these things continue without remedy, the Federal Courts must fall. I would save them by timely remedy." When there was thus presented in Congress the curious spectacle of a Northern Republican advocating the repeal of a measure enacted for the destruction of Nullification and the preservation of the Union, it is no wonder that conservative leading newspapers of the North should have earnestly deprecated speeches of such a nature and should have termed the attempt to impair the Federal Judiciary — "the great bulwark of our safety" — as a "revolutionary step towards subverting the great principles of our Government." [1]

It was in this atmosphere of distrust and antagonism throughout the North, that on January 19, 1859, the Court listened to the argument of the *Booth Cases* by the Attorney-General of the United States, Jeremiah S. Black, no counsel appearing for the State of Wisconsin.[2] On March 7, almost exactly two years from the date of the Dred Scott decision, the judgment of the Court was pronounced by Chief Justice Taney in the most powerful of all his notable opinions. Undeterred by the opposition to its jurisdiction, or by the effect which its decision might have upon the slavery

[1] *National Intelligencer*, Dec. 10, 1858, quoting the *New York Journal of Commerce.*
[2] *Ableman* v. *Booth, United States* v. *Booth,* 21 How. 506. The case of *Ableman* v. *Booth* on which the Wisconsin Supreme Court had made a return to the writ of error had been docketed in the Supreme Court of the United States in due form in 1855, but had been postponed for argument to await the filing of the other case, *In re Booth,* on which the State Court had refused to make return to the writ of error.

issue, the Court remained adamant in upholding the National Government against all efforts at interference with its lawful functions. The rights asserted by the State Court to annul the proceedings of the United States Commissioner, said Taney, and to annul the judgment of a United States District Court, and also to determine that their decision is final and conclusive upon the United States Courts so as to authorize a Clerk to disregard and refuse obedience to a writ of error issued pursuant to the Federal Judiciary Act, were "new in the jurisprudence of the United States as well as of the States, and the supremacy of the State Courts over the Courts of the United States, in cases arising under the Constitution and laws of the United States, is now for the first time asserted and acted upon in the Supreme Court of a State." The Chief Justice then continued with a most vigorous exposition of the supremacy of the Federal jurisdiction in cases contemplated by the Judiciary Act and by the Constitution. The judgment of the State Court, he said, "would subvert the very foundations of this Government. . . . No one will suppose that a Government which has now lasted nearly seventy years, enforcing its laws by its own tribunals, and preserving the Union of the States, could have lasted a single year, or fulfilled the high trusts committed to it, if offenses against its laws could not have been punished without the consent of the State in which the culprit was found." Unless the National Government was supreme in its own sphere, it was evident that it would be "inadequate to the main objects for which the Government was established; and that local interests, local passions or prejudices, incited and fostered by individuals for sinister purposes, would lead to acts of aggression and injustice by one State upon the rights of another, which would ultimately terminate in violence and force, unless there was a common arbiter between them, armed with power enough to protect and guard the rights of all, by appropriate laws, to be carried into execution peacefully by its judicial tribunals." Supremacy must be associated with "permanent judicial authority"; and serious controversies might arise between the authorities of the United States and of the States "which must be settled by force of arms, unless some tribunal was created to decide between them, finally and without appeal. The Constitution accordingly provided, as far as human foresight could provide, against this danger," by conferring upon the Federal Courts the supreme power and jurisdiction. "So long, therefore, as this Constitution shall endure," said Taney, "this tribunal must exist with it, deciding in the peaceful forms of judicial proceedings the angry and irritating controversies between sovereignties, which in other countries have been determined by the arbitrament of force." And he added: "Nor can it be inconsistent with the dignity of a sovereign State, to observe faithfully, and in the spirit of sincerity and truth, the compact into which it voluntarily entered when it became a State of this Union. On the contrary, the highest honor of sovereignty is untarnished faith." With these ringing words in defense of the National supremacy, the Chief Justice concluded the opinion of the Court and announced the reversal of the judgments of the State Courts — an opinion which Marshall himself never excelled in loftiness of tone.

"He has lived long and done much for honor and fame. But here is the summit. He will never surpass the wisdom and value of his recent opinion," was the comment of a Washington newspaper.[1] "It

[1] *The States*, March 11, 1859.

must put an end, for the future, to all contests between the United States and States as to the constitutionality of the Fugitive Slave Law; and all attempts hereafter by State Courts to interfere with officers of the United States in carrying it out will be regarded as revolutionary, and treated as such," said a Democratic paper in New York. "We trust that it will be read with careful, and in the case of men willing to violate the law, with prayerful attention, for the sound law and truthful doctrines it teaches," said an Ohio Democratic paper, which also stated that the Court had well termed Wisconsin's action as "totally illegal and virtually revolutionary." [1] A leading Republican paper in Philadelphia said that: "The conduct of the Wisconsin Court was such as to preclude any other decree. They refused to allow the record to be sent up, thus setting at defiance the established usage, and exhibiting a purpose to disregard the authority of the tribunal of last resort. This is one of the legitimate consequences of the extreme theory of popular sovereignty which will go on augmenting its demands, until judicial decrees, like party platforms, must be subjected to the revision of caucuses, conventions and mobs. Then the reaction will begin and we shall run to the other extreme."

On the other hand, the more extreme Republican press denounced the decision as destined to be quite as notorious as the *Dred Scott Case*, and as "forming a part of the same system of usurpation, tending to the concentration of all power in the Federal Judiciary"; [2] and the *New York Evening Post*, after commending and indorsing the alleged views of Thomas Jefferson and

[1] See *New York Herald*, March 8, 1859; *National Intelligencer*, March 20, 1859; *Cleveland National Democrat*, May 2, March 17, April 25, 1859; *Philadelphia North American*, March 10, 1859.

[2] *New York Tribune*, March 6, April 1, 1859; *New York Evening Post*, March 21, 1859.

of John C. Calhoun, as to the danger of encroachment by the Federal Courts on the States, said that: "Nothing more fatal to the reserved rights of the States, nothing more dangerous to the securities of the individual, can well be conceived, than the authority claimed for it in the recent decision of Judge Taney. . . . The process of the Supreme Court is supreme and final; and no State law or decision of a State Court which interferes with the execution of the Fugitive Slave Act has any constitutional force. Now, so far as this decision is intended to give strength to the Fugitive Slave Act, it is not of much importance; for that Act is very much of a dead letter upon the statute book, the moral sense of the community refusing to execute it in the greater number of cases; but, so far as it asserts a principle, it is an alarming assumption of power. It places the liberty of the citizen, it seems to us, wholly at the disposal of the Federal tribunals, and supersedes every protection which he might claim from the Courts of his own State. . . . No matter whether the Legislature of his State, or the Courts of his State, shall have pronounced the law under which he is arrested, constitutional or not, he is shorn of all guaranties of security, and must bow in silence to the mandate of the Federal officer. The Fugitive Slave Act itself was an enormous stretch of Federal power, and an abrogation, so far as it was itself concerned, of the right of trial by jury; and now we see it compelling another overturn of ancient landmarks, in the virtual denial of one of the oldest and most sacred muniments of jurisprudence." Other Republican papers similarly raised the standard of revolt, and expressed the hope that Wisconsin would not yield obedience to the Court's mandate.

The Wisconsin Legislature almost at once adopted

defiant resolutions declaring the "assumption of jurisdiction by the Federal Judiciary" to be "an act of undelegated power, and therefore without authority void and of no force," "an arbitrary act of power, unauthorized by the Constitution, and virtually superseding the benefit of the writ of habeas corpus and prostrating the rights and liberties of the people at the foot of unlimited power" and further declaring that the principle contended for, that "the General Government is the exclusive judge of the extent of the powers delegated to it, stops nothing short of despotism", and that the several States which formed the Constitution, "being sovereign and independent have the unquestionable right to judge of its infraction; and that a positive defiance of those sovereignties, of all unauthorized acts done or attempted to be done under color of that instrument, is the rightful remedy." [1] The views thus announced were simply a reiteration of the notorious Virginia and Kentucky Resolutions of 1798–1799 and of South Carolina's Nullification doctrine of 1833; and they were so treated in a stirring editorial criticism appearing in the *National Intelligencer:* "So far as this declaration of the Wisconsin Legislature affirms that the mandate of the Supreme Court . . . is 'void and of no force', it was doubtless meant to be nothing more than *brutum fulmen*, as we do not permit ourselves to suppose that the Legislature seriously purpose to raise any practical issue which shall have for its effect to try conclusions with the judicial power of the Federal Government, as exercised through the only tribunal known to the Constitution. . . . As to the second declaration, which under some confusion of diction, purports to deny the right of the Supreme Court to act as the final and ex-

[1] See especially *State Documents on Federal Relations* (1911), by Herman V. Ames.

clusive judge of the meaning and extent of the powers
granted by the Constitution, we need not say that it
is but a rehash of the Resolutions of '98 and '99, which,
after having served their day in Virginia, are found
reappearing in other quarters. . . .   By dint of long
and hard usage, they have come to be somewhat the
worse for wear, and therefore furnish but an indiffer-
ent disguise by which to hide the deformity of Nullification." [1]   The *New York Times* regarded the situation as serious in its possibilities, "since questions
of jurisdiction between the Supreme Court and State
tribunals are in their nature among the most dangerous which are likely to arise in the practical working
of our Government."   While it apprehended no actual forcible conflict in Wisconsin, yet, it said, "similar disputes have heretofore been the most disturbing forces our political machinery has been subject
to, and what has already occurred may happen again.
The remedy must be looked for in mutual forbearance on the part of the General Government from the
exercise of odious and doubtful powers, and on that of the
several States, by acquiescence, where no serious injury
can result."   In spite of conservative advice of this
nature which prevailed generally outside of abolitionist circles, the Supreme Court of Wisconsin refused to
comply with the mandate of the Supreme Court of the
United States.   On September 22, 1859 — six months
after Taney's decision — a motion was made and argued by the United States District Attorney to file
with the State Court Clerk the two mandates from the
Supreme Court.   This motion was not granted, since
Chief Justice Luther S. Dixon and Judge Orsanus Cole
differed in opinion, and the third Judge, Byron Paine,

[1] *National Intelligencer*, April 1, 1859, editorial "The Resolutions of '98 bearing
Fresh Fruit "; *New York Times*, April 11, 1859.

declined to act, having previously been counsel for Booth and elected a Judge for that reason.[1] The Federal Courts were not so easily to be prevented from asserting and enforcing their authority. Booth was again arrested by the United States marshal in March, 1860, and again sued out a writ of habeas corpus in the State Supreme Court. "This case brings the question of State-Rights to an issue," wrote young Carl Schurz, who had been retained as counsel. "We shall now have the final decision of the great contest between the State of Wisconsin and the United States District Court. It is really dreadful that that rascal Booth is involved in this case, and that the great cause has to bear the burden of his sins. But the principles that must be maintained are of so lofty a nature that all other considerations vanish."[2] The State Court was unable to take any action, as Judge Paine felt himself disqualified to sit, and the other two Judges differed in their opinion. Only with the opening of the Civil War was the deadlock broken.[3] But as Schurz wrote later: "The Republican party went to the very verge of Nullification, while the Democratic party . . . became an ardent defender of the Federal power. . . . Thus in the North, as well as in the South, men's sym-

[1] *In re Booth*, 11 Wisc. 498 In *Von Baumbach* v. *Bade* (1859), 9 Wisc. 559, a case in no wise connected with the slavery issue, and involving a State mortgage law, which the Court unanimously held constitutional, Judge Paine in concurring again felt it necessary to set forth his view that the State Court was not bound by decisions of the United States Supreme Court.

[2] *Speeches, Correspondence and Political Papers of Carl Schurz* (ed. by Frederic Bancroft, 1913), II, letter of March 2, 1860.

[3] The final decision in this Booth episode was rendered after the opening of the War, when in June, 1861, the Wisconsin Supreme Court held that the United States District Court had legal jurisdiction of a suit brought against Booth, by the Missouri owner of the slave rescued by Booth, to recover a penalty for such rescue, as authorized by the Fugitive Slave Law, and that a judgment for $1246 levied on Booth's printing press by the United States marshal, Feb. 24, 1857, was a valid judgment, which would not be collaterally attacked in the State Court, on the ground that the Fugitive Slave Law was unconstitutional. *Arnold* v. *Booth* (1861), 14 Wisc. 180.

pathies with regard to slavery shaped and changed their political doctrines and their constitutional theories. In the South, it was State-Rights or the supremacy of the Federal power, as the one or the other furthered the interests of slavery; in the North, it was State-Rights or the supremacy of the Federal power, as one or the other furthered the interests of freedom." [1]

Meanwhile, a similar disregard of the Court's decision was shown in the State of Ohio, where for many years conflicts of jurisdiction between the State and Federal Courts had taken place in the case of fugitive slaves. In the spring of 1859, just after the decision of the *Booth Case*, trials were held in the Federal District Court for the Northern District of Ohio, of the famous *Oberlin Rescue Cases* — indictments for violation of the Fugitive Slave Law. After conviction and sentence of the defendants, the Supreme Court of Ohio, in deliberate defiance of the decision in the *Booth Case*, issued writs of habeas corpus for the defendants then in custody of the United States marshal, and the State Court proceeded to assume the power to decide for itself the constitutionality of the Federal Law involved. Fortunately, its decision was rendered in favor of sustaining the validity of the Law; and thus a direct conflict between the Federal and State authorities was avoided.[2] The opinion, coura-

[1] *Reminiscences of Carl Schurz* (1907), II, 105–115. Schurz wrote that when he published his speeches in 1865, he omitted his speeches in the Wisconsin campaign in 1859, "because a more mature judgment had convinced me that, not indeed the fundamental theory of democracy, but the conclusions drawn from it as to the functions and necessary power of Government, were unsound."

[2] As to these *Oberlin Rescue Cases* — *United States* v. *Simeon Bushnell, United States* v. *Langston* and *Ex parte Bushnell*, 9 Ohio State, 77–325 — see *History of Ohio* (1912), by Emilius O. Randall and Daniel J. Ryan, IV, and see interesting accounts and editorials in *Cleveland National Democrat*, March 17, April 8, 13, 15, 16, 25, 26, 28, 29, 30, May 11, 19, 31, June 6, 10, 1859; *Ohio Statesman*, April 19, 23, 24, 27, 28, 29, May 3, 4, 28, 29, 31, 1859. It may be noted that because of his decision in this case, the very able Chief Justice, Swan, was refused renomination to

geously given by a Republican Chief Justice, resulted,
however, in his defeat for renomination, a few weeks
later, at the instance of Chase, Wade and Giddings,
the abolitionist leaders. The seriousness of the situation was reflected by the statement, commonly made
at the time, that had the Court decided otherwise,
Governor Chase stood ready to use the State troops in
defense of its jurisdiction against the Federal authorities; and, as a Democratic paper said: "A conflict
would have been the consequence, and thus would
civil war have for a time existed; for they may rest
assured that, under no circumstances, would they have
been permitted to carry out their mad, treasonable
design of nullifying the laws of the United States, and
substituting anarchy and misrule in the place of law and
the Constitution." A Republican paper stated, however,
that the law would be obeyed, but only until such time
as the Federal Supreme Court should be reformed.[1]

In Congress, the decision of the *Booth Case* brought
forth denunciations of the Court, nearly as strong as
those which, in 1858, followed the *Dred Scott Case;*
and many speeches were made in defense of the legislation of the various States, known as the Personal
Liberty Laws, enacted for the purpose of nullifying the
enforcement of the Fugitive Slave Law.[2] In a debate
on the subject, Senator Hale stated that for thirty
years the Court had consisted only of politicians, that

the Bench by the Republican Party at its next spring convention — an interesting
example of the evils of a judicial recall system.

[1] *Cleveland National Democrat,* May 31, 1859, and also quoting *Dayton Republican Gazette.* In *ibid.,* May 28, 1859, it was said editorially: "The *Ohio State Journal* thinks that we regard the State of Ohio 'not as a sovereign State but as a mere
Province of the Federal Government.' . . . But as a member of the Federal
Union, the State of Ohio is bound to respect that law. . . . It does not become
the Executive of the State to encourage resistance, nor the Court to meditate its
nullification."

[2] The so-called Personal Liberty Laws had been passed in Maine, New Hampshire, Vermont, Massachusetts, Rhode Island, Connecticut, Michigan, Wisconsin, Iowa and Ohio.

it was now a dangerous department of the Government, that "its history has verified all, and more than all, that Jefferson ever prophesied of it", that its opinion upon political questions should have no weight. "If its encroachments will not be met by Congress they must be met, as Jefferson said, by the action of the State Governments."[1] After praising the past action of Virginia and Georgia in disobeying the mandates of the Court, and after indorsing the alleged views of Jefferson, Jackson and Buchanan as to freedom of Congress from control by the Court's decisions, Hale derided the "new doctrine of the infallibility of the Court now entertained by the Democratic party", which, he said, "after fighting a life-long battle against the Court, had now become great sticklers for the dignity and binding authority of the Court." Senator Doolittle of Wisconsin also indorsed the rebellious actions of Pennsylvania, Virginia and Georgia in the past, and rejoiced that the Supreme Court of Wisconsin had followed their example. While acknowledging the "distinguished ability, industry almost unequalled, honesty of purpose and pure and upright personal character" of Taney, he stated that the tendency of the Chief Justice and of his Court was to absolutism, by the consolidation of all power in that branch of the Government, and that the questions, whether that Court was to be the sole ultimate judge as to the powers delegated by the Constitution to the Federal Government or reserved to the States, and whether upon all constitutional questions the Supreme Courts of the States are inferior and subordinate to the Federal Courts, had always been the battleground of the political contests in this coun-

---

[1] *36th Cong., 1st Sess.* and *App.;* speeches in 1860 of Hale, Feb. 14, Doolittle, Feb. 24, Collamer, March 8, Grimes, Feb. 24, Wade, March 7, Conkling, April 16, 17; see also speeches of Bingham, April 24, in the Senate and of T. B. Florence of April 12, in the House.

try. He admitted that the Republicans hitherto had espoused, and the Democrats opposed, the "Federal doctrine of judicial supremacy"; but now, he asked: "For what purpose have the Democrats set up this judicial Vatican? Why should the leaders of this party interpolate into its creed, this new dogma of the supreme, infallible, and irrevocable doctrine of the Supreme Court?" And he uttered the prediction, that if the power of the Court to decide on the validity of laws for all other departments should be continued, "the days of the empire will commence soon after." Senator Collamer of Vermont said he would not bow down to the Court "as to the inscrutable dispensation of Divine Providence." In the House, Roscoe Conkling, a Republican Congressman from New York (who only twelve years later was offered appointment as Chief Justice), delivered a violent assault on the Court and its "imperial assumptions", stating that "wherever a decision, in the judgment of Congress, is subversive of the rights and liberties of the people, or is otherwise hurtfully erroneous, it is not only the right, but the solemn duty, of Congress to disregard it";[1] and he also cited Jefferson and Jackson as his

[1] Conkling's speech was directed at the statement by President Buchanan in his Third Annual Message to Congress, Dec. 19, 1859, as follows:

"I cordially congratulate you upon the final settlement by the Supreme Court of the United States of the question of slavery in the Territories which had presented an aspect so truly formidable at the commencement of my administration. The right has been established of every citizen to take his property of any kind including slaves into the common Territory belonging equally to all the States of the Confederacy and to have it protected there under the Federal Constitution. Neither Congress nor a Territorial legislature nor any human power has any authority to annul or impair this vested right. The Supreme Judicial tribunal of the country which is a coördinate branch of the Government has sanctioned and affirmed these principles of constitutional law so manifestly just in themselves and so well calculated to promote peace and harmony among the States."

Buchanan, as late as his Fourth Annual Message, Dec. 3, 1860, continued to maintain the correctness and supremacy as law of the Dred Scott decision, saying that "such has been the factious temper of the times", that it has been "extensively impugned before the people and the question has given rise to angry political conflicts throughout the country."

authorities. He advocated "a reorganization and reinvigoration of the Court, with just regard to commercial and political considerations. . . . It is high time that appropriate weight shall be given in the Court and elsewhere to all portions of the country, not excepting those in which a vast preponderance of its wealth, its business and its numbers reside."

Speeches of this nature were commended by radical anti-slavery papers like the *Independent*, which spoke of the "encroachments" of the Judiciary "at the will and instigation of the Slave Oligarchy. . . . The Supreme Court, in the defense of slavery, has become the great teacher of injustice and iniquity, the sapper and miner of our liberties, the great agent of the powers of darkness in debauching the conscience of the country and thus preparing the people to become the victims of the slave despotism." [1]

On the other hand, eloquent defenses of the Court were made in Congress. "We have hitherto debated," said Senator Robert Toombs, of Georgia, "the supremacy of the Federal Courts over the State Courts; but Wisconsin has asserted the supremacy of the State Courts over the Federal Courts. Nobody ever claimed, until Wisconsin, that a State Court, high or low, could seize a case in the Federal Courts and review it. . . . Wisconsin has outstripped all of her delinquent sisters in their disgraceful race of infidelity to the compact." John W. Noell of Missouri, in the House, made a particularly able speech, denouncing those Republicans who, like Conkling, "had raised on the floor of Congress the standard of rebellion to the

---

[1] *Independent*, March 1, 8, 1860; *36th Cong., 1st Sess.*, and *App.*, speeches of Toombs, Jan. 24, Feb. 27, March 7, 1860, speeches of Noell, April 25, Reagan of Texas, Jan. 4, Larrabee of Wisconsin, Jan. 4, 1860.

decrees of the Court. Though that Department still preserves its ancient purity and firmness, it has not kept pace with their progressive fanaticism. Its authority to decide questions of constitutional law is now gravely disputed. . . . These modern Solons have discovered a great distinction between questions which they call political and those which are not political. Every question, while it is pending here is a political question, and every question, when it is transferred to the Judiciary is a judicial question. No law passed by Congress affecting the rights of persons or the rights of property but must be decided upon and enforced by the Judiciary. . . . No man contends that a judgment or opinion of the Federal Judiciary can tie the hands of Congress; but every man who has read the hornbooks of the profession ought to know that, when we enact a law, its validity and constitutionality must be determined by the Judiciary. That determination in this particular instance can only be avoided by rebellion or revolution."

These years of turmoil in politics and of conflict over the Court's decisions affecting the slavery issue, extending from 1854 to 1860, were productive of few other cases of supreme importance in American legal history; and they may be briefly summarized.

With the year 1855, there came to an end the long series of cases in which, for twenty-five years, the Court had been confirming vast numbers of imperfect grants made by Spanish officials in Florida, Louisiana and Missouri prior to the cessions of those territories; and though many of these claims had been of an extremely suspicious character, the Court, in its scrupulous observance of the spirit of the treaties with France and Spain, had preferred to err on the side of justice to the claimant, rather than to give the benefit of the doubt to the Government.[1] But with the disappearance of these cases from its docket, there arose the first of another series which lasted for a further quarter of a century; and in *Cervantes* v. *United States*, 16 How. 619, and *Fremont* v. *United States*, 17 How. 442, general doctrines of law were outlined, on which the Court was to decide the many great Mexican land claims arising in California, Texas and the Southwest territories. In these cases, the Court again showed its anxiety to protect, to the utmost, rights originating under grants from the foreign government with which the United States had concluded a treaty.[2]

On February 19, 1856, in *Murray* v. *Hoboken Land and Improvement Co.*, 18 How. 272, the Court, for the first time since 1819, interpreted the meaning of "due process of law" as contained in the Fifth Amendment.[3] The case, argued with great ability by Benjamin F.

[1] A few claims for very large tracts, where no sufficient identification had taken place before cession, were rejected; see *United States* v. *Kingsley*, 12 Pet. 476, five miles square; *United States* v. *Delespine*, 15 Pet. 319, 92, 160 acres; *United States* v. *Miranda*, 16 Pet. 153, 368,640 acres; *United States* v. *Boisdoré*, 11 How. 63, a tract of 15 by 40 miles; *Doe* v. *Braden*, 16 How. 635, 12,000,000 acres.

[2] The case of the claim of John C. Fremont "of unusual public interest" was argued Feb. 20, 21, 22, 1855, and was described by the *National Intelligencer*, Feb. 26, as follows: "The venerable and learned Mr. Chancellor (George M.) Bibb followed Mr. Jones on the same side in a clear, comprehensive and argumentative address, crowding the merits of the case into the brief space of half an hour. Attorney-General Cushing followed on behalf of the United States, and charmed a large and brilliant audience, during two hours on Wednesday morning, by a discourse of unusual interest and strength, a good portion of it historical, and having the attractiveness of romance, and all of it such as to engross the attention of the Court, the Bar and all hearers. The Attorney-General was replied to, and the argument of the cause concluded, by Hon. John J. Crittenden. Mr. Crittenden brought into the argument, not only legal acumen and research, but all the impassioned eloquence that has distinguished his most powerful efforts, whether in the Senate or before judicial forums, and was listened to with marked attention by a crowded audience of the beauty and intellect at present congregated in the city. ... We presume from all we have heard that the eloquent Kentuckian equalled, if he did not surpass, any previous effort, forensic or Senatorial; he certainly never produced a higher admiration of his powers, or ever received more emphatic applause, from the grave members of the Bench, we believe, as well as the Bar and crowded auditory." See also *ibid.*, March 11, 1855; *Philadelphia North American*, Feb. 21, 1855.

[3] See Johnson, J., in *Bank of Columbia* v. *Okely* (1819), 4 Wheat. 235.

Butler, George Wood and Edgar S. Van Winkle against Ransom H. Gillet, Joseph P. Bradley and A. O. Zabriskie, involved the rights of a purchaser of land sold under a distress warrant issued by the Solicitor of the Treasury against lands of Samuel Swartwout — a former notorious collector of customs at New York, who had defaulted in the sum of $1,479,000. The Court held that such a summary method for the recovery of debts due to the Government from defaulting receivers of the revenue constituted due process, even though no Court trial was provided, inasmuch as such methods were known to the old English law.

At the December Term of 1857, in *Jackson* v. *Steamboat Magnolia*, 20 How. 296, the Court completed the reversal of the former narrow doctrines as to the extent of admiralty jurisdiction entertained by Marshall. The question involved was whether the Federal Court had jurisdiction over a libel for a collision on the Alabama River above tidal flow and wholly within the State of Alabama. The case was twice argued; and the decision upheld the Federal admiralty powers in the most sweeping manner. It is a "remarkable" and "startling assumption of power", said Judge Daniel, again dissenting and fearful of the Court's "indefinite and indefinable pretensions" and the "ceaseless march of central encroachments." In spite of such fears on the part of its dissenting Judge, the Court showed itself zealous to defend the State sovereignty in *Taylor* v. *Carryl*, 20 How. 583, by holding that a vessel attached in a State Court could not be sold by a United States marshal on an order from the United States District Court in a libel for seamen's wages. The case, said Judge Campbell, had been regarded in this Court as one of importance, but it did not present a new question and "is not determinable upon any novel prin-

ciple. . . . It forms a recognized portion of the duty
of this Court to give preference to such principles and
methods of procedure as shall serve to conciliate the distinct and independent tribunals of the States and of the
Union, so that they may coöperate as harmonious members of a judicial system coextensive with the United
States, and submitting to the paramount authority
of the same Constitution, laws and federal obligation.
The decisions of this Court that disclose such an aim,
and that embody the principles and modes of administration to accomplish it, have gone from the Court
with authority, and have returned to it, bringing the
vigor and strength that are always imparted to magistrates, of whatever class, by the approbation and confidence of those submitted to their government." [1]
It is interesting to note that this strong defense of the
State tribunals was uttered on May 18, 1858, and less
than a year before the Court's equally strong defense
of National supremacy in the *Booth Case.*

At the December Term of 1858, important questions
of business law came before the Court. In *Covington
Drawbridge Co.* v. *Shepherd,* 21 How. 112, argued by
Oliver H. Smith against Richard W. Thompson, the
question of the power of a Court in equity to appoint
a receiver for a corporation to collect tolls and hold
them for creditors, was presented for the first time;
and though now so familiar a practice, it was then said
to be a "question of great importance and some difficulty." The Court, however, sustained the power.
The first of a tremendously long line of cases involving
the validity of municipal bonds when held by a bona
fide purchaser was decided in *Commissioners of Knox
County* v. *Aspinwall,* 21 How. 539; and two years

---

[1] The case was twice argued at this Term, first on Dec. 14, 1857, and again on
April 12, 13, 14, 1858, by William M. Evarts against John Cadwalader and Samuel
Hood.

later in this case (24 How. 376), it was held that such bondholders might obtain a mandamus from the Circuit Court to compel an Indiana municipality to levy a tax to satisfy a judgment rendered in a suit on the bonds. This was the first case in the Supreme Court in which a mandamus was issued against a State official.[1] Railroad bonds were also for the first time decided to be negotiable instruments, in *White* v. *Vermont and Massachusetts R. R. Co.*, 21 How. 575, Judge Nelson saying that "within the last few years, large masses of them have gone into general circulation and in which capitalists have invested their money"; and if the quality of negotiability were not conceded to them, the value of such securities "as a means of furnishing the funds for the accomplishment of many of the greatest and most useful enterprises of the day would be impaired."

The December Term of 1859 was a long one, the Court adjourning on May 4, 1860. The Chief Justice and Judge Daniel were both too ill to sit on the Bench, and considerable fear was expressed lest the former might never return. Talk was rife as to the possibility of the appointment by President Buchanan of either the Attorney-General, Jeremiah S. Black, or the former Attorney-General, Caleb Cushing, as Taney's successor;[2] and the weakened condition of the Court gave rise to renewed demand for a relief of the Judges from Circuit duty, so that they might devote more time to clearing the overloaded docket in the Supreme Court. "This reorganization is not a

[1] See also *Aspinwall* v. *Daveiss Co.*, 22 How. 364; *Bissell* v. *Jeffersonville*, 24 How. 287; *Amey* v. *Allegheny City*, 24 How. 364; *Jurisdiction in Mandamus in United States Courts*, by Glendower Evans, *Amer. Law Rev.* (1885), XIX.

[2] *New York Tribune*, Feb. 14, April 27, 1860; *New York Evening Post*, Dec. 14, 1860, said that Taney's resignation was unlikely: "He, like Mr. Buchanan, takes a sort of melancholy satisfaction in being the last incumbent of the office he holds."

boon to the Judges, but a benefit to the public," required by the demand for justice for litigants.[1] At
this Term, the suits involving California land claims
continued to occupy a large proportion of the Court's
time,[2] and few cases of historical importance were decided. Two may be noted, however. In *Sinnot* v.
Davenport, 22 How. 227, an Alabama shipping law was
held to be in conflict with legislation by Congress as
to coasting trade, and therefore unconstitutional;
and again the supremacy of the National Government
was powerfully set forth by the Court. To the argument that the State statute was merely an exercise
of the State police power, Judge Nelson answered that
State legislation enacted in the exercise of an undisputed reserved power must yield to an Act of Congress passed in the exercise of a clear power under the
Constitution. "There has been much controversy,
and probably will continue to be, both by the Bench
and the Bar, in fixing the true boundary line between
the power of Congress under the commercial grant and
the power reserved to the States. But in all these discussions, or nearly all of them, it has been admitted,
that if the Act of Congress fell clearly within the power
conferred upon that body by the Constitution, there
was an end of the controversy. The law of Congress
was supreme."

In *Alabama* v. *Georgia*, 23 How. 505, argued on December 14, 1859, and decided on May 1, 1860, the singular condition was presented of two States of the
Union, on the very eve of their secession, submitting

---

[1] *Philadelphia North American*, March 14, 1859, Feb. 15, 1860.
[2] Among the most important cases won by the Government were *United States* v. *Bolton*, 23 How. 341, involving about 30,000 acres in San Francisco, argued April 2, 1860, by Attorney-General Black and William B. Reed of Philadelphia against J. Mason Campbell and Robert J. Walker; *Luco* v. *United States*, 23 How. 515, involving about 200,000 acres, argued by Caleb Cushing against Edwin M. Stanton. See *New York Tribune*, April 12, 1860.

controversies over their boundary line to the Supreme Court, for decision under the Constitution which they were about to repudiate.[1]

Within three days from the date of this decision, the *Dred Scott Case* developed its most potent consequence, when, on May 3, 1860, the Democratic Party then holding its National Convention at Charleston broke up in dissension, to reassemble six weeks later in two irreconcilable wings and to present two nominees for the Presidency — Stephen A. Douglas and John C. Breckinridge, representing hopelessly irreconcilable views. In thus splitting the Democratic Party, the Dred Scott decision had an even greater effect upon American history than in solidifying the anti-slavery sentiment at the North. When, in 1855, Douglas had succeeded, through the passage of his Kansas-Nebraska Bill, in establishing his doctrine of "squatter sovereignty", the party, united and enthusiastic, had regarded the legislation as a final and practical solution of the slavery question. The language of the statute that it was "the true intent and meaning of this Act not to legislate slavery into any Territory or State or to exclude it therefrom, but to leave the people thereof perfectly free to form and regulate their domestic institutions, subject only to the Constitution of the United States", was believed to fix definitely the principle of non-intervention by Congress with slavery in the States and Territories, which had been adopted in the Compromise of 1850. There was, how-

---

[1] In 1855, an interesting point of practice had been decided; in an original suit between States to establish a boundary line, *Florida* v. *Georgia*, 17 How. 478, the Attorney-General of the United States was permitted to intervene on behalf of the Government and to adduce evidence, examine witnesses and be heard on argument; four Judges (Curtis, McLean, Campbell and Daniel) dissented, contending that to permit such intervention was to allow a suit against a State by the United States which the Constitution did not provide for. It is interesting to note that in this defense of the rights of the State, two Northern Judges joined with two Southern. See for history of this dispute, *Coffee* v. *Groover* (1887), 123 U. S. 1.

ever, an unforeseen ambiguity in this language which
was destined to prove fatal to the Democratic Party.
The intention of Senator Douglas was to give the people of the Territory the right to decide for themselves
on the subject of slavery; but the question soon arose:
Was this right given to the Territorial Legislature or
only to the people of the Territory when framing its
Constitution preparatory to admission as a State?
It was answered when Chief Justice Taney, in his decision in 1857, announced flatly that as Congress had
no power to exclude slavery, so it could not authorize
a Territorial Government to exercise such a power.
"It could confer no power on any local government,
established by its authority, to violate the provisions
of the Constitution." This was a body blow to Douglas' theory of popular sovereignty in the Territories;
and thereafter, his attempts to maintain it were in vain.
Republicans and Democrats alike quoted Taney's
decision against him. The main body of Southern
Democrats, after 1857, insisted that their party platform should embody the exact language of the *Dred
Scott Case*, and should not admit the right of a Territory to deal in any way with the subject of slavery,
except through its Constitution adopted for the purpose of becoming a State. Douglas, however, continued to fight for his pet doctrine, as the only fair
solution of the question; and, in 1859, he wrote that
he could not be the Democratic candidate for President if the party insisted on the principle "that the
Constitution either established or forbade slavery in
the Territories, beyond the power of the people to control it as other property." It was on this issue that
the party divided in 1860 into two opposing factions.[1]

[1] See especially *A History of the American People* (1902), by Woodrow Wilson,
IV; *The Lost Cause* (1867), by Edward A. Pollard; *Life and Times of William
Lowndes Yancey* (1892), by John W. DuBose; *Political History of Secession* (1914),

BOOTH CASE, CONGRESSIONAL ATTACK 357

Had it not been for such division, Lincoln's election might have been doubtful; for the popular vote for the combined opposing candidates in California and Oregon far exceeded, and in Ohio, Indiana and Illinois very nearly equaled, the vote cast for Lincoln; while of the popular vote over the whole country Lincoln received only 1,866,452 as against 2,223,110 cast for his Democratic opponents and 590,636 cast for John Bell, the candidate of the Constitutional Union party. It may fairly be said that Chief Justice Taney elected Abraham Lincoln to the Presidency.

by Daniel Wait Howe; *Our Presidents and How We Make Them* (1900), by A. K. McClure.

The Douglas Platform on slavery was as follows: "That the Democratic party will abide by the decisions of the Supreme Court of the United States on the questions of constitutional law. That . . . during the existence of the Territorial Governments, the measure of restriction, whatever it may be, imposed by the Federal Constitution on the power of the Territorial Legislature over the subject of the domestic relations, as the same has been, or shall hereafter be, determined by the Supreme Court of the United States, should be respected by all good citizens, and enforced with promptness and fidelity by every branch of the General Government."

The Breckinridge Platform was as follows: "That the Government of a Territory organized by an Act of Congress is provisional and temporary, and during its existence all citizens of the United States have an equal right to settle with their property in the Territory, without their rights, either of person or of property, being destroyed or impaired by Congressional legislation. That it is the duty of the Federal Government, in all its departments, to protect, when necessary, the rights of persons and property in the Territories, and wherever else its constitutional authority extends. That when the settlers in a Territory, having an adequate population, form a State Constitution, the right of sovereignty commences, and being consummated by admission into the Union, they stand on an equal footing with the people of other States; and the State thus organized ought to be admitted into the Federal Union, whether its Constitution prohibits or recognizes the institution of slavery."

NOTE. Judge Marvin B. Rosenberry of the Wisconsin Supreme Court stated in *North American Review* (1923), CCXVIII: "It may be of interest to know that the remittitur containing the mandate of the United States Supreme Court in the *Booth Case* has never been filed in the office of the Clerk of the Supreme Court of Wisconsin."

As to conflicts between Federal and State Courts in admiralty matters, see *Rufus P. Ranney*, by E. J. Blander in *Great American Lawyers* (1909), VI, 438.

CHAPTER TWENTY-EIGHT

CIVIL WAR AND CHIEF JUSTICE CHASE

1861–1866

BEFORE the beginning of the December, 1860, Term, Judge Peter V. Daniel died on May 30, 1860, after a service on the Bench of nineteen years. The South was insistent that the new appointee should come from that section of the country; for the Court (exclusive of the Chief Justice) was evenly divided — four from the North and four from the South. Among those urged for the position were William L. Yancey of Alabama, and Alexander H. Handy and Samuel S. Boyd of Mississippi; [1] but the strongest and ablest candidate suggested was William J. Robertson, Judge of the Court of Appeals of Virginia: "The appointment of a successor to Judge Daniel is of very little less importance to the South than the election of the next President," wrote one of Robertson's supporters; and another wrote: "The Court is the last line of defense which, it seems, is now left us." [2] On the other hand,

---

[1] *Franklin Pierce Papers MSS*, see letter of G. M. Davis, Aug. 8, 1860, and S. S. Boyd, Aug. 18, 1860; *Washington Star*, Dec. 17, 1860.

[2] *Correspondence of Robert M. T. Hunter*, in *Amer. Hist. Ass. Rep.* (1916), II. Franklin Minor wrote June 5, 1860: "There may be no danger of a wrong appointment, but still I am filled with solicitude by a rumor which I have heard, that James Lyons is the favorite of Mr. Buchanan. . . . Our friends all believe William J. Robertson of the Court of Appeals is the very man for the place. True as steel and firm as a rock, the South may rely on him with the surest confidence. He is, moreover, in the prime of life, and may live to serve us long, even until the stormy and the evil day may come as it surely will come, if we cannot break our bonds, which I fear we cannot yet. To incorruptible fidelity and unflinching firmness, Robertson adds vast stores of legal learning which will make him a great Judge." William M. Ambler wrote, June 11, 1860: "The vacancy on the Bench of the Supreme Court has caused almost every man of sound State-Rights principles to turn to my friend, William J. Robertson. . . . He is so pure morally and intellectually,

the Republicans, regarding the Court with suspicion, were equally insistent that no further representatives of slavery interests should be appointed; and Charles Sumner wrote at this time (referring to rumors as to Taney's proposed resignation): "I know no man at this time who is fit for the office of Chief Justice. The man to fill it must appear before he is named, must be a messenger, or *vox clamantis*, as Marshall was, and as Taney was not. The drowning honour of that Court is under the water; it must be plucked up by the locks. . . . If the next Chief does not lift the department up, it will go to the bottom." [1] Prominent Republican organs presented the more radical, anti-slavery attitude towards the Court in the following partisan attacks. [2] The *New York Tribune* contended that the Court was the instrument of the slave power, which, "knowing that it would ultimately find no repose in the Legislative and Executive branches of the Government, has long had its eye upon the Supreme Court as its final hiding place from the avenging Spirit of Freedom. . . . When Marshall died, Benjamin F. Butler should have received the appointment. But it was given as a compensation to a politician who had not scrupled to perform a high-handed act at the dictation of the Executive. From that hour, the Court lost caste with the country. Calhoun fixed his eagle eye upon it, and resolved to make it the subservient hack of the negro propaganda. . . . Two new seats were created under Jackson. Van Buren filled them with Catron and McKinley, both extreme slaveholders — the former a respectable jurist, the latter a grovelling

and far abler than (high as he stands) he is yet known to be." See also letter of John Randolph Tucker, June 13, 1860, as to Z. Collins Lee as a candidate.

[1] *Sumner*, III, 335, letter of June 26, 1860.

[2] *New York Tribune*, March 26, 1859; *New York Courier*, Jan. 22, 1861; see also *Philadelphia North American*, March 15, 1859, Jan. 21, 1860.

partisan. And now the Court consisted of five slave-holders and four non-slaveholders with the unscrupulous Taney at its head. And thus it remains to this day. . . . This Court, as now arranged, is scandalously sectional, grossly partial, a mockery of the Constitution, a serf of the slave power, and a disgrace to the country. A truly National Administration will not fail to reform it so as to regain for it the confidence of the people, by adapting it to the ends for which it was created." The *New York Courier* stated that: "The attention of all those of our people who are solicitous to hand down to posterity the inheritance of freedom we received from our forefathers should be drawn to the action of the Supreme Court. Sitting away from popular notice in a secluded nook of the Capitol, we should see that they are not stealthily burrowing under the foundations of the Temple of Liberty. A decided majority of them are the appointees of the party that five sixths of the American people decided against at the last election; and there are no more inveterate sticklers for the predominance of that party in the whole land." It pointed out that three cases involving slavery were likely to be argued at the Term beginning in December, 1860, — one, an appeal from the Territorial Court of Kansas, which might require a decision as to the right of the people of the Territory to exclude slavery therefrom; the second, involving the duty of the Governor of Ohio to honor a requisition from the Governor of Kentucky for a fugitive who had violated the slavery laws of the latter State; the third, the famous *Lemmon Case*, an appeal from the New York Court of Appeals involving the status of a slave brought into that State.[1] This Republican paper, now citing and

[1] The *States and Union*, Jan. 29, 1861, said: "The House accepted yesterday the Senate amendment to the bill admitting Kansas into the Union. Thus the ulti-

adopting views urged in early days by Democrats like John Taylor of Caroline, Jefferson and Calhoun as to the dangers of the exercise of its power by the Court, contended that it had no authority to determine political questions, and spoke of the " delusion abroad as to the power and authority of this Court, that, if continued, may become fatal. It is clear that in all political questions (and the whole subject of slavery outside of a State is such) the decision of the people as to what the Constitution means is above the decision of the Supreme Court, and so the Supreme Court ought to determine, if it be desirous to respect the Constitution and our whole system of government, rather than the demands of party and its own *esprit de corps*."

It was with such fundamental misconceptions prevalent at the North that the Court convened on December 3, 1860, for the Term which was to end in war and in the disappearance of the slavery issue from its docket.[1] Its first session was held in a new Courtroom; and no longer could its surroundings be described as they had been by a newspaper correspondent the previous year: "You walk along a narrow passage lighted with a dim lamp. You enter, and, crowding between two walls of old deal boxes, see a distant glass door, a general gloom. . . . Descending two or three steps, you are ushered into a queer room of small dimensions and shaped overhead like a quarter section of a pumpkin shell, the upper and broader rim crowning three windows, and the lower and narrower com-

mate decision of the Supreme Court will be had upon the question of the right of a Territorial Legislature to abolish slavery."

As to the early stages of the *Lemmon Case*, see especially *Washington Union*, Jan. 1, 1853; *Law Reporter* (1860), XXIII.

[1] *New York Tribune*, Dec. 4, 1860: "The Supreme Court met in their new chamber at noon. Chief Justice Taney and all the Associate Justices were present except Judge Wayne. The Court shortly adjourned, and the Judges proceeded to the White House personally, and paid their respects to the President, and afterwards left their cards for the Vice-President."

ing down garret-like to the floor — the windows being of ground glass, the light trickling through them. . . . We would not speak disrespectfully of the Supreme Court. We recently entered its sacred precincts in company with an irreverent Western lawyer. After gazing around a moment, he exclaimed: 'I don't wonder at that decision in the *Dred Scott Case*. Why! What a potato hole of a place, this! The old men ought to be got up above ground where they can breathe fresh air and see real daylight once in a while!' " [1] The project for the provision of more commodious quarters for the Court had been long under consideration; [2] and finally in 1860, when the new wings were added to the Capitol for the Senate and the House, Congress appropriated $25,000 for the alteration and finishing of the former Senate Chamber for use as a Court-room, with twelve other rooms for the use of the Court, its officers and records. [3]

During this Term beginning in December, 1860, the uncertain political conditions throughout the country and the approach of war cast a gloom over the session.

[1] *New York Tribune*, March 16, 1859.

[2] In 1850, in a report on the extension of the Capitol by Robert Mills, architect, May 1, it was proposed that the Senate should occupy a new Chamber in a new wing and that "the Court should be comfortably and elegantly accommodated in the present Senate Chamber." It was stated that the members of the Court had suffered much from the inconvenience of its Court-room, and from its location, which had proved injurious to health. "The deaths of some of our most talented jurists have been attributed to this location of the Court-room; and it would be but common justice in Congress to provide better accommodation for its sittings." See also *35th Cong., 2d Sess.*, 1579, March 2, 1859; *ibid.*, 2829, June 11, 1860.

Gideon Welles in his diary, March 5, 1863, said: "I subsequently went into the Senate Chamber, a much larger but less pleasant room than the old one, which I first visited in the last days of the second Adams. If the present room is larger, the Senators seemed smaller. My first impressions were doubtless more reverential than those of later times." *The Diary of Gideon Welles* (1911), I, 244.

[3] Act of June 25, 1860; by the Act of April 7, 1866, $6500 was appropriated to fit up rooms in the basement under the new Supreme Court-room for a consultation room for the Court. In a report by the United States Art Commission, Feb. 22, 1860, it was proposed that the new Court-room "may appropriately be decorated with subjects relating to the judicial history of the country." Fortunately, this proposal was never carried out. *Documentary History of the Capitol* (1904), 746.

Frequent references to the situation were made by counsel; and a striking instance of their forebodings occurred in an argument on December 23, 1860, by an eminent lawyer from Texas, George W. Paschal, whose sentiments as reported in the press "produced a profound sensation and brought many of the venerable barristers to their feet to congratulate the Texan upon his patriotic sentiments", when he concluded as follows:[1]

We stand upon the brink of another revolution. . . . The probable indication is that, before the mandate of this Court goes down, Texans may have decreed, so far as in them lies, that this Court has no longer jurisdiction to enforce the Constitution and the laws under which the cause was tried; that the Judge and counsel who tried it and the Germans who have been naturalized are no longer bound by the oaths which they voluntarily took to support the Constitution of the United States, but that all have fallen under a revolution said to be necessary to sever the ties which bind us to the Union, which Texans voluntarily joined and which they now threaten to leave. . . . I own that I have argued the case under the deep melancholy which such events naturally impose. . . . Heaven grant that I may be wrong in my apprehensions and may Texas be long preserved as a member of the Union in which she has had a colossal growth! Already, she has many monuments which chronicle bloody dramas in contending revolutions, and may we find protection for every right which the Union was intended to afford! While we have an ultimate appeal here, I should have no fears.

President Buchanan, having decided to fill the vacancy on the Bench caused by the death of Judge Daniel,

[1] *National Intelligencer*, Dec. 29, 1860; *Chandler v. Von Roeder*, 24 How. 224, decided Jan. 21, 1861. President Buchanan, Dec. 15, 1860, issued a proclamation for a day of fasting and prayer on Jan. 4, 1861, in which he stated: "Hope seems to have deserted the minds of men" and that "God's arm alone can save us from the awful effects of our own crimes and follies!" Referring to this proclamation, the *New York Evening Post*, Dec. 17, 1860, said that Reverdy Johnson made "some appropriate remarks in the Supreme Court, in which that distinguished advocate prays that Heaven may silence the 'whinings of imbecility now discouraging and sickening the honest public heart.' Mr. Johnson is not, it may be remarked, a very ardent admirer of the President's."

and having considered the appointment of Caleb Cushing of Massachusetts, finally, on February 5, 1861, selected for the position Jeremiah S. Black of Pennsylvania.[1] Black was fifty-one years of age; he had served for six years as Judge and Chief Justice of the Pennsylvania Supreme Court, Attorney-General of the United States from 1857 to 1860, and Secretary of State since December 17, 1860. Though a man of hot temper, his legal qualifications were eminent; and had the nomination been made a few months earlier, as had been expected, it would probably have been confirmed. But now, owing to the vacancies in the Senate due to resignation of Senators from seceding States, and further owing to the bitter opposition of Stephen A. Douglas and his followers, confirmation was doubtful. The Republicans, moreover, were insistent that, as the Democrats had turned down Crittenden and Badger whose appointments had been made in the closing days of Whig Administrations, they should now take their own medicine and leave the place to be filled by President Lincoln. The anti-slavery press was savage in its criticism of Black. "In all the extensive range of his most unhappy selections for office, Mr. Buchanan has never hit upon a single nomination more eminently unfit to be made," said the *New York Tribune;* and it alleged that Black had neither the judicial qualities, the vigorous intellect nor the calm or dignified character required for the position, and that the nomination was "a flight of insolence so extraordinary as to partake of some of the most captivating traits of the imagination!" The Senate, by a vote of twenty-five to twenty-six, rejected the nomination on February 21; and while at the very last moment Buchanan considered appoint-

[1] *Philadelphia Press,* Jan. 17, 24, Feb. 5, 6, 28, 1861; *New York Tribune,* Jan. 29, Feb. 7, 20, 1861.

ing either John M. Reed of Pennsylvania or Joseph
Holt of Kentucky, he finally decided to take no further
action.[1]

As soon as President Lincoln was inaugurated, it was
rumored that he intended to appoint the veteran statesman, John J. Crittenden of Kentucky, and this choice
was hailed as highly felicitous. Not only was Crittenden a great lawyer, but he had been recently one of the
most active supporters of an attempt to avert civil
war by means of the famous Crittenden Compromise,
in January, 1861. "His recognition by the Administration would be received with joy all through the Border
States," said one conservative Republican paper. "As
a stroke of policy, the appointment of Mr. Crittenden
at this time will be most fortunate for the future peace
of the country," said another, "as it could hardly fail
to disarm the disunionists in the Virginia Convention
instantly, so far as stripping them of power to work
future mischief in the Border States is concerned. It
would be a practical, tangible explanation of the purpose of the new Administration not to aggress the
South, which every Southern man would instantly
comprehend, despite the intrigues of the disunionists
longer to deceive them on that really now most important point." [2] Opposition to Crittenden, however,

[1] *Executive Journal of the Senate,* XI; *Philadelphia Press,* March 2; *New York Times,* Feb. 20, 1861. One cause of Black's failure was the opinion which he had given as Attorney-General, Nov. 20, 1860, as to the lack of power in the President to prevent a State from seceding; see editorial in *New York Evening Post,* Dec. 10, 1860.

[2] *Philadelphia Press,* March 8, 11, 13, 16, April 5, 9, 1861; *Washington Star,* March 6, 7, 8, 1861; *New York Times,* Feb. 26, March 7, 1861, said: "Nothing would so reassure conservative Southern men as the appointment of Crittenden." *The States and Union,* March 7, said the appointment "would bring considerable strength to the new Administration," and on March 4, it said that the radicals were making "a vindictive effort to rob the Administration of the honor of so wise an appointment" and that Senator Trumbull was Crittenden's most active antago-nist." E. M. Stanton wrote to Buchanan, March 10, 1861, that on the day after the confirmation of the Cabinet, "Mr. Seward sent for me and requested me to draw up a nomination for Mr. Crittenden for Judge of the United States Court. I did

developed among the more radical, anti-slavery Re-
publicans; and the names of Thomas Ruffin of North
Carolina, Joseph Holt of Kentucky and George E.
Badger of North Carolina began to be mentioned.

Meanwhile, the last day of the Court's session on the
momentous eve of war occurred on March 14, 1861,
ten days after Lincoln's inauguration. "The Court
adjourns today. I am now writing in the Supreme
Court-room. If the Court ever reassembles, there will
be considerable change in its organization," wrote
Edwin M. Stanton to Buchanan. "There has been no
further action in respect to the Supreme Judgeship. It
is generally understood that Crittenden will not be
nominated. Judge Campbell has reconsidered his resignation and will not resign immediately. Judge Grier
went home sick, two days ago. Judge McLean is
reported to be quite ill. Lincoln will probably (if his
Administration continues four years) make a change
that will affect the constitutional doctrines of the Court.
. . . The Supreme Court has just decided . . . that
the Federal Government has no power to coerce the
Governor of a State to return a fugitive from justice,
although it is his duty to comply with the demand."
The decision referred to by Stanton as rendered on
this last day of the Term was *Ex parte Kentucky* v.
Dennison, 24 How. 66, in which the State of Kentucky
had brought a petition for mandamus in the United
States Supreme Court to compel the Governor of the
State of Ohio to honor a requisition of the Governor of
Kentucky for the surrender of a violator of a State law
relative to slaves. The Court held that though the

so and gave it to him. My understanding was that the nomination would be immediately sent in. But it has not been sent, and the general understanding is that
it will not be. The rumor is that the red blacks oppose it, and also many of the
Democrats, and that Mr. Holt will be nominated. He appears now to be the chief
favorite of the Republicans." *Works of James Buchanan*, XI.

Constitution provided that "it shall be the duty" of
the Governor of a State to deliver up fugitives from
justice, these words were merely "declaratory of the
moral duty" and that no power was delegated "to the
General Government, either through the judicial department or any other department, to use any coercive
means to compel him." [1]   The decision will strike
most people, said the *New York Evening Post*, "as
much like that message of Mr. Buchanan's, of which
Mr. Seward gave so just and pithy a rendering: 'that
a State has no right to secede, but no one has a right to
prevent it; and that the laws of the United States must
be enforced, but there is no authority to enforce them.'
Justice Taney says, in effect, that the Governor of Ohio
ought to give up the fugitive, but if he will not, there is
no authority to make him do so.   The real point in
question, however, is whether a fugitive demanded by
one State shall be given up by another, when the offence
is no offence against the laws of the State asked to surrender him, or against the law of nations."   Though
the decision gave considerable dissatisfaction to the
slave States, it was rendered at a date too close to the
verge of war to have any effect on the development of
the slavery issue.

Two other decisions rendered at this time were important as showing that the Court was still to be depended
upon to sustain the supremacy of the jurisdiction of the
National Government, which the Chief Justice had so
staunchly upheld in the *Booth Case*, two years before.
In *Freeman* v. *Howe*, 24 How. 450, property attached
by a United States marshal in a suit in a Federal Court
was seized on replevin by a State sheriff on process
issued from a State Court in a suit by bondholders.

[1] *National Intelligencer*, Dec. 18, 1860; *New York Evening Post*, March 14, 15,
1861; see also *National Republican* (Wash.), March 15, 16, 1861.

The Court, through Judge Nelson, said: "No Government could maintain the administration or execution of its laws, civil or criminal, if the jurisdiction of its judicial tribunals were subject to the determination of another. . . . It belongs to the Federal Courts to determine the question of their own jurisdiction, the ultimate arbiter, the supreme judicial tribunal of the Nation."[1] In *Almy* v. *California*, 24 How. 169, involving the validity of a State stamp tax on bills of lading of all gold transported from within to without the State, and argued by Montgomery Blair against Judah P. Benjamin, the Chief Justice had occasion to render an opinion, rejecting his own unsuccessful argument as counsel in *Brown* v. *Maryland* in 1827, and holding that such a tax was a tax on exports within the prohibition of the Constitution.[2]

One month from the date of the adjournment of the Court, the advent of war by the attack on Fort Sumter on April 12 seemed to put an end to all consideration of judicial questions or of judicial appointments Nevertheless, within six weeks after the opening gun was fired, the status of the Judiciary as the defender of the rights of the citizen, in war as well as in peace, became an active issue, when Chief Justice Taney, sitting in the United States Circuit Court, was brought into direct conflict with the President, by his famous decision in *Ex parte Merryman*. In this case, a prominent citizen of Baltimore who had been arrested by the military on a charge of aiding the enemy and who had been imprisoned in Fort McHenry, had obtained a writ of habeas

[1] In *Buck* v. *Colbath*, 3 Wall. 334, the Court said that the *Freeman* v. *Howe* decision "took the profession generally by surprise, overruling as it did the unanimous opinion of the Supreme Court of Massachusetts . . . as well as the opinion of Chancellor Kent."

[2] See as to this case, *Woodruff* v. *Parham*, 8 Wall. 123, 138; *Champion* v. *Ames*, 188 U. S. 321, 349.

corpus from the Chief Justice. The officer in charge of
the prisoner having declined to obey the writ on the
ground that he was authorized by the President to suspend the writ of habeas corpus for the public safety,
Taney at once issued an attachment for contempt.
Its service being prevented by the military, Taney proceeded to file an opinion holding the suspension of the
writ by the President to be in violation of the Constitution, and ordered the Clerk of the Court to transmit
a copy of the opinion to the President.[1] The case
thus involving the powers of the Executive with respect
to the liberty of the citizen excited intense interest
throughout the country.[2] Once more, as in 1857,
criticism and denunciation of the harshest kind were
leveled at the aged Chief Justice ; and many Republican
papers even questioned his loyalty to the Union. "The
Chief Justice takes sides with traitors, throwing around
them the sheltering protection of the ermine," said the
New York Tribune. "When treason stalks abroad in
arms, let decrepit Judges give place to men capable of
detecting and crushing it"; and it stated that Taney's
decision tended "to bring the ermine into contempt
with the great body of loyal citizens. The appropriate
sphere of this writ is the Courts. It is out of place in
the camp. Originally intended to secure the liberty of
loyal men, it would be a gross perversion of its powers

[1] Tyler states in his *Memoir* of Taney that the Chief Justice, as he left the house of
his son, remarked that it was likely that he should be imprisoned in Fort McHenry
before night, but that he was going to Court to do his duty. About the same time,
Judge Treat of the United States District Court in St. Louis issued a writ of habeas
corpus in the case of Capt. Emmet Macdonald, who had been arrested and imprisoned by Gen. Harvey, on charges of treason, and after lengthy arguments an order
for Macdonald's discharge was issued and finally complied with by the Army; see
especially, *Missouri Democrat,* May 16, 23, 24, 27, 28, 29, June 1, 3, 4, 7, 10, 1861;
National Intelligencer, May 29, 1861.

[2] *New York Times,* May 29, 30, 1861; *New York Tribune,* May 29, 30, 31, 1861;
Philadelphia Press, June 5, 6, 1861; *New York World,* May 29, June 5, 1861; *Mis-
souri Democrat,* June 3, 1861, editorial on "Military Despotism as a Bug Bear";
New York Evening Post, May 29, June 4, 1861.

to employ it as the protecting shield of rebels against a constitutional government. . . . No Judge whose heart was loyal to the Constitution would have given such aid and comfort to public enemies. . . . Let us not be afraid of military despotism. . . . Of all the tyrannies that afflict mankind, that of the Judiciary is the most insidious, the most intolerable, the most dangerous." The *New York Times* said that no man knew better than Taney that he was perverting the uses of the writ and prostituting its purposes. "Too feeble to wield the sword against the Constitution, too old and palsied and weak to march in the ranks of rebellion and fight against the Union, he uses the powers of his office to serve the cause of the traitors." The *New York Evening Post* said that Taney was using "his authority and position to the advantage of those who are armed against the Union," and "to serve treason, and embarrass and injure the Government." The *Philadelphia Press* said that Taney's opinion bore every evidence of having been prepared with intention to embarrass the President; and that his sympathies were evidently neither with the Union nor with the President in his efforts to save the Union. "That which curbs tyranny should speed patriotism and crush treason. . . . If his action is an indication of his future course, treason will find a place of refuge, and its abettors encouragement and sympathy, in the Supreme Court." The *Missouri Democrat* spoke of the "meddling and traitorous efforts to thwart the efficiency of the Government in its hour of peril. . . . If the Government will follow up the suspension of the writ of habeas corpus with the dispension of . . . Taney it will be a good riddance for the country."

Derogatory views of this kind were not by any means universal; and many staunch Republican organs com-

mended Taney's action in behalf of personal liberty.[1]
"We are not sorry to see the Judiciary declare its
opinion, or even enter its protest against acts which it
believes to be without authority," said the *Boston
Advertiser*. "If in any point the limits of the Constitution are overstepped, we desire that the excess
should not be overlooked, but that it should be entered
upon the record, to stand as a warning, in more peaceful times yet to come, that here is an act, the necessity
of which was the justification, and which is not to be
made a precedent at any time when the public exigency is less pressing." The *Cincinnati Commercial*,
which had in previous years bitterly assailed Taney,
acknowledged that in this case he had done only what
the law required of him, and that denunciations were
now unjustified; and it stated that, while the offense
committed by Merryman was unquestionably heinous,
"it does appear to us that he could have been held
and punished by the civil power. . . . The very fact
that we are placed in circumstances so critical as to
render the application of the severest remedies sometimes justifiable should guard us against resorting to
military rule. . . . Let us have no dictation from the
Army, so long as we can have justice administered from
her customary seat." The *Baltimore American* took
the same view of the situation. "The plea of State-
necessity may be advanced by the President to justify
himself for so high-handed an act as the suspension of
the writ; . . . but it would not be well for the highest
officer of the Government to justify a plain violation of
the Constitution, while calling out troops to maintain

[1] *Boston Daily Advertiser*, May 30, 1861; *National Intelligencer*, May 30, June 4,
8, 22, 1861; *Cincinnati Commercial*, May 29, June 3, 1861; *Baltimore American*,
May 29, June 4, 1861; The *Washington Star*, May 29, 1861, said that the action
of Chief Justice Taney in this case was probably in accordance with the strict letter
of the law but that it was to be sincerely regretted that he had refused to take into
consideration the revolutionary state of the country.

that same Constitution inviolate. . . . It is eminently proper that a Government which is fighting
to maintain the integrity of the Constitution should interpose no arbitrary action to suspend or interfere with
rights plainly guaranteed under it, if it would have the
support and countenance of its citizens."

While the legal controversy which raged in 1861 over
the constitutional right of the President to suspend the
writ of habeas corpus has never been settled by judicial
decision or public opinion, the right and the duty of
the Chief Justice to issue the writ and to consider the
legal question involved is now universally admitted.[1]
And history has recorded as its verdict that (as stated
by one of his biographers) "there is nothing more
sublime in the acts of great magistrates that give dignity to Governments than this attempt of Chief Justice
Taney to uphold the supremacy of the Constitution and
civil authority in the midst of arms"; and (as another
wrote) : "Taney's action in this case was worthy of the
best traditions of the Anglo-Saxon Judiciary. There
is no sublimer picture in our history than this of the
aged Chief Justice, the fires of Civil War kindling around
him, the President usurping the powers of Congress,
and Congress itself a seething furnace of sectional
animosities, serene and unafraid, while for a third time
in his career, the storm of partisan fury broke over his
devoted head, interposing the shield of the law in the
defense of the liberty of the citizen." [2]

President Lincoln, however, steadfastly adhered to

[1] See among many publications published in 1861 and 1862 on this subject:
The Privilege of the Writ of Habeas Corpus, by Horace Binney; article by Reverdy
Johnson in the *Weekly National Intelligencer*, June 20, 1861; *Habeas Corpus and
the Law of War and Confiscation*, by S. S. Nicholas; *Review of Binney on the Habeas
Corpus*, by J. C. Bullitt; *Habeas Corpus and Martial Law*, by Joel Parker; and see
especially *Suspension of Habeas Corpus during the War of the Rebellion*, by Sydney
G. Fisher, *Pol. Sci. Quar.* (1888), III.

[2] *Roger B. Taney*, by William E. Mikell, in *Great American Lawyers* (1905), IV,
188; *Tyler*, 420-432.

the theory that in time of war the necessities of the emergency were supreme; and accordingly, during the two years following the *Merryman Case*, a series of steps were taken by the President and by the Secretary of War in instituting censorship, military arrest and military trial, violative of the principles laid down by Taney, and which, while possibly justified by war conditions, have since been held to have been in excess of constitutional authority.[1]   Lincoln's theory was eloquently set forth by him in a letter in 1863 as follows: "Thoroughly imbued with a reverence for the guaranteed rights of individuals, I was slow to adopt the strong measures which by degrees I have been forced to regard as being within the exceptions of the Constitution and as indispensable to the public safety. . . . I concede that the class of arrests complained of can be constitutional only when in cases of rebellion or invasion the public safety may require them; and I insist that in such cases they are constitutional wherever the public safety does require them, as well in places in which they may prevent the rebellion extending as in those where it may already be prevailing." [2]   This

[1] See the censorship orders of July 8, Oct. 22, 1861, and Feb. 25, 1862, issued by the Secretary of War and the Secretary of State; the Executive Order of Feb. 14, 1862, by the Secretary of War as to military arrests; the President's Order of April 27, 1861, and his Proclamation of Sept. 24, 1862, suspending habeas corpus; the Suspension of Habeas Corpus Act of March 3, 1863.   Congress by the Act of March 3, 1863, the Act of May 11, 1866, and the Act of March 2, 1867, attempted to confirm and validate the acts of President Lincoln and Secretary Stanton and of military officers acting in accordance with their orders in making military arrests, etc.   These statutes were involved in *Beard* v. *Burts*, 95 U. S. 434, in 1877, and in *Bean* v. *Beckwith*, 98 U. S. 266, in 1878; but the Court did not pass on the question of their constitutionality; see especially *Springfield Republican*, Jan. 9, 1879.

[2] *Complete Works of Abraham Lincoln* (1905), VIII, letter to Erastus Corning, June 12, 1863.   It is interesting to note that one other Court had the courage to deny Lincoln's theories.   The Supreme Court of Wisconsin, the very tribunal which had so long defied Chief Justice Taney's assertion of the supremacy of the National power in the *Booth Case*, in January, 1863, rendered an opinion in *In re Kemp*, 16 Wisc. 359, in which it upheld Taney's views in the *Merryman Case* as "unanswerable", and held that the President had no power to suspend the writ of habeas corpus; see *The Story of a Great Court* (1912), by John B. Winslow.

exaltation of the Executive over the law greatly depressed the aged Chief Justice throughout the remaining years of his life; and he wrote, in 1863, that he saw no ground to hope that the Court would "ever be again restored to the authority and rank which the Constitution intended to confer upon it. The supremacy of the military power over the civil seems to be established, and the public mind has acquiesced in it and sanctioned it." The apprehension so expressed as to the trend of events was unquestionably shared by many Senators and Representatives in Congress, even in the President's own party.[1] Yet such is the sturdiness of the American Judiciary and the vitality of the American belief in and insistence upon the rights of constitutional liberty, that, had the Chief Justice lived but four years after writing his note of pessimism, he would have seen the doctrines laid down by him in the *Merryman Case* strongly upheld. For in *Milligan's Case*, the Court composed largely of Republicans, unanimously joined in denouncing as highly illegal the Executive establishment of military tribunals in States where the civil Courts were open. Never did a fearless Judge receive a more swift or more complete vindication.

On December 2, 1861, when the Court met for its annual session, there were three vacancies; for Judge Daniel's successor had not been appointed, Judge McLean had died on April 4, 1861, and Judge Camp-

---

[1] For a summary of Congressional criticism of the President, see *Lincoln's Despotism*, by Charles Warren, *New York Times*, May 12, 1918. See also *The Diary of Gideon Welles*, I, Sept. 15, 1863: "I think I am not mistaken in my impression that Mr. Chase is one of those who has claimed that the President had the constitutional right to suspend the privilege of this writ, yet he was today sensitive beyond all others in regard to it and proposed relying on the Act of Congress (of March 3, 1863) instead of the constitutional Executive prerogative. He feared if the President acted on Executive authority a civil war in the Free States would be inevitable; fears popular tumult, would not offend Congress, etc. I have none of his apprehensions, and if it is the duty of the President, would not permit legislative aggression, but maintain the prerogative of the Executive."

bell had, with great reluctance, decided that his duty impelled him to follow his State of Alabama out of the Union. While believing in secession as a constitutional right, Campbell had strongly opposed it as a policy; and his efforts through the winter and spring of 1860–1861 to avert war had been active and unremitting.[1] With the outbreak of war, however, he felt that it was his duty to resign, and that his continuance on the Bench would lead to a lack of confidence by the public in his opinions. Accordingly, he wrote to the Chief Justice, April 29, 1861: "Some days ago, I sent through the mail to the President a notice of my resignation. . . . In taking leave of the Court, I should do injustice to my own feeling, if I were not to express to you the profound impression that your eminent qualities as a magistrate and jurist have made upon me. I shall never forget the uprightness, fidelity, learning, thought and labor that have been brought by you to the consideration of the judgments of the Court, or the urbanity, gentleness, kindness and tolerance that have distinguished your intercourse with the members of the Court and Bar. From your hands, I have received all that I could have desired, and in leaving the Court, I carry with me feelings of mingled reverence, affection and gratitude. In the prayer that the remainder of your days may be happy and their end peace, I remain your friend."[2] The loss thus sustained by the Bench was noted by the *National Intelligencer*, which termed Campbell "a learned jurist and a faithful

---

[1] Stanton writing to Buchanan in May, 1861, said that "the *New York Evening Post* is very severe on Judge Campbell, and very unjustly so, for the Judge has been as anxiously and patriotically anxious to preserve the Government as any man in the United States, and he has sacrificed more than any other Southern man, rather than yield to the Secessionists." *John Archibald Campbell* (1920), by Henry G. Connor. The *New York Tribune*, Nov. 27, 1860, said: "Every Judge on the Bench is for the Union." See also *The States and Union*, Jan. 16, 26, 1861.

[2] *Maryland Hist. Mag.* (1910), V.

Judge, who during the entire period of his official service has illustrated the qualities which must adorn the exalted position he was called to fill, and who, in his retirement, will carry with him the admiration of his countrymen."

President Lincoln hesitated at first to fill these vacancies on the Bench. His characteristically just attitude towards the South was shown in his first Message to Congress, December 3, 1861, in which he said: "Two of the outgoing Judges resided within the States now overrun by revolt, so that if successors were appointed in the same localities, they could not now serve upon their Circuits; and many of the most competent men there would not take the personal hazard of accepting to serve even here upon the Supreme Bench. I have been unwilling to throw all the appointments Northward, thus disabling myself from doing justice to the South on the return of peace."[1]

The gloomy conditions under which both the Court and Congress convened at this December Term of 1861 were impressively alluded to by Attorney-General Bates, December 3, in presenting the resolutions of the Bar on the death of Judge McLean:

Since the first organization of this Court, no Term has yet been held under circumstances so gloomy and sorrowful. I look up to that honored Bench and behold vacant seats. Even this august tribunal, the co-equal partner in the government of a great Nation, the revered dispenser of our country's justice, shares with us in feeling the common sorrow, and suffers in the common calamity. It is shorn of its fair proportions, and weakened and diminished in its strength and beauty, by the present loss of one entire third of its competent members. And where are the wise, learned, and

[1] Lincoln pointed out at the same time that the whole judicial system ought to be revised, and that Wisconsin, Minnesota, Iowa, Kansas, Florida, Texas, California and Oregon should be brought within some judicial Circuit, and provided with Circuit Courts.

just men who used to fill those seats? Gone from this
theatre of their fame and usefulness, while all of us remember
them with respect and gratitude, and mourn the loss of their
valuable services. Two of them have been peacefully
gathered to their fathers, and have left their fame safe and
unchangeable beyond the reach of malice, and secure against
accident, embalmed in history, and narrowed by the grave.
And one of them, in the ripe vigor of his manhood, and in
the pride of a noble and highly cultivated mind, has been
swept away from his high position by the turbulent waves of
faction and civil war. And this is not all. Your lawful
jurisdiction is practically restrained; your just power is
diminished, and into a large portion of our country your
writ does not run and your beneficent authority to administer justice according to law is, for the present, successfully
denied and resisted. I look abroad over the country and
behold a ghastly spectacle; a great nation, lately united,
prosperous, and happy and buoyant with hopes of future
glory, torn into warring fragments; and a land once beautiful and rich in the flowers and fruits of peaceful culture,
stained with blood, and blackened with fire. In all that
wide space from the Potomac to the Rio Grande, and from
the Atlantic to the Missouri, the still, small voice of legal
justice is drowned by the incessant roll of the drum, and the
deafening thunder of artillery. To that extent, your just
and lawful power is practically annulled, for the laws are
silent amidst arms. . . . Now, indeed, we are overshadowed
with a dark cloud, broad and gloomy as a nation's pall; but
thanks be to God, the eye of faith and patriotism can discern
the bow of promise set in that cloud, spanning the gloom
with its bright arch, to foreshow the coming of a day of sun-
shine and calm, and to justify our hope of a speedy restoration of peace, and order, and law.

At this Term, few cases of importance were decided,
other than California land claims.[1] In *Jefferson Branch*

[1] See especially *United States* v. *Vallejo*, 1 Black, 541; *United States* v. *Castillero*,
2 Black, 1, involving the title to the rich quicksilver mines in New Almaden, California, decided in 1863. For an elaborate and interesting account of these California land frauds, "a system of extensive frauds with forged grants and perjured witnesses such as the world has seldom witnessed", as Judge Grier said in the *Vallejo
Case*, see arguments of counsel in *De Haro* v. *United States*, 5 Wall. 599, in 1869;

Bank v. *Skelley*, 1 Black, 436, the State of Ohio again attempted to induce the Court to reverse its position as to the power of a State to tax banks, which by a prior statute had been exempted from taxation; but the Court said that though it was aware that its view had not been satisfactory to all persons, "it has been adhered to by this Court in every attempt hitherto made to relax it; and we presume it will be, until the historical recollections, which induced the framers of the Constitution to inhibit the States from passing any law impairing the obligation of contracts, have been forgotten."

Shortly after the opening of the December Term of 1861, the precarious state of health of both Taney and Catron and the consequent retardation of the work of the Court made it imperative that one of the existing vacancies should be filled. Accordingly, on January 22, 1862, President Lincoln appointed in Judge McLean's place Noah Haynes Swayne of Ohio. Swayne was fifty-seven years old; though without previous judicial experience, he held an eminent position at the Ohio Bar, and his appointment had been vigorously urged by Governor Dennison, Senator Sherman and Senator Wade.[1] Appointments to fill the vacancies caused by the death of Judge Daniel and the resignation of Judge Campbell were postponed until Congress should have come to a final decision as to the redistribution of the Circuits, made necessary by the disappearance of the two which comprised the seceding States. It was rumored that the appointees for the new Circuits would be Senator Orville H. Browning of

see also later the notorious McGarrahan claims involved in *United States* v. *Gaines*, 23 How. 326, 1 Wall. 690, 3 Wall. 752; *McGarrahan* v. *Mining Co.*, 96 U. S. 316.

[1] *New York Evening Post*, Jan. 27, 1862; the *New York Tribune*, Jan. 23, 1862, termed Swayne "one of the ablest lawyers in Ohio." Swayne was confirmed by the Senate, Jan. 24, 1862, by a vote of 38 to 1.

Illinois and Caleb B. Smith of Indiana, Lincoln's Secretary of the Interior. Owing to personal opposition to these candidates and to State jealousies, the method of grouping the Western and Southwestern States became a subject of warm controversy in Congress; the House and the Senate adopted different plans; and it was not until the very end of the session, that on July 15, 1862, an agreement was reached and an Act passed reorganizing the Court.[1] To fill one of the new positions the President appointed, on July 16, Samuel Freeman Miller of Iowa. Miller was forty-six years old, an outstanding figure at the Bar west of the Mississippi River, though little known to the country at large, and in no sense a National figure; but his appointment had been vigorously urged by the lawyers of Iowa, Minnesota, Kansas and Wisconsin, by the Governor and Senators and Representatives of Iowa, and by a petition signed by one hundred and twenty-nine out of one hundred and forty Congressmen and twenty-eight out of thirty-two Senators.[2] To the other Judgeship, the President made no appointment for several months. The Bar of Illinois urged the name of Thomas Drummond; that of Michigan, William A. Howard; and

[1] See *37th Cong., 2d Sess.*, July 4, 1862, especially speeches of Senator Trumbull and Senator Wright. The Circuits were finally composed as follows: (6th, Catron's) Ky., Tenn., Ark., Tex., La.; (7th, Swayne's) Ind., Ohio; (8th) Ill., Wisc., Mich.; (9th) Minn., Ia., Kans., Mo. The *New York Tribune*, July 14, 1863, said that by the inclusion of Ohio and Indiana in Swayne's Circuit the opponents of Smith and Browning were successful; that by the union of Wisconsin and Illinois, both Browning and Senator James R. Doolittle (of Wisconsin) were put out of the question, as Michigan was added, in the expectation that its influence would defeat both. "Browning, whose prospects were, until he took ground against the most important Republican measures, considered the best, has been the Jonah of the bill, everybody trying to throw him overboard."

[2] *Samuel Freeman Miller*, by Charles N. Gregory, *Iowa Biog. Series* (1907), *Yale Law Jour.* (1908), XVII; see also article by Horace Stern in *Great American Lawyers* (1908), VI. So little known was Miller that the *New York Tribune* said editorially, July 18, 1862: "Mr. Miller's name is printed 'Samuel' in the despatches but we presume it is 'Daniel F. Miller', the first Whig member of Congress ever chosen from Iowa."

that of Wisconsin, James R. Doolittle. Finally, Lincoln chose his close personal friend, David Davis of Illinois, who was appointed on December 1, and confirmed on December 8, 1862. Davis was forty-seven years of age, and had been for fourteen years a Judge of the Eighth Judicial Circuit in Illinois.[1]

The next spring, by the Act of March 3, 1863, Congress established a new (Tenth) Circuit comprising California and Oregon, and a tenth Associate Judge; and to this position, the President appointed, on March 6, Stephen Johnson Field of California, who was confirmed by the Senate, March 16. Field was forty-six years of age and had served as Judge and Chief Justice of the Supreme Court of California. Though a Democrat in politics, he had been a strong Union man, and his appointment, requested by the whole California delegation, was received with hearty applause throughout the country, regardless of politics — "a fine, general scholar and a thorough lawyer", said the *New York Evening Post*, "probably better acquainted with that mixed system of law, Mexican, Spanish and American, which prevails in California, than any other man in the country. . . . He will long do honor to the position . . . and the Government will have no more determined supporter." [2]

The Term beginning in December, 1862, was a notable one in its effect upon the war. On March 10, 1863, the Court decided the group of cases known as the *Prize Cases*, 2 Black, 635, headed by the *Brig Amy Warwick*.[3] Not only were these the first cases arising

---

[1] *David Davis*, by Thomas Dent, *Amer. Law Rev.* (1919), LIII.

[2] *New York Evening Post*, March 11, 1863; see also *Cincinnati Daily Gazette*, March 14, 1863; *Stephen Johnson Field*, by John N. Pomeroy, Jr., *Great American Lawyers* (1908), VII.

[3] *National Republican*, March 10, 1862, said; "The object of this sitting of the Court was to announce its decision in the great *Almaden Case* and the *Prize Cases*. Besides the counsel for and against the Government there were present a large

out of the Civil War to be decided by this tribunal, but they were far more momentous in the issue involved than any other war case; and their final determination favorable to the Government's contention was almost a necessary factor in the suppression of the war. The problem presented to the Court was how to apply the rules of international and prize law affecting attempts by neutrals to violate a blockade established between separate political powers recognized as belligerents, to the situation presented in this war. The Government of the United States had heretofore acted upon the theory that the war was an insurrection, that there were not two belligerent parties, and that the political integrity of the country had not been modified.[1] The situation was greatly complicated by the facts that Seward as Secretary of State had inserted in his blockade proclamations, provisions unknown to international law; that he had taken the official position that "no war" existed; and that the Government itself was strenuously protesting against any recognition by foreign nations of the Confederacy as a belligerent.[2] If the Court should decide that the principles of international law applying in a war between belligerents did not control in this case, the Government's blockade

number of distinguished lawyers from different sections of the country besides a very intelligent and attentive audience including several ladies. The reading of the *Almaden Case* decision occupied from 11.30 A.M. to 2 P.M."

[1] *William Maxwell Evarts*, by Sherman Evarts, in *Great American Lawyers* (1908), VII.

[2] See *New York World*, March 17, 1863 *Diary* (1863), by Adam Gurowski, II, 146 *et seq.*, Feb. 19, 1863: "The counsel for the English and rebel blockade runners and pilferers find the best point of legal defence, in the unstatesmanlike and unlegal wording of the proclamation of the blockade, as concocted and issued by Mr. Seward, and in the repeated declarations contained in the voluminous correspondence of our Secretary of State, declarations asserting that no war whatever is going on in the Federal Republic. No war, — therefore no lawful prizes in the ocean. So, ignorance and humbug mark every step of this foremost among the pilots of a noble, highminded, but too confiding people. . . . When Mr. Seward penned this doleful proclamation of the blockade . . . he never had before his mind what a mess he generated, what complications might arise therefrom."

would be entirely ineffective.   As Richard H. Dana, one
of the Government's counsel wrote : [1]

These causes present our Constitution in a new and peculiar light.   In all States but ours, now existing or that
have ever existed, the function of the Judiciary is to interpret the acts of the Government.   In ours, it is to decide
their legality.   The Government is carrying on a war.   It
is exerting all the powers of war.   Yet the claimants of the
captured vessels not only seek to save their vessels by denying that they are liable to capture but deny the right of the
Government to exercise war power, — deny that this can be,
in point of law, a war.   So the Judiciary is actually, after
a war of twenty-three months' duration, to decide whether
the Government has the legal capacity to exert these war
powers. . . .   Contemplate, my dear sir, the possibility of a
Supreme Court, deciding that this blockade is illegal !   What
a position it would put us in before the world whose commerce we have been illegally prohibiting, whom we have
unlawfully subjected to a cotton famine, and domestic dangers and distress for two years !   It would end the war, and
how it would leave us with neutral powers, it is fearful to
contemplate !   Yet such an event is legally possible — I
do not think it probable, hardly possible, in fact.   But last
year, I think there was danger of such a result, when the
blockade was new and before the three new Judges were
appointed.   The bare contemplation of such a possibility
makes us pause in our boastful assertion that our written
Constitution is clearly the best adapted to all exigencies, the
last, best gift to man.

The cases were argued for twelve days, February
10–25, by Attorney-General Bates, William M. Evarts
and Charles B. Sedgwick of New York, Richard H.
Dana of Boston, and Charles Eames of Washington,
against James Mandeville Carlisle of Washington,
Daniel Lord and Charles Edwards of New York and
Edward Bangs of Boston.   And the following graphic

[1] *Richard H. Dana* (1890), by Charles Francis Adams, II, 266 *et seq.*, letter of
March 9, 1863.

description of Dana's argument and of its effect upon
the Court was given by an auditor in the Court-room,
recalling "the glow of admiration and delight with
which they listened to that luminous and exquisite
presentation of the status which armed the Executive
with power to use the methods and processes of war to
suppress the great rebellion. Dry legal questions were
lifted into the higher region of international discussion,
and the philosophy of the barbaric right of capture of
private property at sea was, for the first time in the
hearing of most of the Judges then on the Bench,
applied to the pending situation, with a power of reason and a wealth of illustration, and a grace and fe-
licity of style that swept all before them. After Mr.
Dana had closed his argument, I happened to encounter
Judge Grier, who had retired for a moment to the cor-
ridor in the rear of the bench, and whose clear judicial
mind and finely cultivated literary taste had keenly
enjoyed the speech, and, in a burst of unjudicial enthusiasm, he said to me, 'Well, your little *Two Years
before the Mast* has settled that question; there is nothing more to say about it!'" [1] Dana himself wrote
from Washington : "I have every reason to be satisfied
with my argument and its results. The compliments
I have received from the Judges and audience and
counsel are quite too flattering to be put on paper.
They seem to think the philosophy of the law of prize
has been developed for the first time in its bearing on
the present question." And later : "I have won Judge
Grier's heart. He pats me on the shoulder and says
I have cleaned up all his doubts and that it is the best
argument he has heard for five years, etc. The Attorney-General seems quite overcome with his emotion on
the subject, and cannot say enough. Seward is flat-

---

[1] *Richard H. Dana* (1890), by Charles Francis Adams, II, 269-270.

tering, and others." The judgment of the Court was delivered only thirteen days after the close of the argument; and while there was a division in the Court, it was not on political lines; for the three Judges appointed by President Lincoln, Swayne, Miller and Davis, joined with two of the old Court, Wayne and Grier, to make up the majority (Chief Justice Taney and Judges Nelson, Catron and Clifford dissenting). In giving the opinion of the Court, Judge Grier said that: "It is not necessary, to constitute war, that both parties should be acknowledged as independent nations or sovereign States. A war may exist where one of the belligerents claims sovereign rights as against the other . . . and whether the hostile party be a foreign invader, or States organized in rebellion, it is none the less a war, although the declaration of it be 'unilateral.'" It was held that the President's proclamation of a blockade was a lawful exercise of his power to meet and suppress the war, "in the shape in which it presented itself." This decision was greeted by the press of the North with approval and relief.

There had been grave fears lest the Court, composed of a majority of the Judges appointed prior to the war, might embarrass the Administration, by denying the legality of President Lincoln's actions, many of which had been initiated without legislative sanction. A striking illustration of the apprehensions with which the result of the case had been awaited, appeared in an elaborate editorial consideration which the *New York Times* gave to the attitude of the "Copperheads" towards the Courts.[1] It stated that, beginning with the Merryman habeas corpus, appeals to the civil Courts had figured largely in the attempts made to

[1] *New York Times*, March 13, 1863; *New York World*, March 14, 17, 1863; *New York Tribune*, March 13, 1863; *National Republican*, March 11, 1863. See also *Law Reporter* (1863), 737, quoting letter from *Boston Advertiser*, Dec. 18, 1863.

embarrass and weaken the Government. It rejoiced
that hitherto these attempts had failed, and that the
Judges had generally shown a loyal spirit, and had had
"both the heart and head to refuse coöperation with
factious men," and had in habeas corpus proceedings
been content to await the decision of the highest
tribunal before releasing men under military arrest;
and it further rejoiced that the hope of the "Copperheads" "to cast a vast burden upon the Treasury, by
annulling the blockade proclaimed by the President
before the meeting of Congress, is dashed by a decision that the President had a complete right to institute the blockade, without awaiting Congressional
action." It found grounds for expecting the Court to
uphold the legality of the Emancipation Proclamation;
for, it said, "the Court distinctly recognizes the *jus
belli*, the war power, against which so much passionate
declamation has been expended. It is said that the
President may exert this power by proclamation, and
that all the sinews of war may thus be cut. It is difficult to see why the very broad language of the Court
in respect to the proclamation of the blockade does not
involve the constitutional validity of the proclamation
against slave property. . . . It is our firm conviction
that the Supreme Court would indorse the constitutional validity of every important act of the Executive
or of Congress thus far in the rebellion." The *National
Republican* rejoiced that the dissenting opinion of
Judge Nelson had not prevailed, as it left "an unpleasant and unsatisfactory feeling of apprehension that the
powers of the Government, as found in the Constitution,
were not adequate to the high and imperative duties
which devolved upon it, of using all possible means of
crushing the war of the rebellion at the outset."

That the Court was insistent on upholding the arm of

the Government in its war operations was seen in another important decision, rendered on the same day with the *Prize Cases*, March 10, 1863, in *Bank of Commerce* v. *New York*, 2 Black, 620, strongly denouncing any interference by a State with the powers and functions of the National Government. In this case, the State of New York had attempted to tax the capital of a bank, part of which was invested in stock and bonds of the United States. The exercise of such attempted authority was held to be in derogation of the power of the Nation to borrow money, "one of the most important and even vital functions of the General Government . . . a means of supplying the necessary resources to meet exigencies in time of peace or war." While admitting that "there is and must always be a considerable latitude of discretion in every wise government in the exercise of the taxing power", Judge Nelson said that this principle would not warrant the trespass by a State upon the functions of the Nation; that while it might be difficult oftentimes to fix the true boundary between the two systems, "each is sovereign and independent in its sphere of action, and exempt from the interference or control of the other, either in the means employed or functions exercised"; and he added, "influenced by a public and patriotic spirit on both sides, a conflict of authority need not occur or be feared." The hope of the Copperheads "to damage the credit of the Government by subjecting its bonds to State and other local taxation is dashed", said the *New York Times*. The importance of the clear announcement of the principle asserted in this case, just at this period when the financing of the war was becoming increasingly difficult, cannot be overestimated.

That the Court, however, even in time of war, was

not inclined to acquiesce in any extension of National authority which it deemed unwarranted by the Constitution was seen in its attitude towards the provision of the Federal income tax law, imposing a tax upon the incomes of the Judges. In denial of the validity of such a tax, Chief Justice Taney wrote to the Secretary of the Treasury, saying that he would "not by any act or word of mine have it supposed that I acquiesce in a measure that displaces it (the Judicial Department) from the independent position assigned to it by the statesmen who framed the Constitution." The Secretary having ignored this communication, the Court itself, on the day of the decision of the *Prize Cases*, March 10, 1863, ordered a copy of the letter to be entered on its records.[1]

At the December, 1863, Term, it was supposed that the great question of the constitutional power of Congress to issue legal tender paper money would be decided, for a case involving the validity of the Legal Tender Acts was before the Court, on a writ of error to the New York State Supreme Court, *Roosevelt* v. *Meyer*, 1 Wall. 512. By curious mischance, the question was not decided, owing to the fact that the Court held that it had no jurisdiction of the case (although nine years later, it was obliged to admit that its decision had been wrong, and to overrule it). Had the case been decided in 1863, instead of in 1870, it is probable that the Legal Tender Acts would have been held invalid by so large a majority of the Court that no attempt would have been made to reverse the decision, and the Court would have been spared the charges and the temporary discredit, later brought upon it by the rendering of its two contradictory decisions, in 1870 and 1871. The effect of an adverse decision in 1863 upon the methods

[1] *Taney*, 432; *Opinion of the Judges* of Feb. 16, 1863, in 158 U. S. App.

then employed to finance the war presents an interesting field for surmise.

One other case of historical importance with relation to the war may be noted, *Ex parte Vallandigham*, 1 Wall. 243, in which it had been expected that the whole question of the validity of the arrests and military trials ordered by Lincoln and Stanton would be presented for the decision of the Court. The possibility, however, of a conflict between the Court and the Executive on this serious point was averted by a ruling that the Court had no jurisdiction of a petition of habeas corpus issued to a military commission; consequently no decision of the question was made until after the end of the war, in *Ex parte Milligan*, in 1866.

Before the opening of the December Term of 1864, Chief Justice Taney (who had been ill during the whole of the previous Term) died on October 12, 1864. He was then in his eighty-eighth year, and had presided over the Court for more than twenty-eight years. When the Court met on December 7, 1864, resolutions of the Bar were presented by Thomas Ewing, stating that "deeply impressed by the great and good qualities and acquirements and illustrious life" of Taney, they deplored "the decree, inevitable at his advanced age, which had removed him from his place of usefulness, dignity and honor here." [1] In his reply to these resolutions, Judge Wayne, after alluding to the Chief Justice and referring to the body of law built up by his decisions and by those of his predecessor, closed with a patriotic comment upon the war and the duty of the Court in maintaining this great constitutional system

[1] The meeting of the Bar had been held, Dec. 6, 1864, and addresses were made by Thomas Ewing, J. M. Carlisle, Henry Stanbery, Reverdy Johnson and Charles O'Conor. The *National Republican*, Dec. 7, 1864, stated that the resolutions were "read by James M. Carlisle who framed them. Justice Wayne in a low and tremulous voice which was semi-audible replied in behalf of the Court."

of law: "It is truly a system upon which we can rely, as a foundation for securing the rights and independence of the States of this Union and our National Liberty. Gentlemen of the Bar, it is our part to maintain it, and if this shall be done with discretion, and with a spirit exempt from the corruptions of party, our country will again be what it was."

The persistence of the bitterness of partisan feeling which had been aroused by Taney's fatal decision in the *Dred Scott Case* was shown by an entry in the diary of Gideon Welles, the Secretary of the Navy, with reference to a discussion in the Cabinet as to its attendance at Taney's funeral: [1]

I felt little inclined to participate. I have never called upon him living, and while his position and office were to be respected, I had no honors for the deceased beyond those that were public. That he had many good qualities and possessed ability, I do not doubt; that he rendered service in Jackson's Administration is true, and during most of his political life, he was upright and just. But the course pursued in the *Dred Scott Case* and all the attending circumstances forfeited respect for him as a man or Judge . . . for I have looked on him and his Court as having contributed, unintentionally, perhaps, but largely, to the calamities of our afflicted country. They probably did not mean treason, but thought their wisdom and official position would give national sanction to a great wrong.

Many Republican newspapers commented on Taney's death with extreme rancor. The *Independent*, while stating that "a long life of public service in posts of great power and dignity is just ended", and while admitting his "unblemished private life", could not refrain from making the occasion an excuse for a further attack on the "infamous decision" and his "perdurable ignominy", and it repeated the false charge that Taney

[1] *The Diary of Gideon Welles* (1911), Oct. 14, Nov. 26, 1864.

had stated that the negro had no rights which a white man was bound to respect. "This sentence," it said, "will keep the memory of Chief Justice Taney in the popular mind, as long as the memory of slavery endures. It compresses into a single line the whole bloody history and lawless law of slavery. . . . History will expose him to eternal scorn in the pillory she has set up for infamous Judges." [1] The *Cincinnati Gazette* delivered a violent invective on the Dred Scott decision, which it termed "astounding to lawyers and revolting to every humane man"; and it stated that as the Court became successively more "degraded", the Democratic Party "began to set up its decision as a finality. They dragged it into the party arena to decide political questions," in all of which Judge Taney was "as subservient an instrument as in the tyrannical act for which he was rewarded by his place on the Bench." Other papers even questioned Taney's patriotism. Thus, the Washington correspondent of the *Philadelphia Press* wrote that Taney had earned great and just renown, and had been accepted as the best embodiment of a pure and conscientious Justice, until "that fatal decree which in great part has been the source of all our woes. . . . The Supreme Court from that time became a political, if not a party, tribunal, and the awe and veneration that had so long surrounded its Chief were supplanted by suspicion and distrust. . . . Nobody doubts that Taney died with his heart beating for the Rebellion. He scarcely took pains to conceal his feelings. Some of his decisions in

[1] *Independent*, Oct. 20, 1864; *Cincinnati Gazette*, Oct. 14, 20, 1864; *Philadelphia Press*, Oct. 14, 1864; *Philadelphia North American*, Oct. 14, 1864. The *Nation*, April 23, 1885, stated that the story used to be told of Benjamin F. Wade, the radical Republican Senator from Ohio, "that old Ben said he had for many weary years earnestly prayed that the author of the Dred Scott decision might live until a Republican President could name his successor — and he began to fear that he prayed too hard."

the early days of that most murderous revolt were held to be almost partisan. Hence, however we may remember and respect his past excellence, no true friend of the Government can feel that his loss is a National loss." And the *Philadelphia North American* made an equally unwarranted assault, stating that subserviency and partisanship were characteristic of his nature, proofs of which he had afforded "by his efforts to relieve Maryland traitors from arrest. . . . The Nation can feel little regret at his removal from an office which, in his hands, has been so promiscuously used. It is fortunate for the interests of humanity that the President and Senate who must fill the vacancy are devoted to the interests of republican liberty and will suffer no man of that school of politics to which Taney belonged to intrude into the judicial robes of which death has deprived him."

There were, however, many strong Republican papers which were not blinded by passions arising out of the slavery question, and which frankly admitted the greatness of the dead Chief Justice.[1] "He discharged the high duties of his position with a dignity, impartiality, and integrity which have reflected honor on his country, and in a manner which, with one notable exception, have been entirely satisfactory to his countrymen," said the *Washington Chronicle;* and the *New York Tribune*, while terming him "a votary and pillar of the Slave Power", said that though not so wise a man as Marshall, he was still an "able, learned, upright Judge, whose one signal aberration from the line of duty his surviving countrymen will now hasten to forget", and that "it is no more just than generous to question his integrity, nor his sincerity, whatever we may think

[1] *Washington Chronicle*, Oct. 13, 1864; *Missouri Democrat*, Oct. 18, 1864; *New York Tribune*, Oct. 14, 15, 1864; *New York Times*, Oct. 14, 1864; *Ohio State Journal*, Oct. 17, 1864; *Boston Daily Advertiser*, Oct. 14, 1864.

of the quality of his patriotism. . . . It were unjust
to presume that he did not truly and earnestly seek the
good of his country." The *New York Times* spoke of
Taney's "pure, moral character and great legal learning and acumen", and said: "Had it not been for his
unfortunate Dred Scott decision, all would admit that
he had, through all these years, nobly sustained his
high office. That decision itself, wrong as it was, did
not spring from a corrupt or malignant heart. It came,
we have charity to believe, from a sincere desire to
compose, rather than exacerbate, sectional discord.
But yet it was none the less an act of supreme folly, and
its shadow will ever rest on his renown." And the
Boston Advertiser said that, until the Dred Scott decision,
Taney "by his acquirements as a jurist and his grave
deportment seemed the worthy successor of Marshall;
. . . and as the political excitements of the day disappear, and his character as a Judge comes to be read
in the long course of his judgments, rather than in political discussion, we may well believe that his name
will again shine brilliantly and permanently among
those of the greatest of American lawyers and jurists." [1]

That the Democratic papers would eulogize the
Chief Justice was to have been expected; and the
World said that Taney possessed one indispensable
qualification for his position which even his assailants
admitted, "a high and intrepid independence — that
moral fearlessness which is deterred by no obloquy from

[1] That even with Republicans the feelings aroused by Taney's Dred Scott decision
had begun to die down prior to his death is seen from an editorial in *Harper's Weekly*,
Dec. 8, 1860, which stated: "Taney has won high fame. His opinions command
general respect. . . . Within the past year or two, he has, after twenty years
absolution from the strife of politics, been subjected to some animadversion by
members of the Republican party, in consequence of the Dred Scott decision. Without entering upon the controversy involved in this celebrated case, we may close
this brief sketch with the remark that when Judge Taney shall have disappeared
altogether from public life, members of all parties will unite to commend his vast
learning, his unspotted integrity and his remarkable suavity."

stern obedience to honest convictions." The *National Intelligencer* said that he left "a reputation as much distinguished by the superior dignity of his character as by the extraordinary vigor of intellect"; and the *Baltimore Sun* said that the "common opinion of his countrymen bears witness to his faithful performance of the great duties of his station. . . . He will go to his grave, followed by the reverence and regret of the wise, the thoughtful and the virtuous of his generation." [1]

The persistence of the implacable hatred entertained by the radical anti-slavery Republicans towards the Chief Justice was illustrated, four months after his death, by a debate in February, 1865, on a bill which had been introduced by Lyman Trumbull, the prominent Republican Senator from Illinois, for the placing of a marble bust of Taney in the Supreme Court-room (where already busts of Jay, Ellsworth and Marshall had been installed). [2] "I object," said Charles Sumner, "that an emancipated country should make a bust to the author of the Dred Scott decision." To this, Trumbull replied: "A person who has presided over the Supreme Court for more than a quarter of a century and has added reputation to the character of the Judiciary of the United States throughout the world is not to be hooted down, by an exclamation that the country is to be emancipated. Suppose he did make a wrong decision. No man is infallible. He was a great and learned and able man." [3] "The name of Taney," retorted Sumner, "is to be hooted down the page of

---

[1] *New York World*, Oct. 14, 1864; *National Intelligencer*, Oct. 13, 1864; see also Nov. 10, 1864, quoting address of William L. Pryor before the United States Circuit Court in New York, and the response of Judge Nelson; *Baltimore Sun*, Oct. 14, 1864.
[2] *38th Cong., 2d Sess.*, Feb. 23, 1865, 1012 *et seq.*
[3] See editorial in *Springfield Republican*, Jan. 26, 1867, entitled "The Just are Generous", with reference to efforts made in Illinois to defeat Trumbull for reëlection because of his vote on the Taney bust question.

history. . . . The Senator says that he for twenty-
five years administered justice. He administered justice, at last, wickedly, and degraded the Judiciary of
the country and degraded the age." This extreme
attack brought to his defense the warm personal
friend of the late Chief Justice, Reverdy Johnson,
Senator from Maryland, who said: "I cannot fail to
express my astonishment at the course of the honorable
Senator from Massachusetts, which he thinks it, I
suppose, his duty to pursue. If the times in which
we are living are honestly and truly recorded by the
historian, I think the honorable member from Massachusetts will be very happy, if he stands as pure and
high upon the historic page as the learned Judge who is
now no more. . . . The decisions of that learned jurist
are now quoted with approbation everywhere; and
there is not a Judge upon the Bench now (three or four
of them having been selected by the present incumbent
of the Presidential office) who will not say at once that a
brighter intellect never adorned the judicial chair."[1]
Trumbull also defended the dead man's name: "I will
not undertake to institute a comparison between Marshall and Taney. They were great men, both of them
great jurists, and each of them has shed luster upon the
judicial tribunal over which he presided. Each was a
man of great ability, of great learning, of great purity
of character; and I am sorry that the Senator from
Massachusetts should come in with this denunciation of
a man, against whom he can find no fault except that

[1] In a debate over the Territory of Montana bill, March 31, 1864, Johnson had
replied to Sumner's criticism of the Dred Scott decision, in these caustic words:
"I have yet to be advised that the honorable member, either by nature or education,
has attained so much intellectual celebrity, or possesses such transcendent mental
ability as to be able to pronounce *ex cathedra* against a decision pronounced by the
Supreme Court of the United States. There are many men, the equals of the honorable Senator, to say the least, intellectually, who think that that decision was anything but an outrage."

he made an erroneous decision"; and he added with sarcasm: "If the Senator from Massachusetts had presided, or should ever preside, over the Supreme Court of the United States for thirty years, he would be more than man, if he did not make any erroneous decision." Sumner returned to the charge with even more extravagant language, saying that Taney should be "left to the sympathetic companionship of Jeffreys . . . the tool of unjust power. . . . What is the office of Chief Justice, if it has been used to betray Human Rights ? The crime is great, according to the position of the criminal. If you were asked to mention the incident of our history previous to the Rebellion which was in all respects most worthy of condemnation, most calculated to cause the blush of shame, and most deadly in its consequences I do not doubt that you would say the Dred Scott decision and especially the wicked opinion of the Chief Justice. . . . Judicial baseness reached its lowest point on that occasion. You have not forgotten that terrible decision where a most unrighteous judgment was sustained by a falsification of history." Senator Henry Wilson of Massachusetts said that the Dred Scott decision was "the greatest crime in the judicial annals of the Republic", and that Taney was "recreant to liberty and humanity. . . . It is not in the power of the Congress of the United States to affect his reputation with the present or with the coming ages. Laudations, statues and busts will be as impotent as were the eulogies pronounced by a few conservative gentlemen in the Supreme Court-room a few weeks ago." [1] The debate was closed by Sumner — "Taney shall not be represented as a saint by any

---

[1] The *Atlantic Monthly* in February, 1865, said that Taney "will most likely, after the traitor leaders, be held in infamous remembrance" and that he covered "the most glorious pages of his country's history with infamy, and insulted the virtue and intelligence of the civilized world."

vote of Congress, if I can help it." The bill was lost at this session of Congress. Later, however, on January 29, 1874, about a month before Sumner's death, a bill for the busts of Chase and Taney was passed without debate, and they were duly placed in the Court-room.

History has recorded a very different verdict upon his place in the annals of the legal history of the country from that which Sumner and Wilson endeavored to establish. "Before the first term of my service in the Court had passed, I more than liked him; I loved him," said Judge Miller, later. "And after all that has been said of that great good man, I always stand ready to say that conscience was his guide, and sense of duty his principle." "Few Judges have had wider experience, and none, perhaps, more capable of forming a sound and unimpassioned judgment," said Judge Dillon. George Ticknor Curtis, one of the counsel who had argued before Taney in behalf of Dred Scott, writing only fourteen years after Taney's death, paid the following handsome and judicious tribute to his qualities: "He was indeed a great magistrate, and a man of singular purity of life and character. That there should have been one mistake in a judicial career so long, so exalted, and so useful, is only proof of the imperfection of our natures. . . . If he had never done anything else that was high, heroic and important, his noble vindication of the writ of habeas corpus and of the dignity and authority of his office against a rash minister of state, who, in the pride of a fancied Executive power, came near to the commission of a great crime, will command the admiration and gratitude of every lover of constitutional liberty, so long as our institutions shall endure." [1] And a sane and temperate review

[1] *Samuel Freeman Miller*, by Charles N. Gregory, *Yale Law Journ.* (1908), XVII; *A Great Judicial Character — Roger Brooke Taney*, by Charles N. Gregory, *ibid.*

of Taney's life in a leading law journal, written only eight years after his death, thus portrayed his position in legal annals. "He presided over the Supreme Court of the United States for upwards of twenty-eight years. To borrow the suggestive words of Cushing: 'He had inducted into office nine Presidents of the United States; and as he stood on that historic eastern front of the Capitol, the Republic's giant steps, in the lofty dignity of his great form and office, year after year witnessing and assisting at the rise and fall of parties, of Administrations, of dynasties, all else seemed to be transitory as day and night, evanescent as dream-spectres, whilst he and it were stable and monumental alone in this government.' His professional career was nearly contemporaneous with the judicial career of Chief Justice Marshall. Together they filled that high office for more than sixty-three years, and may be said to have built up the great structure of Federal juris-prudence, of which the foundation only was laid by their predecessors. . . . Upon all points of new prac-tice, he almost uniformly, even when very infirm and unable to write other opinions, delivered the judgment of the Court. The stability, uniformity, and com-pleteness of our National jurisprudence is largely to be attributed to the fact that, for sixty-three years, only two persons presided over the Supreme Court and that, when its business accumulated and the docket became crowded, Chief Justice Taney possessed that organizing genius which rendered the practice complete and sys-tematic. His judicial Associates speak with profound respect of his value in the consultation-room; and it is the concurrent voice of all whose professional avo-cations brought them into personal relations with him

(1908), XVIII; *Laws and Jurisprudence of England and America* (1895), by John F. Dillon, 167; *Curtis*, I, 239–246; *Amer. Law Rev.* (1873), VII, 327–328.

that there was a sweetness and benignity, a courtesy of the heart as well as of the manner, and a simple kindliness, especially to the younger members of his profession, which rendered him a conspicuous example for all Judges to imitate. The patient and untiring attention which he always gave to counsel while addressing the Court is worthy of perpetual remembrance. . . . Whatever opinion posterity may form of the greatness of the Judge, there can be but one as to the purity of his heart and his earnest fidelity to his own understanding of his duty. He was twice the object of general denunciation by large multitudes of his countrymen. . . . It is doubtless too soon to expect cool and fair judgment upon one who on such different occasions, so conspicuously opposed popular sentiment. It is an unhappy American custom to charge treason and baseness upon those who differ from us on great questions of policy and law. . . . The calmer judgment of posterity may, perchance, say that, as an abstract question of constitutional law, the Chief Justice rightly interpreted the law as it was, and that the dissenting voices only proclaimed what it should have been. Revolution has confirmed their dissent, and, if amendment was needed, the sword has amended the construction now."

As soon as the death of Taney was announced, agitation as to his successor became active, and the probability of a Republican Chief Justice was hailed with delight by the supporters of the Union. "So old Taney is dead," wrote Col. Charles Francis Adams. "These fatal Ides of November bid fair to see the Executive, Legislative, Judiciary and Army of this country working in one harmonious whole like the strands of a cable. It is a pleasant vision. I at least feel confident it will be realized. However that election may result, one thing is settled: the darling wish of Taney's last day is doomed not to be realized. It was not reserved for him to put the veto of the law on the Proclamation of Emancipation. I suppose Chase will succeed him, and I do not know that we have any better man. If he does, he will have a great future before him in the moulding of our new constitutional law." Charles Sumner had already written to Lincoln, urging the importance of having the war measures sustained by the Court, and saying that "from this time forward the Constitution must be interpreted for liberty, as it has thus far for slavery." [1] "There is an opportunity now to restore to the office the high character given it by Jay and Marshall, and to lay a cornerstone of regenerated and reconstructed Union," said a prominent Republican organ; and another expressed the hope that the appointment would be made, not in payment of any personal or political debt, but as "the crowning grace of a career of exalted and beneficent public service"; for, it said, "notoriously the Bench of the Supreme Court is not so strong as it was forty years ago, and emphatically it needs to be reënforced and elevated in the opinion of the Nation." The press, in general, assumed that Lincoln would appoint Salmon Portland Chase of Ohio, who had resigned as Secretary of the Treasury, in the preceding June. "The country expects the President to fulfil the wishes of the people by the appointment of Chase," said the *Independent*.[2] Chase had, moreover, very strong supporters in his

---

[1] *A Cycle of Adams Letters* (1920), letter of Oct. 15, 1864; *Sumner*, IV, letter to Francis Lieber, Oct. 12, 1864; the *Detroit Free Press*, Oct. 17, 1864, said that Taney's death has been "looked for with anxiety by the malignant partisans of Mr. Lincoln. One of their schemes has been to abolitionize the Supreme Court."

[2] *Cincinnati Gazette*, Oct. 20, 1864; *New York Tribune*, Oct. 18, 1864; *Independent*, Oct. 30, 1864; the *New York Herald*, on the other hand, said, Oct. 16, 1864, that: "A worse selection could not be made. The position requires a lawyer of profound attainments. Chase is but a dabbler in legal lore. It requires a man of calm judgment and unbiased opinion. Chase is a partisan!"

Cabinet colleague, Edwin M. Stanton, and in the three prominent Senators, Wilson and Sumner of Massachusetts and William P. Fessenden of Maine. The President, notwithstanding his many differences of opinions with his "imperious Secretary", had always preserved a high and unshaken opinion of his great ability. Long before Taney's death, he had said: "Chase is about one and a half times bigger than any other man I ever knew", and had stated that: "There is not one man in the Union who would make as good a Chief Justice as Chase; and, if I have the opportunity, I will make him Chief Justice of the United States." [1] But Lincoln was uneasy lest Chase's well-known ambition for the Presidency should lead him to mingle politics with law, if he were placed upon the Bench. To Senator Wilson, who had remarked to him that he could afford to overlook Chase's harsh words, Lincoln had replied: "Oh, as to that, I care nothing. . . . I have only one doubt about his appointment. He is a man of unbounded ambition and has been working all his life to become President. That he can never be; and I fear that if I make him Chief Justice, he will simply become more restless and uneasy, and neglect the place, in his strife and intrigue to make himself President. If I were sure that he would go on the Bench and give up his aspirations and do nothing but make himself a great Judge, I would not hesitate a moment." [2] And to George S. Boutwell, Lincoln said: "There are three reasons in favor of his appointment, and one very strong reason

---

[1] *Salmon Portland Chase* (1899), by Albert Bushnell Hart; *Abraham Lincoln* (1890), by John C. Nicolay and John Hay, IX.

[2] *Abraham Lincoln* (1890), by John C. Nicolay and John Hay, IX; *Reminiscences of Sixty Years in Public Affairs* (1902), by George S. Boutwell, II, 29. In an editorial in the *Independent*, May 15, 1873, on Chase's death, it is said that: "Mr. Lincoln hesitated to appoint him, only because as he said, he (Chase) had the Presidential maggot in his brain, and he (Lincoln) never knew anybody who once had it to get rid of it."

against it. First, he occupies the largest place in the public mind in connection with the office; then we wish for a Chief Justice who will sustain what has been done in regard to emancipation and the legal tenders. We cannot ask a man what he will do, and if we should, and he should answer us, we should despise him for it. Therefore, we must take a man whose opinions are known. But there is one very strong reason against his appointment. He is a candidate for the Presidency and if he does not give up that idea, it will be very bad for him and very bad for me." Some of his opponents urged that Chase was too old; but as he was only fifty-six, while at the time of their respective appointments, Taney had been fifty-nine, Rutledge fifty-five and Ellsworth fifty, there was little force in this criticism. Other rival candidates of legal eminence had strong advocates. Judge Swayne, then on the Court, was extremely desirous of promotion, and was vigorously urged by Lincoln's personal friend Judge David Davis, and by the Postmaster-General, Dennison. Montgomery Blair, the former Postmaster-General, was also an ardent candidate, and was supported by the Secretary of State, William H. Seward, and by the Secretary of the Navy, Gideon Welles.[1] Chase himself believed that Edwin M. Stanton would be appointed. There was a suggestion of the promotion of Judge Wayne, and Judge William Strong of Pennsylvania was considered.[2] The New York and Massachusetts Bars were supporting

[1] Charles Sumner wrote, Aug. 8, 1865: "Montgomery Blair complained to Seward that he had not pushed him for the Chief Justiceship against Chase. Seward said that he had 'presented his papers' and that Blair was 'his candidate.' Blair thought that if Seward had been much in earnest, he could have prevented Chase's nomination." *Sumner*, IV.

[2] The *National Intelligencer*, Dec. 6, 1864, quoted a Kentucky paper as saying that the appointment of Wayne would be "a suitable acknowledgment of his pure patriotism in a crisis so trying to his allegiance to the Constitution and Union which so many other distinguished Southern men have proved unfaithful to." *Amer. Law Rev.* (1881), XV, 130.

William M. Evarts of New York, and Chase, himself, acknowledged Evart's qualifications, writing characteristically: "Evarts is a man of sterling abilities and excellent learning, and a much greater lawyer than I ever pretended to be. The truth is, I always thought myself much overestimated. And yet, I think I have more judgment than Evarts, and that, tried by the Marshall standard should make a better Judge, while he might, tried by the Story standard." Chase himself had long been anxious to obtain the appointment, but he was unwilling to become an active applicant; and he wrote to his warmest and most effective supporter, Charles Sumner of Massachusetts: "I have feared that the President might suppose that I have some agency in the representations which reach him favorable to my appointment. If he has, I hope you will disadvise him of the impression. I would not have the office on the terms of being obliged to ask for it." Many leading Republicans, however, opposed Chase, and delegations appeared even from Ohio in protest against him, arguing that he had ardent political ambition and that he would use the Bench merely as a stepping-stone to the Presidency, and that he was not of judicial temper.[1]

While the President postponed acting upon the appointment until a month after the close of the Presidential campaign in November, the importance of the choice to be made, and "the duty of filling the Supreme Bench with a man who shall revive Marshall" was pointed out to him in frequent articles in the press. The *Independent* said: "That Court will be called upon,

[1] The *New York World* and *New York Herald* opposed Chase; while the *New York Tribune* and *Independent* warmly favored him. The *Independent*, Dec. 15, 1868, said that Thurlow Weed and James Gordon Bennett came to Washington to consult with Montgomery Blair (Chase's bitterest foe) to see if the nomination could not be prevented.

before long, to deal with the most momentous questions it can ever handle — questions involving the dearest rights of millions of human beings, the sacred honor of the Government, and the entire future of the Republic. If the next Chief Justice of the United States should have either a wrong head or a wrong heart — if he could be another Taney — who could measure the far-reaching extent of such a National calamity? There is one man whose appointment will fulfill the general expectation — Chase. Will the President hesitate about his duty? We believe not." [1]   Writing November 26, 1864, Gideon Welles described the situation in an interesting manner, though in his estimate of Chase, allowance must be made for Welles' strong personal prejudices: [2]

The question of Chief Justice has excited much remark and caused quite a movement with many. Mr. Chase is expecting it, and he has many strong friends who are urging him. But I have not much idea that the President will appoint him, nor is it advisable he should. I had called on the President on the 23rd and had some conversation, after dispatching a little business, in regard to this appointment of Chief Justice. He said there was a great pressure and a good many talked of, but that he was now preparing his message and did not intend to take up the subject of Judge before the session commenced. "There is," said he, "a tremendous pressure just now for Evarts of New York, who, I suppose, is a good lawyer?" This he put inquiringly. I stated that he stood among the foremost at the New York Bar; perhaps no one was more prominent as a lawyer. "But that," I remarked, "is not all. Our Chief Justice must have a judicial mind, be upright, of strict integrity, not too pliant; should be a statesman and a politician." By politician I did not mean a partisan. (I said) that it appeared to me the occasion should be improved to place at the head of the Court a man, not a partisan, but one who was impressed with the principles and doctrines which had brought this Administration into power, that it would conduce to the public welfare and his own comfort to have harmony between himself and the judicial department, and that it was all-important that he should have a Judge who would be a correct and faithful expositor of the principles of his Administration and policy after his Administration shall have closed. I stated that among the candidates who had been named, Mr. Montgomery Blair, it appeared to me, best conformed to those requirements; that the President knew the man, his ability, his truthfulness, honesty and courage.

Welles also wrote that Postmaster-General Dennison had said that Chase and Lincoln "could not assimilate, and that, were Chase in that position — a life tenure — he would exhibit his resentment against the President, who, he thinks, has prevented his upward official career. . . . He never forgets or forgives those who have once thwarted him." A few days later, Welles wrote that: "Gov. Morgan thinks Chase will be appointed Chief Justice, but I do not yet arrive at that conclusion. The President sometimes does strange things, but this would be a singular mistake, in my opinion, for one who is so shrewd and honest — an appointment that he would soon regret."

Finally, Lincoln made his decision; and magnanimously overlooking all personal considerations he elevated Chase to the Chief Justiceship, on December 6, 1864. "It took Congress, as it did the country, somewhat by surprise," wrote a Washington correspondent, "because the President had so conducted himself within a fortnight as to create the impression that he would not decide the matter at once. Mr. Lincoln is a humorous man, and he seems to have enjoyed the pleasant surprise of Mr. Chase's friends and the confusion of his enemies. He kept his secret

well, if it is a fact, as some of his friends claim, that he
has never thought of appointing any one else. . . . A
day or two before the nomination was made out, Mr.
Lincoln said to a very intimate friend: 'Mr. Chase's
enemies have been appealing to the lowest and meanest
of my feelings. They report ill-natured remarks of
his upon me and my Administration. If it were true
that he made them, I could not be so base as to allow
the fact to influence me in the selection of a man for the
Chief Justiceship.' " No better illustration of Lincoln's
high-mindedness and nobility of soul can be found
than in this nomination; for as Welles wrote: "The
President told Chandler, of New Hampshire, who
remonstrated against such selection, that he would
rather have swallowed his buckhorn chair than to have
nominated Chase." That Lincoln evidently did not
consult his Cabinet as to this important appointment
is seen from another entry in Welles' diary, on December 6 :[1]

Shortly after leaving the Cabinet, I heard that Chase had
been nominated to, and confirmed by, the Senate as Chief
Justice. Not a word was interchanged in the Cabinet respecting it. . . . I hope the selection may prove a good one.
I would not have advised it, because I have apprehensions
on that subject. Chase has mental power and resources,
but he is politically ambitious and restless, prone to, but not
very skillful in, intrigues and subtle management. If he
applies himself strictly and faithfully to his duties, he may
succeed on the Bench, although his mind, I fear, is not so
much judicial as ministerial. He will be likely to use the
place for political advancement, and thereby endanger confidence in the Court. He, though selfish, stubborn sometimes, wants moral courage and frankness, is fond of adula-

[1] *Welles*, II, 195–197, *Independent*, Dec. 15, 1864. A letter to the *Cincinnati
Gazette* said, Dec. 6, 1864, that the appointment of Chase was written out by
Lincoln in his own hand; that the first persons informed were Senator Sherman,
and Hugh McCulloch; and that it was not known to any one else, even to the
President's Secretary, until it was sent in to the Senate.

tion, and with official superiors is a sycophant. I hope the President may have no occasion to regret his selection.

The appointment was received with very varied feelings by the public. On December 15, Welles wrote: "Chase's appointment gives satisfaction to Sumner and a few others; but there is general disappointment. Public sentiment had settled down under the conviction that he could not have the position. Sumner helped to secure it for him. . . . Sumner declares to me that Chase will retire from the field of politics and not be a candidate for the Presidency. I questioned it, but Sumner said with emphasis it was so. He had assured the President that Chase would retire from party politics. I have no doubt Sumner believes it. What foundations he has for the belief, I know not, though he speaks positively and as if he had assurance. My own convictions are that, if he lives, Chase will be a candidate and his restless and ambitious mind is already at work. It is his nature." By the press of the country, in general, the appointment met with approbation.[1] "The eminent qualifications which Mr. Chase brings to this exalted position will be recognized by all citizens without distinction of party, among whom purity of character in combination with distinguished intellectual endowments are held in honor," said the *National Intelligencer*. Even the Democratic *New York World* said that the appointment "will be generally endorsed by the public opinion of the country as the most suitable that could have been made." The *Boston Advertiser* commented with

[1] *Washington Star*, Dec. 7, 1864: "The nomination will strike the country generally as one eminently fit to be made." *Philadelphia Press*, Dec. 8, 1864; *Boston Daily Advertiser*, Dec. 8, 1864; *New York World*, Dec. 7, 1864. The *New York Evening Post*, Dec. 6, 1864, termed him "calm, deliberate, just . . . long intimately acquainted with the whole class of subjects which are likely to engage in the coming time the attention of the Court."

much fairness as follows: "Enemy as well as friend has admitted his dignity and force of character, his intellectual power and grasp, and the immoveable strength of his convictions of right. . . . It was urged by many, and with some force, while this appointment was still in doubt, that in filling such a place, the President's choice should properly fall upon some man of legal eminence, rather than anybody whose name had long been connected with politics, and that by such a course, Mr. Lincoln might do something towards raising the Supreme Judicial tribunal of the Nation above the embittered discussion of the past few years, and give it something like its former hold upon the confidence of men of all parties. Mr. Lincoln, however, in making this appointment from political life rather than with reference to professional distinction alone, has followed a long line of precedents on both sides of the water. . . . Jay, Ellsworth, Marshall and Taney . . . were all men whose political career had given them a position and rank which mere preëminence at the Bar seldom brings. Mr. Lincoln, like former Presidents, preferred to call to that station a statesman who has already secured the attention and respect, if not the friendship, of the whole country, trusting, as they did with such eminent success, that the judicial capacity and high merit of the man would, in the sequel, secure besides these advantages, the confidence of all classes and parties."

There were some who, as stated in the foregoing editorial, were apprehensive of the appointment as savoring too much of politics, and who feared that Chase's absence from the Bar since 1850 and his service in the Senate and in the Cabinet had withdrawn him from legal pursuits, and had rendered him less able to cope with the modern developments of the law.

Some also believed that he would find it difficult to disassociate his opinions from political considerations, in view of the fact that many questions on which he must now pass had been before him when in Executive office. "I dined with him," wrote Hugh McCulloch, "a couple of weeks after the coveted honor had been conferred upon him, and I was pained by discovering that he was far from being satisfied. . . . High as the position was, it was not the one to which he had really aspired. To him it seemed like retirement from public life." [1]

Few of the forebodings of his opponents were justified, and the prediction that politics would influence his decisions proved especially false. For though with this appointment, President Lincoln had practically reconstituted the Supreme Court as it existed prior to the war (five of the members being his appointees — Swayne, Miller, Davis, Field and Chase, — and these five becoming a majority of the Court on the death of Judge Catron, six months later), nevertheless, those politicians who hoped for a partisan administration of justice by the Court with its new Judges were disappointed. Again it was shown to the American people that even in time of stress, the men who ascended the Supreme Bench, dropped their "politics when they assumed the black robes." And again it was found, as has been well said by Chase's biographer, that, precisely as the Republican appointees of Jefferson and Madison had failed to conform to the Presidential hopes that they would modify the Federalism of the

[1] *Men and Measures of Half a Century* (1888), by Hugh McCulloch, 186–187; John Sherman in his *Recollections of Forty Years* (1895), II, 340, states that in September, 1864, Chase was his guest for a day or two; "He was evidently restless and uneasy as to his future. I spoke to him about the position of Chief Justice. . . . He said it was a position of eminence that ought to satisfy the ambitions of any one but for which few men were fitted."

Court under Washington and Adams, so now, the reconstituted Court, "inherited the spirit of its predecessors; it continued to hold fast to its time-honored principles on public law and private rights, rather than to set up a new régime; and Chase's influence bore for caution and restraint, and not for radical changes." His own view of the necessity of eliminating all political considerations was set forth in a letter during the Johnson impeachment proceedings, when he wrote that he wished his name permanently disconnected from the Presidency: "I must dismiss every thought which might incline the scale of judgment either way. Do what I may, I cannot hope to escape imputations. I only hope to avoid giving any just occasion for them. The rest I leave cheerfully to Him who alone judgeth righteously." [1]

It must be admitted, however, that, in spite of the expression contained in this letter, Chase retained his ambition to succeed to the Presidency, and he was undoubtedly desirous of receiving the nomination both in 1868 and in 1872. While this ambition never influenced his judicial decisions, it seriously impaired the popular confidence in his impartiality and weakened the effect of some of his opinions. There was one further obstacle to his complete eminence in his position, which was referred to by Hugh McCulloch: "He had not been in the active practice of the law for twenty years, nor had he been able during that period to devote any time to legal studies. . . . So that when he went upon the Bench, he was unfamiliar with the work which he was called upon to perform. . . . He did have to work much harder in the investigation of legal questions,

[1] *Private Life and Public Services of Salmon Portland Chase* (1874), by Robert B. Warden, letters of March 2, 10, 1868; *Salmon Portland Chase* (1899), by Albert Bushnell Hart.

and in the preparation of opinions, than any of his Associates." Though he gradually developed great legal capacities as a Judge, Chase's own modest attitude towards his qualifications was strikingly expressed in a letter written three years after his appointment: "I never expected great success in any position I have occupied. My surprise at the degree of it that I have achieved has been greater, perhaps than any other man's. And now I still less hope for much success as a Judge. I came to the Bench too late and from too active pursuits to think of emulating any of my great predecessors. It will suffice if the duties of my position are performed according to the measure of my ability and circumstances."

On Thursday, December 15, 1864, at eleven in the morning, Chief Justice Chase took his seat on the Bench. "The scene was one to be remembered for a lifetime, yet it was of the simplest character," wrote a Washington correspondent. "There was a crowd of spectators present; but next to Mr. Chase, one man, himself a spectator, was the most interesting figure in the group of celebrated persons there. It was Charles Sumner. He stood leaning against one of the composite pillars at the right of the Justices, evidently agitated by the reflections suggested by the scene. It was in that very chamber, and the Senator looked down upon the spot, where Brooks made his murderous assault upon him but a few years ago; and now what a change! An abolitionist, and one glorying in the name, is Chief Justice; while of all the bloody men who participated in the intended murder (either actively or passively) scarcely one is alive; and the two or three who are, have sunk to obscurity. This is the revenge that time brings to the virtuous. When I saw Mr. Chase stand there in the highest place upon that Bench, already

THE SUPREME COURT IN 1865

Left to right: Davis, Swayne, Grier, Wayne, Chief Justice Chase, Nelson, Clifford, Miller, Field.

honoring it by his majestic presence, I was satisfied that Providence had ordered events more wisely than men could have done, in making Abraham Lincoln President, and Salmon P. Chase, Chief Justice."

On February 1, 1865, six weeks after the new Chief Justice took his seat, an event occurred in the Court which must have stirred his soul to its depths, when he reflected on the long years during which he had struggled in behalf of the negro; for on that day, the first negro lawyer — John S. Rock of Massachusetts — was admitted to practice before the bar of the Court. The dramatic event was thus described by an earnest anti-slavery man:[1] "The black man was admitted. Jet black, with hair of an extra twist — let me have the pleasure of saying, by purpose and premeditation, of an aggravating 'kink' — unqualifiedly, obtrusively, defiantly 'Nigger' — with no palliation of complexion, no let-down in lip, no compromise in nose, no abatement whatever in any facial, cranial, osteological particular from the despised standard of humanity brutally set up in our politics and in our Judicatory by the Dred Scott decision — this inky-hued African stood, in the monarchical power of recognized American Manhood and American Citizenship, within the bar of the Court which had solemnly pronounced that black men had no rights which white men were bound to respect; stood there a recognized member of it, professionally the brother of the distinguished counsellors on its long-rolls, in rights their equal, in the standing which rank gives their peer. By Jupiter, the sight was grand! 'Twas dramatic, too. At three minutes before eleven o'clock in the morning, Charles Sumner entered the Court-room, followed by

[1] *Independent*, Dec. 22, 1864, Feb. 9, 1865, quoting *New York Tribune*. Gideon Welles wrote in his diary, Feb. 3, 1865: "A negro lawyer has been presented by him (Sumner) to practice in the Supreme Court and extra demonstrations of that kind have been made by him and Chief Justice Chase."

the negro applicant for admission, and sat down within the Bar. At eleven, the procession of gowned Judges entered the room, with Chief Justice Chase at their head. The spectators and the lawyers in attendance rose respectfully on their coming. The Associate Justices seated themselves nearly at once, as is their courteous custom of waiting upon each other's movements. The Chief Justice, standing to the last, bowed with affable dignity to the Bar, and took his central seat with a great presence. Immediately the Senator from Massachusetts arose, and in composed manner and quiet tone said: 'May it please the Court, I move that John S. Rock, a member of the Supreme Court of the State of Massachusetts, be admitted to practice as a member of this Court.' The grave to bury the Dred Scott decision was in that one sentence dug; and it yawned there, wide open, under the very eyes of some of the Judges who had participated in the judicial crime against Democracy and humanity. The assenting nod of the great head of the Chief Justice tumbled in the corse and filled up the pit, and the black counselor of the Supreme Court got on to it and stamped it down and smoothed the earth to his walk to the rolls of the Court." It is a noteworthy fact that the status of the negro, even at that date, had continued so unsettled, that the new member of the Supreme Court Bar was obliged, after his admission, to go to the Provost Marshal to obtain a permit, before he could return to Massachusetts — no negroes being then allowed to leave Washington without a license from the military authority.

Within a year after Chase's accession, his progress in his judicial office was described in a letter from Washington as follows:[1] "The Chief Justice is hale and

[1] *Independent*, March 29, 1866.

hard at work, busy in downright earnest with his grave duties. Rising early, he attacks his books, examines his briefs, ponders his points of law and often before breakfast has done a fair day's work. Mr. Chase has signally realized his early ambition to attain to the one official position, which I know him to regard as the loftiest in our American system of government. During the few months immediately after his appointment, he found the studious and meditative life of the Judge so great a contrast to the exciting labors of a cabinet minister, that a man of his executive genius could not but feel a temporary irksomeness, as from a loss of customary muscular exercise. His shoulders at first did not feel weight enough in his gown. But he soon brought his faculties into such harmony with his office that he now takes up each new case, with a freshness of spirit that shows how a total change in one's intellectual habits in mature years may prove one of the best methods of keeping an elderly gentleman from growing old."

In view of the tremendous number of cases arising out of the war, during the ten years following the appointment of Chase as Chief Justice, it was of inestimable value to the country to have at the head of the Court not only a great lawyer, but a great statesman who had served both in Congress and in the Cabinet, and who was thoroughly and practically familiar with the business administration and economic and military problems of the Government. As had been predicted on his appointment, Chase brought "to the complicated and embarrassing questions growing out of the war and the subsequent reconciliation of divided sections . . . a large wisdom, a discerning but impartial judgment, and the sincerest patriotism, a love for the whole Nation and for all its parts, and a resolute will that neither an overgrown centralization of power in the

Federal head, nor an anarchical claim of absolute
sovereignty in the component States shall vitiate and
defeat" the long-established system of American
government.[1] With such a man at its head, and in
view of the conditions of the times, it was but natural
that, for the first six years after his accession to the
Bench, the trend of the Court's decisions should be
distinctly Nationalistic in character, sustaining the
powers of the Government to the fullest extent. The
first important task which fell to Chase's lot was the
development of the American prize law, in a series
of about thirty noted cases. As early as January 30,
1865, in *The Circassian*, 2 Wall. 135,[2] and in the more
famous cases of the *Bermuda*, the *Springbok* and the
Peterhoff in the two succeeding years, the Court established the famous doctrine of "continuous voyage"
and "ulterior destination." In the *Bank Tax Cases*,
2 Wall. 200, in 1865, and in a long series of cases later,
the Court was required to consider the constitutionality
of the great National banking system and the validity of
the numerous State statutes which sought to tax the
notes and operations of the National banks and the capital of State banks invested in United States Government stock or bonds. In all these cases, the Court consistently held that investments in Government securities
could not be taxed by the States, and that shares in the
National banks could only be taxed by permission of
Congress — such National banks being an agency of the
National Government whose operation could not legally be impeded by State action.[3]

[1] *New York Evening Post*, Dec. 8, 1864.
[2] See especially as to this case an editorial in the *New York World*, March 17, 1863.
[3] See also *Bank of Commerce* v. *Commissioner*, 2 Black, 620; *Bank Tax Cases*,
2 Wall. 200; *Van Allen* v. *Assessors*, 3 Wall. 573; *Society for Savings* v. *Coite*, 6
Wall. 594; *Provident Institution for Savings* v. *Massachusetts*, 6 Wall. 611; *Bank* v.
The Supervisors, 7 Wall. 26; *Austin* v. *The Aldermen*, 7 Wall. 694; *National Bank*
v. *Commonwealth*, 9 Wall. 353; *Lionberger* v. *Rouse*, 9 Wall. 468.

In 1866, the Court enhanced the National power by an important decision in *The Moses Taylor* and in *The Hine* v. *Trevor*, 4 Wall. 411, 555. In these cases, it was held for the first time that the grant of admiralty jurisdiction to the District Courts by the Judiciary Act of 1789 was exclusive, and that State laws conferring remedies *in rem* could only be enforced in these Courts. The result of the decision was to deprive the State Courts, especially in the West, of an immense class of cases relating to maritime contracts, collisions and other torts, over which they had hitherto exercised jurisdiction.

In 1867, another phase of the development of the principle that a State might not impede or embarrass the Government or impair the rights of the United States' citizens under the Constitution was presented by the decision in *Crandall* v. *Nevada*, 6 Wall. 35, in which a tax imposed by the State of Nevada upon every person leaving the State by railroad or stage coach or vehicle transporting for hire, was held invalid. It was declared that all citizens had a right to pass from State to State and to come to the seat of the Government, and that "this right is in its nature independent of the will of any State over whose soil he must pass in the exercise of it." That the Court had not yet fully realized the broad scope of the Commerce Clause of the Constitution was illustrated in this case by the fact that it refused to hold the statute invalid under that Clause; and it stated that "the tax does not itself institute any regulation of commerce of a National character or which has a uniform operation over the whole country." [1]

[1] Four years later, in 1871, in *Ward* v. *Maryland*, 12 Wall. 418, the Court held a State tax discriminating against non-resident traders invalid, as repugnant to the provision of the Constitution guaranteeing State citizens all the privileges and immunities of citizens in the several States; but here again it found it unnecessary to decide whether the tax infringed on the right of Congress to regulate interstate commerce. See also *Woodruff* v. *Parham*, 8 Wall. 123; *Hinson* v. *Lott*, 8 Wall. 148, in 1869; and *United States* v. *Wheeler*, 254 U. S. 281 in 1920.

Other than these decisions on National supremacy, the Court's chief work, in 1867 and the immediately ensuing years, in connection with the war was the settlement of the legal effect of the existence of a state of war upon business conditions. Its effect upon the running of the statute of limitations was considered in *Hanger* v. *Abbott*, 6 Wall. 532, and on contracts and trading with or for the enemy and on debts to an enemy in *Coppell* v. *Hall*, 7 Wall. 542. The important financial and tax legislation of the war was upheld in *Pacific Insurance Company* v. *Soule*, 7 Wall. 433, in which the nature of a "direct tax" under the Constitution was carefully elucidated in connection with the internal revenue laws.[1] The general power of the Government to expropriate property other than enemy property, in time of war and immediate public exigency, and the validity of the statutes which provided for the disposition of captured and abandoned cotton and for its sale and deposit of proceeds in the United States Treasury to meet the claims of any owners who could prove they had not adhered to the cause of the enemy were upheld, in 1871, in the noted case of *United States* v. *Russell*, 13 Wall. 623, and in about twenty cases during the succeeding fifteen years.[2] Another series of about thirty cases (decided over a period of twelve years) involved the statutes enacted for the confiscation and conservation of enemy property, the constitution-

---

[1] In *Bennett* v. *Hunter*, 9 Wall. 326, there was involved the first instance, since the early years of the Republic, of the imposition by Congress of a direct tax on land apportioned among the States.

[2] Act of March 12, 1863, and Act of July 2, 1864. See *The Constitution and the War Power — War Claims against the United States*, by William Lawrence, *Amer. Law Reg.* (1874–75), N. S. XIII, XIV; *The Rebellion*, by R. McPhail Smith, *Southern Law Rev.* (1873–74), II, III; *The Late Civil War and its Effect on Civil Remedies*, by William A. Maury, *Amer. Law Reg.* (1875), N. S. XIV; *Constitutional Foundation of War Claims for Property*, by William B. King, *Amer. Law Reg.* (1881), N. S. XX; *Some Legal Aspects of the Confiscation Acts of the Civil War*, by James G. Randall, *Amer. Hist. Rev.* (1912), XVII; *Captured and Abandoned Property during the Civil War, ibid.* (1913), XIX.

ality of which were upheld in another notable opinion, in 1871, *Miller* v. *United States*, 11 Wall. 268.[1] The legal status of the Confederate States and of their legislation during the war was settled by the Court, as early as 1870, in *Hickman* v. *Jones*, 9 Wall. 197, in which it held the Confederate Government to be "simply an armed resistance to the rightful authority of the sovereign"; and all its acts were held invalid so far as they were in aid of the rebellion. While the more radical Republican leaders were insistent that all legislation of every kind enacted by the various States of the Confederacy were illegal and void, the Court took a more conservative and rational view; and in *Horn* v. *Lockhart*, 17 Wall. 570, in 1873, it decided that the acts of the several Confederate States "so far as they did not impair or tend to impair the supremacy of the National authority or the just rights of citizens under the Constitution, are, in general, to be treated as valid and binding. The existence of a state of insurrection and war did not loosen the bonds of society or do away with civil government."

[1] Act of July 13, 1861; Act of August 6, 1861; Act of July 17, 1862; see especially *McVeigh* v. *United States*, 11 Wall. 259, in which the right even of an enemy to be heard in proceedings under the confiscation laws was upheld; and for the facts of this very extraordinary cause, see *New York Herald*, April 23, May 7, 1873.

NOTE. It is stated in *A Casket of Reminiscences* (1884), 433, by Ex-Senator Henry S. Foote, that President Lincoln, in 1864, had actually offered the Chief Justiceship to Judge Swayne, when the vacancy should occur, and that Swayne released Lincoln from the pledge, when later it seemed advisable to appoint Chase. Chase wrote to W. G. Brownlow, June 14, 1866: "I have become a Judge, in which office I confess myself less at home than when a co-operator with the friends of Union and freedom in the grand cause of human progress. But both as a Judge and as a citizen, I feel a profound interest in the complete restoration of the Union and the perfect re-establishment of civil order." *Ibid.*, 422.

CHAPTER TWENTY-NINE

THE MILLIGAN CASE

1866-1867

ALTHOUGH, from 1861 to 1870, the Court had consistently upheld the authority of the National Government, had widened the scope of jurisdiction of the Judiciary of the United States and had strictly limited the sovereignty of the States whenever they appeared to trespass on the National domain, it was destined to become the object of the most serious and determined attack by the very political party which favored such extension of National power.

The death of President Lincoln occurred on April 15, 1865, at the close of the December, 1864, Term; and with that Term, there ended a period of five years during which the Court had been absolutely free from the partisan criticism prevalent during the decade from 1850 to 1860. In 1866, however, political attack was renewed in a most violent form, as the Court became gradually involved in the fierce conflict then ensuing between President Johnson and the Congress over Reconstruction policies. The Republican opponents of the President were determined to abolish the military and civil State Governments in the South, instituted by Johnson under his Executive authority. They were insistent upon the establishment of a purely military control by legislative enactment, until the States should be reorganized and admitted back into the Union upon acceptance of such conditions as Congress should choose to impose. But, while confident of their power to prevail over the President's antagonism to their measures, the radical Republicans were apprehensive as to the attitude of the Court. Since no one of the forms of Government for the South proposed by them had any express constitutional sanction, and since it was openly stated by the President and his supporters that the validity of any such legislation would be challenged, it was evident that the Court might become the final arbiter of the situation; and in such event, the Radical Republicans were very doubtful as to the views of the Chief Justice. It was reported in the press that he did not approve their course in Congress; and it was well known that President Lincoln himself had expressed some fear lest Chase on the Bench might not support his war policies. "Lincoln hesitated," wrote Hugh McCulloch, "for some days, while the matter was under consideration, to send his name to the Senate, under the apprehension that he might be somewhat rigorous in his judgment of some of the Executive acts, and especially those of the Secretary of War, if suit should be brought involving questions that could only be settled by the Supreme Court. Knowing that my relations with Mr. Chase were intimate, he sent for me one day, and after explaining the nature of his fears, asked me what I thought about them. 'Why, Mr. President,' I replied, 'you have no reason for fears on that score. Mr. Chase is in the same box with yourself and Mr. Stanton. He favored and advised, as he himself has informed me, the dispersion by force of the Maryland Legislature, and if anything more illegal than that would have been has been done, I have not heard of it.' " [1] Shortly before Lincoln's death, and less than three months after the appointment of the new Chief Justice, it appears that he had received further intimations that Chase's views as to the legality of military trials would be adverse to the Administration, for his Secretary of the Navy, Gideon Welles, wrote in his diary :

Feb. 21, 1865. I found the President and Attorney-General Speed in consultation over an apprehended decision of Chief Justice Chase, whenever he could reach the question of the suspension of the writ of habeas corpus. Some intimation comes through Stanton, that His Honor the Chief Justice intends to make himself felt by the Administration, when he can reach them. I shall not be surprised, for he is ambitious and able. Yet on that subject, he is as much implicated as others.

Feb. 22, 1865. Met Speed at President's a day or two since. He is apprehensive Chase will fail the Administration on the question of habeas corpus and State arrests. The President expresses, and feels, astonishment. Calls up the committals of Chase on those measures. Yet I think an adroit intriguer can, if he chooses, escape these committals. I remember that on one occasion when I was with him, Chase made a fling which he meant should hit Seward on these matters, and as Seward is, he imagines, a rival for high position, the ambition of Chase will not permit the opportunity to pass, when it occurs, of striking his competitor. There is no man with more fierce aspirations than Chase, and the Bench will be used to promote his personal ends. Speed and myself called on Seward on Monday, after the foregoing interview with the President. Seward thinks Chase, if badly disposed, cannot carry the Court, but this is mere random conjecture.

At the time of the trial of the assassins of Lincoln before a military commission sitting in the District

[1] *Springfield Weekly Republican*, April 7, 1866, quoting a Washington correspondent of the *Cincinnati Commercial; Men and Manners of Half a Century* (1888), 186, 187, by Hugh McCulloch; *The Diary of Gideon Welles* (1911), II, 242, 245, 246.

of Columbia, the attitude of some of the other Judges of the Court had disturbed the Radical leaders in Congress, who feared lest the Court should issue writs of habeas corpus and discharge the prisoners. Welles recorded in his diary, July 17, 1865, that Secretary of War Stanton, in his characteristic, arbitrary fashion, wanted the prisoners sent to the Dry Tortugas in the South, "where old Nelson or any other Judge would not try to make difficulty by habeas corpus." The Judges had also drawn upon themselves the criticism of the Radicals, by their refusal to sit in the Circuit Courts in the Southern States, so long as those States were governed by military authority. Though the Federal District Judges in Virginia, Mississippi and Alabama held Court during 1866, Chief Justice Chase and his Associates had declined to sit on Circuit until, as he said, "all possibility of claim that the judicial is subordinate to the military power is removed, by express declaration of the President"; and it was not until June 6, 1867, that he opened in North Carolina the first Circuit Court to be held in the Southern States.[1] The refusal of the Chief Justice to hold Court in Virginia, thereby preventing the trial of Jefferson Davis for treason, gave particular offense to the Radical Republicans.[2]

As a consequence of this distrust both of the Pres-

[1] Under the Judiciary Act of July 29, 1866, the Supreme Court Judges lost their Circuit Court jurisdiction in the Southern States; but this was restored by the Act of March 2, 1867. Cases appealed from Southern States were heard for the first time at the December, 1866, Term of the Supreme Court, there being then twenty-nine pending; see *New York Herald*, Dec. 13, 1866. See Chase's address to the Bar, *Amer. Law Rev.* (1867), I, 745.

[2] One of Davis' counsel, George W. Brown, wrote to Franklin Pierce, Jan. 10, and July 14, 1866: "Whether or not a trial will ever take place is wholly uncertain, dependent on the turn political affairs may take. The Radicals have insisted on a trial, because they thought that something might be gained for their party, very erroneously, I believe. It is a strange and anomalous condition of

ident and of the Court, the first move which Congress made was to reduce the membership of the Court. After the number of Associate Judges had been increased to nine, in 1863, to provide a new Circuit Court for the Districts of California and Oregon, and after appointment of Judge Field, the Court had consisted of six Democrats and four Republicans. On the appointment of Chase in 1864, the Court had become evenly divided in political character; and after Judge Catron had died, May 30, 1865, the Judges appointed by President Lincoln constituted a majority of the Court (Chase, Swayne, Miller, Field and Davis). President Johnson had nominated, on April 16, 1866, to fill the vacancy caused by Catron's death, Henry Stanbery of Ohio, a close personal friend, then Attorney-General of the United States, a Republican and a lawyer of high eminence. "A most excellent appointment, and it is to be hoped that he will be promptly confirmed. His power of legal analysis, close reasoning, accuracy of statement and concise and forcible expression have justly placed him at the head of the present Bar of the Supreme Court," said a prominent Republican paper.[1] The Senate, however, was determined to curb the President in every move; and fearing that he might have the opportunity to make further appointments to the Bench,

---

things that the Court which has indicted him refuses to bail him, because he is held by the military arm of the Government; and the Chief Justice will not hold Court in Virginia, until martial law is formally revoked. He had no such scruples about holding Court in Maryland, when martial law was carried out with a strong hand. . . . The real difficulty, no doubt, is that Ch. J. Chase does not choose to recognize Virginia as legally in the Union, by going to Richmond and holding Court there." *Franklin Pierce Papers MSS.* See also *Harper's Weekly*, Nov. 25, 1865, quoting Chase as saying that "it was not becoming the Courts of the United States to sit in regions still subordinate to military law." The *Springfield Weekly Republican*, Jan. 13, 20, Feb. 3, 24, April 7, 1866, assailed Chase for his attitude as to Davis, and said he had "White House on the brain. . . . No man has fallen more in public esteem, in public confidence."

[1] *Philadelphia Inquirer*, April 18, 1866.

it passed a bill, moved by Lyman Trumbull of Illinois, providing for the reduction of the number of Associate Judges to seven. To the question asked in the House whether "this bill abolishes the Judge whose appointment the President sent to the Senate the other day", it was stated by Wilson of Iowa that such was its effect as well as purpose.[1] By this Act of July 23, 1866, the Court became nine in number, and by the death of Judge Wayne on July 5, 1867, it was further reduced to eight.

Meanwhile, before the passage of this Act affecting the membership of the Court, that body had seemed to justify the fears of the Republican leaders, by rendering a decision at the very end of the Term, on April 3, 1866, which came as a staggering blow to the plans for the use of the military forces in the process of Reconstruction then being matured by Congress. In *Ex parte Milligan*, 4 Wall. 2, the Court held that the President had no power to institute trial by military tribunal during the war in localities where the civil Courts were open. At first, the country at large did not realize the fateful breadth of the decision, and the press paid little attention to it, since, on this date, the Court confined itself to a mere announce-

[1] *39th Cong., 1st Sess.*, Feb. 26, July 10, 18, 1866. See criticism of this action of Congress in *Democracy in the United States* (1868), by Ransom H. Gillet. The *American Law Review* (1867), I, 206, said: "There seems to have been no serious opposition to the law, which was in no sense a political measure, however much political feelings may have aided its passage. We are constrained, however, to doubt the wisdom of it. Ten Judges is too large a number for any Court; but, when we consider the great extent of the country, the distances which Judges have to travel, the advantage of having every section of the Union represented, if possible, in this tribunal, — it is a matter of serious inquiry, whether the number of Judges can be much reduced, without our incurring greater evils than that of the bulkiness of the Bench. Nor does the Act strike us as opportune, if we allow the abstract wisdom of it. In consequence of the great number of vacancies which have taken place of late years, there are many Judges of brief experience upon the Bench. The older ones have reached an age at which we cannot expect much more service from them; and the result of the recent law may be, that, ere long, the entire South will be without a Judge on this Bench, and the country east of the Allegheny Mountains have but two, who must bear the chief burden of all maritime cases."

ment of its judgment, without setting forth its reasoning. Nevertheless, its full effect was at once apparent to President Johnson and to the Radical Reconstructionists in the Senate; and Welles recorded in his diary:

April 2, 1866: The President inquired as soon as the subject was taken up whether any facts were yet public in relation to the decision of the Supreme Court in the Indiana cases.

April 6, 1866: The decision of the Supreme Court in the Indiana Cases, — Milligan, Bolles and others — was discussed. Attorney-General Speed could not state exactly the points. The Judges do not give their opinions until next winter. They seem to have decided against the legality of military commissions. I inquired what should be done in Semmes' case, which had been long pending. Little was said, and the President said he would see me after the session, and I therefore remained. He remarked that there was a somewhat strange state of things. . . . The Courts were taking up some of the cases for treason and were showing themselves against military commissions. He therefore thought it would be as well to release Semmes on parole.

On December 17, 1866, at the beginning of the next Term, however, when the Judges delivered their opinions in full, the decision became at once the subject of the most violent and virulent attack, as well as of extravagant praise, by the different factions throughout the country. This *Milligan Case* had arisen in the following manner. A previous attempt had been made, in 1864, to secure an opinion from the Court as to the legality of the military commissions constituted by President Lincoln. Application had been made to the Court for a writ of habeas corpus in the case of the notorious Clement L. Vallandigham, who had been arrested and held for military trial. No decision, however, had been rendered on the point desired to be tested; for the Court held, in *Ex parte Vallandigham*, 1 Wall. 243, on February 15, 1864, that it had no power to issue such a writ to a military commission, since under the Judiciary Act its appellate jurisdiction extended only to judicial Courts. Within a short time after this decision, however, another case was initiated, in which the Court would be required to face and settle the issue. One Milligan had been arrested on order of the General commanding the military district of Indiana and tried, in October, 1864, by a military commission on a charge of conspiracy against the Government, giving aid and comfort to the rebels, initiating insurrection, disloyal practices, and violating the laws of war. He was found guilty, and was sentenced to be hung on May 19, 1865. On May 10, 1865, he petitioned the United States Circuit Court in Indiana for a writ of habeas corpus; and the Judges disagreeing certified the question of law to the Supreme Court. The case was argued on March 6 to 13, 1866, only two months after the adoption of the Fourteenth Amendment by Congress, and at a time when legislation based on the continuance of military control was still under debate.[1] Impressive, eloquent and impassioned pleas were made by David Dudley Field, General James A. Garfield and Jeremiah S. Black for the prisoner,[2] and by Attorney-

---

[1] The resolution for this Amendment passed the Senate, Jan. 8, and the House, Jan. 13, 1866; see *History of the Fourteenth Amendment* (1908), by Horace S. Flack.

The Civil Rights Act was enacted April 6, 1866, over President Johnson's veto.

[2] See Address of Levi March in *Reminiscences of J. S. Black* (1887), by M. B. Clayton, 131: "Of the arguments the most powerful is that of Jeremiah S. Black, which has been described as 'indisputably the most remarkable forensic effort before that august tribunal, delivering his address without a solitary note of reading from a book, and yet he presented an array of law, fact and argument, with such remarkable force and eloquence as startled and bewildered those who listened to him. . . . Freedom was his client. The great cause of Constitutional Liberty hung upon that single life.'"

General James Speed, Henry Stanbery and Benjamin
F. Butler for the Government. On April 3, 1866,
within the short space of three weeks after the argument, the Court rendered its decision, unanimously
holding the military commission authorized by the
President to have been unlawful. A majority of the
Court — Judges Field and Davis (appointed by Lincoln) and Nelson, Grier and Clifford (appointed in
pre-war days) — took the occasion to state their further
opinion that neither the President nor Congress possessed the power to institute such a military commission, except in the actual theater of war, where the
civil Courts were not open. There being thus injected into the case a question which did not arise
on the facts, four Judges — Chief Justice Chase and
Judges Miller, Swayne (appointed by Lincoln) and
Wayne (appointed by Jackson) — filed a dissenting
opinion refusing to regard the power of Congress as
subject to such limitations. The opinion of the
Court, holding Lincoln's military tribunal illegal, was
delivered by Lincoln's personal friend, Judge Davis.
"No graver question was ever considered by this
Court, nor one which more nearly concerns the rights
of every American citizen when charged with crime,
to be tried and punished according to law," he said.
"The Constitution of the United States is a law for
rulers and people, equally in war and in peace, and
covers with the shield of its protection all classes of
men, at all times, and under all circumstances." Its
provisions cannot "be suspended during any of the
great exigencies of government. Such a doctrine
leads directly to anarchy or despotism. . . . Martial
rule can never exist where the Courts are open, and
in the proper and unobstructed exercise of their jurisdiction." Hence the military commissions were held

illegal.[1] In a dissenting opinion agreeing with the majority on the actual question involved, but contending that Congress had the power to institute military commissions, the Chief Justice said: "We cannot doubt that, in such a time of public danger, Congress had power, under the Constitution," to make such provisions for military trial; and he stated that the civil Courts "might be open and undisturbed in the execution of their functions, and yet wholly incompetent to avert threatened danger, or to punish with adequate promptitude and certainty, the guilty conspirators. . . . The power of Congress to authorize trials for crimes against the security and safety of the National forces may be derived from its constitutional authority to raise and support armies and to declare war, if not from its constitutional authority to provide for governing the National forces."

This famous decision has been so long recognized as one of the bulwarks of American liberty that it is difficult to realize now the storm of invective and opprobrium which burst upon the Court at the time when

---

[1] The subsequent facts as to the petitioner in the *Milligan Case* are of interest. His sentence of hanging on May 19, 1865, was suspended on May 10, pending his petition to the Court; and it was commuted to life imprisonment by President Johnson on June 21, 1865. He was confined in the Ohio Penitentiary by order of Gen. Hovey, the military commander of the District of Indiana, and was released on April 10, 1866, after the decision of the Supreme Court. On March 13, 1868, he brought an action for damages against Gen. Hovey in the State Court, which, under the Removals Act, was removed to the Federal Circuit Court by Hovey. While it was pending there, the *Cincinnati Enquirer*, on May 18, 1871, expressed the editorial hope that Milligan's suit would be upheld: "It would be a healthy, political sign to show that there was a limit to military usurpation; and that even the President of the United States cannot give an order, or enforce a decree, against the law of the land, and that his illegal orders are no protection to his subordinates. This is a lesson that military tyrants and usurpers should be taught, if we would preserve any remnant of liberty in the land." The jury, after a charge from Judge Thomas Drummond, rendered a verdict in Milligan's favor, but awarded him only nominal damages, since under the two years' statute of limitation he could only recover for damages for confinement between March 13 and April 10, 1866. See also *Humphrey* v. *McCormick* (1866), 27 Ind. 144; and *Washington Weekly Chronicle*, March 16, 1867.

it was first made public.[1] By the Reconstructionists, the decision was regarded as a reversion to the theory of constitutional law held by opponents of the Union; they claimed that the Court's doctrine, if applied in war time, would have resulted in the loss of the war; and they asserted that the Court had now joined hands with President Johnson in an effort to destroy the Congressional plans for Reconstruction. An illustration of this feeling as to the majority opinion is to be seen in a letter written to Chief Justice Chase by John Jay: "If, as the public begin to fear, their denial of the powers of Congress is any index to the view they are prepared to take of the great questions that will come before them in reference to Reconstruction, our situation is certainly a grave one . . . to surmount the formidable opposition, no longer of an obstinate President defying the will of the people, but of an Executive furnished with a constitutional standpoint, by the Supreme Judiciary giving validity to his acts, and checkmating Congress at the most eventful moment by denying its powers and annulling its legislation. I cannot yet consent to believe that we are brought into this dilemma, and that appointees of Mr. Lincoln are ready to imitate the late Chief Justice, in making the Court the chief support of the advocates of slavery and the Rebellion." [2] The virulence of attack upon the Judges can only be appreciated by a comprehensive perusal of the editorials of the day, of which the following are illustrative.[3]

[1] See *Salmon Portland Chase* (1899), by Albert Bushnell Hart. The Washington correspondent of the *New York Times* wrote, Dec. 27, 1866: "There is much confusion in the public mind as to what the Court actually did decide, and the publicity of the decision is anxiously looked for, especially as the Court, in order to prevent an imperfect synopsis of the decision from going forth, denied the reporters present the usual privilege of taking notes." The decision in full was given to the public through the press for the first time on Jan. 1, 1867.

[2] *Amer. Hist. Ass. Rep.* (1902), II, letter of Jan. 5, 1867.

[3] *New York Times*, Jan. 3, 1867; *Indianapolis Daily Journal.* Jan. 2, 1867,

"In the conflict of principle thus evoked, the States which sustained the cause of the Union will recognize an old foe with a new face," said the *New York Times*. "It is the old dogma of rigid construction as applied to the National Government and liberal construction as applied to the States on the one hand, and on the other, the common sense doctrine that the Constitution provides for the permanence of the Union, and for such an exercise of authority by Congress as may be necessary to preserve the National existence. . . . The Supreme Court, we regret to find, throws the great weight of its influence into the scale of those who assailed the Union and step after step impugned the constitutionality of nearly everything that was done to uphold it. . . . The whole Copperhead press exults over the decision. . . . They shelter themselves behind Justice Davis and his Associates, and indirectly renew their assault upon the policy that dictated and guided the war for National unity. . . . The newly declared reliance of the President and the Southern States upon the interposition of the Supreme Court has a certain apparent justification in this decision." The *Indianapolis Journal* said that the decision was "such as to create misgivings in the mind of the patriotic people who saved the Nation from destruction at the hands of rebels." Admitting that, under some circumstances, a decision against military tribunals "would be an invaluable defense to popular liberties, here it is intended only to aid the Johnson men, and is so clearly a forerunner of other decisions looking to a defeat of Republican ascendancy and to a restoration of Southern domination, that the indignation against the Court is just

Cleveland Herald, Jan. 3, 4, 5, 7, 1867; *Independent*, Jan. 10, 1867; *Cincinnati Commercial*, Jan. 3, 4, 5, 1867.

and warranted." But, it concluded, "the Court cannot enforce its reactionary dogmas upon the people. The decision carries no moral force, and cannot bind coördinate departments." The *Cleveland Herald*, speaking of "the late alarming pronunciamento called a decision of the Supreme Court" termed it a "judicial tyranny." "The Milligan decision now occupies the most prominent place in the political situation," it said. "A new and most mischievous weapon has been placed in the hands of those who oppose the great Union party." It stated that, had the decision been made early in the war, "our country would have been compelled to pass through an ordeal of blood and turmoil that would have shaken society in all its phases to its centre, even had not the rebellion been successful in overthrowing the Government. . . . If the doctrine avowed by the majority be sound, this Government is but a wisp of straw. . . . It is well enough to talk about the military power being subservient to the civil, when the civil power can stand; but when war has trodden down the civil power, he is either a traitor or a granny who hesitates as to employing the military power, either its bayonets or its Courts, to preserve the life of the Nation. The minority, as in the *Dred Scott Case*, will receive the thanks of all loyal men who would seize any means within reach to save a government from the hands of traitors who could subvert it, while its timid defenders were poring over dusty, musty tomes, seeking the proper civil remedy." It "has produced a profound impression," said the *Independent*. "It virtually declares that Lincoln's assassins suffered a juridico-military murder. . . . We regard it as the most dangerous opinion ever pronounced by that tribunal. . . . Nor shall we waste criticism on the verbose sophistries with which they labor to conceal the iniquitous doctrines propounded. . . . So far as it bears upon the actual points in issue and is a determination of the case under review, it will be yielded to. Beyond this, it will be treated as a mere partisan harangue, unseemly, because of the source whence it emanated . . . a sorry attempt of five not very distinguished persons to exhibit themselves as profound jurists, whereas they have only succeeded in proving themselves to be very poor politicians. We regret this decision on many grounds. The Supreme Court had begun to recover the prestige tarnished by the Dred Scott decision. . . . The recent decision restores the Court to the bad eminence it occupied when Taney dictated its decrees, and will again withdraw from it that entire confidence which a loyal people would fain repose in its adjudications." The *New York Herald* was especially savage on the Court, and, in a series of editorials, demanded its reformation. "The decision in the Indiana Case may be according to the strict letter of the Constitution," it said. "But in adhering to the strict letter, we must go back to President Buchanan's decision, that he could find no authority in the Constitution to interfere with a seceding State. . . . It is in this view of the Indiana decision, ignoring the vital necessities of the Government during the Rebellion, that a reconstruction of the Supreme Court, adapted to the paramount decisions of the war, looms up into bold relief, on a question of vital importance. . . . As the Court now stands, away behind the war, we hold that there is good reason to fear that its judgments, yet to come, in regard to the doings of Congress during and since the war, including the abolition of slavery and the creation of our present National

debt, if not provided for in season, may result in a
new chapter of troubles and disasters to the country." Again it said: "This two-faced opinion of
Mr. Justice Davis is utterly inconsistent with the
deciding facts of the war, and therefore utterly preposterous. These ante-diluvian Judges seem to forget that the war was an appeal from the Constitution
to the sword. . . . This constitutional twaddle of
Mr. Justice Davis will no more stand the fire of public opinion than the Dred Scott decision." [1] "It is
a marvelous fact," said the *Cleveland Herald*, "that
each of the two decisions of our Federal Supreme
Court which has gone the farthest to sustain slavery
and to paralyze the arm of our Government in putting
down the rebellion — to wit the *Dred Scott Case* and
the *Milligan Case* — was a decision falling under the
title of an *ipse dixit*, a mere extra-judicial assertion
of the Judges." "Like the Dred Scott decision, it
is not a judicial opinion; it is a political act. . . .
The Dred Scott decision was meant to deprive slaves
taken into a Territory of the chances of liberty under
the United States Constitution. The Indiana decision operates to deprive the freedmen, in the late
rebel States whose laws grievously outrage them, of
the protection of the freedmen's Courts," said *Harper's Weekly*. That this decision, which has since
been recognized by all men as the palladium of the
rights of the individual, should at the time of its rendition have been so generally compared with the *Dred
Scott Case* is a striking commentary on the passionate
political conditions of that era.[2]

[1] *New York Herald*, Dec. 19, 20, 23, 1866, Jan. 2, 8, 1867. In a later editorial,
Jan. 5, it termed the Court "a relic of the past, nine old superior pettifoggers,
old marplots, a formidable barrier to the consummation of the great revolution."

[2] *Cleveland Herald*, Jan. 4, 1867; *Harper's Weekly*, Jan. 19, 1867, editorial entitled "The New Dred Scott." See also *New York Times*, Jan. 3, 1867, and
numerous papers comparing the *Milligan Case* to the *Dred Scott Case*.

The most virulent assault upon the Court was made
by John W. Forney, in the *Washington Chronicle*, the
semi-official organ of the Republican Senate, and the
constant opponent of the *National Intelligencer* which
supported President Johnson. "The decision cannot
fail to shock the sensibilities and provoke the severe
rebuke of loyal men everywhere," it said in one of
its earliest criticisms of the Court. "The exultation of the rebel *Intelligencer* over it will awaken a
jubilant echo throughout rebeldom, and the hearts of
traitors will be glad by the announcement that treason, vanquished upon the battlefield and hunted from
every other retreat, has at last found a secure shelter
in the bosom of the Supreme Court." This was very
extreme and unjustifiable language, and the personal
attack on the Judges' character very properly met
with indignant protest from many men who, though
disagreeing with the Judges' opinion, were eager to
defend their loyalty. Nevertheless the *Chronicle* continued, for a month, to launch a series of violent attacks on Judge Davis and on the Court, which were
widely copied and imitated.[1] "We have not met a
Republican who does not speak with contempt of
the language of Justice Davis," it said. "The people have said, if it is not lawful to whip traitors, we
will make it so. . . . The denial of Congressional
power has elicited universal condemnation from the
people of the country. And the fact that this denial
was wholly uncalled for, was well calculated to inspire mistrust of the motives which induced the Judges
to drag it into their decision. The masses of the

---

[1] *Washington Chronicle*, Dec. 19, 22, 29, 1866, and *passim* through January,
1867, and see *Philadelphia Press* and *Philadelphia North American*, *passim* (the
latter saying that President Lincoln had "made a mistake in appointing a Judge
of the fatal name of Davis"); and furious attacks on the Court and on Chief Justice Chase in *New York Tribune*, *passim*.

American people are not behind these five Judges, in their reverence for the Constitution and their re-gard for the rights of the citizen; but they will not assent to an interpretation of that instrument, which places the rights of the individual before the safety of the whole people." Again, it said that: "Time and reflection have only served to strengthen the conviction of the partisan character of the decision and the apprehension that it is the precursor of other decisions in the interest of unrepentant treason in the support of an apostate President." To the Court, as a co-conspirator with President Johnson and as a dangerous and reactionary factor in the Government, it devoted several editorials, in the last of which it stated that the decision "has not startled the country more by its far-reaching and calamitous results than it has amazed jurists and statesmen by the poverty of its learning and the feebleness of its logic. It has surprised all, too, with its total want of sympathy with the spirit in which the war for the Union was prosecuted, and necessarily with those great issues growing out of it, which concern not only the life of the Republic but the very progress of the race, and which, having been decided on the battle-field, are now sought to be reversed by the very theory of construction which led to rebellion."

While these criticisms of the *Milligan Case* decision vastly outweighed the applause, the more conservative Republicans and the Democrats hailed it as a triumph of the rule of law over lawlessness.[1] "The laws are no longer silenced by the clash of arms. The supreme tribunal of the country has vindicated their assaulted majesty," said the President's organ,

[1] *National Intelligencer*, Dec. 13, 18, 20, 25, 27, 28, 31, 1866, Jan. 1, 3, 11, 15, 17, 1867; *Nation*, Jan. 10, 1867.

the *National Intelligencer*, on the day after the decision; and it continued with the following memorable words, which rang through the country: "They are disloyal, who, under the pretense of preserving the liberties of the citizen, have disregarded the obligations of the organic law. They are disunionists, who, claiming to fight for the Union, have trampled upon its fundamental bond. And, as in war times, these monopolists of patriotism denounced those who upheld the sacred liberties of the citizen as guaranteed by the Constitution, so now, in the midst of peace, they assail those who maintain the rights of the States as guaranteed by that same instrument. But the Supreme Court has evermore made such an assault upon the rights of the citizen impossible; and we doubt not that, in due time, it will extend its broad aegis over the violated commonwealths of the South." In later editorials, it termed the decision of greater moral weight than any ever rendered, since "neither in the breadth of the issue, the extravagance of contemporary heresies on the subject, nor in the magnitude of the stake could any law cause before that Court compare with this. . . . It establishes the rights of the citizen on an impregnable basis. It is not Milligan, the alleged conspirator, who is set free; but Milligan, citizen, tried by an illegal tribunal. . . . It is not the crime of treason which is shielded by this memorable decision, but the sacred rights of the citizen that are vindicated against the arbitrary decisions of military authority. Above the might of the sword, the majesty of the law is thus raised supreme." And to the "wild attacks of partisan malevolence and malice", and to the diatribes of the Senators, the *Chronicle* and the Bureau of Military Justice and others, calling for impeachment of the

Judges and for reconstruction of the Court, it said: "We defend now the people against the anarchical schemes of those who, in overriding the Court, fearfully imperil our liberties, by striving to impair the public respect for law and for an impartial Judiciary. The anarchists who would destroy the public confidence in the Constitution and its Supreme Court are as dangerous, as the revolutionists who sought to withdraw from that jurisdiction." The *Nation*, Republican in its views, remarked that President Lincoln had "at times seemed to revel in the breach of Acts of Congress, and did so with the approval of a large portion of the public" and that the chief criticism of President Johnson had been his exaltation of Executive power; and it stated that the very men who had previously denounced Presidential usurpation were now talking of "impeaching the Judges for doing what they were bound to do before God and man, come what might. . . . We hope this whole matter, grave and important as it is, will open the eyes of the public to the great danger there is that the breaches of law and of propriety, into which overzeal on behalf of the right now carries us, may be, one day, used against it, in defense of the wrong. It is not very long, since there was a majority in the United States on the side of wickedness, and we may all live to see it again; if we should, we may have sore need, for our own protection, of all the forms and traditions of the law and the Constitution." The *Springfield Republican*, which had been a strong antislavery paper, but which was now less radical in its Republicanism, said that the decision had been "strangely misunderstood and perverted", and that "to suspect such men as Judges Chase, Davis and Wayne of assenting to any doctrine that shall cripple the power of the Government to suppress rebellion is preposterous. . . . The Milligan decision is simply a reaffirmation of the sacred right of trial by jury. To deny principles so well established and so essential to liberty and justice would not be progress, but a long step backwards towards despotism." It pointed out that the decision would not necessarily operate to prevent action of Congress in Reconstruction, since "the application of the decision of the Court to the Southern States must be governed by opinions of the conditions. The President has proclaimed them at peace, and the civil law in full force. Those who believe that the war is still going on will call for the perpetuation of military Courts." And it very sanely stated its belief that "attempts to excite popular alarm or partisan animosity are false and foolish, and so palpably so that they cannot succeed. The Democrats want very much to be the sole champions of the Constitution and the Supreme Court, and they will not achieve that honor. . . . No good citizen can regret that the Constitution and laws are again declared supreme. If either are faulty or behind the spirit of the age, the people are sovereign, and the process of amendment is easy and direct." [1]

The Democratic papers naturally applauded the decision.[2] "It is both a triumphant vindication of the Democratic party and a happy augury of the future," said the *New York World*. "This decision on a matter which was the main topic of controversy

---

[1] *Springfield Republican*, Jan. 2, 5, 1867. This paper was one of the few which had recognized the importance of the decision, when rendered in the preceding April; and it had then rejoiced, April 7, 1866, that it would end the "senseless clamor for the military trial of Jefferson Davis and other rebel leaders."

[2] *New York World*, Dec. 18, 19, 21, 25, 1866, Jan. 5, 12, 1867; *Baltimore Sun*, Dec. 22, 1866; *Richmond Enquirer*, Dec. 20, 24, 27, 28, 1866. *Detroit Free Press*, Jan. 8, 11, 1867.

between the Democratic Party and its opponents during the war is the final judgment of the law, as it will be the verdict of history, that the obloquy heaped upon Democrats for their opposition to the arbitrary exertion of authority was undeserved, . . . that the arbitrary proceedings against which they protested were as lawless as they were high-handed. . . . There is always a period of peril to civil liberty. . . . The fact that the Supreme Court has escaped the servile contamination of the times, and pronounces an independent opinion which vindi-cates a party so traduced and maligned as the Democ-racy, is full of encouragement." The *Baltimore Sun* rejoiced at the Court's emphatic declaration that the Constitution is the supreme law in war as well as in peace. "With that single sentence the miserable plea of military necessity is torn from human liberty, and men feel again that the chains of despotic power are utterly riven. . . . The great writ of habeas corpus is no longer an idle phrase." It asserted that the decision had greatly increased the confidence of the people in the Court. "Fanaticism, feeling the sting of death in the decision, has already raised a clamor for the overthrow of the Court; but fast an-chored in the affections of the American people that tribunal will resist the assaults directed against it, and continue the tranquil and sure arbiter of right." And it said that the decision "needing no commen-tary, and by its piercing force of truth and logic admitting of no refutation . . . ought to be read by every man who has pride in the name of an American citizen."

That the newspapers in the late Confederate States should rejoice at the decision was also natural; but if there were readers of the *Richmond Enquirer* of the year 1821 who were alive on December 27, 1866, they must have been astounded to read in its columns, on the latter date, an article highly praising the Supreme Court of the United States for its exercise of the function of testing the constitutionality of legislation, and for its position as one of the needful checks and balances of Government. "It has inspired us with new hope for the future of our institutions," it said. "It could not have been foreseen that the Judiciary both in England and America would have proved, in the main, so pure and incorruptible, so elevated above the passions of the hour, and so fearless and efficient in checking the usurpations of power proceeding from other departments. . . . Now that the Supreme Court has come to the rescue of the Constitution, the future is lighted with signs of good cheer." Later, it pointed out the remarkable freedom from partisan action, as shown by the decision of the Chief Justice, "a high priest of radicalism", and of his Republican Associates, defending the Constitution in direct opposition to the political measures advocated by their Party; and it expressed the ardent hope that the Judges would stand firm, though they had been "reproached as enemies, if not traitors, to their party, threatened with reconstruction, threatened with demolition, insulted, abused and defied. . . . If the authority of the Constitution shall be vindicated, the South is safe and the end of her troubles approaches."

The view expressed by the Democratic press undoubtedly represents, in general, the verdict of history on the immortal opinion of Judge Davis in support of the right of the citizen to protection against arbitrary military action. But there has always been considerable sympathy with the sentiments entertained by the Republicans towards that part of the decision of the four Judges which distinguished the question of Congressional power from Executive usurpation; and an eminent jurist wrote with much reason, fourteen years after the decision: "The minority opinion is the only view which can reconcile jurisprudence with political science, law with policy. It is devoutly to be hoped that the decision of the Court may never be subjected to the strain of actual war. If, however, it should be, we may safely predict that it will necessarily be disregarded. In time of war and public danger, the whole power of the State must be vested in the General Government, and the constitutional liberty of the individual must be sacrificed, so far as the Government finds it necessary for the preservation of the life and security of the State. This is the experience of political history and the principle of political science." [1] That the doctrine asserted by the majority is "calculated to cripple the constitutional powers of the Government and to augment the public dangers in times of invasion and rebellion" (in the words of Chief Justice Chase) is so unquestionable as to excuse both those who were confronting the problems of Reconstruction in 1867, as well as those who may in the future be called on to deal with internal war problems in this country, for hoping for a reversal of the Court's decision on this point. But whatever may be the view as to the law so laid down, there was a serious and well-founded criticism of the propriety of the Court's action in expressing any opinion whatever on the power

[1] *Political Science and Constitutional Law* (1890), by John W. Burgess, I, 250–252. "Political science would confer, and, as it appears to me, the Constitution does confer, the power of determining when and where war exists, upon those bodies who represent the whole United States, who wield the power of the United States and upon whom the Constitution casts the responsibility of the public defence against both the foreign and the domestic foe."

of Congress; and a leading law journal expressed very ably the views of the Bar at the time:[1]

On the main point at issue, all the nine Judges agreed. It is rare that the whole Court agrees on any constitutional question; it is still more rare when the Court agrees to decide an important question in opposition to Executive authority and the current of popular feeling; and such unanimity is too precious a thing to be hid under a bushel. Had this unanimous opinion been given simply and directly, it would have established for ever a solid principle of law, on which, in all troublous times, the country would have relied. It would have been a strong defence against all assaults upon the liberties of the people. It would have commanded universal respect, and would have enlisted in its support the sound judgment and the common sense of the Nation. But the Court did not deliver a unanimous opinion. They divided on a point which was not before them for adjudication. . . . Had they in truth, simply adhered to their plain duty as Judges, they could have united in one opinion on this most important case. We deem the course they saw fit to adopt matter for great regret. Instead of approaching the subject of the powers of the coördinate branches of the government as one of great delicacy, which they were loath to consider, but which they felt bound to pass upon because it was involved in the righteous decision of the cause before them, yet concerning which they had nothing to do, and would have nothing to say, except so far as it was necessary to the determination of that cause, they have seemed eager to go beyond the record, and not only to state the reason of their present judgment, but to lay down the principles on which they would decide other questions, not now before them, involving the gravest and highest powers of Congress. They have seemed to forget how all-important it is for the preservation of their influence that they should confine themselves to their duties as Judges between the parties in a particular case; how certainly the jealousy of the coördinate departments of the government and of the people would be excited by any attempt on their part

[1] *American Law Review* (April, 1867), I, 572.

to exceed their constitutional functions; and how, the more a case before the Supreme Court assumes a political aspect, the more cautious should the Judges be to confine themselves within their proper limits. . . . But, however much the Supreme Court may have provoked criticism, none the less is much of that criticism to be deprecated. And the most alarming feature in such criticism is not indignation that the Judges have decided from political prepossessions, but a feeling that they are to blame if they do not — a feeling that a Judge of the Supreme Court of the United States who gives judgment contrary to the wishes, for the time being, of a majority of the people, or, at any rate, contrary to the wishes of an Administration which raised him to the Bench, is liable to the same just censure that waits upon a politician who has left the party to which he has pledged himself, and votes with the opposition; that a Judge is in fact, a representative to carry out the wishes of a political party. Against this degradation of the judicial office we protest. For what is the Supreme Court mainly established but that it may be a tribunal of last resort, composed of men uninfluenced by Executive or Legislative power or popular impulse, who may do justice, free, as far as the lot of humanity admits, from party passion or political expediency?

The apprehensions of the Radical Republicans as to the disastrous effect of the *Milligan Case* decision upon their policies were fully confirmed by the steps which were taken by the President and by the action of some of the Federal Judges, immediately following the publication of the opinion. President Johnson regarded it as an indorsement of his policy to put an end to military government in the South as soon as possible; and he at once issued orders dismissing all trials of civilians by the military then pending in Virginia and in other States in which the Republicans were claiming that a condition of war still existed; and a similar action was taken by Judge Hall of the United States District Court in Delaware in ordering the release on habeas corpus of four men convicted of murder of Union soldiers by a military Court in South Carolina.[1] Though the Court spoke of Indiana and any State where the Courts have been open and unobstructed, said the *New York Herald*, "the President insists that the decision applies as well to Virginia as to Indiana, and eager to please the white blood-hounds of the Old Dominion, he orders the dismissal of a military tribunal engaged in trying the murderer of a black man. There is no warrant for such a cruel inference; but the President will not wait, but wishes with unseemly haste to issue his order to all departmental commanders on rebel soil *to respect the decision of the Court.*" The Radical Republicans were even more disturbed by the realization that the logical result of the decision was to declare illegal the trial and conviction of Lincoln's assassins, and to constitute the execution of Payne, Atzerott, Herold and Mrs. Suratt, little more than lynching. "It virtually declares that they suffered a juridico-military murder," said the *Independent.*[2] That their apprehensions were justified became evident when, within a week after the Milligan decision in December, 1866, applications were made to Judge Wayne and to Chief Justice Chase for a writ of habeas corpus by one of these prisoners

---

[1] See especially as to this case *Boston Daily Advertiser*, Feb. 8, 1867. The *Nation* said, Jan. 3, 1867: "Mr. Johnson has at last found what he imagines to be a snug and safe harbor for his 'policy.' The Supreme Court has come to his aid, and has already declared military commissions illegal — thus putting an end to military interference with the action of the local authorities at the South — and it is fully believed will take strong conservative ground in several cases now before it."

[2] *New York Herald*, Dec. 23, 28, 1866; *Independent*, Jan. 3, 1867. See *Life of Lyman Trumbull* (1913), by Horace White. The Washington correspondent of the *Boston Daily Advertiser*, Dec. 27, 1866, said: "Good lawyers here give it as their opinion that the late decision renders the Secretary of War, the Judge Advocate General and all the members of the Court which tried the assassins, liable to prosecution; while Secretary Stanton holds that it overthrows the Freedmen's Bureau, and renders the Army wholly powerless in the South."

at the Tortugas convicted by military commission.[1] Though Chase denied the application, he based
his refusal only on the ground that he had no power
to issue such a writ outside his own Circuit; and
therefore the question of the legality of the military
trial of the prisoner still remained open. This episode
brought about an active debate in the House of Representatives in Congress, on January 3, 1867, on a
resolution that the Committee on the Judiciary should
report on the advisability of a repeal of the habeas
corpus law of March 3, 1863, so as "to prevent the
Supreme Court from releasing and discharging the
assassins of Mr. Lincoln and the conspirators to
release the rebel prisoners at Camp Douglas in
Chicago." Of the excited political atmosphere at
Washington, a Western correspondent wrote: "The
President holds that this decision applies to every rebellious State as well as to the loyal; and the blood-
hounds are loose all over the South, and the freedmen must take their chances. I am informed on very
respectable authority that one at least of the majority
Judges in the decision of the Court is very nervous
over the result of this blunder. The Justice I refer
to was a personal friend of Mr. Lincoln, and claimed
to be at that time a staunch Republican. He shud-
ders as he sees the cruelties that are to be perpetrated
all over the South under his decision, but it is too
late. If a case could properly come before the Court,
it would be found that a majority do not hold that
military tribunals are unconstitutional in the rebel-

[1] See *Indianapolis Daily Journal*, Jan. 3, 1867; *Springfield Republican*, Dec.
29, 1866; *Boston Daily Advertiser*, Dec. 21, 25, 1866; speech of Reverdy Johnson, Jan. 25, 1867, *39th Cong., 2d Sess.*, 730. It appears that another application
for habeas corpus by this prisoner was contemplated later, in 1867, when Judge
Wayne should for the first time hold Court on Circuit in Florida, but it was not
made, and the prisoner was pardoned by President Johnson in Feb., 1869. See
Life of Samuel A. Mudd (1906), by Nettie Mudd, letters of Jan. 15, March 25, 1867.

lious States, for Congress holds that they are still in a belligerent condition. . . . Should the Court, however, by any other decision show that it is irrevocably wedded to pro-slavery ideas, to a sympathy for rebels — then a future Congress will reorganize the Court." [1] Another correspondent wrote: "Thaddeus Stevens today visited several of the Departments, and with General Schenck had a long interview with Secretary Stanton. . . . He has a great contempt for the Supreme Court's decision in the *Milligan Case*. He does not favor the project of impeaching several of the Justices, but wants to impeach the President, from whom all the evils flow. General Grant had a long interview with Secretary Stanton today upon the effect of the recent decision of the Supreme Court upon military commissions. It renders the Freedman's Bureau and Civil Rights bills a nullity, and while it is allowed to stand, orders will be issued to prevent any conflict of authority under it. Secretary Stanton, General Geary, General Palmer and all the other army officers who have been on military commissions are hourly liable to criminal arrest and trial. Senator Trumbull who drew up both the above bills agrees with the Supreme Court. The decision creates intense excitement and it is now claimed by the President that the Constitutional Amendment abolishing slavery will yet be declared a nullity. A movement that will be started tomorrow for the impeaching of several of the Justices will meet

---

[1] *Cleveland Herald,* quoting *Detroit Tribune,* Jan. 2, 1867; see also *Cincinnati Commercial,* Jan. 5, 1867. The *Springfield Republican,* Dec. 29, 1867, said: "All the copperheads and secessionists of this vicinity have jumped to the conclusion that under the recent decision of the Supreme Court military tribunals are unconstitutional in the rebellious States. The language of the decision warrants no such inference. . . . One or two of the Judges who supported the recent decision are said to be not a little nervous over the use the President is making of it at the South."

with favor in the House, where there are a number of military men ready to take the strongest ground against judicial usurpation; but in the Senate, there are no soldiers, and any move like impeachments would be hopeless before the present Senate. Mr. Stevens is preparing some stringent measures to protect the country from the evil tendencies of the Supreme Court."

These accounts were not exaggerated; for the reports of statements made by the President that the Supreme Court was prepared to follow its Milligan decision to its logical consequences and to hold unconstitutional any legislation which contemplated the government of the Southern States by military force, aroused the Republican leaders in Congress to a consideration of means of curbing the Court.[1] The measure most vigorously urged upon them was a reorganization of the Court, the argument for which was strongly set forth as follows by *Harper's Weekly*: "The people have decided that Congress has supreme authority in time of war and must necessarily be judge when and where and how to exercise it. They have decided that States which rebel have not a continuous right to resume at their pleasure their functions in the Union, but are to resume them upon such terms as the victorious loyal people in Congress may deter-

[1] "The President is said to have conferred with several Judges of the Supreme Court in regard to the positions assumed by Congress towards the Southern States, when he announced to the Commissioner from South Carolina, Mr. Wetherby, that the Supreme Court would declare the Amendment unconstitutional, and is thought to have spoken by the card," wrote the Washington correspondent of the *Columbus Morning Journal* (Ohio), Jan. 1, 1867; see also *New York Tribune*, Jan. 1, 1867. But as to this, the *Nation* rightly said, Jan. 3, 1867: "Statements of what 'is said' are of little value unless we know who 'said it.' It is very unlikely that President Johnson knows anything more about the way in which the Supreme Court is likely to decide on any of the great questions of the day than anybody else. The Judges may not be 'sound' on the Reconstruction question, but most of them, at least, still retain a strong sense of judicial propriety, and find better occupation than talking over their decisions with Mr. Johnson."

mine. . . . It is plain that if Congress passes laws the Supreme Court declares unconstitutional and which the President, as Commander-in-Chief, refuses upon that ground to execute, the situation would be critical. But the remedy is obvious and it is not revolutionary. . . . If the Supreme Court undertakes to declare that the people of the United States, at the end of a long and fearful war in which they saved the Government, can do nothing to secure that Government from similar assaults hereafter, let the Supreme Court be swamped by a thorough reorganization and increased number of Judges. . . . The question in regard to the Supreme Court need not be misunderstood. It is not, whether in time of peace in loyal States the civil Courts shall be supreme, which nobody questions. It is, whether loyal men or rebels shall reorganize the Union. . . . The remodeling of the Court may truly be called an extreme measure, to be adopted only in most extraordinary cases, as that which would arise if the five Judges should deliberately undertake to nullify the will of the majority of the people of the United States in reorganizing the Union." [1] This recommendation for a re-formation of the Court, which had been advocated also by the *New York Herald*, was opposed, however, both by Republicans and Democrats, as a "desperate and disgraceful" device to "pack" the Court; and it was pointed out that the Constitution stood in the way of abolition of the Court, and that even if the Judges should be removed, or additional Judges created, it would rest with President Johnson to make the new appointments.

While this measure, therefore, did not secure support in Congress, the debates, during December, 1866,

[1] *Harper's Weekly*, Jan. 19, Feb. 9, March 2, 1867.

and January, 1867, over other bills directed against the Court were long-continued and bitter. The discussion was opened by Reverdy Johnson in the Senate, defending the Court from the infamous charge made against the Judges by the *Washington Chronicle*.[1] "The opinion of the majority was given by a man whose character, public and private, stands beyond possible reproach, placed upon that high tribunal by the lamented late President, loyal throughout the civil contest in which we have been engaged," Johnson said. "The editor to whom I allude thought proper to say that treason had found a refuge in the bosom of the Supreme Court of the United States. I am sure no Senator on this floor will justify such an attack. . . . They (the Judges) will stand upon the character which long lives of honor and integrity have earned for them, while their assailant will reap all the reward to which he may be entitled by such an assault"; and Johnson continued by terming the decision as "not to be surpassed in my judgment, by any opinion pronounced by any Judge in any former case in that tribunal." To this, Thaddeus Stevens, the most savage of the Reconstructionists, retorted that, in his opinion, the decision, "although in terms not as infamous as the Dred Scott decision, is yet far more dangerous in its operation upon the lives and liberties of the loyal men of this country. . . . If the doctrine enunciated in that decision be true, never were the people of any country, anywhere, or at any time, in such terrible peril as are our loyal brethren at the South"; and he spoke of "murderers that were being turned loose under the Milligan decision."

John A. Bingham of Ohio, in the House, proposed

---

[1] *39th Cong., 2d Sess.*, 210, 251, 269, speech of Johnson, Dec. 20, 1866, Jan. 4, 1867, speech of Stevens, Jan. 3, 1867. See also *Life of Thaddeus Stevens* (1913), by James A. Woodburn.

"sweeping away at once the Court's appellate jurisdiction in all cases"; and he said: "If, however, the
Court usurps power to decide political questions and
defy a free people's will, it will only remain for a
people, thus insulted and defied, to demonstrate that
the servant is not above his lord, by procuring a
further Constitutional Amendment and ratifying the
same, which will defy judicial usurpation, by annihilat-
ing the usurpers, in the abolition of the tribunal
itself." [1]

Thomas Williams of Pennsylvania urged a bill for
the concurrence of all the Judges in any opinion on
a constitutional question. "This bill, if passed into
a law," a newspaper advocate said, "will practically
relieve the Supreme Court of any further interference
with Congress in the business of Southern Reconstruction, and it may then operate in a remarkable
change of Southern sentiment; for it appears that
the main reliance of the intractable, ruling classes
of the South now is in the Supreme Court. . . . Nor
are these things the mere expedients of party for party
purposes. They are the demands of a great revolution, which cannot be resisted but which must run its
course." [2]

In the midst of the debates over these measures
affecting the Court, the Radical Reconstructionists,
who desired to see all participants in the cause of the
Confederacy treated as traitors and denied any civil
rights or privileges, were still further enraged by two
decisions of the Court, rendered on January 14, 1867,

[1] *39th Cong., 2d Sess.*, 249, 286, 501 *et seq.*, Jan. 3, 4, 16, 21, 23, 1867. This suggestion of limiting the appellate jurisdiction of the Court was first made by the
leading Republican paper in the West, the *Chicago Tribune*. It also suggested
a statutory requirement of the concurrence of eight Judges; see *New York World*,
Jan. 21, 1867, in criticism of this proposal.
[2] *New York Herald*, Jan. 23, 1867; see *Cleveland Herald*, Jan. 28, 1867, approving a bill requiring concurrence of two thirds of the Judges.

in *Cummings* v. *Missouri* and *Ex parte Garland*, 4 Wall. 277, 333, — decisions which revealed the Court as wholly unaffected by the tumult raised by its Milligan decision, and which displayed its freedom from prejudices arising from the late war and its utter fairness towards those engaged in it.[1] The first case involved the validity of the provisions of a State Constitution requiring certain persons (a minister of the gospel in the instant case) as a prerequisite to engaging in their pursuits, to take an oath that they had not supported, aided or favored by act or word the cause of the Confederacy; the second case involved an Act of Congress of January 24, 1865, and a Rule of Court adopted in March, 1865, in pursuance of the Act, requiring a similar oath before an attorney should be admitted or allowed to practice before the Court. In the first case, David Dudley Field, Montgomery Blair and Reverdy Johnson argued for the petitioner against John B. Henderson and G. P. Strong for the State of Missouri. In the second, Reverdy Johnson and Matt H. Carpenter argued for the petitioner and Augustus H. Garland (who was later Attorney-General of the United States) also filed a brief *pro se;* the Attorney-General, James Speed, appeared for the Government. The Court held the requirement of the oath in both cases to be unconstitutional; but again it was closely divided. The four Judges appointed prior to the war — Wayne, Grier, Nelson and Clifford — joined with Judge Field, in holding that the framers of the Constitution intended to guard against such "excited action of the

---

[1] The *New York World*, the *Washington Chronicle* and other papers announced as early as Dec. 8, 1866, that the constitutionality of the ironclad oath case had been decided by the Judges in conference, by a majority of five to four against the radicals." But the *New York Herald* stated, Dec. 10, 1866, that: "Chief Justice Chase denied the rumor." See also *National Intelligencer*, Dec. 13, 1866.

States, under such influences as these"; that "the
Constitution deals with substance, not shadows. Its
inhibition was levelled at the thing, not the name.
It intended that the rights of the citizen should be
secure against deprivation for past conduct by legislative enactment, under any form, however dis-
guised." Accordingly, the statutes were held invalid as imposing a form of punishment forbidden
by the constitutional prohibition against bills of attainder and *ex post facto* laws. On the other hand,
Lincoln's appointees — the Chief Justice and Judges
Miller, Swayne and Davis — supported the legislation as a desirable protection of the country against
disloyal men, and as fixing proper qualifications for
the practice of professions; and they denied that the
statutes were either bills of attainder or *ex post facto*
laws within the meaning of the Constitution.[1]

The attacks on these decisions were again of the
most violent character. The *Washington Chronicle*
said that they had been made "the fortification behind which impertinent rebels may renew or continue their war upon the Government", and that
"dangerous in the encouragement they have extended
to traitors, they have nevertheless produced a reaction, which will not stop until the exact relation of
that tribunal to the other departments of the Government is absolutely and irrevocably fixed." The *New
York Herald* stated that they were of the highest importance in their political aspect, and it again urged
a reconstruction of the Court, "to secure such interpretation of the Constitution as will proclaim the
great fixed fact that the war for the Union was neither
a blunder nor a failure but a great revolution." *Harper's Weekly* said that they were merely "another

[1] See *American Law Review* (1867), I, 575.

proof of the disposition of the Court to withstand the National will and reverse the results of the war." [1] On the other hand, the *New York World* said: "The decisions are an additional proof of the Court's superiority to party passions and popular clamor"; the *Detroit Free Press* congratulated the people "that their liberties are safe as against the despotic and treasonable contentions of Congress, at least until a bloody revolution has overthrown the Supreme Court or until its independence and usefulness is destroyed in some more insidious but perhaps more dangerous manner"; and the *National Intelligencer* said that: "It may suit the purposes of corrupt and unscrupulous partisans, alike in the press, the forums and the pulpit, to impugn the motives of the learned Judges who interpret the organic law of the Nation under a solemn sense of their responsibilities; but the plain people will not believe that they can be swerved from their sworn duty, by any sinister or improper inducements. Full of years, and full of honors, with no other ambition than to live in history as the wise and well qualified guardians of those principles which, embodied in the Constitution, constitute at once the boast and safeguard of the Nation, they are as incapable of being seduced into partial, much less political, decisions, as they are incapable of being intimidated by the threats of brawling politicians or the coarse vituperation of unprincipled editors. In an era of revolutionary convulsion, they yield neither to the passions of the mob, nor the invective of the

[1] *Washington Chronicle*, Feb. 16, 1867; *New York Herald*, Jan. 16, 1867; *Harper's Weekly*, March 2, 1867; *New York World*, Jan. 15, 1867, charging Chief Justice Chase, in dissenting in these cases, as "acting a most unworthy and responsible part", "acting with a bias", since he had already advised President Lincoln in regard to them; *Detroit Free Press*, Jan. 16, 1867; *National Intelligencer*, Jan. 15, 1867; the *Springfield Weekly Republican*, Jan. 19, 1867, noted with gratification that the division of the Judges was not based on political lines.

demagogue. . . . We simply congratulate the country
that though, amid the clash of arms, the sacred rights
of the citizen were somewhat infringed, yet, with the
return of peace, the Constitution is vindicated in all
its fullness and integrity."

The effect upon Congress was to strengthen the
demand for legislation to curb the Court; and George
S. Boutwell of Massachusetts at once introduced a
bill in the House to nullify the Court's decision by
providing that it should be a rule in all the Courts
of the United States that no person who had been
engaged in the Rebellion or supported its cause should
act as an attorney in those Courts.[1] "It is an offence
to the dignity and respectability of the Nation," he
said, "that that tribunal, under the general authority
vested in it under the Constitution and the laws, does
not protect itself from the contamination of rebels
and traitors, until the rebellion itself shall be suppressed and those men shall be restored to their former rights as citizens of this country. The Supreme
Court failing in the performance of this high and
self-protecting duty, the time has arrived when the
Congress of the United States, by whose breath alone
the Supreme Court enacts rules of any sort, or admits any man to the office of counsellor or attorney
at its Bar, should assume exact and specific authority
to declare by solemn law, that men who have been
guilty of murder or treason or bribery, or who have
raised their arms to strike down the Government of
this country, shall not participate in the administration of the laws of the land, until they are absolved
from their crimes."

[1] *39th Cong., 2d Sess.*, Jan. 22, 1867, 646–673; *Springfield Republican*, Jan. 26,
1867; *Philadelphia Inquirer*, Jan. 24, 1867; see also the accounts of this bill in
New York World, Jan. 24, 1867; *National Intelligencer*, Jan. 15, 1867; *Boston
Daily Advertiser*, Jan. 23. 1867.

The bill did not meet with warm support, even in the Republican press. "The bill is an attempt to neutralize the decision of the Court. It strikes the country as designed to place these two branches of the Government in direct and open antagonism but that Act itself will probably prove a nullity. Congress is not the final judge of the validity of its own acts, and cannot make itself so, while there is a Constitution and a Supreme Court," said the *Springfield Republican*. On the other hand, the *Philadelphia Inquirer* warned the Court that either it would be obliged "to succumb, or to take the high ground that it is beyond Congressional control in matters of detail and practices connected with the organization of the Court. It would be of dangerous consequence for the Judges to assume any such view; as the Court is, as to administration, constituents, and regulation, entirely within the authority of Congress and the laws."

Boutwell's bill and other corrective measures failed of adoption. Nevertheless, the radical attitude of the majority portended trouble for the future, and was truthfully described by a Democratic Congressman, when he said in one of the debates that, since the decisions of the Court were "in irreconcilable conflict with all the leading measures and policies of the dominant party in Congress, and, by the plainest logical sequence, pronounce judgment of condemnation against them all in advance, hence arises the growing hostility of radicalism towards that great tribunal. The country may well anticipate an early attempt by the radical despotism, that now claims to be the 'Nation' and to measure its power by its own will, to reduce that last citadel of National safety to its control, and to make the Judges mere clerks, to record as law the edicts of party and caucus."

CHAPTER THIRTY

RECONSTRUCTION

1867–1869

THOUGH exceedingly apprehensive as to the attitude of the Court toward its proposed Reconstruction legislation, Congress did not allow itself to be deflected from its firm purpose to adopt such measures as it believed imperative. Accordingly, in March, 1867, it proceeded to enact a series of statutes (over the constitutional objections raised by Presidential veto), providing for military government in the Southern States.[1]

Within three weeks after their passage, the long-expected attempt to obtain a ruling of the Court upon the validity of military government in time of peace was consummated, when, on April 5, 1867, a motion was made by Robert J. Walker, Augustus H. Garland and William L. Sharkey for leave to file an original bill in equity in the Supreme Court on behalf of the State of Mississippi, to enjoin "Andrew Johnson, a citizen of the State of Tennessee and President of the United States and his officers and agents appointed for that purpose, and especially E. O. C. Ord, assigned as military commander of the district . . . from executing or in any manner carrying out the Acts of March 2,

[1] See Act of March 2, 1867; Act of March 23, 1867; Act of July 19, 1867; Act of March 11, 1868; and the Act of June 25, 1868. See also *History of the Reconstruction Measures of the 39th and 40th Congresses 1865–68* (1868), by Henry Wilson; *Military Government of Southern Territory*, by A. H. Carpenter, *Amer. Hist. Ass. Rep.* (1900), I.

and 25, 1867.[1] Attorney-General Stanbery objected
to the filing of the bill on the ground that it contained
"matter not fit to be received." The occasion was
thus described by one who was present. "Those who
attended the Court-room were witnesses to one of the
most significant and remarkable scenes which ever
occurred in any hall of justice. William L. Sharkey
and Robert J. Walker as counsel for the people of the
State of Mississippi rose in their places and asked
leave to file an injunction, restraining the President
and military commanders from enforcing the Reconstruction Act, on the ground of its unconstitutionality.
For the first time in the history of any nation, the legal
representatives of the participants in an organized rebellion, defeated in the field, were permitted to appear
in Court, not to defend their clients on trial, but to ar-
raign and deny the authority of the law-making power,
and to plead anew the issues of the cause already decided by the sword. After accepting the terms of surrender, they propose in the Supreme Court to test the
very right admitted by their surrender. No greater
effrontery on the part of insurgents and rebels against
legal authority has ever been witnessed; and no instance on the part of any other government can be
quoted, as this in which the highest tribunal of the

---

[1] Ex-Judge John A. Campbell, over six months before, was preparing a suit to test
the validity of the military tribunals which had been established by President Johnson in Mississippi. In a letter to Benjamin R. Curtis, July 22, 1866, Campbell
wrote that he had just been to Washington in connection with the case of a super-
vising agent of the Treasury not connected with the military service and charged
with appropriating captured cotton and "in the clutches of a military commission
at Mobile. It was a good case to try the potency of these 'new minted judicatures',
as Prynne styled Strafford's military commissions that were trying men 'by an arbitrary, summary, illegal and martial proceeding, without any lawful presentment
or trial by a sworn, impartial able jury, diametrically opposite to the fundamental
laws, customs, great charters, statutes of the realm, and inherent liberty of the subject.' . . . I hope that D——, who is not a guilty criminal, will be allowed a trial
by a Court and not delivered over to the military commission's tender mercies.
The record in his case is a curious specimen of 'Military Justice' of which I am told
there is a Bureau at Washington." *Benjamin R. Curtis MSS.*

country patiently sits to hear arguments, which, if admitted, would declare the war for the Union to have been unjust and oppressive." And the *Independent's* Washington correspondent wrote : "A few rebel leaders of the proscribed class are trying to break down the Reconstruction Act through the Supreme Court. . . . They cannot succeed. . . . Congress found a way to carry its plans into execution against the opposition of the President, and it is able to sense means to carry out its purposes if the Supreme Court puts itself in the way. The proceedings yesterday in Court indicate that the President will execute the Act and that he will give no open encouragment to the rebel Governors." [1] On April 12, the power of the Court to exercise jurisdiction over the President was argued. The petitioners relied on Chief Justice Marshall's decision in the Burr treason trial, sixty years previous, sustaining the right of the Court to issue a *subpoena duces tecum* to President Jefferson. The Attorney-General argued vigorously as to the extraordinary results which would follow from an attempt by the Judiciary to control the acts of the Executive. "The scene was the most notable that has been witnessed in the Chamber of the Supreme Court for a long time," wrote a newspaper correspondent. "One marked the intellectual face of Mr. Trumbull, the fine forehead and weak mouth of Charles O'Conor, the

[1] *Independent*, April 10, 1867; the *New York Herald*, April 6, 1867, printed an editorial headed "Mississippi before the Supreme Court. The Old Southern Twaddle but a most important movement"; and said that the decision "will at all events, from the gravity of the subject, be waited for with the deepest interest by all parties." The *New York World*, April 4, 11, 1867, said it thought the Court would evade the issue, and that it did not suppose Sharkey himself had "any sanguine hope of success." The *Springfield Republican*, April 13, 1867, said that "Judge Sharkey denies that the President had anything to do with his attempt. . . . He says that he does not know the President's opinion on the subject, and when he notified him of his intention to petition for an injunction the President expressed neither approval nor disapproval."

See *Reconstruction and the Constitution* (1902), by John W. Burgess, 144 *et seq.*

Mephistophelian features of Montgomery Blair, the cunning eyes of Robert J. Walker, the classic profile of Roscoe Conkling, the white hair and florid countenance of Judge Sharkey, the mastiff jaws of Reverdy Johnson, Ex-Senator Harris genial and dignified, the Attorney-General bland and courteous, Mr. Cowan seemingly troubled with self-consciousness, the Ex-Attorney-General, Mr. Black, jocular and uneasy, and Governor Jenkins of Georgia grave and courtly. . . . The Attorney-General spoke an hour and was listened to with the closest attention throughout. Tall, spare, angular in action, of the sweetest personal courtesy, Mr. Stanbery is a most unique type of an old-fashioned gentleman, admired by his friends and seemingly respected by everybody. . . . The Attorney-General's manner was quite as impressive as his language. . . . He spoke with a clear voice, and held the fixed notice not only of the audience and of the attorneys but of every member of the Supreme Bench." Walker's argument was described as of little interest and as "adroit and specious." "Small, dapper, with a squatty appearance, sharp of feature and sharp of voice, with foxy manners and blinking eyes, Mr. Walker is quite as unique in his way as the Attorney-General. Equally easy and courteous, he lacks Mr. Stanbery's frankness and earnestness." Another correspondent wrote: "The Supreme Court presented a striking scene. It was crowded with distinguished officials, great lawyers and curious civilians. Two rebel States, which for four years fought with all their ability to overthrow the Government and to escape from its control, appeared in the Court to claim that during all that four years of cruel war, they were States in the Union and entitled to the same immunities and privileges as New York, Ohio and any of the loyal

States. This was a fine illustration of the humility of our 'conquered rebels.'" To this criticism, the *New York World* replied : "The South has heretofore refused to recognize the Supreme Court as the ultimate arbiter between the States and the Federal Government in disputed questions. The present applications ought, therefore, instead of the reprobations they have called forth in some quarters, to be accepted in a spirit of congratulation, as a signal token of the great change public opinion has undergone in the South." [1]

Although the *Independent's* correspondent stated that: "There is but one opinion here among men of all parties, as to the result; the Court will refuse to grant leave; this tribunal, already suspecting that, as now constituted, it is regarded as a diseased member of the body politic, will not run the risk of amputation by touching the edged tools of Sharkey and Walker," there were others who were not so confident as to the Court's action; and Francis Lieber wrote to Charles Sumner: "I imagine that at no time in our history have there been so many ears pricked up, in all portions of our country, for a coming decision, as at present, for the decision of the Supreme Court. . . . As it appears to me, the Court has only to decide between two laws presumed to conflict — a necessary consequence of an enacted (or written) Constitution. It leads to many inconveniences; but where parties contend, justice must be done. If we could obtain some archangels to sit, after each Congress, to decide on the laws of Congress, then we might make consti-

[1] *Boston Daily Advertiser*, April 13, 1867; *Independent*, April 16, 17, 1867; see *Philadelphia Inquirer*, April 13, 1867, for full report of the arguments of counsel; *New York World*, April 17, 1867. *Harper's Weekly*, April 20th, 1867, in an editorial headed "Rip Van Winkle in the Supreme Court", said that the arguments set forth in great amplitude "the old fallacy, thoroughly exposed and exploded, that once a State, always a State", and termed them "a desperate effort to undo in a Court the decision of a war."

tutionality a general question; but, with all respect for
our Supreme Court, or for many of the Judges at least, I
have never seen the angelic wings penetrating the gown."[1]

On April 15, 1867, within three days after the argument, the Court, through the Chief Justice, rendered
a decision in which it avoided the delicate issue as to
its power to control Executive acts in general, and
contented itself with holding that, inasmuch as the
actions involved in this case were not ministerial and
required Executive discretion, the Court "has no jurisdiction of a bill to enjoin the President in the performance of his official duties, and no such bill ought to
be received by us."[2]

Undiscouraged by this failure, counsel for the States
of Georgia and Mississippi made another attempt to test
the validity of the Reconstruction legislation by asking leave to file bills praying for injunctions to restrain
Secretary of War Stanton and General Grant from executing the provisions of the Reconstruction Acts, and
setting forth that the design of these Acts was to annul
the existing State Governments and to subject the people to military rule.   The Court deciding to allow these
bills to be filed, on consent of the Attorney-General,
they were set down for immediate argument.[3]   Con-

---

[1] *Life and Letters of Francis Lieber* (1882), letter of April 14, 1867.

[2] *Mississippi* v. *Johnson*, 4 Wall. 475.

[3] See *Cleveland Herald*, April 15, 27, 1867: "Sharkey's New Rebellion, as developed in the Supreme Court today, drew forth a motley audience, who crowded
the Court-room. . . . Most of them were rebels and sympathizers who did not
look as if they were aware that the late rebellion was over. . . .   The clear, strong
argument of the Attorney-General seemed easily to overbear the formidable array
of legal talent engaged in this new crusade against the peace of the country —
Ewing, Johnson, Black, O'Conor, Edgar Cowan, Sharkey, Walker." See also
especially *Philadelphia Inquirer*, April 17, 1867; *Boston Daily Advertiser*, April 16,
18, 19, 1867.   The *Springfield Weekly Republican*, April 20, 1867, said that: "There
is no expectation that the Court will grant the injunction prayed for, whatever
may be the opinions of the Judges as to the constitutionality of the law. Even if
the Court should grant the petition, final action will not be taken till next December, and by that time Reconstruction will have been completed in nearly every
Southern State. We have no doubt the Southern people prefer to have it so."

servatives and Radicals alike approved this course, both believing that it was better that the Court should say at once whether it would take jurisdiction in this manner over the Reconstruction question. And the Radicals expressed the view that, if the Court should now decide against the bill at the present Term : "The whole South will understand at once that the Court will not step in between Congress and rebels, not at present certainly, and not early enough in any event to do any good or harm. As a matter of course, in due time, a case can be made up in one of the inferior Courts against the Military Act; but a decision of the Supreme Court could not be reasonably expected before 1869. By that time the rebellious States will be thoroughly reconstructed." [1] The case was elaborately argued on April 26, May 1, 3, 6, 1867, by Charles O'Conor of New York and Robert J. Walker of Mississippi in behalf of the States. They were opposed by Attorney-General Stanbery, who, though stating that personally he was opposed to the Reconstruction measures, nevertheless, made an exceptionally powerful argument against the jurisdiction of the Court over the purely political question presented by the bills in equity before it. "The little Court-room was filled but not at any time crowded. One fourth of the spectators were ladies, some of them well-known secessionists," wrote a correspondent. "The attendance of young and unknown lawyers was quite large. For the rest, there was Chief Justice Cartter of the District Court, shrewd and practical in every feature; good old Tom Ewing with his bald head and jovial double chin; Senator Morgan, grave and dignified; the Secretary of the

[1] *Independent,* April 25, 1867. On May 2, it said: "There is but one way for the Court to obtain jurisdiction of the Reconstruction Acts and that is by appeal from a State Court. To do this will take so long that the South can obtain no relief."

Treasury, bland and unruffled; Thomas J. Durant, the sad-faced and thin featured New Orleans Unionist; Judge Black, with his sardonic smile and white eyebrows and black wig; rugged Joshua Hill, the Georgia Loyalist; and a goodly number of white-haired Washington Rebel sympathizers." [1]

Only ten days later, the Court rendered a decision dismissing the suits, and holding that they called for an adjudication on rights, not of persons or property, but of a political character, of sovereignty, of corporate existence as a State, and that it had no jurisdiction over such a controversy — *Georgia* v. *Stanton*, 6 Wall. 50. "Undoubtedly, it is no light matter," said the *Nation*, "that the highest Court in the land should thus disclaim the power of enquiring into the constitutionality of an Act of Congress destroying the government of ten States. For it must be observed that every word of Mr. Stanbery's argument would be just as applicable if Massachusetts, instead of Georgia, were the complainant, and if Congress had undertaken to overthrow a State government which it at the same time admitted to be perfectly legitimate. No State in the Union, therefore, can rely upon the Supreme Court for protection against the usurpation of Congress. This is a grave fact which deserves serious consideration, and yet, notwithstanding all the perils of such a decision, it is clear that it is justified by reason and ex-

---

[1] *Boston Daily Advertiser*, April 27, 1867; see also especially *Philadelphia Inquirer*, April 29, 1867; *Nation*, May 2, 9, 16, 1867; *Harper's Weekly*, May 11, 1867. Welles wrote in his diary, April 29, 1867: "The injunction cases in behalf of Georgia and Mississippi have been before the Court and are still pending. Attorney-General and Mr. O'Conor made arguments on Friday. The latter is evidently more of a lawyer than statesman, studies law more than Constitution, cases more than governmental principles. Nothing will be got from the Court, I apprehend, and there are embarrassments in the case. The Attorney-General's position cannot be subscribed to in all respects. Why O'Conor and his associates make no use of the recent decision of the Court in Milligan's case, I don't understand. Congress under color of law, cannot invest brigadiers with power to abolish jury trial or to suspend the privilege of habeas corpus in time of peace."

perience. . . . Purely political controversies are, of all things, the least amenable to the jurisdiction of a Court. The origin and existence of a State, the existence and justice of a war, or the validity of a revolutionary change in the form of government, are all of them questions which no nation ever allowed Courts to determine. . . . The immediate results of the decision just rendered by the Court are unqualifiedly beneficial. Even if the suit had been merely entertained without a decision upon the merits, the effect upon the South must have been injurious, while it is difficult to estimate the mischief that might have been wrought by the entire success of the complainant. It could not have saved the State from the ultimate control of Congress, and it would have introduced new elements of evil into the conflict. We think that every intelligent Southerner — certainly every shrewd lawyer or politician — feels relieved by the decision. Certainly, it is a cause for congratulation among all friends of regulated liberty. The speedy reorganization of the South under the Reconstruction Act is now made all but certain." The *Springfield Republican* said that the decision was "what all sensible persons expected. . . . The Court is not going to establish so dangerous a precedent." [1]

One last attempt was now made by counsel for Mississippi to amend their bill so as to show a property interest in the State in matters affected by the actions of the defendant military commanders; but this motion was denied by an equally divided Court; Wayne, Clifford, Nelson and Field being in favor of granting

[1] *Nation*, May 23, 1867; *Springfield Weekly Republican*, May 18, 1867. The *Philadelphia Inquirer*, May 17, 1867, spoke of "those remarkable geniuses, Sharkey and Walker . . . the first to imagine that an Act of Congress might be nullified by the special injunction of a Court of equity — an original doctrine which the Court have not yet comprehended." See also for an interesting criticism of Black's argument, *Washington Weekly Chronicle*, May 18, 1867.

leave to amend, the Chief Justice, Swayne, Miller and Davis being opposed. Owing to the absence of Judge Grier, who, had he been present, would have probably favored the motion, the question whether the Court could interfere with the Reconstruction legislation in order to protect the public property of a State remained undecided; and Congress was left with a free hand.[1] While the decision of the Court, that it would not take jurisdiction when the facts of the case involved only political and not personal or property rights, enounced no new doctrine of law, the Democrats throughout the country were inclined to believe that the Court was evading its responsibilities by refusal of jurisdiction, and criticized it for its course. "What is to become of the Supreme Court of the United States — the conservative branch of the Government?" wrote James Buchanan. "When I recall the names of the pure, able and venerable men who have filled the office of Chief Justice from John Jay to Roger B. Taney, and witness the efforts of the present Chief Justice to drag the judicial ermine through the dirt to propitiate radicals, I cannot help thinking we have fallen on evil times. But I am now an old fogy." [2]

Though the Reconstruction legislation had thus become safe from injunction, its constitutionality was brought before the Court at the next Term, in December, 1867, in an unexpected manner, through the operation of a statute recently enacted by Congress for the protection of Federal officials and other loyal persons against adverse action by the Courts and officials in the late Confederate States. Under this new

[1] *Boston Daily Advertiser*, May 17, 1867; the *Springfield Weekly Republican*, May 18, 1867, said that the motion to amend by asking for an injunction against Gen. Ord's taking possession of the Mississippi State Treasury, was denied by a divided Court, the names of the Judges being withheld. "All legal obstacles to Reconstruction are now removed."

[2] *Works of James Buchanan* (1910), XI, letter of June 11, 1867.

Act of February 5, 1867, appeals from the Federal Circuit Courts to the Supreme Court in habeas corpus cases, which had hitherto been allowed in a very limited class of cases, were now extended to "all cases where any person may be restrained of his or her liberty, in violation of the Constitution or of any treaty or law of the United States." By an ironic stroke, this Act designed to enforce the Reconstruction measures was now seized upon as a weapon to test their validity. An editor named McCardle, who had been arrested and held for trial by a military commission in Mississippi under authority of one of the first Reconstruction Acts, petitioned for a writ of habeas corpus in the Federal Circuit Court, and after an adverse decision took an appeal to the Supreme Court. On January 10, 1868, Jeremiah S. Black, counsel for McCardle, moved that the case be advanced for speedy hearing. Attorney-General Stanbery stated to the Court that, as he had already officially advised the President that the Reconstruction Laws were unconstitutional, he could not act on behalf of the Government, and that he had so notified the commanding military officials concerned. On January 17, the Court granted the motion and set the case for the first Monday in March. "This decision," said a leading Republican paper, "gives satisfaction to the Radicals, as they hope by that time to have affairs in such condition in the States of Mississippi and Alabama that, even if the Court decides the Reconstruction Acts unconstitutional, it will not seriously impede the work in those States." [1] It was reported that the Judges were divided on the question

---

[1] See especially as to the proceedings in this case, *Indianapolis Journal*, Jan. 18, 1868; *Chicago Republican*, Jan. 11, 17, 18, 22, 1868. On Feb. 1, it said that: "The speech of Jerry Black was an extremely bitter copperhead harangue on State-Rights and the unconstitutionality of the Reconstruction laws. He evidently argued the McCardle case *con amore.*"

of advancing, as follows — Judges Grier, Clifford, Nelson, Davis and Field, against Chief Justice Chase, Judges Swayne and Miller; and the newspapers believed that there would be a similar division on the constitutionality of the laws. Before the final hearing, however, vigorous arguments were heard by the Court, on January 31 and February 1, on its right to take jurisdiction of the case under the new habeas corpus statute, Jeremiah S. Black, David Dudley Field and William L. Sharkey appearing for McCardle, and Matt H. Carpenter, Lyman Trumbull and James Hughes for the Government.

Meanwhile, rumors that the Court intended to hold the Reconstruction Laws invalid,[1] and the fact that the impeachment of President Johnson was already being discussed, had convinced the Reconstructionists in Congress of the necessity of some form of action which should save their imperiled legislation. Accordingly, with the intent of averting such an adverse decision by the Court, the Judiciary Committee of the House reported a bill to provide that, in any case involving the validity of a law of Congress, two thirds of the Judges must concur in an opinion adverse to the law.[2] In the debate which ensued, the Court was warmly defended by John V. L. Pruyn of New York and Samuel S. Marshall of Illinois, the latter stating that he con-

---

[1] The *Springfield Republican*, Jan. 10, 1868, speaking of the rumor that the Court was to hold the laws invalid by a vote of five to three, said: "It is not easy to understand why Congress should be disturbed about it. Mr. Stevens always said that these Acts and much other legislation for the South were 'outside of the Constitution', and the only real support has been found in the supposed right of Congress to exercise the war power over conquered States. Of course, the Constitution recognizes no such power." *Ibid.*, Jan. 25, 1868.

[2] *40th Cong., 2d Sess.*, 478 *et seq*. The bill was stated by Thomas Williams, Jan. 13, 1868, to be a copy of a bill introduced in the last Congress "which seemed at the time of its introduction to startle the profession, and, to some extent, the country at large." See especially speech by Wilson of Iowa, Jan. 14, 1868, 492–498, attacking Judges Swayne and Chief Justice Chase and defending Judge Field and the Court against Radicalism.

sidered the bill "revolutionary and dangerous . . . one of the worst of the revolutionary measures brought forward to subvert and destroy the institutions of our country, which have caused such widespread gloom and despondency. . . . This measure is hurried through here this morning to prevent an adjudication of the validity of their motley Reconstruction Acts. . . . It is a confession of guilt on the part of the majority. It is evident that they feel and know in their hearts that their legislation will not bear investigation by a legal tribunal, made up now principally of members of their own party, placed there by their own favored President." George W. Woodward of Pennsylvania declared that Congress had no power to prescribe the number of Judges necessary for a decision, or to dictate to the Court how it should decide constitutional questions. On the other hand, in support of the measure, Rufus P. Spalding of Ohio declared that "for everything except its official life, that tribunal must look to an Act of Congress"; and John A. Bingham of Ohio, in a savage onslaught, urged that as Congress had full power over the Court, it could even limit its number to three, of which two or even three should be required as a quorum.[1] The bill passed the House by a vote of one hundred and sixteen to thirty-nine, and it was warmly supported by the Radical Republican press.[2] "There is danger of an adverse

[1] James F. Wilson of Iowa proposed to amend the Committee amendment as follows: "Provided however, that if any Circuit or District Court of the United States shall adjudge any Act of Congress to be unconstitutional or invalid, the judgment, before any further proceeding shall be had upon it, shall be certified up to the Supreme Court of the United States and shall be considered therein, and if upon consideration thereof, two thirds of all the members of the Supreme Court shall not affirm such judgment, the same shall be declared and held reversed." This new modification was defeated by a vote of twenty-five to one hundred and twenty-four.

[2] *Independent*, Jan. 23, 1868; *Harper's Weekly*, Feb. 1, 1868; *Indianapolis Journal*, Jan. 25, 1868; *Washington Weekly Chronicle*, Jan. 25, 1868.

decision from the Supreme Court. Let the bill pass prohibiting a bare majority from declaring any Congressional Act void," said the *Independent*. "It is needed now, never more than at this moment; and the fact that it is needed is no argument against the propriety of passing the bill, as some timid people contend; " and it even charged that: "The Supreme Court is at this hour the guilty confederate of Andrew Johnson. The country will rejoice to see it checkmated." *Harper's Weekly* argued, in support of the measure, that: "If the Court shall decide against the validity of the Legal Tender Act, that the War was fought on an unconstitutional basis, and that the Southern States are still in the Union . . . results that cannot be contemplated without extreme solicitude would follow, and it is wholly unsafe to leave these questions to the decision of a bare majority of the Judges. . . . The regulation in question in no manner interferes with the stability of the Court, except to promote it. It leaves the whole judicial power in the tribunal, and only regulates it so as to prevent a capricious judgment. The independence of the Judge is not interfered with." The *Indianapolis Journal* regretted that the bill had not been introduced at an earlier date, when it would not provoke such partisan feeling; but it said that it was never of so great importance as now. "The Reconstruction Acts are full of the rights and liberties of millions of men; and to have these stricken down, by the decision of some old fossil on the Supreme Bench whose political opinion belongs to a past era, would be an outrage on humanity." It urged that a two-thirds requirement would lift judicial decisions into universal respect, while the present close divisions exposed the Court to imputations of partisanship. The *Washington Chronicle*, urging the passage of the bill, said that owing to the Court's action in the *McCardle Case*, which had created "a feeling of just and general resentment . . . the new peril of the Republic is grave; but the remedy is sure and drastic, and it ought to be applied without waiting or shrinking."

These views, however, were not shared by the country at large; and the general public was opposed to so revolutionary an attempt to interfere with the Judiciary.[1] A leading paper in the West, the *Chicago Republican*, said that Congress was attempting to override the Supreme Court, the National Executive and every judicial tribunal in the country; that Congress should "check injustice and oppression on its own part." And it further stated that it could never "sit by quietly and see a hand lifted against the Court or the Constitution, whether by our National Congress or by Southern traitors", and that such were the views of nine tenths of the Republicans in the Northwest. "The people are not in favor of this Supreme Court bill. Let Congress avoid all doubtful or violent measures of legislation. . . . It must not meddle with the constitutional rights and privileges of the people, nor of their Executive or Supreme Judiciary. . . . Regarding, as they do, the Supreme Court as the judicial bulwark against tyranny and injustice on the part of either President or Congress, they will never permit this safeguard against oppression to be swept away. The people will be found as prompt to resent usurpation on the part of Congress as of Johnson." Other papers asked if the Republican leaders in Congress wished to justify the charge of the Democracy that they are bound upon usurpation and revolution. The

[1] *Chicago Republican*, Jan. 15, 24, 25, 27, 31; in the latter issue it stated that the *Cincinnati Gazette, Detroit Tribune, Cleveland Herald, Albany Evening Journal*, and fifty other Republican papers were opposed to the bill. See also *Nation*, Jan. 16, 30, Feb. 20, 1868; *Springfield Republican*, Jan. 13, 18, 25, Feb. 1, 1868.

Springfield Republican remarked sarcastically, but per-
tinently : "If the Supreme Court should decide the
two-thirds law to be unconstitutional, and by a two-
thirds vote, what is to be done next? This is a poser.
There seems to be nothing for it but to suspend the action of the Court on constitutional questions, during
the existence of the present Congress." The *Nation*
opposed the bill as an attempt by Congress to manipu-
late the Court to suit a particular exigency, the only
effect of which would be to weaken the Court's influence.
Pointing out that, hitherto, the opponents of the Court
had been found among the partisans of State-Rights,
it said that : "It is more than strange, it is pitiable,
to find the National men of the present day repeat-
ing the State arguments so often used by their adver-
saries. To remove the legislation of Congress from the
reach of all jurisdiction is simply impossible. . . . If
the Judges of the Nation are silenced, those of the
States will be left entirely uncontrolled. . . . Remove
the supervisory function of the National Judiciary and
these laws will become the sport of local partisanship ;
upheld in one commonwealth, they will be overthrown
in another, and all compulsive character will be lost.
. . . To restrict their jurisdiction and weaken their
moral power is, therefore, to sacrifice in a most unnecessary manner that department of the Government
which, more than any other, will make National ideas
triumphant, not only in the legislation of today but in
the permanent convictions of the people."

Gideon Welles displayed his apprehensions as a conservative Republican over this attitude of the Radicals as follows:

Jan. 13, 1868: In the House, under the discipline and
stimulation of the Radical leaders, there is manifested a
revolutionary and violent spirit. Part of the conspiracy

is a scheme to change the character of the Supreme Court, which Stevens and his fellows find is against them.

Feb. 18, 1868: In their war upon the Court, the Radicals under the lead of Trumbull, have under consideration an act prohibiting the Court from passing judgment on political questions, and they have now a bill declaring what are political questions. These usurpations and intrigues strain our government.

In the Senate, there now appeared some hesitation on the part of the Republican leaders to enact the House bill for the requirement of a concurrence of two thirds of the Judges; and Democratic Senators made the charge (with considerable reason) that the Republicans suspected that, even with such a requirement, the Reconstruction Laws would be held unconstitutional. After several postponements, the bill was finally dropped. Later, another more extreme measure, originating with Thaddeus Stevens in the House and expressly forbidding the Supreme Court to take jurisdiction in any case in law or equity arising out of the Reconstruction Acts, was introduced by Lyman Trumbull in the Senate; but that body, doubting the political expediency of creating such a precedent, finally took no action.[1] The wisdom of this course was well pointed out by the *Nation*: "If this game of 'exceptions', as an instrument of party warfare, be once fairly entered on, we venture to say that, in the course of the next twenty years, the constitutionality of half the statutes at large would be withdrawn from the cognizance of the Supreme Court. It is, luckily, three years before the Democrats can get the upper hand in

[1] *40th Cong., 2d Sess.*, 2127, March 26, 1868. It is to be noted that are solution was introduced into the House to investigate a statement appearing in the *Washington Evening Express* of Jan. 29, 1868, to the effect that Judge Field had openly declared the Reconstruction law to be invalid. *Chicago Republican,* Feb. 6, 7, 1868. These statements were later proved false.

Congress; but when they do, there will be some wonder-
working legislation."

On February 10, 1868, the Court made public for the
first time its full opinion (delivered by Judge Nelson)
in the cases brought by the States of Georgia and Mississippi against Secretary Stanton and General Grant,
which it had dismissed in the preceding May.   The
first sentiment of the Republicans as to this opinion
was that it would dispose of the *McCardle Case*,[1] which
they assumed would also be regarded by the Court as
involving a mere political question.   "Not only is the
supremacy of the Court declared to be judicial supremacy, but the issues arising out of the Reconstruction
legislation of Congress are pronounced to fall within
the political domain, upon which the tribunal has no
right to enter.   In vain will ex-rebels look to the judicial department of the United States to aid them in
their wicked scheme of insubordination and resistance,"
was the exultant comment of the *Chicago Tribune;* and
the *Chicago Republican*, remarking the unanimity of the
Judges, said that: "It must exert a powerful influence
in repressing the stubbornness and confidence of the
ex-rebels in their reactionary schemes.   They must
now feel that Congress is sole master of the political
situation. . . .   Disregard of the distinctions between
political and judicial powers would convert the Supreme
Court into a political council and board of control.
. . .   It would confer on the Supreme Court, powers
too gigantic and terrific, too dangerous to the peace
of the United States."   On the other hand, the *Nation*
correctly pointed out that: "The judgment is mainly
important, as showing the reluctance of the whole
Court to meddle in Reconstruction, or in any way

---

[1] *Chicago Tribune*, Feb. 12, 1868; *Chicago Republican*, Feb. 11, 12, 1868; *Nation*,
Feb. 13, 1868; *Springfield Republican*, Feb. 12, 22, 1868.

throw itself across the track of Congress or of the Executive, and ought to make some of the 'sons of thunder' who have been abusing it for the last month a little ashamed of their work. But it does not, it seems to us, remove all grounds for anxiety as to the *McCardle Case;* for Judge Nelson in several places suggests the inference that a bill showing that the Act of Congress in some way infringed on rights of persons or property might be differently treated."

On February 3, 1868, one week before the publication of its opinion in the Georgia and Mississippi cases, and only one week after the argument of *Ex parte Mc-Cardle*, 6 Wall. 318, the Court, contrary to general public expectation, rendered its decision upholding its jurisdiction of the latter case, and on March 2, arguments were begun before it. "I spoke two and a half hours today, and as well as I expected or hoped to do," wrote Senator Mathew Hale Carpenter (one of the Government counsel) to his wife. "I am praised nearly to death. I had half of the Senate for an audience. Miller's face was as the face of an angel, radiant with light and joy. Davis and Field looked troubled. Nelson, Clifford and Grier, dead against me. But I shook them up and rattled their dry bones." [1] Meanwhile, the Impeachment Trial of President Johnson had been initiated and on March 5, in the midst of the McCardle argument, Chief Justice Chase was withdrawn from the Bench in order to preside over the Senate. [2] On March 9, the Court took the case under advisement. [3] Three days later, Con-

---

[1] *Mathew Hale Carpenter as a Lawyer*, by Henry D. Ashley, *Green Bag* (1894), VI: "When Carpenter finished, Secretary of War Stanton, with tears in his eyes, exclaimed fervently: 'Carpenter, you have saved us.'"

[2] The House had voted for impeachment, Feb. 24, 1868; the first proceedings in the Senate took place on March 5; the trial began March 13, and the first vote was taken May 16.

[3] As to this case, see especially *New York Herald*, March 4, 14, 1868, publishing

gress finally decided to intervene and to render any decision of the case impossible. In spite of the fact that, owing to Chase's absence, the Court might be desirous of postponing a decision until the next Term, the Radicals in Congress were fearful and resolved to take no chances. On March 12, 1868, there was pending in the House a harmless and unimportant Senate bill to extend to the Court's appellate jurisdiction in cases involving customs and revenue officers. Unanimous consent had been obtained by Robert C. Schenck of Ohio for its consideration, on the statement that it was a mere routine matter; and while the Democrats were thus thrown off their guard by this assertion, James F. Wilson of Iowa, without any explanation or debate, introduced an amendment entirely repealing the appellate jurisdiction of the Court under the Habeas Corpus Act of 1867, and further prohibiting the exercise of any jurisdiction by the Court on appeals which had been or might be taken.[1] The amendment was agreed to without comment or objection, and the bill as thus amended by the House went back to the Senate. Then, for the first time, the moderate Republicans and the Democrats awoke to the fact that they had been deceived. Benjamin M. Boyer of Pennsylvania charged that the House had been disarmed by Schenck's remarks and induced to accept an amendment not genuine. He charged that it had

David Dudley Field's argument in full; *Chicago Republican*, March 5, 6, 7, 10, 1868; *Indianapolis Journal*, March 6, 10, 1868. The *Springfield Republican's* Washington correspondent wrote, March 5, that it was considered certain that the case would not be decided until the next Term.

[1] In *Social Forces in American History* (1911), by A. M. Simons, 300–301, it is stated: "On the 27th of March, 1868, Congress passed a law threatening the members of the Supreme Court with fines and imprisonment, if they interfered with the carrying out of such legislation, and notifying that body that this legislation was not subject to review as to its constitutionality. The Court and Congress completely punctured the bubble upon which the autocratic power of the Court rests." Such a statement as to the character of the statute enacted is incorrect, for it made no provision for fines and imprisonment.

been smuggled through, to prevent a test of the constitutionality of the Reconstruction Acts; and while admitting that the minority had not been wide enough awake, and had been caught napping, he thought that it would have been more manly to have introduced such a measure for free discussion.[1]   Schenck, in reply, boldly and frankly avowed that his purpose had been to deprive the Court of its power and jurisdiction, saying that he had lost confidence in the majority of that tribunal, and that: "They usurp power, whenever they dare to undertake to settle questions, purely political, in regard to the status of the States and the manner in which those States are to be held subject to the law-making power.   And if I find them abusing that power, by attempting to arrogate to themselves jurisdiction under any statute that happens to be upon the record from which they claim to derive that jurisdiction, and I can take it away from them by a repeal of that statute, I will do it. . . .   Now I hold that the Supreme Court, arrogating to themselves the pretension to settle not merely judicial but political questions, and trampling upon the principle of the decision made in the case of the Dorr Rebellion and upon every other decision of that kind, are, the majority of them, proceeding step by step to the usurpation of jurisdiction which does not belong to them.   And I hold it to be not only my right, but my duty as a Representative of the people, to clip the wings of that Court."

In the Senate, the amendment to its bill was concurred in, with no explanation or debate, on March 12, 1868, by a vote of thirty-two to six, with sixteen Senators absent.   A request by Charles R. Buckalew of Pennsylvania for information as to the purpose of the amendment received only a very brief reply by George

[1] *40th Cong., 2d Sess.*, 1859, 1881 *et seq.*, March 12, 14, 1868.

H. Williams of Oregon, which did not in any way explain its real purpose; and a request by Buckalew for postponement of action was refused.[1] Within a very few days, however, after the passage of the bill through both Houses, the fact that Congress had been practically tricked into passing, without debate, a measure of the utmost importance burst with a shock upon the country. Welles wrote in his diary:

March 14, 1868. It is evident that the Radicals in Congress are in a conspiracy to overthrow not only the President but the Government. The impeachment is but a single act in the drama. . . . By trick, imposition and breach of courtesy, an Act was slipped through both houses, repealing the laws of 1867 and 1789, the effect of which is to take from the Supreme Court certain powers and which is designed to prevent a decision in the *McCardle Case.* Should the Court in that case, as it is supposed they will, pronounce the Reconstruction Laws unconstitutional, the military governments will fall and the whole Radical fabric will tumble with it. Only one course can prolong the miserable contrivance, and that is a President like Wade, who will maintain the military governments regardless of Courts, of law, or right. Hence, I have very little expectation that the President will escape conviction. His deposition is a party necessity, and the Senators have not individually the strength, ability, nor honesty, to resist the Radical caucus decision, which Stevens, Ben Butler, and other chief conspirators sent out.

"The country is in the hands of Congress. That Congress is the Radical majority, and that Radical majority is old Thad Stevens. Government by the people has its glories!" said the *New York Herald*, with sarcasm, but with truth.[2] But the Radical Republican press was exultant. "The passage of that little

---

[1] *40th Cong., 2d Sess.,* 2095, March 25, 1868; see speech of Senator Thomas A. Hendricks explaining the method by which the bill passed the Senate.

[2] *New York Herald*, March 14, 1868; *Independent*, March 19, April 21, 1868; *Springfield Republican*, March 27, 1868.

bill which put a knife to the throat of the *McCardle Case* was a splendid performance. . . . Congress will not abandon its Reconstruction policy to please any Court, because it sincerely believes that the welfare of the Nation depends upon the success of that policy," said the *Independent*. "This Congress will not brook opposition from the Court in political matters. The safety of the Nation demands that Congressional Reconstruction shall be successful; and if the Court interferes, the Court will go to the wall. This language sounds harsh and indecorous to fossil ears, no doubt." And the *Springfield Republican* said: "Congress does not intend to permit the Supreme Court to overthrow it or revive rebellion, if it can help it."

Although his impeachment trial had already begun, the President did not hesitate, even at this desperate moment in his career, to meet the Congressional attack upon the Court with a vigorous determination to uphold the honorable status of that tribunal; and on March 25, he sent to Congress a powerfully worded veto of the bill, in which he stated:

Thus far during the existence of the Government, the Supreme Court of the United States has been viewed by the people as the true expounder of their Constitution, and in the most violent party conflicts, its judgments and decrees have always been sought and deferred to with confidence and respect. In public estimation, it combines judicial wisdom and impartiality in a greater degree than any other authority known to the Constitution; and any act which may be construed into, or mistaken for, an attempt to prevent or evade its decisions on a question which affects the liberty of the citizens and agitates the country cannot fail to be attended with unpropitious consequences. It will be justly held by a large portion of the people as an admission of the unconstitutionality of the act on which its judgment may be forbidden or forestalled, and may interfere with that willing acquiescence in its provisions which is necessary for the harmonious and efficient execution of any law.

When the question of passing the bill over the veto arose in the Senate, opportunity was at last given for a thorough debate as to its purpose, and its supporters were worsted on the argument.[1] Lyman Trumbull, who was largely responsible for its enactment, attempted to argue that there was no case pending before the Supreme Court under the Habeas Corpus Act of February 5, 1867. This bill, he said, was not a very important measure; and at all events the "liberties of the people had been pretty well preserved for three quarters of a century, without the Act of 1867 in any of its provisions; and all the securities that were ever afforded until within the last year are left just as they always have been."[2] To this rather disingenuous argument, James R. Doolittle of Wisconsin replied very forcibly that, if there was no case pending before the Supreme Court which would be affected by the bill, why did the bill make specific provisions for repeal of jurisdiction in all pending cases? "Why undertake to take away the jurisdiction of the Court? The truth is, and we may as well look it square in the face, it is because men know that these acts will be decided to be unconstitutional. . . . I say it is because they fear it; because they know that the constitutionality of the measures is in-

---

[1] 40th Cong., 2d Sess., 2095, 2115, 2127, 2165, March 25, 26, 1868.

[2] The *Chicago Republican*, March 27, 1868, attempted a similar and false-hearted defense of the bill, saying that the Habeas Corpus Act of 1867 was only intended "to counteract the spirit of rebel persecution that sought to inflict vengeance upon Union whites and blacks under the forms of law" and that "probably, through the expensiveness of its processes, it had been little resorted to. Indeed the ingenuity of disloyal men threatens to make it an instrument for promoting their nefarious ends. Congress has, therefore, decided to remove from them this source of embroilment. Another reason justifying its repeal is that the whole time of the Supreme Court is already occupied in its consideration of cases naturally and properly arising, and that it would be impolitic to encumber the docket with unnecessary causes."

volved, and they fear that the decision will be against their constitutionality." Trumbull's position in regard to this bill was a delicate one, for he was counsel for the Government in the *McCardle Case* and had full knowledge of the issues involved. William M. Stewart of Nevada, therefore, came to his aid with a vicious attack upon the Court and its motives. Stewart was no more fortunate, however, in the explanation which he proffered as to the necessity for this bill; since, after stating that it was required because of the crowd of cases arising under the Act of 1867, he was obliged to admit, on being pressed for details, that he knew of only one pending case — McCardle's. In a masterly speech on the whole subject of habeas corpus, Senator Thomas A. Hendricks of Indiana taunted the "brave Senators" who were "afraid of the decision of the Court. . . . You did claim to the country that the Administration of Mr. Lincoln was entitled to its confidence; and are there not five Judges out of eight whom Mr. Lincoln appointed and whom you confirmed; and at the head is there not Chief Justice Chase, distinguished as a party leader? Then, with a Supreme Court, five out of eight appointed by Mr. Lincoln and confirmed by these honorable Senators that I am addressing, and only three of the Old Court left, you say you cannot afford to risk this question before that Court. Why? Let that question be answered." Senator Reverdy Johnson also replied with force to Stewart's attacks on the Court, and said that it was "dangerous to inculcate the belief that Courts can be governed by political and party motives." Senator Willard Saulsbury of Delaware charged that the passage of the bill was an act of "despotism"; Senator Thomas F. Bayard of Delaware termed it a "confession of fear"; and Senator Charles R. Buckalew of

Pennsylvania spoke of Trumbull's "feeble and fruit-
less denial" of the real purpose of the Act. But though
the merits of the debate were wholly with the defenders
of the Court, the bill passed the Senate on March 26,
1868, over the President's veto, by a vote of thirty-three
to nine (with twelve Senators absent); it passed the
House on March 27, by a vote of one hundred and
fifteen to fifty-seven, and became the Act of March 27,
1868. Thus was consummated an action which has
been, with justice, characterized as "an abominable
subterfuge on the part of Congress and a shameful
abuse of its powers." [1]

Meanwhile, during the eighteen days between the
close of the argument in the *McCardle Case* and the
final passage of this bill, there was much excitement
over the question whether the Court would proceed
to render its decision, regardless of the pendency of
the bill taking away its jurisdiction.[2] Gradually, it
became apparent that the Court intended to await
the final outcome of the bill, and, as the Republican
papers stated, that it did not choose "to run a race
with Congress", since "it would hardly have been
consistent with the dignity of the country and the respect due to the other branches of the Government to
proceed with the matter until the President had either
approved or vetoed the bill, and the Congress had acted
on the veto." [3] "The Supreme Court, acting with

[1] *Reconstruction and the Constitution* (1902), by John W. Burgess, 196–197.

[2] The *Boston Post's* Washington correspondent wrote that it was believed that
the Court would decide the case, "in defense of its own dignity, and to show that
the Court cannot be trifled with by reckless partisans who flippantly speak of
'clipping the wings of the Court.' It is well ascertained that Justices Chase,
Nelson, Grier, Clifford, Davis and Field believe the Reconstruction Acts to be unconstitutional. . . . The decision is made up, and they have the power and the
right to deliver it. Whether they have the nerve to be an independent Judiciary
remains to be seen." See *New York Tribune*, March 19, 1868.

[3] The *Indianapolis Journal*, March 18, 1868, said: "The Copperheads contend
that so far as the *McCardle Case* is concerned, having already been argued before

more discretion and better taste than the President,"
said the *Springfield Republican*, "bows down to the will
of Congress, and has postponed the *McCardle Case* till
Congress has more definitely settled the Reconstruction question. No announcement to this effect has
been publicly made, but it is known that the Court
has made the decision, only Justices Field and Grier
voting for an immediate decision." This delay by the
Court was the subject of much criticism by the Democrats, who asserted that it was seeking to evade its
responsibilities. When the bill was finally passed over
the President's veto, the Court was immediately confronted with the necessity of deciding whether Congress had the power to abolish its right to adjudicate
pending cases. On Monday, March 30, Jeremiah S.
Black moved that the case be set down for argument
on this important question, and the Court after some
hesitation agreed to hear it on April 2. Counsel, however, not being prepared to proceed on so short a notice,
a majority of the Judges (Grier and Field dissenting)
decided that no further date would be fixed and that
the whole matter must be postponed until the next
Term, and it was so ordered. At the same time, the
Court refused to take up the pending case of *Georgia*
v. *Grant*, a new bill in equity filed by the State to enjoin the enforcement of military action.[1]

---

the Court, the bill is *ex post facto* and cannot apply." The *Chicago Republican*,
April 7, 1868, said that the case was not considered at the first consultation day,
Saturday, March 13, and that before the next one, the Court had learned of the
passage of the bill on March 12; see also *Indianapolis Journal*, April 7, 1868; *New
York Herald*, March 20, 1868; *Springfield Republican*, March 28, 1868; speech
of Reverdy Johnson, *40th Cong., 2d Sess.*, 2095. The *Chicago Republican*, March
24, 1868, said: "The Democrats are abusing the Supreme Court soundly for not
rendering decision, since the announcement is made, on authority of the Court,
that a decision will not be made for some time."

[1] *Indianapolis Journal*, March 28, 1868. In this case, on Feb. 8, 1868, David D.
Field moved for leave to file a new bill in equity; leave was granted March 16; see
also *New York Tribune*, March 21, 28, 1868.

The Reconstruction cases were thus disposed of, for another year. But the revolutionary methods which had been employed by Congress in accomplishing its purpose and the evident reluctance of the Court to face the issue dismayed and disheartened the conservative portion of the community. So strongly did Judge Grier feel over the postponement of the *McCardle Case* that, on conclusion of Black's argument on March 30, he filed in writing the following stout protest : [1]

This case was fully argued in the beginning of this month. It is a case which involves the liberty and rights, not only of the appellant, but of millions of our fellow citizens. The country and the parties had a right to expect that it would receive the immediate and solemn attention of the Court. By the postponement of this case, we shall subject ourselves, whether justly or unjustly, to the imputation that we have evaded the performance of a duty imposed on us by the Constitution, and waited for Legislative interposition to supersede our action, and relieve us from responsibility. I am not willing to be a partaker of the eulogy or opprobrium that may follow. I can only say,

Pudet hoc opprobrium nobis
Et potuisse dici et non potuisse repelli.

or, literally translated, I am ashamed that such opprobrium should be cast upon the Court, and that it cannot be refuted.

This action by Grier was made the subject of considerable comment, and extreme Republican papers termed it "an unseemly exhibition . . . a breach of judicial decorum, for which there is no excuse unless it was caused by aberration of mind or dotage, . . . an extra-judicial opinion of an extraordinary character tantamount to accusing his Associates on the Bench

---

[1] *Indianapolis Journal*, April 2, 3, 1868; *Chicago Republican*, April 3, 1868; *National Intelligencer*, March 31, April 6, 1868. Grier's statement is reported in slightly differing phraseology in the various papers.

of malversation in office." There was, nevertheless, a very general feeling throughout the country that the Court had evaded an issue. "It must be confessed," said the *Springfield Republican*, "that the course of the Supreme Court has not been creditable to that body as the embodiment of the highest judicial authority of the Nation. Justice Grier seems to have been especially sensitive to the unfavorable effect the action of the Court in postponing the decision would have on its reputation and influence, and when the case was called, read a brief document, strongly phrased, expressing his sense of the shame and dishonor which the Court had incurred. He had held no counsel with his Associates, and his action took both them and the public by surprise, and still causes much excited comment at Washington." Benjamin R. Curtis wrote that: "Congress, with the acquiescence of the country, has subdued the Supreme Court, as well as the President." And Welles in his diary took a despairing view of the situation :

March 20, 1868. The Judges of the Supreme Court have caved in, fallen through, failed in the *McCardle Case.* Only Grier and Field have held out like men, patriots, Judges of nerve and honest independence. These things look ominous and sadden me. I fear for my country when I see such abasement. Fear of the usurping Radicals in Congress has intimidated some of these Judges, or like reckless Democratic leaders, they are willing their party should triumph through Radical folly and wickedness. These are indeed evil times ! Seward has on more than one occasion declared that he controlled Judge Nelson. Whether he is, or has been, intriguing in the matter, or taken any part is a problem. The action of Congress, and particularly the Senate in taking from the Supreme Court certain powers to prevent a decision in the *McCardle Case* is shameful, and forebodes an unhappy future to the country. There is no exercise of reason, judgment, intelligence or patriotism by the Radical majority on any subject whereby their party is affected. Truth, justice, right, law and Constitution are broken down and trampled under foot by Senators. I say this in sorrow.

The *National Intelligencer* said that Grier's protest was rendered "with a manifestation of much emotion", and that it was an "everlasting memorial" to his honor. " Well does he anticipate the inevitable imputation of weak evasion of a duty, whose obligation is inexorable in proportion to the peril threatened by its performance."

While there was some justification for the view that the Court had not been firm in its stand, it must be admitted that, in view of the fact that the Chief Justice was presiding in the Impeachment Trial of the President, it was probably wiser on the part of the Court to postpone arguments on so important an issue until there should be a full Court; and the intimations that its action was influenced by the political situation were clearly unfair, in view of its previous courageous action in sustaining its jurisdiction over the case.[1] That the Court could not escape the issue presented to it by Congress had been shown, four days before its adjournment, when an original petition for habeas corpus was presented to it, in a case arising in Florida where two men were held by the military for the murder of a negro. This case would inevitably require a decision on the Reconstruction Laws, at the next Term.[2]

---

[1] Chief Justice Chase wrote his views in a letter in September, 1868, as follows: "I hold my old faith in universal suffrage, in Reconstruction upon that basis, in universal amnesty, and in inviolate public faith; but I do not believe in military government for American States, nor in military commissions for the trial of American citizens, nor in the subversion of the Executive and Judicial Departments of the General Government by Congress." *Green Bag* (1902), XIV.

[2] This case (not reported) of *Ex parte Martin and Gilly*, in which a writ was granted, returnable at the December, 1869, Term, seems not to have been pressed; for references to it, see *Chicago Republican*, March 28, 1868; *Indianapolis Journal*, March 28, April 1, 1868; *National Intelligencer*, March 31, 1868.

With the passage of the Act of March 27, 1868, Congress reached the limit of its attacks upon the Court. A reaction in favor and support of that tribunal at once arose. The acquittal of President Johnson, in May, 1868, broke the power of the Radicals. Both Congress and the country at large acquired a cooler and saner point of view. Many of the Southern States, reluctantly accepting Reconstruction as an ineluctable fact, ratified the Fourteenth Amendment and were readmitted to participate in the Government. And finally, in the spring of 1869, several decisions of the Court itself seemed to give assurance that there would be no judicial overthrow of Congressional plans.

Encouragement appeared to be first afforded when the Court dismissed from its docket the indictment of Jefferson Davis for treason. For four years, the question whether the Southern participants in the Civil War were guilty of treason had been involved in this case, and had never been decided authoritatively in any other case in the Federal Courts. Davis had been captured on May 10, 1865, and had been indicted in the District of Columbia, and later in the United States District Court in Virginia; but as it had been generally felt that a trial "in the hotbed of treason by a jury of sympathizing traitors would be a transparent farce",[1] he had been kept by the military authorities in Fortress Monroe. Finally, on October 12, 1866, Attorney-General Stanbery advised his transfer to the civil authorities; on refusal of compliance by the military, his transfer was ordered by the District Court on a

[1] *Philadelphia Inquirer*, May 12, 1866; see especially *ibid.*, April 10, May 17, June 8, 13, 1866, May 8, 11, 13, 15, 1867, for full account of the various proceedings; see also *Cleveland Herald*, May, 1867, *passim*. See *Notes* of Col. W. G. Moore, Private Secretary to President Johnson, in *Amer. Hist. Rev.* (1913), XIX, giving account of a Cabinet Meeting of May 7, 1867, at which the President ordered the War Department to turn Davis over to the civil authorities.

writ of habeas corpus, May 12, 1867, and he was released on bail. While the Radical Republicans were
confident that all "Rebels" were traitors, there had
been grave doubts expressed by many at the North
(including most of the Bar) whether a military officer of the Confederate Government could legally be
held to be guilty of treason. Many others, like Horace
Greeley, had believed it to be bad policy to press the
point, and had advocated the release of Davis.[1] Many,
however, had urged that the trial should be pressed in
order that the question of law might be finally decided.
"The trial of Mr. Davis, if it can be conducted in a
satisfactory manner, will have some important and
beneficial results. An honest jury cannot fail to find
the prisoner guilty, as far as the mere facts are concerned," said the *Nation* in 1867. "The real controversy will be before the Court, to determine whether
those facts constitute treason. No authoritative decision has yet been rendered upon that question. The
only convictions for treason against the United States,
so far as we are aware, took place in California and
Kentucky before the United States District Courts....
The Kentucky convict was a citizen of Kentucky and
could only have made his case worse by justifying under
the authority of Tennessee and a seceded and foreign
State. The California party was made up of nonde-
scripts from various Nations and States, all of them
residents of California and therefore clearly without
excuse for hostile acts. But no Court has yet had an
opportunity to determine whether the commander of

---

[1] To Greeley, Chief Justice Chase wrote, June 26, 1867, advising him to read
Webster's reply to Hayne, and saying: "You will find no hint that nullifiers, pursuing their nullification to civil war, ceased to be traitors, on becoming engaged in
such a war."

The *American Law Review* (Jan., 1867), I, 387, said that "the continued postponement of the trial of this State prisoner has been the subject of bitter
altercation."

a regular army, conducting war against the United States upon equal terms and in the name of a hostile government, can be convicted of treason." [1]

Owing to the unwillingness of Chief Justice Chase to hold Court in Virginia while the military authorities were in control, and to many other reasons, the trial did not occur until December 3, 1868. By that time, the war passion against Davis had died down; the interest in the law of treason had dissipated; and the adoption of the Fourteenth Amendment had given rise to another question in the case, namely, whether the provision for disqualification for office established by the third clause of that Amendment was intended to exclude any other form of punishment for the acts to which it referred. Chief Justice Chase and District Judge Underwood, sitting in the District Court, had differed in opinion on this latter new question of law, and the case had accordingly been certified to the Supreme Court, December 5, 1868. Finally, on February 19, 1869, the Government not wishing to press the case further, it was dismissed from the docket — a disposition of the affair which commended itself to the Bar and to the general public; "and so a ridiculous farce ends," said *Harper's Weekly*. [2]

Soon after the end of the *Davis Case*, the *McCardle Case* was reached for final argument, on March 19, 1869, on the question of the power of Congress to prohibit the Court from deciding a pending case; and on April 12, the Court rendered a unanimous decision that the statute had taken away its jurisdiction, and that therefore it could not proceed to pronounce judgment.

---

[1] *Nation*, May 10, 1867.

[2] The certificate of division was filed in the Supreme Court, Dec. 7, 1868; *Trial of Jefferson Davis*, by David K. Watson, *Yale Law Journal* (1915), XXIV; *Harper's Weekly*, Jan. 30, 1869; *Amer. Law Rev.* (Jan., 1869), III, 368; *Springfield Weekly Republican*, Nov. 28, Dec. 26, 1868, Jan. 2, 1869.

"Judicial duty," said the Chief Justice, "is not less fitly performed by declining ungranted jurisdiction than in exercising firmly that which the Constitution and the laws confer." While appellate jurisdiction of the Supreme Court, he held, was not derived from Acts of Congress but from the Constitution, yet it was conferred "with such exceptions and under such regulations as Congress shall make." Congress had chosen to make a specific and positive exception in this case; and the Court was "not at liberty to inquire into the motives of the Legislature." *Ex parte McCardle*, 7 Wall. 506. On the same day, the Court rendered an opinion in a most important case involving the status of the seceding States, — *Texas* v. *White*, 7 Wall. 700; and while it did not actually decide the question of the validity of the Reconstruction Laws, its general language gave much encouragement to their supporters. In this case, the State of Texas, through its Governor, brought an original suit in equity to enjoin the payment of certain State bonds owned by the State prior to the war and negotiated by the Confederate State Government. The first question presented to the Court was: "Is Texas a State of the Union, and as such, capable of bringing suit?" It was contended by the defendants that Texas, having seceded and not yet being represented by Senators and Representatives in Congress, was still out of the Union. This was the position which Thaddeus Stevens and other Radicals had taken in Congress. It was also contended that a Governor elected before the passage of the Reconstruction Acts was illegally elected and incapable of authorizing suit. The Court, by Chief Justice Chase, held that it was unnecessary to inquire into or pronounce judgment upon "the constitutionality of this legislation so far as it relates to military authority or to the paramount authority of Congress"; that the ordinance of secession by Texas was a nullity; that Texas had always remained a State of the Union within the purview of the Constitution, which, in the memorable words of Chase, "in all its provisions looks to an indestructible Union, composed of indestructible States. When, therefore, Texas became one of the United States, she entered into an indissoluble relation." While her obligations to the Union remained the same, her relations after secession changed, and "these new relations imposed new duties upon the United States. The first was that of suppressing the rebellion. The next was that of reëstablishing the broken relation of the State with the Nation." This duty Congress had the power and the duty to perform, under the provision of the Constitution guaranteeing to the States a republican form of Government. But as the President had appointed a provisional Government, which was in actual operation when Congress passed its Reconstruction Acts, and which had authorized this suit, the Court held that the suit was instituted by a competent authority and by a State of the Union. As to the right of the bondholders in the case, the Court held that it must be determined by the purposes for which the bonds were negotiated; that while Texas was legally always a State of the Union, it did not follow that all her actions and laws, while in fact a member of the Confederacy, were to be held valid; and that statutes which were "necessary to peace and good order among citizens" might be valid, but that those passed in furtherance or support of the rebellion, were to be regarded as absolutely void.[1]

---

[1] The case was argued by George W. Paschal and R. T. Merrick against James Hughes, Albert Pike, Robert W. Johnson, J. M. Carlisle, P. Phillips, S. S. Cox and J. W. Moore. See *The Case of Texas* v. *White*, by William W. Pierson, *Southwestern Hist. Quart.* (1915), XVIII, XIX.

This decision has constituted one of the landmarks in American history. It settled forever the question whether a State could legally secede, and it confirmed the permanence of the Union. Nevertheless, it has frequently been considered logically unsatisfactory in its reasoning; and the dissenting opinion of Judges Grier (concurred in by Swayne and Miller) seems more easily to be supported, when he said that the status of Texas was "to be decided as a political fact, not as a legal fiction. . . . If I regard the truth of history for the last eight years, I cannot discover the State of Texas as one of these United States. . . . I am not disposed to join in any essay to prove Texas to be a State of the Union when Congress have decided that she is not. . . . Politically, Texas is not a State in this Union. Whether rightfully out of it or not is a question not before the Court." The decision came, however, as a welcome solution to a greatly vexed and debated question; and Chase's opinion, though adverse to the extreme claims of Thaddeus Stevens and the Radicals, who deemed the seceding States entirely out of the Union and properly subject to any legislation Congress chose to enact, was equally adverse to the claim of the Democrats, who held that Congress had no power whatever to withhold from these States any of the rights which they had possessed before the war. The general views and plans of the more moderate Reconstruction statesmen were in complete consonance with the language of the opinion; and the growing fears lest the Court would interfere with their plans were thus allayed. An able opinion rendered by Attorney-General Hoar, following the decision of *Texas* v. *White* and sustaining the legality of military trials in Texas, gave further comfort to the Reconstructionists. "The Act of March 2, 1867, is, in my opinion," said Hoar, "a legislative declaration that in Texas the war which sprang from the rebellion is not to all intents and purposes ended;" and he held that other statutory legislation and judicial declarations recognizing the end of the war were "not inconsistent with the proposition that, for some purposes, the rights of war are not ended." [1]

In spite of these judicial decisions, and in spite of the action of Congress in abolishing the Court's appellate jurisdiction in habeas corpus proceedings instituted under the Act of 1867, it appeared in the fall of 1869 that there was still a possibility that the Court might be required to render a decision on the legality of the Reconstruction Laws. On October 15, 1869, the case of *Ex parte Yerger*, 8 Wall. 85, was brought up for argument by Philip Phillips and J. M. Carlisle against Attorney-General Ebenezer R. Hoar. This suit was a petition for habeas corpus originally made to a Federal Circuit Court in Mississippi by another editor, who had been imprisoned by the military, but who on denial of his writ had taken an appeal to the Supreme Court, under the provisions of the original Judiciary Act of 1789, and not under the repealed Act of 1867.

One week after the argument, the Court, through the Chief Justice, rendered a decision exhaustively reviewing the Court's powers under the various habeas corpus statutes, and upholding its jurisdiction of this appeal, under the old Act of 1789. By this unexpected ruling, the road was left open for a full argument of the whole question of the Reconstruction legislation, when the case should be reached for hearing on the merits. With such a situation confronting them, the Radicals in Congress determined upon their most radical move against the Judiciary. On December 9,

---

[1] See *Amer. Law Rev.* (Dec., 1869), IV, opinion of Hoar to the Secretary of War, in *Weaver's Case*, May 31, 1869.

1869, Senator Trumbull reported a bill which was entitled "to define the jurisdiction of the Supreme Court
in certain cases", but which was in reality a bill to destroy the constitutional function of the Court — a bill
which was aptly termed the "bright, consummate
flower of the military doctrine." [1]   It declared that no
civil government existed in Virginia, Mississippi and
Texas and that none should be recognized by the Executive or by the Judiciary until Congress should decide; it further declared that the Reconstruction Laws
were "political in their character, the propriety or validity of which no judicial tribunal was competent to
question", and it prohibited the Supreme Court "from
entertaining jurisdiction of any case growing out of
the execution of said Acts"; and it suspended all appeals growing out of such execution, either in habeas
corpus cases or otherwise.

While this bill was welcomed by the Radical Republicans, conservative men of both parties felt that the
proposed action was far too extreme.   One of the leading Western Republican papers, expressing its opposition and regret at this renewal of attack on the Court,
stated that Congress had "no power to arbitrarily and
conclusively decide what issues the National Judiciary
cannot take into consideration", and that the Court
must possess the power to determine what questions
are political merely, and what questions involve per-

---

[1] *New York World*, Dec. 10, 11, 1869. Section 1 of this bill provided that: "Under
the Constitution, the judicial power of the United States does not embrace political power, or give to the judicial tribunals any authority to question the decisions
of the political departments of the Government on political questions; and it is
hereby declared that all Courts of the United States in the administration of justice shall be bound by the decisions of the political departments of the Government
on political questions." Section 2 provided that: "It rests with Congress to decide
what Government is the established one in a State, and that it is hereby, in accordance with former legislation, declared that no civil State Government exists
in Virginia, Mississippi, or Texas." *41st Cong., 2d Sess.*, 167 *et seq.*, speech of
Trumbull, Dec. 16, 1869.

sonal rights and liberties. The power of the Courts to decide the question of constitutionality "arises out of the circumstances of the necessity to decide which of two laws shall prevail." And it concluded with this striking praise of the Court: "If this country possesses an able, experienced, conscientious and universally satisfactory Bench, it is to be found in our Supreme Court. It makes its decisions under the eyes of the whole legal fraternity. If a conspicuous error should be committed, it could not escape detection; and the exposure, through the press of the country, would be entirely equal to the error committed. As yet, no one has presumed to question the purity of the motives which have obtained hitherto in the adjudication of mooted questions." [1] The *New York World* said: "If Congress can force the judicial power to yield to it, the Constitution is annulled; if it is in the power of Congress to say that any law of the United States can be made, into whose constitutional validity, when a case arising under it has taken a judicial form, the judicial power shall not inquire, then Congress is above the Constitution, and all its restraints, prohibitions and injunctions are so much waste paper. . . . The design is to emancipate Congress from all constitutional restraints which arise under any power that Congress chooses to assert is political in character." And the *Nation* asked: "If a majority of Congress is sure not to do wrong, why have any Constitution at all? Why restrain this body of sages by any restrictions whatever? Why not let them make their own Constitution, every session? Indeed, why administer any oath of office?" And it said further that there existed no

[1] *Chicago Republican*, Dec. 11, 1869; *ibid.*, Dec. 15, said that: "Trumbull's bill will hardly become law in its present form. It does not meet with much favor, but it may increase in popularity." *New York World*, Jan. 9, 1870.

need of such a measure to check any supposed tendency of the Court to usurp Congressional power; that the dangers of this, "feared by our democratic fathers, have proved not to have a particle of foundation. Indeed the Judiciary is the branch of the Government and the only one which has been steadily declining in influence and authority during the last fifty years. Nearly every tendency of the day has told against the increase of its power, while there is hardly one which has not helped to increase the power of the Executive and the Legislature."

But there were Senators who desired to go even further than Trumbull, and on December 13, Senator Charles D. Drake of Missouri delivered a violent speech advocating a bill to provide that no Court created by Congress should have any power to adjudge invalid any Act of Congress, and to prohibit the Supreme Court in its appellate jurisdiction from affirming any such judgment of invalidity by an inferior Court — "a bill to abolish the Constitution," said the *New York World*.[1] "It is the distinguishing function of a Judicature to declare the law, no Court, high or low, being able to decide any case without deciding at the same time what is the law applicable to that case. This results from the very essence of the judicial function, nay, it is inseparable from the nature of things. If the laws appertaining to the question in litigation are contradictory, it is obvious that the Court must decide which law is valid and which null, before it can reach a rule for rendering justice to the parties." The *Nation* opposed Drake's bill, on the ground that "the action of Congress of late years has not been such as

---

[1] *Nation*, Dec. 2, 16, 23, 1869; *New York Herald*, Dec. 15, 1869; *Independent*, Dec. 16, 1869; *Chicago Republican*, Dec. 8, 1869. The *New York Times*, Dec. 14, 1869, in an account of the debate, stated that Drake's speech was not favorably received in the Senate. *41st Cong., 2d Sess.*, 2, 87 *et seq.*

to entitle it to this supreme power." The *New York Herald*, speaking of the "riotous spirit which prevails in law-making bodies where one side has an overwhelming majority", said very sanely: "The framers of the Constitution seem to have supposed that the best Congress we could ever get would still be composed of human creatures, and that, in virtue of its humanity, Congress might be liable to err. They supposed also that the representatives of the people would be drawn from all the fields of national activity, that they would be merchants, miners, farmers, ship carpenters, shoemakers, schoolteachers, bankers, drovers, etc., and that Congress might, therefore, be an assembly not learned in the law. Whilst, therefore, the crude decrees of such a body might oppress any man in his rights, it was determined that the people should always have an appeal to a given number of men who have made the law the study of a lifetime." Even the radical *Independent* was inclined to believe that there was no immediate necessity for either Trumbull's or Drake's bill, and that the Court would "hardly make a contest with Congress. Its action last winter proved that it does not choose to measure its strength with the National Legislature. It looked, one month ago, as if Mr. Chase and his Associates were bent on precipitating a decision against the Reconstruction Acts, and as if Yerger would be set free; but the Court will pause in its course, while Congress acts on the measure, for it very well knows where victory lies in such a controversy. . . . If Congress takes from it jurisdiction in political questions and it refuses to obey, Congress can impeach and remove the Court. But it will not come to that. The good sense of a majority of the Justices will avert any such conflict." The *Chicago Republican* made the following eloquent defense of the Court: "A more dangerous, not to say absurd, attempt to destroy the Courts and make Congress supreme could not be conceived. . . . What is this but declaring Congress as the supreme authority of the Nation, placing the country under an oligarchy, none the less despotic because the people themselves elected its members? The Courts, sitting in calm isolation, removed from partisan prejudices and often exciting passions of the hour, were especially instituted as checks and balances against attempted usurpation by either the Executive or the Legislative departments, to prevent wrong or harm from hasty and inconsiderate legislation, or from misconception or wrongful appropriation of power by the Executive. . . . The truth is, Mr. Drake's proposition is in outrageous repugnance to the whole genius of republican government; and he will find, we believe, but few sympathizers with his revolutionary scheme, either in Congress or among the people. We cannot give up our Courts at present, even though experience has shown that they are not always infallible. They are safer to trust to, in matters of Constitution and law, than a tribunal selected as Congress is."

Meanwhile, before Congress took any action on the bills, a situation had arisen in the Court itself (as will be described in the next chapter) which made action seem less necessary. Moreover, by agreement between Yerger's counsel and the Attorney-General, stipulations were entered into by which Yerger was to be protected from the military, and his case became, therefore, a moot one which required no argument at the present time.[1] Thus, this hotly contested legal ques-

---

[1] See *New York World*, Dec. 2, 1869, Jan. 9, 1870. Later, Congress took cognizance of the case, and the House requested information as to the delay in the execution of Yerger's sentence. See *Washington Chronicle*, Feb. 5, 1870. The final disposition of this case was reported in the *New York Times*, March 12, 1870.

tion of the validity of the Reconstruction Laws disappeared from the Court's history, without any express decision.[1]

"In the Supreme Court today (March 11) Mr. Phillips stated that the counsel for Yerger, who was convicted by a military commission of the killing of Col. Crane and sentenced, having received authentic information that the military authorities had turned over the prisoner to the civil authorities of the State of Mississippi, the object of the petition was fulfilled, and therefore he moved that it be dismissed." In February, 1870, another case arose in the Court which might have called for a decision on the Reconstruction Acts, when George R. Kennedy, tried by military commission in Texas on charge of murder, applied to the Court for a writ of habeas corpus. See *Boston Daily Advertiser*, Feb. 19, 1870.

[1] It was not until as late as 1875 that the Court (whose membership by that date had been considerably changed) gave an intimation in *Raymond* v. *Thomas*, 91 U. S. 712, that it might possibly hold the Reconstruction Acts to be lawful, but the case was actually decided on a subordinate point.

The Committee Bill referred to on p. 466, *supra*, was: "That no cause pending before the Supreme Court of the United States which involves the action or effect of any law of the United States shall be decided adversely to the validity of such law, without the concurrence of two thirds of all the members of said Court in the decision upon the several points in which said law or any part thereof may be deemed invalid." The Bill proposed by Thomas Williams of Pennsylvania was: "That in all cases of writs of error from and appeals to the Supreme Court of the United States where is drawn in question the validity of a statute of or an authority exercised by the United States or the construction of any clause of the Constitution of the United States, or the validity of a statute of, or an authority exercised under, any State on the ground of repugnance to the Constitution or laws of the United States, the hearing shall be had only before a full bench of the Judges of said Court and no judgment shall be rendered or decision made against the validity of any statute or any authority exercised by the United States except with the concurrence of all the Judges of said Court." This Williams Bill was apparently reported by the Judiciary Committee in 1867; for so Benjamin N. Boyer of Pennsylvania stated, *39th Cong., 2d Sess.*, p. 685.

As to investigation of Senator Trumbull's part as counsel in the *McCardle Case*, see debate in the Senate, March 15, 1872, *42d Cong., 2d Sess.* A bill to restore appeals in habeas corpus cases passed the House Jan. 15, 1874, *43d Cong., 1st Sess.*, and see debate, Jan. 15, 28, 1874, as to the fraudulent method of the passage of the Repeal Act of 1868.

CHAPTER THIRTY-ONE

THE LEGAL TENDER CASES

1869–1871

THE disposition of the *Yerger Case*, in December, 1869, having removed all present danger of any judicial decision on Reconstruction, another question then came to the front, — the validity of the war legislation making the paper currency (the Treasury notes) legal tender. Though the first of these Legal Tender Acts had been passed as early as February 25, 1862, by a singular chance, no decision as to its validity had yet been reached in 1869. The constitutional issue had been involved in a case which came up on writ of error to the New York State Court, in 1863, *Roosevelt* v. *Meyer*, 1 Wall. 512, but the Court had decided in that year that it had no jurisdiction under the Judiciary Act.[1] In 1865, however, the question was presented in a case in which the Court had undoubted jurisdiction on writ of error to the Kentucky Court of Appeals, *Hepburn* v. *Griswold*, 8 Wall. 603, and it was first argued at the December Term of 1867. On the suggestion of Attorney-General Stanbery as to the great public importance of the question, a reargument was ordered for the next Term, with leave to the Government to be represented; and accordingly on December 10, 1868, it was reargued by Benjamin R. Curtis and Attorney-General William M. Evarts, against Clarkson N. Pot-

---

[1] Nine years later, in 1872, the Court held that this decision had been erroneous, and accordingly overruled it. *Trebilcock* v. *Wilson*, 12 Wall. 687.

ter.[1] The probable action of the Court had been the
subject of long and excited debate in the community.
On the one side, were the National and the State banks,
the mortgagees and creditors who demanded payment
in gold; lined up with these interests were those men
who, on principle, denied the right of the Federal Government to make paper currency legal tender, and opposed legalized cheating through the enforced payments of debts in depreciated currency. On the other
side, were the railroads, the municipal corporations, the
mortgagors of land and other debtors who now sought
to pay, with a depreciated legal tender currency, debts
contracted on a gold basis before the war; and with
these interests, there were associated all those men who
felt strongly that the Government ought not to be deprived of a power which they considered so necessary
to its existence in time of war. But while, as a war
measure, issue of legal tender may have been necessary,
there is no doubt that most thoughtful men believed
that its evils outweighed its benefits, and agreed with
the *Nation*, when it said that "the prevailing laxity in
commercial morals, the rise of notorious cheats into
position of fame and wealth, and the prostration at
their feet of large masses of private property, is largely
due, not simply to the spirit of speculation bred by the
issue of irredeemable paper, but to the sanction given
by the law to the wholesale cheating by fraudulent
debtors which was the direct result of the Legal Tender
Act."

Practically every State Court which had considered
the question had upheld the constitutionality of the
law; there was little expectation by the public or by

[1] The *Springfield Republican*, Feb. 15, 1868, stated that on Feb. 14, the Attorney-
General had read to the Court a letter from Secretary of the Treasury McCulloch
asking him to appear, and had stated that he had had no time to prepare and
wished a postponement.

the Bar that the Court would do otherwise.[1] Soon
after the argument, however, the rumor spread that
its decision would be adverse; and thereupon, strong
appeals were made in the press that, in view of the
ruinous consequences of such a ruling, the Court
should postpone decision.[2] An interesting editorial in
the *Chicago Republican* strongly indorsed this rather
preposterous suggestion, saying: "The gloomy prospect
which presents itself to anyone contemplating the results
of an adverse decision ought to convince Judges, who at
the same time are statesmen, that a decision should not
be given, if adverse. . . . It is plainly the general
wish of the country that this tardy and ruinous wisdom
of the Supreme Court should not now work universal
ruin, if the decision is to be adverse to the constitutionality of the Act. Let the petty cases be dismissed
and no decision be given. Harmless inaction is better
than a dangerous act."[3]

While unable to arrive at a decision in this case during the December, 1868, Term, the Court did decide
several cases in which it passed upon subordinate aspects of this question. In *Lane County* v. *Oregon*, 7
Wall. 71, it considered whether Congress had the power
to make the paper war currency legal tender in payment
of taxes to a State, and while intimating that Congress
could not so interfere with the State taxing power, it
held that the Legal Tender Acts were not to be con-

[1] *Nation*, Feb. 10, 25, 1869: "The Judges of most of the State Courts to whom
it has been submitted, being in closer dependence on popular opinion than they
have ever been before, have not unnaturally shrunk from what seemed the tremendous responsibility of gainsaying what so many good men had been saying,
and the best part of the community believing for so long, on such an exceedingly
delicate subject as the value and power of the currency actually in use."

[2] *Chicago Republican*, Dec. 11, 14, 21, 1868.

[3] This editorial also stated that a written opinion was obtained, though with
great difficulty, from members of the Court in favor of the validity of the Legal
Tender Act, at the time of its passage; and that it is now stated that "its authors
will be glad to rewrite it, by a decision declaring the Act void."

strued as so providing.   In *Bronson* v. *Rodes* and *Butler* v. *Horwitz*, 7 Wall. 229, 258, the Legal Tender Acts were held not to apply to obligations calling specifically for payment in gold and silver coin.

One reason for the delay in the decision of the *Legal Tender Cases* had undoubtedly been the fact that, at this time, the Court had been reduced in number to eight Judges by the operation of the Act of 1866 (passed to deprive President Johnson of the opportunity of filling expected vacancies), and hence there was danger of an even division of the Court on the question.   This situation was now changed by the accession of Grant to the Presidency, and the consequent enactment of a statute (the Act of April 10, 1869), increasing the number of the Court to nine, and authorizing the President to nominate an additional Judge at the next session of the Senate.   At the same time, Congress had at last provided a long-desired and long-contested judicial reform, by establishing a new Circuit Court system with nine new Circuit Judges, but without entirely relieving the Supreme Court Judges of Circuit duty.[1]   To fill these new positions, President Grant made nine appointments, based largely on the recommendation of his Attorney-General, Ebenezer Rockwood Hoar of Massachusetts;[2] and on December 14, 1869, he appointed Hoar to the vacancy on the Supreme Bench.   "It is a gratifying proof of the increased respect in which the Supreme Court is held that we do not hear of any attempt to foist upon it, under the

[1] As late as 1866, the *American Law Review*, I, 307, had rejoiced over the failure of the passage of Circuit Court bills introduced in Congress, April 2, 1866, March 5, 1867 (see *39th Cong., 1st Sess.; 40th Cong., 1st Sess., Senate Special Sess.*) and had said: "We trust that so mischievous a measure will never receive the assent of Congress.   Mr. Webster more than once defeated similar propositions. . . .   It has been well designated as a bill to prevent the Justices of the Supreme Court from ever learning any law."

[2] See *New York Times*, Dec. 9, 1869, for detailed criticism of the Circuit Court appointments.

provisions of this Act, a partisan Judge," said the
Nation. "There seems to be a general agreement of
opinion that no such appointment should be made.
The reiterated assertions that the Attorney-General is
to have the place show the general feeling about it.
The present Chief Justice has been 'in politics' quite
enough. . . . If Judge Hoar is appointed, the appointment will be an admirable one." And it further pointed
out that, in the year of the Reconstruction excitement, in 1868, the Court had "touched the lowest point
in its career; and now that the spirit of conservation
has begun to reign again, the important problem of the
hour is to bring back harmony and justice into the affairs
of the country", that the Court was the agency best
calculated to assist in the work, that its hands must be
strengthened, and that apparently popular respect for
the judicial function had begun again to appear. "As
Congress and the President fell, so the Court arose in
regard and esteem. The balance is at length in a fair
way of being restored, and one more illustration furnished of the inherent excellence of the system of checks
and balances which lies at the root of American politics.
Thus one day may the future historian of America, for
the instruction of generations to come, carve the lessons
of the recent history of the Judiciary." Hoar's nomination was commended on all sides by the public and
the press. "His distinguished abilities are conceded
and his elevation to the Supreme Bench is received with
profound satisfaction by all," said the *New York Times*.
"One of the best that could have been made," said
Harper's Weekly, and it mentioned his "vigorous independence, soundness of judgment, masculine good
sense and legal learning." [1] That he was supremely

[1] *Nation*, Dec. 2, 1869, Jan. 6, 1870; *New York Times*, Dec. 16, 1869; *Harper's
Weekly*, Jan. 1, 1870; *Amer. Law Rev.*, IV, 380. See also *Washington Chronicle*,

fitted for the position by his legal qualifications, all admitted. He was fifty-three years of age and at the height of his vigor; he had been Judge of the Massachusetts Supreme Court, and an able Attorney-General of the United States; he was also in thorough sympathy with Grant's policies. But in the Senate, the nomination met with hearty opposition from many causes. Some Senators believed that a lawyer from the South, particularly Thomas J. Durant of Louisiana, should have been appointed; others were disgruntled over the nominees recommended by Hoar for Circuit Judges; to many Senators, Hoar's brusque manners had given great offense; others resented his opposition to the Johnson impeachment; others disliked his support of Civil Service Reform.[1] He was supported by

Dec. 15, 1869, saying it "will generally be accepted as an appropriate selection, comparatively young, possessing the required learning and ability."

[1] *Harper's Weekly*, Jan. 1, 1870, said that the real ground of objection must be his "hearty contempt of the system that makes the whole civil service party plunder." On Jan. 8, it said that the Senate's virtual rejection of Hoar was reported by the *New York Times* to be due to a "sense of the affronts Senators and Representatives have received at his hands. . . . He has no one to blame for his discomfiture but himself." "This means," said the *Weekly*, "that Mr. Hoar has refused to be a mere party tool." The *Independent*, Feb. 10, 1870, said: "Nobody can deny that the Attorney-General is an able lawyer and a genuine radical. The Senate disliked him personally and looked with disfavor upon the selection of a Northern man for a Southern Circuit." The *New York Herald*, Dec. 21, 1869, stated that the Senate contrasted the "polished politeness of Evarts, and dignified but courteous bearing of Stanbery with the supercilious contempt of Hoar to his superiors." George F. Hoar in his *Autobiography of Seventy Years* (1903), said: "Judge Hoar strenuously insisted that the Judges of the newly created Circuit Courts of the United States should be made up of the best lawyers, without Senatorial dictation. President Grant acted in accordance with his advice. The constitution of the Circuit Court gave great satisfaction to the public. But leading and influential Senators, whose advice had been rejected and who were compelled, by the high character of the persons nominated, to submit and did not venture upon a controversy with the President, were intensely angry with the Attorney-General. The result was that when he was nominated by the President for the office of Associate Justice of the Supreme Court of the United States, he was rejected by the Senate. A few Senators avowed, as a pretext for their action, that there was no Judge on the Bench from the South, and that the new appointee ought to reside in the Southern Circuit. But these gentlemen all voted for the confirmation of Mr. Justice Bradley, a most admirable appointment, to whom the same objection applied." See also especially *Springfield Weekly Republican*, Dec. 26, 1869, Jan. 1, 1870, giving the causes of Hoar's rejection.

Senator Trumbull but opposed by Conkling, Edmunds, Carpenter, by the carpet-bag Senators from the South and by the Democrats. "In the whole proceedings," said the *Nation*, "the Democrats alone can be justified or excused. To them, Judge Hoar is the principal representative of a system they believed to be unconstitutional and outrageous."

While this fight was pending in the Senate, the President was given an opportunity to make another appointment. Judge Grier, who, in his seventy-sixth year and after twenty-three years' service, had become mentally and physically enfeebled, took advantage of the recent statute increasing the Judges' salaries and authorizing retirement on half pay, and sent in his resignation on December 15, 1869, to take effect, February 1, 1870. A petition was at once signed by a large majority of the Senate and of the House and presented to the President, asking that the vacancy be filled by the appointment of the late Secretary of War, Edwin M. Stanton of Pennsylvania.[1] Grant, while reluctant to make this nomination and while desiring to appoint Judge William Strong of Pennsylvania, saw a chance of conciliating the Senate with regard to Hoar; and accordingly, on Sunday, December 19, 1869 (Stanton's fifty-fourth birthday), he called on him, offered him the position and sent in his name, the next day, to the Senate, where he was promptly confirmed by a vote of forty-six to eleven. The appointment was received by the country with great differences of opinion. Though Stanton had been an able lawyer, his tempera-

[1] Judge Grier had suggested to Grant that Joseph P. Bradley of New Jersey be appointed his successor. *Independent*, Dec. 23, 1869. The *Springfield Republican* as early as Nov. 27, 1869, had urged Stanton's appointment, and it said, Dec. 26, that "as Gen. Grant never got on well with Stanton when he was in the War Department, and had some prejudice to conquer in order to bring him up to this appointment, it must have been quite a gratifying interview to the old war horse of the Army Department."

ment was such as to make him a doubtful acquisition to the Bench; for he was arbitrary, overbearing, masterful and utterly lacking in judicial poise. Nevertheless, the Republicans hailed his choice with delight, and termed it "the equivalent of a Constitutional Amendment." The *Washington Chronicle* "thrilled with joy" and said that no statesman had a firmer hold on the affections of the people. The *Chicago Republican* said it would "give general satisfaction" and that he "had few peers at the Bar." The *Springfield Republican* said that "justice is his strong point." The *New York Times* spoke of the "general congratulations" and of his "sturdy integrity, intellectual acumen and force, unswerving patriotism, high legal reputation, tireless energy." "It is a recognition of his illustrious service to his country, in the performance of which he was equalled for energy, courage and genius by no other statesman or hero of the war. . . . The peer of Bismarck in executive force, we believe that . . . he will attain a judicial eminence second to none ever achieved in the same judicial station. God bless Edwin M. Stanton!" said the *Independent*.

The Democratic press raged at the appointment. The *New York World* said that: "His enemies (and no one ever had a greater number) think him a passionate, violent and headstrong man, malignant, despotic and utterly unscrupulous. . . . His apologists have never denied that he has an impetuous temper and overbearing manners. . . . There has never been any difference of opinion between his foes and his partisans, respecting the general type and structure of his character, which is as far removed as possible from dispassionate calmness, judicial impartiality and reverence for strict law. No one could be more out of place than such a hasty, violent, imperious zealot on the bench of the Supreme Court." The *New York Herald* stated, more fairly, that while he was fully qualified as a lawyer for the position of Judge, and while he had been honest, earnest, active, firm, resolute, decisive and efficient in the War Office, "the man of all men for the part he had to play, . . . it may be said that he was rough, imperious, despotic, cruel and offensive in many things."

Of the independent papers, the *Nation* was inclined to be hopeful. "There are many signs," it said, "that the Supreme Court is recovering from the temporary loss of influence and dignity inflicted on it by the Dred Scott decision and the events of the war. The general excellence of the President's appointments to the new Circuit Judgeships, capped by the bestowal of the vacant seats in the Supreme Court itself on Judge Hoar and Mr. Stanton, and the increase of salaries which is now pending in Congress, are all signs of a healthy reaction in the public mind as to the inestimable value of an upright, independent and honored Judiciary." Whatever Stanton's fitness may or may not have been, his sudden death from heart trouble, on December 24, four days after his nomination, put an end to the discussion. "In him, the bench of the Supreme Court loses a Judge of large experience and learning, of perfect integrity and of unflinching courage in the discharge of duty," said the *American Law Review*. "And at this time, when there is so manifest a disposition in many of our public men to undervalue the duties and to encroach upon the province of the Judiciary, and to throw aside men, confessedly fitted by character, learning, and experience to adorn the Bench, for trivial and unworthy causes, we deem that the country has suffered an irreparable loss." [1]

---

[1] *Nation*, Dec. 23, 1869; *Amer. Law Rev.* (1870), IV, 394; see *Chicago Republican*, Dec. 22, 25, 1869; *Independent*, Dec. 23. 30. 1869; *New York Times*, Dec. 21, 25,

As the Senate had not confirmed Hoar, and as, after January 8, 1870, it was certain that it would not do so, the President had still two appointments to make.[1] For the Grier vacancy, Benjamin H. Brewster of Pennsylvania, and Judge George P. Fisher of Delaware were urged; and in place of Hoar, Thomas J. Durant of Louisiana and Senator Charles D. Drake of Missouri. "What the country wants is purity, honesty, ability and fearless radicalism," said the *Independent*. "The country distrusts lawyers, when it comes to questions of loyalty and human rights. What we want now is two or three sincere and obstinate radicals on the Bench . . . with a sincere, profound belief in the equality of human rights." [2] Very early in January, the President had informed visitors that he had decided to appoint Judge Strong to the Grier vacancy; [3] but the

27, 1869, stating that: "The commission of Mr. Stanton as Associate Justice had not been signed at the time of his death, but in the course of the day the President appended the signature and sent the paper to the widow as a mark of respect." *Washington Chronicle*, Dec. 25, 1869; *New York Herald*, Dec. 25, 1869; *New York World*, Dec. 22, 1869. On Dec. 24, the *World* published an editorial containing invective against Stanton of the most extreme nature; and after his death, it said, Dec. 25: "When Mr. Stanton's character is viewed in its true light, he will be regarded as the most faithful personal embodiment of the passionate and vindictive spirit of the period in which he acted;" see *Springfield Weekly Republican* stating, Jan. 1, 1870, that the *World's* rancor against Stanton was due to the latter's refusal to give a pass, in 1864, to a *World* correspondent, to whom he said: "No favor can be given here to a treasonable newspaper."

[1] See *New York Times*, Jan. 8, 10, 1870; *Ebenezer Rockwood Hoar* (1911), by Moorfield Storey and Edward W. Emerson. James Russell Lowell wrote to Hoar: "Don't let your name be withdrawn. Let the responsibility lie with the knaves who hate you for your impregnability and haven't the courage to say so." Hoar's nomination was finally defeated by the Senate, Feb. 3, 1870, by a vote of 24 to 33.

[2] The *Nation* said, Feb. 16, 1870: "We are informed that it was in contemplation to urge Mr. Durant of New Orleans for the Judgeship which Mr. Hoar did not get. Mr. Durant is, and was before the war, a leading member of the Louisiana Bar, was a staunch Union man during the war and a man of the highest character, both professional and personal. His appointment would supply what is greatly needed — a Civilian on the Supreme Bench. The want of any Judge versed in Civil Law is often severely felt in appeals from Louisiana, Texas and California."

[3] *Independent*, Jan. 6, Feb. 10, 1870; *New York Times*, Jan. 10, 1870; *New York Herald*, Jan. 20, 1870, *Nation*, Jan. 6, 1870. The *Springfield Weekly Republican*, Jan. 15, 1870, stated that Strong had been definitely selected and that he had long been "a prominent and honored citizen . . . and will be a real addition to the working ability and legal character of the Court."

hope was generally expressed that he would not repeat what the *Nation* termed "an act of very doubtful propriety" and "a dangerous precedent", when the President had nominated Stanton to the Supreme Bench "long before any vacancy existed, the immediate result of which was the curious spectacle of a Judge dead and buried in state while his predecessor sits on the Bench and goes to the funeral."

During all this time, when the question of filling the vacancies was pending, the Court had been withholding making public a decision at which it had arrived; for on November 27, 1869, four Judges had agreed in holding the Legal Tender Act unconstitutional as applied to contracts made before its passage, and Judge Grier, who had at first declared himself in favor of the Act, had finally changed his view and agreed with the majority. As three Judges dissented, the rendering of the opinion was delayed until the varying views could be definitely reconciled. In the meanwhile, however, the Court, on December 13, 1869, decided the important case of *Veazie Bank* v. *Fenno*, 8 Wall. 533, argued for the State banks by Reverdy Johnson and Caleb Cushing and by Attorney-General Hoar for the Government. In this case, the power of Congress to restrain by taxation the circulation of State bank notes as currency was upheld, as an appropriate means under the Constitution of providing a National currency for the country. Chief Justice Chase held the tax was not a direct tax; and stated that without this power of taxation, the Government's "attempts to secure a sound and uniform currency for the country must be futile." That the tax was so excessive as to indicate a purpose on the part of Congress to destroy the franchise of the State bank, he held was a matter which the Court could not consider. "The power to tax may be exercised oppressively upon persons, but the responsibility of the Legislature is not to the Courts, but to the people, by whom its members are elected." [1] From the broad construction given to the "necessary and proper" clause of the Constitution by the Chief Justice in this case, the country was led to believe that he would render a similar favorable decision in the *Legal Tender Case* then pending.[2] No definite knowledge, however, as to the actual decision at which the Court had arrived in the previous November leaked out; and on January 4, 1870, the *New York Times* stated that: "From all that can be learned of the matter, it is reasonably certain that no decision will be reached during the present Term. No consideration has yet been had in the case by the Court, and inasmuch as the Court will be reorganized by the addition of two new members, it is altogether probable that the cases will be ordered to be reargued before a decision is made." On January 21, the *New York World* stated that in the three important litigations arising out of the war, the *Legal Tender Case*, the *Cotton Tax Case* [3] and the *State Test Oath Case*, the

---

[1] James M. Beck in *Nullification by Indirection, Harv. Law Rev.* (1911), XXIII, said that *Veazie* v. *Fenno* first announced the doctrine "that the Judiciary is without power to prevent the nullification of the rights of the States by the exercise of Federal powers for unconstitutional purposes." See also *McCray* v. *United States* (1904), 195 U. S. 27; *The Extension of Federal Control through the Regulation of the Mails*, by Lindsay Rogers, *Harv. Law Rev.* (1913), XXVII; *Power of Regulation Vested in Congress*, by Max Pam, *ibid.* (1910), XXIV.

[2] The *Cincinnati Daily Chronicle*, Dec. 15, 1869, stated that the decision "must settle the validity of the Legal Tender Law." The *New York World*, Dec. 16, 1869, said as to this decision that "there was a manifest indecorum in Judge Chase's taking part, as he was the real author of the scheme for taxing State banks out of existence"; and that his opinion "was an elaborate defense of his own policy when he was Secretary of the Treasury. He is the father of the present system of National Banks. He was the instigator of the tax whose manifest design and real effect was to cripple and crush the rival State institutions", and that his sense of propriety should have led him not to sit.

[3] This case, *Farrington* v. *Saunders*, involving the question whether the Cotton Tax was a "direct tax" had been argued, Dec. 8, 9, 1869, by Philip Phillips, Albert Pike, R. W. Johnson, W. L. Sharkey, James Hughes, John A. Campbell, Benjamin R. Curtis and Robertson Topp against Attorney-General E. R. Hoar. See *New York Herald*, Dec. 9, 1869. It was not decided until 1871, when by an evenly divided

opinions of the Court would probably be adverse. "Great anxiety," it said, "is felt in reference to these decisions; and the expectation that the decision adverse to these Acts would irritate the Radicals in Congress has made some go so far as to impute timidity, as one of the reasons that there is not a full Court. The idea is thus obtaining currency that the Court will not have the nerve to perform their duty in these cases, and that these important cases will be suffered to sleep as they have done for so many months." The want of justification for this charge of lack of nerve on the part of the Court was seen, when within two weeks, on February 1, 1870, the Court rendered a decision in the *Test Oath Case* upholding by a four to four division the validity of the Missouri statute.[1] On Saturday, January 29, 1870, the Court had met in conference and adopted the form of its final opinion in the *Legal Tender Case*; but that the speculative surmises of the press as to its action in this latter case were far from accurate may be seen from the *New York Tribune's* statement of February 1, that a consultation had been held and that "there is ground for believing that the decision will not go into the question of the constitutionality of the law,

Court, the decision of the lower Court upholding the validity of the tax was affirmed; it is not reported in *Wallace Reports*. See *67th Cong., 2d Sess.*, March 13, 1922.

[1] This case, *Blair* v. *Thompson & Ridgely* (not reported in *Wallace Reports*), had been begun in 1866 to test the constitutionality of a Missouri statute depriving all persons of a right to vote who did not take an oath that they had not participated in hostilities against the Nation or the States. See *New York World*, Jan. 9, 21, Feb. 2, 1870. The *Independent* said, Feb. 10, 1870: "Mr. Chase gave his vote in favor of the constitutionality of the oath and saved it from overthrow. This shows two things, first that he is not a modern Democrat; and second that he is not seeking a nomination to the Presidency from the Democratic party." See also *New York Times*, Feb. 1, 1870; *New York Tribune*, Feb. 1, 1870, for a full report of the case. It was argued by Montgomery Blair against Senator Drake. The Judges divided — Nelson, Grier, Clifford and Field against the statute, Chase, Swayne, Davis and Miller for it; see *Boston Daily Advertiser*, Feb. 1, 1870. On the same day, the Court by another four to four decision (not reported) upheld the validity of the Act of Congress forbidding suits against United States officers who took or destroyed property in the South as a war measure. See especially *Springfield Republican*, Feb. 2, 4, 1870; *Boston Daily Advertiser*, Feb. 2, 1870.

but will decide that all contracts made previous to the passage of the act contemplated payment in gold." [1] The Court had intended that its opinion should be delivered on Monday, January 31, when Judge Grier would still be a member of the Court and would be one of the five Judges constituting the majority; but out of deference to the minority, who wished for further time to prepare their dissenting opinions, the matter was postponed for a week.[2] On February 7, Chief Justice Chase announced the opinion of the Court, which was concurred in by Judges Nelson, Clifford and Field, with Judges Miller, Swayne and Davis dissenting, — *Hepburn* v. *Griswold*, 8 Wall. 603.

On the underlying principles of law, both the majority and the minority agreed in accepting Marshall's statement of the implied powers of Congress as set forth in *McCulloch* v. *Maryland*. The Chief Justice, however, held that the attempt to impart the quality of legal tender to the Government paper currency was not "an appropriate and plainly adapted means for carrying on war"; and that the argument by which the legality of the statute was defended carried the doctrine of implied powers too far, and "asserts that whatever in any degree promotes an end within the scope of a general power, whether, in the correct sense of the word, appropriate or not, may be done in the exercise of an implied power. . . . Undoubtedly, among means appropriate, plainly adapted, really calculated, the Legislature has unrestricted choice." But it was for the Court to determine whether the means adopted came within that category. He held, moreover, that "a law not made in pursuance of an express power,

[1] *New York Tribune*, Feb. 1, 4, 1870; see also *Boston Journal*, Feb. 2, 1870, which said that the opinion "will carefully avoid the question of the constitutionality of the Act itself;" *Independent*, Dec. 23, 1869.
[2] See statement of Chief Justice Chase in *Knox* v. *Lee*, 12 Wall. 457.

which necessarily and in its direct operation impairs the obligation of contracts, is inconsistent with the spirit of the Constitution." And finally, referring indirectly to his own support of this law when Secretary of the Treasury, he said: "It is not surprising that amid the tumult of the late civil war, and under the influence of apprehensions for the safety of the Republic almost universal, different views, never before entertained by American statesmen or jurists, were adopted by many. The time was not favorable to considerate reflection upon the constitutional limits of Legislative or Executive authority. If power was assumed from patriotic motives, the assumption found ready justification in patriotic hearts. Many who doubted, yielded their doubts; many who did not doubt were silent. . . . Not a few who then insisted upon its necessity, or acquiesced in that view, have, since the return of peace, and under the influence of the calmer time, reconsidered their conclusions." Accordingly, so far as the Legal Tender Act applied to contracts made before its passage (which was the only question actually involved in this case), the Court held the Act unconstitutional. The reasoning, however, contained in the Chief Justice's opinion was equally applicable to cases of contracts executed after the passage of the law and would render it equally invalid as to them. The minority, after reviewing the conditions of the war when the Act was passed, held that "this law was a necessity, in the most stringent sense in which that word can be used"; and they described the war in terms which have a very modern sound, as "a war which, if we take into account the increased capacity for destruction introduced by modern science and the corresponding increase of its cost, brought into operation powers of belligerency, more potent and more expensive than any that the world has ever known."

Apart from the question of impairing obligation of contract, the real difference between the majority and the minority was simply one of fact, *viz.* whether Congress might, within the bounds of reason, have considered the issue of legal currency to be "necessary" for the carrying on of the war.

At first, the decision was not regarded as of great consequence, as its effect was supposed to be confined merely to cases of contracts made before the war. "The decision is not unexpected," said the *New York Times*, "and in no manner involves the constitutionality of the law itself. . . . There will be hardship, undoubtedly, and in some instances injustice; but the judgment of the Court rests upon an intelligible, if not an agreeable or entirely defensible principle, the promulgation of which constitutes another reason for the restoration with all convenient speed of specie payments." [1] "This decision is of much less consequence than it would have been if it had been rendered five years sooner," said the *Independent*. "In 1870, it is not a means of protection or redress, but only a message of condolence." "It would have been of great importance had it been 'more timely,'" said the *New York World*. The *Washington Chronicle* said that while the decision was "an insidious assault upon the great measure which saved the country during the rebellion", it was not likely to work any serious injury. "The confidence in the greenbacks is too great to be shaken by judicial decision." The *New York Herald*, which also

---

[1] The *New York Times*, Feb. 8, 1870, said: "There was a great deal of perturbation and much confusion at the Capitol today at the announcement. . . . The Court-room was crowded; but little satisfaction was obtained in listening to the reading of the decision . . . by the Chief Justice, as he was almost wholly inaudible;" see also *Washington Chronicle*, Feb. 12, 1870; *Independent*, Feb. 10, 17, 1870; *New York Herald*, Feb. 8, 9, 16, 22, 1870; on Feb. 24, it said: "The decision does not foreshadow a decision denying the validity of the act. . . . There is not a vestige of probability that the Court will go a step further."

favored the greenbacks and opposed the National banks,
at first took this restricted view of the opinion and said
that the Court had avoided holding the Legal Tender
Act unconstitutional as to present contracts — a decision which would have "involved the whole country
in financial chaos and the Government perhaps in bankruptcy and repudiation. . . . We have no fears that
the Supreme Court will risk, for a long time to come, a
decision against our greenback currency as legal tender."
And it stated that with the new members on the Court.
it expected a favorable decision. "The Court, even
when most strongly seasoned with State-Rights, has
carefully avoided any disturbing collision with Congress." The *Nation* said, presenting what was probably
the view held by most thoughtful men: "There is little
question, whatever be the objections to the decision on
general grounds, that it will accelerate the return of
specie payments and give a useful fillip to the moral
sense of the country, and especially of the knavish portion of the public. . . . Legal tenders are one thing;
depreciated legal tenders are another thing; and no
Court can be expected to declare cheating lawful, unless
it is plainly and unmistakably obliged to do so by
the recognized decrees of the sovereign authority. . . .
The Court can very well say, and does say, that it knows
nothing of legislative necessity, but that it does know
that nothing but express direction would justify it in
declaring lawful and justifiable the evasion of a clear
moral obligation." As to the opinion of the dissenting
Judges, it said: "The strong point of Judge Miller's
argument is, as might be expected, what is the Chief
Justice's weakest — the impropriety of taking from
Congress and committing to a Court of Justice a task
so plainly legislative in its nature as the decision what
means are necessary and proper to the performance of

a duty, so complex, so delicate and so full of unforeseen contingencies . . . as the government of a great Nation during a great war, even within the limited sphere prescribed by our written Constitution. . . . And yet if the interpretation of a written Constitution is not committed to Judges, what use is it? If the majority can do whatever they choose to declare constitutional, what better is it than the revocable charters which absolute sovereigns in Europe amused themselves by granting, for some years after 1815?"[1]

The views of the other side were presented by *Harper's Weekly,* which said that: "It is dangerous to deprive ourselves of an essential means of warfare and defense on such delusive grounds. It will soon appear that the Legal Tender Act cannot safely be dispensed with. Its constitutionality is clear, and it should remain with Congress to decide when it shall be inoperative. The Court has overstepped the just line of its authority, and attempted to restrict Congress in this matter, when the framers of the Constitution decided to leave them free of such restriction." The *New York Times* stated that: "The effect of the decision, if allowed to stand, upon the future of the country if it shall unfortunately be involved in war, will constitute its worst feature. It strips the Nation of one of its means of warfare and defense."

As soon as it became evident that, though the case before the Court involved only the effect of the Act upon contracts made before its passage, the reasoning of the majority opinion was such as to make it unconstitutional both as to contracts entered into after, as well as before, a strong movement arose in the community to urge the Court to grant a rehearing, or to

[1] *Nation,* Feb. 10, 17, 1870; *Harper's Weekly,* March 19, April 16, 1870; *Springfield Weekly Republican,* Feb. 11, 18, 1870; *New York Times,* Feb. 12, March 8, 1870.

review the whole question on argument of other cases
pending on the docket.[1] Those who believed the decision to be disastrous not only in its financial, but in
its governmental effect, were encouraged in this movement by the fact that at last the two long-pending
vacancies in the Court had been filled and the appointees confirmed. For on February 7, on the same day
and at the very time when Chief Justice Chase was
reading his opinion in the *Legal Tender Case*, President
Grant sent in to the Senate the names of William Strong
of Pennsylvania to fill Grier's place, and of Joseph P.
Bradley of New Jersey to fill the new Judgeship for
which Hoar's name had already been rejected.[2] The
legal qualifications of both were eminent; and while
they were believed to favor the necessity of a strong
National Government, both were entirely free from
political entanglements, or suspicion of political activity or ambition. Strong was sixty-two years of age,
and had been for eleven years a Judge of the Supreme
Court of Pennsylvania. Bradley was fifty-seven years
of age; he had been highly prominent at the Bar of
New Jersey, which regardless of party had urged his
appointment, and though a Republican, he had been
earnestly recommended to the President, in the previous
December, by a Democratic Judge, Grier.[3]

---

[1] The *Nation*, March 24, 1870, said that the scheme for reversing the decision
grew out of the notorious dislike of the Senators for Chief Justice Chase and out
of efforts of moneyed corporations. "So far as the public is concerned, there has
not been a breath of popular discontent to justify any political movement; and
yet grave men have doubted the result; Senators have fully expressed their opinion that the decision must be reversed; Congressmen have furiously denounced
it as rivalling the Dred Scott decision in bad preëminence."

[2] See *Amer. Law Rev.*, IV, 394, saying that Hoar's rejection was a scandal, and
that the reasons given by the Senate as to the tartness and acerbity of Hoar's manners were puerile and trivial.

It may be noted that Bradley had a middle initial "P", but no middle name.

[3] The *New York Tribune*, Feb. 9, 1870, said: "General Grant has nominated
very good lawyers for the Supreme Court, but none truer or fitter than Bradley";
see also *New York Times*, Feb. 8, 1870.

The coincidence that the appointments were made on the day of the rendering of the adverse Legal Tender decision soon gave rise to a story, which later had much currency, that "Grant packed the Court" for the purpose of obtaining a reversal of the decision. The charge has been conclusively answered many times, but still occasionally crops out in attacks on the Court.[1] The facts themselves disprove the accusation. Both Judges were nominated on recommendation of Hoar, who later formally stated that their views on the Legal Tender issue had nothing to do with his recommendation. Strong's appointment had been decided on, fully a month before February 7; and Bradley's had been urged on the President and favorably considered, before Hoar's own appointment in the previous December.[2] The President himself formally stated that he had no advance knowledge as to the decision of the Court, and members of his cabinet later stated the same thing. The newspapers of the time clearly show that there was no leak as to the decision, for their published forecasts were inaccurate.[3] Since practically every State Court (except Kentucky) and every prominent Republican lawyer held the view that the Legal Tender Act was constitutional it would have been impossible for the President to find any State Judge or any lawyer

[1] See *Nation*, April 7, 1870, March 7, 1872. In its issue, April 11, 1872, it stated that it considered that Hoar (the Ex-Attorney-General) had fully answered the charges; *ibid.*, April 5, 1872, Nov. 9, 1876. See especially for full statement, *The Charge of Packing the Court against President Grant and Attorney-General Hoar* (1895), by George F. Hoar; see also Hoar's speech, April 1, 7, 1874. *43d Cong., 1st Sess.*

[2] The *New York Herald*, Dec. 16, 1869, said that Strong's name was being considered for Grier's place; see also *New York Tribune*, Feb. 7, 1870; *New York World*, Feb. 15, 1870, saying that Bradley was Grant's original choice before he appointed Hoar.

[3] See Washington correspondent of *Boston Daily Advertiser*, writing Feb. 6, 1870. That at least one prominent statesman, however, had advance knowledge is seen from George S. Boutwell's statement in his *Reminiscences of Sixty Years* (1902), IV, 209, that Chase told him of the Court's conclusion "two weeks in advance of the delivery of the opinion."

of his own party who differed from Strong and Bradley
in the view which they later expressed on the Supreme
Bench.   Moreover, if Grant had desired to "pack the
Court", it would have been far easier to do so by appointing some Judge more acceptable to the Radicals
than the conservative Strong, and also by appointing
a carpet-bag Judge from the South instead of Bradley;
for it was known at the time of the appointments that
Strong was not popular, and that Bradley's confirmation
by the Senate would be very doubtful, owing to the
prevalent sentiment that at least one vacancy should
be filled by a Southern lawyer.   "Bradley's nomination
is a surprise," said the *New York Tribune's* Washington
correspondent, "and the comments of Senators make
the opinion general that both are looked upon with disfavor.   In regard to Judge Strong, the time of his nomination is very inopportune, on account of the decision
of the Supreme Court just rendered on the *Legal Tender
Cases.*   That decision has stirred up the more radical
members of the Republican party in Congress and especially the Senate. . . .   Judge Strong they think a
man as conservative as either Chase or Field. . . .
Bradley lacks a National reputation"; and the *New
York Herald* said that "the Senate vigorously inveigh
against Bradley.   The carpet-bag Senators are particularly ferocious on the appointment of Bradley . . .
and demand to have a man from their own section.
A pure Southerner is their ultimatum.   Bradley, though
personally acceptable to every Republican Senator,
notwithstanding his conservative record, carries with
him the same objection as Hoar as to locality."   There
was "universal feeling of surprise" at Bradley's appointment and "Northern and Southern Senators have
strongly urged the President to withdraw it," said the
New York World.   While Strong was finally confirmed

by the Senate on February 18, Bradley's nomination
was postponed, awaiting action on a bill then pending
in Congress requiring Judges to reside in the Circuit
to which they were appointed; but it was finally confirmed on March 21, by a vote of forty-six to nine,
receiving the support of the Democrats and the opposition of the Southern Republicans.[1] The best evidence
that the Democrats did not then suppose that Grant
was "packing the Court" appears to be the highly
flattering editorial comment of the *New York World* on
Judge Bradley. "By this result, the Court gains an
accomplished jurist, and the carpet-baggers are dis-
gracefully defeated in their scheme of foisting upon
the highest judicial tribunal in the land one of their
own class. . . . The Democratic Senators, have, from
the first, hailed the nomination of Mr. Bradley as that
of one so respectable and worthy, though a Republican,
that the wonder grew how Grant ever came to pick
him out. . . . He is in all respects worthy of it. We
confidently look to him and to Judge Strong as active
allies with the Chief Justice and his conservative
brethren in keeping the great tribunal of the land up
to the mark where Marshall and Taney left it. Mr.
Bradley goes on the Bench utterly untrammelled."

On March 25, four days after confirmation of the
Judges, Attorney-General Hoar produced a sensation
by moving in the Supreme Court that two of the *Legal
Tender Cases*, *Latham* v. *United States* and *Deming* v.
United States, then pending and which involved contracts made after the passage of the Act be taken up for
argument. While predictions had been current that

---

[1] *New York Herald*, Feb. 8, 18, 1870; *New York World*, Feb. 9, 1870, March 1,
3, 1870. On March 2, Bradley's name came up in the Senate and after speeches
by the Southern Senators opposing him, action was postponed. *New York World*,
March 22, 23, 1870; *Boston Daily Advertiser*, March 22, 1870, described fully the
confirmation and the opposition of Southern Senators and of Thayer of Nebraska.

such an attempt would be made, and while the Radical Republicans and the Greenbackers were threatening dire results politically and financially, unless the Court should reopen the question, nevertheless, the general public had assumed that the question of constitutionality was to be considered as completely settled in the *Hepburn Case*.[1]   Hence, when on April 1 the Court announced that the cases would be heard on April 11, on all the questions involved, thus reopening the *Hepburn Case*, the action produced a marked sensation in the community;[2] and there was much sympathy expressed with the vigorous dissent filed by Chief Justice Chase, and Judges Nelson, Clifford and Field.   The Court's reasons, however, for granting a rehearing were well stated later by Judge Strong, 12 Wall. 529: "It would be difficult to over-estimate the consequences which must follow our decision.   They will affect the entire business of the country, and take hold of the possible continued existence of the government.   If it be held by this Court that Congress has no constitutional power under any circumstances, or in any emergency, to make treasury notes a legal tender for the payment of all debts (a power confessedly possessed by every independent sovereignty other than the United States), the Government is without those means of self-preservation which, all must admit, may, in certain contingencies, become indispensable, even if they were not when the Acts of Congress now called in question were enacted.   It is also clear that if we hold the Acts invalid as applicable to debts incurred or transactions which have taken place since their enactment, our decision must cause, throughout the country, great business derangement, widespread distress and the

[1] See *Nation*, March 24, 1870.
[2] See *Boston Daily Advertiser*, April 2, 1870.

rankest injustice. . . . These consequences are too
obvious to admit of question."

Of course, the answer to all this was, that the Court
should not concern itself with "consequences", but
only with the question of constitutional limits, regardless of results produced. There was, however, popular
support in many directions, chiefly based on financial
reasons, for the Court's action in ordering a rehearing;
while the argument that the authority in the Government was requisite for the public security was naturally
an appealing one. *Harper's Weekly*, which favored
reargument, issued this warning to the Court: "The
relations of the Court to Congress, as prescribed in the
Constitution, constitute a powerful reason for the utmost delicacy in the treatment of questions of Congressional power. . . . Far be it from us to wish to limit
in any degree the perfect independence of the Judiciary,
as we regard this freedom as the sheet-anchor of our
safety; but prudence requires that a tribunal, subjected
so materially to the power of Congress by the fundamental law, should continue to use the same delicacy
in questions affecting Congressional power which governed the Court when Marshall presided over its deliberations. Its dignity and usefulness will always be
promoted by extreme caution. The exhibition of this
care will command public confidence, and prevent ex-
tremities in providing for the *regulations* which Congress is empowered to make." The *Nation*, on the
other hand, stated that there was danger to the Court in
the process through which it was now going, and that it
would never long survive the loss of popular respect:
"We find very little difference of opinion in the press
as to the gross impropriety (to use a very mild term)
of the reopening of the Legal Tender decision. It is,
in every way one looks at it, a blunder." It feared,

moreover, that this was a beginning of refusal by parties affected by a decision to accept any ruling as final; and it said that "the country ought to speak out boldly against these disgraceful beginnings."[1] The *Springfield Republican* said that it still hoped that "the country is to be spared this great wrong and scandal of a reversal."

Whatever may have been the popular view in 1870, there is no doubt that ever since that era the Court's action in reopening its first decision has been regarded as a very grave mistake — and a mistake which for many years impaired the people's confidence, not in the honesty, but in the impartiality and good sense of the Court. Not only was the Court's action unfortunate, but the manner in which it was taken caused an unpleasant degree of friction, — an instance of which on April 11, 1870, was described by a Washington correspondent as follows: "There was a very lively scene at the Supreme Court this morning, the oldest lawyers practicing there having witnessed nothing like it in their day." Counsel during the argument of the Latham and Deming appeals having stated that when Evarts was Attorney-General an order had been made by the Court that these cases should abide the result in the *Hepburn Case*, Attorney-General Hoar now denied that there had been any such order, and "the Chief Justice here interrupted to say that according to his recollection such an order had been made. This was said with evident feeling and Justice Miller remarked with equal feeling that he knew of no such order. Justice Nelson came to the rescue of the Chief Justice, and Justice Davis spoke up, saying that he concurred with Justice Miller. The Chief Justice repeated his statement with emphasis

[1] *Harper's Weekly*, April 16, 1870; *Nation*, April 7, 14, 21, 28, 1870; *Springfield Republican*, April 8, 1870.

and hardly suppressed passion, and then upon the suggestion of Judge Davis, who remarked that it was not worth while to bandy words, it was decided that the cases might go over to next Monday. The Attorney-General meantime bowed to the recollection of the Chief Justice, and merely expressed his regret that in a matter of this importance there was no record."[1] This action of the Court, however, in reopening the question had no immediate effect; for on April 18, 1870, the counsel for the appellants in the *Latham and Deming Cases* moved to dismiss their appeals, and after some discussion and variance of opinion, the motion was granted.[2] The *American Law Review* expressed the hope, which was shared by most conservative men, that the question was finally settled and would not be disturbed in the Court: "The inferior Courts throughout the country have been adapting their opinions to the decision pronounced in *Hepburn* v. *Griswold*, and declaring contracts made previous to the passage of the Legal Tender Act, payable in gold. This has gone so far that we observe in our recent exchanges one or two reported decisions following *Hepburn* v. *Griswold*. To upset *Hepburn* v. *Griswold* now would be to upset all these subsequent

---

[1] *Boston Daily Advertiser*, April 12, 1870. On April 13, it said that the affair had been the subject of a good deal of talk among lawyers present and that the Chief Justice showed strong passion. "It is evident that there is a state of feeling in the Court by no means pleasant." *Amer. Law Rev.* (1870), V, 158, 366; the *Nation*, April 14, 1870, spoke of "an unseemly squabble on the bench in open Court."

Chase prepared a memorandum in which he made allegations that the Judges who formed the minority in the *Hepburn Case* and who now were part of the majority of the Court had agreed that the *Hepburn Case* decision should settle all the other cases pending. This raised a point of bad faith on the part of his associates, and learning that they were prepared to deny it, Chase withdrew his memorandum. Later its substance appeared in a biography; whereupon in 1901, Charles Bradley in *Miscellaneous Writings of the late Hon. Joseph P. Bradley* (1902) published for the first time a statement written by Judge Miller and signed by the majority of the Court, April 30, 1870, giving a detailed statement of all facts concerning these cases, which completely disproved Chase's allegation; see also *Green Bag* (1902), XIV, 203.

[2] *Latham and Deming's Appeals*, 9 Wall. 145; *Boston Daily Advertiser*, April 22, 1870.

adjudications; and that the business interests of the country can demand such chronic vacillation in the law as this would imply, we cannot believe. And this, too, is a minor point. The great objection to opening the Legal Tender decision is, that the Supreme Court cannot do it without degrading itself in the eyes of all intelligent men; and this fact, we should think the new members of the Court would recognize, quite as distinctly as the old. We believe we express the opinion of every unbiased lawyer throughout the United States, when we say that the reopening of the *Legal Tender Cases* would be a terrible blow at the independence and dignity of the profession."

There was, moreover, a general relief over the withdrawal of the appeals, since it seemed apparent that, if the decision should be reversed, a political movement might be initiated to reverse this second decision, by adding still more Judges to the Court; and thus the question of the Judiciary might be injected into the approaching Presidential campaign. All hopes, however, that the issue might be considered settled were dashed when, on April 30, 1870, the Court ordered the reargument of the case of *Knox* v. *Lee*, 12 Wall. 457, which had been already argued in November, 1869, and which involved primarily the confiscation law of one of the Confederate States. At the reargument on February 23, 1871, counsel for both sides admitted the validity of the Legal Tender Acts so far as they affected this case, and did not raise the point; but at its close, Clarkson N. Potter, who had argued the *Hepburn Case*, asked to be heard on the constitutional question; and the Court, over the dissent of Judges Clifford, Nelson and Field, ordered a second reargument by Potter and Attorney-General Akerman, on the constitutional question. The matter being thus reopened, and heard on April 18, 19, 1871, the Court rendered a decision, ten days later, on May 1, reversing *Hepburn* v. *Griswold* and sustaining the Legal Tender Acts in the broadest possible manner, as a valid exercise by Congress of the war power, in respect to all contracts whether made after or before the passage of the Acts.   In this opinion, the new Judges Strong and Bradley united with the former minority, Swayne, Miller and Davis, while the Chief Justice, Nelson, Clifford and Field dissented and reaffirmed their previous decision.

This reversal by the Court of a decision which had been rendered only fifteen months before was regretted on all sides, both by many who agreed with its conclusion as well as by those who held the contrary view. "It is a grievous mistake," said the *Springfield Republican*.   "It will greatly aggravate the growing contempt for what has long been the most respected and the most influential department of our government, its Judiciary." "The present action of the Court," said the *Nation*, "is to be deplored, first, because this sudden reversal of a former judgment which had been maturely considered after full argument, will weaken popular respect for all decisions of the Court including this last one; second, because the value of a judgment does not depend on the number of Judges who concur in it — Judges being weighed, not counted, and because of the rehearing of a cause, in consequence of the number of Judges having been increased, is peculiarly, and for obvious reasons, objectionable, where the number is dependent on the will of the very body whose acts the Court has to review, and which in this very case it is reviewing; and third, because the Judges who have been added to the Bench since the former decision are men who were at the Bar when that decision was rendered, and were interested professionally and personally in having a different decision. We do not mean to insinuate that this has affected their judgment, but we do say that it is not enough for a Judge to be pure; he must be likewise above suspicion; that is, he must not only be honest, but must give no man any reason for thinking him otherwise than honest." [1]   Many who believed in their absolute honesty felt that the new Judges, as a matter of propriety, should have refrained from taking part in the decision; and they agreed with the *New York Tribune*, which said that the assurance given by various papers that the new Judges divested themselves absolutely of their railroad interests in going upon the Bench did not touch the point of the complaint. "It was an essentially improper thing that a recent and earnest paid advocate of the constitutionality of the Legal Tender Act should take his seat upon the Supreme Bench to decide its constitutionality. Let him be as pure as snow, he cannot, for this, escape condemnation. . . . It will not be easy to restore public respect and reverence for the tribunal which this decision has sacrificed." With this violently Republican paper, the equally violent *New York World* joined in assailing the decision and reiterating the charge, which had been made in the previous year, that the Court had been "packed" — a charge which, as noted above, has since been completely exploded. "The decision provokes the indignant contempt of thinking men. It is generally regarded not as the solemn adjudication of an upright and impartial tribunal, but as a base compliance with Executive instructions by creatures of the President placed upon the Bench to carry out his instructions." And in this curious combination of news-

[1] *Nation*, April 27, 1871; *New York Tribune*, May 1, 2, 1871; *New York World*, May 3, 8, 1871; *New York Times*, May 3, 1871; *New York Herald*, May 3, 1871; *Springfield Republican*, May 5, 1871; *Harper's Weekly*, May 20, 1871; *Cincinnati Enquirer*, May 6, 8, 10, 1871.

paper opinion, the *New York Evening Post* joined, declaring that the decision was the voice of the Administration, and not of the law, and that under this practice of reconstituting the Court, if tolerated, "the Constitution and its interpretation cease to limit the National Government and become just what the appointing power choose to make them."

On the other hand, an equally curious combination of diverse political and other interests defended the decision. "Happily for the country, the opinion of the Chief Justice did not prevail," said the *New York Times*. "The country will be satisfied," said the *New York Herald*. That the character of the new Judges "forbids any suspicion of other than the best motives in their action", was the view of *Harper's Weekly;* and it added (with some extravagance of statement) that the chief class of person who would regard the decision "with profound disgust" was "all those who wish to see the powers of the National Government against its enemies weakened." And the *Cincinnati Enquirer*, a Democratic advocate of greenbacks, stated that the people of the country would be benefited by the decision, though the Republican charges against the Republican Judges were "very mortifying to every American who has pride in the honor of his country and in the integrity of the Judiciary." There was thus presented the singular spectacle of strong adherents of National power opposing a judicial opinion which voiced most extreme limits of such power, and ardent advocates of a non-centralized Government praising a decision which vastly increased the authority of the National Government.

In the year following its decision in the *Legal Tender Cases*, the Court once more upheld in the most extreme terms the powers of the National Government in its relation to the States. In *United States* v. *Tarble*, 13 Wall. 397, a State Commissioner of Wisconsin had issued a writ of habeas corpus discharging a man held by the United States Army for trial by military tribunal on charge of desertion. The Court held, on March 11, 1872, that if on application for habeas corpus made to a State official it should appear by the return that the petitioner was "confined under the authority or claim and color of authority of the United States by an officer of the Government", the writ must be refused; and that the State official had no power to issue a writ under such conditions. "Whenever any conflict arises between the enactments of the two sovereignties, or in the enforcement of their asserted authorities, those of the National Government must have supremacy until the validity of the different enactments and authorities can be finally determined by the tribunals of the United States. This temporary supremacy, until judicial decision by the National tribunals, and the ultimate determination of the conflict by such decision, are essential to the preservation of order and peace, and the avoidance of forcible collision between the two Governments." It is interesting to note that a Democratic Judge, Field, wrote this opinion, reasserting the National supremacy previously voiced by a Democratic Chief Justice in the *Booth Case* while the Republican Chief Justice, Chase, dissented in an opinion strongly upholding the powers of the States.

In 1873, in *Olcott* v. *Supervisors*, 16 Wall. 678, the Court reaffirmed its adherence to a doctrine, which it had first announced in 1864, and which, upheld throughout this critical post-war period, probably had a more important effect upon the commercial development of the country than any other of the Court's extensions of National power. This was the doctrine

by virtue of which the Federal Courts were held to be
vested with power to disregard the decisions of State
Courts on the validity of the issue of municipal bonds.
The decision asserting this power arose out of economic conditions which had prevailed for a long period
prior. From 1840 to 1860, the States of the Union, especially in the Central West, had run riot in authorizing municipalities to vote money and to issue bonds,
and the constitutional power to extend such aid to
public corporations had been, in general, upheld by the
State Courts.[1] Gradually, the extensive frauds committed by both the officers of municipalities and by
officers of the railroads, the enormous loans made to
corporations which failed to fulfill the objects for which
the money was loaned or granted, produced a revulsion
of feeling; counties, cities and towns entered on a course
of repudiation, and State Courts reversed or overruled
their previous judgments and denied the power of the
Legislatures to authorize municipalities to issue such
bonds. Such were the conditions, therefore, which
existed, when, in 1864, the case of *Gelpcke* v. *Dubuque*
came before the Court on appeal from a Circuit Court
of the United States. The State Supreme Court of
Iowa had, in many opinions from 1853 to 1859, sustained
the validity of municipal bonds issued in aid of railroads; but in 1860, it had given an opinion overruling
all the previous cases. Suit being brought on bonds
issued by a city while the former State decisions prevailed, it was contended by counsel for the city that the
Court must adhere to its established doctrine of following the latest construction of a State Constitution made
by a State Court. But by adopting such a rule in these

---

[1] See especially description of these conditions by Judge Jeremiah S. Black in
Sharpless v. *Mayor*, 21 Pa. St. 147; *Amer. Law Reg.* (1853), II; in *Ritchie* v. *Franklin County*, 22 Wall. 67, in 1875, Judge Davis referred to "the well known mania of
the people to run in debt for public improvements."

cases, the Court would give countenance to repudiation, and would bring untold losses upon thousands of innocent bondholders who had invested their money on the faith of apparently established law. To deal with such a situation, the Court apparently had but three possible courses open to it; either to follow the latest State decisions; or to follow the earlier decision on the ground that it was, in fact, the "latest *settled* adjudication"; or to hold that the question was one of commercial law, and that in accordance with its decision in *Swift* v. *Tyson*, it would determine all such questions for itself regardless of the law of the State. Instead of following either of these courses, however, the Court decided the case on an entirely new ground; and in a noted opinion by Judge Swayne held that where a contract was valid by the law of a State as expounded by its Judiciary at the time it was made, it could not be impaired, either by subsequent action of a Legislature or decision of a State Court, and that this rule "rests upon the plainest principles of justice." While not unmindful of the importance of uniformity in the decisions of the Court, and those of the highest local Courts, "we shall never", he said, "immolate truth, justice, and the law, because a State tribunal has erected the altar, and decreed the sacrifice." And in later cases, it held that "such a rule is based upon the highest principles of justice." While it was difficult to reconcile this equitable doctrine with the duty imposed on Federal Courts by the Thirty-Fourth Section of the Judiciary Act to follow the laws of the State, and while from time to time the Court advanced varying grounds for its action,[1] nevertheless, it continued for the

---

[1] The Court's theory of impairment of obligation of contract by judicial decision was reiterated in *Olcott* v. *Supervisors*, 16 Wall. 678, in 1873, and *Township of Pine Grove* v. *Talcott*, 19 Wall. 666, in 1874, but was gradually abandoned until

next twenty years consistently to disregard opinions of
the State Courts denying the validity of these municipal
railroad aid bonds, to formulate its own commercial
law on the subject and to discountenance every form
of attempted repudiation of debt.[1] While the doctrine
thus firmly asserted by the Court had an inestimable
effect upon the material and moral prosperity of the
country in restoring confidence in a class of securities
which were an indispensable factor in the development
of municipal and industrial enterprises, it became, on
the other hand, a somewhat serious factor in the history
of the relations of the Court to the American people.
For owing to the pronounced feelings of hostility to the
Federal Judiciary which these bond decisions aroused
through the Central West, popular confidence in, and
support of, the supreme tribunal were weakened, at the
precise time when such confidence and support were especially needed. These bond decisions were rendered
during the partisan and passionate contests which centered around Reconstruction legislation, and at the very
period when the Court was being made the subject of

---

it was entirely repudiated in 1888 in *New Orleans Waterworks* v. *Louisiana Sugar
Co.*, 125 U. S. 18, 30.   See *Impairment of Contract by Judicial Decisions*, by Conrad
Reno, *Amer. Law Rev.* (1889), XXXII.   Prof. James B. Thayer upheld the decision
on the ground that it was a rule adopted by the Court to shape its discretion in matters arising in the Federal Circuit Courts in suits based on diverse citizenship and involving the construction of State laws and Constitutions, and termed it a just and
wholesome one.   *The Scope of Gelpcke* v. *Dubuque, Harv. Law Rev.* (1891), IV;
ibid. (1898), VIII.

[1] See *Municipal Corporations* (1874, 2d ed.) by John F. Dillon, sec. 416; *The
Rule in Gelpcke* v. *Dubuque*, by John M. Read (Chief Justice of Pennsylvania),
Amer. Law Rev. (1875), IX; *Railroad Aid Bonds in the Supreme Court*, by James
F. Mister, *Amer. Law Reg.* (1878), N. S., XVII; *Statutory Powers in Bond Cases*,
ibid. (1881), N. S., XX; *Municipal Bonds*, by Frank W. Hackett, *Harv. Law Rev.*
(1891), V; see also *Law of Municipal Bonds*, in *Southern Law Rev.* (1876), N. S.,
II; (1881), VII: "The Supreme Court has upheld the right of holders with a strong
hand, and has set a face of flint against repudiation, even when made on legal
ground deemed solid by the State Courts, by municipalities which had been deceived and defrauded.   That such securities have any general value left is largely
due to this course of adjudication and to the reliance felt by the public that it will
stand firmly by its doctrines."

most violent attacks in Congress and in the press.
That the Court had taken a position in the bond cases
which must bring it into disfavor with large portions of
the public had been predicted at the outset by Judge
Miller, in his strong dissenting opinion in the *Gelpcke
Case*; and the fulfillment of his prophecy was seen in the
numerous clashes which ensued during the next thirty
years, and which resulted in bringing before the Court
for its decision during that period approximately three
hundred municipal bond cases — a larger number than
on any other subject presented for its consideration.[1]

[1] Judge Davis said in *Thomson* v. *Lee County*, 3 Wall. 327, in 1866: "There is
hardly any question connected with this species of securities that has not been discussed and decided by the Court." This statement showed curiously little appreciation of the troubles that were to face the Court, since in succeeding years the Court
had before it about three hundred cases involving such bonds. Of these cases,
sixty-five arose in Illinois; fifty in Missouri; twenty-five in Iowa; twenty-two in
Kansas; eighteen in Wisconsin; fourteen in New York; eleven in Indiana; nine
each in Kentucky and Tennessee; the others being scattered over eighteen States;
none, however, arising in New England.

NOTE. An interesting account of the argument in the first *Legal Tender Case*
by Judge Isaac F. Redfield of Vermont appeared in the *American Law Register*
(April, 1869), XVII: "The opening argument in favor of the validity of the law was
made by Judge Curtis in his clearest, purest, happiest vein, as nearly perfect in
matter and manner as it is possible for us to conceive a law argument to be. Mr.
Townsend of New York and Mr. Potter occupied parts of two days in reply, placing
the main force of the argument on the ground of the impolicy and injustice of the
law, and upon the early history of the Government and the Constitution, as showing both the improbability that the Constitution was intended to receive any such
construction, and, as far as practicable, the fact that such was not the purpose of
its framers or of those who adopted it. The gentlemen commanded a good degree
of attention, and made themselves, on the whole, very interesting. The Attorney
General, Mr. Evarts, closed the argument with his usual copiousness of learning
and fullness of illustration. The only possible exception one can make to his
manner of arguing causes in banc is that he is, if possible, too deliberate. . . . But
bating this single and unimportant drawback . . . it must be admitted that he
presents one of the best models of forensic eloquence at present to be found in this
or perhaps any other country. The argument of Judge Curtis fell far within the
limits of one hour and it commanded the most undivided and unflagging attention
to the last moment, and as a presentation of the legal argument, and it aspired to
nothing else, it was certainly of a most uncommon and unrivalled character. But
the general style of argument in this Court is losing much of that conversational
air which gave it such charm thirty years ago, and which still prevails to a great
extent in Westminster Hall. The present style of forensic debate there is more
like that of Pinkney and Emmet and Lowndes than the school that followed these
great masters of forensic eloquence which was far less ornate and discursive. . . .
Each has its advantages and its followers. But the present style of forensic debate
in America, is rather French than English. . . ."

CHAPTER THIRTY-TWO

THE SLAUGHTERHOUSE CASES AND THE DEATH OF CHASE

1873

As the preceding chapters have shown, the period of Chase's Chief Justiceship had constituted an era of Nationalism, and the pronounced trend of the Court was significantly noted at this time in a review of the first digest of decisions of the Federal Courts: "The great increase in the strength and influence of the Federal Government, which has been the natural consequence of the triumph over a gigantic rebellion, is nowhere more clearly evinced than in the enhanced interest felt by the Bar of the whole country in the decisions of the Federal Courts . . . or in the newly felt importance of the Federal Judiciary." [1]   With the year 1873, however, there came a distinct reaction from this extreme Nationalism.   That the Court from 1870 to 1873 was receding somewhat from the almost unvaried support which it had theretofore given to Congressional power had been seen in the increased instances in which it had exercised its function of declaring Federal legislation to be violative of the Constitution.   While in the eighty-one years from 1789 to 1869, only four Acts of Congress had been declared invalid, in the four years from 1870 to 1873, six of such Acts were held unconstitutional.[2]   Signs of a reaction in favor of the State

---

[1] *Western Jurist*, II, 319, review of *Brightly's Digest*.

[2] *Marbury* v. *Madison* (1803), 1 Cranch, 137; *Dred Scott* v. *Sandford* (1857), 19 How. 393; *Gordon* v. *United States* (1865), 2 Wall. 561; *Ex parte Garland* (1867), 4 Wall. 333; *Hepburn* v. *Griswold* (1870), 8 Wall. 603; *United States* v. *De Witt*

powers had appeared as early as 1870, when, two months after the first *Legal Tender Case* decision, the Court upheld, in *Thomson* v. *Union Pacific R. R.*, 9 Wall. 579, the right of a State to tax the property of a railroad even when built with Government money and acting as a Government agency. Attorney-General Hoar had argued eloquently against such an interference, saying: "It is a military, postal and commercial road and came out of the throes of the rebellion. It was designed to promote the unity and indivisibility of our people . . . a work which more than any other ever undertaken by the Government tends to consolidate peace and to maintain the dignity and reflect the glory of the nation." The Court, however, by Chief Justice Chase, held that while taxation of the agency is taxation of the means employed by the Government, "there is a clear distinction between the means employed by the Government and the property of agents employed by the Government. . . . Taxation of the agency is taxation of the means; taxation of the property of the agent is not always, or generally, taxation of the means." In the absence of interposition by Congress to protect this property from State taxation, it held that it must be assumed that the State power to tax was not being employed so as to defeat or hinder the operation of the National Government.[1]

Another sign of reaction came in 1871, when, one month before the second *Legal Tender Case* decision, the Court had occasion, in *Collector* v. *Day*, 11 Wall. 113,

(1870), 9 Wall. 41; *Justices* v. *Murray* (1870), 9 Wall. 274; *Collector* v. *Day* (1871), 11 Wall. 113; *United States* v. *Klein* (1872), 13 Wall. 128; *United States* v. *B. & O. R. R.* (1873), 17 Wall. 322.

[1] See *Union Pacific R. R.* v. *Peniston*, 18 Wall. 5, decided Dec. 15, 1873, in which the same decision was made as to a railroad chartered by Congress; see *United States* v. *Union Pacific R. R.*, 91 U. S. 72; *United States* v. *Burlington & Mo. River R. R.*, 98 U. S. 334; *Platt* v. *Union Pacific R. R.*, 99 U. S. 48; *Union Pacific R. R.* v. *United States*, 99 U. S. 402; *Union Pacific R. R.* v. *United States*, 104 U. S. 662; *Union Pacific R. R.* v. *United States*, 117 U. S. 355.

to consider the right of Congress to impose in time of war an income tax on the salary of a State judicial officer. It had held that the sovereignty of a State could not thus "be crippled, much less defeated by the taxing power of another Government. . . . The exemption rests upon necessary implication, and is upheld by the great law of self-preservation; as any government, whose means employed in conducting its operations, if subject to the control of another and distinct government, can exist only at the mercy of that government." This decision, said the *Cincinnati Enquirer*, "that the States have rights which are as sovereign as those of the General Government, and that the maintenance of their political dignity and sovereignty is as essential to good order and the perpetuity of free institutions as is the maintenance of the political dignity and sovereignty of the Federal Government, knocks the pins from under the trestle work the Republicans have been erecting, and over which they hoped to march the people from a land of freedom to one of despotism." [1]

It was with the decision of the famous *Slaughterhouse Cases*, 16 Wall. 36, in 1873, however, that the change in the attitude of the Court became most marked. In these cases, the Court, in construing for the first time the scope of the Fourteenth Amendment, rendered a decision which profoundly affected the course of the future history of the country.

Though the Amendment had been proclaimed to be in force July 28, 1868, nearly five years had elapsed before the question of its construction had been presented for determination by the Court. [2] These *Slaugh-*

[1] *Cincinnati Enquirer*, May 6, 1871; *New York World*, May 2, 11, 1871; the *New York Tribune*, April 29, May 3, 1871, attacked the decision.

[2] See 10 Wall. 273, in 1870, when the Court considered in the *Slaughterhouse Cases*, the effect of a writ of error as a supersedeas. The first case in which the applicability of this Amendment was urged was *Worthy* v. *Commissioners*, 9 Wall.

terhouse Cases had been pending since 1870; they had
been argued in January, 1872, but as Judge Nelson was
absent,[1] and as there was a division of opinion among
the Judges, they were argued again, on February 3, 4, 5,
1873, with supreme ability by John A. Campbell
against Matt H. Carpenter and Thomas J. Durant,
Jeremiah S. Black and Charles Allen.[2] The facts in
these cases presented a situation which clearly called
for relief, if the Federal Courts had any power to grant
it. The "carpet-bag" Legislature of Louisiana, undoubtedly under influence of corruption and bribery,
had passed a statute which granted a monopoly of the
slaughterhouse business within certain parishes of New
Orleans in favor of one corporation, and which deprived
over one thousand persons of the right to engage in that
business. There had been a general feeling of outrage
throughout the community, and the right of a State to
establish such a monopoly was vigorously challenged.[3]
Theretofore, the legal questions presented would have
been purely of State concern and for exclusive decision
by the State Courts. Now, it was contended by the
opponents of the monopoly that rights guaranteed by
the Fourteenth Amendment had been violated by the
State statute, and that it not only abridged the privileges and immunities of citizens of the United States,

611, but the Court on Feb. 7, 1870, held that the point was not properly claimed in
the State Court and dismissed the case for lack of Federal jurisdiction appearing in
the record.

[1] Judge Nelson resigned Nov. 28, 1872, at the age of eighty and after twenty-
seven years' service on the Court (see 14 Wall. ix). To succeed him, President
Grant was urged and expected to appoint a Judge from the South, either Thomas
J. Durant of Louisiana or Judge Duvall of Texas; he was also urged to appoint
William M. Evarts of New York (*Harper's Weekly*, Dec. 14, 1872); but he finally
appointed Dec. 11, 1872, Ward Hunt of New York, a man sixty-two years of age,
and a Judge of the New York Court of Appeals.

[2] Campbell had appeared before the Court for the first time since his resigna-
tion, in *Waring* v. *Mayor*, 8 Wall. 110, on Oct. 12, 1869. As to his part in the
Slaughterhouse Cases, see especially *John Archibald Campbell* (1920), by Henry
G. Connor.

[3] See *Reconstruction in Louisiana after 1868* (1918), by Ella Lonn.

but deprived them of their property without due process of law, and denied to them the equal protection of
the laws; it was further argued that it constituted an
involuntary servitude, in violation of the Thirteenth
Amendment.   Two months after the second argument,
the opinion of the Court was rendered by Judge Miller,
on April 14, 1873, Judges Clifford, Davis, Strong and
Hunt concurring.   It stated that it was "impressed
with the gravity of the questions raised", and recognized the "great responsibility" of the decision; that
"no questions so far-reaching and pervading in their
consequences, so profoundly interesting to the people of
this country, and so important in their bearing upon the
relations of the United States and of the several States
to each other, and to the citizens of the States and of the
United States, have been before this Court during the
official life of any of its present members" (*i.e.* since
1858).   After considering the history of the Fourteenth
Amendment, the evil which it was designed to remedy,
and its "pervading spirit", the Court held that the
Louisiana statute did not violate the Amendment in any
particular; that if the right claimed by the plaintiff to
be freed of monopoly existed, it was not a privilege or
immunity of a citizen of the United States as distinguished from a citizen of a State; that the Amendment,
in defining a citizen of the United States, did not add
any additional privileges and immunities to those which
inhered in such citizens before its adoption, that it was
only rights which owed their existence to the Federal
Government, its National character, its Constitution
or its laws, that were placed under the special care of
the National Government; that it was not intended to
bring within the power of Congress or the jurisdiction
of the Supreme Court, "the entire domain of civil rights
heretofore belonging exclusively to the States"; and

that to hold otherwise would "constitute this Court a perpetual censor upon all legislation of the States on the civil rights of their own citizens." [1]   Such, very briefly stated, was this momentous opinion. That the decision, so far as it concerned the provision of the Amendment forbidding the States to abridge the privileges and immunities of a citizen, rendered that clause a practical nullity, was pointed out by the dissenting Judges (Field, Swayne, Bradley and Chief Justice Chase). The construction given by the majority of the Court made of this clause, they said, "a vain and idle enactment which accomplished nothing, and most unnecessarily excited Congress and the people on its passage"; for "with privileges and immunities pertaining only to citizens of the United States *as such*, no State ever could have interfered by its laws", and no new constitutional provision was required to inhibit such interference. The supremacy of the Constitution and laws of the United States always controlled any State legislation of that character, even before the Fourteenth Amendment. Accordingly, the dissenting Judges were of opinion that the Amendment must be given such a construction as to render it of some effect; and they held that the monopoly was a "flagrant and indefensible violation of the rights of many for the benefit of a few"; that grants of exclusive privileges of this kind were "opposed to the whole theory of free government and it requires no aid from any bill of rights to render them void", and that a right of a citizen had been vio-

[1] "The privileges of American citizenship on American soil, as distinguished from those of State citizenship, were hardly thought of until the Civil War had done its nationalizing work. They would have remained largely a matter of sentiment then, had it not been for the new conditions and controversies precipitated by the enfranchisement of the colored race. By fundamental alterations in our Constitution, they have acquired a new dignity and power; but their ultimate range and scope have been left for the future to determine, by the slow growth of National institutions." *The Citizens of the United States*, by Simeon E. Baldwin, *Yale Law Journ.* (1893), II, 83: *Maxwell* v. *Dow* (1900), 176 U. S. 581.

lated which was entitled to protection under the Amendment. "By the Constitution, as it stood before the War," said Judge Swayne, "ample protection was given against oppression by the Union, but little was given against wrong and oppression by the States. That want was intended to be supplied by this Amendment. Against the former this Court had been called upon more than once to interpose. Authority of the same amplitude was intended to be conferred as to the latter. But this arm of our jurisdiction is, in these cases, stricken down by the judgment just given."

"The decision was given to an almost empty Courtroom and Bar," wrote a Washington correspondent, the next day, "and has as yet attracted little attention outside of legal circles, although the Judges of the Court regard the case as the most important which has been before them since the Dred Scott decision. The opinion of Mr. Justice Miller is held by the Bar to be exceedingly able, while passages in it were regarded as striking examples of judicial eloquence." [1] It was but a short time, however, before the Bar and the general public began to realize the immense scope of the decision. To the Radical Reconstructionists it came as a tremendous shock and disappointment; for their intent in framing the language of the Amendment was directly contrary to the narrow construction now placed upon it by the Court. Though the country at large may not have understood, at the time of the passage of the Fourteenth Amendment, the full purpose of its very general phraseology, the Radical leaders in Congress had had very definite ideas in drafting and submitting it to the people. Not only did they desire punishment of the South (to be achieved through the second, third and fourth sections, which were easily understood by the people) and

[1] *Boston Daily Advertiser*, April 16, 1873.

the elevation of the negro to the plane of equality with
the white man (which was to be achieved by section five,
as well as by the Thirteenth and Fifteenth Amendments),
but they also intended, by section one, to centralize in
the hands of the Federal Government large powers,
hitherto exercised by the States. The interval between
the adoption of the Thirteenth Amendment and the
proposal of the Fourteenth had been marked by legislation in the Southern States, designed, under the guise
of repressing vagrancy and regulating contracts of employment, to keep the negroes in a state of subjection;
and in order to gain control over the negro situation in
the South, wide extension of Federal power, and withdrawal of power previously vested in the States, were
deemed necessary. As has been said: "They desired
to nationalize all civil rights; to make the Federal
power supreme; and to bring the private life of every
citizen directly under the eye of Congress. This intention of the Radicals, though too much involved for the
people in general to comprehend, was quite generally
understood by the leading editors in the North and in
the South and by the party leaders on both sides."[1]
The feelings of those Republicans who had taken part
in framing the Amendment were clearly shown by their
comments on the decision. Senator George S. Boutwell,
who had been a member of the Committee on Recon-

[1] *The Fourteenth Amendment and the States* (1912), by Charles Wallace Collins,
45. Prof. John W. Burgess said in *Political Science and Constitutional Law* (1890),
I, 325: "They intended to occupy the whole ground, and thought they had done
so. The opposition charged that these Amendments would nationalize the whole
sphere of civil liberty; the majority accepted the view; and the legislation of
Congress for their elaboration and enforcement proceeded upon that view." See
39th Cong., 1st Sess., 2530–2542. James G. Blaine in his *Twenty Years of Congress*
(1884–1886), II, 419, said that by the decision "the Amendment has been deprived,
in fact, of the power which Congress intended to impart to it."

See *The Adoption of the Fourteenth Amendment*, by Horace Edgar Flack (1908);
The Fourteenth Amendment (1898), by William D. Guthrie; *Contemporary American History* (1914), by Charles A. Beard; *The Fourteenth Amendment and the Slaughterhouse Case*, by William L. Royall, *Southern Law Rev.* (1879), N. S., IV, 558.

struction, said that the Court had "erred in holding that there were two classes of rights, National and State." Senator Timothy O. Howe declared that "the American people would say, as they had said about the Dred Scott decision, that it was not law and could not be law." Senator Roscoe Conkling stated that the Drafting Committee had intended to include within the scope of the Amendment, not only the negro struggling upward from bondage, but also corporations and business interests struggling for emancipation from legislative interference. Senator George F. Edmunds, who also took part in framing the Amendment, said later: "There is no word in it that did not undergo the completest scrutiny. There is no word in it that was not scanned, and intended to mean the full and beneficial thing it seems to mean. There was no discussion omitted; there was no conceivable posture of affairs to the people who had it in hand which was not considered. And yet it was found upon the first attempt to enforce its first clause . . . that the Court, by a division of five to four, radically differed in respect both to the intention of the framers and the construction of the language used by them."

Those Radical Republicans, who opposed the decision from a partisan standpoint, were joined in their denunciation by a large number of Democrats, more especially in the West, who, though sympathizing with the views of the Court in regard to the relations of the Nation and the States, nevertheless deplored the decision from an economic and social standpoint, in the support which it gave to State-created monopolies. Typical of this form of critic was the *Cincinnati Enquirer*, which feared that the "degeneracy of the Court" was displayed by this decision upholding "a law passed by a so-called Legislature, elected by the bayonet and through the agency of the most degraded and ignorant portion of the population . . . to reward particular favorites. . . . We are astonished at this decision of the Court for which hitherto we have had the greatest respect. We could not have believed it possible that they could have had any hesitancy as to their duty. . . . It gives a legal sanction to the consummation of an outrage on individual rights that is almost unparalleled. It seems to us that, in view of the alarming precedent which has been set, the Court cannot maintain its opinion, but must recede from it. It is truly the monopolists' decision." It pointed out that the Fourteenth Amendment, originally designed for oppressing the Southern people, was now, as construed by the Court, only shelter for fraud and outrage, and not only "powerless for good, but powerful to harm." The opinion, it said, "will create a prejudice against the continued existence of a tribunal that has such little regard for the interests of the public. Not since the war, nor during it, was there so dangerous a precedent established as by this decision, which gives to a political body the authority to create monopolies of a few persons to tyrannize over and rob the many, forever." [1] The *Southern Law Review* also assailed the Court for sustaining a "menacing monopoly created by a corrupt and ignorant carpet-bag State Government."

Opinions of this nature, however, were not generally shared; for it was seen by most of the press and by the Bar that the decision did not, in reality, sanction monopolies, but simply established the proposition that the subject of local monopoly was for the States to deal with and not for the Federal Government; [2] and this was un-

[1] *Cincinnati Enquirer*, April 16, 17, 1873; *The Slaughterhouse Cases, Southern Law Rev.* (1874), III; *The Fourteenth Amendment, ibid.* (1878), N. S., IV.

[2] The *Chicago Tribune*, April 18, 19, 1873, said: "The decision of the Court, while it indirectly sustains this monopoly, does not turn upon this point. The ques-

doubtedly in accord with the temper of the times. The country was tiring of the extensions, and, in some circumstances, usurpations of Federal power which had been the natural outcome of war and of war necessities. The decision marked the end of the great centralizing, Nationalistic movement, and the beginning of a reaction towards the enhancement of the powers of the States. "It is important," said the *Nation*, "as showing that the Court is recovering from the war fever and is getting ready to abandon sentimental canons of construction." [1] "No one for a moment can suppose that the Amendments were ratified with any such revolutionary purpose," said the *Independent;* and the *New York World* said that the gist of the question before the Court was "whether those Amendments had changed the previous relations of the States to the Federal Government. The Court very properly decided that they had not. . . . Nothing is clearer than that the new Amendments, fairly interpreted, leave all the broader relations between the States and the Federal Government unchanged and untouched. . . . The joint design of them all was to bleach the negro into a political white man, to raise the African to the level of the Caucasian in his civil and political rights. . . . Such suits would never have been thought of, if certain shallow people had not gone crazy about the scope of the Fourteenth Amendment. There is no limit to the follies which have clutched at that Amendment for support. The

tion of monopoly was not before the Court at all, as is assumed by the *Missouri Democrat* and some other journals."

[1] *Nation*, April 24, 1873; *Independent*, May 22, 1873; *New York World*, April 16, 1873; *New York Times*, April 16, 1873; *Boston Daily Advertiser*, April 17, 1873; *Philadelphia Press*, April 17, 1873; *Chicago Tribune*, April 18, 19, 1873. William L. Royall in *Southern Law Review* (1878), N. S., IV, said: "The truth is that when this Amendment came before the Court for construction, the minds of patriotic men were filled with alarm at the centralizing tendency of the government . . . and those who wish well to their country looked with sorrowing eyes upon the prospect that the ancient landmarks of the States were to yield before the advancing strides of our imperial despotism."

women's-rights people have claimed that it ordains
female suffrage. A Chicago she-attorney claims 'that
it admits her to the Bar.' Certain New Orleans
butchers assert that it gives them the right to land and
slaughter animals in any part of that city they please.
But the Supreme Court has decided, really, but too fal-
teringly, that its only legal effect is to make full-fledged
citizens of negroes, but leaving the government of the
country in all other respects precisely the same as if the
Constitution had stood as first adopted, and no negro
had ever left his native Africa. . . . That the Court did
not strike a bolder note in declaring this sound doctrine
is to be accounted for by their consciousness that they
were running counter to the impetuous hostility of the
Republican party to the constitutional rights of the
States." The *New York Times* said that it was "calculated to throw the immense moral force of the Court
on the side of rational and careful interpretation of the
rights of the States and those of the Union. It is calculated to maintain, and to add to the respect felt for,
the Court, as being at once scrupulous in its regard for
the Constitution and unambitious of extending its own
jurisdiction. It is also a severe, and we might almost
hope a fatal, blow to that school of constitutional lawyers
who have been engaged, ever since the adoption of the
Fourteenth Amendment, in inventing impossible consequences for that addition to the Constitution." The
New York Tribune termed it "a most important decision", and said that it "set up a barrier against new
attempts to take to the National Government the adjustment of questions legitimately belonging to State
tribunals and Legislatures." The *Philadelphia Press*
said that it would "clear away a tolerably dense legal
fog"; and the *Boston Advertiser* said that a contrary decision "would constitute this Court a perpetual censor

upon all State legislation concerning the rights of its citizens. A doctrine so subversive of ancient and fundamental principles cannot be set up, unless by language too plain to be capable of any other interpretation." The *Chicago Tribune* said that the decision plainly indicated two things: "That the Court will not construe the Constitutional Amendments as upsetting State Governments; and that the people of every State must look to their own protection against monopolies, when they frame their Constitution and elect their Legislatures, and not come to the Courts afterwards and ask them to undo what the Legislative authority has done." Of the soundness of the decision, it said that there could be no doubt: "The Constitutional Amendments, beyond their estoppel of the States from enslaving the negro or depriving him of the privilege of the elective franchise and the other rights of white men, cannot interfere with State-Rights. Any other interpretation of these Amendments would be glaringly in conflict with historical facts. . . . The Federal Government thus becomes absolute in its jurisdiction, and State Governments only exist or exercise their powers by its suffrance. . . . The principal value of this decision grows out of the fact that it clearly and unmistakably defines the province of the Constitutional Amendments, and will hereafter put a quietus upon the thousand and one follies seeking to be legalized by hanging on to the Fourteenth Amendment. . . . The decision has long been needed, as a check upon the centralizing tendencies of the Government and upon the determination of the Administration to enforce its policy and to maintain its power, even at the expense of the constitutional prerogatives of the States. The Supreme Court has not spoken a moment too soon or any too boldly on this subject."

Sentiments like these, widely expressed in the North, the East and the West, afford an interesting illustration of how far the pendulum had swung away from centralization and towards the most extreme State-Rights views held by the Democratic Party before the war.

An opinion similar to that of the daily press was also held by the *American Law Review*, which said: "In its results it is of untold importance to the future relations of the different members of our complex system with the whole. The line which separates the Federal Government from the States, and which of late years has trenched on what are called the reserved rights of the latter, was never so precisely defined as to make trite or tiresome new descriptions of its position; and the interpretation of the Thirteenth, Fourteenth, and Fifteenth Amendments to the Constitution of the United States, which was called for by attempts to apply their letter, if not their spirit, to new states of fact not contemplated by the Congress nor the Legislatures that made them, is the latest and one of the most important acts of government, growing out of the war. It is noteworthy that, while the Executive Department keeps Casey in New Orleans, and sends its soldiers to regulate the internal politics of Louisiana, the Judicial Department remits to the people of that State, to its Courts and Legislature, the custody of the privileges and immunities of its citizens." [1]

The development of the law since the date of this great decision has, on the whole, justified its wisdom, and Judge Miller's opinion has justly been regarded as one of the glorious landmarks of American law. The defeated counsel, John A. Campbell, in after years, admitted that it was "probably best for the country that the case so turned out"; and another Southerner,

[1] *American Law Review* (July, 1873), VII, 732.

John S. Wise, said at the celebration of the Centennial of the Court: "That decision did more than all the battles of the Union to bring order out of chaos. . . . When war had ceased, when blood was stanched, when the victor stood above his vanquished foe with drawn sword, the Supreme Court of this Nation planted its foot and said: This victory is not an annihilation of State Sovereignty but a just interpretation of Federal power." Finally, the words of Judge Moody, in 1908, may well be quoted: "Criticism of the case has never entirely ceased, nor has it ever received universal assent by members of this Court. Undoubtedly, it gave much less effect to the Fourteenth Amendment than some of the public men active in framing it intended, and disappointed many others. On the other hand, if the views of the minority had prevailed, it is easy to see how far the authority and independence of the States would have been diminished, by subjecting all their legislative and judicial acts to correction by the legislative and review by the judicial branch of the National Government." [1]

Had the case been decided otherwise, the States would have largely lost their autonomy and become, as political entities, only of historical interest. If every civil right possessed by a citizen of a State was to receive the protection of the National Judiciary, and if every case involving such a right was to be subject to its review, the States would be placed in a hopelessly subordinate position; and the ultimate authority over the citizens of the State would rest with the National Government. The boundary lines between the States and the National Government would be practically abolished, and the rights of the citizens of each State would be irrevocably

---

[1] *Twining* v. *New Jersey* (1908), 211 U. S. 78; see also *Samuel Freeman Miller*, by Horace Stevens, *Great American Lawyers* (1908), VI.

fixed as of the date of the Fourteenth Amendment, without power in the State to modify them, and with power in the Supreme Court of the Nation to review any State statute asserted to be in violation of such rights, even if such statute affected solely a matter of State policy. Inasmuch as about eight hundred cases have been before the Court since 1873, involving State statutes under the due process clause of the Fourteenth Amendment, it is impossible to conceive of the amount of litigation on which that Court would have been called to pass, if State legislation involving every possible civil right of a State citizen could also have been brought before it under the privilege and immunity clause.[1]

Though the case presented two other questions arising under the Fourteenth Amendment — whether the State legislation deprived the plaintiffs of life, liberty and property without due process, and whether it denied them equal protection of the laws,—the Court's opinion gave to these points very slight attention. As to the first point, the Court simply said : "The argument has not been much pressed. . . . It is sufficient to say that under no construction of that provision that we have

[1] "Never was the Court truer to itself, truer to the Constitution." *Politics and the United States Supreme Court*, by Walter D. Coles, *Amer. Law Rev.* (1893), XXVII.

On the other hand, the opposite view has been expressed by Prof. John W. Burgess in *Political Science and Constitutional Law*, I, 228–230. Writing in 1890, he termed it "an ominously important decision. . . . Coming at the time when the reaction had begun to set in against the pronounced Nationalism of the preceding decade, it partook of the same, and set the direction towards the restoration of that particularism in the domain of civil liberty, from which we suffered so severely before 1861, and from which we are again suffering now. From whatever point of view, I regard the decision . . . from the historical, political, or juristic, it appears to me entirely erroneous. It appears to me to have thrown away the great gain in the domain of civil liberty won by the terrible exertions of the nation in the appeal to arms. I have perfect confidence that the day will come, when it will be seen to be intensely reactionary and will be overturned." See also *Judicial Constitutional Amendment*, by Frederic R. Coudert, *Yale Law Journ.* (1904), XIII; and see Everett V. Abbott, who says in his *Justice and the Modern Law* (1913), that the *Slaughterhouse Case* was "obviously erroneous, and we may safely conclude that it would not be rendered today."

ever seen, or any that we deem admissible, can the re-straint imposed by the State of Louisiana upon the exercise of their trade by the butchers of New Orleans be held to be a deprivation of property within the mean-ing of that provision." In view of later decisions of the Court relative to the extent of the State police power over liberty and property, it may well be doubted whether the decision might not have been otherwise, had the case been argued more fully on the point of due process and had the facts been more clearly stressed; for one of the dissenting Judges, Field, always insisted in subsequent cases, that the question whether the stat-ute involved had any real relation whatsoever to the police power had not been properly presented or con-sidered. As to the other point argued in the case, the Court held that the Amendment grew out of the negro question and was to be interpreted as dealing almost solely with it. "We doubt very much whether any action of a State not directed by way of discrimination against the negroes as a class, or on account of their race, will ever be held to come within the purview of this provision," said Judge Miller. It is interesting to note that this prediction has been utterly falsified; since the protection granted by this clause of the Amendment has been sought by litigants almost wholly in cases involving social and economic State legislation, and very seldom in cases presenting discrimination against negroes.

A particularly fortunate circumstance in the decision of this case was the fact that no criticism could be based on the political or sectional attitude of the Judges. For the Democrat, Judge Field, and the Republican, Chief Justice Chase, both of whom were of the moderate State-Rights school, were joined by the pronouncedly Nationalistic Republican Judges, Bradley and Swayne, in delivering the minority opinion directed against the power of the State; while in favor of the State authority were found three Republicans, Judges Miller, Strong and Hunt, Judge Clifford, a Democrat, and Judge Davis whose political views were tending towards the Democracy.

A practical application of the doctrine of the *Slaughter-house Cases* was made in another case decided at the same time at this Term, *Bradwell* v. *The State*, 16 Wall. 130, in which a refusal of the Supreme Court of Illinois to license a woman to practice law was held not to violate the Fourteenth Amendment, inasmuch as the right to practice law in a State Court was not a privilege or immunity of a citizen of the United States as that term was construed by the Court. Judge Bradley (Swayne and Field concurring) agreed with the result but not with the grounds of the decision, saying (in language probably unacceptable to the women suffragists) that every citizen was not qualified for every calling, and hence that "in view of the peculiar characteristics, destiny and mission of women, it is within the province of the Legislature to ordain what offices, positions and callings shall be filled and discharged by men, and shall receive the benefit of those energies and responsibilities, and that decision and firmness which are presumed to predominate in the sterner sex." [1]

[1] The *Nation* said, April 24, 1873: "It is a rather ludicrous illustration of the character of the woman movement that a prominent female agitator should have seized the opportunity to prove the fitness of her sex for professional life, by taking for her first important case one which she must have known the Court would decide against her, unless she supposed that they were likely to be influenced by personal solicitation and clamor, or else that they were all gone crazy." The *Boston Daily Advertiser*, April 16, 1873, said: "Judge Bradley's opinion seemed to cause no little amusement upon the Bench and on the Bar." See also *Death of Myra Bradwell*, *Amer. Law Rev.* (1896), XXX, 254.

In 1877, the Supreme Court of the United States denied the application of a woman lawyer, Mrs. Belva A. Lockwood, for admission to practice as an Attorney in that Court, the Chief Justice saying, Nov. 6, that he had been instructed by the Court to announce the following decision: "By the uniform practice of the Court,

Two weeks after participating in these momentous decisions, and on the last day of the Term, Chief Justice Chase delivered an opinion in another case, *Osborne* v. *Mobile*, 16 Wall. 479, which again marked the tendency towards a reaction in favor of the State Sovereignty now apparent in the Court; and in upholding a State license tax on express companies doing business partly outside the State, the Chief Justice said that, while it was always difficult to draw the line as to unconstitutionality, "it is as important to leave the rightful powers of the State in respect to taxation unimpaired as to maintain the powers of the Federal Government in their integrity" — a sentiment which should have gratified the strongest believer in the upholding of State-Rights by the Court.[1]

Ten days later, Chase died suddenly, on May 7, 1873. For over two years, he had been in feeble health, due to a paralytic shock. He had served for eight years, through a notable period filled with political passions, in which only the most determined and rugged honesty of mind and purpose could have held the Court to the courageous course which it had pursued. "The nine annual Terms through which he has presided constitute a judicial period of little less importance than that period of constitutional interpretation which it was the

from its organization to the present time, and by the fair construction of its rules, none but men are admitted to practice before it as attorneys and counsellors. This is in accordance with immemorial usage in England, and the law and practice in all the States until within a recent period; and the Court does not feel called upon to make a change, until such a change is required by statute, or a more extended practice in the highest Courts of the States." The result of this was the enactment by Congress of the Act of Feb. 15, 1879, making women eligible for admission to practice. See *Amer. Law Rev.* (1877), XI, 367.

[1] George W. Julian in his *Political Recollections* (1884), said: "After the Presidential election (1872), I went to Washington where I met Chief Justice Chase in the Supreme Court and accepted an invitation to dine with him. He looked so wasted and prematurely old, that I scarcely knew him. He was very genial, however, and our long political talk was exceedingly enjoyable. It seemed to afford him much satisfaction to show me a recently reported dissenting opinion of his, in which he reasserted his favorite principle of States'-rights."

fortune of Chief Justice Marshall to fill," said the *Nation*, in a very just summary of his work. "For many years to come, the decisions of these nine Terms will be referred to by lawyers, legislators and constitutional students more than any others. In them, the late Chief Justice will always appear prominent and never far from right. He brought to the Court no store of legal learning, but he brought comprehensive views, considerable power of generalization and a just sense of constitutional rights and judicial responsibility . . . firm, liberal, and just; and his judicial services will be more highly esteemed when it is more clearly perceived that they uniformly tend to the maintenance of those principles which are the basis of National integrity, personal or political." "Mr. Chase was an ambitious man; he wished to please people and to gain their support, but he would not sacrifice to this object one jot of his convictions," said the *Independent*.[1]

At the opening of the Court on October 23, 1873, resolutions of the Bar were presented, to which Judge Clifford made a noble response. In view of the many political attacks which had been made upon Chase, Clifford's comment is of peculiar interest: "From the first moment he drew the judicial robes around him, he viewed all questions submitted to him as a Judge in the calm atmosphere of the Bench, and with the deliberate consideration of one who feels that he is determining issues for the remote and unknown future of a great people." He spoke especially of the "candor and self control" which enabled him, over the "pride of opinion", to change his views on the subject of legal tender.

It was generally supposed that Chase's successor would be chosen from six men, Benjamin R. Curtis,

[1] *Nation*, May 15, 1873; *Independent*, May 15, 29, 1873. See also *Chief Justice Chase*, by Isaac F. Redfield, *North Amer. Rev.* (April, 1876), CXXII.

William M. Evarts, E. Rockwood Hoar, Lyman Trumbull, William B. Groesbeck or Judge Miller. The latter's appointment would have especially pleased the country; for not only did he possess one of the ablest judicial minds, but his breadth of view and sturdy common sense had particularly commended him.[1] Many papers, like the *Chicago Tribune*, urged the President to appoint such a man as Evarts, to select a jurist from the ablest and most distinguished lawyers, and "to disregard paltry considerations of locality or party service." President Grant, however, after a delay of six months, finally offered the position to his close personal friend and supporter, Roscoe Conkling, the Senator from New York. Writing to him, November 8, 1873, he said: "When the Chief Justiceship became vacant, I immediately looked with anxiety to some one whose appointment would be recognized as entirely fitting and acceptable to the country at large. My own preference went to you at once." Conkling was hardly fitted for the position, either by the extent of his practice or the eminence of his legal acquirements; and probably wisely for his own reputation, he declined the honor.[2] Thereupon, December 1, Grant nominated his Attorney-General, George H. Williams of Oregon. The nomination surprised not only the whole Bar, but the whole country; and the *American Law Review* expressed the general feeling in a temperate article as follows: "Mr. Williams has, within a few years, been called to

---

[1] *Chicago Tribune*, May 8, 16, 1873; *Amer. Law Rev.* (1873), VII, 749, VIII, 159; *Independent*, May 29, 1873.

[2] *Life and Letters of Roscoe Conkling* (1889), by Alfred R. Conkling. *Harper's Weekly* looked more favorably on Conkling's legal attainments than did most of the Bar, saying, Dec. 13, 1873: "Senator Conkling, whose name is now oftenest mentioned in connection with the office, is forty-five years of age, and has quite as much reputation as a lawyer as either of the Chief Justices at the period of their appointment, and is probably a better speaker than any of them were at any period of their career." But see *Nation*, May 22, Oct. 2, 1873; *Independent*, Nov. 27, 1873, presenting a contrary view.

fill, in rapid succession, some of the most exalted places under our government; as a Senator, as a member of the Joint High Commission, and lastly, as the official head of the American Bar, he has had ample opportunity for the display of great talents, and in all these positions he has acquitted himself in such a manner as neither to invite distinguished praise, nor, except in the *Pacific Railroad Case*, to provoke much adverse criticism. If the public have seen in him, as yet, little to justify his selection for the high promotion with which the President has honored him, they have seen nothing to indicate that in his hands the dignity of his great office will be lowered or its powers used unworthily. Indeed, while it would be idle to deny that the nomination was a disappointment to all who had hoped that the seat of Marshall might be filled by a fitting successor, yet that disappointment was tempered by a sense of relief that the country had at least escaped the mortification of seeing in that honored place a man destitute alike of judicial temper and judicial experience, whose only claim to it was derived from active and unscrupulous service as a political partisan. Of Mr. Williams' judicial experience, there is little to say. He was born in 1823, and was admitted to the Bar in New York. Three years afterwards, in 1847, he was elected Judge of the first judicial district of Iowa, and in 1853, he was appointed Chief Justice of Oregon Territory, — an office which he held till 1857, when he declined a reappointment, as he then left the Bench to begin his political career. Such a training does not of necessity give that familiarity with questions of the class upon which the Supreme Court is called to pass, which we have been taught to consider desirable; but it is calculated at least to free the mind from narrowing local influences. We cannot conclude without expressing our regret that the President, in making this, the most important appointment of his Administration, has not improved the opportunity to make such a choice from the eminent lawyers of the country as the people had a right to expect." "It is rather odd, it must be admitted," said the *Nation*, "that the chief of a Court which has to pass on the most complicated controversies of a great commercial country should be chosen from the Bar of a frontier State like Oregon. . . . Mr. Williams, if not able and learned, is laborious, painstaking and respectable; and as things go, his appointment will create a feeling of relief."

The comments of the press were apologetic, many frankly condemnatory, and all indicating clearly that the selection was not regarded as a fit one. "The general feeling of the public is that the President might and should have done better, with such names as Evarts, Cushing, Curtis, Hoar — to say nothing of the present members of the Supreme Court," said the *Independent*, and it expressed the hope that the Senate would refuse to confirm. "The country cannot afford to have any second-rate man, or any one whose qualifications are not beyond dispute, placed at the head of the Supreme Court." "The nomination surprised and disgusted every lawyer in the United States who has the honor of his profession at heart. It fell like a blow upon every respectable member of the Federal Judiciary," said the *Springfield Republican*.[1]

[1] *Amer. Law Rev.* (Jan., 1874), VIII; *Nation*, Dec. 4, 1873; *Independent*, Dec. 11, 25, 1873. Williams had only recently been defeated in the very important *Credit Mobilier Case*, in the Circuit Court in Connecticut, where he had argued against giants of the Bar like Benjamin R. Curtis, William M. Evarts and Sidney Bartlett. "The appearance made by Mr. Williams in this case was very unfortunate, and does not reconcile the Bar throughout the country to his nomination." *Nation*, Dec. 11, 1873; *Springfield Republican*, Jan. 2, 1874; *New York Herald*, Jan 4, 6, 1874, quoting press opinion through the country; *New York Tribune*, Jan. 2, 1874; *New York Evening Post*, Jan. 5, 1874. *Harper's Weekly* was at first favorable to Williams, see Dec. 20, 1873, Jan. 3, 1874.

George H. Williams himself in his *Reminiscences*, in *Yale Law Journ.*, VIII,

Within a week, the sentiment of the country and of the Bar had become so clearly that of protest that the Senate Judiciary Committee, which had at first reported favorably on the nomination, called back its report for further investigation. Williams himself, however, claimed that he had been viciously slandered, and his friends urged confirmation as a vindication. Nevertheless, it was reported in the newspapers that Senator Conkling was to propose a bill in the Senate to abolish the office of Chief Justice as a Presidential appointment, and to make it the duty of the Associate Judges to elect the presiding Chief Justice from their number — such a measure being deemed a happy expedient "to let Mr. Williams down gracefully and save the Republican party the blemish of a scandal." One Senator said that there was no need of a bill to abolish the Chief Justiceship, for the nomination of Williams had already done that. Finally, after the New York Bar Association had passed resolutions protesting the nomination, and stating that it "disappoints the just expectation of the legal profession and does not deserve the approval of the people, for the reason that the candidate proposed is wanting in those qualifications of intellect, experience and reputation which are indispensable to uphold the dignity of the highest National Court, and to maintain general respect for the law in the person of the officer who presides over its administration," [1] President Grant yielded, and, at Williams' own request, withdrew the nomination on January 8, 1874.

written in 1899, said: "I was favorable to the appointment of Justice Miller, but the President was unwilling to discriminate between the Judges on the Bench. . . . Conkling would have made a splendid Chief Justice. . . . The President nominated me without my knowledge or consent. . . . Suffice to say that the reasons for the Republican opposition to me in the Senate were not such as were given to the public by the newspapers."

[1] *New York Tribune*, Jan. 8, 1874, said it hoped the President had learned a lesson. The *New York Herald*, Jan. 7, 8, 1874, said that the President was immensely surprised at the unfavorable reception of Williams' nomination by the country.

Grant's next nomination for Chief Justice caused even more of a surprise and sensation; for on January 9, he nominated another close personal friend, Caleb Cushing. Unlike Williams, Cushing was a man pre-eminently qualified by legal attainments for the position. He had been Attorney-General of the United States, Judge of the Supreme Judicial Court of Massachusetts, and as a profound jurist, he probably excelled either Marshall or Taney or Chase; but he was a man of exceedingly unstable character, and in politics had been successively "a Whig, a Tyler man, a Democrat, a Constitutional Conservative in the confidence of Johnson, and a Republican." While vigorous both mentally and physically, he was, nevertheless, in his seventy-fourth year. His appointment appears to have been largely due to Grant's desire to recognize the services of the American counsel at the Geneva Arbitration, at the head of which had been Cushing and Evarts. While the nomination was objectionable to the Senate, still the completeness with which Cushing fulfilled the legal requirements of the office would probably have led to confirmation, had action been taken at once, even though the Radical Republican press violently protested against such action on this "incongruous" and "objectionable" nomination (as the *Tribune* termed it). "Simply because he is a familiar and serviceable friend, Gen. Grant proposes to place at the head of the Supreme Court, to decide upon questions involving the National sovereignty and the civil rights acquired by the war and consecrated by the late Amendments to the Constitution, a pro-slavery Democrat whose views have been notoriously in opposition to those by virtue of which the war was carried on"; [1] but,

[1] *New York Herald*, Jan. 10, 13, 15, 1874; *New York Tribune*, Jan. 10, 12, 13, 14, 15, 1874; *Harper's Weekly*, Feb. 7, 1874; *Nation*, Jan. 15, 1874.

it added caustically: "The fear of a worse thing may induce the Senate to accept this." So too, the *Nation* said that while admitting that Cushing stood in the front ranks for legal ability and learning, "the President has at last entered the small circle of eminent lawyers, and then with great care has chosen the worst man in it. His entering the circle was a result of the public feeling caused by the appointment of an utterly unfit man of doubtful reputation like Williams; his selection of Mr. Cushing, a consequence of his fixed policy of making public appointments on private considerations. As to Mr. Cushing, it may be said on the one hand, that he is past the age at which the law contemplates a Chief Justice retiring, is of a crafty nature and erratic temperament, and more renowned for shrewdness and learning than respected for talents and integrity; on the other hand, he is more active in body and mind than many a man of half his years, and like Chief Justice Taney may live to be eighty-eight. . . . We believe that it would be found, if the truth were known, that a good deal of the favor with which the nomination was at first received at Washington was due to the fear felt by those who are behind the scenes, that, if he was rejected, a worse man might be produced."

Before the Senate acted, a curious turn of fortune supplied it with an excuse for rejection. Some years previous, the Government had purchased from a Confederate agent, who had fled to Canada, three trunks of Confederate official documents, many of which had been found useful in defense of suits brought by alleged loyal men in the South on claims against the Government. Among these papers, there now was found a letter written by Cushing to Jefferson Davis, as President of the Confederacy, on March 21, 1861, recommending to his attention a young man who was then returning to

Texas. It was a simple, friendly letter and contained no proof of disloyalty on Cushing's part, nor could there be any doubt whatever of Cushing's full sympathy and action with the Union cause, throughout the war. But this letter, "an astounding development" as it was termed, afforded sufficient ground for an outcry against his confirmation; [1] and Grant was forced to withdraw the nomination, on January 13. That Cushing would have made an able Chief Justice was the opinion of Charles Sumner, who supported him and who wrote, January 15, the following interesting commentary: [2]

I should never have nominated or recommended Cushing as Chief Justice, but I was called to consider, his name being before the Senate, if I could vote for his rejection. Now, I know him well, having seen him for the last ten years constantly; and I know his positions on questions in which I am deeply interested. I trust him absolutely, and believe, if the occasion had occurred, he would have vindicated our ideas judicially far better than any probable nominee of Grant. I do not talk in the dark, for I have talked with him on these questions and have seen his sympathy with me. You know that I do not cherish old differences and animosities. How many have I seen advanced to the front who were once bitterly the other way! Knowing Cushing as I did, would it not have been mean and craven for me to turn against him, or to skulk in silence? This is not my way with

[1] The *Springfield Weekly Republican*, Jan. 16, 1874, stated that, according to the Washington correspondent of the *New York Herald*, the letter was found by a clerk, who took it to Gen. Townsend; that it then passed to President Grant through Gen. Belknap; that Grant saw nothing objectionable in it; that then Senator Sargent of California got hold of it; and that, after Senators Boutwell and Conkling had voted for Cushing in Executive Session, Sargent rose and read the note; whereupon, Senators Cameron and Carpenter said that they could not vote for Cushing, and action was postponed so that the President might be communicated with.

[2] *Sumner*, IV, 588, letter to F. W. Bird, Jan. 15, 1874. See *Reports, Reporters and Reporting*, Southern Law Rev. (April, 1879), for a remarkable description of the causes of the rejection of Williams and of Cushing by the Senate. In *Timothy Otis Howe*, by Duane Mowry, *Green Bag* (1903), XV, it is said that Howe, then Senator from Wisconsin, was offered the position of Chief Justice by Grant, but that he declined, not wishing to make a vacancy in the Senate for the election of a Democrat.

friends. Such is not my idea of friendship. But no earthly friendship could make me put in jeopardy our cause. I confess that I am glad of the sensibility shown for the safeguards of Reconstruction. . . . But what shall we do with other possible nominees? Who will vouch for B. R. C.(urtis)? And who will vouch for some accepted Republicans with whom technicality is a peril to principle?

There was now much anxiety on the part of the Bar as to the President's next action. "The country warned by two such experiences will await with unusual alarm Grant's third choice; but there is no further room for surprise," said the *Tribune*. "After the previous shocks, the people are prepared to accept, with something like equanimity, any appointment which should not be scandalous." Those who were close to Grant believed that he would appoint either the Solicitor General, Benjamin H. Bristow of Kentucky, or Morrison R. Waite of Ohio who had been one of the counsel at the Geneva Arbitration. The President fulfilled their expectation by sending to the Senate on January 19, the name of the latter. Waite was confirmed on January 21, by a vote of sixty-three to six. He was then in his fifty-eighth year, and had no previous judicial experience; his legal practice had been chiefly in Ohio; he had been admitted to practice in the Supreme Court during the previous year, but had argued no case there. The appointment was greeted with a sense of relief, but with no enthusiasm.[1] "He is an

[1] *New York Tribune*, Jan. 17, 20, 21, 1874, quoting opinions of the press; *Nation*, Jan. 22, 1874. *Amer. Law Rev.* (April, 1874), VIII, said: "His reputation in Ohio is that of a learned, upright and able lawyer. He presided over the constitutional convention of Ohio at the time of his appointment, and was with Mr. Evarts and Mr. Cushing of counsel for the United States at the Geneva Arbitration, where his services, though unaided by a prestige like theirs, were not less valuable than those of his distinguished associates. He comes to the Bench with no entanglements of personal ambition, and no judicial record with which perforce he must be consistent; and we welcome him, with the assurance that whatever he accomplished for the more full and perfect exposition of the law, will meet with the hearty support of the profession. Chief Justice Waite has had this rare experience, that

honest man and a fair lawyer and that is as much as we can reasonably expect from the President;" "a perfectly respectable man." "The President has with remarkable skill avoided choosing any first rate man. . . . On the whole considering what the President might have done and tried to do, we ought to be very thankful and give Mr. Waite a cordial welcome." Such were some of the newspaper comments. "The general feeling both inside and outside the Bar will be one of profound relief, shading into cordial approbation," said the *Springfield Republican*. "Contrasting what is, with what might have been, we congratulate the President upon his good choice, and the country upon its good fortune." "Waite is that luckiest of all individuals known to the law," said Judge Hoar, "an innocent third party without notice." "I do not hesitate to say that there were scores of lawyers in Ohio who would have been regarded by members of his profession as being as well if not better qualified," said McCulloch. "He was little known outside of the State. He had not been ranked among the great lawyers of the country." [1]

On March 4, 1874, Waite assumed his office, and served for fourteen years, to the great satisfaction of the Bar and of the public. [2]

twice — in being elected to preside over the constitutional convention of Ohio, and in being confirmed as Chief Justice — he has had all the votes of each party in his favor."

[1] *Springfield Weekly Republican*, Jan. 23, 1874; *Men and Manners of Half a Century* (1888), by Hugh McCulloch, 352; *Morrison R. Waite*, by Benjamin Rush Cowen, *Great American Lawyers* (1909), VII.

[2] With Waite's Chief Justiceship, the Court began its lengthened annual service, the beginning of the session in each year having been advanced from the first Monday in December to the second Monday in October, under the provisions of the Act of Jan. 24, 1873.

As to the *Slaughterhouse Case* decision, see esp. articles in *Southern Law Rev.* (1874), IV; *ibid.* (1879), IV, N. S.

For details of the appointment and withdrawal of Cushing, see *The Life of Caleb Cushing* (1923), II, by Claude M. Fuess.

CHAPTER THIRTY-THREE

CHIEF JUSTICE WAITE AND THE FOURTEENTH AMENDMENT

1874–1878

THE years of Waite's Chief Justiceship covered President Grant's second term and the Administrations of Hayes, Garfield, Arthur and Cleveland. The problems of the war and its aftermath had been largely settled before he came upon the Bench; but new and grave economic and social questions now presented themselves. These years saw the growth of the Western States and the immense development of the material resources of the country, and gave rise to a multitude of decisions on subjects of political and industrial importance — the new phases of the regulation of interstate commerce, of the transcontinental railroads and of the telegraph, railroad receiverships, the Granger legislation, control of public utilities and rates, the relation of the States to the liquor traffic, strikes and anarchist riots, polygamy, anti-Chinese legislation, superintendence and status of the Indian wards of the Nation, repudiation of State and municipal debts, the constitutionality of Federal laws enacted for the protection of the negro, the right to sue State officials and the scope of the Eleventh Amendment, the liability of agents of the Federal Government to respond for tortious acts and Federal protection of such agents for acts done in pursuance of their duties. It was fortunate for the country that the molding of its destiny in these various directions fell upon the shoulders of a Court containing Judges of such strength of mind and character and of such breadth of vision as Waite, Miller, Field and Bradley. And the general public confidence in the Court was shown by the fact that, for over ten years after Waite's accession, it was substantially free from serious attack, either in Congress or in the press. When it is recalled that in every year from 1850 to 1873 (with the exception of the five years of the war) there had been Congressional legislation proposed in serious derogation of the Court's powers, the practical immunity from assault which occurred from 1873 to 1884 is a notable feature in its history.

One advantage which accrued to the Court during this period was the comparatively slight change in its membership; for during the first eight years of Waite's Chief Justiceship, from 1873 to 1881, there were but two vacancies. And as more than a majority of the Judges (Waite, Clifford, Field, Miller, Swayne, Bradley and Hunt) continued to serve throughout this period, the policy of the Court remained unusually stable and continuous. In 1875, an effort was made to induce the Chief Justice to allow his name to be considered for the coming Presidential nomination; but he finally refused, writing: [1]

[1] *Toledo Commercial*, Nov. 27, 1875; *New York Times*, Nov. 27, 1875. It appears that Judge Miller entertained similar views as to the propriety of a Judge of the Supreme Court becoming a Presidential candidate, see *Washington Chronicle*, Aug. 28, 1874, stating: "When the name of Justice Miller was urged in certain Republican journals, he very promptly authorized a publication in the *New York Times* that under no circumstances would he allow himself to be a candidate for any political office; that when he accepted his judicial position he abandoned political aspirations, and that he believed it inconsistent with the dignity or purity of the Bench, for Judges to allow themselves to become possible or probable candidates for any political office, however distinguished or honorable." The *Central Law Journal*, Sept. 3, 1874, said: "It is not improbable that the popular confidence in the integrity of the highest Court of the Nation may have been to some extent impaired, within the last few years, by the knowledge that some of its members were possible, or even probable, candidates for the Presidency. Whenever the integrity of the Bench is subject, in any considerable degree, to the misgivings of in-

The office came to me covered with honor, and when I accepted it, my chief duty was not to make it a stepping-stone to something else, but to preserve its purity, and, if possible, make my name as honorable as that of my predecessors.   No man ought to accept this place unless he shall take a vow to leave it as honorable as he found it.   There ought never to be any necessity for rebuilding from below. All addition should be above.   In my judgment, the Constitution might wisely have prohibited the election of a Chief Justice to the Presidency.   Entertaining such a view, could I properly or consistently permit my name to be used for the promotion of a political combination as now suggested? If I should do so, could I at all times and in all cases remain an unbiased Judge in the estimation of the people?

"Chief Justice Waite, who has been talked of as a candidate for the Presidency, has made a really valuable contribution to political literature, not only by declining to allow his name to be used for any such purpose, but by pointing out the gross impropriety of making the Bench of the Supreme Court a stepping-stone to something else," said the *Nation;* and this paper very strikingly pointed out the necessity for the preservation of the utmost possible public confidence in the Court. "The strain, indeed, which the increase and conglomeration of wealth are likely to put on judicial integrity and judicial reputation, is certainly greater than that to which they were exposed through the pressure of royal influence.   The influence of the new temptation is far more subtle, and far less alarming to judicial virtue, and far harder to discover.   The growth of riches is creating powerful bodies of persons whose interest in legislation and judicial decisions is enormous, whose assiduity never tires, and who can often accomplish

telligent hope, it is a public misfortune. The repose of society requires that the popular judgment should rest with confidence in the impartiality of the Bench; and this cannot be, if the Bench comes to be looked upon as a stepping-stone to political preferment."

their object just as well by pretending they are able to corrupt officers as by acknowledging that they have corrupted them. The Rings never admit that any man is pure. . . . The stronger and more daring they grow, the more necessary it is that Courts of Justice should be fortified against them; and a Court of Justice is never fortified as long as it is not above suspicion. The Supreme Court is above suspicion thus far, and there is no such dearth of Presidential candidates as to make it excusable to expose it to even a shadow of a doubt." [1]

The first vacancy during Waite's régime was brought about by the withdrawal of Judge David Davis, who after a service of fifteen years, had been elected Senator from Illinois, January 25, 1877, and who resigned as Judge on March 4, 1877, after the inauguration of President Hayes. His retirement from the Bench was not entirely unwelcome, for his participation in politics and public affairs, particularly his acceptance in 1872 of the nomination for the Presidency by the Labor Reform Party, had caused considerable comment and disapproval.[2] For Davis' place, there were many eager candidates — Senator Isaac P. Christiancy of Michigan, Senator Timothy O. Howe of Wisconsin (who had been prominently mentioned for Chief Justice, before Waite's appointment), John H. Caldwell of Arkansas, Circuit Judge Thomas Drummond of Illinois, Circuit Judge John F. Dillon of Iowa. The

---

[1] *Nation*, Dec. 2, 1875. *Harper's Weekly*, Nov. 27, 1875, also commented on the "essential impropriety of the effort to draw the Supreme Bench into every Presidential contest", and added: "Chief Justice Waite fulfils his duties with quiet dignity. When he took his seat, it was the general conviction that political ambition no longer sat upon the highest Bench, and the country would be spared the spectacle that had pained it."

[2] *Harper's Weekly*, Oct. 28, 1871, stated that it was reported that Davis was to be Democratic candidate for President; *ibid.*, April, 1872, "The Presidential Fever on the Bench." See also *Nation*, Feb. 1, 1877, stating that there should be a Constitutional Amendment making Judges ineligible to political office.

South urged William Frierson Cooper (Chancellor of Tennessee), Herschell V. Johnson of Georgia and Benjamin H. Bristow of Kentucky (ex-Secretary of the Treasury.[1] At one time, President Hayes had definitely decided on Bristow; but as there was strong opposition to him in the Senate, Hayes finally appointed on March 29, 1877, Bristow's law partner, John Marshall Harlan of Kentucky. Harlan was but forty-four years old; he had held no high judicial office, but for four years had been State Attorney-General.[2] Three years elapsed before another vacancy occurred. In 1880, Judge Strong resigned, after a comparatively brief service of ten years. In his place, President Hayes appointed on December 15, 1880, William B. Woods of Georgia, the first Judge from the South since the appointment of Judge Campbell, twenty-eight years before, in 1852. Judge Woods was fifty-six years old and had been United States Circuit Judge for the Fifth Circuit for twelve years.[3]

For the first six years after Waite became Chief Justice, the tendency of the Court was one of reaction from the extreme Nationalistic doctrines which had in general prevailed in the opinions delivered during and after the war. Beginning with the *Slaughterhouse Cases* in 1873, and continuing until about 1880, the decisions showed a marked tendency to uphold the powers of the States. This was particularly apparent in the cases involving the Fourteenth Amendment. Though the main purpose of the framers of that Amendment had been to cut

[1] *New York Tribune*, March 7, 1877; *New York World*, March 7; *Southern Law Rev.* (1877), N. S., III; *Philadelphia Press*, March 16, 1877; *Boston Post*, March 10, 1877, strongly opposed Bristow and urged Drummond.

[2] President Hayes wrote in his diary, March 12, 1878: "The most important appointments are the judicial. They are for life, and the Judiciary of the country concerns all interests, public and private. My appointments will bear examination;" and on March 26, 1878, referring to a bitter attack on him by Senator Howe, Hayes wrote: "His grievance is the failure to appoint him Judge."

[3] Woods was confirmed on Dec. 21, 1880, by a vote of 39 to 8.

down the State police power and to confer on the National Government the right to restrain the States in its exercise, the course of the decisions of the Court had been, with very little variation, to controvert the purpose of the Amendment, to belittle its effect, to magnify the police power and to give it an excessively wide range.[1]

Within a year after Waite's accession, the Court affirmed its adherence to the doctrine of the *Slaughterhouse Case*, by holding in *Minor* v. *Happerset*, 21 Wall. 162, in 1875, that the Fourteenth Amendment did not add to the privileges and immunities of a citizen of the United States, and that suffrage, not being a right belonging to a citizen of the United States, was not infringed by the action of a Missouri official in refusing to register a woman as a voter. Since rights pertaining to a citizen of the United States as such were few in number,[2] and since the Court had already, in 1869, held in *Paul* v. *Virginia*, 8 Wall. 168, that a corporation was not a "citizen", it now became evident that the Privilege and Immunity Clause of the Amendment, as construed by the Court, afforded slight protection to an individual, and no protection to a corporation, affected by oppressive State legislation. Consequently, litigants and their counsel began to take appeals to the Supreme Court, based on the Due Process Clause. Two ques-

---

[1] *Political Science and Constitutional Law* (1890), by John W. Burgess, I, 211 *et seq. A New Nation*, by Hollis R. Bailey, *Harv. Law Rev.* (1895), IX; *Twining* v. *New Jersey* (1908), 211 U. S. 78. It is somewhat difficult to assent to the theory propounded in *Constitutional Opinions of Justice Holmes*, by Felix Frankfurter, *Harv. Law Rev.* (1916), XXIX, 190, in which the writer contends that Judge Field's dissenting opinion in the *Slaughterhouse Cases* narrowing the scope of the State police power gradually became the prevailing doctrine of the Court, " until in *Allgeyer* v. *Louisiana*, 165 U. S. 578, in 1897, we reach the crest of the wave. The break came and the tide turned. The turning point is the dissent in the case of *Lochner* v. *New York*, 198 U. S. 45, 75, in 1905."

[2] See *McCready* v. *Virginia* (1877), 94 U. S. 391, in which a right to plant oysters in a State was held not a right pertaining to a United States citizen; so of a right to bear arms, in *Presser* v. *Illinois* (1886), 116 U. S. 252.

tions were usually presented by these cases — one whether the act by which the State interfered with the citizen constituted a lack of "due process", the other whether such act fell within the legal meaning of the word "deprive" in connection with life, liberty or property. The cases of State interference with life or liberty generally presented only the question of "due process" and involved methods of judicial or administrative procedure, or of regulation or restriction of an individual's vocation or avocation; while State interference with property might involve questions either of "due process" or of "deprivation", and generally arose out of the exercise of the police power or of the power of taxation or eminent domain.[1] Very few of the cases arising under the Amendment, prior to the death of Chief Justice Waite, in 1888, presented the question of the meaning of the word "deprive"; still fewer involved State legislation restrictive or corrective of business or labor conditions or of social activities. It was not until after the accession of Chief Justice Fuller that the great function of the Court, in upholding the progressive and experimental, social and economic legislation of modern times, was developed. Under Chief Justice Waite, the application of this Clause of the Amendment was chiefly involved in cases arising under State tax laws, and in connection with judicial procedure and changes in administrative and judicial statutes of the States. Of the latter class of cases, one of historic interest arose in the *Chicago Anarchists Case, Ex parte Spies*, 123 U. S. 131, in 1887.[2] The former

[1] See *Popular Law Making* (1910), by Frederic J. Stimson, 129.

[2] See *Anarchists Case*, by William H. Dunbar, *Harv. Law Rev.* (1888), I; Note on writ of error in *Fielden's Case, Amer. Law Rev.* (1890), XXIV, 301; see also *Fielden v. Illinois*, 143 U. S. 452, in 1891; see interesting article on *The Due Process Clause and the Substance of Individual Rights*, by Robert P. Reeder, *Amer. Law Reg.* (1910) N. S., XLIX, contending that the clause should not be applied to substantive rights, but only to questions of procedure.

class of cases, presenting the question of due process in tax legislation, arose very early. The first four (between 1876 and 1878) involved Reconstruction legislation in Louisiana on taxation, jury trial and betterment assessment, and the Court sustained the law in each instance. During the next ten years, tax and betterment laws of Connecticut, Pennsylvania, California, New Jersey and Kentucky and New York were sustained.[1]

As an illustration of the inadequate appreciation of the scope of the possibilities of the Fourteenth Amendment, it is interesting to note that, though, between 1868 and 1873, numerous State statutes attempting to tax property outside the State had been held to be unconstitutional, in no one of these cases was the Court's decision based on the ground that such a statute was violative of the Fourteenth Amendment.[2] In each, the Court founded its doctrine on the general underlying principles of government; "where there is jurisdiction neither as to person nor property, the imposition of a tax would be ultra vires and void," said Judge Swayne in *St. Louis* v. *Ferry Company*, 11 Wall. 423. Similarly in the famous case of *Loan Association* v. *Topeka*, 20 Wall. 655, as late as 1875, in which the constitutional validity of a State statute authorizing taxation to pay city bonds issued in aid of a bridge factory corporation was involved, neither the counsel nor the Court invoked the Fourteenth Amendment, though it was clearly applicable. Judge Miller, in holding the statute invalid, made the

---

[1] *Kennard* v. *Louisiana* (1876), 92 U. S. 480; *Walker* v. *Sauvinet* (1876), 92 U. S. 90; *Pearson* v. *Yewdall* (1877), 95 U. S. 294; *Davidson* v. *New Orleans* (1878), 96 U. S. 97; *Kirtland* v. *Hotchkiss* (1879), 100 U. S. 491; *Kelly* v. *Pittsburgh* (1881), 104 U. S. 78; *Hagar* v. *Reclamation District* (1884), 111 U. S. 701; *Provident Institution etc.* v. *Jersey City* (1885), 113 U. S. 506; *Wurts* v. *Hoagland* (1885), 114 U. S. 606; *Spencer* v. *Merchant* (1888), 125 U. S. 337.

[2] See *Railroad Company* v. *Jackson* (1869), 7 Wall. 262; *Cleveland etc. R. R.* v. *Pennsylvania* (1873), 15 Wall. 300; see also *Pennoyer* v. *Neff* (1878), 95 U. S. 714.

classic observation that "to lay, with one hand, the power of the government on the property of the citizen and with the other to bestow it upon favored individuals to aid private enterprises and build up private fortunes, is none the less a robbery because it is done under the forms of law and is called taxation. This is not legislation. It is a decree under legislative forms." But he decided the case, not on the ground that there was lack of "due process", but that there was a limitation on the power of taxation "which grew out of the essential nature of all free governments", — "implied reservations of individual rights, without which the social compact could not exist, and which are respected by all governments entitled to the name."[1] A resort to the general principles of free governments for the foundation of a Federal legal doctrine was a hazy and unsatisfying method of dealing with the case.[2]

That the Court intended to proceed very cautiously in its interpretation of the phrase "due process" was shown by its opinion in *Davidson* v. *New Orleans*, 96 U. S. 97, in 1878, in which Judge Miller stated that: "Apart from the imminent risk of a failure to give any definition which would be at once perspicuous, comprehensive and satisfactory, there is wisdom, we think, in the ascertaining of the intent and application of such an important phrase in the Constitution, by the gradual

[1] Frederic N. Judson in *The Judiciary and the People* (1913), said: "This opinion in the *Loan Association Case*, though rendered after the Fourteenth Amendment, was not based upon the guarantees of individual rights therein contained. We shall see in the discussion of this Amendment that its construction has really rendered academic this invocation of natural law; as both of the instances cited by Judge Miller of violation of domestic and property rights would be annulled under the due process of law."

[2] Three years later, in *Davidson* v. *New Orleans*, 95 U. S. 97, Judge Miller, in a case of writ of error to a State Court said, in declining to hold a State law violative of the Fourteenth Amendment: "It may possibly violate some of those principles of general constitutional law of which we could take jurisdiction, if we were sitting in review of a Circuit Court of the United States, as we were in *Loan Association* v. *Topeka*."

process of judicial inclusion and exclusion, as the cases prosecuted for decision shall require, with the reasoning on which such decision may be founded." He admitted that "if it were possible to define what it is for a State to deprive a person of life, liberty and property without due process of law, in terms which would cover every exercise of power thus forbidden to the State, and exclude those which are not, no more useful construction could be furnished by this or any other Court to any part of the fundamental law." But he warned suitors and counsel that the phrase clearly did not include a case where a party had, by the laws of the State, "a fair trial in a Court of Justice, according to the mode of proceeding applicable to such a case." Gradually, later, the Court's attitude towards the phrase "due process" crystallized into sustaining any proceeding authorized by a State Legislature which was not arbitrary and which in general preserved principles of justice and fairness; and it might finally be summed up in the phrase "giving a square deal." [1] How little inclined the Court was to restrict changes in legal procedure was shown in *Hurtado* v. *California*, 110 U. S. 516, in 1884, in which the Court was confronted with a new and vitally important question — whether the Due Process Clause prevented a State from dispensing with indictment by a grand jury in cases of felony. In a memorable opinion by Judge Matthews, one of the landmarks of our law, it was held that the State powers were not so restricted, and that the phrase "due process" in the Fourteenth Amendment was intended only to secure "those fundamental principles of liberty and justice

---

[1] See *infra*, 466–467, "Amid the labyrinth of decisions . . . the principle that has guided the Court is that the object of the Amendment was to prevent arbitrary action. Action is not arbitrary if the discrimination is founded upon a reasonable basis and has relation to the subject matter of the legislation." *Judicial Construction of the Fourteenth Amendment*, by Judge Francis J. Swayze, *Harv. Law Rev.* (1912), **XXVI**.

which lie at the base of all our civil and political institutions"; but that it was not intended to confine State
legislation simply to those forms and proceedings which
had been sanctioned by usage. "To hold that such a
characteristic is essential to due process of law, would
be to deny every quality of the law but its age, and
to render it incapable of progress or improvement. It
would be to stamp upon our jurisprudence the un-
changeableness attributed to the laws of the Medes and
Persians. . . . This flexibility and capacity for growth
and adaptation is the peculiar boast and excellence of
the common law. . . . Any legal proceeding enforced
by public authority, whether sanctioned by age and custom or newly devised in the discretion of the Legislative
power, in furtherance of the general public good, which
regards and preserves these principles of liberty and
justice, must be held to be due process of law."

On the question as to what action of a State was to be
held to "deprive" a person of his property, the Court
limited very decidedly the scope of the protection which
the Fourteenth Amendment had been expected to provide, by holding in a series of cases that an act which
came within the scope of the State police power could
not be termed a deprivation of property. In the first
case presenting this issue, *Bartemeyer* v. *Iowa*, 18 Wall.
129, which had been argued with the *Slaughterhouse
Cases*, but which was not decided until a year later, the
Court upheld, in 1874, a State liquor law prohibiting
sale of liquor owned at its passage, as a proper exercise
of the police power. Thirteen years later, in 1887, an
even more radical prohibition law was upheld in *Mugler*
v. *Kansas*, 123 U. S. 123, argued by George G. Vest
against Joseph H. Choate; and the Court practically
asserted that statutes passed in the exercise of the State
police power would be upheld in every case unless the

statute "purporting to have been enacted to protect the public health, the public morals, or the public safety has no real or substantial relation to these objects, or is a palpable invasion of rights secured by the fundamental law."[1]

The anti-Chinese ordinances of San Francisco served as a means of further developing the limits of the State police power. In 1885, a municipal ordinance of San Francisco prohibiting laundry work at night, but in reality directed solely against the Chinese, was held by Judge Field to be constitutional, in *Barbier* v. *Connolly*, 113 U. S. 27. It was held that the Fourteenth Amendment was not designed "to interfere with the power of the State, sometimes termed its 'police power', to prescribe regulations to promote the health, peace, morals, education, and good order of the people, and to legislate so as to increase the industries of the State, develop its resources and add to its wealth and prosperity." And in *Soon Hing* v. *Crowley*, 113 U. S. 703, Judge Field, in sustaining a similar ordinance, held that the liberty guaranteed by the Constitution was "liberty regulated by just and impartial laws", and he also held that the motives which inspired the ordinance could not be inquired into by the Courts so long as its enforcement was undertaken without unjust discrimination. A Pennsylvania statute suppressing the manufacture of oleomargarine was held not to constitute a deprivation of either liberty or property, in *Powell* v. *Pennsylvania*, 127 U. S. 678, in 1888. In two cases, the Court sustained State regulation of the operation of railroads as being within the police power, and not a deprivation of property, though imposing considerable expense on the roads, *Railroad Co.* v. *Richmond*, 96 U. S. 521, in 1878, and

---

[1] See also *Foster* v. *Kansas* (1884), 112 U. S. 201; *Schmidt* v. *Cobb* (1886), 119 U. S. 286; *Kidd* v. *Pearson* (1888), 128 U. S. 1.

Missouri Pacific Ry. Co. v. *Humes*, 115 U. S. 512, in 1885.

But it was in the class of cases involving the power of the State to regulate the rates and charges of railroad and other corporations, that the Court most profoundly affected the course of American history. By the *Granger Cases* decided in 1877, the proponents of the Amendment, who had intended to provide a sweeping protection of civil rights against State aggression, saw its operation reduced by judicial construction to a very narrow field. For a correct understanding of the revolutionary and historic decision in these *Granger Cases*, the whole economic history of the country in the eight years following the Civil War must be carefully studied. Briefly stated, the cases originated as follows. During the years 1870–1871, there had swept through the Central West a movement known as the Grange, directed largely against the railroads and other large semi-public corporations such as the grain elevators. Somewhat coincident with the Greenback movement, it was the result of the high rates and undue discriminations by railroads and of the corporate financial excesses, abuses and legislative corruptions of the period.[1] "The State must either absorb the railroads or the railroads will absorb the State" was the Granger cry; and from it there originated radical legislation in Illinois, Wisconsin, Minnesota, Iowa and other of the States of the Central West, fixing maximum rates for the railroads, and (in Illinois) for grain elevators, and imposing heavy fines and triple to quintuple damages, attorneys' fees and costs on any corporation failing to comply with the rates fixed by the State. As described by a leading Western paper

[1] See *The Rise of the Granger Movement, The Outcome of the Granger Movement,* by Charles W. Pierson, *Popular Science Mo.* (1887), XXXII; *Class Struggles in America* (1907), by A. M. Simons; *The Granger Movement* (1913), by Solon Justus Buck.

WAITE AND FOURTEENTH AMENDMENT 575

in 1877 : "This legislation had its origin in the unquestionable extortions of the railways. For several years following the war, the majority of the roads were run on the principle that there must be dividends amounting at least annually to ten per cent." This resulted in the least possible service and in excessive rates, especially where there was no competition. "The accommodation of the public was left out of sight altogether; and the monopoly, standing on the high ground of irrepealable charters and vested privileges, was defiant and unyielding. The outraged popular feeling at last took form in the way of public meetings, conventions and organizations, which in due time resulted in legislative enactments." [1] The significance and importance of this Granger movement was that it aroused the attention of the American people to the fact that there was a railroad problem which free competition could not solve. Moreover, it constituted the first considerable attempt to use representative government as a means of limiting the power of property owners to manage their business in their own way.[2] " The railroad corporations were in fact rapidly assuming a position which could not be tolerated," wrote a prominent authority on railroad problems. "Sheltering themselves behind the Dartmouth College decision, they practically undertook to set even public opinion at defiance. . . . In other words, they thoroughly got it into their heads that they as common carriers were in no way bound to afford equal facilities to all, and indeed that it was in the last degree absurd and unreasonable to expect them to do so.

[1] *Chicago Tribune*, March 3, 1877. "In the matter of railroad abuses, no region has felt the shoe pinch more than has the portion of the West traversed by the great trunk lines system. A few cents' fluctuation in grain rates made all the difference to the farmers between a good and a losing year." *State Legislation Regulating Railroad Traffic*, by Charles C. Savage, *Amer. Law Reg.* (1884), N. S., XXIII.

[2] *Railroads, Their Origin and Problems* (1885), by Charles Francis Adams; *Undercurrents in American Politics* (1915), by Arthur T. Hadley, 68, note.

The Granger method was probably as good a method of approaching men in this frame of mind as could have been devised." [1]

The railroads and investors very reasonably regarded the legislation with the greatest alarm. "That it has effectually destroyed all future railroad enterprises, no one who is acquainted with its effect in money centers will for a moment doubt," wrote the president of one of the roads in April, 1874. To test the validity of these various Granger laws, suits had been promptly instituted by the railroads and other corporations affected, as early as 1871; but for various reasons they were not reached for argument in the Supreme Court until the fall of 1875. Meanwhile, the panic of 1873, combined with unscrupulous manipulation and unskillful management, had left the railroads of the country in a disastrous financial condition. As a Western newspaper said in 1877, describing the changed conditions: "The panic had altered the complexion of the railroad monopoly. It revolutionized the transportation business. It had reduced railway securities and railway credits. It had put one half the railway mileage of the country into practical bankruptcy. . . . Railroads have become an article of merchandise, sold regularly at auction, not by capital stock but according to value, including a preferred portion of debt. The expenses of running railroads have been reduced; dividends are fewer and smaller. Retrenchment has become essential to life. . . . The rates have so fallen that the popular complaint which led to State legislation no longer exists." [2] Since, therefore, the reasons for the Granger laws were

[1] *The Railroad Question* (1899), by William Larrabee (Ex-Governor of Iowa).
[2] *Chicago Tribune*, March 3, 13, 1877. Defaults in railroad bonds prior to 1873 were $134,684,600 by thirty-seven railroad companies; up to 1876 defaults amounted to $814,416,000 by two hundred and one companies. The total bonded railroad debt in 1876 was $2,175,000,000; so that the percentage of default was 30.7%.

disappearing, through reform of their own methods by the railroads, and since the existence of these laws had retarded railroad extension and development by reason of the distrust of investors in railroad securities, and since some of the States had already modified their legislation, there was little belief in the general community that the laws would be upheld by the Court. The conservative and business element, especially in the East, had violently denounced the laws for many years, and had expressed confidence in their overturn by the Court. In 1874, the *Nation*, stating that the matter was soon to come on for argument, said that it was "of the last importance that it should be there determined not only correctly but in such a way as to inspire public confidence in the decision. The Court, for the first time almost in its history, is out of politics. The Judges are not Democrats or Republicans; nor are they divided, as the country once was, on the question of internal improvements. Since the lamentable fiasco of the Legal Tender decision, the Court has shown a marked tendency to conservatism and self-respect. In construing the new Amendments to the Constitution, it has shown a very laudable determination to cling to old and well-settled maxims of interpretation. The country will look with deep interest to its decision in this case."[1] An able writer in the *American Law Review* in 1875, after a thorough review of the constitutional questions, pronounced the State laws to be clearly invalid,[2] and he concluded: "The late war left the average Amer-

---

[1] Editorials in the *Nation:* Sept. 24, 1874, *The Right to Confiscate;* Oct. 29, 1874, *How Will the United States Supreme Court Decide the Granger Cases?* Jan. 28, 1875, *The Farmers and the Supreme Court,* stating that the existence of the Potter Law in Wisconsin affects financing of the railroads and pointing out the inconsistency of the position of the farmers, since "formerly, in order to invalidate bonds issued by counties, they asked that railroads be held purely private enterprises, and now they want them held to be public highways, entitled to only such tolls as the public deems reasonable." See also editorial, Jan. 27, 1876, *The Granger Collapse.*

[2] *The Potter Act at Washington, Amer. Law Rev.* (Jan., 1875), IX.

ican politician with a powerful desire to acquire property from other people, without paying for it. A succession of schemes, too familiar to recapitulate here, have been tried, and, after hard struggles, have been defeated by the honest common sense of the community. We have sufficient faith in the speedy clarification of ideas, among the honest advocates of the so-called Granger laws, to feel confident that this assault upon private property will soon lose their support, and be publicly classed with the exploded fallacies of repudiation and unlimited greenbacks, before the illegality of the Potter law is adjudicated at Washington. When that decision is reached, we believe it will then be received with general favor throughout the whole country. It is necessary, in order to restore public confidence in the rights of private property now severely shaken." Later, it stated that it had never believed "that a movement would succeed in America which was really directed, not against abuses, but against the rights of property. . . . When the Grangers had once proclaimed that their object was to 'fix rates' . . . it was perfectly clear that the Granger movement was rank communism."

Some of the so-called *Granger Cases*, which related to railroad rates, were argued in October and November, 1875; other of the railroad cases, together with the grain elevator case, were argued in January, 1876. Very able counsel appeared in opposition to the constitutionality of the State legislation — amongst them, Orville H. Browning, Frederick T. Frelinghuysen, William M. Evarts, Charles B. Lawrence, B. C. Cook, E. W. Stoughton and John W. Cary. In the principal case, *Munn* v. *Illinois*, 94 U. S. 113, there was involved an Illinois statute, enacted in 1871, in compliance with a provision of the Illinois Constitution (adopted in 1870) requiring the Legislature to pass laws "for the protection of producers, shippers and receivers of grain and produce." This statute, fixing the maximum charges on storage of grain in all grain elevators and public warehouses, was now vigorously attacked as a deprivation of life, liberty and property without due process of law, in violation of the Fourteenth Amendment.

On March 1, 1877, the Court rendered its decision, through Chief Justice Waite. It pointed out that the question presented by this case was the meaning of the word "deprive" as used in the Amendment, and that to determine its signification, "it is necessary to ascertain the effect which usage has given it, when employed in the same or a like connection." After a long historical discussion, the Court finally reached the conclusion that the law was as follows : that when property had become clothed with a public interest, the owner must submit to be controlled by the public for the common good; and the general test as to the character and status of property was stated to be that : "Property does become clothed with a public interest when used in a manner to make it of public consequence, and affect the community at large. When, therefore, one devotes his property to a use in which the public has an interest, he, in effect, grants to the public an interest in that use, and must submit to be controlled by the public for the common good, to the extent of the interest he has thus created." Applying this test to the grain elevator business, the Court pointed out that such business, established twenty years prior, had assumed immense proportions, was practically a monopoly, and affected the whole commerce in grain of seven or eight States of the West. "It is a business in which the whole public has a direct and positive interest. . . . It presents, therefore, a case for the application of a long-known and well-established principle in social science, and this statute

simply extends the law so as to meet this new development of commercial progress." That the power might
be abused, the Court said, was no argument against its
existence. "For protection against abuses by Legislatures, the people must resort to the polls, not to the
Courts." Judge Field alone dissented, stating that it
appeared to him "that the Court holds that property
loses something of its private character when employed
in such a way as to be generally useful. . . . The doctrine . . . that whenever one's property is used in such
a manner as to affect the community at large, it becomes by that fact clothed with a public interest . . .
appears to me to destroy, for all useful purposes, the
efficacy of the constitutional guaranty." He pointed
out that the public had an interest in many private enterprises and business, in the sense in which the Court
had used the term, and that to uphold the right of the
public to regulate the prices and rates of such business
would destroy all rights of private property.

On the same day that the Court sustained the grain
elevator rate law, it upheld the validity of the laws of
Illinois, Wisconsin, Iowa and Minnesota fixing maximum rates for passengers and freights on all railroads
operating in those States.[1] While in these cases the
laws had been claimed not only to violate the Fourteenth Amendment, but also the Commerce Clause and
the Impairment of Obligation of Contract Clause of the
Constitution,[2] the Court held that the State police
power was supreme in respect to regulation of these
public corporations; that the State legislation passed
by virtue of that power did not infringe any provision

---

[1] *Chicago, Burlington & Quincy R. R.* v. *Iowa,* 94 U. S. 155: *Peik* v. *Chicago &
Northwestern R. R.,* 94 U. S. 164; *Chicago, Milwaukee & St. Paul* v. *Ackly,* 94 U. S.
179; *Winona & St. Peter R. R.* v. *Blake,* 94 U. S. 180.

[2] See *Charter Contracts and the Regulation of Rates,* by Charles G. Fenwick, *Mich.
Law Rev.* (1911), IX.

of the Federal Constitution; and that the corporations being "engaged in a public employment affecting the public interest" had been and were subject to legislative control as to rates, from the moment of their incorporation. Judge Field, again dissenting, said that the questions presented were "of the gravest importance, and their solution must materially affect the value of property invested in railroads to the amount of many hundreds of millions, and will have a great influence in encouraging or repelling future investments in such property." He regretted that though the Court had an opportunity to define the limits of the power of a State, "so that on the one hand the property interests of the stockholder would be protected from practical confiscation, and on the other hand, the people would be protected from arbitrary and extortionate charges", the Court had not done this, but had simply applied the doctrine of the *Grain Elevator Case*. The decision, he said, "in its wide sweep practically destroys all the guaranties of the Constitution and of the common law."

Though the decision of the *Granger Cases* did not result in the destruction of private business, as Judge Field prophesied, it was, nevertheless, revolutionary in the history of law; it permanently turned the economic and social development of the United States; and it established forever the power of the States over the corporations and over monopolizing wealth. That these results were fully appreciated at the time is clearly shown in the contemporary newspaper criticism. "These decisions seem to make the broadest possible affirmation of the right of the State to regulate its own commerce, and their importance can hardly be overestimated," said the *New York Tribune*, and in another editorial on "Property and the Supreme Court", it stated that the decision showed that: "The limits within which public opinion is tending to confine the power of expropriation for reasons of public utility are extremely vague and liberal. . . . The statement of these doctrines will, no doubt, startle many people, especially in the Eastern Section of the country, though it is really a logical result of the general principle of expropriation. . . . It is an advanced guard of a sort of enlightened socialism." The *Nation* feared that the decision would give a strong stimulus to threatening, "striking" legislation; it pointed out that investors must pay close attention to the consequences of the decision; it deplored the assumption that "a common carrier is *ex vi termini* a common rogue"; but it finally concluded that though "two years ago, the judgment would have created a good deal of excitement and probably have had a serious effect on the market value of railroad property in the States from which the appeals were taken, since then, the hostility to the railroads, in States in which the legislation fixing rates originated, has disappeared; and the Granger Movement itself, as a political force has collapsed, so that the decision is not now likely to have any marked immediate influence."[1] Other conservative papers of the East hotly attacked the decision as supporting "oppression", "thievery", and "brigandage" by State Legislatures, and as semisocialistic in its tendencies; and their view was summed up, six years later, by a noted jurist, in the statement that the decision in the *Munn Case* "stands a menace to business and material interests of all kinds. No other decision has ever been made in the course of our judicial history — not even excepting the notorious *Dred Scott Case* — which threatens such disastrous consequences to the future welfare and prosperity of the country.

[1] *Nation*, March 8, 1877; see *ibid.*, also March 29, 1877, editorial on "Management of Corporations", describing the panic in England over American railway securities.

. . . The *Elevator Case* directly strikes at the stability of private property, at rights which lie at the very foundation of modern society and civilization. . . . By the demagogues who are conducting the agitation now going on throughout the country, it is confidently appealed to and relied upon to sustain the yet more communistic and destructive legislation which they demand." [1]

It should also be noted that a part of the contemporary criticism of the decision was due to the political antagonisms which had arisen from the actions of the Hayes-Tilden Electoral Commission, on which Judges Bradley, Miller and Strong and Judges Field and Clifford had been sitting, in the month prior to the date of the decision. The decision in the *Granger Cases* was announced by the Court, on March 1, 1877, the day before the election of President Hayes by Congress as a result of the action of that Commission. The partisan excitement caused by this election and by the inauguration of Hayes led some newspapers to assert that public confidence in the Judges had been weakened, and that the country would be the less willing to accept the doctrines laid down by the Court.

The American Bar in general was undoubtedly startled at the sweeping character of the doctrines asserted in the decision.[2] The *American Law Review* termed them "the most important that have ever been made, in defining the power of the States, though the

[1] *The Supreme Court and State Repudiation*, by John Norton Pomeroy, *Amer. Law Rev.* (Sept., 1883), XVII.

[2] In 1886, William P. Wells, in an address on *The Dartmouth College Case* before the American Bar Association, said: "These decisions assert principles which have not received, and as we believe, cannot receive the assent of the most weighty professional opinion." *Amer. Bar Ass. Report* (1886); *Amer. Law Rev.* (1877–78), XI, 602, XII, 359.

For an excellent description of the conditions leading up to these *Granger Cases* and of the decisions themselves, see *The Granger Cases and the Police Power*, by James K. Edsall, *Amer. Bar Ass. Report* (1887).

discussion leaves something to be desired, and the judgment of the Bar seems to be a good deal divided." It admitted, however, that upon the whole, the decision was justified. "It is very true that the 'police power' is open to the suspicion of being a convenient phrase to cover acts, which cannot be justified by the letter of the Constitution, but which are nevertheless deemed necessary. On the other hand . . . if railroads and elevators have a constitutional right to charge what they please, it is just as truly a right to destroy the property of others as a right to make noxious vapors would be. In such cases, it is immaterial that there is no statutory monopoly, so long as there is actual power on one side and actual dependence on the other."

While opposed by the ultra-conservative part of the community, the decisions were highly approved by many prominent Eastern newspapers. The *Springfield Republican* derided the fears of papers like the *Nation*, and highly praised the decision. " This language is a complete answer to those who have claimed that the Grange policy was a policy of spoliation and robbery. It was a harsh policy, a foolish policy in the extreme to which it was carried for a brief season; but it was undertaken on a just principle, the principle that the great agricultural industry of the Western States had a paramount interest in the manner in which railroads and grain elevators were managed." Answering the "old wail, the Wall Street nonsense, that the decision renders railway capital insecure", it pointed out that: "It was the waste, extravagance and inflation of the railroad-building era which have ruined railroad enterprises and rendered capital invested insecure. . . . The idea of the railroads was that, no matter how many rings fattened off from construction accounts, the communities using the roads would be bound to pay the interest on their inflated cost, forever. The people revolted and we don't blame them. Nevertheless, the bankruptcy which has overtaken the railroads of the country since 1873 has been due far less to the Granger legislation than to the collapse of the credit of new railroads from natural causes." Of the practical effect of the decision, it said: "Viewed in the broad and future aspect, the greatly increased strictness of railroad supervision which is the fruit of the Grange era will render railway capital more secure, instead of less so. It secures a degree of publicity of railroad affairs which was never before attempted." Of the immense importance of the legal doctrines enounced, it said: "What seemed 'thieving' and 'brigandage' proves to have been the vindication of the power of the State over all the public interests in its borders, not merely by the decision of the Supreme Court, but by the revolution in the attitude of Legislatures to corporate power — from a servile deference to a sharply critical and almost inquisitorial sovereignty." [1] The *New York Herald* said that "the decision is equivalent to a revolution in the railroad business and . . . has brought safety to the country and salvation to the railroads." It hailed with gratification the settlement of the "right of absolute control by the representatives of the people." "The time had come when either the people would govern the railroads, or the railroads would govern the people. The Supreme Court has come to the rescue, and now both the public and the railroads are safe." It pointed out that the decision had really increased the value of railroad investments, for the railroad financiers must now "cease their incessant warfare for through traffic and turn their attention to their true source of strength and profit, their local business." And it added, with some-

[1] *Springfield Republican*, March 13, 14, 1877; *New York Herald*, March 11, 1877.

what undue optimism: "There is no chance that the people will oppress the railroads. . . . The public is always just, in the long run. Any unfair treatment of railroads by legislation will be fought by the press, and eventually remedied by the people." And the general sentiment of the community was well summed up, later, by the *Independent*: "It is safer and better for the public interest that the final power to determine the toll rates of railroads should be lodged in the Legislature of a State than in a private corporation that is practically a monopoly. . . . The knowledge on their part that the Legislature can interpose its power to correct abuses is well calculated to restrain their cupidity and cause them to deal fairly and properly with the general public." [1]

The newspapers of the West, and especially in the States where the problem of railroad rate regulation had been the most vital question, naturally greeted the decisions with warm approval. The *Chicago Tribune*, while admitting that, because of financial changes, the controversy at one time so angry had lost much of its consequence, stated that, nevertheless: "The decisions of the Court are no less important, as determining the principle of constitutional power. Railroads and the people will now both recognize the principle as settled, and with such unanimity by the Courts as to preclude all probability of a change, during the next half century." [2] And it further pointed out that "no man need

[1] *Independent*, May 17, 1883.

[2] *Chicago Tribune*, March 3, 13, 1877. The *Milwaukee Sentinel*, March 6, 1877, said: "Had it not been for the rush of great events during the past week, no little stir would have been created by the announcement of the decisions. . . . We believe that the *Sentinel* might be excused for glorifying itself at this result. When the subject was being agitated, the infallible press, which term includes such papers as the *Nation*, and the great dailies of New York, Chicago and elsewhere, which assume to be Courts of last resort with respect to all such questions, vehemently protested that no power existed in the Legislatures of the States to pass such laws. The *Sentinel* alone contended for the existence of such a power. . . . In recompense for the bitter denunciation which it thus brought upon itself, it has had the satisfaction of seeing its view endorsed." See *Wisconsin State Journal*, March 8, 1877.

fear for his property in railroads, so long as those rail-roads recognize and act upon the principle that the true interest of both public and corporations is for the latter to depend for their profits on the magnitude of their business, and not upon the extortionate character of their rates." The Western papers further regarded as the most striking and most beneficial phase of the decisions, "the breaking down of the extreme doctrine of vested rights asserted in the *Dartmouth College Case* . . . that parent of many evils, public and private." [1] "The decisions in the *Granger Cases* have not been made too soon. They are the preliminary steps to the uprooting of the doctrine that temporary Legislatures may enact irrepealable or unalterable laws to bind peoples and States indefinitely. These decisions indicate that the reign of chartered monopolies has reached its end, and that we are approaching a recognition of the inalienability of the political or governmental powers of the State. The sooner this recognition is made, the better for the corporations and for the Government. It will cheapen special franchises; it will take from Governments the corrupting inducement to grant perpetual privileges," said the *Chicago Tribune*. The *St. Paul Pioneer Press* said that the decisions "amount to a complete revolution of what, a few years ago, was regarded as the established law of corporations", — a revision due to "the rapidly growing power of these corporations, and the unlimited powers of oppression which they would enjoy, if the logical results of the *Dartmouth College Case* were insisted upon by the Courts." It was pointed out, however, by this newspaper that the result of the decisions might be twofold, and that, while they cured an evil, they also made possible grave injury to the legitimate business. On the one hand, "it is

---

[1] *Chicago Tribune.* March 10, 1877; *St. Paul Pioneer Press*, March 13, 24, 1877.

justly regarded as a great public blessing that the monstrous doctrine has been overthrown, that one Legislature granting a charter with special privileges to a railroad corporation could bind all subsequent Legislatures and build up a power as sovereign as the State itself, and forever beyond the reach of governmental control, and place the public at the mercy of the corporation"; on the other hand, it said, "the decision places the corporations at the mercy of the Legislatures, deprives the capital invested in railroads of all security, and by transferring the control of their property interests from the corporation to the State Legislature, renders it liable to be at any time confiscated by ignorant, capricious or vindictive legislation." To guard against such disastrous effect upon railroad credit, and to protect and encourage legitimate investments of capital, this paper urged that the State Constitution be amended, "so as to limit the power of the Legislature to regulate railroad fares, by the common law principle that they are entitled to reasonable compensation, to be judicially ascertained." [1] Similar views were expressed in the East by the *New York Times*, that "the objection properly held is, that if each State may decide for itself what rates are reasonable, the holders of railroad stocks and bonds can have no guarantee against the application of a measure which might practically amount to con-

[1] *St. Paul Pioneer Press*, March 13, April 5, 1877: "Railroads must be placed on some new foundation in the organic law of the State which, while leaving them subject to legislative control, will place such limitations on legislative regulation of railroads, as shall protect the capital invested in them from being put to hazard or subjected to confiscation by legislative bodies, and from the perpetual peril of legislative passion, ignorance or caprice." See also *ibid.*, editorial, March 24, 1877: "There can be no question that this decision must be disastrous to all the railroad interests of the West; for it places their whole financial foundation on the shifting sands of legislative caprice. How can it be expected that capitalists will invest their money in railroads, when this decision deprives them of any control whatever over their investments, and subjects the capital they put in, to the hazard of being swept away at any moment by the breath of demagoguery? Its calamitous effects are already beginning to manifest itself." *Ibid.*, April 5, 1877.

fiscation, . . . and great properties may be placed at the mercy of a power which is essentially capricious"; and it continued: "The tendency towards meddlesome legislation to the prejudice of the rights and property is rendered more obnoxious, by the failure to exercise a legitimate authority in their behalf." Accordingly, it argued that the States, having now absolute power over the railroads, should enact legislation directed at the evils of railroad financing, and at the policies "fraught with disaster" which had prevailed in financial circles, such as improper leases, stock watering and secrecy of accounts and operations.[1]

Moreover, as has been well pointed out, a more powerful force than that of the Courts was working to protect the railroads, the investors and the public. As soon as the capitalists found that certain States would not allow them to earn interest on railroad investments, they refused to invest more money in those States. No new roads were constructed; the equipment that wore out was not replaced. While the rates at which wheat was carried to market remained low, a great deal of wheat did not get carried to market at all, owing to lack of the physical means of transportation. The Legislatures could prevent high charges, but they could not prevent deficient service; and deficient service was a worse evil than high charges. Under these circumstances the farmers found themselves compelled to allow to the railroads a fair profit.[2] Consequently, the very men who had been most active in passing rate laws, from 1870 to 1874, were the readiest to repeal them, in 1878; and even in the States where the Granger policies had taken firmest root, the sentiment developed rapidly in favor of constructive legislation, which should both

---

[1] *New York Times*, March 29, 1877.
[2] *Undercurrents in American Politics* (1915), by Arthur T. Hadley, 70–71.

protect the public from railroad extortion and abuses, and the railroads from unjust or confiscatory laws. "The laws were finally repealed, not because the people had tired of them or regarded them unwise or unjust," wrote a Granger advocate, "but because it was hoped that the Commission system would prove more efficient. It was offered as a compromise measure, and was accepted as such by the railroad managers, who, in their eagerness to rid themselves of the restrictions imposed by the Granger laws, gave every assurance of complete submission to the requirements of the proposed legislation." [1]   This compromise, embodying the new view of the public in dealing with the railroad problem, took the shape of statutes constituting State Railroad Commissions with power to fix rates after due investigation, and to frame and administer other regulatory provisions.[2] When the validity of such statutes finally came before the Court, the composition of that tribunal had been greatly changed by death and resignation; and the trend of its decisions was far more Nationalistic than it had been in the early years of Waite's Chief Justiceship. Hence, in 1886, when the case of *Stone* v. *Farmers Loan & Trust Co.*, 116 U. S. 307, was decided, the validity of a Mississippi statute providing for a railroad commission with full regulatory powers was sustained; but the Court further held that, even though the railroad charter granted a specific power to the corporation to fix its tolls and charges, this provision was subject to the implied condition that such charges must be reasonable; and for the first time it intimated that the question of what was a reasonable rate might be for the Courts to

---

[1] *The Railroad Question* (1899), by William Larrabee.

[2] *State Legislation Regulating Railroad Traffic*, by Charles C. Savage, *Amer. Law Reg.* (1884), N.S., XXIII; *Constitutionality of Railroad Commissions*, by Charles C. Savage, *Amer. Law Rev.* (1885), XIX; see also *Filley* v. *Railroad* (1881), 5 Fed. 641.

decide, and not (as Waite himself had stated nine years previously) solely for the Legislature. "From what has thus been said it is not to be inferred that this power of limitation or regulation is itself without limit. This power to regulate is not a power to destroy, and limitation is not the equivalent of confiscation. Under pretense of regulating fares and freights, the State cannot require a railroad corporation to carry persons or property without reward; neither can it do that which in law amounts to a taking of private property for public use without just compensation, or without due process of law." By this significant sentence, the corporate interests of the country and the Bar were given warning that the powers which the *Granger Cases* had recognized as possessed by the State Legislatures were by no means as unlimited as had been generally supposed. Two years later, in 1888, in *Dow* v. *Beidelman*, 125 U. S. 680, the Court remarked that the facts of the case did not present "such confiscation as amounts to a taking of property without due process of law." Finally, in 1890, thirteen years after the *Granger Cases*, the Court held in *Chicago, Milwaukee & St. Paul R. R.* v. *Minnesota*, 134 U. S. 418, that not only was the reasonableness of rates a question for ultimate judicial decision, but also that any determination of rates by legislative sanction which deprived a railroad of the right to judicial investigation of their reasonableness was invalid. As has been said, the Court "repudiated the doctrine of uncontrolled rights on the part of the Legislature to make rates, as emphatically as it repudiated the doctrine of uncontrolled rights on the part of agents of the corporation in the *Granger Cases.*" [1] Judges Bradley, Gray and Lamar dissented,

---

[1] *Railway Passenger Rates* (1891), by Arthur T. Hadley; *Railway Transportation, its History and its Law* (1885), by Arthur T. Hadley.

on the ground that the decision overruled the *Granger Cases* (which it undoubtedly did); they held that the only limitations on the power of the Legislature to determine the reasonableness of rates was that its action must constitute "due process", that is, that it must not be arbitrary or fraudulent; and they further held that the Fourteenth Amendment did not forbid the taking of property for public uses without just compensation, but only the taking without due process. While it was generally felt that the opinion of the dissenting Judges was the more correct as a matter of strict law, nevertheless, this decision of the Court in 1890 was undoubtedly the more in accord with the general trend of judicial decisions and the temper of the times.[1] "Nothing has done more to sustain the value of American railroad securities," wrote a well-known jurist in 1895, "or to create greater confidence therein than the knowledge that beyond and above the sovereign power of the State, there is the supreme authority of the Nation over interstate as well as foreign commerce, while beyond and above that is the ultimate final doctrine of vested rights which neither State nor Nation, jointly or separately, can invade or impair."[2] On the other hand, the radical, anti-corporation portion of the community regarded the decision with some anx-

[1] See especially *The Railroad Question* (1899), by William Larrabee; and for a comprehension of the interest in the subject at this time, see *Railroads, Their Origin and Problems* (1878), by Charles Francis Adams; *The Railways, the Farmer and the Public* (1885), by Edward Atkinson; *The People and the Railways* (1888), by James Appleton Morgan; *The Relation of the Railroads to the People*, etc. (1881), by Marshall M. Kirkham; *The Railways and the Republic* (1886), by James F. Hudson; *Railway Secrecy and Trusts* (1890), by John M. Bonham; *The West and the Railroads*, by Sidney Dillon, *North Amer. Rev.* (1891), CLIII; *Railway Rates and Government Control* (1892), by Marshall M. Kirkham.

[2] *Federal Restraints upon State Regulation of Railroad Rates*, by William L. Dana, *Harv. Law Rev.* (1895), IX; and as to this whole railroad rate question, see especially *Contemporary American History* (1914), by Charles B. Beard, 71 *et seq.*; *The Legal, Legislative and Economic Battle over Railroad Rates*, by William W. Cook, *Harv. Law Rev.* (1921), XXXV.

iety. It noted that Judge Brewer, a newly-appointed Judge, had disclaimed all belief in the correctness of the Munn decision and had said that "the paternal theory of government is to me odious."[1] "We have even reason to believe that unless the people of the United States are on the alert, as railway managers always are, there is, with further changes in the personnel of the Court, danger of its deviating from the sound principles of law laid down in its decision in the *Granger Cases*," wrote Governor Larrabee of Iowa.

While that portion of the Court's decision in *Munn* v. *Illinois* which announced the State power to fix corporate rates was, for many years, the point on which public interest centered, it was soon realized by the Bar that the broad views announced, relative to the classes of business subject to the exercise of such power, were likely to have an even more extensive and revolutionary effect upon the course of legal and economic history. In 1888, James Bryce wrote that the *Granger Cases* "evidently represent a different view of the sacredness of private rights and of the powers of a Legislature, from that entertained by Chief Justice Marshall and his contemporaries. They reveal that current of opinion, which now runs strongly in America, against what are called monopolies and the powers of incorporated companies. . . . The Court feels the touch of public opinion."[2] As early as 1891, in an article entitled "A New Constitutional Amendment", it was said: "In a commercial emergency, the oracles of the law have been approached. . . . They now give forth a response, which startles lawyers and laymen. . . . For the first time, it is appreciated that there has lain dormant for a century a vigorous principle of the common law, an element of

[1] Brewer, J., in *Budd* v. *New York*, 143 U. S. 517.
[2] *The American Commonwealth* (1888), by James Bryce, I, 267.

Anglo-Saxon government, which, in the hands of an aristocracy, has often been an instrument of wrong and oppression, and which may, in the hands of the people, effect a despoliation of property owners, surpassing the encroachments of the Crown at the worst periods of English history. . . . Years ago, the Court introduced the Slavery struggle with the Dred Scott decision. To-day, it may be that it has introduced the property struggle, with the decision of *Munn* v. *Illinois*. . . . The principle is one which can only be regarded with anxiety and alarm by conservative minds. Speculation falters in guessing at the uses to which it may be put in experimental legislation by those who believe in the theory of State control. . . . A learned ex-Judge of one of the Federal Courts remarked on reading the opinions : 'If this Government is to endure, the views expressed in the dissenting opinion of Mr. Justice Field must be adopted as the law of the land.' " [1] On the other hand, it was said that though the *Munn Case* seemed to "strike a telling blow at individualism and lends a strong support to the socialistic ideas of the day", yet that "the doctrine may be regarded rather as an effort of individualism to stem the rising tide of combination, rather than as socialistic, a stand made by the individual rather than a move forward of socialism." [2]

In spite of all apprehensions and of Judge Field's foreboding, the State Legislatures refrained for many years from unduly extending their control of private business ; and the Court had occasion to apply the doc-

[1] *A New Constitutional Amendment*, by Charles C. Marshall, *Amer. Law Rev.* (1891), XXIV, stating that the case had been "conspicuous for a torrent of adverse criticism." Everett V. Abbot in *Justice and the Common Law*, in 1913, said : "The *Granger Cases* are still to be justified. . . . Public interest and public right are two very different things."

[2] *The Doctrine of the United States Supreme Court of Property Affected by a Public Interest, and its Tendencies*, by W. Fred Fisher, *Yale Law Journ.* (1895), V.

trine of "business clothed with a public interest", to but few businesses, other than those involved or discussed in the *Granger Cases*.[1] Nevertheless, the right of control still remained where it was placed by the Court in 1877; and the existence of such a right in a State Legislature served as a warning, and as a check on corporate pretensions. Until the year 1914, however, it was generally regarded by law writers that under this decision, any business in which there was a virtual monopoly as a permanent condition inherent in the nature of things, might at any time be subjected by the Legislature to a regulation of its charges, the conditions which might produce such virtual monopoly being various — natural limitations such as available sources of supply, restricted opportunities of access, necessity of conduct of business within a certain location, difficulties in distribution, large scale of the business and absence of effectual substitutes.[2] In 1914, a momentous decision of the Court in a case involving the regulation of fire insurance seemed to broaden the foundation of power

[1] For later discussions of the principles involved, see *Budd* v. *New York* (1892), 143 U. S. 517: *Brass* v. *North Dakota* (1894), 153 U. S. 391; *Covington etc. Turnpike Road Co.* v. *Sandford* (1896), 164 U. S. 578; *Smyth* v. *Ames* (1898), 169 U. S. 466, *Cotting* v. *Kansas City Stockyards Co.* (1901), 183 U. S. 79. It is interesting to note that Judges Brewer and Field dissenting in the *Budd Case*, in 1892, fifteen years after the *Munn Case*, expressed the belief that the Court would abandon its doctrine. Twenty years have elapsed since the *Budd Case*, without any change of the Court's doctrine. See also *Block* v. *Hirsh*, 41 Sup. Ct. Rep., April 18, 1921.

[2] This was practically the explanation of the *Granger Case* given a year later by Judge Bradley in the *Sinking Fund Cases*, 99 U. S. 700, 747, in 1878, "that when an employment or business becomes a matter of such public interest and importance as to create a common charge or burden upon the citizen; in other words, when it becomes a practical monopoly, to which the citizen is compelled to resort, and by means of which a tribute can be exacted from the community, it is subject to regulation by the legislative power." See also *Social Reform and the Constitution* (1911), by Frank J. Goodman; *Increased Control of State Activities by Federal Courts*, by Charles A. Moore, *Proc. Amer. Pol. Science Ass.* (1901); *The Coal Mines and the Public*, by Heman W. Chaplin (1902); *The Coal Mines and the Law*, by Bruce Wyman, *Green Bag* (1902), XIV; *A Word More as to the Coal Mines*, by Heman W. Chaplin, *Green Bag* (1902), XIV; *Control of the Market*, by Bruce Wyman (1901); *Public Service Company Rates and the Fourteenth Amendment*, *Harv. Law Rev.* (1901), XV; *Popular Law Making* (1910), by Frederic J. Stimson.

of State regulation, and to base it purely on the "public
interest" requiring such a regulation, as determined by
the Legislature.[1] But, while the legislative power of
regulation was, until recent years, extended to few additional cases of private business "clothed with a public interest", it was applied to a large number of varied corporate interests the control of which has been justified
by the semi-public nature imparted to them by the possession of special franchises; and the extent of the
authority of the State Legislatures to regulate the
charges of water, gas, electric light, telephone, street
railway, bridge, turnpike, irrigation, ore-carrier and
numbers of other like corporations has been the subject
of a mass of litigation and decisions by the Court.[2]

Having thus, as early as 1877, limited both the Privilege and Immunity Clause and the Due Process Clause
of the Fourteenth Amendment, the Court under Chief
Justice Waite gave also a restricted meaning to the
Denial of the Equal Protection of the Laws Clause.
About ten decisions were rendered involving this portion of the Amendment; but in only one case was the
action of the State found to come within its proscrip-
tion.[3] In *Missouri* v. *Lewis*, 101 U. S. 22, the Court
stated that all that this Clause meant was "that no person or persons shall be denied the same protection of the
laws which is enjoyed by other persons or other classes
in the same place under like circumstances." In 1886, a
case was decided in which the country expected that the

[1] *German Alliance Insurance Co.* v. *Kansas*, 233 U. S. 389; see especially *Business
Jurisprudence*, by Edward A. Adler, *Harv. Law Rev.* (1914), XXVIII; *Labor, Capital and Business at Common Law*, by Edward A. Adler, *ibid.* (1916), XXIX; *Notes
on the Federal Power to Regulate Commodity Prices, Cong. Rec.*, June 16, 1917.

[2] See *Spring Valley Waterworks* v. *Schottler*, 110 U. S. 347, as early as 1884; and
see *Public Service Company Rates and the Fourteenth Amendment*, by Nathan
Mathews, Jr., and William G. Thompson, *Harv. Law Rev.* (1901), XV.

[3] In *Yick Wo* v. *Hopkins* (1886), 118 U. S. 356; see also *Missouri* v. *Lewis* (1880),
101 U. S. 22; *Fire Ass. etc.* v. *New York* (1886), 119 U. S. 110; *Hayes* v. *Missouri*
(1887), 120 U. S. 68; *Dow* v. *Biedelman* (1888), 125 U. S. 680; *Pembina Mining Co.*
v. *Pennsylvania* (1888), 125 U. S. 181.

Court would finally settle a great question long agitated in the community : how far, under the Amendment, a State might impose upon corporations a different system of taxation from that imposed upon individuals. The question had been argued with supreme ability by George F. Edmunds, William M. Evarts and Roscoe Conkling in 1882 and 1886, in two cases involving California taxes on the Southern Pacific Railroads. The decision of the Federal Circuit Courts had been opposed to the corporation tax involved. "If confirmed by the Supreme Court, it will add greatly to the protective usefulness of the Fourteenth Amendment," said the *Independent*. "It will impose a restriction upon the taxing power of the States, adapted to guard against abuses of the power, and promote the general interests of justice among the people." [1] The question was not decided at this time, in 1886, since the case was disposed of on another point; but Judge Field in a concurring opinion stated his regret that the Court had not passed on the question whether, in the tax assessment involved, "an unjust discrimination had been made between the corporation's property and the property of individuals, to its disadvantage, thus subjecting it to an unequal share of the public burdens, and to that extent depriving it of the equal protection of the laws." "At the present day," he said, "nearly all great enterprises are conducted by corporations, and a vast portion of the wealth of the country is in their hands. It is, therefore, of the greatest interest to them, whether their property is subject to the same rules of assessment and taxation as the property of natural persons. . . . The question

[1] *County of San Mateo* v. *Southern Pacific R. R.* (1885), 116 U. S. 138; *Santa Clara County* v. *Southern Pacific R. R.* (1886), 118 U. S. 394; *Independent*, Nov. 30, 1882; *New York Tribune*, Dec. 19, 1882; *New York World*, Jan. 23, 1883, giving high praise to Conkling's argument, and speaking of the "novel aggression of sandhill radicalism upon corporation and capital, as embedded in the Constitution of California."

is of transcendent importance, and it will continue to
come here, until it is authoritatively decided, in harmony with the great Constitutional Amendment, which
insures every person, whatever his position or association, the equal protection of the law; and that necessarily implies freedom from the imposition of unequal
burdens under the same conditions." In later years,
the Court finally disposed of the question by confirming
fully the power of the State to discriminate between
corporations and individuals in methods of taxation.[1]

It is interesting to note that throughout the period of
Chief Justice Waite's term of office, the Court evinced
considerable apprehension at the number of cases which
were being presented to it under the Fourteenth Amendment. As early as 1878, at a time when less than
twenty cases had involved the Amendment, the Court
gave the following warning, through Judge Miller, in
Davidson v. *New Orleans*, 96 U. S. 97: "It is not a little
remarkable, that while this provision has been in the
Constitution of the United States, as a restraint upon
the authority of the Federal Government, for nearly a
century, and while, during all that time, the manner in
which the powers of that Government have been exercised has been watched with jealousy, and subjected
to the most rigid criticism in all its branches, this special
limitation upon its powers has rarely been invoked in
the judicial forum or the more enlarged theater of public
discussion. But while it has been a part of the Constitution, as a restraint upon the power of the States,
only a very few years, the docket of this Court is crowded
with cases in which we are asked to hold that State

[1] It is interesting to note that it was not until the year 1886, in this case of *Santa Clara County* v. *Southern Pacific R. R.*, 118 U. S. 394, that the Court for the first time expressly recognized a corporation to be a "person" within the meaning of the Fourteenth Amendment; and a distinct decision to that effect was made in 1888 in *Pembina etc. Mining Co.* v. *Pennsylvania*, 125 U. S. 181.

Courts and State Legislatures have deprived their own citizens of life, liberty or property without due process of law. There is here abundant evidence that there exists some strange misconception of the scope of this provision as found in the Fourteenth Amendment. In fact, it would seem, from the character of many of the cases before us, and the arguments made in them, that the clause under consideration is looked upon as a means of bringing to the test of the decision of this Court the abstract opinions of every unsuccessful litigant in a State Court of the justice of the decision against him, and of the merits of the legislation on which such a decision may be founded." And in 1885, in *Missouri Pacific Railway Co.* v. *Humes*, 115 U. S. 512, the Court, through Judge Field, expressed "its increased surprise at the continued misconception of the purpose of the provision"; and it again asserted that the "hardship, impolicy, or injustice of State laws is not necessarily an objection to their constitutional validity", and that "this Court is not a harbor where refuge can be found from every act of ill-advised and oppressive State legislation." So long as the State's action is not purely arbitrary, and the enforcement of the law is "attended with the observance of those general rules which our system of jurisprudence prescribes for the security of private rights, the harshness, injustice or oppressive character of the law will not invalidate them as affecting life, liberty or process without due process of law."

These expressions of alarm, while scarcely required by the actual number of cases then presented, were later to be justified. For while less than seventy cases were decided under that Amendment in the sixteen years between 1873 and 1888 inclusive, about seven hundred and twenty-five were so decided in the thirty years from 1888 to 1918.

CHAPTER THIRTY-FOUR

THE CIVIL RIGHTS ACTS

1875–1884

WHILE the scope of the Fourteenth Amendment and the degree of its application to the financial, economic and social legislation of the period were thus being gradually developed by Chief Justice Waite and his Associates, the greatest growth of this branch of the law did not begin until after Waite's death in 1888. The meaning and effect of that Amendment, however, so far as it concerned the negro race for whose protection it had been primarily adopted, were fully and definitely settled by Waite and his Court, in a series of eight cases between 1876 and 1884.[1]

The conservative and restricted interpretation which the Court, under Chief Justice Chase, had placed on the Privilege and Immunity Clause of the Amendment had given a warning to the extreme Reconstructionists

---

[1] It may be noted that the Thirteenth Amendment was proclaimed to be in force, Dec. 18, 1865; the Fourteenth, July 28, 1868; the Fifteenth, March 30, 1870. The statutes passed in enforcement of the Amendments were as follows: the Civil Rights or Enforcement Act of April 9, 1866; the Civil Rights or Enforcement Act of May 31, 1870, Act of Feb. 28, 1871; the Ku Klux Act of April 20, 1871; the Civil Rights Act of March 1, 1875. See *Documentary History of Reconstruction* (1906), by Walter L. Fleming; *The Federal Enforcement Acts*, by William W. Davis, *Studies in Southern History and Politics* (1914); *Essays on the Civil War and Reconstruction* (1904), by William A. Dunning; *Reconstruction, Political and Economic* (1907), by William A. Dunning.

In April, 1872, the Civil Rights Enforcement Act of April 9, 1866 (passed prior to the Fourteenth Amendment) was considered in *Blyew* v. *United States*, 13 Wall. 581, but its constitutionality was not passed upon. This Act had been held constitutional in cases in the Federal Circuits Courts by Judge Swayne, in Kentucky in 1866, and by Chief Justice Chase, in Maryland in 1867, and Horace White said in his *Life of Lyman Trumbull* (1913), 274–275, that: "If either of these cases had been taken to the Supreme Court on appeal at that time, the Civil Rights Act of 1866 would doubtless have been upheld by that body."

that their hopes as to the validity of National Legislative protection to the negro might be dashed. When the additional Civil Rights Act of 1875, which directly penalized discrimination against the negro in public conveyances, hotels and elsewhere, was under debate in Congress, it was pointed out in the press that its validity was highly doubtful. "There can be little doubt," said the *Nation*, "that if it were not for the fatal habit we have fallen into since the war of regarding the Central Government practically above the law and the Constitution, whenever the negro is concerned, the mere suggestion of the constitutional points ought to have killed the bill forever. It is plainly unconstitutional. . . . The Fourteenth Amendment has twice come before the Supreme Court; and on neither of these well-known occasions was the decision of the Court of such a character as to lend much encouragement to those who believe the new Amendments to have introduced very revolutionary principles as to the relations of the States to the General Government. . . . In the light of these decisions, it may safely be inferred that the Supreme Court must look with extreme suspicion upon a law, upsetting the domestic law of States on the subject of schools, of common carriers, of innkeepers, and substituting for them the new and strange system invented by the authors of this bill. In the interest of the negro, we trust that it may never reach the Court. Deeply as we sympathize with his wrongs, we have no expectation or hope of seeing them righted, by hounding on his old masters to acts of violence and lawlessness, by the passage of equally violent and lawless Acts of Congress. The Reconstruction period is ended, and the negro in future will occupy such a position as his industry and sobriety entitle him to. Such bills as the one we have been considering do nothing for him but turn his friends into enemies." [1] The probable action of the Court was thus correctly prophesied; for within a year after this Civil Rights Act of 1875 passed, two decisions were rendered which entirely demolished the Radical Reconstructionist plan of protecting the rights of the negro by direct Federal legislation. On March 27, 1876, the Court, in *United States v. Reese*, 92 U. S. 214, held unconstitutional sections three and four of the earlier Civil Rights Enforcement Act of May 31, 1870, which penalized inspectors in State elections for refusing to receive and count votes and for obstructing any citizen from voting. In an opinion rendered by Chief Justice Waite, the Court held that under the Fifteenth Amendment, Congress had only power to enforce "by appropriate legislation" the right to exemption from discrimination in the exercise of the elective franchise on account of race, color or previous condition of servitude; that the statute in question was not confined to such a limited class of discrimination, but extended broadly to all discriminations and obstructions; that, so construed, it was an unconstitutional interference with the rights of the States. To the old argument against the Court's power to overthrow an Act of Congress, the Chief Justice replied that, while Congress was supreme within its legislative sphere, the Courts, "when called upon in due course of legal proceedings, must annul its encroachments upon the reserved powers of the States and the people." The decision in this case had been long looked for with much anxiety by those opposed to Federal interference in State elections; and the care with which the Court considered the case was shown by

[1] *Nation*, Sept. 17, 1874; see also *The Constitutionality of the Civil Rights Law*, by William Archer Cooke, *Southern Law Rev.* (July, 1875), N.S., I, 193: "There may be a partisan feeling moving the spirit of the law; in a legal sense, we have nothing to fear from it if the same feeling does not invade the Bench."

the fact that while it was argued, January 13, 1875, by Attorney-General Williams and Solicitor-General S. F. Phillips against the veteran Henry Stanbery and B. F. Buckner, the Court reserved its decision for fifteen months. Concomitant with this case, the Court rendered another decision which came as a heavy blow to those who were seeking to protect the negro voter. In *United States* v. *Cruikshank*, 92 U. S. 542, indictments had been found for conspiracy under section six of the statute, which forbade any person "to injure, oppress, threaten or intimidate any citizen, with intent to prevent or hinder his free exercise and enjoyment of any right or privilege granted or secured to him by the Constitution or laws of the United States." Frauds and violence against the negroes in Louisiana State elections were involved in this case; and the defendants were charged with conspiring to prevent citizens in the enjoyment of their right to peaceably assemble with others, of their right to petition for redress of grievances, of their right to bear arms and of their right to vote; also with conspiring to falsely imprison and murder and thus deprive citizens of their lives and liberty without due process of law. Arguments had been heard in March, 1875, the Attorney-General and the Solicitor-General appearing for the Government, and David Dudley Field, Reverdy Johnson, Philip Phillips, John A. Campbell and R. H. Marr for the defendants. The decision, handed down, over a year later, was a notable victory for the defendants' eminent counsel. The Court held that the various rights so set up were not rights which citizens enjoyed by virtue of, or which were secured to them by, the Constitution of the United States; and hence, the actions set forth in the indictment did not come within the purview of the statute. "The right of the people peaceably to assemble for lawful purposes existed long before the adoption of the Constitution . . . and always has been one of the attributes of citizenship under a free government," the Court said. "It was not, therefore, a right granted to the people by the Constitution." This same was held true as to the right to bear arms. With respect to the right to due process, while the Fourteenth Amendment prohibits a State from denying due process, the Amendment does not add anything to the right which a citizen already possessed. "It simply furnishes an additional guaranty as against any encroachment by the States upon the fundamental rights which belong to every citizen as a member of society. . . . The power of the National Government is limited to the enforcement of this guaranty." The right to vote was held to come from the States only, and it was only right of exemption from discrimination on account of race or color under the Fifteenth Amendment, which came from the United States. Inasmuch as the indictments did not allege such discrimination, they could not be upheld. "We may suspect," said the Court, "that race was the cause of the hostility, but it is not so averred."

The practical effect of these decisions was to leave the Federal statutes almost wholly ineffective to protect the negro, in view of the construction of the Amendments adopted by the Court, the lack of adequate legislation in the Southern States, and the extremely limited number of rights which the Court deemed inherent in a citizen of the United States, *as such*, under the Constitution. The decisions, nevertheless, were believed by all, except the Radical opponents of the South, to be wise and to open the door for more sane and liberal methods of dealing with the negro problem in the South. " The fatal defect in the legislation consists in an assumption, which, if it were true, would revolutionize our whole system of government, and as remarked by the Supreme Court, clothe Congress at its discretion with jurisdiction in respect to the entire domain of civil rights heretofore belonging exclusively to the States," said the *Independent*. "To assume State powers as the method of punishing and preventing wrong in the States would be an experiment with our political system that had better be omitted. The ostensible end will not justify it. Southern questions, so far as they are purely State questions, must be left to the States themselves, and to those moral influences which finally shape the course of legislation. The General Government cannot authoritatively deal with them, without producing more evils than it will remedy." [1] It further pointed out that, as the Court did not concur with the underlying theory on which the statutes were based, namely, that the Amendments gave to Congress the power to enact ordinary police legislation penalizing trespasses and crimes committed by individuals in the States, the decision should serve as a warning to Congress to keep within the scope of its constitutional powers. Similarly, the *New York Times* said that the source of a good many blunders made in the legislation was "the tendency to confound the right which one citizen must respect in another with the rights whose enjoyment the State must guarantee to all its citizens. The United States have neither the power nor the obligation to do police duty in the States, a fact which both Judges and Legislators have committed serious mistakes in ignor-

[1] *Independent*, April 6, 13, 1876; *New York Times*, March 8, 29, 1876; *New York Tribune*, March 29, 1876; *New York Herald*, March 28, 1876. *Chicago Tribune*, March 22, 29, 1876; *New York World*, March 28, 1876; *Harper's Weekly*, March 20, 1875, at the time of the argument.

ing." That the decision marked the commencement
of a new era in the exercise of legislative power, and
formed, like the *Slaughterhouse Case* decision, a curb
on the breadth of power theretofore asserted by Congress was ably pointed out by the *New York Tribune.*
"During and since the war, Congress has often acted
as if it were supreme, not merely within but outside
of its constitutional limitations. For some error in
this direction, there was much excuse. A powerful
party persistently tried to make the Constitution of the
United States the left wing of Lee's army. The same
party had so construed the Constitution as to make
it the bulwark of slavery." Under such conditions,
public opinion rejected the theory that in time of war
the Nation did not have full power to defend itself,
and supported Congress in its asserted power to adopt
any measure which it deemed necessary to public welfare. But, after the war, said the *Tribune,* "greedy
and malignant partisanship began to demand, as necessary to the public welfare, measures which were only
needful for the maintenance of unworthy or corrupt
men in power. Of these measures, the Enforcement
Act was one of the most odious. Under it, shameful
abuses have been perpetrated; " and it concluded impressively: "It will now lie dead upon the statute
book, to remind future generations of Americans that
no conceivable abuse of the Constitution by one party
can justify disregard of the Constitution by the other." [1]

The more partisan Republican papers, like the
Chicago Tribune, regarded the decisions with mixed
views. After saying that "for clearness of thought
and trimness of expression" the opinions would "commend the new Chief Justice to the confidence of his
countrymen", it stated that it was "fortunate, in so

[1] See also *Springfield Republican,* March 28, 29, 1876.

far as it restrains Congress from enacting penal legislation in elections beyond the power conferred upon it by the Constitution, the infraction of which would be seriously dangerous, no matter what party were in power. But it is unfortunate, in so far as it may, for a time, open up the opportunity for serious abuses, and perhaps terrorism in the South. . . . The present law, being practically inoperative, will exercise no restraint upon those who desire to interfere with the votes of the colored people at the South. The necessity for further and proper legislation, to carry into effect the provisions of the Fifteenth Amendment, will be another reason, however, for renewed effort on the part of the Republican Party to regain control of Congress." The Democratic papers of course applauded the decision. "It may be described as the final and authoritative enunciation of the doctrine of the duality of the American system of Government and the dual nature of American citizenship," said the *New York World*.

The Radical Reconstructionists and their press saw, with anger and dismay, their whole scheme of legislation overthrown; and, as one party organ said, under the Court's construction, the statute was "only a pretense, keeping a promise to the colored man's ear and breaking it to his hope", and "if the Amendments, intended to secure all citizens of the United States from legal discriminations on account of color, fail to express their intention, the blunder is unprecedented."

But both supporters and opponents agreed in the view that the opinions rendered in the cases proclaimed the new Chief Justice a great lawyer. "Chief Justice Waite, in this decision and in the terms of its utterance, has vindicated his disposition and capacity to emulate the fame of Jay, Marshall and Taney," said the *New York World;* and the *New York Times* said : "So far as they may be regarded as reflecting his influence upon the Court, they afford abundant evidence that his appointment was a judicious one, adding strength and dignity to that great tribunal. . . . The decisions deal with constitutional questions of the highest order, and deal with them in a way to render still more firm the confidence of the people in the impartiality and wisdom of the Court, and to enhance the value of that department of the Government as a means of securing the rights of citizens. It is the highest function of the Supreme Court to interpret the National Constitution."

Viewed in historical perspective now, however, there can be no question that the decisions in these cases were most fortunate. They largely eliminated from National politics the negro question which had so long embittered Congressional debates; they relegated the burden and the duty of protecting the negro to the States, to whom they properly belonged; and they served to restore confidence in the National Court in the Southern States. As an eminent Southern lawyer has said: "When the decision was reached and the prisoners were released, the utmost joy succeeded [in Louisiana], and with it a return of confidence which gave best hopes for the future. . . . What gave satisfaction to the South and strength to bear the affliction in which they found themselves was the determination of the Court to maintain the true character of the Government, and to hold, notwithstanding the excited feeling growing out of the war, that the existence of the States, with powers for domestic and local government including regulation of civil rights, the rights of persons and property, was essential to the perfect working of our complex form of government." [1]

---

[1] *Fifty Years' Experience in Practice at the Bar*, address of Carleton Hunt. LL. B., at a meeting of the Louisiana Bar Association, June 6, 1908.

A year after these decisions, President Hayes partially adopted the policy of leaving the South to work out its problems free from National interference, by withdrawing the regular army from Louisiana and South Carolina in April, 1877. An attempt by the Democratic Congress to repeal the Civil Rights Enforcement Acts was vetoed in 1877 by the President; but the Democratic success in the election of 1878 brought about a two years' fight for such repeal, and a bill was actually passed, as a rider to an Appropriation Act, forbidding the United States marshals to use military forces in the execution of election laws. It was not until 1894, under President Cleveland, that the chief obnoxious provisions of the Enforcement Acts were finally abolished.

Meanwhile, the extent to which the Fourteenth Amendment could be invoked for the protection of the negro was being further explained by other decisions of the Court. In 1880, in *Strauder* v. *West Virginia*, 100 U. S. 303, the Court reiterated that the chief design of the Amendment "was to protect an emancipated race and to strike down all possible legal discriminations"; and it held that a State statute which confined jury duty to white persons violated the Amendment, by failing to secure to negroes the equal protection of the laws guaranteed to them by the National law and Constitution. The validity of the section of the Civil Rights Act, which authorized removal into the United States Courts when the equal rights of a citizen were denied in the State Courts, was upheld by the Court on the ground that, as the Amendment provided that Congress might enforce it by appropriate legislation, removal of cases into United States Courts had been "an acknowledged mode of protecting rights, ever since the foundation of the government." [1] That Congress still possessed some power of protecting the negro against discrimination was shown in *Ex parte Virginia*, 100 U. S. 339, in 1880, a case which involved the actions of one Coles, a County Court Judge of Virginia held in custody on a Federal indictment charging him with excluding negroes from jury service. The Court held that he was not entitled to release on a petition for habeas corpus to the Judge of the United States District Court. "A State acts by its legislative, its executive or its judicial authorities," said the Court. "It can act in no other way. The Constitutional provision, therefore, must mean that no agency of the State, or of the officers or agents by whom its powers are exerted, shall deny to any person within its jurisdiction the equal protection of the law." Since the Amendment was enacted to secure equal rights, and since Congress was given power to enforce its provisions against the State, "such legislation must act upon persons, not upon the abstract thing denominated a State, but upon the persons who are the agents of the State in the denial of the rights which were intended to be secured." Strong dissents were filed by Judges Field and Clifford, who denied that Congress had the power "to exercise coercive authority over judicial officers of the States in the discharge of their duties under the State laws." They claimed that such power would reduce the States "to a humiliating and degrading dependence upon the Central Government; engender constant irritations, and destroy that domestic tranquillity which it was one of the objects of the Constitution to ensure. . . . Those who regard the independence of the States in all their re-

[1] See the *Nation*, March 4, 1880; see also *Virginia* v. *Rives*, 100 U. S. 313, limiting the operation of the Removals Act to action of a State official occurring prior to trial; *Bush* v. *Kentucky*, 107 U. S. 110.

served powers . . . cannot fail to view with the gravest apprehension for the future" an indictment of a State Judge in a Federal Court.[1] If this decision, said the *Nation*, "is to be carried to its logical results, (it) implies a long, and we may add, an unexpected stride in the direction of centralization."

In *Neal* v. *Delaware*, 103 U. S. 370, the Court held that the Fifteenth Amendment *ipso facto* rendered inoperative the provisions of the Constitution and laws of Delaware, in force at the time of its adoption, restricting jurors to white persons qualified to vote; and that the absence of any statute, in conflict with the Fifteenth Amendment since its adoption, constituted a presumption "that the State recognizes as its plain duty" the binding force of the Amendment. The Court found, therefore, that there was no denial of equality by the State, and hence no right of the defendant to remove his case into a United States Court. But on the facts presented, showing an actual discrimination against negroes in the drawing of the jury by State officers, it held that "the refusal of the State Court to redress the wrong by them committed was a denial of a right secured to the prisoner by the Constitution and laws of the United States," and it reversed the judgment of the State Court.

[1] The final outcome of this case was interestingly commented on by the *Nation*, March 25, 1880: "One of the Virginia Judges, Judge Hill, whose indictment for not summoning negroes on juries has been sustained by the late decision of the United States Supreme Court has been, at Lynchburg, tried before Judge Rives and a jury composed of ten white and two colored men, and acquitted without argument, the evidence against him having completely broken down. We presume that what brought him into trouble was the difficulty which exists in many parts of the South of finding negroes mentally and morally qualified to sit on juries. Those who think the chief end of Courts of law is the dispensing of justice between litigants and between the State and criminals, and not the exemplification of social and political equality will feel that a certain amount of discretion in making up juries must be lodged somewhere, and that if those who are engaged in the duty and give the necessary guarantees as to character, are to be pursued criminally whenever their use of discretion does not satisfy local politicians, far more valuable things than any man's right to be summoned on a jury will suffer seriously."

In 1883, however, the Court rendered two decisions which practically put an end to attempts on the part of the Federal Government to settle the negro question by means of indictments in the Federal Courts. In *United States* v. *Harris*, 106 U. S. 629, which involved the constitutionality of section two of the Ku Klux Act of April 20, 1871, making it criminal for two or more persons to conspire or go in disguise upon the highway or upon another's premises for the purpose of depriving any persons of the equal protection of the laws and privileges and immunities under the laws, the Court held the section invalid, as unwarranted by the provisions of any of the Amendments, which, in granting to Congress the power to enforce their provisions, did not authorize Congress to legislate directly as to the acts of private persons.[1] In the *Civil Rights Cases*, 109 U. S. 3, decided October 15, 1883, the Civil Rights Act of March 1, 1875, was finally held unconstitutional. This statute had made it a crime for any person to deny full and equal enjoyment of the accommodation of inns, public conveyances and places of public amusement. The Court, through Judge Bradley, held the law to be beyond the power of Congress, and again stated that the Fourteenth Amendment did not invest Congress with power to legislate on subjects which are within the domain of State legislation, or to create a code of municipal law for the regulation of private

[1] The *Nation*, April 20, 1871, at the time of the passage of this Ku Klux Act had accurately predicted the decision of the Court as to its validity, and had said : "Its central idea develops itself into a plan by which the United States Courts may exercise full criminal and civil jurisdiction over any and all acts of violence to the person and property of private citizens; by which, in short, Congress and the National tribunals may assume and wield a complete police power throughout the States." See *contra*, *Amer. Law Rev.* (1870), V, 249. After the decision of the case, the *Nation* said, Aug. 31, 1882, that for its "disloyal" view of the subject in 1871, "we were severely criticised, at the time, by those who, like the late Mr. Sumner, thought that what the country wanted was 'the centralization of liberty' and 'the imperialism of equal rights.' Nevertheless, the view we advanced is precisely that now laid down by the Supreme Court."

rights, but only authorized Congress to enforce its provisions by "appropriate legislation for correcting the effect of such prohibited State laws and State acts and thus to render them effectually null, void and innocuous." In other words, the legislation which Congress was authorized to adopt was "not general legislation upon the rights of the citizen, but corrective legislation." Congress could not step into the domain of local jurisprudence and lay down rules for the conduct of individuals in society towards each other. The Court further held that refusal of accommodation to a negro could not be justly regarded as imposing any badge of slavery or servitude upon him; and it said that "it would be running the slavery argument into the ground, to make it apply to every act of discrimination which a person may see fit to make as to the guest he will entertain"; hence the statute could not be upheld as a proper means of enforcing the Thirteenth Amendment. An interesting and vivacious dissenting opinion was given by Judge Harlan, who regarded the statute as clearly valid under the Thirteenth Amendment, and said that he could not "resist the conclusion that the substance and spirit of the recent Amendments of the Constitution have been sacrificed by a subtle and ingenious verbal criticism."

"The decision settles the point forever, that the Fourteenth Amendment merely adds new limitations upon State action to those already existing in the Constitution, and does not change in any way the fundamental structure of the Government," said the *Nation*; and the *Independent* said: "It is important for both the State and the Federal Government to keep within the sphere assigned to it. In this way, and in no other way, can our duplicate system of government be harmoniously and successfully worked;" and it stated that though "several leading colored men have expressed great indignation and disappointment, the Court is clearly right. The question as to the class of rights involved belongs exclusively to the States. There is the proper place to look for a remedy against any abuse of these rights." [1] *Harper's Weekly* said that the decision commended itself to every intelligent mind and showed the groundlessness of the fears, recently expressed, of a "dangerous centralizing tendency in the government." It stated that the decision was in strict accord with "the true doctrine of National supremacy, with distinctly defined State authority — one of the great traditions of the Supreme Court"; and that since the "long and terrible Civil War sprang from the dogma of State sovereignty, invoked to protect and perpetuate slavery, it was natural that, at its close, the tendency to magnify the National authority should have been very strong, and especially to defend the victims of slavery. . . . In a calmer time, the laws passed under that humane impulse are reviewed, and when found to be incompatible with strict constitutional authority, they are set aside. It is another illustration of the singular wisdom of our constitutional system." "The Court has been serving a useful purpose in thus undoing the work of Congress," said the *New York Times*; and it urged this memorable word of warning to all those who were inclined to look to the National Government for aid against local abuses, which should be cured locally. "The fact is, that, so long as we have State governments, within their field of action we cannot by National authority prevent the consequences of misgovernment. The people of the State are dependent on their own civilized ideas and

---

[1] *Independent*, Feb. 1, Oct. 25, 1883; *New York World*, Jan. 23, 1883; *Harper's Weekly*, Feb. 3, 1883; *New York Times*, Jan. 24, 1883; *New York Herald*, Jan. 30, 1883.

habits for the benefits of a civilized administration of laws."

On March 3, 1884, in *Ex parte Yarborough*, 110 U. S. 651, that portion of the Civil Rights Acts punishing conspiracy "to injure, oppress, threaten or intimidate any citizen in the free exercise or enjoyment of any right or privilege secured to him by the Constitution or laws of the United States", was upheld as a valid exercise of the power granted to Congress to enforce the Fifteenth Amendment — an Amendment which the Court said "does, *proprio vigore*, substantially confer on the negro the right to vote, and Congress has the power to protect and enforce that right." But the Court further held that, independently of this Amendment, it was "essential to the healthy organization of the government itself", that Congress should have the power to protect the citizens in the exercise of such constitutional rights.[1] The case in question involved serious interference in Georgia with negro-voting at a Congressional election; but, as Judge Miller pointed out, there were other forms of interference with elections fully as serious, against which Congress must have power to protect the Government, viz., bribery:

If the recurrence of such acts as these prisoners stand convicted of are too common in one quarter of the country, and give omen of danger from lawless violence, the free use of money in elections, arising from the vast growth of recent wealth in other quarters, presents equal cause for anxiety. If the Government of the United States has within its constitutional domain no authority to provide against these evils, if the very sources of power may be poisoned by cor-

---

[1] "The Ku Klux Klan gets no encouragement from the Supreme Court. It was decided yesterday, in the well known Ku Klux Cases that the Federal Government has power to prevent fraud and intimidation at elections. The most remarkable thing about these cases is that the question should ever have been raised." *New York Tribune*, March 4, 1884. But for a limitation of the power of Congress in respect to punishment of election offenses, see *James* v. *Bowman*, 190 U. S. 127, in 1903.

ruption or controlled by violence and outrage, without legal
restraint, then, indeed, is the country in danger, and its
best powers, its highest purposes, the hopes which it inspires
and the love which enshrines it, are at the mercy of the
combinations of those who respect no right but brute
force on the one hand, and unprincipled corruptionists on
the other.

This case in 1884 was the last in which the scope of
the Civil War Amendments was considered while Waite
was Chief Justice; and the decisions of the Court, in
the twenty years since Waite's death, have not added
substantially to the doctrines established. That the
interpretation given by the Court to the Amendments
was a surprise to many statesmen, and a disappointment to those who saw, or thought they saw, in them
a more comprehensive chart of liberty, has been frequently pointed out. "It was information that was
new to the framers . . . when they were told that by
those Amendments it was not intended to add anything
to the rights of one citizen as against another; that
it was not designed to enable Congress to legislate
affirmatively or directly for the protection of civil
rights, but only to use corrective and restraining
measures as against the States so as to secure to the
black race the right to be dealt with as equals. It
was information that was new, as well as unwelcome,
that the provisions creating National citizenship and
prohibiting the abridgement of the privileges thereof
. . . added nothing to existing rights, but simply provided additional guarantees for such as already existed."
Nevertheless, as a historian of the Court has well said:
"Now, after the lapse of years, when the temper and
spirit in which the text of the Amendments was penned
have cooled and the views of men have matured, it
is seen that the value of the Court as the great con-

servative department of the Government was never greater than then." [1]

As a result of the above cases, the effect of the Amendments upon the negro race may be summed up as follows. The first section of the Fourteenth Amendment is a prohibitory measure, and the prohibitions operate against the States only, and not against acts of private persons; the fifth section only gives Congress power, by general legislation, to enforce these prohibitions, and Congress may, within bounds, provide the modes of redress against individuals when a State has violated the prohibitions; and though Congress cannot act directly against the States, Congress may regulate the method of appeal to United States Courts by any person whose right under the Amendment has been affected by action of the States. As to the Fifteenth Amendment, though theoretically it is capable of being enforced to a certain extent by direct Congressional action, Congress has, in fact, taken few steps towards such enforcement; and only a few acts of a State or of a State officer have been found by the Courts to violate it. Meanwhile, the Southern States, by constitutional and statutory provisions, which have been in general upheld by the Court, have found methods of limiting the negro right to vote.[2] Of the

---

[1] See Address of Samuel Shellabarger at the Bar Meeting, on March 26, 1888, on the death of Chief Justice Waite, 126 U. S. app.; *History of the Supreme Court of the United States*, by Hampton L. Carson (1889), 485.

[2] *The Fourteenth Amendment and the States* (1912), by Charles Wallace Collins, 67; *Is the Fifteenth Amendment Void?* by A. W. Mason, *Harv. Law Rev.* (1910), XXIII; *Legislative and Judicial History of the Fifteenth Amendment* (1909), by John Mabry Mathews; *The Fifteenth Amendment*, by William C. Coleman, *Columbia Law Rev.* (1910), X; *Constitutionality of Race Distinctions and the Baltimore Negro Segregation Case*, ibid. (1911), XI. See *American Political Ideas* (1920), by Charles E. Merriam: "In 1890, Mississippi began the process of constitutional limitation of the right to vote which has been carried on until the colored vote in the South has been rendered almost ineffective. This result has been brought about by means of educational requirements, property qualifications and the poll tax. The so-called 'grandfather' clauses were instituted and the whites excluded by other provisions were included by stipulating that descendants of those who

Enforcement Laws enacted in the Reconstruction period, only a small part remain even nominally in force. Of the forty-seven sections of the three statutes, forty-two have either been repealed directly, or rendered obsolete by such laws as the Disabilities Act of 1898, or declared invalid by the Court; and as has been well said, they have disappeared, because "they were in fact out of joint with the times. They did not square with public consciousness, either North or South. They belonged logically to a more arbitrary period. They fitted a condition of war, not of peace, and suggested autocracy, rather than a democracy." [1]

While the Court was thus greatly restricting the National authority under the War Amendments to the Constitution, its trend towards the enlargement of the field and importance of the sovereignty of the States and especially of the State police power was also clearly marked by the doctrine which it now announced in cases arising under the Impairment of Obligation of Contract Clause of the Constitution. As early as 1878, in *Beer Co.* v. *Massachusetts*, 97 U. S. 25, it had shown that it was prepared to go to great lengths in sustaining State legislation interfering with corporate charters; but it was not until 1880 that, in *Stone* v. *Mississippi*, 101 U. S. 814, it rendered the decision which greatly modified the doctrines of the *Dartmouth College Case* as to the degree of control over its cor-

---

were voters in the year 1867, might be registered." South Carolina adopted such provisions in 1895, Louisiana in 1898, Alabama in 1901, North Carolina and Virginia in 1902, Georgia in 1908. In general, the Supreme Court has upheld these provisions; see *Williams* v. *Mississippi* (1898), 170 U. S. 213; *Giles* v. *Harris* (1903), 189 U. S. 475. In *Guinn* v. *United States* (1917), 238 U. S. 347, however, the "grandfather" clause of Oklahoma was held unconstitutional. See also *The Right of the Federal Courts to Punish Offenders against the Ballot Box*, by D. H. Pingrey, *Amer. Law Reg.* (1890), XXXVII; *Racial Discrimination*, by D. H. Pingrey, *ibid.* (1892), XL.

[1] *The Federal Enforcement Acts*, by William W. Davis, *Studies on Southern History and Politics* (1914).

porations retained by a State; and while admitting
that the doctrines of that case had "become so im-
bedded in the jurisprudence of the United States as
to make them, to all intents and purposes, a part of
the Constitution itself", it nevertheless read into those
doctrines an exception which, never before so distinctly
announced, produced a profound effect on the relations of the State toward its corporations.[1] The facts
of the case were as follows: lotteries had been illegal
in Mississippi prior to 1867, but in that year the "carpet-bag" government chartered a lottery corporation
in consideration of the payment of further sums and a
percentage of its receipts; when the people of Mississippi adopted their Constitution in 1868, "with a
view to the resumption of their political rights as
one of the United States", they embodied in it a
prohibition of all lotteries. This Constitution, it was
claimed by the corporation, was an impairment of the
obligation of its contract with the State. The case
was argued by Philip Phillips against A. M. Clayton
and Van H. Manning. The Court, in a notable opinion by Chief Justice Waite, held that the existence of
any contract which might be impaired depended on the
authority of the Legislature to bind the State; and
that while the Legislature might make irrevocable
grants of property and franchises, it could not "bargain away the public health or the public morals",
i.e. its police power. "Government is organized with
a view to their preservation, and cannot divest itself
of the power to provide for them. . . . The contracts
which the Constitution protects are those that relate
to property rights, not governmental." Hence, it

[1] See previous cases, *Boyd* v. *Alabama* (1877), 94 U. S. 645; *Beer Co.* v. *Massachusetts* (1878), 97 U. S. 25, and *Northwestern Fertilizing Co.* v. *Hyde Park* (1878),
97 U. S. 659; see, however, *New Orleans* v. *Houston* (1886), 119 U. S. 265, where
the Louisiana Constitution itself protected the lottery.

held that a corporation accepting a lottery charter only acquired a permit or license, which was subject to future legislative or constitutional control or withdrawal, if deemed advisable or necessary for the public morality. This doctrine that a State Legislature might not, by contract, limit the future exercise of the State police power over the subject matter of the contract was again set forth in *Butchers Union etc. Co.* v. *Crescent City Co.*, 111 U. S. 746, in 1884. In this case, Louisiana had in 1869 granted to a slaughterhouse company a twenty-five year monopoly (a monopoly which the Court had sustained in the *Slaughterhouse Cases* in 1873), but under the provisions of the State Constitution of 1879, which forbade the existence of a monopoly, the State granted slaughtering rights to another corporation. The Court held that, since the original monopoly had been created by the State in its exercise of the police power, the State might, in behalf of public health, alter its view and destroy such a monopoly, and that its action did not impair the obligation of the contract contained in its prior law. This decision undoubtedly went to great extremes in upholding the authority of the States over rights granted by corporate charters; and it was viewed with apprehension by the conservative portion of the public. "The Supreme Court of the United States has just made a new anti-monopoly decision which is of great importance in its bearing on rights of property and contracts under the Constitution," said the *Nation*. "The curious thing in this case is, that there is nothing on the face of the opinion to show that the public health in New Orleans would be at all safer with the slaughterhouse business in the hands of several companies, than in the hands of one. The Constitutional Amendment, moreover, is distinctly directed at the 'monopoly' feature of the contract; and, as far as we can see, the only effect of the case is to give any State the right to destroy the obligation of the most solemn contracts, provided the Judges at Washington can extract from its action some shadow of a reason, growing out of what they regard as the cause of 'health' or 'morals.' This is a wide definition of the police power, and gives the Supreme Court and the State Legislatures a power of interference with contracts and property, such as nobody ever dreamed they possessed. Take this decision in connection with that on the legal tender question, and compare the two. Is it not plain that the Judges have adopted a latitudinarian system of construction, which may make lawyers and laymen alike look forward, with less apprehension than they otherwise would, to the infusion of some new blood into the Court, as the consequence of a change of parties?" [1]

[1] *Nation*, Aug. 28, 1884. It is interesting to note that it took thirteen years before the Ku Klux Law was held invalid. An earlier attempt to test the law in a case from South Carolina failed by reason of defect in procedure, see *United States* v. *Avery* (1872), 13 Wall. 251; *Boston Post*, March 22, 1872. As to the first case brought to enforce this law, see *Albany Law Journ.*, III, July 8, 1871.

As to later cases, involving rights of negroes, see *Pace* v. *Alabama* (1882), 106 U. S. 583; *Bush* v. *Kentucky* (1883), 107 U. S. 110; *Mills* v. *Green* (1895), 159 U. S. 651; *Gibson* v. *Mississippi* (1896), 162 U. S. 565; *Murray* v. *Louisiana* (1896), 163 U. S. 101; *Plessy* v. *Ferguson* (1896), 163 U. S. 537; *Cummings* v. *Board* (1899), 175 U. S. 528; *Wiley* v. *Sinkler* (1900), 179 U. S. 58; *Carter* v. *Texas* (1900), 177 U. S. 442; *Swafford* v. *Templeton* (1902), 185 U. S. 487; *Torrence* v. *Florida* (1902), 188 U. S. 519; *Brownfield* v. *South Carolina* (1902), 189 U. S. 426; *Giles* v. *Harris* (1903), 189 U. S. 475; *Rogers* v. *Alabama* (1904), 192 U. S. 26; *Giles* v. *Teasley* (1904), 193 U. S. 146; *Martin* v. *Texas* (1905), 200 U. S. 316; *Hodges* v. *United States* (1906), 203 U. S. 81; *Berea College* v. *Kentucky* (1908), 211 U. S. 45; *Thomas* v. *Texas* (1908), 213 U. S. 278; *Marbles* v. *Creecy* (1909), 215 U. S. 63; *Franklin* v. *South Carolina* (1910), 218 U. S. 161; *McCabe* v. *A. T. & S. F. R. R.* (1914), 235 U. S. 151; *Buchanan* v. *Warley* (1917), 245 U. S. 60.

CHAPTER THIRTY-FIVE

INCREASE OF NATIONALISM

1881–1887

AFTER a period of seven years without substantial alteration of the personnel of the Court, three changes occurred in the years 1881 and 1882, which seem to have had a profound effect upon the future tendency of its decisions. On January 21, 1881, Judge Swayne resigned, at the comparatively youthful age of seventy-six, and after nineteen years of judicial service;[1] and on March 14, 1881, President Garfield appointed in his place Stanley Matthews of Ohio. Matthews was fifty-six years old; he had served as a United States Attorney under President Buchanan, and had been a Republican Senator from Ohio from 1877 to 1879. He had been previously appointed to a place on the Court by President Hayes in the closing days of his Administration; but the Senate, for political reasons and because of newspaper charges that he was too closely allied with corporate interests, had failed to confirm him. This second nomination was again the subject of great criticism and opposition; but the Senate, finding insufficient grounds for any of the charges, confirmed his appointment on May 12, by the close vote of twenty-four to twenty-three. As has so often happened, later events proved Matthews to be a wise and

---

[1] See note on the death of Swayne, June 8, 1884, *Amer. Law Rev.* (1884), XVIII, 693.

THE SUPREME COURT IN 1882

Standing: Wood, Gray, Harlan, Blatchford. *Seated:* Bradley, Miller, Chief Justice Waite, Field, Matthews.

upright jurist, and he "lived to hear his detractors sound his praise." [1]

In the same year, on July 25, 1881, Judge Clifford died, at the age of seventy-eight after twenty-three years on the Bench; [2] and in his place President Arthur appointed Horace Gray of Massachusetts, on December 19, 1881. Gray was confirmed, the next day, by a vote of fifty-one to five; he was then fifty-three years of age, and had served as Judge of the Supreme Judicial Court of Massachusetts since 1864, and as Chief Justice since 1873. [3] In 1882, Judge Hunt, who had been incapacitated from serving on the Bench for the past five years, resigned; and President Arthur, to the surprise of most of the Bar, filled the vacant position by the appointment of Roscoe Conkling of New York, on February 24, 1882. This action raised

[1] Hayes sent the name of Matthews to the Senate, Jan. 26, 1881. See violent editorials against Matthews in the *New York Sun*, Jan. 27, Feb. 1, 2, 4, 9, 11, 12, 16, 19, March 7, 19, 23, 24, 29, May 12, 13, 1881; see also *Stanley Matthews*, by Charles T. Grove, in *Great American Lawyers* (1908), VII. In *Life of Rutherford Birchard Hayes* (1914), by Charles R. Williams, II, 327, note, it is said that "the appointment of Matthews was received by a large part of the press with a storm of disapproval because Mr. Matthews had been a corporation attorney. Mr. Matthews proved on the Bench that Mr. Hayes' judgment of his character and fitness was altogether sound."

[2] The *Nation*, July 28, 1881, said as to Clifford: "His mental faculties had been impaired for some time previous to his death, and his place on the Bench has been practically vacant, in consequence. He refused to resign, however, in the hope that the election of a Democratic President might render certain the appointment of a Democratic successor. . . . As a Judge, his industry and conscientious accuracy were remarkable, as well as the rigidity of his political convictions. . . . His partisanship, however, was chiefly the result of the narrow legal view of the relation of the States to the General Government which the old-fashioned New England Democrat always took, and bore no resemblance to the bitter and unscrupulous spirit of faction with which the politics of our day threatens to taint the Judiciary." The *Boston Daily Advertiser*, July 26, 1881, said as to Clifford: "Without brilliant qualities, he had what was far more serviceable, unfailing good sense, clear judgment, boundless capacity for labor, a capacious memory and great love of justice." See also *Amer. Law Rev.* (1881), XV, 686. For a violent expression of the views of Clifford's political opponents, see letters of "Warrington" in *Springfield Weekly Republican*, April 1, 1868, Dec. 18, 1869.

[3] See *Amer. Law Rev.* (1882), XVI, 137; the *Nation*, Dec. 22, 1881, spoke of Gray's "conspicuous fitness for the position"; and see especially tributes to Gray after his death by Charles Francis Adams and by George F. Hoar, in *Mass. Hist. Soc. Proc.*, 2d Ser., XVI, XVIII.

a storm of disapproval. "No nomination could have surprised the country more," said *Harper's Weekly.* "The nomination of Gray has been received with universal approval, that of Conkling with universal amazement," and it stated that Conkling's career as a politician had not inspired the country with confidence in him as a magistrate, and that he was "singularly unfitted to be a Judge." "Mr. Conkling is a lawyer only in name," said the *Nation*, "and must make a poor Judge. He has passed his life in politics. . . . Legal learning, he has not. . . . The mystery is deepened when we reflect that he has been offered the Chief Justiceship of the same Court once before, and declined it as beneath his notice." While this criticism of Conkling's legal ability was probably unfair, nevertheless, his political career had not won for him the confidence of the community. Conkling, however, after being confirmed by the Senate on March 2, by a vote of thirty-nine to twelve, settled the controversy by declining the position. Thereupon, on March 13, 1882, President Arthur, to the complete satisfaction of the Bar, appointed Samuel Blatchford of New York. Blatchford, who was confirmed, March 27, was sixty-two years of age, and had been Judge of the United States District and Circuit Courts in New York since 1867.[1]

Judge Woods died in 1881, and to succeed him President Cleveland appointed Lucius Quintus Cincinnatus Lamar of Mississippi, on December 6, 1887. After opposition in the Senate, Lamar was confirmed, on January 16, 1888, by a vote of thirty-two to twenty-eight; he was sixty-two years of age, and though he had no judicial experience, he had been a professor

[1] *Harper's Weekly*, March 11, 26, 1882; *Nation*, March 2, 1882; *Amer. Law Rev.* (1882), XVI, 335, for article on Blatchford; see also *Nation*, April 23, 1885, "The President and the Judiciary."

of law, a United States Senator from 1875 to 1885, and Secretary of the Interior for the previous three years. It may also be noted that he was the first Democrat appointed on the Court since Judge Field in 1862, and the first Judge who had served in the Confederate Army.

With these changes in its composition, the Court began to show a decided reaction from the policy which it had maintained from 1872 to 1880, with respect to the sovereign powers of the States. A marked disposition to enhance the powers of the National Government by a liberal construction of the Constitution, and to widen the scope of the jurisdiction and powers of the National Judiciary became increasingly apparent; and this distinctly Nationalistic era in its history continued for the next ten years.

With respect to one class of cases, however, those involving the Commerce Clause of the Constitution, the Court had shown from the outset a tendency to limit strictly the sovereignty of the States. With the immense development of the railroad and telegraph systems of the country, the increased facility for the doing of interstate business and the multiplication of commercial corporations after the Civil War, this Clause of the Constitution began to assume an importance in the history of the law which it had never before attained. Up to 1840, the number of cases in Court requiring its construction had only been five, and up to 1860 only twenty, while the subjects of legislation involved had been practically confined to navigation, immigration, slavery and the sale of liquor. By 1870, the number had increased to thirty, in 1880 to seventy-seven, and in 1890 to one hundred forty-eight, involving a great variety of topics — State action relative to peddlers, liquor, railroads, and telegraphs and immigration and quarantine (both seaboard and internal), and manifold forms of taxation.[1]

Under Chief Justice Chase, only a few interstate commerce cases had been considered, but in each the Court had taken a pronounced stand in favor of State regulation; and in the case which had the most important effect upon the business of the country, the Court had relegated to the States complete control over the great insurance companies of the country, by holding in *Paul* v. *Virginia*, 8 Wall. 168, in 1869, that the negotiation of insurance policies and contracts and the business of insurance was not "commerce" within the purview of the Constitution.

From the beginning of Chief Justice Waite's term of office, however, the Court reversed its policy and upheld the National authority over commerce in practically every case of importance coming before it. In 1873, the Commerce Clause was held to impose considerable limitation on the taxing powers of the States. In *Philadelphia & Reading R. R.* v. *Pennsylvania*, 15 Wall. 232, a tonnage freight tax was held invalid as being a regulation of interstate commerce, when applied to freight originating or carried outside the State: "It is of National importance," said Judge Strong, "that over that subject there should be but one regulating power, for if one State can directly tax persons or property passing through it, or tax them indirectly by levying a tax upon their transportation, every other may; and thus commercial intercourse between States remote from each other may be destroyed. The produce of Western States may thus be effectually excluded from Eastern markets, for though it might bear the imposition of a single tax, it would be crushed under

[1] These figures are taken from *The Commerce Clause of the Federal Constitution* (1898), E. Parmalee Prentice and John G. Egan.

the load of many." The effect of this decision upon the development of the great transcontinental trade, and the unrestricted movement of wheat, ore and coal in this country cannot be overestimated. At the same time, the Court, by its decision in the second case of *Philadelphia & Reading Railroad* v. *Pennsylvania*, 15 Wall. 232, showed that it was not inclined to defeat the State's power to tax, any further than was absolutely necessary; and it upheld a State tax on the gross receipts of railroads, notwithstanding that such receipts were made up in part from freights transported in interstate commerce. "It is not everything that affects commerce that amounts to a regulation of it within the meaning of the Constitution," said Judge Strong. "The ultimate effect of the tax may be to increase cost of transportation, but it is not a tax on transportation itself." Judges Miller, Field and Hunt, however, dissented, holding that a tax on gross receipts was in fact for the privilege of transportation within the border of the States, and they laid down "the broad proposition that by no device or evasion, by no form of statutory words, can a State compel citizens of other States to pay to it a tax, contribution or toll, for the privilege of having their goods transported through that State" and that "the full recognition of this principle is essential to the harmonious future of this country. . . . The interstate commerce today far exceeds in value that which is foreign, and it is of immense importance that it should not be shackled by restrictions imposed by any State in order to place on others the burden of supporting its own government, as was done in the days of the helpless Confederation."

In 1876, the Court held unconstitutional a Missouri statute imposing a license tax on persons peddling goods of foreign origin, in *Welton* v. *Missouri*, 91 U. S. 275; but it still declined to lay down any general rule as to the extent of the scope of the interstate commerce clause, saying that: "It would be premature to state any rule which would be universal in its application to determine when the commercial power of the Federal Government over a commodity has ceased, and the power of the State has commenced. It is sufficient to hold now that the commercial power continues until the commodity has ceased to be the subject of discriminating legislation by reason of its foreign character." [1] In the same year, the Court greatly enhanced the powers of the National Government by upholding the exclusive right of Congress to regulate the subject of immigration as a question of National concern susceptible only of a uniform rule; and in *Henderson* v. *New York* and *Chy Lung* v. *Freeman*, 92 U. S. 259 and 275, it held invalid laws of New York, Louisiana and California, affecting that subject. [2] One result of this decision was the enactment of the first general Immigration law, the Act of August 3, 1882; another was the aggravation of the Anti-Chinese agitation in California, and the disturbances arising out of this troublesome question. The *Nation* indorsed the Court's action, as "sound and wholesome", and stated that since the question of immigration was National, not local, and since State regulation produced confusion and injustice, Congress alone must regulate; but it pointed

[1] In connection with the class of discriminatory legislation involved in this case, see *Commercial Retaliation Between the States*, by Edward B. Whitney, *Amer. Law Rev.* (1885), XIX.

[2] The *New York World*, March 22, 26, 1896, opposed the decision as an infringement of the right of the State to protect itself against pauperism. The *New York Times*, March 21, 24, 29, pointed out that since immigration had been held to be a subject which concerned all the States, Federal legislation was now an imperative duty and that Congress must "take some action giving to the States the protection which they cannot provide for themselves." See also *Edye* v. *Robertson*, 112 U. S. 580.

out that "it appears from the Anti-Chinese outbreak on the Pacific Coast that the decision is felt in California to be a blow at the defences erected by that State against the Mongolian invasion." [1] The continuance of the agitation produced by this decision resulted in the negotiation of the Treaty with China of October 5, 1881, and in the later Chinese Exclusion Acts of 1882, 1884 and 1888. A similar class of State statutes restricting commerce was held invalid in *Inman Steamship Co.* v. *Tinker*, 94 U. S. 238, in 1877, in which a tonnage fee imposed by New York on all vessels entering its ports was held to violate the prohibition of the Constitution against the imposition of a tonnage tax by a State. Judge Swayne, stating that the Commerce Clauses of the Constitution "had their origin in a wise and salutary policy", said that: "The confusion and mischiefs that would ensue if this restriction were removed are too obvious to require comment. The lesson upon the subject taught by the law before us is an impressive one." In 1878, a Missouri statute prohibiting the entry into the State between certain months of the year of any Texas or Mexican cattle, was held in *Hannibal & St. Joseph R. R.* v. *Husen*, 95 U. S. 465, to be an interference with interstate commerce. The Court said that a State "may not, under the cover of exerting its police powers, substantially prohibit or burden either foreign or interstate commerce . . . beyond what is absolutely necessary for its self-protection", and it stated that, as the range of the police powers "sometimes comes very near to the field committed by the Constitution to Congress, it is the duty of the Court to guard vigilantly against any needless intrusion." This case, in connection with the case on the immigra-

---

[1] See also *Foster* v. *New Orleans* (1877), 94 U. S. 246.

tion law of New York decided two years prior, showed a distinct advance in the disposition of the Court to restrict the doctrine of the application of the State police power in matters of interstate commerce. A Reconstruction statute of Louisiana requiring all carriers to give equal rights in their conveyances to all persons without discrimination on account of race or color was held invalid, as a regulation of interstate commerce, in *Hall* v. *De Cuir*, 95 U. S. 485, the Court saying, "if the public good requires such legislation, it must come from Congress and not from the States." The right of a State to grant a charter to a telegraph corporation to the exclusion of another such corporation doing an interstate business was denied, in 1878, in *Pensacola Telegraph Co.* v. *Western Union Telegraph Co.*, 96 U. S. 1, Chief Justice Waite saying that the powers granted to Congress by the Constitution "are not confined to the instrumentalities of commerce, of the postal service known or in use when the Constitution was adopted, but they keep pace with the progress of the country, and adapt themselves to the new developments of time and circumstances. . . . As they were intrusted to the General Government for the good of the Nation, it is not only the right but the duty of Congress to see to it that intercourse among the States and the transmission of intelligence are not obstructed or unnecessarily encumbered by State legislation. The electric telegraph marks an epoch in the progress of time. In a little more than a quarter of a century it has changed the habits of business, and become one of the necessities of commerce. It is indispensable as a means of intercommunication, but especially is it so in commercial transactions." The fact that Congress, by the Act of July 24, 1866, had authorized any telegraph company to construct its line along any of the military or post roads of the United States was held to "amount to a prohibition of all State monopolies in this particular." This decision, said a prominent law journal "promises to rank in importance with *Gibbons* v. *Ogden* and the *Dartmouth College Case*."[1] The limits on the power of a State to interfere with interstate commerce carried on by drummers were set forth in an able opinion rendered in 1887 in *Robbins* v. *Shelby County Taxing District*, 120 U. S. 489, in which it was stated that "in the matter of interstate commerce the United States are but one country and must be subject to one system of regulations and not to a multitude of systems." The right of a State to prohibit the introduction of liquor from other States by a common carrier was denied in *Bowman* v. *Chicago and Northwestern Ry. Co.*, 125 U. S. 465, in 1888, and an Iowa statute on the subject was held invalid as a regulation of interstate commerce.

Each of these cases marked an advance of National power, and the "centralizing tendencies of the Court" were the subject of much comment by law writers.[2] In fact, there was substantially but one class of cases affecting interstate commerce in which the State powers were upheld, namely, those involving the right of the State to control its bridges, wharves and ferries.[3]

[1] *Southern Law Rev.* (1878), N. S., IV.

[2] *Recent Centralizing Tendencies in the Supreme Court*, by Frederic P. Powers, *Pol. Sci. Qu.* (1890), V.

[3] See *Gilman* v. *Philadelphia* (1866), 3 Wall. 713; *Escanaba, etc. Co.* v. *Chicago, Wiggins Ferry Co.* v. *East St. Louis*, and *Parkersburg, etc. Co.* v. *Parkersburg* (1883), 107 U. S. 678, 365, 691; *Willamette Iron Bridge Co.* v. *Hatch* (1888), 125 U. S. 1; and see also *Miller* v. *New York* (1883), 109 U. S. 385, in which a bill in equity to enjoin the construction of the Brooklyn Bridge on the ground of its being an obstruction to navigation was dismissed, the Court holding that Congress had authorized the structure and that Congress had plenary power over navigation under the Commerce Clause. For an interesting commentary on the Court's recession from its position in the *Wheeling Bridge Case*, in favor of the rights of the States, see *The Commerce Clause and the State*, by A H. Wintersteen, *Amer. Law Reg.* (1889), XXXVII.

None of the Court's decisions on the Commerce Clause, however, so seriously impaired the power of the State or so potently affected the future of the country, as its final decision, in 1886, settling the extent of the control of a State over railroad rates. While National regulation of all railroad rates by virtue of the power contained in the Commerce Clause had been urged by eminent jurists as early as the year 1874, as the only adequate remedy for the evils then existing in the railroad situation, the country and the Courts were not as yet prepared for what then seemed a radical measure.[1] Nevertheless, that such National control was contemplated as an eventual possibility was very interestingly shown in an opinion rendered by Judge Bradley in 1875, in *Baltimore and Ohio R. R.* v. *Maryland*, 21 Wall. 456. In this case, the railroad charter granting a right to build a branch between Baltimore and Washington, fixed the maximum fare at $2.50 and provided that one fifth of the passenger receipts should be paid to the State. It was urged by the railroad that this was an unconstitutional interference with interstate commerce. The Court, however, held to the contrary, and in answer to the query, "has the public no remedy against such exorbitant fares and freights exacted by a State or by a railroad or steamship company?" said that if any "system of exactions be established in these States, as materially to impede the

---

[1] *Railroad Legislation*, by C. F. Adams, Jr., *Amer. Law Rev.* (1867), II; *Legislative Control of Railroads*, by S. S. Wallace, *Southern Law Rev.* (1874), III; *Legislative Control of Railroads*, by F. L. Wells, *Western Jurist* (1877), XII, saying: "Of late years, this has become a very important question, accidents on railroads and abuses practiced are becoming so numerous." *The Federal Power over Commerce* (1892), by W. D. Lewis; *The Commerce Clause of the Constitution* (1908), by F. H. Cooke; *Law of Interstate Commerce* (1905), by F. N. Judson; *Regulation of Commerce under the Federal Constitution* (1907), by T. H. Calvert; *American Railroad Rates* (1905), by Walter C. Noyes; *Law of Railroad Rates Regulation* (1905), by Joseph H. and Bruce Wyman. *The Legal, Legislative and Economic Battle over Railroad Rates*, by William W. Cook, *Harv. Law Rev.* (1921), XXXV

passage of produce, merchandise, or travel from one part of the country to another, it is hardly to be supposed that the case is a *casus omissus* in the Constitution. Commercially, this is but one country, and intercourse between all its parts should be as free as due compensation to the carrier interest will allow. This is demanded by the 'general welfare' and is dictated by the spirit of the Constitution at least. Any local interference with it will demand from the National Legislature the exercise of all the just powers with which it is clothed." Whether Congress had the power "to establish and facilitate the means of communication between the different parts of the country, and thus to counteract the apprehended impediments referred to," Judge Bradley said, "is a question which has exercised the profoundest minds of the country. . . . But it is to be hoped that no occasion will ever arise to call for any general exercise of such a power, if it exists." [1] In 1877, in the *Granger Cases*, Chief Justice Waite had distinctly stated that until Congress should act, the States had plenary control of rates, whether interstate or intrastate, "so far as they are of domestic concern", and that State regulation of railroads operating within a State was valid, "even though it may indirectly affect those without the State." While the correctness of this statement was widely doubted by many members of the Bar, and received strong criticism in legal journals, it was accepted generally as the law, until, in 1886, in *Wabash, St. Louis and Pacific Ry. Co.* v. *Illinois*, 118 U. S. 557, the Court practically overruled the *Granger Cases* in this respect, and held that a State had no power to regulate railroad rates for transportation within the

[1] See especially *Regulation of Interstate Traffic on Railways by Congress*, by Isaac F. Redfield, *Amer. Law Reg.* (1874), XXII; *Federal Restraints upon State Regulation of Railroad Rates*, by William F. Dana, *Harv. Law Rev.* (1895), IX.

State, when that transportation was a part of an interstate commerce transaction. "The decision is of the
highest importance," said the *Nation*. "It utterly
demolishes the pretension of State Legislatures and
railroad commissions. . . . The principles are very
clearly stated, and are fundamental to the existence
of the Union and to the existence of trade." [1] As a
result of this decision, the railroad question became a
truly National problem, and there arose an imperative
demand for National regulation. That such regulation
of this vitally important means of communication between the States should have been deferred until so
late a date as 1887, and that control of railroads crossing State boundary lines should so long have been left
exclusively with the States, are singular facts in our
National development. From the year 1822, when it
enacted the Cumberland Road Bill (which was vetoed
by President Monroe) until the year 1862, Congress
had undertaken to exercise its constitutional power to
regulate interstate commerce in only two classes of
subjects — construction of interstate bridges and extension of admiralty jurisdiction. In 1862, Congress incorporated the various Pacific Railroad Companies;
but as its exercise of authority in these cases was supposed by many legislators and jurists to arise out of
the "war power" or to be based on the Post-roads
Clause of the Constitution, the scope of the Commerce
Clause in connection with incorporation and regulation
of railroads remained still an unsettled question. [2]

---

[1] *Nation,* Oct. 26, 1886.

[2] In *United States* v. *Union Pacific R. R. Co.* (1875), 91 U. S. 72, the Court said
that, at the time of the railroad's charter in 1862, "the war of the rebellion was
in progress; and the country had become alarmed for the safety of our Pacific
possessions, owing to complications with England"; that the road was a military
necessity to protect an exposed frontier; that it was intended to open up "vast
unpeopled territory lying between the Missouri and the Sacramento Rivers which
was practically worthless without the facilities afforded by a railroad"; that it

In 1866, a mild and tentative move was made towards the exercise of its power of National regulation when Congress, at the instance of the railroads themselves, passed an act authorizing railroad companies chartered by the States to carry passengers, freight, etc., "on their way from any State to another State, and to receive compensation therefor, and to connect with roads of other States so as to form continuous lines for transportation of the same to the place of destination." In 1873, Congress provided that "no railway within the United States whose road forms any part of a line or road over which cattle, sheep, swine or other animals shall be conveyed from one State to another", should confine animals for longer than twenty-eight hours without unloading for water, rest, and feeding. In the same year, the Senate authorized the Select Committee on Transportation Routes to the Seaboard to investigate and report "upon the subject of transportation between the interior and the seaboard." This Committee reported that the existing defects and abuses were insufficient facilities, unfair discrimination and extortionate charges — the latter due to stock-watering, capitalization of surplus earnings, construction rings, extravagance and corruption in management and consolidations of companies. In 1874, a bill moderately regulating railroads was passed in the House. In 1878, John H. Reagan of Texas introduced in the House a bill to regulate railroad companies engaged in interstate commerce. In 1885, the Senate appointed a committee to investigate the subject of regulation of interstate commerce by railroads,

was necessary for the transportation of the mails, and army and Indian supplies; that it was not then conceived possible to be built by private resources alone; and that though it had actually been built "at less cost of time and money than had been considered possible, no argument can be drawn *from the wisdom that comes after the fact.*"

which reported, January 18, 1886; and as a result of this action, Congress enacted the Interstate Commerce Commission Act of February 4, 1887, and President Cleveland appointed the first Commission, with Judge Thomas M. Cooley as its Chairman. This was the first broad exercise of Congressional power over interstate common carriers — a power which, fifteen years later, was destined to be so greatly extended. It is to be noted that this initial step was regarded with grave apprehensions by the State-Rights Democrats.[1] "I dread to set in motion a doubtful and dangerous power, which will soon become a factor of immense influence in the party politics of the Republic," said Senator Morgan of Alabama, in the debates:

If Congress, instead of holding the States in check by a constant distrust or denial of their powers, will open their way to the full and free control of the men and corporations engaged in domestic commerce, through civil and criminal laws, and will hold over the States its corrective authority so as to prevent any of them from doing injustice to the other States or their people, the States will soon settle all the knotty problems about long and short hauls, pools, drawbacks, bribes and bonuses, and will close the doors of their penitentiaries upon those who offend against their laws, made to secure the people against wrong and the honest freedom of commerce against injustice and obstruction. . . . I admit all that has been said about the wrongs and injustice that people have suffered through the overbearing insolence and oppression of the railroad companies. Their greed is destructive to the people, and the governments, from whom they derived their powers; but in finding a remedy for this evil, I neither wish to find for the people a new master, remote from them and their influence, in the Congress of the United States, nor to place in the hands of that master a power over their trade and traffic, more dangerous than the power of the railroad companies.

[1] *49th Cong., 2d Sess.*, 400, Jan. 6, 1887.

In 1888, twenty-five years after the first National railroad charter had been granted, the Court, in a striking opinion by Judge Bradley, upheld the power of Congress to establish highways and bridges from State to State as essential to its complete control and regulation of interstate commerce — *California* v. *Central Pacific R. R.*, 127 U. S. 1. Thus was settled the great question of Internal Improvements, which, since the early years of the Nation, had been a topic of such sharp political division.[1]

In connection with National control of railroads under the Commerce Clause, such National regulation received a further extension, through the development of substantive doctrines of equity and commercial law in the decisions of the United States Courts. By reason of the financial crisis, the Granger legislation, and the corrupt manipulations of promoters and stock-jobbers, applications to these Courts for the appointment of receivers and for the liberal exercise of this extraordinary jurisdiction in behalf of judgment creditors, bondholders and mortgagees, increased enormously in number between 1871 and 1878. "No branch of equity jurisprudence has developed more rapidly during the past three years than the law of receivers," said a leading law review in 1876, and another spoke of "the magnitude of the proportion of railroad litigation."[2] In 1879, Chief Justice Waite remarked in *Fosdick* v. *Schall*, 99 U. S. 235, that: "Rail-

[1] See *Power of Congress to Enact Incorporation Laws*, by Victor Morawetz, *Harv. Law Rev.* (1913), XXVI; and see especially, *Wilson* v. *Shaw* (1907), 204 U. S. 24.

[2] See *Right of Action against Receivers*, by James L. High, *Southern Law Rev.* (1876), N. S., II; *Receivers of Railways*, by Leonard Jones, *ibid.* (1878), N. S., IV; *Rights of Material Men Against Mortgages*, *ibid.* (1881), N. S., VII; *Liability of Receivers, Western Jurist* (1876), X; *High on Receivers* (1876); *Claims and Equities Affecting the Priority of Railroad Mortgages*, by Leonard A. Jones, *Amer. Law Rev.* (1878), XII; *Liabilities Incurred by Receivers of Railroads*, *ibid.* (1883), XVII; *Railroad Receiverships, ibid.* (1886), XIX; *Law of Railroads and Other Corporate Securities* (1879), by Leonard A. Jones.

road mortgages and the rights of railroad mortgagees
are comparatively new in the history of judicial proceedings. They are peculiar in their character and
affect peculiar interests." And he pointed out that,
in receivership proceedings in equity, concessions from
strict legal rights must oftentimes be made, to secure
advantages that would operate for the general good of
all interested. "This results almost as a matter of
necessity from the peculiar circumstances which sur-
round such litigation." The case was an interesting
example of the flexibility of the law of equity and its
adaptation to new and modern conditions of life and
business; for the Court held that a railroad receiver
might be authorized to pay debts incurred for labor,
supplies, and permanent improvements, in priority
to the claims of the mortgage bondholders. In 1881,
the whole subject of railroad receivership was given
thorough consideration by the Court in *Barton* v.
Barbour, 104 U. S. 126, in which the question was involved whether a railroad receiver could be sued without permission of the Court appointing him. The
Court, in holding that such permission must be obtained, stated that railroad insolvencies and receiverships presented a "new and changed condition of
things"; that unlike the procedure with reference to
insolvent banks, insurance and manufacturing companies, where receivers were appointed to wind up the
company and distribute the assets, a railroad receiver
was appointed, as a rule, to continue the operation
of the railroad; that the public was vastly interested
in such a receivership, and it was because of this public right that a Court's receiver should not be interfered with by suits maintained in another jurisdiction.
Judge Miller dissented, saying that: "The rapid ab-
sorption of the business of the country of every char-

acter by legally authorized corporations, while productive of much good to the public, is beginning also to develop many evils. Not the least of these evils arise from the failure to pay their debts and perform the duties which by the terms of their organization they have assumed." He pointed out that in his Circuit, of the fifty or more railroads, "hardly half a dozen have escaped the hands of the receiver"; that the receiver rarely paid the debts of the company, but frequently injured prior creditors by creating new and superior liens on the property. He believed that no authority or principle could be found to support the Court's decision, and that a plaintiff injured by the operation or breach of contract by a receiver ought to be allowed to sue such receiver in any Court which had jurisdiction.[1]

In 1884, a new form of receivership was originated in the Circuit Courts in the *Wabash Railroad Cases*, through an application made for the first time by the railroad company itself for the appointment of a receiver. This new precedent was soon followed by most railroads in financial straits. The result of this new and modern development of an old equitable doctrine was an enormous increase in the work of these Courts and the assumption of new duties and new responsibilities, presenting many novel questions for decision, and, above all, requiring the control of railroads to be taken from the hands of State commissions and State officials and placed in the custody and direction of the judicial branch of the National Government.[2]

[1] For an early case of the appointment of a receiver to wind up a corporation, see *Covington Drawbridge Co.* v. *Shepherd* (1858), 21 How. 112, and *White Water Valley Canal Co.* v. *Vallette* (1859), 21 How. 414; for one of the earliest cases of appointment of a receiver to run a railroad, see *Bronson* v. *La Crosse and Milwaukee R. R.* (1864), 1 Wall. 405.

[2] See *Wabash R. R.* v. *Central Trust Co.*, 22 Fed. 272, 29 Fed. 623, in 1884; and *Quincy, etc. R. R.* v. *Humphreys* (1892), 145 U. S. 82, *New-Fashioned Receiverships*, by D. H. Chamberlain, *Harv. Law Rev.* (1896), X.

One further form of regulation of the railroads found expression in a series of important cases, in which the extent of the liability of railroad corporations and of other common carriers was settled by decision of the Judiciary, without legislation by Congress. In 1873, in *Michigan Central R. R.* v. *Mineral Springs Manufacturing Co.*, 16 Wall. 318, the Court held that, though a railroad might limit its common law liability by special contract assented to by the consignor, an unsigned general notice on the back of a receipt did not constitute such a contract, even though taken by the contractor without dissent. The parties were not on an equality in their dealing with each other, said Judge Davis: "The law, in conceding to carriers the ability to obtain any reasonable qualifications of their responsibility by express contract, has gone as far in this direction as public policy will allow. To relax still further the strict rules of common law applicable to them, by presuming acquiescence in the conditions on which they propose to carry freight when they have no right to impose them, would, in our opinion, work great harm to the business community." In *New York Central R. R.* v. *Lockwood*, 17 Wall. 357, in a notable opinion by Judge Bradley, the Court held that a common carrier could not stipulate for exemption from responsibility for the negligence of himself or his servants; that the customer had no real freedom of choice, no reasonable and practicable alternative; that the corporations were in a position to control the business, and it was against public policy to allow them to use this public position as a means to exempt themselves from liability for negligence. "The carrier and his customer do not stand on a footing of equality. The latter is only one individual of a million. He cannot afford to higgle or stand out and seek redress in the Courts. His business will not admit such a course." [1] In 1876, in *Bank of Kentucky* v. *Adams Express Co.*, 93 U. S. 174, it was held that public policy would not permit an express company to contract for exemption for loss by fire caused by the negligence of its agent, a railroad company: "The foundation of the rule is, that it tends to the greater security of consignors, who always deal with such carriers at a disadvantage." In 1884, in *Hart* v. *Pennsylvania R. R.*, 112 U. S. 331, the Court upheld a form of contract confining the carrier's liability to a certain valuation of the shipment, even in case of loss by negligence. In 1880, in *Pennsylvania Co.* v. *Roy*, 102 U. S. 451, the liability of a railroad for injury to a passenger riding in a Pullman car was first adjudicated; and in *Pickard* v. *Pullman Southern Car Co.*, 117 U. S. 34, in 1886, the nature of the sleeping car business was considered, in a case holding invalid a statute of Tennessee taxing sleeping cars running in interstate commerce. In 1884, the fellow-servant rule (established in this country in 1841) was considered in *Chicago, Milwaukee and St. Paul R. R.* v. *Ross*, 112 U. S. 377, in which it was held that the rule should not be extended to apply to persons having supervision or control; and that, therefore, a train conductor was not a fellow servant with other train employees. In

---

[1] Again in *Southern Express Company* v. *Caldwell* (1875), 21 Wall. 264, the Court considered the question of public policy in relation to common carriers, upholding a clause in an express company contract requiring claims for loss or damages to be made within ninety days. "Common carriers do not deal with their employers on equal terms," said Judge Strong. "There is, in a very important sense, a necessity for their employment. . . . In fact, they are without competition, except as between themselves, and that they are thus is, in most cases, a consequence of advantages obtained from the public. It is, therefore, just that they are not allowed to take advantage of their powers, and of the necessities of the public to exact exemptions from that measure of duty which public policy demands. But that which was public policy a hundred years ago has undergone changes in the progress of material and social civilization. There is less danger than there was of collision with highwaymen. Intelligence is more rapidly diffused. It is more easy to trace a consignment than it was. . . . The business of common carriers is more increased and subdivided. . . . Thus his hazard is greatly increased."

1886, it was held in the *Express Cases*, 117 U. S. 1, that railroad companies were not required at common law to furnish to all express companies equal facilities for doing business upon their passenger trains.

While National control over the instrumentalities of interstate commerce was thus being enhanced and supported by judicial decision, the Court, since 1879, had shown its increasingly Nationalistic tendencies in other directions in a series of important cases.

On May 5, 1879, it rendered a decision in the *Sinking Fund Cases*, 99 U. S. 727, in which it announced for the first time the wide extent of the control which the Government might exercise over corporations chartered by Congress. While the Impairment of Obligation of Contract Clause in the Constitution applied only to the States, it was contended by the railroads, party to these suits, that the Due Process Clause contained in the Fifth Amendment constituted an equally strong limitation upon the power of the Federal Government, and that this latter clause rendered invalid the Act of May 7, 1878, by which statute Congress had amended the charter of the Union Pacific Railroad by requiring it to establish a sinking fund with the United States Treasury for the redemption of the Government loan.   The Court, at the outset of its opinion rendered by Chief Justice Waite, remarked that it was indisputable that "the United States are as much bound by their contracts as are individuals.   If they repudiate their obligations, it is as much repudiation, with all the wrong and reproach that term implies, as it would be if the repudiator had been a State or a municipality or a citizen."   It, nevertheless, laid down the very broad rule that, under the power to amend the charter, which it had expressly reserved, Congress retained the

power to establish by amendment, "whatever rules
Congress might have prescribed in the original charter
for the government of the corporation in the administration of its affairs", so long as the amendment should
act prospectively and not upon past and executed transactions. And it held that the sinking fund provision
was sustainable, on the ground that "it is a reasonable
regulation of the administration of the affairs of the
corporation, and promotive of the interests of the public and the corporators. It takes nothing from the
corporation or the stockholders which actually belongs to them. It oppresses no one, and inflicts no
wrong. It simply gives further assurance of the continued solvency and prosperity of a corporation in
which the public are so largely interested, and adds
another guaranty to the permanent and lasting value
of its vast amount of securities." The conclusion thus
reached was strongly opposed by three Judges, Field,
Strong and Bradley, each of whom in a separate dissenting opinion displayed his fear that the Court's
decision would encourage repudiation of contracts.
Judge Strong said that the doctrine was a very grave
and dangerous assertion. "It is especially dangerous
in these days of attempted repudiation, when the good
faith of the Government is above all price." Judge
Bradley said that: "The initiation of this species of
legislation by Congress is well calculated to excite
alarm. It has the effect of announcing to the world and
giving it to be understood that this Government does
not consider itself bound by its engagements. It sets
the example of repudiation of Government obligations.
It strikes a blow at the public credit. It asserts the
principle that might makes right. It saps the foundation of public morality." Judge Field said that the
decision would "tend to create insecurity in the title

to corporate property in this country. It, in effect, determines that the General Government, in its dealings with the Pacific Railroad Companies, is under no legal obligation to fulfil its contracts, and that whether it shall do so is a question of policy and not of duty." "I am aware," he said, "of the opinion which prevails generally that the Pacific railroad corporations have, by their accumulation of wealth, and the numbers in their employ, become so powerful as to be disturbing and dangerous influences in the legislation of the country; and that they should, therefore, be brought by stringent measures into subjection to the State. This may be true; I do not say that it is not; but if it is, it furnishes no justification for the repudiation or evasion of the contracts made with them by the government. The law that protects the wealth of the most powerful, protects also the earnings of the most humble; and the law which would confiscate the property of the one would in the end take the earnings of the other."

"This decision lays down certain fundamental principles which we are glad to see again affirmed by the tribunal of highest authority," said the *Nation*. And it criticized Judge Bradley's dissenting opinion as "extremely acrimonious", and said that "such language from a Judge, who joined in reversing the Legal Tender decisions and in laying down the doctrine that Congress may legislate backward indefinitely upon contracts between citizens, is not calculated to promote harmony between the legislative and judicial branches of the Government, or to make an agreeable impression on the public mind." The *Springfield Republican* also considered that the Court had "gone to the root of the matter and taken the general ground, towards which its decisions have been long tending, that grants of rights and privileges by the Federal Government are revocable, unless an express covenant to the contrary is made." [1]

Announced at a time when corporate pretensions and assumptions of power were rapidly mounting, and when corporate corruption of Legislatures was flagrant, this decision, confirming in the Federal Government enormous powers of control over corporate charters, constituted a warning, not only to railroads, but to all corporations doing an interstate business that, if the Government should ever assume to regulate them by enforcing National incorporation, the scope of its regulation would be subject to few limitations.[2] The decision served also as a complete answer to the charges which had been made from time to time, after the Legal Tender decision, that the Bench had been filled with "railroad attorneys" for the purpose of obtaining decisions favoring these corporations.[3] The absurdity of this charge had been clearly demonstrated when, in 1877, the Court decided the *Granger Cases* sustaining the State maximum rate laws, against the violent opposition of all the railroads and financial interests of the country. The criticism of the Court had, however, broken out again when, on January 6, 1879, only four months before the decision in the *Sinking Fund Cases*, the Court

---

[1] *Nation*, May 8, Nov. 13, 1879; *Springfield Republican*, May 7, 1879.

[2] An interesting illustration of the power which Congress reserves to itself in granting charters appears in *Newport and Cincinnati Bridge Co.* v. *United States* (1882), 105 U. S. 470, in which a corporation constructing a bridge across the Ohio River at Cincinnati obtained permissive legislation from Congress containing a reservation by Congress of its right to withdraw its assent. The Court held that the franchise thus obtained "was a species of property, but from the moment of its origin was dependent on the will of Congress", and the company ran the risk of its withdrawal. It was, of course, possible that this power might be abused by Congress, but "for protection against unjust or unwise legislation, within the limits of recognized legislative power, the people must look to the polls and not to the Courts."

[3] See *History of the Supreme Court of the United States* (1912), by Gustavus Myers, 528–577, written from the Socialist point of view.

held in *United States* v. *Union Pacific R. R.*, 98 U. S.
569, that the Government had no right to recover for
itself or its stockholders the enormous sums lost through
the notorious Credit Mobilier frauds in 1864–1866,
attendant on the securing of amendments to the railroad charter, and through the corrupt construction,
coal and Pullman Car contracts made by the officers
and promoters. These frauds had caused a National
scandal and had resulted in a Congressional investigation in 1872, and the passage of the Act of March 3,
1873, under which the Attorney-General was directed
to institute a suit in equity against stockholders and
others who secured stock not paid-up or illegal profits
from contracts made with themselves, to compel the
restoration of unlawfully obtained property to the corporation or to the Government, "whichever shall in
equity be held entitled thereto." The suit so brought
finally reached the Supreme Court in 1876, when it
was exhaustively argued, and a reargument was had
in 1878. Of the charges (which for the purposes of
the case were admitted by the demurrer to be true)
the Court, in its decision, said that "more unmitigated
frauds were never perpetrated on a helpless corporation
by its managing directors than are set forth in this
bill." Yet, as the Court pointed out, the frauds were
committed against the corporation itself, and against
such innocent stockholders as had paid in full for their
stock, but not against the Government. The corporation, however, was not seeking relief in Court, and
"as to the directors and stockholders who took part
in these fraudulent contracts they are *particeps criminis*
and can have no relief. This class probably included
nine-tenths in value of the stockholders." But the
Government, on the other hand, was not in a position
to obtain relief in equity; it was a creditor under its

contract with the railroad and under its mortgage, and must be supposed to have guarded its rights thereunder. To the Government's contention that it was a trustee for the public and had visitorial powers to correct frauds, the Court answered that such powers could be exercised only in relation to municipal, charitable and religious corporations, or to restrain a private corporation from *ultra vires* acts. To the argument that the Government's rights should be liberally construed, in view of the liberal aid which it had given to the railroad, the Court stated that "it was a wise liberality for which the Government has received all the advantages for which it has bargained, and more than it expected", and though the corporation "since it has grown to a vigorous manhood . . . may not have displayed the gratitude which so much care called for . . . it is but another instance of the absence of human affections which is said to characterize all corporations." And the Court added that "a Court of Justice is not called on to inquire into the balance of benefits and favors on each side of this controversy, but into the rights of the parties as established by law, as found in their contracts, as recognized by the established principles of equity, and to decide accordingly." There was no doubt that the Court was entirely correct in holding that no recognized principle of law authorized the maintenance of any such suits, and as the *Springfield Republican* rightly said: "The Credit Mobilier suit came to the end foredoomed. To turn a bad trade into a good one by means of a subsequent lawsuit is a task as hopeless for Congress as for anybody." This decision, putting an end to the Government's effort to make the guilty parties disgorge for the benefit of a badly looted railroad and a cheated government, was highly unsatisfactory to the

country.[1] That the Court, however, did not intend
to allow the guilty to escape, in a case properly maintainable at law, was seen in *Wardell* v. *Railroad Co.*,
103 U. S. 651, in 1881, in which one of the fraudulent
coal contracts made between the Union Pacific Railroad and a prospector, in the benefits of which contract
the railroad directors were to share under the guise of
a separate corporation to whom the contract was assigned, was held to be "utterly indefensible and illegal.
. . . Their character as agents forbade the exercise
of their powers for their personal ends against the interest of the company." [2] And that the Court was also
fully aware of the corrupt lobbyism prevalent in that
era, and that it did not intend to allow any of the parties
participating in such illegal actions to recover in suits
arising therefrom had been shown by its decision, four
years before, in 1875, in *Trist* v. *Child*, 21 Wall. 441.
In this case, involving a contract for legal services in
relation to the passage of an Act of Congress, the Court
had said : "The foundation of a republic is the virtue
of its citizens. They are at once sovereigns and subjects. As the foundation is undermined, the structure
is weakened. When it is destroyed, the fabric must
fall. Such is the voice of universal history." After
pointing out that the contract was to obtain the passage
of a law to pay a private claim without reference to
its merits, " by means, which, if not corrupt, were
illegitimate", Judge Swayne had continued (undoubtedly referring to the Credit Mobilier) : "If any of the

[1] *Springfield Republican*, Jan. 7, 1879. *The Independent*, Dec. 4, 1873, had said
at the time of the defeat of the Government in the Circuit Court in this case that
"the best lawyers in Congress last Winter stated that a suit brought in a respectable Court could have no other result. The country may as well understand
that when Congress, through lobbying or otherwise, makes improper grants to corporations, the Courts cannot rectify the end."

[2] In 1891, in *Griswold* v. *Hazard*, 141 U. S. 260, the Court upheld a judgment for
over sixteen million dollars against the president of the Credit Mobilier, and others.

great corporations of the country were to hire adventurers who make market of themselves in this way to
procure the passage of a general law, with a view to
the promotion of their private interests, the moral
sense of every right-minded man would instinctively
denounce the employer and employed as steeped in
corruption, and the employment as infamous. . . .
The same thing in lesser legislation, if not so prolific
of alarming evils, is not less vicious in itself, nor less
to be condemned." The country applauded this decision. "The whole American people will cordially
thank the Supreme Court for its authoritative expression that services of this kind cannot be the basis
of any valid contract for compensation," said the
American Law Review. The *Nation* said that while
it remained to be considered whether the decision
would "prove effective to remove wholly, or in any
considerable degree, the grossly evil practices which
it so strongly condemns", nevertheless, the opinion was
stated in "very plain language, coming from the highest tribunal in this country, and language very much
needed at this time. . . . The Supreme Court has been
at the pains to say, in a manner not likely to be forgotten or misunderstood, that all and the best of the
present lobby business in Congress is pernicious, immoral and void; and it has also indirectly read the
Court below a pretty strong lecture upon the impropriety of a judicial tribunal lending its aid to carry out
these nefarious transactions. . . . A disorganized, incompetent Congress is a continuing, abiding demand
for a lobby, and it is a demand which has not hitherto
failed, and will not hereafter fail, to produce a supply.
Whoever wishes the lobby annihilated must first see
to it that the business of Congress shall be conducted
in such a way that it can, with reasonable certainty,

be done without a lobby. . . . The conclusion of the whole matter is, that special legislation breeds a lobby, and a lobby breeds fraudulent claims and the corruption of Congress." [1]

In two cases in 1880, the Court took another advanced step in proclaiming a far greater field for Congressional legislation than had hitherto been supposed to exist under the Constitution, when it upheld in sweeping terms the authority of the National Government to protect by legislation its own functions, agencies and sovereignty. In *Ex parte Siebold*, 100 U. S. 371, the Court upheld convictions for ballot stuffing at Congressional elections in Baltimore and Cincinnati, and held valid those sections of the Enforcement Laws of May 31, 1870, and February 28, 1871, which made it a Federal crime for a State election officer at a Congressional election to neglect to perform any duty required of him by State or Federal law. In *Tennessee v. Davis*, 100 U. S. 257, an even greater extension of National authority was promoted when the Court sustained the constitutionality of the Act of July 13, 1866, providing for the removal into the United States Courts of any civil suit or criminal prosecution begun in a State Court against a Federal officer acting under any Federal revenue law. The defendant, a deputy

---

[1] *Lobbying at Washington*, *Amer. Law Rev.* (1875), IX; *Nation*, April 22, 1875. An agreement to divide fees with a Government officer for securing an appointment as counsel was emphatically denounced in 1880 in *Meguire* v. *Corwine*, 101 U. S. 108: "No legal right can spring from such a source," said Judge Swayne. "They are the sappers and miners of the public welfare and of free government as well. The latter depends for its vitality upon the virtue and good faith of those for whom it exists, and of those by whom it is administered. Corruption is always the forerunner of despotism." The duty of a Government officer to refrain from pecuniary interest in its contracts was forcibly set out by Judge Field in *Oscanyon* v. *Winchester Arms Co.*, 103 U. S. 261, in a suit by the Turkish Consul-General in 1881. "All such positions are trusts to be exercised from considerations of duty and for the public good. Whenever other considerations are allowed to intervene and control their exercise, the trust is perverted and the community suffers. . . . Personal influence to be exercised over an officer of Government, in the procurement of contracts, . . . is not a vendible article in our system of law and morals."

collector, being indicted for murder in the State Court, alleged that the killing was in self-defense and while engaged in discharge of his official duties, and he sought to remove his trial into the United States Court. The Court held that Congress had power to authorize such removal, as indispensable to the enforcement of the National laws and to the supremacy of the National Government in their execution. This decision, said the *Nation*, "practically destroys State Sovereignty with regard to criminal law in a class of cases in which it has hitherto always been supposed to be intact." When this case was considered with *Ex parte Virginia*, in this same year, holding that a State Judge who discriminated against negroes in the impaneling of a jury was indictable under the Civil Rights Act, it was not astonishing that these decisions were profoundly disturbing to those who opposed centralizing tendencies. "They have attracted but little attention at the North," said the *Nation*, "but at the South these decisions have been received with many expressions of hostility, as being aimed at what is left of the once cherished doctrine of State-Rights. They are really, however, of as much importance to one region as to another, and are destined, unless we are much mistaken, to play a prominent part in the future constitutional development of the country. . . . Important and far-reaching changes have been brought in the relation of the State to the General Government." And the *American Law Review* also pointed out how vividly the *Siebold Case* illustrated a growing disposition to enhance the importance of the National Government.[1]

Another form of the extension of the protecting arm of the United States Government to its officials was upheld in *Ex parte Curtis*, 106 U. S. 371, in 1882. This

[1] *Nation*, March 4, 11, 25, 1880; *Amer. Law Rev.* (1881), XV.

case which involved the constitutionality of the Act of August 15, 1876, prohibiting solicitation of money for political purposes from officers or employees of the United States, had aroused great public interest, owing to the scandals growing out of the political assessments levied in the Garfield Presidential campaign. The Court ruled that the law was clearly within the just scope of legislative power, as its object "was to protect the classes of officials and employees provided for, from being compelled to make contributions for such purposes, through fear of dismissal if they refused." The newspapers very generally endorsed this decision and its "calm, luminous and vigorous language"; and referred to "the outspoken popular disapproval of the past assessments, the whole system of which must be rooted out." [1] "Political assessments should be legally proscribed. This is the imperative demand of public sentiment," said the *Independent;* and the *Philadelphia North American* said that it would be received "with little surprise and with very general satisfaction. . . . It constitutes an important step in the direction of civil service reform."

In 1884, the Court delivered the most sweeping opinion as to the extent of Congressional power which had ever theretofore been rendered, when the question of the constitutionality of the Act of Congress, enacted after the war, making Treasury notes legal tender was presented for the first time in *Juilliard* v. *Greenman,* 110 U. S. 421. The right to issue legal tender notes had been sustained in *Knox* v. *Lee*, in 1871, as an exercise of the war power under the Constitution; but that case had not definitely settled the status of notes issued

---

[1] See *Independent*, Dec. 14, 28, 1882; *New York Tribune*, Dec. 20, 27, 1882; *New York Times*, Dec. 19, 1882; *Philadelphia North American*, Dec. 20, 1882; and see also editorials on the decision in practically all the New York, Boston and Chicago papers.

in time of peace. Meanwhile, since 1872, the composition of the Court had been greatly changed, death
or resignation having removed from the Bench, Chief
Justice Chase, and Judges Nelson, Davis, Strong,
Swayne and Clifford, and their places having been
taken by Chief Justice Waite, and Judges Blatchford,
Harlan, Woods, Matthews and Gray, while of the
former Court only Judges Field, Miller and Bradley
still remained. The case now presented had been pending in the Court for five years. It was finally argued
on January 2, 1884, by Senator George F. Edmunds
and William Allen Butler, against Benjamin F. Butler,
James McKeen and Thomas H. Talbot.[1] On March 3,
1884, the Court rendered a decision, through Judge
Gray, which was concurred in by all the Judges except
Field, and held in the broadest terms that the words
"necessary and proper" in the Constitution "include
all appropriate means which are conducive or adapted
to the end to be accomplished, and which in the judgment of Congress will most advantageously effect it";
that under its power "to borrow money", Congress
might "issue the obligations of the United States in
such form, and impress upon them such qualities as
currency for the purchase of merchandise and the
payment of debts . . . as accord with the usage of
sovereign governments"; that the power of making

[1] See *Nation*, May 29, 1879: "Messrs. Butler and Chittenden have undertaken
to bring before the Supreme Court, by means of a test case, the power of Congress
to issue or keep afloat legal tender paper money in time of peace. . . . The contention is that the Act of May 31, 1878, directing reissue of legal tender, is unconstitutional." The *Nation* said, Jan. 8, 1880: "The Supreme Court has denied Mr.
Edmunds' motion to advance the Butler-Chittenden legal tender case on the calendar, on the ground that it will not hear constitutional cases in the absence of a full
Bench. Judge Hunt's place is now vacant, and we shall therefore have to wait for
it to be filled before the case can come up. This is perhaps a wise rule, in view of
what happened in the *Hepburn* v. *Griswold* case; but we hope it is not true that
Court, as it now stands, is equally divided on this point, and that the new Justice
will have the casting vote, for, if so, the temptation to find out the opinion of the
lawyer who is nominated, before he gets the nomination, will be strong, if not irresistible."

paper money, issued for such purposes, legal tender for
the payment of private debts was "universally understood to belong to sovereignty, in Europe and America,
at the time of the framing and adoption of the Constitution"; that the power to make the notes of the
Government a legal tender in payment of private debts
"being one of the powers belonging to sovereignty in
other civilized nations, and not expressly withheld
from Congress by the Constitution", the impressing
of such legal tender quality was "an appropriate means,
conducive and plainly adapted" to the execution of
express powers granted to Congress by the Constitution. "Such being our conclusion in matter of law,
the question whether at any particular time, in war
or in peace, the exigency is such . . . that it is, as
matter of fact, wise and expedient to resort to this
means is a political question, to be determined by Congress when the question of exigency arises, and not a
judicial question, to be afterwards passed upon by the
Courts." Judge Field in dissenting, lamented that:
"What was in 1862 called the 'medicine of the Constitution' has now become its daily bread. So it always
happens that whenever a wrong principle of conduct,
political or personal, is adopted on the plea of necessity, it will be afterwards followed on a plea of
convenience. . . . From the decision of the Court
I see only evil likely to follow." The extraordinary
length to which the decision carried the implied powers
of Congress, and especially the announcement of the
doctrine that the National Government possessed all
powers belonging to other sovereignties, unless withheld by express constitutional restriction, elicited
vigorous criticism from many newspapers and jurists.[1]

[1] Charles Francis Adams in his *Memoirs of Horace Gray* termed the decision:
"One of the most significant and far-reaching changes ever worked by judicial
construction in constitutional jurisprudence. Largely as the result of his influence,

The financial and industrial effect of the decision also disturbed a large portion of the public who were unconcerned with the radical legal doctrine asserted by the Court. The decision of Judge Strong in the *Legal Tender Cases* of 1871 "strained the Constitution to its extremest limits, and was far from being satisfactory to the legal minds of the country", said the *Independent*, shortly before the decision. "If now the Supreme Court should substantially sustain the Greenback theory as to the legal tender power of Congress, . . . it would seem to us to be creating a new Constitution by the process of interpretation, . . . an improper and dangerous straining of language." [1] After the decision, which more than confirmed its worst apprehensions, the *Independent* said that it was "evident that a very radical change of opinion has occurred in the Court", which it did not consider an improvement, and it termed the Court's new doctrine "a dangerous theory, which makes a new Constitution, in the process of interpreting it." "The decision makes the Constitution . . . different from what it has been supposed to be for now nearly a century. Nobody, until the exigency created by the late war, ever dreamed that Congress had any power to make the debt obligations of the Government a legal tender in the discharge of private contracts; and then it was done on the ground solely of an imperative necessity. . . . The Court now excludes all circumstances and all limitations. . . . This mode of construction, if applied in other relations, would sweep away all the reserved powers of the States, and, at the pleasure of

as exercised and expressed in this case . . . the National Legislature was clothed with broad and undefined Parliamentary powers, covering practically the whole field of sovereignty, in all matters where the exercise of such power was not expressly inhibited to it." *Mass. Hist. Soc. Proc.*, 2d Ser., XVI, XVIII.

[1] *Independent*, Oct. 25, 1883, March 13, 20, 1884.

Congress, reduce them to the condition of mere municipalities." The *New York Times* strongly denounced the decision as one "which, while it must command obedience, cannot command respect, a decision weak in itself and supported by reasoning of the most defective character, inconsistent with the previous decisions of the Court on like issues, and singularly, almost ridiculously, inconsistent with the traditional interpretation of the Constitution, with the spirit of that instrument and its language"; and it stated that the Court had evolved a doctrine "directly opposed to the words of the Constitution, avowedly based upon the theory of sovereignty held at a time when there was not a considerable republic in the world, and bestowing upon Congress a power which it did not dare to claim in stress of war." And the *Louisville Courier Journal* said that the decision had introduced "a new régime. The whole constitutional bulwark is destroyed at one stab, and unbridled license in currency legislation is submitted for constitutional restraint." After stating that it was not clear to a plain democratic mind that foreign customs ought to be a guide to American Judges, in construing American law, it charged that the Court had "violated the letter and spirit of the Constitution", and had "consulted its own conception of political and economic expediency, instead of the commands of the organic law." The *Nation*, in an editorial entitled "A New View of the Constitution", said : " The system of construction adopted in this case is one which weakens the Court itself and enlarges the power of Congress, and makes a long stride in the direction of centralization. . . . The rule adopted by the Court enables Congress to do what it pleases, makes it the judge of what is appropriate to the exercise of the implied powers of the Constitution, and makes the only limit of these the general doctrine of 'sovereignty', which is either one of arbitrary power, or at the best the authority enjoyed by the English Parliament." An eminent writer in the *American Law Review* spoke of Judge Gray's novel contribution to law in his statement that Congress has powers "incidental to sovereignty"; and he concluded : "It is permitted to those who revere the Court and the Constitution, and believe in public honor, to hope that in future decisions that Court will recur to the doctrines and guidance of Madison, Marshall and Webster, on this question, and restore to our country the blessings of real, honest, constitutional money. . . . Senator Bayard has well said that the Supreme Court has put B. F. Butler on his feet." And a Mississippi Greenbackian wrote that "we feel a just pride in the fact that the Supreme Court has fully sustained our views." [1] Another jurist said, with a pessimistic prophecy which subsequent events did not fulfill : "The Court has fallen, and it is not probable it can ever again act as an effective check upon the popular will, or should it attempt to do so, that it can prevail."

Some newspapers, while regretting not only the legal doctrines of the decision but the encouragement which it would give to inflation of the currency and radical paper money legislation, felt that, as a practical question, Congress could be trusted to deal sanely with the situation. "Fortunately, for the country, the decision involves for the present a theoretical question only," said the *Boston Advertiser*, "but some day the

---

[1] *The Legal Tender Question,* by H. H. Neill, *Pol. Sci. Qu.* (1886), I; *The Legal Tender Decisions of 1884,* by D. H. Chamberlain, *Amer. Law Rev.* (1884), XVIII; see *ibid., A Reply,* by Thomas H. Talbot; *Nation,* March 6, 20, 1884; *Legal Tender,* by James B. Thayer, *Harv. Law Rev.* (1887), I; Brooks Adams in *Atlantic Monthly* (1885), LV; *Harper's Weekly,* March 15, 1884; *New York Tribune,* March 4, 17, 1884; *New York Times,* March 4, 1884; *Boston Daily Advertiser,* March 4, 1884; *Louisville Courier Journal,* March 5, 11, 1884; *Cincinnati Enquirer,* March 4. 6, 1884; see also *Philadelphia Press,* March 4, 1884; *Philadelphia North American,* March 12, 1884.

question will be severely practical, and then the country must look to Congress rather than to the Supreme Court for the determination of what constitutes sound money." *Harper's Weekly* stated that, since the Court was composed of "a body of very able lawyers and of conservative and patriotic men, and as there is at present no very strong party feeling or pressure of any kind", this opinion must be regarded with great respect and of very great weight. Nevertheless, it could not be regarded but as surprising, it said, that the Court should apparently assert "that the power of Congress is as supreme as that of Parliament, except that it cannot exercise powers expressly withheld." Still, though the decision "recognizes in Congress the constitutional authority of indefinite inflation, the practical reply to the possible peril of such a recognition is that Congress would never have hesitated to use such authority, if it had felt strong enough and had believed that the exigency demanded the action. In an emergency, Congress has always exercised supreme National powers, and the true conservative restraint upon its action lies in the intelligence and honesty of the country." The *New York Tribune* said that: "Timid observers will probably think that this is a dangerous decision, and anti-monopolists will doubtless flatter themselves that it contains the promise of the issue of fiat money, whenever they can get control of Congress. But there is practically no reason for fear, or rejoicing either, for that matter." Later, this paper expressed the hopeful view that, while the decision had been described as "a public misfortune", reviving the greenback agitation and exposing the country to complete debauchment of the currency, "whenever a majority in Congress can find a convenient excuse for inflation, this, however, is not an opinion warranted by past experience. The greenback agitation died out, not because the people supposed the issue of legal tenders unconstitutional, but because they discovered that the legal tender quality was of no use. . . . (The people and Congress) are not restrained, . . . except by a sense of duty and intelligent care for the consequences. But those restraints ought to be the more powerful, since it appears that the honor and welfare of the Nation depend, not upon any supposed fences by which the people may be penned in, but upon their own good faith and good sense."

In only a few of the more radical Democratic papers was any endorsement of the decision to be found. Representative of these was the *Cincinnati Enquirer*, which termed it one of the most important judicial decisions ever made in this country, "the effects of which will be greater for the good of the toiling millions than those of any other decision made by the Supreme Court. The fact that all the Members of the Court joining in the opinion have been Republicans and were appointed by Republican Presidents bars the money-power from saying it was a Democratic party decision. We are sorry to say that Justice Field dissented from this most righteous determination. . . . By the true friends of the people, Republicans and Democrats, who bore the brunt of battle with the money-power, this edict of our Supreme Court will be received with utmost satisfaction. We will hear no more of inflationists and the 'rag-baby.' "

One immediate effect of the decision was the introduction into Congress of resolves for a Constitutional Amendment to limit the powers of Congress as to the issue of legal tender notes, such measures being proposed by Thomas F. Bayard of Delaware and A. H. Garland of Arkansas in the Senate, and Orlando B.

Potter and Abram Hewitt of New York in the House. "The decision has already become a subject of political discussion, and he must be blind to the profound significance of the great question which has been opened by that decision who fails to see that in some form it must become a fruitful source of agitation," said a leading Democratic paper, which strongly opposed the decision. "People should insist upon having clearly defined constitutional metes and bounds to protect their liberties and rights, instead of depending upon the caprices of the unlimited sovereignty which the Supreme Court dwells upon with such complacency. . . . Without strict limitation, Government becomes a despotism, and as it has steadily moved in the direction of centralization and 'the highest sovereignty', the Republican party has been marking all the stages of its progress by fragments of these safeguards, these muniments of the fundamental law." And an equally strong Republican opponent, referring to the proposed Amendments, said that they showed that the decision had attracted deserved attention by Congress.[1]

Coming only a few months before the Presidential election of 1884, when the Democratic party was returned to power after twenty-four years, the decision may be said to have marked the climacteric of the broad tide of Nationalism which had, with ebbs and flows, been sweeping over American constitutional law.

[1] *Louisville Courier-Journal*, March 11, 1884; *Independent*, March 20, 1884.

Potter's Amendment provided that Congress should not have power to make anything but "gold or silver coin a tender in payment of debts, except after a declaration of war, when the public safety may require it." Bayard's and Hewitt's Amendments were similar except as to the last clause. Garland's Amendment limited the issue of legal tender notes to $350,000,000 except on a two-thirds vote of each House. *48th Cong., 1st Sess.*, 1745, 1756, March 10, 1884. See also *The Proposed Amendments to the Constitution*, by Herman V. Ames, *Amer. Hist. Ass. Rep.* (1896), II.

In 1886, the rights of the United States Government even within the territorial boundaries of the States were broadly upheld in *Van Brocklin* v. *Tennessee*, 117 U. S. 151, in which the power of a State to tax real estate belonging to the National Government was unequivocally denied.[1] And another example of the National control within State boundaries was given, when the Court sustained the plenary right of the National Government to legislate in control and for the protection of its tribal Indian wards located in a State, in *United States* v. *Kagama* (1886), 118 U. S. 375.[2]

In 1887, the Court extended even farther the implied powers contained in the Constitution, by upholding, in *United States* v. *Arjona*, 120 U. S. 479, the validity of the statute punishing the counterfeiting of notes and bonds of foreign governments. It held that, as international comity required that protection be afforded to such foreign securities, and as failure to give such protection would create under international law a right of complaint, "a law which is necessary and proper to afford this protection is one that Congress may enact, because it is one that is needed to carry into execution a power conferred by

---

[1] In 1876, in *Kohl* v. *United States*, 91 U. S. 367, the right of the United States to take land by eminent domain within a State was first upheld, Judge Strong saying that the right is "the offspring of political necessity; and it is inseparable from sovereignty, unless denied to it by its fundamental law. . . . It is a right which may be exercised within the States, so far as it is necessary to the enjoyment of the powers conferred upon (the United States) by the Constitution"; and that though it was true that this power of the Federal Government "has not heretofore been exercised adversely, the nonuser of a power does not disprove its existence."

[2] See also *United States* v. *43 Gallons of Whiskey* (1876), 93 U. S. 188. That an Indian born a member of one of the Indian tribes was not a citizen of the United States, even though he had severed his tribal relation, was held in 1884, in *Elk* v. *Wilkins*, 112 U. S. 94. "The National legislation has tended more and more towards the education and civilization of the Indians, and fitting them to be citizens," said Judge Gray. "But the question whether any Indian Tribes or any members thereof have become so far advanced in civilization that they should be let out of the state of pupilage and admitted to the privileges and responsibilities of citizenship, is a question to be decided by the Nation whose wards they are and whose citizens they seek to become, and not by each Indian for himself."

the Constitution on the Government of the United States exclusively. There is no authority in the United States to require the passage and enforcement of such a law by the States. Therefore, the United States must have the power to pass it and enforce it themselves . . . or be unable to perform a duty which they owe to another nation, and which the law of nations has imposed on them as part of their international obligations." Having in the *Legal Tender Case*, in 1884, deduced a power in Congress from its possession by other sovereignties, the Court now held, in 1887, that Congress must be held to possess a power, because of the fact that the States did not possess it. The decision was an interesting example of the very broad views of the Constitution at which the Court had arrived.

The *American Law Review* (1885), XX, 202, said, after President Cleveland's election: "It will not be any harm if a little of the strict-constructionist leaven gets into the Court, during the next four years. The public is not satisfied with the Legal Tender decision of 1884, and is not prepared to sanction the doctrine that Congress can do anything except make a man a woman, or a woman a man." But for apparent reiteration of Judge Gray's doctrine, see White, C. J. in *Billings* v. *Bennett* (1914), 232 U. S. 306.

For early doubts as to the power of Congress to regulate railroads under the Commerce Clause, see resolutions and speeches of Clayton and Morton in the Senate, Jan. 20, 27, 1874, *43d Cong., 1st Sess.*, 775, 941; McCrary's bill in the House, Jan. 23, 1874, *ibid.*, 993. And see *United States* v. *Stanford* (1896), 161 U. S. 412, 427, for a statement as to the objects of the various Pacific Railroad charters and grants.

CHAPTER THIRTY-SIX

EXPANSION OF JUDICIAL POWERS

1885-1889

In 1885, the Court rendered a decision which marked a new era in the development of the domain of National power and which restricted in a large measure the sovereignty of the States. Since the case of *Osborn* v. *Bank of the United States* in 1824, there had been practically no instance in which the Courts of the United States had sustained an action against a State official for administering an unconstitutional law. On the contrary, attempts to sue such officials had been discountenanced and defeated in many cases, on the ground that they were in violation of the Eleventh Amendment prohibiting suits against a State. Between 1875 and 1885, however, conditions had arisen in many States in this country which made of the Eleventh Amendment simply a shield for State dishonesty. Owing to the devastation due to the Civil War, the corruption of their "carpet-bag" Legislatures and the financial depression after the panic of 1873, many Southern States had attempted to default in the payment of bonds issued or guaranteed by them. The extent of this repudiation had become a National scandal. "Today more than $100,000,000 and, if we include interest, more than $200,000,000 are due to creditors from repudiating States. . . . The whole country is in disgrace by reason of this horrid spectacle," said the *Independent*, in 1883. "Public morality has suffered from the foul contagion. Municipal corporations have caught the disease. . . . Repudiation is simply the highwayman's morality. When practiced by States, it is power against right. As an exhibit of sovereignty, it is the sovereignty of rascality. State repudiation in this country is a criminality that has behind it millions of offenders. The people are the State and control its action." [1] The Court, nevertheless, in almost every attempt made to enforce compliance by a State with its obligations, was confronted with the Eleventh Amendment. Though determined to uphold principles of honesty in business and to enforce rigidly the Impairment of Obligation of Contract Clause of the Constitution in suits involving private individuals, it had thus far met with an insuperable obstacle in suits involving State officials. The situation was well illustrated by three cases decided in 1883. In *Louisiana* v. *Jumel*, 107 U. S. 711, the Court upheld the right of the State and its officers to be exempt from a mandamus suit requiring officials to apply funds in the State Treasury to payment of State bonds. Judges Field and Harlan vigorously dissented, stating that they would continue to do so, "until the prohibition inserted in the Constitution, as a barrier against the agrarian and despoiling spirit which both precedes and follows a breach of public faith, is restored to its original vigor"; otherwise,

[1] *Independent*, May 3, 1883, Feb. 19, April 30, 1885; *The Supreme Court and State Repudiation*, by John N. Pomeroy, *Amer. Law Rev.* (1883), XVII; see *Can States be Compelled to Pay Their Debts?* by Bradley T. Johnson, *Amer. Law Rev.* (1878), XII; *Suing the State*, by George M. Davie, *Amer. Law Reg.* (1884), XXXII; *The Eleventh Amendment*, by Allen C. Braxton, *Virg. Bar Ass.* (1907), XX; *The Eleventh Amendment*, by William D. Guthrie, in *Magna Carta* (1914); *Suability of States by Individuals*, by Judge Jacob-Trieber, *Amer. Law Rev.* (1907), XLI; *The Eleventh Amendment and the Non-Suability of a State*, by A. H. Wintersteen, *Amer Law Rev.* (1896), XXX; *Suit Against a State*, by A. D. Lauer, *Amer. Law Reg.* (1893), XLI; *Georgia Bar Ass. Report* (1896), 171; *Washington State Bar Ass. Report* (1887), 127.

they said, "public faith will be the synonym of public dishonesty." [1] In *Cunningham* v. *Macon & Brunswick R. R.*, 109 U. S. 446, the Court held that a bill in equity by mortgage bondholders to foreclose on a railroad whose bonds had been endorsed by the State of Georgia, which had been taken possession of by that State, could not be maintained, since the State was an indispensable party and could not be sued. [2] In *New Hampshire* v. *Louisiana*, 108 U. S. 76, the Court refused to sanction an attempted evasion of the Eleventh Amendment by creditors who had assigned their bonds to a State which accepted them simply for the purpose of bringing suit. [3]

While these decisions were undoubtedly wise and in full conformity with the Constitution, they profoundly disturbed the conservative element of the community, which saw in them only encouragement for future municipal and State defaulters; and they even evoked a demand for the abolition of the Eleventh Amendment. "We do not believe in the wisdom or justice of this Amendment at all," said the *Independent*. "It ought to be amended out of the Constitution. . . . The repudiation of State debts under the cloak of this Amendment has become the shame and disgrace of our country, and the proper remedy to arrest this enormous evil is to give to the Federal Courts the power which the Eleventh Amendment took away, and authorize Congress by appropriate legislation to carry that power into full and complete

[1] The premium bond troubles of Louisiana were also involved in *New Orleans Board of Liquidation* v. *Hart* (1886), 118 U. S. 136; see *Wolff* v. *New Orleans* (1881), 103 U. S. 358; *Louisiana* v. *Pilsbury* (1882), 105 U. S. 278.

[2] Creditors of South Carolina were held to be similarly remediless in 1886, in *Hagood* v. *Southern*, 117 U. S. 52.

[3] See, however, *South Dakota* v. *North Carolina*, 192 U. S. 286, in 1904, in which a State was allowed to recover on bonds of another State. As to this case see *John Archibald Campbell* (1920), by Henry G. Connor, and see also severe attack by Camm Patteson in *Virginia Law Reg.* (1905), X, 855.

effect." [1] "The Supreme Court should be able to compel a State to pay its debts. With this power lodged in the Supreme Court and lodged in Congress, the system of State repudiation would come to an end, greatly in the interests of justice." A resolve was actually introduced in the House for the repeal of the Eleventh Amendment and for the grant to Congress of the power to provide by appropriate legislation for enforcement of the obligation of contracts entered into by any of the States of the Union. [2] Fortunately, no such radical move was found necessary; for the Court, in 1885, finally enounced a doctrine as to suits against State officials which, to a certain extent, relieved the situation, and marked a new era in the relations of the National Judiciary and the States. The case in which this momentous decision was made was one of a long series from 1881 to 1887, involving the notorious Mahone-Riddleberger legislation in Virginia, by which that State had practically repudiated $11,000,000 out of a refunded debt of $30,000,000, had cut in half the interest on its outstanding bonds, and had repealed the provisions of law which made coupons on its bonds receivable in payment of taxes. [3] This violation of the State's express agreement with its bond and coupon holders had been held by the Court, in 1881, in *Hartman* v. *Greenhow*, 102 U. S. 672, to be invalid as an impairment of obligation of contract; and in an answer to

---

[1] *Nation*, March 8, 1883; *Independent*, Feb. 1, March 15, 1883.

[2] *47th Cong., 2d Sess.*, 1356, Jan. 19, 1883. The Amendment was introduced by William R. Moore of Tennessee. It provided for rescinding the Eleventh Amendment and that "The Congress shall have power to provide by appropriate legislation for the legal enforcement of the obligation of contracts entered into by any of the States of the Union."

[3] For details of this and subsequent legislation and the litigation arising out of it, see *Nation*, April 30, 1885; see also *Independent*, March 29, April 5, 12, 19, 1882; *History of the Virginia Debt Controversy* (1897), by William R. Royall; *The Readjuster Movement in Virginia* (1917), by Charles C. Pearson; *The Constitutionality of Repudiation*, by D. H. Chamberlain, and *A Reply*, by John S. Wise, *North Amer. Rev.* (1884), CXXXVIII.

the argument that legislation as to receipt of taxes, binding future Legislatures, might result in crippling the power and resources of the State in time of war or other great calamity, Judge Field had said, quoting the Virginia Court of Appeals: " 'At such a time, however, the honored name and high credit secured to a State by unbroken faith, even in adversity, will, apart from all other considerations, be worth more to her in dollars — incalculably more — than the comparatively insignificant amount of interest on a portion of the public debt enjoyed by breach of contract.' The Court thus expressed a great truth, which all just men appreciate, that there is no wealth or power equal to that which ultimately comes to a State when in all her engagement she keeps her faith unbroken." In an effort to avoid the force of this decision, Virginia had proceeded to pass legislation imposing such restrictions upon bondholders as practically to destroy the commercial value of the bonds and coupons; and when bondholders declined to comply with these new restrictions, the State officers attempted to distrain their property in payment of taxes. It was at this point that the Court, in 1885, proclaimed a doctrine which relieved the situation, and which made the provisions of the Eleventh Amendment far less onerous than they had been hitherto supposed to be. In *Poindexter* v. *Greenhow*, 114 U. S. 270, it pointed out that there was a clear distinction between a suit against a State or a State official to compel it or him to perform an obligation of the State, and a suit against a State official to recover damages for an act performed in carrying out an unconstitutional State law; and that no official could claim exemption from personal responsibility for acts committed under such an invalid law. Accordingly, it sustained a suit in detinue against a city treasurer, and held that the treasurer could not justify, under an unconstitutional State statute, his action in seizing property after the tax-payer had made a valid tender of coupons in payment of his tax.   There is an important distinction between the government of a State and the State itself, and governing officials within the sphere of their agency are the State, but outside of their agency are lawless usurpers, individual trespassers, said Judge Matthews, in substance.   "This distinction between the government of a State and the State itself is important.   To deny it or blot it out obliterates the line of demarcation that separates constitutional government from abso-lutism, free self-government based on the sovereignty of the people, from that despotism, whether of the one or the many, which enables the agent of the State to declare and decree that he is the State, to say '*L'État, c'est Moi.*' . . . How else can these principles of individual liberty and right be maintained, if, when violated, the judicial tribunals are forbidden to visit penalties upon individual offenders, who are the in-struments of wrong, whenever they interpose the shield of the State?   The doctrine is not to be toler-ated.   The whole frame and scheme of the political institutions of the country, State and Federal, protest against it.   Their continued existence is not compatible with it.   It is the doctrine of absolutism, pure, simple and naked; and of communism, which is its twin; the double progeny of the same evil birth."   Judges Bradley, Miller, Gray and the Chief Justice dissented, saying that: "A State can only act by and through its constituted authorities and it is represented by them in all the ordinary exhibitions of sovereign power. It may act wrongly; it may act unconstitutionally; but to say that it is not the State that acts is to make

a misuse of terms, and tends to confound all just distinctions. It also tends, in our judgment, to inculcate
the dangerous doctrine that the Government may be
treated and resisted as a usurpation whenever the
citizen, in the exercise of his private judgment, deems
its acts to be unconstitutional." They asserted that
against unconstitutional oppression by the State or
its officers, the citizen had sufficient redress by habeas
corpus, by defense to prosecutions, by injunction or by
mandamus; but this right, they said, is "a very different thing from the right to coerce the State into a fulfillment of its contracts." That these suits were attempts
to coerce the State, they held to be plain. "It is useless to deceive ourselves by an adroit use of words,
or by a train of metaphysical reasoning. . . . This is
the first time, we believe, since the Eleventh Amendment was adopted, in which a State has been coerced
by judicial proceedings at the suit of individuals in
the Federal Courts." [1]

With this decision and similar decisions in the next
year, 1886, there began a new epoch in the relation of
the Federal and State powers. "It marks another revolution in constitutional construction, which will be
regarded by some as a virtual change of the Constitution itself, and by others as an adaptation of conflicting parts to the broad requirements of justice,"
said the *Nation;* and it added, with considerable
grounds for the statement: "Since the State can act
only through its agents, of whom the tax collector is

[1] See *Antoni* v. *Greenhow* (1883), 107 U. S. 760, and the comment on this case in
Nation, March 8, 1883; *Ex parte Crouch, Ex parte Royall* (1884), 112 U. S. 178,
181; *Allen* v. *Baltimore & Ohio R. R. Co.* (1885), 114 U. S. 311; *Carter* v. *Greenhow*, 114 U. S. 317; *Pleasants* v. *Greenhow*, 114 U. S. 323; *Marye* v. *Parsons*, 114
U. S. 325; *Barry* v. *Edmunds* (1886), 116 U. S. 550; *Royall* v. *Virginia* (1886),
116 U. S. 572; *Stewart* v. *Virginia* (1886), 117 U. S. 612; *Ex parte Royall* (1886),
117 U. S. 241. See also *Nation*, April 23, May 7, 1885, Feb. 4, 11, March 4, 1886;
Ex parte Ayers (1887), 123 U. S. 443; *McCullough* v. *Virginia* (1898), 172 U. S. 102.

one, the point [made by the Court] seems to be forced, and although in accord with principles of justice, yet practically a change of the Constitution and one of exceeding gravity." A few weeks later, the *Nation* pointed out how largely the partisan line had broken down in the Court, in the consideration of the broad issue. "The question of State-Rights in its most extreme form was directly involved in this matter, and it might have been expected that the strong Republican bias of our highest Bench would have produced a close approach to unanimity against the traditional Democratic side of that issue. It certainly might have been supposed that the one representative of the Democratic party in the Court would plant himself firmly upon the Eleventh Amendment. . . . In point of fact, Judge Field took the contrary ground, while it was from the lips of a Republican Judge, speaking for three party associates, as well as himself, that there issued a rather heated protest against the attempt of the Court to treat the Eleventh Amendment as a mere jingle of words, to be slurred over by cunning subtleties and artificial methods of interpretation, so as to give it a little compliance, without regarding its substantial meaning." Still later, the *Nation* pointed out with great force, "the great triumph of honesty over fraud", and the immense importance of these cases in bringing constitutional law into conformity with morals. "If they are accepted without resistance, they will make the first victory of the Supreme Court over a really recalcitrant and angry State. . . . Until the present time, the United States has never been victorious in its Judiciary department over a State determined to defy it. . . . There have been many other cases before the Supreme Court in which acts of State Legislatures have been declared unconstitutional and

void, but never, when the State has used all its civil
power, its intellect and obstinacy, backed finally by
a united public opinion, to frustrate the constitutional
demands of hated creditors.   These decisions are, then,
the first absolutely peaceable triumph of the Constitution and its honest principles over the narrowness,
bitterness and often dishonesty of local popular will,
and as such they form an epoch in constitutional history.   It is a triumph of the regular power of the National Government over the irregular power of the
State."

While there were, in subsequent years, some vacil-
lations and inconsistencies in the decisions of the Court
involving State officials, the principles laid down in the
various *Virginia Coupon Cases* have been, in general,
the foundation for an extension of National power over
the States which has had a profound effect on the course
of American law.[1]

In this connection, it should be noted that, in spite
of its tendency to uphold the authority of the Nation
in the exercise of political power, the Court showed
itself as determined to defend the rights of an individual, when trespassed upon by an officer of the National Government, as when injured by the action of a
State officer; and in a memorable opinion in 1882, it
had applied to the National Government itself the
same principles of distinction between the right to sue
a Government officer for his personal illegal acts and
the right to sue the Government itself, which it later
applied to the State.   In *United States* v. *Lee*, 106 U. S.
196, the son of Gen. Robert E. Lee sued to recover
possession of eleven hundred acres known as the Arlington estate, which was formerly the property of

---

[1] *Public Service Rates and the Fourteenth Amendment*, by Nathan Mathews, Jr.
and William G. Thompson, *Harv. Law Rev.* (1901), XV.

Mrs. Lee as heir of her grandfather, George Washington Custis Lee.   This estate had been bid in by the United States Government at a tax sale during the Civil War, and later used as a National Cemetery, being in the possession and under the control of the defendants in this case, who were military officers placed in charge by the President.   In the lower Court, the Attorney-General of the United States, Charles Devens, had, without making the United States a party to the suit, filed a motion to dismiss, on the ground that the property belonged to the Government and was in actual possession of its officers, and that therefore the Court was without jurisdiction to entertain the suit.[1]   The Court, in a notable opinion rendered by Judge Miller, considered with great fullness the doctrine of immunity of the Government from suits without its consent, and held that this immunity did not apply when suit was brought against Government officials in unlawful possession of property.   "No man in this country is so high that he is above the law.   No officer of the law may set that law at defiance, with impunity.   All the officers of the Government, from the highest to the lowest, are creatures of the law and are bound to obey it."   "Shall it be said," he asked, "that the Courts cannot give a remedy when the citizen has been deprived of his property by force, his estate seized and converted to the use of the government without lawful authority, without any process of law and without compensation, because the President has ordered it and his officers are in possession?"   To sanction this would be to sanction tyranny.   "The evils supposed to grow out of the possible interference of judicial action with the exercise of powers of the Government

[1] The case was argued March 10–13, 1882, reargued Oct. 18, 19, 1882, and decided Dec. 4, 1882.   William J. Robertson, W. J. Shipman and S. F. Beach appeared for Lee.

essential to some of its important operations, will be seen to be small indeed compared to this evil." Moreover, said Judge Miller, answering the arguments of the Attorney-General: "Hypothetical cases of great evils may be suggested by a particularly fruitful imagination in regard to almost every law upon which depend the rights of the individual or of the Government, and if the existence of laws is to depend upon their capacity to withstand such criticism, the whole fabric of the law must fail." And he concluded with a striking characterization of the Judiciary, as inherently the weakest of the three branches of the Government: "Dependent as its Courts are for the enforcement of their judgments, upon officers appointed by the Executive and removable at his pleasure, with no patronage and no control of purse or sword, their power and influence rest solely upon the public sense of the necessity for the existence of a tribunal to which all may appeal for the assertion and protection of rights guaranteed by the Constitution and by the laws of the land, and on the confidence reposed in the soundness of their decisions and the purity of their motives. From such a tribunal no well-founded fear can be entertained of injustice to the Government, or purpose to obstruct or diminish its just authority." In accordance with its opinion, the Court, finding the tax sale illegal, gave judgment for the Lee heirs and ousted the Government from possession. An elaborate dissenting opinion, concurred in by Chief Justice Waite and Judges Bradley and Woods, was given by the new Judge, Gray, in which it was contended that the suit was simply an action, "to invade the possession of the sovereign and to disregard the fundamental maxim that the sovereign cannot be sued."

Though the decision is now regarded as one of the

glories of American law, there were varied views taken
of it at the time of its rendition. The greater part of
the Bar, however, shared in the feelings which were
very strikingly expressed in the *New York World* that :
"All self-respecting Americans will rejoice to learn
that the Supreme Court has restored to the heirs of
General Robert E. Lee the Arlington estate, which
for twenty years past has been lawlessly and violently
held by the Government without a penny of compensation to the owners. . . . The decision is of especial
interest and importance at this time, as reaffirming
conspicuously the supreme sovereignty of the Law,
'the State's collected will', above all the heats and
fluctuations of popular and sectional passion. The
highest tribunal of the Union by its decision, in short,
has recognized the wisdom and solidity of a response
made by Judge Shipman to one member of the Court,
during the proceedings — a response which will, let
us hope, become proverbial in American thought and
speech. 'Do I understand your position to be,' said
one of the Supreme Court Judges to Judge Shipman,
'that if the title to a piece of land on which the Government has set up a lighthouse should be disputed, the
claimant might bring an action of ejectment, and if
successful, remove the lighthouse?' 'Certainly,' replied the intrepid lawyer. 'That is my position. Far
better extinguish all the lighthouses in the land than
put out the light of the Law.' " [1]

The decision appealed also to independent journals
like the *Springfield Republican*, as being "very sensible
law"; and while it "greatly modifies the doctrine that
the Government cannot be sued by the private citizen,
it correspondingly strengthens the safeguards of pri-

[1] *New York World*, Dec. 5, 1882; *Springfield Republican*, Dec. 7, 1882; *Amer-
Law Rev.* (1883), XVII, 444; *New York Commercial Advertiser*, Dec. 5, 1882. See
also *Philadelphia Press*, Dec. 6, 1882.

vate right in property. . . . It was in one of the
most despotic of those monarchies in the last century
that the stubborn miller, whose windmill adjoined,
and still adjoins, the palace of Frederick the Great,
replied to the covetous efforts of his Majesty to get
possession, 'There are still Courts in Berlin, sire', and
he relied on the Courts to protect him, as they did."
On the other hand, a writer in the *American Law Review* expressed the view that the decision was an infringement on the sovereignty of the United States,
and that the rule that the Government cannot be sued
has had "its vitality almost wholly emasculated, by the
further ruling that the principle cannot be invoked
by any officer of the Government against whom, in
the discharge of his duty, an action is brought. The
reasoning of the majority is certainly forcible, even
plausible; but that of the minority through Mr. Justice Gray is invincible. . . . The majority opinion
goes so far that a recoil will be the natural result."
And a paper of extreme views on the subject of the
war bitterly attacked the decision, which, it said,
"will strike the man who fought to preserve that very
Court, and the bones of whose comrades lie whitening
on these plains, with something like a feeling of disgust, if not amazement. . . . The argument used by
the Court in granting possession was, in brief, that
public officers, acting under the power of sovereign
prerogative while the Government was repelling treason, were answerable, after that treason had been
crushed, to judicial authority. That authority now
revokes the action of the Government done under
peculiar and, we think, justifiable circumstances. The
future action of this Government's officers will be
watched with interest."

Concomitant with the policy of the Court in setting

its face against State repudiation of its bonded obligations was its firm condemnation of all attempts by States to avoid compliance with their solemn legislative contracts in corporate charters containing exemptions from State taxation. While holding that such charters must be construed with utmost strictness against the corporations, and that no exemption from taxation was to be established by implication or other than by the most express phraseology, it continued to adhere to its doctrine, first enounced in 1854, that it was competent for a State Legislature to grant to a corporation an irrevocable tax exemption and that such a grant could not be impaired by a subsequent Legislature. This doctrine had always met with powerful resistance from State officials, and had been the subject of constant and numerous dissents by members of the Court itself. Nevertheless, in 1878, it had been reaffirmed in an eloquent opinion rendered by Judge Swayne in *Farrington* v. *Tennessee*, 95 U. S. 679. "Contracts," he said, "mark the progress of communities in civilization and prosperity. They guard, as far as possible, against the fluctuations of human affairs. They seek to give stability to the present and certainty to the future. They gauge the confidence of man in the truthfulness and integrity of his fellow-man. They are springs of business, trade and commerce. Without them, Society could not go on. Spotless faith in their fulfillment honors alike communities and individuals. Where this is wanting in the body politic, the process of descent has begun, and a lower plane will be speedily reached. To the extent to which the defect exists among individuals, there is decay and degeneracy. . . . A Republican government can have no foundation other than the virtue of its citizens. When that is largely impaired, all is in peril. It is needless to lift the veil and contemplate the future of such a people. History but repeats itself. The trite old aphorism that 'honesty is the best policy' is true alike of individuals and communities. It is vital to the highest welfare." [1] But while still refusing to invalidate these tax exemptions, the Court plainly showed, in the trend of its decisions, a reflection of the public sentiment which was being aroused by the arbitrary, corrupt and monopolistic activities of many of the corporations of the day. For as in the *Granger Cases* and in the *Sinking Fund Case* it evidenced its intention to strengthen the control of both State and National Governments over such corporations, so now it displayed an equally marked tendency to restrict the scope of corporate tax exemptions and to uphold the State's denial of their legal existence, wherever possible. As Judge Brown said, later: "Exemptions from taxation are not favored by law. . . . It is not too much to say that Courts are astute to seize upon evidence tending to show that such exemptions were not intended, or that they have become inoperative by changes in the original constitution of the companies." [2] Here, as elsewhere throughout the law, the Court was responsive to the spirit of the times and to the new and constantly increasing demand for the subordination of private rights and privileges to the interests of the public welfare.

[1] See *Nation*, Jan. 2, 1879; *Washington University* v. *Rowe* (1869), 8 Wall. 439, and *Humphrey* v. *Pegues* (1873), 16 Wall. 244; *Exemption from Taxation by Legislative Contract*, by James F. Colby, *Amer. Law Rev.* (1878), XIII.

[2] *Yazoo & Miss. River Valley R. R.* v. *Adams* (1901), 180 U. S. 1, 22; see also especially *Morgan* v. *Louisiana* (1876), 93 U. S. 217; *Washington University* v. *Rouse* (1869), 8 Wall. 439; *Humphrey* v. *Pegues* (1873), 16 Wall. 244; *Sioux City Street Ry. Co.* v. *Sioux City* (1891), 138 U. S. 98; *Ford* v. *Delta & Pine Land Co.* (1897), 164 U. S. 662; *Grand Lodge of Louisiana* v. *New Orleans* (1897), 186 U. S. 143; *Covington* v. *Kentucky* (1899), 173 U. S. 231; *Legislative Tax Exemption Contracts*, by Ernest W. Huffcut, *Amer. Law Rev.* (1891), XXIV; *The Nature of Tax Exemptions*, by Frank J. Goodnow, *Columbia Law Rev.* (1913), XIII.

Another form of repudiation continued to be sternly discountenanced by the Court, in a long series of opinions in which it declined to modify its doctrine, announced as early as 1863, with reference to municipal ¦bonds, valid when issued but subsequently held illegal by State Courts. During Chief Justice Waite's term of service, nearly two hundred cases involving such bonds were decided by the Court, and in very few instances were the efforts of the municipalities to escape payment successful. Attempts to avoid payment of bonds, by the creation of a new municipal corporation in place of the corporation issuing the bonds, were dealt with by the Court in *Barkley* v. *Levee Commissioners* and *Broughton* v. *Pensacola*, 93 U. S. 258, 266, in 1876; and an attempt by the city of Mobile to escape payment of its debts, by dissolution of the municipal corporations and legislative creation of a new corporation containing less territory but substantially the same population and property, was defeated in *Mobile* v. *Watson*, 116 U. S. 289, in 1886.[1] In *Louisiana* v. *Pilsbury*, 105 U. S. 278, the contract contained in bonds issued by the city of New Orleans was held to be impaired by extraordinary legislation which provided for bonds the time of whose payment both as to principal and interest was to be determined by chance in a lottery.[2]

---

[1] A singular case involving the failure of a county in Missouri to pay its bonds was *Findlay* v. *McAllister* (1885), 113 U. S. 104, in which a bondholder was held to have good cause for an action for damages against persons conspiring as "the Taxpayers' Association of Scotland County" to prevent by threats, etc. sale of property seized under levy. To hold otherwise, said Judge Woods, "would allow an organized band of conspirators fraudulently and maliciously to obstruct and defeat the process of the Courts and render a judgment nugatory and worthless. Such a conclusion would be contrary to the principles of the common law and of right and justice."

[2] In a few cases, the Court found itself forced so to construe the law and the Constitution as to permit municipalities to escape payment of their honest debts; but in most of such instances, it expressed its regret that such should be the result of its decision. In *Meriwether* v. *Garrett* (1880), 102 U. S. 472, it held that the public

One result of this firm policy of the Court in requiring cities and counties to pay their debts was to awaken in parts of the country — notably in Missouri, Iowa, Kansas, Wisconsin, Michigan and the Southern States — a considerable feeling of hostility, which led to the introduction of a bill in Congress, in 1878, providing that no municipal or public corporation should be sued in the United States Courts. Such jurisdiction, it was said, "leads to centralization" and "deprives a State of a free and right exercise of its sovereignty." Congress took no action; and the general public agreed with the *Nation* in saying that : "Instead of interfering to make repudiation easy for these bodies, it is the plain duty of Congress to arm the National Courts with whatever additional powers are necessary to be used in bringing them to a sense of their legal obligations." [1] The antagonism to these Courts, on account of their decisions in the municipal bond cases committing county officials to jail for refusal to levy taxes to pay bonds, remained active in several States for many years; and as late as 1893 the Governor of Missouri sent a message to the State Legislature, reviewing the situation with respect to such imprisoned officials, and recommending that action should be taken by the State "to assert the outraged dignity of the State against usurpation of power by the Federal Judiciary." [2]

property and taxes of the City of Memphis, whose charter had been repealed and whose property was in the hands of a receiver appointed by the State, were not liable to respond to a suit for payment by bondholders; Judges Strong, Swayne and Harlan dissented on the ground that the State receivership legislation, "certainly very extraordinary and unprecedented in the history of the country", was an impairment of the obligation of the contract contained in the bonds issued by the city. See also *Amy* v. *Shelby County Taxing District* (1885), 114 U. S. 387; *Louisiana* v. *New Orleans* (1883), 109 U. S. 285.

[1] *Nation*, Jan. 2, 1879. "The Federal Judiciary and the Repudiators." The *Nation*, on Aug. 8, 1878, had made a suggestion that Congress appropriate no public money for the benefit of counties guilty of fraud or refusing to pay interest on their loans", citing certain counties and townships in Kansas as "shameless defaulters."

[2] *Amer. Law Rev.* (1893), XXVII, 393.

While the Court, between 1878 and 1889, was thus steadily strengthening the political and governmental powers of the Nation and its control over the industrial and economic interests of the country, these powers and this control were being further enhanced by the immense increase in litigation which came within the jurisdiction of the inferior Courts of the United States — an increase caused, not merely by the growth of subjects of litigation, but also by the extension of National jurisdiction through Congressional action. Mention has already been made of the volume of cases in these Courts which arose out of municipal bond repudiation, out of the Reconstruction Laws, out of the enlargement of the scope of admiralty, out of State railroad regulation, out of railroad receiverships, and out of the insistence by litigants on testing the validity of State statutes under the Fourteenth Amendment.[1] Notwithstanding all this increased burden upon the United States Courts, Congressional legislation, between 1867 and 1885, had opened still further fields of jurisdiction.

An early attempt by Congress to enlarge the jurisdiction of the Supreme Court itself had been defeated by a decision of vast importance rendered by the Court, in 1875 in *Murdock* v. *Memphis*, 20 Wall. 590, a case which involved a question whose decision seemed destined to affect profoundly the whole subsequent legal

---

[1] The increase in litigation in the United States Courts had resulted in demands for reorganization of the National Judiciary system and for relief of the Supreme Court from its overcrowded docket. Projects of relief introduced in Congress at various times from 1876 to 1884, failed to pass, though advocated by the American Bar Association and by the Bar in general. It was not until the Circuit Court of Appeals Act of 1891 that any adequate remedial legislation was secured. See articles in *Amer. Law Rev.* (1876), X; (1884), XVIII; (1889), XXIII; *Amer. Law Reg.* (1881–82), XXIX, XXX (1884), XXXII; *Nation*, Feb. 10, 1876, May 18, 1882, April 24, 1884; *North Amer. Rev.* (1881), CXXXII; and see especially full summary of the effort for reform of the Judiciary system, *Amer. Bar Ass. Journ.* (1921), VII, 24 *et seq.*

history of the country and which arose as follows. By the Act of February 5, 1867, Congress in amending the original Judiciary Act of 1789, had enacted (among other changes) a new section in place of the famous Twenty-Fifth Section relative to writs of error to State Courts. It had omitted the last clause of the old Act which had in express terms limited the power of the Supreme Court, in reversing the judgment of a State Court, to a consideration of errors on the face of the record and of errors respecting Federal questions only. The issue presented was, whether Congress, by this omission, intended that the Court should, on future writs of error, examine into *all* errors in the record, whether respecting Federal questions or otherwise. If the Court should decide that this was the intention, not only would its work be enormously increased, but the class of matters coming within its jurisdiction and presented for decision would be revolutionized. Such was the importance of the case that, after it had been first argued, January 21, 1873, by W. J. Scott and J. B. Heiskell against W. T. Otto, B. M. Estes, J. M. Carlisle and J. D. McPherson, it was reargued at the request of the Court on April 2, 3, 1873, by the same counsel and by Philip Phillips and Benjamin R. Curtis, who "in response to the invitation of this Court", appeared as *amici curiae*. The contention was made by counsel that the new statute was passed just after the overt acts of rebellion had been suppressed by the force of Federal arms, but while it was uncertain how far the spirit of opposition, though covert, yet remained both alive and active, and that the new statute showed an apprehension that Federal justice would be obstructed by local and State animosities and revenges, and that the record in State Courts might artfully suppress the fact that Federal questions had been actually adjudicated. It was pointed out that other Congressional legislation about the same time, providing for extension of the right of habeas corpus and for removal into the United States Courts in case of the existence of local State prejudice, showed a general intention on the part of Congress to enlarge the jurisdiction of those Courts. That these contentions were correct, and that it was the real intention of Congress to provide, by this amendment, that every question passed on by the State Court should be open for reconsideration in the Supreme Court, is highly probable. Undoubtedly, the whole trend of the legislation of the period sustained this view. The Court, nevertheless, in an opinion by Judge Miller rendered on January 11, 1875, over one and a half years after the argument, held that Congress, by dropping the clause from the old Judiciary Act, had not intended to change the law as it had existed for eighty years; and that, if it had actually intended such a change, it would have legislated in express and affirmative terms.[1] In reaching this conclusion, it is evident that the Court was largely influenced by a consideration of the alarming results which would have followed from the opposite interpretation of the statute. For it stated that if a party could bring here, for decision on all matters involved, any case from a State Court, by merely raising a Federal question, and if the Court, on examination in conference, finding the Federal question clearly untenable, were obliged to examine the rest of the record and decide all points involved, it would follow that there would be "no conceivable case so insignificant in amount or unimportant in principle that a perverse and obstinate man may not bring it to this Court by

[1] See *The Enforcement of State Law by State Courts*, by Henry Schofield, *Illinois Law Rev.* (1908), III.

the aid of a sagacious lawyer raising a Federal question in the record — a point which he may be wholly unable to support by the facts, or which he may well know will be decided against him, the moment it is stated." Hence, it said, it would require "a very bold reach of thought, and a readiness to impute to Congress a radical and hazardous change of a policy vital in its essential nature to the independence of the State Courts, to believe that that body contemplated or intended" such a result. Judge Bradley in dissenting, believed that Congress did intend exactly this "radical" change, however unwise it might be, and that the omission of the original clause from the Judiciary "meant something and effected something." [1]

While this decision restricted the jurisdiction of the United States Courts, the legislative policy which Congress had adopted during the war, and which it now continued to pursue, led to extension of such jurisdiction in many directions. By the Acts of March 3, 1863, and of April 9, May 11, and July 27, 1866, Congress had authorized the removal into these Courts of any prosecution in a State Court based on acts committed under National authority in suppressing the Rebellion; and these statutes had been vigorously upheld in *Mayor of Nashville* v. *Cooper*, 6 Wall. 247, in 1868, the Court saying: "It is the right and the duty of the National Government to have its Constitution and laws interpreted and applied by its own judicial tribunals. . . . The decisions of the Courts of the United States, within their sphere of action, are as conclusive as the laws of Congress made in pursuance

[1] For other examples of decisions by which the Court sought to relieve itself of the rapidly growing volume of cases on its docket, see *State Railroad Tax Cases* (1876), 92 U. S. 575, in which a rule was laid down to govern the granting of injunctions against State tax laws by the Circuit Courts; and see *Hawes* v. *Oakland* (1882), 104 U. S. 450, laying down the rule for suits brought by stockholders against their own corporations; *Huntington* v. *Palmer* (1882), 104 U. S. 482.

of the Constitution.   This is essential to the peace of
the Nation, and to the vigor and efficiency of the government." [1]   By the Act of March 2, 1867, Congress
gave to plaintiffs the right to remove a case from the
State Courts under certain conditions, that right having
theretofore been confined to the defendants; and the
Court held, in *Chicago & Northwestern Railway Co.* v.
Whitton, 13 Wall. 270, in 1872, that such a right of
removal was not properly an exercise of appellate
jurisdiction, "but rather an indirect mode by which
the Federal Court acquires original jurisdiction of the
cause"; and that there was no constitutional objection to such a provision, "where a plaintiff discovers,
after suit brought in a State Court, that the prejudice
and local influence, against which the Constitution
intended to guard, are such as are likely to prevent him
from obtaining justice."

By the Act of March 3, 1875, passed two months
after the decision in *Murdock* v. *Memphis*, Congress
still further enlarged the powers of the Circuit Courts
by granting to them for the first time jurisdiction in
all suits arising under the Constitution and laws of
the United States.   This statute greatly increased
the classes of cases removable from the State into the
National Courts; and since, in cases taken on writ of
error or appeal from the Circuit Court to the Supreme
Court, all questions whether Federal or State, presented on the record were passed upon by the latter
Court, Congress thus practically enabled that Court
to review matters, which the decision in *Murdock* v.
Memphis had tended to eliminate from its consideration.   Naturally, the United States Courts soon be-

[1] See *Justices* v. *Murray* (1870), 9 Wall. 274, in which the Court held that so
much of the Act of March 3, 1863, as authorized removal of a case after judgment,
for retrial in the Federal Court on the facts and the law, was unconstitutional, as
a violation of the Seventh Amendment; as to this case, see *New York Times*, March
21, 1870.   See also *McKee* v. *Rains* (1870), 10 Wall. 22.

came overwhelmed with litigation.[1] Examples of two classes of cases which were thus brought within the National control, were illustrated by decisions in the following important cases, in 1884 and 1885. In *Ames v. Kansas*, 111 U. S. 449, which was an action brought by the State of Kansas to invalidate the consolidation of one of its corporations, the Kansas Pacific Company, with the Union Pacific Railway Company, the Court held that a suit brought by a State in a State Court was removable into the Circuit Court; and that the fact that the Supreme Court had original Federal jurisdiction of suits by a State did not exclude Congress from granting similar jurisdiction to inferior Federal Courts. "It rests with the Legislative department of the government to say to what extent such grants shall be made," said Chief Justice Waite, "and it may safely be assumed that nothing will ever be done to encroach upon the high privileges of those for whose protection the constitutional provision was intended." In the *Pacific Railroad Removal Cases*, 115 U. S. 1, the Court held that a suit against a railroad chartered by the United States

[1] Early Removal Acts had grown out of fear of prejudice in State Courts against the National Government. See Act of Sept. 24, 1789, Act of Feb. 2, 1815, Act of March 9, 1815, Act of April 27, 1816, growing out of opposition of New England to the War of 1812; Act of March 2, 1833, growing out of nullification in South Carolina; Act of July 27, 1866, and Act of March 2, 1867, growing out of conditions in the Southern States; see also Civil Rights Act of March 1, 1875. *Gordon v. Longest*, 16 Pet. 97, in 1842 was the first instance in which a State Court refused to a party a right to remove his cause to the Circuit Court of the United States; and the Court had said in that case: "One great object in the establishment of the Courts of the United States and regulating their jurisdiction was to have a tribunal in each State presumed to be free from local influence, and to which all who were non-residents or aliens might resort for legal redress. But this object would be defeated if a State Judge, in the exercise of his discretion, may deny to the party entitled to it a removal of his cause."

See *Removal of Cases*, by J. F. Dillon, *Southern Law Rev.* (1876), II; *Removal of Suits from State to Federal Courts*, by Allen B. Magruder, *Amer. Law Rev.* (1878), XIII. *Removal of Causes from State Courts to Federal Courts*, by John F. Dillon was published in 1877, and a third edition in 1881, of which the *American Law Review* (1881), XV, said: "The expansion of the monograph, from 105 pages in 1877 to 168 pages in 1881, illustrates the appalling growth of case law in this country, and the strong tendency of the Federal Judiciary to assert vigorously their own jurisdiction"

arose "under the laws of the United States", and was therefore removable into the Circuit Court. The decision had important results in the Western States, as it transferred the trial of tort cases to a large extent from the State to the United States Courts.[1]

The enhancement of the National power through these Removal Acts and the ensuing decisions of the Court aroused a considerable sentiment of jealous opposition in the States, and their resentment at the extent to which litigants, especially corporations, took advantage of the right to remove suits into the United States Courts led to the enactment in many States of statutes providing that no corporation should be permitted to do business within the State, without first filing an agreement not to remove any case from a State Court. The constitutional validity of these State laws was tested as early as 1874, and in *Home Insurance Co.* v. *Morse*, 20 Wall. 445, such an act of Wisconsin relative to fire insurance companies was held invalid, the Court deciding that both individuals and corporations had a right to appeal to the Courts of the United States, which right was protected by the Constitution; and in 1887, this doctrine was reaffirmed in *Barron* v. *Burnside*, 121 U. S. 186, in which the Court held invalid a statute of Iowa relative to removal of suits by foreign corporations. The decision was attacked by many writers as hostile to the interests of the Western States, which had "particularly suffered from foreign corporations, especially railroad and insurance." [2]

Another enlargement of the powers of the National

[1] See also for construction of the Removals Act of 1875, *Starin* v. *New York* (1885), 115 U. S. 248; *Detroit* v. *Dean* (1883), 106 U. S. 537.

[2] *Recent Centralizing Tendencies in the Supreme Court*, by Frederic P. Powers, *Pol. Sci. Qu.* (1890), X. It has not been easy to reconcile the various opinions of the Court on the right of the States to legislate as to removals — see *Doyle* v. *Continental Insurance Co.* (1877), 94 U. S. 535; *Donald* v. *Phil. & Reading R. R.* (1916), 241 U. S. 329; *The Constitutionality of Statutes Prohibiting Resort to the Federal Courts*, by Frank Lacy, *Amer. Law Rev.* (1909), XLII.

Judiciary was made by Congress by the Act of March 3, 1885, in which it restored the right of appeal to the Supreme Court in cases of habeas corpus arising out of the restraint of any person in violation of the Constitution or laws of the United States. This right of appeal had been in abeyance for seventeen years, ever since the Act of February 5, 1867, granting such an appeal had been repealed in 1868, at the time of the *McCardle Case.* The effect of this repeal, enacted in the passionate era of Reconstruction, had been disastrous in many ways, and most especially since it left final action in habeas corpus cases with the District and Circuit Judges, unrestrained by decisions of the Supreme Court. These inferior Court Judges, particularly in the Southern and Western States, had gone to so great lengths, in the issue of writs on behalf of persons restrained by State authority, that their assumption of power had greatly alarmed those who believed in the necessity of preserving intact the respective lines of National and State authority. The Federal Judges have asserted power "to annul the criminal judgments of the State Courts, and to pass finally and conclusively upon the validity of the criminal codes, the police regulations, and even the Constitutions of the States", wrote a noted jurist in 1884.[1]

[1] *Abuses of the Writ of Habeas Corpus,* by Seymour D. Thompson, *Amer. Law Rev.* (1884), XVIII; *Abuse in Habeas Corpus Cases by Federal Judges, Amer. Law Rev.* (1896), XXX, 254; *Report of Committee on the Judiciary,* March 8, 1884, *Amer. Law Reg.* (1884), XXXII. See *Ex parte Parks* (1876), 93 U. S. 18, for history of habeas corpus in the Federal Courts. By the original Judiciary Act of 1789, the power of the Federal Judges to issue writs of habeas corpus did not extend to persons restrained by State authorities or unless in custody under or by color of the authority of the United States or committed for trial before some Court of the United States. The first extension arose out of Nullification in South Carolina, the right of habeas corpus being extended by the Act of March 2, 1833, to any persons restrained "from any act done or omitted to be done in pursuance of a law of the United States or on any order of any Judge or Court thereof." The next extension arose out of the conflict with Great Britain in the *McLeod Case,* when by Act of Aug. 29, 1842, foreigners, restrained by a State or other Court in violation of international rights, were given right to habeas corpus, with appeal to the

Consequently, Congress was called upon for action, and
a bill was reported restoring the right of appeal to the
Supreme Court, the House Committee on the Judiciary
stating in its report that: "The jurisdiction assumed
by Federal Judges, if allowed to continue, and continue
unrestrained and unquestioned, cannot fail to bring
the two judicial systems into serious and powerful
conflict unless the State Courts shall tamely submit
to be shorn of the jurisdiction they have exclusively
exercised since the Government existed. . . . With
this right of appeal restored, the true extent of the Act
of 1867 and the true limits of the Federal Courts and
Judges under it will become defined, and it can then
be seen whether further legislation is necessary." [1]

During the entire fifteen years of Waite's term of
office, the Court's growing hesitation to limit the powers
of the National Legislature was further illustrated by
the fact that in only eight cases did it exercise its function of declaring Acts of Congress unconstitutional.
Three of these cases related to Reconstruction legislation, already noted. Of the other five, only one —
the *Trade Mark Cases*, 100 U. S. 82, decided in 1879 —
had an important effect upon the history or development of the country; in this case the Act of Congress
providing for registration of trademarks was held invalid, on the ground that its scope was not confined to
the only subject on which Congress had power to legislate, namely, commerce between the States and with
foreign nations; and the Court again expressed its
regret at being obliged to take this action, saying that:
"A due respect for a coördinate branch of the govern-

Supreme Court. The Reconstruction Act of Feb. 5, 1867, extended right of habeas
corpus to "all cases where any person may be restrained of his or her liberty in
violation of the Constitution or of any treaty or law of the United States."
  [1] See as to this Act of March 3, 1885, *Ex parte Royall* (1886), 117 U. S. 241; *Cunningham* v. *Neagle* (1890), 135 U. S. 1.

ment requires that we shall decide that it has transcended its power, only when that is so plain that we cannot avoid the duty." [1] Nevertheless, though the Courts' action in this respect was highly circumspect, it gave rise, at this period to a more careful and scholarly examination into the legal and historical basis for the exercise of the power of the Court to pass upon the validity of an Act of Congress, than had hitherto been made. As will be recalled, the existence of this power had been attacked by the Democrats (the Republicans of those days) in 1802 and again in 1819, and by the Republicans in 1857 and 1867, but on all these occasions the attack had been made by politicians and had been based on political prejudices. In 1885, the basis of the power became subject to investigation and consideration by jurists of distinction ; and a number of valuable articles were written presenting each side of this controversy—the beginning of a long line of publications which has lasted to the present day.[2]

---

[1] The cases holding Federal statutes unconstitutional during Waite's term were : *United States* v. *Reese* (1876), 92 U. S. 214, one of the Reconstruction laws; *United States* v. *Fox* (1878), 95 U. S. 670, a statute making criminal actions wholly within the domain of the State police power, such as the fraudulent incurring of debts; *Trade Mark Cases* (1879), 100 U. S. 82; *Kilburn* v. *Thompson* (1881), 103 U. S. 168, a House Resolution punishing a witness for contempt, in relation to a matter over which Congress had no jurisdiction to inquire; *United States* v. *Harris* (1883), 106 U. S. 629, a Reconstruction law; *Civil Rights Cases* (1883), 109 U. S. 3, a Reconstruction law; *Boyd* v. *United States* (1886), 116 U. S. 616, an internal revenue law, held to violate the Fourth and Fifth Amendments, as to which see especially *New York World*, March 31, 1876; *Callan* v. *Wilson* (1888), 127 U. S. 540, a District of Columbia statute held to deprive persons of rights to trial by jury. As to the striking feature of the cases, that the Court did not divide on political lines, since in all these cases a Republican Court set aside Republican legislation, see *Address of George F. Hoar*, before the *Virginia Bar Ass.*, *Virg. Law Reg.* (1899), IV, and *The Supreme Court of the United States*, by Charles Hume, *Amer. Law Rev.* (1899), X, 411.

[2] See *Relation of the Judiciary to the Constitution*, by William M. Meigs, *Amer. Law Rev.* (1885), XIX; *A Plea for the Constitution of the United States of America Wounded in the House of its Guardians* (1886), by George Bancroft; *Observations on Mr. George Bancroft's Plea for the Constitution* (1886), by Richard C. McMurtrie; *Judicial Power and Unconstitutional Legislation*, by Brinton Coxe, pub. posthumously in 1893; *The Legislature and the Courts*, by Charles B. Elliott, *Pol. Sci. Qu.* (1890), V.

CHAPTER THIRTY-SEVEN

CHIEF JUSTICES FULLER AND WHITE

1888–1918

On March 23, 1888, Chief Justice Waite died at the age of seventy-one and after fourteen years' service on the Court.[1] "While impartial criticism may not assign to him the extraordinary rank in the esteem of the profession attained by his predecessors," said John Randolph Tucker at the Bar Proceeding on his death, "yet it may with entire truth be affirmed that in the soundness of his judgment, in the diligence of his research, in the clearness of his statements of legal principles and in the tact and skill displayed in the conduct of the business of the Court, he was a worthy successor. . . . It must be confessed that the period of service covered by his term was more fraught with difficulties, more full of new responsibilities and demanded more labor, learning and ability than in any previous period." Waite's great contribution to American law and to American history was of course his expounding of the scope of the War Amendments; and of this phase of his career a most striking account was given by Samuel A. Shellabarger, at the Bar Proceedings. He stated that just before the vote on the confirmation of Waite, Senator Sumner had asked him about Waite's character, saying: "I hesitate. I fear we stand at an epoch in the country's life, in the midst of revolution in its constitutional progress, at a nascent stage in the development of some of its institutions;

[1] See 126 U. S. App. proceedings of the Bar, March 26, 1888.

and I long for a Chief Justice like John Marshall, who
shall pilot the country through the rocks and rapids in
which we are." "I asked Mr. Sumner," said Shellabarger, "to point the President to a few John Marshalls
standing 'in waiting', and I would guarantee the immediate nomination of at least one of them to the Chief
Justiceship. Mr. Sumner said he would require some
time to 'look around.' . . . As neither the time nor
the spirit in which the new Amendments were gendered
nor the text of these Amendments was characterized
by eminent conservatism, therefore to many of us who
engaged in framing these Amendments, the nomination
of Waite 'gave pause.' When, therefore, Waite's
great opinions construing these Amendments came, one
in *Minor's Case* in 1874, holding that the Fourteenth
Amendment does not add to the privileges and immunities of American citizens but simply adds guarantees
for the protection of privileges theretofore existing,
and especially when the great opinion appeared in
1876 in *Cruikshank's Case*, also holding that the Fourteenth Amendment adds nothing to the rights of one
citizen against another, and . . . that these framers did
not design to enable Congress to legislate affirmatively
and directly for the protection of civil rights, but only
to use corrective and restraining legislation as against
the States, ... many of the framers of these Amendments received information regarding their intentions,
which was new, and was not calculated to allay the
apprehensions with which they saw Chief Justice Waite
go upon the Bench. Still I am bound to say now,
when the lapse of years has matured men's views and
cooled their feelings regarding the results of the late
war, and succeeding decisions have explained and
supplemented these early decisions and have guarded
against what was believed to be their erroneous tend-

encies, that I am inclined to think the judgment of
history will be, that he has been, in the main, steadily
right regarding these Amendments, especially in view of
the restraining effect of the later decisions. I am inclined to think that the position in which is now left
the power of the National Government in providing
for the defence of the civil and political rights of the
people, as members of the Nation, especially as that
position is defined in such cases as *Ex parte Virginia,
Ex parte Siebold, Strauder* v. *West Virginia,* and other
later and kindred decisions, is safe and is conservative
of our institutions; and that the great Court of which
Chief Justice Waite has been so long the head will be
entitled to, and will receive, the gratitude and veneration of the people of this Republic, in the generations
to come, for having guided the Republic safely through
many perils and for having fixed its institutions upon
high, just and stable foundations."

As Waite's successor, President Cleveland, after considering Judge Miller, John G. Carlisle of Kentucky
and many others, finally decided upon the appointment
on May 2, 1888, of Melville Weston Fuller of Illinois.
Fuller, who was fifty-five years of age and who had had
no previous judicial experience, was confirmed by the
Senate on July 20, 1888, by a vote of forty-one to
twenty. Fuller's Chief Justiceship lasted twenty-two
years, his death occurring on July 4, 1910, in his seventy-
seventh year. His successor was Edward Douglass
White of Louisiana, who had been an Associate Judge
on the Court since 1894, and who served as Chief
Justice until his death on May 19, 1921.

The period covered by the Chief Justiceships of
Fuller and White is too recent and too clearly within
the view of living men to warrant detailed description,
nor can an adequate account be written until the lapse

of time shall afford a true historical perspective.   No attempt, therefore, is made here to present more than a sketch in broad outlines of the general course of the Court's status and decisions, in the thirty years from 1888 to 1918, with especial reference to their connection with the history of the country.[1]   These years were a period of unprecedented National growth.   They presented a vast variety of legal questions arising out of the new status of the United States as a world power and in control of territorial possessions, as well as out of the multitudinous attempts by State Legislatures and by Congress to solve by legislation the complex social and economic problems of modern times.

The cases involving constitutional questions presented to the Court fall in general into three broad classes : first, those involving the debatable ground between the sphere allotted to the National Government by the Constitution and that reserved to the States; second, those involving the respective rights of individuals and the States in their relations to each other; third, those involving the powers of the National Government under the Constitution over matters relating to which either the States have no authority or have authority only until Congress shall have decided to legislate.[2]   With respect to the first and second classes, the bulk of the cases have arisen under the Commerce Clause and the Fourteenth Amendment.

In interpreting the Fourteenth Amendment, while the Court has shown a consistent and progressive tendency to uphold the legislation of the States, it has developed no new principle which was not already

---

[1] The extent to which the new legal problems and decisions engaged public attention has been indicated in this chapter by copious citation of articles in leading law journals, all of which (with the exception of three) came into existence during the period from 1888 to 1918.

[2] See *Judicial Constitutional Amendment*, by Frederic R. Coudert, *Yale Lau Journ.* (1904), XIII.

established or foreshadowed before the death of Waite. Its work has been largely in applying settled principles to new conditions and to new forms of legislation.

With respect to the Commerce Clause, on the other hand, there has been an immense development of the law, and an expansion of National power through affirmative action of Congress in new directions which had not been dreamed of prior to Waite's death. It is for this new tendency and for the increase of National functions under other clauses of the Constitution, especially in relation to the control of the mails, the taxing power, and the acquirement and government of new territorial possessions that the thirty years since 1888 have been a notable era in the history of American law. As early as 1885, Judge Thomas M. Cooley wrote: "Everything gravitates to Washington, the highest interests and the most absorbing ambitions look to the National Capital for gratification; and it is no longer the State, but the Nation that in men's minds and imagination is an ever-present sovereignty." In 1887, Judge Miller said: "While the pendulum of public opinion has swung with much force away from the extreme point of State-Rights doctrine, there may be danger of its reaching an extreme point on the other side." "The ceaseless accumulation of power" in the National Government became the theme of law writers throughout the years from 1890 to 1910. "The tendency in the country towards a centralization of power is increasing; the field of the National Government is constantly widening; a Unity is growing out of a Union, and the primary source of all this nationalizing power is the Commerce Clause," wrote Judge Walter E. Noyes in 1907; and three years later, James M. Beck wrote: "The insistence upon the reserved rights of the States has become little more than a political

platitude. There is little, if any, real popular sentiment of sufficient strength to protect the States against
the encroachment of the Federal Government. . . .
Men have been trained by imperative economic influences to look to the Central Government as the real
political government, and to the States as little more
than subordinate provinces, useful for purposes of
local police regulation and nothing more. This tendency seems to be in the very nature of events. It is
the work of no especial political party or of any political
leader. . . . The American people think Nationally
and not locally, as they once thought locally and rarely
Nationally." [1]

The first great case sustaining the National power,
decided after the accession of Chief Justice Fuller, was
the *Chinese Exclusion Case, Chae Chan Ping* v. *United
States*, 130 U. S. 581, in 1889, in which the Act of
October 1, 1888, prohibiting entry of Chinese laborers
and in violation of the Treaty with China was upheld
as within the power of Congress.[2] This case was

---

[1] *History of Michigan* (1885), by Thomas M. Cooley, 271; *A New Nation*, by
Hollis R. Bailey, *Harv. Law Rev.* (1895), IX; James Bryce in his *American Commonwealth* (1888), I, wrote: "It is clear that the development of the Constitution as between the Nation and the States has not yet stopped and present appearances suggest that the centralizing tendency will continue to prevail." See also
Recent Centralizing Tendencies in the Supreme Court, by Frederic P. Powers, *Pol.
Sci. Qu.* (1890), V; *The Commerce Clause and the State*, by A. H. Wintersteen,
Amer. Law Reg. (1889), XXXVII; *Politics and the United States Supreme Court*,
by Walter D. Coles, *Amer. Law Rev.* (1893), XXVII; *The Power to Regulate Interstate Commerce and the Police Powers of the State*, by Herbert B. Shoemaker, *ibid.*
(1895), XXIX; *Judicial Centralization*, by L. H. Pool, *Yale Law Journ.* (1902),
XI; *Development of the Commerce Clause*, by Walter C. Noyes, *ibid.* (1907), XVI;
Nullification by Indirection, by James M. Beck, *Harv. Law Rev.* (1910), XXIII.
Simeon E. Baldwin in his address to the American Political Science Association in
1912 on *The Progressive Unfolding of the Power of the United States*, asked: "How
far will this process of expansion go?" *Amer. Pol. Sci. Rev.* (1912), VI; *Expansion
of Federal Power*, by Judge Francis L. Smith, *Virginia Law Reg.* (1911), XVII.

[2] *The Chinese Exclusion Cases*, by M. J. Farrelly, *Amer. Law Rev.* (1894), XXVIII;
see for practical application of the doctrine, *United States* v. *Sing Tuck* (1904), 194
U. S. 161; *United States* v. *Ji Toy* (1905), 198 U. S. 253; *Chin Low* v. *United States*,
208 U. S. 8; *Administrative Action in Immigration Proceedings*, by Thomas R.
Powell, *Harv. Law Rev.* (1908), XXII; *The Control of Immigration as an Admin-*

followed by the extreme decision made in *Fong Yue Ting* v. *United States*, 149 U. S. 698, three years later, in 1893, in which the power of a sovereign nation to forbid the entrance of foreigners or to expel or deport them was upheld as absolute and unqualified, and the Act of May 5, 1892, was held valid.[1] This opinion by Judge Gray seemed to justify the old Alien Law of 1798, and there was a strong dissent by the Democratic Judges Fuller and Field, and by Judge Brewer, who stated that it was "a blow against constitutional liberty", and that it contained within it "the germs of an assertion of unlimited and arbitrary power, in general incompatible with the immutable principles of justice, inconsistent with the nature of our government."

In 1890, in *Geofroy* v. *Riggs*, 133 U. S. 258, the Court broadened the field of National action by holding that it was within the scope of the treaty power to regulate alien inheritance of lands in the States.[2] The power of the President to direct the United States marshals to afford protection to the lives of the Federal Judges was upheld, in 1890, in *Cunningham* v. *Neagle*, 135 U. S. 1; and a marshal who shot a man in defense of Judge Field, though given no statutory authority, was held to be acting "in pursuance of a law of the United

istrative Problem, by Paul S. Pierce, *Amer. Pol. Sci. Rev.* (1909), III; *Administrative Decision in Connection with Immigration*, by Louis F. Post, *ibid.* (1916), X.

That Congress, however, cannot regulate the citizenship of a Chinaman was held in *United States* v. *Wong Kim Ark* (1898), 169 U. S. 649.

[1] In 1912, in *Zakonaite* v. *Wolf* (1898), 226 U. S. 272, the deportation of alien prostitutes under the Act of Feb. 20, 1907, was upheld; and see *Hoke* v. *United States* (1913), 227 U. S. 308; and see *Keller* v. *United States* (1909), 213 U. S. 138, as to the limit of Congressional power over aliens in this country.

[2] These decisions culminated in *Missouri* v. *Holland* (1920), 252 U. S. 416, upholding the Migratory Bird Treaty with Canada; see also *National Supremacy, Treaty Power* v. *State Power* (1913), by Edward S. Corwin; *Federal Treaties and State Laws*, by C. N. Gregory, *Michigan Law Rev.* (1907), VI; *The Treaty Power and Its Relation to State Courts*, by William C. Coleman, *Amer. Law Rev.* (1909), XLIII; *The Extent of the Treaty-Making Power*, by William E. Mikell, *Amer. Law Reg.* (1909), LVII.

States." This was the broadest interpretation yet given to implied powers of the National Government under the Constitution.[1] The plenary power of Congress over the Territories was upheld in broad terms in *Corporation of Latter Day Saints* v. *United States*, 136 U. S. 1, sustaining the statute annulling the charter of the Mormon Church, the Court reaffirming a decision, rendered five years before, holding that the "people of the United States as sovereign owners of the National Territories have supreme power over them and their inhabitants."[2] The announcement of the Original Package doctrine, in *Leisy* v. *Hardin*, 135 U. S. 100, as applicable to articles in interstate commerce was regarded as the "most crushing blow against the rights of the States which has ever been dealt by that tribunal."[3] At the same time it was made clear in *Chicago, Milwaukee & St. Paul R. R.* v. *Minnesota*, 134 U. S. 418, that the right of the State to regulate corporate rates, established by the *Granger Cases* in 1878, was not unlimited, but was confined to a right to fix reasonable and nonconfiscatory rates and reviewable by the Court under the Due Process Clause.[4]

In 1892, the National power received further expan-

---

[1] *Power of the General Government to Protect its Officers and to Control Anarchy*, by Joseph B. Thompson, *Amer. Law Rev.* (1901), XXXV.

[2] Polygamy was prohibited by Congress in 1867 but the statute remained a dead letter until the Edmunds Act in 1882, and the Tucker Act in 1887. Utah was admitted as a State in 1895, under an Act forbidding polygamous and plural marriages. For other cases as to the Mormon Church and polygamy, see *Reynolds* v. *United States* (1879), 98 U. S. 145; *Miles* v. *United States* (1881), 103 U. S. 304; *Clawson* v. *United States* (1885), 114 U. S. 477; *Murphy* v. *Ramsay* (1885), 114 U. S. 15; *Cannon* v. *United States* (1885), 116 U. S. 55; *Snow* v. *United States* (1886), 118 U. S. 346; *United States* v. *The Late Corporation of the Church of Jesus Christ of Latter Day Saints* (1893), 150 U. S. 145. See also *Independent*, Jan. 16, 1879, May 6, 1886, as to argument of G. T. Curtis for overruling of *Reynolds* v. *United States; Nation*, April 23, 1885.

[3] *Amer. Law Rev.* (1890), XXIV, 474, 490.

[4] See also *Budd* v. *New York*, 143 U. S. 517, in 1892; *Legal Theories of Price Regulation*, by Arthur T. Hadley, *Yale Law Journ.* (1892), I; *Can Prices be Regulated by Law?* by William D. Lewis, *Amer. Law Reg.*(1893), XXXII; *A New Canon on Constitutional Construction*, by Richard C. McMurtrie, *ibid.*

sion through the decision in *Ex parte Rapier*, 143 U. S. 110, upholding the power of Congress to exclude lotteries from the use of the mails; and the extent of the scope of this clause of the Constitution relative to postroads was illustrated, twelve years later, in 1904, by a decision upholding the fraud-order legislation, *Public Clearing House* v. *Coyne*, 194 U. S. 497.[1] In 1892 also, the power of the United States to sue a State in order to fix boundaries — a power which had been vigorously denied in the debates in Congress succeeding the Mexican War, — was upheld in *United States* v. *Texas*, 143 U. S. 621.

In 1893, the Court restated and reiterated the doctrine which Judge Story had originated, in 1842, in *Swift* v. *Tyson*, that upon questions of general commercial law the Court would ascertain the law for itself and would not be bound by State decisions. Year by year, and especially since *Burgess* v. *Seligman*, 107 U. S. 20, in 1883, the Court had developed this formulation of a body of National law, distinct from State law and applicable in the National Courts, until it had become a distinct factor in the increase of National power. Now, in *Baltimore & Ohio R. R.* v. *Baugh*, 149 U. S. 368, it applied its doctrine in a case involving the question whether certain railroad employees fell within the fellow-servant rule under the general law, rather than within the rule as applied in the State. Judge Field wrote a vigorous dissent, terming the doctrine "an invasion of the authority of the State, and to that extent a denial of its independence." Eight years later, the doctrine received a notable application and extension when Judge Brewer announced, in *Western Union Tel. Co.* v. *Call Publishing Co.*, 181 U. S. 92,

[1] See *The Expansion of Federal Control Through the Regulation of the Mails*, by Lindsay Rogers, *Harv. Law Rev.* (1913), XXVII; *The Power of the States to Interfere with the Mails*, by Lindsay Rogers, *Virg. Law Rev.* (1916), III.

that "the principles of the common law are operative
upon all interstate commercial transactions, except so
far as they are modified by Congressional enactment";
and in *Kansas* v. *Colorado*, 206 U. S. 46, in 1907, the
Court said that "the Court is practically building up
what may be not improperly called Interstate Common
Law." [1]

In 1894, the growing power of the National Government over the railroads was shown when a railroad rate
order of a Texas State Commission was held invalid in
Reagan v. *Farmer Loan & Trust Co.*, 154 U. S. 362. [2]

The year 1895 was notable for the decision of three
great cases in which the public took the liveliest interest. In the first, decided January 21, the Court passed
for the first time on the application of the Sherman
Anti-Trust Act to commercial corporations, and in
United States v. *E. C. Knight Co.*, 156 U. S. 1, — the
Sugar Trust Case, — held that, on the facts presented,
the corporations involved in the combination refining
sugar were not engaged in interstate commerce. The
result was a disappointment to those who relied on the
Act as a destroyer of the trusts. The second case
involved the constitutionality of the Income Tax imposed in the Wilson-Gorman Tariff Act in President
Cleveland's Administration, *Pollock* v. *Farmers' Loan
and Trust Co.*, 157 U. S. 429, 158 U. S. 601; and the
unfortunate circumstances attending this case aroused
further bitter attacks upon the Court. At its first
decision, April 8, 1895, the Court held a tax on real

[1] *The Common Law Jurisdiction of the United States Courts*, by Alton B. Parker,
Yale Law Journ. (1907), XVII; *Relation of Judicial Decisions to Law*, by Alexander
Lincoln, *Harv. Law Rev.* (1907), XXI; *The Common Law of the Federal Courts*, by
Edward C. Eliot, *Amer. Law Rev.* (1902), XXXVI; *Decisions of the Federal Courts
on Questions of State Law*, by William M. Meigs, *Amer. Law Rev.* (1911), XLV;
see especially for criticisms of the extent of the doctrine, Holmes, J., dissenting
in *Kuhn* v. *Fairmont Coal Co.*, 215 U. S. 349, in 1910.

[2] *The Right of the Public to Regulate Charges*, by Walter Clark, *Amer. Law Rev.*
(1897), XXXI.

estate income unconstitutional, unless levied in the manner required for a direct tax; as to other income, the Court was evenly divided, Judge Jackson being absent owing to illness. A reargument being ordered, a second decision was made May 20, 1895, in which Judge Jackson (three months before his death) participated; but owing to the fact that Judge Shiras changed his mind after the first decision, the Court, by a vote of five to four, held the whole tax invalid.[1] Violent criticism followed this event (the result of which was the adoption of the Sixteenth Amendment, in 1913).[2]

Equally violent assaults upon the Court followed from a decision rendered, seven days later, in the third great case, *In re Debs*, 158 U. S. 564. For the past five years, legal questions growing out of labor strikes had been presented more and more frequently to the inferior Federal Courts through applications for injunctions, chiefly by owners and Federal receivers of railroads. In 1893, the Supreme Court had for the first time been called upon to deal with the subject in *Pettibone* v. *United States*, 148 U. S. 197, arising on an indictment for conspiracy to impede the administration of justice, by obstruction of processes issued by an inferior Federal Court in the serious strike and riots which took place, in 1899, in the Cœur d'Alenes in Idaho. The *Debs Case* grew out of the great Pullman strike and

[1] See *Amer. Law Rev.* (1895), XXIX, 524, 489, 742: "The Sugar Trust decision and the Income Tax decision counterbalance all the good it has done in seventy years . . . a wound inflicted on the rights of the American people;" *Pollock* v. *Farmers' Loan & Trust Co.*, by Francis R. Jones, *Harv. Law Rev.* (1895), IX; *The Constitutionality of the Income Tax*, by William D. Lewis, *Amer. Law Reg.* (1895), XXXIV; *What is Now an Indirect Tax*, by Louis D. Richardson, *ibid.*

[2] *Recent Constitutional Amendments*, by Gordon E. Sherman, *Yale Law Journ.* (1913), XXIII; *The Income Tax and the Constitution*, by Edward B. Whitney. *Harv. Law Rev.* (1907), XX; *Direct Taxes under the Constitution*, by Charles T. Bullock, *Pol. Sci. Qu.* (1900), XV; *The Income Tax Amendment*, by E. R. A. Seligman, *ibid.* (1910), XXV; *The Income Tax Amendment*, by Dwight W. Morrow, *Columbia Law Rev.* (1910), X.

riots of 1894, and its decision, on May 25, 1895, is to be regarded as one of the datum posts in American legal history. The Court, in a notable opinion by Judge Brewer, upheld an injunction issued by the lower Court, restraining the defendant from obstructing trains engaged in interstate commerce or in carrying the mails. "The strong arm of the National Government may be put forth to brush away all obstructions to the freedom of interstate commerce or the transportation of the mails," said Brewer. "If the emergency arises, the army of the Nation, and all its militia, are at the service of the Nation to compel obedience to its laws." While holding that the Government had a property right in the mails sufficient to warrant its suing in equity, he stated that the Court did not care to place its decision upon this ground alone. "Every government, entrusted by the very terms of its being with powers and duties to be exercised and discharged for the general welfare, has a right to apply to its own Courts for any proper assistance in the exercise of the one and the discharge of the other. . . . Whenever the wrongs complained of are such as affect the public at large, and are in respect of matters which by the Constitution are entrusted to the care of the Nation, and concerning which the Nation owes a duty to all the citizens of securing to them their common rights, then the mere fact that the Government has no pecuniary interest in the controversy is not sufficient to exclude it from the Courts or to prevent it from taking measures therein to fully discharge those constitutional duties."

This decision, sustaining President Cleveland's energetic action in employing both the military and civil forces of the Government to end the strike, caused a great sensation, and was widely indorsed by conservative and patriotic men, as a strong support to the

stability of the Nation. Such an application of National power to a labor situation, however, was a long
step towards centralization of authority; and as a legal
writer said, while "all must applaud the promptness
and vigor with which the Federal power acted, saving
the country perhaps from a reign of anarchy and blood-
shed. . . slowly but inevitably one after another of
these State police powers is being brought within the
limits of Federal jurisdiction." [1] The decision gave
great offense to certain labor elements in the community; and as it was rendered only a week after the decision in the *Income Tax Case*, it was criticized as an
illustration of the prejudice of the Court in favor of
capital.

The public discussion and hostility which grew out
of these three decisions in 1895, each of which was
asserted to have been in favor of "the propertied
class", was signalized by the insertion of a plank in the
platform adopted at the National Convention of the
Democratic Party in Chicago in 1896, which, in that
campaign of somewhat hysterical political passion, was
termed an anarchical attack on the Judiciary. In
reality, the plank was an extremely mild expression of
views, when compared with many former criticisms
which had been made in conservative newspapers and
law journals. [2] The general situation, however, and

---

[1] *Federal Power to Regulate Interstate Commerce and the Police Powers of the State,*
by Herbert B. Shoemaker, *Amer. Law Rev.* (1895), XXIX; *Use of the Army in Aid
of the Civil Power,* by C. M. Lieber, *ibid.* (1898), XXXII; see also note as to President Cleveland's authority to use the army, *ibid.* (1896), XXVIII.

[2] See *Amer. Law Rev.* (1896), XXX, 579, as to the Democratic platform. The
controverted plank was as follows: "We declare that it is the duty of Congress
to use all the constitutional power which remains after that decision, or which may
come from its reversal by the Court as it may hereafter be constituted, so that the
burden of taxation may be equally and impartially laid, to the end that wealth
may bear its due proportion of the expenses of the government. . . . We denounce
arbitrary interference by Federal authorities in local affairs as a violation of the
Constitution of the United States and as a crime against free institutions, and we
especially object to government by injunction as a new and highly dangerous form

especially the Income Tax decision, produced a re-awakening of the type of assault on the Court which had appeared successively in 1821, 1833, 1857, 1868, 1885 — namely the demand that the Court should be shorn of its alleged "usurped" power to pass upon the validity of Acts of Congress. All the fallacious arguments which had been used in previous eras were reproduced, and, as formerly, reiterated without any attempt to ascertain the historical facts as to the "usurpation", and as to the contemporary view of *Marbury* v. *Madison* in this respect.[1] Most violent and voluble of all the Court's critics was Governor Sylvester Pennoyer of Oregon, who wrote : "We have during this time been living under a government not based upon the Federal Constitution, but under one created by the plausible sophistries of John Marshall. The Supreme Court has not contented itself with its undisputed judicial prerogative of inter-preting the laws of Congress which may be ambiguous, but it has usurped the legislative prerogative of de-claring what the laws shall not be. Our constitutional government has been supplanted by a judicial oligarchy. The time has now arrived when the government should be restored to its constitutional basis. The duty is plain and the road is clear. If Congress at the next session would impeach the nullifying Judges for the usurpa-

---

of oppression by which Federal Judges, in contempt of the law of the States and rights of citizens, become at once Legislators, Judges and executioners; and we approve the bill, passed at the last session of the United States Senate and now pending in the House, relative to contempts in Federal Courts, providing for trials by jury in certain cases of contempt."

[1] *The Income Tax Decision and the Power of the Supreme Court to Nullify Acts of Congress,* by Sylvester Pennoyer, *Amer. Law Rev.* (July, 1895), XXIX; *The Case of Marbury* v. *Madison,* by Sylvester Pennoyer, *ibid.* (1896), XXX; *Due Process of Law,* by T. W. Brown, *ibid.* (1898), XXXII; see in defense of the Court, *Origin of the Supreme Judicial Power,* by Robert L. Fowler, *ibid.* (1895), XXIX; *The Supreme Court as Expounder of the Constitution,* by T. C. Rosenberger, *ibid.* (1896), XXX; *The Judiciary, its Growing Power and Influence,* by Boyd Winchester, *ibid.* (1898), XXXII; *The Jurisdiction to Declare Void Acts of Legislation,* by Richard C. McMurtrie, *Amer. Law Reg.* (1893), XLI.

tion of legislative power, remove them from office, and instruct the President to enforce the collection of the income tax, the Supreme Court of the United States would never hereafter presume to trench upon the exclusive powers of Congress; and thus the Government, as created by our fathers, would be restored, with all its faultless outlines and harmonious proportions." Another critic, a prominent Georgia lawyer, wrote on the "Aggressions of the Federal Courts", including among them, the issue of injunctions in criminal matters, the decision of the *Neagle Case*, the interference with municipal governments by Federal injunctions and receiverships, the annulment of statutes, the permission of corporations to sue in Federal Courts, the control of State railroad rate legislation, labor injunctions and the *Debs Case*, the *Sugar Trust Case*, the "jailing of Sovereign States", and Federal Court management of railroads.[1]

Coincident with these attacks on the Supreme Court, there had arisen severe criticisms of the extension of the power of the National Judiciary through its increasingly wide exercise of equity jurisdiction and extensive employment of injunctions. "Government by injunction" had become a term of judicial opprobrium constantly echoed by the laboring class.[2] The abuse of

[1] *Aggressions of the Federal Courts*, by John W. Akin, *Amer. Law Rev.* (1898), XXXII. Camm Patteson in *Judicial Usurpation of Power*, *Virginia Law Reg.* (1905), X, said: "The greatest danger which threatens the American Republic, is the judicial usurpation of power. . . . The fatal extension of the power of the process of injunction was the greatest step of all. It tore down and trampled under foot the chief protection of our liberty. . . . The so-called protection of the United States mail was used as a mere pretext to cover the unauthorized usurpation of power."

[2] *Protest against Administering Criminal Law by Injunction — the Debs Case*, by William D. Lewis, *Amer. Law Reg.* (1894), XLII; see especially symposium on labor injunctions in *Chicago Times Herald*, Sept. 19, 1897; *Government by Injunction*, by Charles N. Gregory, *Harv. Law Rev.* (1898), XI; *Strikes and Trusts*, *Amer. Law Rev.* (1893), XXVII; *The Modern Use of Injunctions*, by Frederic J. Stimson, *ibid.* (1895), X; *Injunction in the Federal Courts*, by William A. Woods, *Yale Law Journ.* (1896), VI; *Government by Injunction*, by W. G. Peterkin, *Vir-*

Federal railroad receiverships was a source of complaint in the business world. State Legislatures, lawyers and Judges questioned the freedom of assumption of jurisdiction by the United States Circuit Courts — "the innate viciousness of a receivership régime." [1]

Discussions had also arisen, in connection with the situation, as to the advisability of some statutory change in the doctrine evolved by Chief Justice Taney in the *Letson Case*, in 1844, under which corporations were held citizens of the State of their charter for purpose of suit in the Circuit Courts on grounds of diverse citizenship. This doctrine had never met full acceptance by Judges of the Court, and with the enormous development of corporate activities, and of "tramp" corporations, it had become more and more unpopular, since it resulted in the removal of almost all important litigation against corporations into the Circuit Courts and out of the State jurisdictions. A bill had been introduced in Congress in 1894 to restore the law as to the right of corporations to sue in such Courts to its status at the time of Marshall's decision in the *Deveaux Case*, in 1804. Congress failed to act, though strong arguments were made in the law journals of the country against retention of this privileged position for corporations.[2]

ginia Law Reg. (1898), III: *Strikes and Courts of Equity*, by William D. Lewis, *Amer. Law Reg.* (1898), XLVI; *The Court's View of Injunction in Labor Disputes*, by G. G. Groat, *Harv. Law Rev.* (1908), XXIII; *Injunctions Against Strikes, and Boycotts*, by James W. Bryan, *Amer. Law Rev.* (1906), XL.

[1] *Memorial of the Legislature of South Carolina on Receivers of Railroad Corporations and the Equity Jurisdiction of United States Courts*, in *Amer. Law Rev.* (1894), XXVIII; *The Court Management of Railroads*, by Seymour D. Thompson, *ibid.* (1893), XXVII; *Criticisms of the Federal Judiciary*, by Judge William H. Taft, *ibid.* (1895), XXVIII; *Railroad Receiverships in the Federal Courts*, by Judge Henry C. Caldwell, *ibid.* (1896), XXX; *New Fashioned Receiverships*, by D. H. Chamberlain, *Harv. Law Rev.* (1896), X; *Mandatory Injunction*, by Judge Jacob Klein, *Harv. Law Rev.* (1898), XII; *Suits Against Receivers*, by W. A. Coutts, *Amer. Law Rev.* (1904), XXXVIII; (1905), XXXIX; *Jurisdiction of Federal Equity Courts*, by Benjamin F. Keller, *ibid.* (1913), XLVII.

[2] *Congress Should Abrogate Federal Jurisdiction Over Corporations*, by Alfred

In 1896, the Court announced the broadest definition of the right of Congress to legislate for the general welfare when it sustained the taking by eminent domain of the Gettysburg battlefield for a National cemetery, in *United States* v. *Gettysburg Electric Ry. Co.*, 160 U. S. 668: "Such a use," said the Democratic Judge, Peckham, "seems necessarily, not only a public use, but one so closely connected with the welfare of the Republic itself as to be within the powers granted to Congress by the Constitution for the purpose of protecting and preserving the whole country." This decision, taken in connection with the *Debs Case*, showed that the Court was practically prepared to support any action taken by the National Government and reasonably necessary for its self-preservation and welfare.

In this same year, a decision upholding the payment to claimants of the sugar bounty granted by the McKinley Act aroused severe criticism, since the Court, while expressly declining to rule on the validity of the bounty legislation, held the claim under the circumstances to be one which Congress had power to recognize and pay, *United States* v. *Realty Co.*, 163 U. S. 274. "The Nation, speaking broadly, owes a 'debt' to an individual, when his claim grows out of general principles of right and justice; when, in other words, it is based upon considerations of a moral or merely honorary nature, such as are binding on the conscience or

Russell, *Harv. Law Rev.* (1893), VII; *Federal Jurisdiction in Case of Corporations*, by Seymour D. Thompson, *Amer. Law Rev.* (1895), XXIX: Judge William H. Taft vigorously controverted the position taken in the foregoing articles, see *Criticisms of the Federal Judiciary*, *Amer. Law Rev.* (1895), XXIX; see also *Jurisdiction of Federal Courts in Actions in which Corporations are Parties*, by Judge Jacob Trieber, *ibid.* (1905), XXXIX; *A Legal Fiction with its Wings Clipped*, by Simeon E. Baldwin, *ibid.* (1907), XLI; *Jurisdiction of Federal Courts over State Corporations*, by P. J. Altizer, *ibid.* (1909), XLIII; *The Supreme Court and Enforcement of State Laws by State Courts*, by Henry Schofield, *Illinois Law Rev.* (1908), III; *Should Federal Courts Ignore State Laws*, by Henry E. Mills, *Amer. Law Rev.* (1900), XXXIV.

the honor of an individual, although the debt could obtain no recognition in a Court of law." This decision was attacked as "a departure from the ancient tenets of law"; as "partisan and class favoring"; "dangerous and revolutionary"; "if not hastily repudiated it may work an epoch like Dred Scott . . . the one decision denying the rights of man, the other violating the rights of the whole people." [1]

In 1897, the Court, to the shock of the business world, for the first time announced, in *United States* v. *Trans-Missouri Freight Ass.*, 166 U. S. 290, that railroad pools were illegal under the Sherman Act directed against combinations in restraint of interstate trade; [2] eleven years later, when the case of *Loewe* v. *Lawlor*, 208 U. S. 274, was decided in 1908, the labor-unions were equally shocked to find that a labor boycott obstructing the free flow of commerce between the States came also within the prohibition of the Sherman Act.[3]

In 1899, there began the long series of cases growing out of the Spanish War, which occupied much of the attention of the Court during the next six years. The first to be decided were a group of prize cases in which various important points of international law were settled.[4] These were followed, in May, 1901, by the

---

[1] *Constitutionality of a Bounty on Sugar*, by William D. Lewis, *Amer. Law Reg.* (1892), XXXI; *Sugar Bounty Cases*, by Joseph Wheless, *Amer. Law Rev.* (1896), XXX; *Sugar Bounty Cases*, by H. Campbell Black, *ibid.* (1895), XXIX; *Sugar Bounties*, by Charles F. Chamberlayne, *Harv. Law Rev.* (1892), V; and see *Field* v. *Clark* (1892), 143 U. S. 649; *Ship Subsidies and Bounties*, by H. F. Robinson, *Columbia Law Rev.* (1902), II.

[2] *Case of the Trans-Missouri Freight Association*, by G. S. Patterson, *Amer. Law Reg.* (1897), XLV.

[3] *The Danbury Hatters Case, Its Possible Effect on Labor Unions*, by Theodor Megaarden, *Amer. Law Rev.* (1915), XLIX.

[4] *The Pedro* (1899), 175 U. S. 354; *The Buena Ventura* (1899), 175 U. S. 384; *The Paquete Habana* (1900), 175 U. S. 677, 189 U. S. 453; *The Adula* (1900), 176 U. S. 361; *The Panama* (1900), 176 U. S. 535; *The Benito Estenger* (1900), 176 U. S. 568; see *The Law of Blockade*, by Charles N. Gregory, *Yale Law Journ.* (1903), XII; *Recent Developments and Tendency of the Law of Prize*, by Henry M. Holt, *ibid.*; *The Doctrine of Continuous Voyage*, by Charles B. Elliott, *ibid.* (1903),

notable cases, lasting until 1905, in which the status and constitutional rights of Cuba, of the newly acquired territory of Porto Rico and the Philippines and of Hawaii were at last definitely settled.[1] "This judicial drama of truly Olympian proportions" constituted by far the most important fact in the Court's history during the period since Waite's death, and has been interestingly summarized as follows.[2] "When the Spanish War had resulted in the cession to the United States of Porto Rico and the Philippines, the question of their constitutional status at once arose. It entered immediately into the political arena, and in the Presidential campaign of 1900 divided, with the cry of 'Imperialism', political parties and their adherents. The discord which it created in the judicial forum was no less pronounced. The *De Lima*, *Dooley* and *Bidwell Cases* presented in concrete form the questions whether the Island of Porto Rico, after its cession by Spain,

XIII; *Right of a Belligerent to Destroy a Captured Prize*, by Francis T. Swayze, *Harv. Law Rev.* (1904), XVIII; *Doctrine of Continuous Voyage*, by Charles N. Gregory, *ibid.* (1910), XXIV; *Questions of International Law Involved in the Spanish War*, by W. W. Goodrich, *Amer. Law Rev.* (1898), XXXII; *Rights of Belligerents and Neutrals from the American Point of View*, by Alexander P. Morse, *Amer. Law Reg.* (1898), XLVI.

[1] *Neeley v. Henkel* (1901), 180 U. S. 109; *De Lima v. Bidwell* (1901), 182 U. S. 1; *Downes v. Bidwell* (1901), 182 U. S. 244; *Dooley v. United States* (1901), 182 U. S. 222; *Dooley v. United States* (1901), 183 U. S. 151; *The Diamond Rings* (1901), 183 U. S. 176; *Hawaii v. Mankichi* (1903), 190 U. S. 197; *Kepner v. United States* (1904), 195 U. S. 100; *Dorr v. United States* (1904), 195 U. S. 138; *Trono v. United States* (1905), 199 U. S. 521, and *Rasmussen v. United States* (1905), 197 U. S. 516; *Porto Rico v. Tapia* (1918), 245 U. S. 639. The tremendous interest taken in the decision by the Court as to the status of the new territories is illustrated by the enormous number of articles in the law journals, 1899–1905, citation of which is not practicable; but see *The Causes and Results of our War with Spain from a Legal Standpoint*, by Judge Elmer B. Adams, *Yale Law Journ.* (Dec., 1898), VIII; *The Final Phase of the Insular Tariff Controversies*, by Henry M. Hoyt, *ibid.* (1905), XIV; *The Legal Status of the Philippines*, by Lebbeus R. Wilfrey, *ibid.*; *The Hawaiian Case*, by Emlin McClain, *Harv. Law Rev.* (1904), VII; *The Decisions of the Supreme Court in the Insular Cases*, by John W. Burgess, *Pol. Sci. Qu.* (1901), XVI; *The Insular Cases*, by Carman F. Randolph, *Columbia Law Rev.* (1901), I; *The Insular Decisions of 1901*, by Edward B. Whitney, *ibid.* (1902), II.

[2] See *Edward Douglass White*, by John W. Davis, *Amer. Bar Ass. Journ.* (1921), VII.

THE SUPREME COURT IN 1899

Standing: Peckham, Shiras, White, McKenna. *Seated:* Brewer, Harlan, Chief Justice Fuller, Gray, Brown.

ceased to be 'foreign country', within the meaning of
the existing tariff laws of the United States; and secondly, to what extent, if at all, the island fell within the
revenue clauses of the Constitution, and the requirement that duties, imposts and excises should be uniform throughout the United States. The division of
opinion on the Court was sharp and pronounced. The
first view was that of Mr. Justice Brown, alone. He
plowed a lonely furrow and held that, while Porto Rico
had ceased to be 'foreign country' within the meaning
of the Dingley Act, yet, as to future legislation (the
Foraker Act of April 12, 1900), the uniform clause did
not apply; that Porto Rico became by the cession 'territory appurtenant' to the United States, but not a part of
it; and that even over continental and contiguous
territory, the Constitution went only as the result of
express Congressional action. As against this, Chief
Justice Fuller and Justices Harlan, Brewer, and Peckham maintained that Porto Rico, at least upon the
ratification of the treaty, became a part of the United
States, and as such could be dealt with only in the
manner which the Constitution provides; or, in the
language of the hour, the 'Constitution follows the
flag.' Between these two extremes were to be found
Justices White, McKenna, Shiras and Gray, who maintained that the government of the United States has
power to acquire and hold territory without immediately incorporating it into the United States, and that
Congress can determine when acquired territory has
reached that state where it is proper that it should enter
into and form a part of the American family; and that
Porto Rico, though not a foreign country in an international sense, since it was subject to and under the
sovereignty of the United States after the treaty of
cession, continued to be foreign to the United States in

a domestic sense because it had not been incorporated
into the United States, but was merely appurtenant
thereto as a possession.   These views were defended
with a wealth of reasoning and a warmth of argument
worthy of the greatness of the issue, but with the curious
result that the judgment in the *De Lima* and *Dooley
Cases* was concurred in, though for wholly different
reasons, by Justices Brown, Harlan, Brewer, Peckham
and the Chief Justice ; while that in the *Downes Case*
was supported by Justices Brown, White, McKenna,
Shiras and Gray. . . .   Judge White's 'idea of incorporation' was destined to prevail. . . .   In *Hawaii* v.
Mankichi, in 1903, the constitutional guaranties of
trial by jury were held inapplicable to the Hawaiian
Islands, Justice White taking occasion for himself and
Justice McKenna to reiterate their views in *Downer* v.
Bidwell, and Justices Fuller, Brewer, Harlan and Peckham filing the customary dissent.   A year later came the
case of *Dorr* v. *The United States* in which the opinion
written by Justice Day, who meanwhile had come upon
the Bench, held that the right of trial by jury was not
extended by the Federal Constitution, without legislation and of its own force, to the Philippine Islands,
ceded to the United States by Spain, but not incorporated into the United States by Congressional action. . . .   Finally, in *Rasmussen* v. *United States*,
the question arose with reference to Alaska, and at last
Justice White, writing for a clear majority of the Court,
was able to repeat with authority the views he had all
along maintained. . . .   Justice Harlan, although concurring in the instant result, nailed his colors to the
mast on the main question and went down fighting to
the last.   Years later, in speaking of the controversy,
Chief Justice White evidenced the depth of his conviction by the remark, 'Why, sir, if we had not decided

as we did, this country would have been less than a Nation!' " The capsheaf of the doctrine of incorporation was applied in *Porto Rico* v. *Tapia*, in 1918, when the Court held that rights guaranteed by the Constitution might be withheld by Congress from an unincorporated territory even though Congress had granted United States citizenship to the inhabitants of such territory.

Growing out of the Spanish War, there were also a series of important cases, decided from 1899 to 1901, in which the Court sustained (in all but one) the power of the United States to levy taxes of various kinds in the nature of an excise or stamp tax, including a tax on transmission of property by death.[1]

In 1903, the decision in the great *Lottery Case*, *Champion* v. *Ames*, 188 U. S. 321, gave an enormous impetus to the extension of National power over interstate commerce, and the decision in *Perry* v. *Haines*, 191 U. S. 17, by which the Federal Admiralty jurisdiction was for the first time held to extend to inland canals, greatly broadened the field of the National Courts.[2]

In 1904, the decision in *Northern Securities Co.* v. *United States*, 193 U. S. 197, deciding the Sherman Act to be applicable to the case of a holding company, for the first time showed that this law had teeth.[3] In

---

[1] See *Knowlton* v. *Moore*, 178 U. S. 41, in 1900; *Nicol* v. *Ames*, 173 U. S. 509, in 1899; in *Fairbank* v. *United States*, 181 U. S. 283, in 1901, a stamp tax on a foreign bill of lading was held unconstitutional.

[2] "It treated the profession and the country with a general surprise . . . jealousy and alarm." *Amer. Law Rev.* (1903), XXXVII, 911.

[3] *The Northern Securities Co.*, by Edward B. Whitney, *Yale Law Journ.* (1902), XI; *A Reply*, by D. H. Chamberlain, *ibid.* (1903), XIII; *Northern Securities Case*, by Christopher C. Langdell, *Harv. Law Rev.* (1903), XVI, XVII; see press comments on the *Northern Securities Case*, in *Amer. Law Rev.* (1904), XXVII. *Northern Securities Case*, by Carman F. Randolph, *Columbia Law Rev.* (1903), III; *Northern Securities Decision*, by George F. Canfield, *ibid.* (1904), IV; *The Supreme Court and the Sherman Anti-Trust Act*, by William F. Dana, *Harv. Law Rev.* (1903), XVI; *The Northern Securities Decision*, by Henry W. Biklé, *Amer. Law Reg.* (1904).

Buttfield v. *Stranahan*, 192 U. S. 470, the Court upheld a statute vesting wide regulative power in an Executive Department. By holding that Congress had legislated on the subject "as far as was reasonably practicable", and that it had the power "to leave to Executive officials the duty of bringing about the result pointed out by the statute," the Court vastly increased the extent of Executive authority. This tendency of Congress to vest the Executive with power to make regulations, as a substitute for specific legislative enactment, has of late years been the source of considerable adverse criticism.[1]

In 1905, State sovereignty was greatly impaired by a decision in *South Carolina* v. *United States*, 199 U. S. 437, that State agents selling liquor must pay a Federal license tax. "Under the assumed necessity of protecting the taxing power of the Government of the United States," said Judge White dissenting, "it establishes a doctrine which in its potentiality strips the States of their lawful authority. . . . The ancient landmarks are obliterated and the distinct powers be-

LII. In *Minnesota* v. *Northern Securities Co.*, 184 U. S. 540, in 1902, the Court had held that a State can have no power to sue one of its own citizens in an original suit in the United States Supreme Court. A decision as to the legality of the company was not made, therefore, until the Government suit was decided in 1904.

[1] But see *The Administrative Powers of the President*, by John A. Fairlie, *Michigan Law Rev.* (1903), II; *The Administrative Law of the United States*, by Frank J. Goodnow, *Pol. Sci. Qu.* (1904), XIX; *Conclusiveness of Administrative Determination in the Federal Government*, by Thomas R. Powell, *Amer. Pol. Sci. Rev.* (1907), I; *Administrative Exercise of Legislative and Judicial Power*, by Thomas R. Powell, *ibid.* (1912, 1913), XXVII, XXVIII; *Jurisdictional Limitations upon Commission Action*, by Bruce Wyman, *Harv. Law Rev.* (1914), XXVII; *Judicial Determination by Administrative Commissions*, by Charles W. Needham, *Amer. Pol. Sci. Rev.* (1916), X; *The Land Department as an Administrative Tribunal*, by Charles P. Pierce, *ibid.*; see also *Monongahela Bridge Co.* v. *United States* (1910), 216 U. S. 177; *Some Powers and Problems of the Federal Administrative*, by Jasper Y. Brinton, *U. of P. Law Rev.* (1913), LXI; *Administrative Legislation*, by John A. Fairlie, *Michigan Law Rev.* (1910), XVIII. *Judicial Review of Administrative Action by the Federal Supreme Court*, by G. E. F. Albertsworth, *ibid.* (1921), XXXV; *Judicial Review of Administrative Findings*, by Nathan Isaacs, *Yale Law Journ.* (1921), XXX; *Judicial Review of Commissioners*, by Lawrence Curtis, 2nd, *Harv. Law Rev.* (1921), XXXIV.

longing to both the National and State Governments are reciprocally placed the one at the mercy of the other, so as to give to each the potency of destroying the other."

In this year, 1905, the decision in *Lochner* v. *New York*, 198 U. S. 45, holding the New York bakers' ten-hour-law unconstitutional — one of the very few cases in which the Court has ever held invalid any State legislation designed to protect the laboring class for the welfare of society — aroused widespread public discussion, and evoked another series of attacks, such as had taken place, ten years previously, in 1896, over the Court's alleged exercise of an usurped power in passing upon the validity of statutes. It is to be noted that its critics wholly failed to distinguish between the act of holding a State statute void, and the act of holding a Congressional statute void. Not only are these two functions utterly distinct but they have different constitutional bases, and different arguments to support them.[1]

[1] See Introductory Chapter, *supra*, 14–19. Some of the attacks on the Court's power were: *Judicial Usurpation of Power*, by Camm Patteson, *Virginia Law Reg.* (1905), X; *The Great Usurpation*, by William Trickett, *Amer. Law Rev.* (1906), XL; *Judicial Dispensation from Congressional Statutes*, by William Trickett, *ibid.* (1907), XLVI; paper by Judge Walter Clark, April 27, 1906, *Amer. Law Reg.*, LIV; *Government by Judiciary*, by L. B. Boudin, *Pol. Sci. Qu.* (1911), XXVI; *The Usurped Power of the Courts*, by Allan L. Benson, *Pearson's Mag.* (1911), XVI; *Usurpation of Power by Federal Courts*, by James B. McDonough, *Amer. Law Rev.* (1912), XLVI; *Government by Judges*, by Walter Clark, *Sen. Doc. 610, 63d Cong., 2d Sess.* (1914); *Withdrawing Power from Federal Courts to Declare Acts of Congress Void*, by Sen. Robert L. Owen, *Sen. Doc. 737, 64th Cong., 2d Sess.* (1917); *Back to the Constitution*, by Walter Clark, *Amer. Law Rev.* (1916), L; *Annulment of Legislation by the Supreme Court*, by Horace A. Davis, *Amer. Pol. Sci. Rev.* (1913), VII; *Judicial Control over Legislation*, by Jackson H. Ralston, *Amer. Law Rev.* (1920), LIV; Theodore Roosevelt in *The Outlook*, Dec. 17, 1910, April 15, 1911, Jan. 6, Feb. 24, March 21, 1912.

Some defenses of the Court were as follows: *The Supremacy of the Judiciary*, by A. Ingles Clark, *Harv. Law Rev.* (1903), XVII; *Written and Unwritten Constitutions in the United States*, by Emlen McClain, *Columbia Law Rev.* (1906), VI; *The Supreme Law of the Land*, by Blackburn Esterline, *Amer. Law Rev.* (1906), XL; *Some Recent Attacks on the American Doctrine of Judicial Power*, by William M. Meigs, *ibid.*; *The Irreconcilable Conflict*, by Judge Robert G. Street, *ibid.* (1907), XLI (see especially list of articles, p. 695); *The Function of the Judiciary*, by Percy

In 1907, in the great case of *Kansas* v. *Colorado*, 18.}
U. S. 125, s. c., 206 U. S. 46, involving the rights of two
sovereign States and of the Nation in the flow of an
interstate stream, the Court restated the basic relations
between the two forms of sovereignty in a Federal
Government. This case had an important bearing
upon the National power in relation to the subject of
conservation, in holding that the United States had no
power to interfere with the appropriation or use of any
water within a State, except so far as might be necessary
to prevent interference with or obstruction of navigable
waters, or except so far as it occurred on Government
land, and that it had no right over the general subject
of reclamation of arid lands within the States.[1]

In 1908, two cases in which Federal statutes were
held invalid as beyond the power of Congress under the

Bordwell, *Columbia Law Rev.* (1907), VII; *The Growth of Judicial Power*, by William F. Dodd, *Pol. Sci. Qu.* (1909), XXIV; *Congress and the Supreme Court*, by H. C. Bowman, *ibid.* (1910), XXV; *The Establishment of Judicial Review*, by Edward A. Corwin, *Michigan Law Rev.* (1910), IX; *A Government of Law or a Government of Men?* by Horace H. Lurton, *North Amer. Rev.* (1911), Vol. 193; *Is it Usurpation to Hold as Void Unconstitutional Laws?* by W. G. Hastings, *Green Bag* (1908), XX; *The Federal Censorship of Legislatures*, by Frederick Green, *ibid.* (1913), XLVII; *The American Doctrine of Judicial Power in Its Early Origin*, by William M. Meigs, *ibid.; Constitutional and Extra-Constitutional Restraints*, by Robert P. Reeder, *U. of P. Law Rev.* (1913), LXI; *Unconstitutional Law and Federal Judicial Power*, by C. H. Burr, *ibid.* (1913), LX; *The Fundamental Law and the Power of the Courts*, by Herbert Pope, *Harv. Law Rev.* (1913), XXVII; *The Judicial Bulwark of the Constitution*, by F. E. Melvin, *Amer. Pol. Sci. Rev.* (1914), VIII; *Judicial Power to Declare Legislative Acts Void*, by Oscar Haller, *ibid.* (1914), XLVIII; *The Process of Judicial Legislation*, by Morris P. Cohen, *ibid.; The Supreme Court, Usurper or Grantee*, by Charles A. Beard, *Pol. Sci. Qu.* (1912), XXVIII; *Power of the Supreme Court to Declare Acts of Congress Unconstitutional*, by Charles B. Stuart, *Sen. Doc. 708, 64th Cong., 2d Sess.* (1917); *The Power of Courts to Declare a Statute Void*, by George W. Williams, *Amer. Law Rev.* (1918), LII. See also the *Causes of Popular Dissatisfaction with the Administration of Justice*, by Roscoe Pound, *Amer. Bar Ass. Rev.* (1903); *Courts and Legislation*, by Roscoe Pound, *Amer. Pol. Sci. Qu.* (1913), VII; *The Supreme Court and the Constitution* (1902), by Charles A. Beard; *The Courts, the Constitution and Parties* (1912), by Andred C. McLaughlin; *The Power of the Federal Judiciary over Legislation* (1912), by J. Hampden Dougherty; *The Doctrine of Judicial Review* (1914), by Edward S. Corwin.

[1] *Suits between States, Kansas* v. *Colorado*, by Carman F. Randolph, *Columbia Law Rev.* (1902), II; *Conservation and the Constitution*, by W. B. Bosley, *Yale Law Journ.* (1911), XX.

Commerce Clause produced some criticism of the
Court — *The Employers' Liability Cases*, 207 U. S. 463,
and *Adair* v. *United States*, 208 U. S. 161 — the latter
case involving the law prohibiting railroad discrimination against union labor. The decision that regulation of employment with reference to union conditions
had no reasonable relation to interstate commerce
caused much surprise and well-justified antagonism.
"The inability of the Supreme Court to find any connection between the membership of a labor union and
the carrying on of interstate commerce seems inex-
plicable," wrote Richard Olney.[1] There is little doubt
that with further enlightenment of the Court as to conditions this decision will be and should be overruled.

In this same year, 1908, the power of the National
Judiciary was vitally enhanced by a decision which
caused much well-grounded apprehension among the
States.[2] Although in *Hans* v. *Louisiana*, 134 U. S. 1, in
1890, the Court had gone far in sustaining the non-
suability of a State either by one of its own citizens or
by citizens of another State, and in even overruling
Chisholm v. *Georgia*, nevertheless, the twenty years
since the death of Waite had witnessed a rapidly increasing series of cases in which suits had been sustained
to restrain State officials from carrying out State laws
alleged to violate the Constitution.[3] In 1891, an

[1] *Discrimination against Union Labor — Legal?* by Richard Olney, *Amer. Law Rev.*
(1908), XLII; *The Living Law,* by Louis D. Brandeis, *Illinois Law Rev.* (1916), X.
[2] *The Eleventh Amendment,* by William D. Guthrie, *New York Bar Ass.* (1908);
Magna Carta (1916), by William D. Guthrie.
[3] *Rolston* v. *Crittenden* (1887), 120 U. S. 390; *Pennoyer* v. *McConnaughty* (1891),
140 U. S. 1; see also *Ex parte Tyler* (1893), 149 U. S. 164; *Reagan* v. *Farmers' Loan
& Trust Co.* (1891), 154 U. S. 362; *Scott* v. *Donald* (1897), 165 U. S. 58; *Smyth*
v. *Ames* (1898), 169 U. S. 466; *Prout* v. *Starr* (1903), 188 U. S. 537; *Missouri,
Kansas & Texas Railway Co.* v. *Hickman* (1901), 183 U. S. 53; *Chandler* v. *Dix*
(1904), 194 U. S. 590; *Fargo* v. *Hart* (1904), 193 U. S. 490; *McNeill* v. *Southern
Railway Co.* (1906), 202 U. S. 543; *Mississippi Railroad Commission* v. *Illinois,
etc. Co.* (1906), 203 U. S. 335. And see *Cavanaugh* v. *Looney* (1918), 248 U. S. 453.
North Carolina v. *Temple* (1890), 134 U. S. 22, and *Fitts* v. *McGhee* (1899), 172

injunction had been granted to restrain the Governor, Secretary of State and State Treasurer of Oregon as State Land Commissioners from selling certain land under an unconstitutional statute. In 1894, an injunction was granted to restrain the Railroad Commission and the Attorney-General of Texas from enforcing the State Railroad Rate law by instituting suits for penalties. In 1897, State constables of South Carolina were enjoined from enforcing an unconstitutional State dispensary law; and judgment was allowed against the Secretary of State of South Carolina for damages for illegal possession of land under color of a South Carolina statute. In 1898 and in 1903, the Attorney-General of Nebraska was enjoined from enforcing against the Union Pacific Railroad an unconstitutional railroad rate law of that State. In 1901, the Board of Railroad & Warehouse Commissioners of Missouri were involved in a suit. In 1904, an attempt was made to restrain the Auditor-General of Michigan from assessing alleged illegal taxes; and the State Auditors of Indiana were restrained by injunction from assessing the American Express Company under an unconstitutional tax statute. In 1906, the State Corporation Commission of North Carolina was enjoined from enforcing orders as to delivery of cars on private sidings by railroad companies; and an injunction was upheld against the enforcement by the Mississippi Railroad Commission of an order requiring railroads to stop mail trains at county seats.[1] The climax of these decisions was

U. S. 516, were practically the only suits against State officials which the Court had deemed to constitute suits against the State and hence not maintainable.

[1] See *Suits Against a State*, by Joseph Wheless, *Amer. Law Rev.* (1900), XXXIV; *Suability of States by Individuals*, by Judge Jacob Trieber, *ibid.* (1907), XLI; *Suits Against States*, by William Trickett, *ibid.*; *The Increased Control of State Activities by the Federal Government*, by Robert P. Scott, *Amer. Pol. Sci. Rev.* (1909), III; *The Progressive Unfolding of the Power of the United States*, by Simeon E. Baldwin, *ibid.* (1912), VI.

reached, in 1908, in *Ex parte Young*, 209 U. S. 123, when the Court decided that the Attorney-General of the State of Minnesota could be enjoined from bringing any proceedings to enforce against the Northern Pacific Railroad in the State Courts the State Railroad Rate Law, and could be fined for contempt if he disobeyed the injunction. "We recognize and appreciate to the fullest extent the very great importance of this case," said Judge Peckham, "not only to the parties now before the Court, but also to the great mass of the citizens of this country, all of whom are interested in the practical working of Courts of justice throughout the land, both Federal and State, and in the proper exercise of the jurisdiction of the Federal Courts as limited and controlled by the Federal Constitution and the laws of Congress." The decision aroused harsh criticism throughout the country. The Legislature of Nebraska and the Association of Attorneys-General sent memorials to Congress demanding legislation; President Roosevelt in his Annual Message in 1907 had referred to the existing discontent over the situation; and finally Congress enacted a statute, in 1910, forbidding the issue of an injunction against a State officer based on the unconstitutionality of a State statute, unless after hearing in a Court of three Federal Judges, one of whom should be a Supreme Court or Circuit Court Judge.

In 1910, the rights of the States over corporations doing an interstate business were considerably restricted by decisions in *Western Union Tel. Co.* v. *Kansas*, and *Ludwig* v. *Western Union Tel. Co.*, 216 U. S. 1, 146, in which for the first time it was made clear that there were limits to the power of a State to tax a foreign corporation for the privilege of engaging in interstate business. These cases and the further decisions in the same year in *International Text Book*

Co. v. *Pigg*, 217 U. S. 91, holding that transmission of instruction by correspondence was interstate commerce, and that a foreign corporation engaging in such business could not be required by a State to obtain a license, led many lawyers and economists to believe that the situation thus created must lead, either to placing interstate business corporations under State control by Congressional legislation like the Wilson Liquor Act, or to National licensing of such corporations or to National incorporation.[1]

On July 4, 1910, Chief Justice Fuller died after twenty-two years' service. During the first ten years of his Chief Justiceship, the composition of the Court itself had been subjected to frequent changes; a vacancy occurring nearly every year. At the death of Chief Justice Waite in 1888, the Court had consisted of Judges Miller, Field, Bradley, Harlan, Gray, Blatchford, Lamar and Matthews. Judge Matthews died on March 22, 1889; and in his place President Harrison appointed, on December 4, 1889, Judge Field's nephew, David Josiah Brewer of Kansas, who was confirmed, December 18, by a vote of fifty-three to eleven. Brewer was fifty-two years old and had been Judge of the Supreme Court of Kansas for fourteen years and Judge of the United States Circuit Court since 1884. Judge Miller died on October 14, 1890, after twenty-eight years' service; and in his place Harrison appointed Henry B. Brown of Michigan, December 23, 1890. Brown was fifty-four years old and had been a Judge of the United States District Court for fifteen years. Judge Bradley died on January 22, 1892, after twenty-two years' service; and in his place Harrison appointed, July 19, 1892, George Shiras, Jr., of Pennsylvania, who

---

[1] *Constitutional Law in 1909–1910*, by Eugene Wambaugh, *Amer. Pol. Sci. Rev.* (1910), IV; *State Taxation of Interstate Commerce*, by H. T. Davenport, *Pol. Sci Qu.* (1911, 1912), XXVI, XXVII.

was confirmed July 26, after strong opposition. Shiras was sixty years old and had had no previous judicial experience. The next year, Judge Lamar died, January 24, 1893, and Harrison selected as his fourth appointment to the Court, Howell E. Jackson of Tennessee, February 2, 1893, who was confirmed February 18. Jackson was sixty years old and had been a United States Circuit Court Judge; he was the first Democrat appointed by a Republican President, since Judge Field, in 1861. Within another year, Judge Blatchford died on July 7, 1894. The vacancy led to a long and bitter struggle between President Cleveland and Senator Hill of New York, the former appointing successively William B. Hornblower on September 19, 1893, and Wheeler H. Peckham, on January 22, 1894. In each case, through "Senatorial courtesy", the Senate refused to confirm, rejecting Hornblower, January 15, 1894, by a vote of twenty-four to thirty, and Peckham, February 16, 1894, by a vote of thirty-two to forty-one. Three days after the rejection of Peckham, President Cleveland filled the vacancy on February 19, 1894, by appointing Edward Douglass White, of Louisiana, who was confirmed the same day.[1] White was forty-eight years old, had been Judge of the Supreme Court of Louisiana from 1876 to 1879, and United States Senator since 1891. Judge Jackson died on August 8, 1895, after a service of but two years; and on December 3, 1895, Cleveland appointed Rufus Wheeler Peckham of New York — a man fifty-seven years of age, who had been a Judge of the New York Court of Appeals from 1870 to 1886. Judge Field resigned on October 12, 1897 (to take effect December 1), having served on the Bench thirty-four years and seven months. President

---

[1] See notes in *Amer. Law Rev.* (1894), XXVII, 273, as to White, the Senate, and Courtesy of the Senate.

McKinley appointed, on December 16, 1897, Joseph McKenna of California, who was confirmed January 21, 1898, after strong opposition. McKenna was fifty-five years old; he had been three times a Member of Congress and had served as Judge of the United States Circuit Court, and for six months as Attorney-General of the United States. McKinley had no further opportunity to make an appointment, as the Court remained unbroken for four years. On July 9, 1902, Judge Gray resigned; and President Roosevelt appointed, on August 11, 1902, Oliver Wendell Holmes, Jr., of Massachusetts, — a man sixty-one years of age who had been Judge of the Massachusetts Supreme Judicial Court since 1882, and Chief Justice since 1899.[1] Judge Shiras resigned February 23, 1903, and Roosevelt appointed in his place, William R. Day of Ohio, February 19, 1903. Day was fifty-three years old and had been Secretary of State from May, 1898, to February, 1899, when he had been appointed Judge of the United States Circuit Court. Judge Brown resigned, May 28, 1906, and Roosevelt appointed, December 3, 1906, William H. Moody of Massachusetts. Moody was fifty-two years of age, and had been a Congressman, Secretary of the Navy and Attorney-General. Judge Peckham died, October 24, 1909, and in his place President Taft appointed Horace H. Lurton of Tennessee, who was confirmed, December 20, 1909. Lurton was sixty-five years old and had been a Judge of the United States Circuit Court.

To succeed Chief Justice Fuller, President Taft decided to promote to the vacant position at the head of the Court, Edward Douglass White, who had served as an Associate Judge since his appointment by President

---

[1] See *Oliver Wendell Holmes, the Jurist*, by Leonard A. Jones, *Amer. Law Rev.* (1902), XXXVI; and see *ibid.*, 437 *et seq.* for personal description of the Judges on the Court in 1902.

Cleveland, in 1894, and who was then sixty-five years of age. The appointment, made on December 12, 1910, was notable, not only because it was the first promotion of a Judge of the Court to the Chief Justiceship since the appointment of Judge Cushing in 1796, but because a Republican President was broad-minded enough to promote a Democratic Judge.

The slight importance, however, which was to be attached to the party designations of the Judges upon the Court was never better illustrated than during Fuller's Chief Justiceship. As was pointed out by one of the law journals upon his death : "In view of the number of vacancies which will be filled by President Taft and the Senate, and the many statements which have been made concerning the political importance of these appointments, in more than eighteen years since the decision in *Field* v. *Clark*, in 1892, there has been but one case which involved a question of constitutional law and in which all the Republican members of the Court took one position and all the Democratic members took a contrary position; that case (*Snyder* v. *Bettman*, 190 U. S. 249, in 1903) was whether a Federal inheritance tax, which was collected while the property was in the hands of an executor, could constitutionally be applied to a bequest to a municipality for public purposes; the Court upheld the tax, against the dissents of the Chief Justice and Justices White and Peckham; this decision will not be of much practical importance, until the people of the United States have become far more eager to make bequests to municipalities than they are today." [1] There was only one other case during those eighteen years in which all the Republican Judges approved the decision and all the

[1] *Chief Justice Fuller*, by Robert P. Reeder, *Amer. Law Reg.* (1911), LIX. Prior to *Field* v. *Clark*, see only *In re Neagle* (1890), 135 U. S. 1; *Handley* v. *Stutz* (1891), 139 U. S. 417; *United States* v. *Texas* (1892), 143 U. S. 621, in 1892.

Democratic Judges disapproved — *United States* v. *Shea*, 152 U. S. 178, in 1894, a case from the Court of Claims. In the cases as to which the most political excitement raged, the *Insular Cases* and the *Northern Securities Case*, Republican and Democratic Judges united in both the majority and the minority opinions, and, as so often in the past, the mental attitude of the Judge had far more to do with the conclusions of his opinion than had his political attitude. Certainly no decision could have been forecast by a consideration of party lines in the Court.

Chief Justice White's first Term was signalized by the decisions, on May 15, 1911, of the great *Standard Oil Co.* and *American Tobacco Co. Cases*, 221 U. S. 1, 106, under the Sherman Anti-Trust Act, which produced a profound sensation in the country and revived the hopes, somewhat shaken by previous decisions, that the National power was adequate to deal with the trusts.

In 1911, the Court for the first time gave real effect to the Thirteenth Amendment prohibiting slavery or involuntary servitude, by holding a peonage law of Alabama to be in conflict with its provisions, *Bailey* v. *Alabama*, 219 U. S. 219.[1]

In 1912, it was clearly shown that the Court was not grasping for power, when, in *Pacific States Telephone and Telegraph Co.* v. *Oregon*, 223 U. S. 118, it decided that the right of the State to adopt the initiative and referendum was a political and not a judicial question, and therefore non-justiciable by the Court. "It is the Government, the political entity, which is called to the bar of the Court," said Chief Justice White, "not for the purpose of testing judicially some exercise of power assailed on the ground that its exertion has

[1] See also *Reynolds* v. *United States* (1917), 235 U. S. 133.

injuriously affected the rights of an individual because
of repugnancy to some constitutional limitation, but to
demand of the State that it establish its right to exist
as a State, republican in form." Such an issue was
held not to be within the reach of judicial power.

In 1913, Congressional power to legislate as to the
newspaper press of the country by prescribing publication of details of ownership was upheld, as incidental
to its control of the mails and postroads; and by this
decision in *Lewis Publishing Co.* v. *Morgan*, 229 U. S.
288, a fertile field for National legislation was opened
up, advantage of which will undoubtedly be taken in
the future.

In 1913, also, the National power over railroads
received a tremendous impetus through the opinion
rendered in the *Minnesota Rate Cases*, 230 U. S. 352, in
which there was asserted more clearly than hitherto the
power of Congress to legislate as to intrastate railroad
rates when intimately connected with interstate rates.
"The execution by Congress of its constitutional power
to regulate interstate commerce is not limited by the
fact that intrastate transactions may have become so
interwoven therewith that the effective government of
the former incidentally controls the latter. . . . If the
situation has become such, by reason of the inter-
blending of the interstate and intrastate operations of
interstate carriers, that adequate regulation of their
interstate rates cannot be maintained without imposing
requirements with respect to their intrastate rates which
substantially affect the former, it is for Congress to
determine, within the limits of its constitutional
authority over interstate commerce and its instruments,
the measure of the regulation it should supply." [1]   The

---

[1] *Power of Congress to Regulate Railway Rates*, by Victor Morawetz, *Harv. Law
Rev.* (1905), XVIII; *Railroad Rate Regulation*, by Adelbert Moot, *ibid.* (1906),

next year, the power of Congress to regulate long and short hauls was upheld in the *Intermountain Rate Cases,* 234 U. S. 476.

In 1914, the doctrine of the *Granger Cases* received a restatement, and the scope of the State police power, especially with reference to the regulation of corporate rates, was defined in exceedingly broad terms in *German Alliance Insurance Co.* v. *Kansas,* 233 U. S. 389.[1] In 1915, the power of the National Executive received a notable extension, when, in *United States* v. *Midwest Oil Co.,* 236 U. S. 459, President Taft's action in withdrawing public lands from settlement without express statutory authority was upheld, on the ground that a long-continued practice, known to and acquiesced in by Congress, implied authority. In the same year, the power of the Court to determine controversies between States and to enforce its decree against a State was finally settled, in *Virginia* v. *West Virginia,* 238 U. S. 202. The Fifteenth Amendment was for the first time given real effect when the "Grandfather Clause" of the Oklahoma Constitution was held to violate it, in *Guinn* v. *United States,* 238 U. S. 347. The right of Congress absolutely to prohibit the introduction of any article in

XIX; *Power of Congress to Prescribe Railroad Rates,* by Frank W. Hackett, *ibid.* (1907), XX; *The Power of Congress to Regulate Commerce,* by Frank J. Goodnow, *Pol. Sci. Qu.* (1910), XXV; *The Minnesota Rate Cases,* by John Bauer, *Pol. Sci. Qu.* (1914), XXIX; *The Minnesota Rate Cases,* by Hannis Taylor, *Harv. Law Rev.* (1913), XXVII; *The Commerce Clause and Intrastate Rates,* by William C. Coleman, *Columbia Law Rev.* (1912), XII; *The Minnesota Rate Cases and the 14th Amendment,* by Charles W. Collins, *Amer. Law Rev.* (1914), XLVII; *The Evolution of Federal Regulation of Intrastate Rates — The Shreveport Rate Cases,* by William C. Coleman, *Harv. Law Rev.* (1914), XXVIII; *The Vanishing Rate-Making Power of the States,* by William C. Coleman, *ibid.* (1914), XIV; *The Minnesota Rate Cases and the Fourteenth Amendment,* by William C. Coleman, *Amer. Law Rev.* (1914), XLVIII; *Federal Control of Intrastate Railroad Rates,* by Harry W. Biklé, *U. of P. Law Rev.* (1915), LXIII.

[1] *The United States Supreme Court and Rate Regulation as Affected by the Distribution of Governmental Powers in the Constitution,* by Robert P. Reeder, *Amer. Law Reg.* (1909), LVII; *United States Supreme Court and Rate Regulation,* by Douglas D. Storey, *U. of P. Law Rev.* (1916), LXIV.

foreign trade was upheld, in *Weber* v. *Freed*, 239 U. S. 325, and *Brolan* v. *United States*, 236 U. S. 216.

In 1916, the effect of the Income Tax Amendment was construed in *Brushaber* v. *Union Pacific R. R.*, 240 U. S. 1. The power of the States to obstruct or deny removal of cases into the United States Courts was again restricted and redefined in *Donald* v. *Philadelphia and Reading Coal & Iron Co.*, 241 U. S. 329.[1]

In 1917, the power of Congress to regulate the instrumentalities of interstate commerce received a radical extension, when the Court upheld the Adamson Eight-Hour Law, in *Wilson* v. *New*, 243 U. S. 332.[2]

In the years succeeding the accession of White to the Chief Justiceship, the composition of the Court rapidly changed, Judges Peckham, Brewer, Harlan, Lurton, Lamar and Hughes leaving the Bench within the space

---

[1] See *supra*, III, 408.

[2] The original plan of this book did not contemplate the consideration of any cases later than 1917; but in order to show the steady development and judicial support of the powers of the National Government, during the years 1918 to 1921, the following cases should be noted.

The Selective Service Act was upheld in *Selective Draft Cases*, 245 U. S. 366, and *Goldman* v. *United States*, 245 U. S. 474, in 1918. The Espionage Act was upheld in *Schenck* v. *United States*, 249 U. S. 47, and *Debs* v. *United States*, 249 U. S. 211, in 1919, and in *Schaefer* v. *United States*, 251 U. S. 466, in 1920, and in *Milwaukee Publishing Co.* v. *Burleson*, 255 U. S. 407, in 1921. The Government wartime control of railroads was upheld in *Northern Pacific R. R.* v. *North Dakota*, 250 U. S. 135, and the Government wartime control of telegraph and telephones in *Dakota Central Telephone Co.* v. *South Dakota*, 250 U. S. 163, in 1919. The Wartime Prohibition Act was upheld in *Hamilton* v. *Kentucky Distilling Co.*, 251 U. S. 146, and in *Ruppert* v. *Caffey*, 251 U. S. 264, in 1919.

The national power to regulate by treaty the subject of migratory birds was upheld in an epoch-making decision in *Missouri* v. *Holland*, 252 U. S. 416, in 1920. The Volstead Prohibition Act and the 18th Amendment were upheld in *National Prohibition Cases*, 253 U. S. 350, in 1920. The 19th Amendment was upheld in *Hawke* v. *Smith*, 253 U. S. 221, 231, in 1920. The Farm Loan Act of 1916 was upheld in *Smith* v. *Kansas City Title Co.*, 255 U. S. 180, in 1921. The Trading with the Enemy Act was upheld in *Stoehr* v. *Wallace*, 255 U. S. 239, in 1921.

The chief Acts of Congress held invalid were four: the Child Labor Law of 1916, in *Hammer* v. *Dagenhart*, 247 U. S. 251, in 1918; the Income Tax Law of 1916, taxing stock dividends, in *Eisner* v. *Macomber*, 252 U. S. 189, in 1920; the Income Tax Law of 1919, taxing salaries of United States Judges, in *Evans* v. *Gore*, 253 U. S. 245, in 1920; and the Lever Food Control Act of 1917, in *United States* v. *L. Cohen Grocery Co.*, 255 U. S. 81, in 1921.

of seven years — President Taft having an opportunity
to appoint five Judges, a majority of the Court, and
President Wilson, three. On March 28, 1910, Judge
Brewer died after a service of twenty years and in his
place, Taft appointed Charles Evans Hughes of New
York, who was confirmed May 2, 1910. Hughes was
forty-eight years of age and had been Governor of
New York, but had had no previous judicial experience.
On November 20, 1910, Judge Moody resigned, and in
his place Taft appointed Willis Van Devanter of
Wyoming, who was confirmed December 15, 1910.
Van Devanter was fifty-one years old and had been
an Assistant Attorney-General and Judge of the United
States Circuit Court. On December 15, 1910, the
appointment of Joseph Rucker Lamar of Georgia was
confirmed to fill the vacancy caused by the promotion
of Judge White. Lamar was fifty-three years old,
and had served upon the Supreme Court of Georgia.
Judge Harlan died on October 14, 1911. To the vacant
place, President Taft appointed on February 19, 1912,
Mahlon Pitney of New Jersey, who was confirmed
March 13, 1912. Pitney was fifty-four years old and
had been Judge of the Supreme Court and Chancellor
of New Jersey. Judge Lurton died on July 12, 1912,
and President Wilson appointed on August 19, 1914,
James Clark McReynolds of Tennessee, a man fifty-
two years of age who had served as Attorney-General
for a year and a half. Judge Lamar died on January
2, 1916, and in his place Wilson appointed on January
28, 1916, Louis D. Brandeis of Massachusetts, who was
confirmed on June 1, 1916, by a vote of forty-seven to
twenty-two, after a long and bitter contest. Brandeis
was fifty-nine years old and had had no previous
judicial experience. On June 10, 1916, Judge Hughes
resigned in order to accept his nomination as Republican

candidate for the Presidency, and in his place Wilson appointed on July 14, 1916, John H. Clarke of Ohio, a man fifty-eight years of age, who had served as Judge of the United States District Court.[1]

During these thirty years from 1888 to 1918, there were two radical extensions and two restrictions of the Court's jurisdiction through Congressional action. By the Act of March 2, 1907, appeals by the Government in criminal cases were authorized on rulings by inferior United States Courts on demurrer, plea in abatement and motion to quash.[2] By the Act of December 23, 1914, the Court was authorized to review on certiorari, cases in the State Courts in which the decision is against the validity of a State statute claimed to violate the Constitution. This was the first important change in the Twenty-Fifth Section of the Judiciary Act of 1789; and it had long been advocated by the American Bar Association. It enabled the Court in the future to take jurisdiction in such cases as the *Ives Case*, in which the New York Court of Appeals had held the Workmen's Compensation law of that State repugnant to the Constitution, and in similar cases in which the State Courts had hitherto been less progressive in their constitutional doctrines and more inclined to hold State laws invalid.[3] By the Act of 1891 establishing the

---

[1] Chief Justice White died, May 19, 1921; and to succeed him, President Harding appointed William Howard Taft, June 30, 1921.

[2] The statute had been recommended as early as 1902 by Attorney-General Knox. It was enacted largely through President Roosevelt's insistence, after the decision by Judge Humphreys in *United States* v. *Armour & Co.*, 142 Fed. 808, holding the packers, indicted under the Meat Inspection Law, to be entitled to immunity because of having testified before the Bureau of Corporations; see also *59th Cong., 2d Sess.*, debate in Senate, Feb. 4, 13, 1907; *United States* v. *Sanges* (1892), 144 U. S. 310, in which it was held that the United States has no power to sue out a writ of error in a criminal case.

[3] Prior to 1825, the decided cases averaged 24 a year; from 1826 to 1830, 58; in 1836 there were 37 cases disposed of; in the five years from 1846 to 1850, an average of 71. In the October, 1890, Term, there were 1816 cases on the docket and the Court disposed of 617; in the October, 1891, Term, there were 1582, of which 496 were disposed of, and at this time it took three years to reach a case for

Circuit Court of Appeals, Congress afforded a marked relief to the Court by restricting its appellate jurisdiction; and by the Court of Customs Appeals Act of 1909, the Court was further relieved of customs cases.

argument. *The Needs of the Supreme Court*, by William Strong, *North Amer. Rev.* (1895), CXXXII; and see 140 U. S. App. as to the effect of the Act of 1891.

NOTE. There has been much misunderstanding as to the exact scope of the decisions in the *Insular Cases;* and many statements have been made not only by laymen but also by historians and lawyers that the Court held in these cases that the Constitution did not apply to, or was not extended to, the insular possessions. A concise summary of the Court's position is contained in Chief Justice Taft's decision in *Balzac* v. *Porto Rico* (1922), 258 U. S. 298 (affirming *Porto Rico* v. *Tapia* (1917), 245 U. S. 639), as follows: "The Constitution of the United States is in force in Porto Rico as it is wherever and whenever the sovereign power of that government is exerted. This has not only been admitted but emphasized by this Court in all its authoritative expressions upon the issues arising in the *Insular Cases,* especially in the *Downes* v. *Bidwell* and the *Dorr Cases.* The Constitution, however, contains grants of power, and limitations which, in the nature of things, are not always and everywhere applicable, and the real issue in the *Insular Cases* was not whether the Constitution extended to the Philippines or Porto Rico when we went there, but which ones of its provisions were applicable by way of limitation upon the exercise of executive and legislative power in dealing with new conditions and requirements. The guaranties of certain fundamental personal rights declared in the Constitution, as, for instance, that no person could be deprived of life, liberty, or property without due process of law, had, from the beginning, full application in the Philippines and Porto Rico."

CHAPTER THIRTY-EIGHT

COMMERCE AND THE POLICE POWER

1888-1918

In all this development of the National sovereignty during the thirty years after the death of Chief Justice Waite, one feature deserves more detailed comment, namely the awakening of Congress to the realization of the vast power wrapped up in the Commerce Clause, its increasing exercise of that power, and the breadth of the decisions by which the Court has sustained such exercise of power.[1]

As was said in 1907: "The development of the power was for one hundred years rather in a negative way than in a positive way. The Court was called upon to say what the States could not do, instead of what Congress could do — except as the one necessarily followed from the other. . . . The tendency in this country towards a centralization of power is increasing. The field of the National Government is constantly widening. . . . A Unity is growing out of a Union, and the primary source of all this Nationalizing power is the Commerce Clause."[2]

The first important exercise by Congress of its power under the Commerce Clause, was the Interstate Commerce Act of 1887; but while this law was construed

---

[1] For an early appreciation and fear of this tendency, see *The Supreme Court and Interstate Commerce*, by Charles A. Culbertson, *Amer. Law Rev.* (1890), XXIV.

[2] *The Constitutional Opinion of Justice Holmes*, by Felix Frankfurter, *Harv. Law Rev.* (1916), XXIX; *Development of the Commerce Clause in the Federal Constitution*, by Judge Walter C. Noyes, *Yale Law Journ.* (1907), XVI.

and applied by the Court in a vast number of cases, it was not until six years later that Congress took further advantage of its constitutional powers to regulate common carriers engaged in interstate and foreign commerce, by the passage of the Safety Appliance Act of 1893 (further developed by the Acts of 1896, 1908 and 1911); and by the Harter Act of 1893 regulating bills of lading and the liability of sea-carriers.[1] In 1903, however, the enactment of the Elkins Act was followed by a series of statutes regulating such carriers — the Automatic Coupler Act of 1903, the Hours of Service Acts of 1907 and 1916, the Employers' Liability Acts of 1905 and 1908, the Carmack Amendment of 1906,[2] the Hepburn Act of 1906,[3] the Interstate Express Company Act of 1906, the Transportation of Explosives Act of 1909, the Mann-Elkins Act of 1910 regulating also telegraph, telephone and cable companies, the Boiler Inspection Acts of 1911 and 1915, the United States Shipping Board Act of 1916 regulating carriers by water, the Bills of Lading Act of 1916, the Adamson Act of 1916 regulating hours of labor and wages of railroad employees, the Car Service Act of 1917. All of these statutes, except the first Employers' Liability Act, were upheld by the Court.[4] In sustaining the power of Congress over carriers, it reached an extreme point when, in the *Adamson Law Case* in 1917, it upheld the right to fix wages and hours of labor in case of an emergency and for the purpose of keeping

[1] *The Harter Act; Recent Legislation in the United States Respecting Bills of Lading*, by Everett P. Wheeler, *Amer. Law Rev.* (1899), XXXIII; *The Harter Act*, by Frederick Green, *Harv. Law Rev.* (1902) XVI.

[2] See *Adams Express Co.* v. *Croninger* (1913), 226 U. S. 491.

[3] *United States* v. *Delaware & Hudson Co.* (1909), 213 U. S. 366; *Constitutional Questions Involved in the Commodity Clause of the Hepburn Act*, by William D. Lewis, *Harv. Law Rev.* (1908), XXI; *Recent Problems on Railway Legislation*, by William Z. Ripley, *Pol. Sci. Qu.* (1912), XXVII.

[4] *The National Employers' Liability Act*, by Jacob Trieber, *Amer. Law Rev.* (1915). XLIX.

interstate traffic open and continuous.[1] "A majority of
the Court has established a doctrine the application of
which it is to be hoped the good sense of Congress will
strictly confine within the limits of an urgent necessity."
This comment, written shortly after the decision, probably expresses the general view of the public.

The second important exercise by Congress of its
power under the Commerce Clause was an attempt on
its part to exercise the National authority for the
purpose of enlarging the powers of the States. By the
decisions of the Court in *Bowman* v. *Chicago & Northwestern R. R.*, 125 U. S. 465, in 1888, and in *Leisy* v.
Hardin, 135 U. S. 100, — the *Original Package Case* — in
1890, which denied the validity of State prohibition
laws affecting intoxicating liquors during the period of
interstate transportation, the power of the States to
enforce their liquor legislation effectively had been
seriously impaired — "an invasion by the Federal
Government of State domain and a National destruction of State prohibition." [2] By the Wilson Act of
1890, Congress restored to the States their control over
liquor upon its arrival within the State; but this statute
resulted in little benefit to the prohibition States, since,
while the Court held it constitutional, it also held that

---

[1] See *Wilson* v. *New* (1917), 243 U. S. 332; *The Constitutionality of the Eight-
Hour Railroad Law*, by M. H. Lauchheimer, *Columbia Law Rev.* (1916), XVI; *Due
Process and the Adamson Law*, by Thomas R. Powell, *ibid.* (1917), XVII; *Railway
Strikes and the Constitution*, by Arthur F. Ballantyne, *ibid.*; *The Adamson Act
Decision*, by Frank W. Hackett, *Amer. Law Rev.* (1918), LII; *The Supreme Court
in the Adamson Law*, by C. W. Burr, *Minnesota Law Rev.* (1918), I; *The Adamson
Law Decision*, by C. K. Burdick, *Cornell Law Qu.* (1917), II; *The Supreme Court
and the Adamson Law*, by Thomas R. Powell, *U. of P. Law Rev.* (1917), LXV.

[2] See *The Law Governing an Original Package*, by John B. Uhle, *Amer. Law Reg.*
(1890), XXXVIII; *Recent Centralizing Tendencies in the Supreme Court*, by Frederic P. Powers, *Pol. Sci. Qu.* (1890), V; see also *Amer. Law Rev.* (1890), XXIV,
474, 490; *Lyng* v. *Michigan* (1890), 135 U. S. 161; *Eilenbecker* v. *Plymouth Co.*
(1890), 134 U. S. 31; *In re Rahrer* (1891), 140 U. S. 545; *Crowley* v. *Christensen*
(1890), 137 U. S. 86; *Rhodes* v. *Iowa* (1898), 170 U. S. 412; *Vance* v. *Vandercook
Co.* (1898), 170 U. S. 438; *Adams Express Co.* v. *Iowa* (1905), 196 U. S. 147; *Louisville & Nashville R. R.* v. *Cook Brewing Co.* (1912), 223 U. S. 70.

the word "arrival" meant not physical arrival within the State but commercial arrival by delivery to the consignee, the status of interstate transportation not being concluded until such delivery. The same doctrine as to the want of power in the States to interfere with the objects of interstate transportation when in their original packages was applied by the Court to State legislation on the subjects of oleomargarine and cigarettes.[1] For thirteen years, the National power over liquor transportation growing out of this Original Package doctrine reigned supreme. "The Interstate Commerce Clause, intended to be a harmonizer among the States, has been made a weapon of offense by which the liquor producing States have compelled prohibition States to receive intoxicating liquors willy-nilly, and thus have made the enforcement of local prohibition laws substantially impossible," said Assistant Attorney-General Denison, in 1914. "So there has arisen what amounts to a direct offensive warfare by the Federal Government, in alliance with certain States, against the domestic, social and economic policies of other States." To put an end to this situation, Congress passed the Webb-Kenyon Act of 1913, penalizing the shipment or transportation of liquor intended to be received, possessed or sold either in original package or otherwise in violation of State laws. Though the constitutionality of this law was doubted by President Taft and by most of the Bar, it was supported by the Court in decisions which gave greatly added scope to the power of Congress to transfer its authority to the

[1] See *Schollenberger* v. *Pennsylvania* (1898), 171 U. S. 1, as to a State oleomargarine law; and see the Oleomargarine Act of 1902 restoring control to the States; *Austin* v. *Tennessee* (1900), 179 U. S. 343; *Cook* v. *Marshall Co.* (1905), 196 U. S. 261; *The Latest Phase of the Original Package Doctrine*, by Shackelford Miller, *Amer. Law Rev.* (1901), XXXV; *What is the Original Package Doctrine*, by Morris M. Townley, *ibid.*; *The Original Package Ineptitude*, by William Trickett, *Columbia Law Rev.* (1906), VI.

States.[1] The Reed Amendment of 1917, also supported by decisions of the Court, was the culmination of this form of National legislation.[2]

The third important example of the exercise by Congress of its power under the Commerce Clause, the Sherman Anti-Trust Act of 1890, has been the subject of extensive judicial construction, from 1895 until the present day. At first, the meaning of the terms of this Act was supposed by Congress to be free from doubt, and though there was some criticism by the Bar, an article in a law journal in 1893 expressed the general view: "The Act has been criticised because it contains no definition; but the common law terms used in it seem to be sufficient. The language is searching and the provisions are drastic." This confidence in the clarity of the language of the Act was soon dispelled. Owing to the unfortunate manner in which the facts were alleged and proved in the first decided case, *United States* v. *E. C. Knight Co.*, 156 U. S. 1, the opinion, holding the operations of the sugar refiners involved to be legal, served to discourage further attempts to invoke the statute in relation to commercial business. Decisions followed, in 1898 holding railroads to be subject to the law, in 1904 holding stockholding corporations to be within its purview, in 1908 holding combinations of laborers in a boycott to be liable under the law.[3] In 1911, twenty-one years

---

[1] *Clark Distilling Co.* v. *Western Maryland R. R.* (1917), 242 U. S. 311; *The Webb Act*, by Allen H. Kerr, *Yale Law Journ.* (1913), XXII; *State Rights and the Webb-Kenyon and the Liquor Law*, by Winfred T. Denison, *Columbia Law Rev.* (1914), XIV; *Unlawful Possession of Liquor and the Webb-Kenyon Act*, by Lindsay Rogers, *ibid.* (1916), XVI, and see especially long list of articles on the Webb-Kenyon Act cited in *Decisions of the Supreme Court, 1914–1917*, by Thomas R. Powell, *Amer. Pol. Sci. Rev.* (1918), XII.

[2] *The Reed Bone-Dry Amendment*, by J. K. Graves, *Virginia Law Rev.* (1917), IV; *United States* v. *Hill* (1918), 248 U. S. 420; *United States* v. *Simpson* (1920), 252 U. S. 465; *Life, Liberty and Liquor*, by Lindsay Rogers, *Virginia Law Rev.* (1919), VI.

[3] *Strikes and Trusts*, *Amer. Law Rev.* (1893), XXVII. For discussion of the Trusts and the Sherman Act at varying stages in its early career, see the following

after the passage of the Act, decisions in the *Standard Oil Co.* and *American Tobacco Co. Cases*, 221 U. S. 1, made more clear the general scope and limitations of the National control of combination in restraint of interstate trade.[1] Later decisions have not materially extended the National power. When it appeared that unreasonable restraint and improper methods by which the restraint was attained or maintained were to be controlling features in determining the legality of the corporate combination, it became more and more the general belief that the National power over these interstate combinations should be exercised in regulation, rather than in destruction, and that the economic evils — the evils of monopoly control and unjust and unfair business methods — must be remedied, without attacking the principle of mere combination. It was largely on this theory that the Clayton Act and the Act establishing the Federal Trade Commission were adopted, in 1916.[2] In addition

articles: *The Economic and Social Aspects of Trusts*, by George Gunton, *Pol. Soc. Qu.* (1888), III; *"Monopoly" under the National Anti-Trust Act*, by William F. Dana, *Harv. Law Rev.* (1894), VII; *Federal Trust Regulation*, by Carman F. Randolph, *Pol. Sci. Qu.* (1897), XII; *Federal Anti-Trust Law*, Report of Committee on Jurisprudence and Law Reform, *Amer. Bar Ass. Rep.* (1897), *Amer. Law Rev.* (1897), XXXI; *The Anti-Trust Act, The Case of the Trans-Missouri Traffic Association*, by William D. Guthrie, *Harv. Law Rev.* (1897), XI; *Anti-Trust Legislation*, by Frederick H. Cooke, *Amer. Law Rev.* (1899), XXXIII; *Trusts*, by J. B. Clark, *Pol. Sci. Qu.* (1900), XV.

[1] *The Supreme Court and the Anti-Trust Act*, by Victor Morawetz, *Columbia Law Rev.* (1910), X; *The Sherman Anti-Trust Law*, by M. S. Hottenstein, *Amer. Law Rev.* (1910), XLIV; *Has the Sugar Case been Overruled?* by Stuart Chevalier, *ibid.; The Standard Oil Decision*, by H. A. Wilgus, *Michigan Law Rev.* (1911), IX; *The Federal Anti-Trust Act*, by Robert L. Raymond, *Harv. Law Rev.* (1910), XXIII; *"Anti-Trust" Legislation and Litigation*, by William B. Hornblower, *Columbia Law Rev.* (1911), XI; *The Standard Oil and Tobacco Cases*, by Robert L. Raymond, *ibid.* (1911), XXV; *The Oil and Tobacco Cases*, by Albert H. Walker, *Amer. Law Rev.* (1911), XLV; *The Recent Trust Decision*, by H. R. Seager, *Pol. Sci. Qu.* (1911), XXVI; *Recent Interpretation of the Sherman Act*, by George W. Wickersham, *Michigan Law Rev.* (1911), X; *The Supreme Court and the Sherman Anti-Trust Act*, by Harold Evans, *Amer. Law Reg.* (1911), LIX; *The Standard Oil Case ana American Tobacco Cases*, by Harold Evans, *U. of P. Law Rev.* (1912), LX; *The Federal Anti-Trust Act*, by Roland L. Foulke, *ibid.* (1913), LXII; *What the Sherman Anti-Trust Act has Accomplished*, by Alfred Hayes, *Amer. Law Rev.* (1913), XLVII.

[2] *Unfair Competition*, by W. H. S. Stevens, *Pol. Sci. Qu.* (1914), XXIX; *The New Anti-Trust Act*, by Henry R. Seager, *ibid.* (1915), XXX; *The Federal Trade*

Congress legislated regarding monopolies and restraint of trade by enacting sections 73 to 77 of the Wilson Tariff Act in 1894 as to combinations of importers, and in the Panama Canal Act of 1912, forbidding ownership by common carriers of competing water lines, and in the Hepburn Act of 1916 making it unlawful for a railroad to transport, except for its own needs, any article manufactured, mined or produced by it directly or indirectly.

Until the year 1903, Congress had confined the exercise of its powers under the Commerce Clause almost entirely to the subject of intoxicating liquor, common carriers and trusts. In that year, however, the decision of the Court in the great case of *Champion* v. *Ames,* 188 U. S. 321, upholding the Act of 1895 by which Congress forbade all transportation of lottery tickets in interstate commerce, disclosed the existence of a hitherto unsuspected field of National power. While the Court expressly stated that, in sustaining the right absolutely to prohibit interstate commerce in lottery tickets, it must not be understood to uphold a general right to exclude any and all articles from such commerce, nevertheless, the reasoning on which the opinion was based left a very wide discretion to Congress. Hitherto, it had been largely left to the States under the exercise of the police power to decide each for itself what articles of commerce should or should not be brought within the State or produced within the State for transportation elsewhere. Now the Court announced the doctrine that Congress might decide to what extent and under what regulations such articles might be transported. The decision caused much uneasiness among those who feared the vesting of such

broad powers in the National Government and such
extinction of the State police powers; and many
sympathized with Chief Justice Fuller's remark in his
dissenting opinion that "our form of government may
remain, notwithstanding legislation or decision, but, as
long ago observed, it is with governments, as with
religions, that the form may survive the substance of
the faith." Many agreeing with the author of an
article entitled: "Is Congress a Conservator of the
Public Morals?", stated that the decision was to be
viewed with alarm.[1] "The case is of extraordinary
interest and of far-reaching consequence. The Court
has unfolded a vast power wrapped up in the Commerce
Clause," said another writer. "The police powers of
the State are extinct, so far as their exercise bears upon
any of the subjects entrusted to Congress by the Constitution, notably upon intercommunication with the
States or with foreign parts. In the execution of the
powers over commerce and over the mails, Congress
may enact laws which regulate the internal affairs of
States that are not in any way dependent upon or
connected with communication with the exterior,"
wrote another. The practical result of the case was
the creation of a Federal police power — the right to
regulate the manner of production, manufacture, sale
and transportation of articles and the transportation of
persons, through the medium of legislation professing
to regulate commerce between the States. Congress
took very swift advantage of the new field thus opened
to it. In 1903 and 1905, it passed the Animal Contagion Disease and the enlarged Animal Quarantine

[1] See *Amer. Law Rev.* (1904), XXXVIII; *Three Constitutional Questions*, by
Alfred Russell, *ibid.* (1904), XXXVII; *Is There a Federal Police Power?* by Paul
Fuller, *Columbia Law Rev.* (1904), IV; *The Exclusive Power of Congress to Regulate
Interstate and Foreign Commerce*, by David W. Brown, *ibid.*; *Latest Development
of the Interstate Commerce Power*, by Edward B. Whitney, *Michigan Law
Rev.* (1902), I.

Acts; in 1906, the Pure Food Act; in 1905 and 1906, the Metals Hallmark Acts; in 1905, 1912, 1915 and 1917, the Plant Quarantine Acts; in 1907, the Meat Inspection Act; in 1909 and 1914, the Narcotics Acts; in 1910, the White Slave Traffic Act; in 1910, the Insecticide Act; in 1912, the Apple-Grading Act and the Adulterated-Seed Act; in 1913, the Serums and Toxins Act; in 1916, the Warehouse Act and the Grain Standards Act; in 1916, the Child Labor Act.[1]

All this legislative activity in fields theretofore reserved to State action was the subject of constant comment by legal writers,[2] and the pendency in Congress of bills to regulate child labor in the States by debarring the products of such labor from interstate transportation presented the question as to the limits of Congressional power in a new light. "The new proposition is this," said Attorney-General Knox in 1907, "that Congress has the power to regulate commerce, including its instrumentalities, *and likewise* power to regulate the persons by whom articles of commerce are produced in respect to matters not connected with commerce . . . , to prohibit articles of value, which are in themselves innocuous and which are lawfully made or produced in a State, for reasons not affecting interstate commerce."[3]

[1] See *Hipolite Egg Co.* v. *United States* (1911), 220 U. S. 45, sustaining the Pure Food Act; *Hoke* v. *United States*, 227 U. S. 308, sustaining the White Slave Traffic Act; and *United States* v. *Jin Fuey Moy* (1916), 241 U. S. 394, sustaining the Narcotics Act of 1914.

[2] *Power of Congress to Regulate Commerce*, by Frank J. Goodnow, *Pol. Sci. Qu.* (1910), XXV; *Powers of Regulation Vested in Congress*, by Max Pam, *Harv. Law Rev.* (1910), XXIV; *Federal Control of Interstate Commerce*, by George W. Wickersham, *ibid.* (1910), XXIII; *Nature and Scope of the Power of Congress to Regulate Commerce*, by Frederick H. Cooke, *Columbia Law Rev.* (1911), XI; *The Exclusive Power of Congress over Interstate Commerce*, by Charles W. Needham, *ibid.*

[3] *The Exclusiveness of the Power of Congress over Interstate and Foreign Commerce*, by James S. Rogers, *Amer. Law Rev.* (1905), LIII; *Recent Developments in the Law Relating to Interstate Commerce*, by Morris M. Cohn, *Amer. Law Rev.* (1908), XLII; *The Development of the Federal Power to Regulate Commerce*, by Philander C. Knox, *Yale Law Journ.* (1908), XVII; *Power of the States over Commodities Excluded by Congress from Interstate Commerce*, by Lindsay Rogers, *Yale Law Journ.* (1915).

Fear of this legislative trend was expressed before the American Bar Association in 1917 : "This case was undoubtedly the Pandora's box from which burst forth with amazing speed and ever-increasing velocity the tendency to federalize and centralize, beyond the dreams of Alexander Hamilton, a government whose centripetal forces had already been too greatly strengthened as a result of the Civil War. It was the beginning of that steady, unending, unceasing movement in Congress to stretch far beyond its real meaning and far beyond what any fair construction, however liberal, warranted the Commerce Clause of the Constitution. This movement has progressed so steadily, has been pressed so persistently, and has gone so far that it threatens to utterly annihilate our dual system of government, to utterly destroy the police powers of the several States, and finally to be about to deprive our people of the inestimable blessings of local self-government, unless it be checked speedily and sharply."[1] That there was a limit to Congressional power under the Commerce Clause was finally settled by the Court in *Hammer* v. *Dagenhart*, 247 U. S. 251, in 1918, when it held the Child Labor Law of 1916 unconstitutional.[2]

While, however, the so-called National police powers may be restricted under the Commerce Clause, it is to be noted that there seems to be very little restriction on the extent to which the National Government may regulate, under the taxing power, the production, manufacture, sale and transportation of articles within the States. As early as 1869, it was held, in *Veazie Bank* v.

XXIV; *Congressional Prohibition of Interstate Commerce*, by Thomas I. Parkinson, *Columbia Law Rev.* (1916), XVI; *Working towards a Federal Domain*, by R. L. Schuyler, *Pol. Sci. Qu.* (1913), XXVII.

[1] *The Regulation of Commerce Between the States*, by Thomas W. Hardwick, *Amer. Bar Ass. Rep.* (1917).

[2] But see *The Federal Power to Regulate Child Labor*, by William D. Lewis, *U. of P. Law Rev.* (1914), LXII.

Fenno, 8 Wall. 533, that the taxing power might be exercised for the purpose of destroying or regulating the thing taxed; and in 1904, this doctrine received further affirmation in the decision in *McCray* v. *United States*, 195 U. S. 27, involving the Oleomargarine Act.[1] The number of subjects, the manufacture and sale of which Congress has regulated in great detail is large and constantly increasing, of which the following statutes are an example — the Oleomargarine Acts of 1886 and 1902; the Filled Cheese Act of 1896; the Mixed-Flour Act of 1898; the White Phosphorus Match Act of 1912; the Harrison Narcotic Act of 1914; the Cotton Futures Act of 1916.

While it has thus upheld Congressional powers of affirmative action under the Commerce Clause, and under the provisions of the Constitution relating to post-roads and taxes, and has thus developed a so-called National police power, the Court has demonstrated an equally strong desire to uphold State legislation passed in the exercise of the State police power, whenever such legislation could be construed as no interference with the authority of the National Government. State laws challenged as violative of the Fourteenth Amendment and enacted under the police power generally involve mere questions between the State and the individual. But those State laws which are challenged as in conflict with the Commerce Clause often present questions of the respective rights of the State and of the National Governments. The difficulty of drawing the line between permissible protection of the public welfare by the State and unlawful encroachment

[1] See also *Cornell* v. *Coyne* (1904), 192 U. S. 418; *Federal Taxation of Interstate Commerce*, by Simeon E. Baldwin, *Harv. Law Rev.* (1908), XXII; *Nullification by Indirection*, by James M. Beck, *ibid.* (1910), XXIII; *Power of Regulation Vested in Congress*, by Max Pam, *ibid.* (1910), XXIV; *May Congress Levy Money Exactions Designated as "Taxes" Solely for the Purpose of Destruction?* by John B. Waite, *Michigan Law Rev.* (1908), VI.

on the Nation's power to regulate commerce has been recognized by the invention of the popular phrase, "the twilight zone."[1]

The police power of a State, so far as the Federal Constitution is concerned, ultimately means that degree of interference with individual freedom of action or with use of private property in the interest of the public welfare, which the Judiciary considers not to be arbitrary, or not to be unduly violative of National rights in commerce between the States, at any given time and in the light of prevailing conditions. It is the judicial interpretation of the concept of private property, the fixing of the metes and bounds to the use of such property and to the liberty of the individual.[2] By the Legislature primarily, but by the Judiciary finally, individual rights are adjusted to existing social and economic conditions, through the settlement of the question of how far governmental regulation may, without compensation, impose burdens on property or action. As a consequence, the idea of vested rights in any well governed community must develop correspondingly to the ever changing conditions of time and place. It is in the progressive recognition and application of this principle that the Court has performed one of its greatest services.

State statutes regulative or restrictive of individual

[1] The boundary line between the State police power and the Commerce Clause has been the subject of a vast amount of discussion; for early articles, see *What is the Test of a Regulation of Foreign or Interstate Commerce?* by Louis M. Greeley, *Harv. Law Rev.* (1887), I, stating that "no class of cases is more perplexing"; *Police Power and Interstate Commerce*, by William R. Howland, *ibid.*, IV, attacking the decision in *Leisy* v. *Hardin; The Relation of the Police Power of the States to the Commerce Power of the Nation*, by Charles C. Binney, *Amer. Law Rev.* (1891), XXV.

[2] *Property and Contract* (1918), by Richard T. Ely, I, 205–226, II, 699. See *What is the Police Power?* by Walter W. Cook, *Columbia Law Rev.* (1907), VII; *The Sociological Interpretation of Law*, by Joseph H. Drake, *Michigan Law Rev.* (1918), XVI: "The invocation and application of the police power is nothing more than an appeal to the sociological method of interpreting our Constitution and laws."

property or action, and passed under alleged authority
of the State police power, have been attacked in the
Court in almost six hundred cases during the past
thirty years. The bulk of these statutes were claimed
to violate the Fourteenth Amendment; the remainder
were claimed by the parties affected to constitute an
interference with National control of commerce. With
comparatively few exceptions of importance, the Court
has upheld the validity of the State legislation.[1] Between the years 1889 and 1918 inclusive, it has decided
about 790 cases, in which statutes were attacked under
the Due Process and the Equal Protection of the Law
Clauses of the Fourteenth Amendment. Of these, 422
involved State statutes passed under the police power;
196, State statutes passed under the taxing power; and
172, State statutes prescribing administrative or judicial procedure. Of these 422 cases arising under the
police power (being those which involved the new and
progressive social and economic legislation of modern
times), the Court held the statutes unconstitutional in
53 cases, two thirds of which, however, involved the
rates and regulation of public-service corporations; of
the remainder, 2 involved municipal improvements;
5, anti-trust laws; and only 14 involved legislation
affecting the general rights and liberties of individuals.
The decision in only 2 of these 14 cases involving what
has been termed "social justice" legislation aroused any
widespread criticism, one being *Lochner* v. *New York*, in
1905, which, if not now practically overruled, is certain
in the near future to be disregarded by the Court; [2]

[1] See for detailed synopsis of cases to the year 1912, *The Progressiveness of the
United States Supreme Court*, by Charles Warren, *Columbia Law Rev.* (1913), XIII,
reprinted as *Sen. Doc. 30, 63d Cong., 1st Sess.* (1913); *A Bulwark to the State
Police Power*, by Charles Warren, *Columbia Law Rev.* (1913), XIII; *The Honor
Roll of the Police Power*, by B. L. Mayes, *Amer. Law Rev.* (1916), L.

[2] But see *Police Power and Civil Liberty*, by S. Whitney Dunscumb, Jr., *Columbia
Law Rev.* (1906), VI, terming the Court a "bulwark of American liberty", because

the other was *Coppage* v. *Kansas*, 236 U. S. 1, decided in 1915, in which a Kansas law forbidding employers to coerce, require or influence employees not to join or remain in labor-unions was held invalid — a decision which, with the increasing development of the aspect of the social desirability of labor-unions, is likely to be overruled.[1]

A similar record was made in cases in which the State statutes were challenged under the Commerce Clause of the Constitution, and in which the Court has upheld the State legislation as within the scope of the police power in substantially all cases involving State statutes promotive of "social justice." Under the Commerce Clause, the Court decided 216 cases, of which 142 involved statutes passed under the police power, and 94 under the taxing power In these 142 cases arising under the police power, the Court held the State statutes unconstitutional in 46, of which 24 were corporation regulation laws, 9 were liquor and cigarette laws, and only 13 were general progressive legislation. In no one of these 13 cases was there any strong criticism of the decision.

It may fairly be said that the support which the Court has thus given to the police power of the States has been one of the most remarkable features of its career. Certainly a litigant who hopes to overturn the deliberate judgment of a State Legislature as expressed in this form of legislation has a very scanty hope of assistance from the Court.[2]

of this decision. Lawyers and laymen alike have progressed far from such an opinion at the present time.

[1] *The Living Law,* by Louis D. Brandeis, *Illinois Law Rev.* (1916), X; "In the *Coppage Case,* the Supreme Court showed the potency of mental prepossessions."

[2] A more detailed statement of laws upheld by the Court will serve to make this even clearer. Of laws regulating sales of pure food and other merchandise and the conduct of mercantile business, the Court has upheld the law in 32 cases challenged under the Fourteenth Amendment and in 11 challenged under the Commerce Clause; and in only 5 cases has it held a law unconstitutional. Laws

So long as it shall adhere to the course which it has followed from 1889 to 1918, there will be no possible justification for the demand for recall of Judges or of judicial decisions — a cry which was, at its origin, based purely on ignorance of the facts as to the Court's decisions.[1] At present, the demand made by certain labor organizations for the abolition of the Court's power to pass upon the constitutionality of statutes seems based wholly on the claim that the Court has

regulating wages it has upheld in 12 cases; relating to employees' injuries in 9 cases under the Fourteenth Amendment, and 1 under the Commerce Clause; workmen's compensation laws in 5 under the Fourteenth Amendment, and in 1 under the Commerce Clause; other labor laws in 8 cases under the Fourteenth Amendment, and 1 under the Commerce Clause. In only 3 cases has it held a State statute regarding labor unconstitutional. (*Lochner* v. *New York* (1905), 198 U. S. 45; *Coppage* v. *Kansas* (1915), 236 U. S. 1; *Truax* v. *Raich* (1915), 239 U. S. 33; but see also *Adams* v. *Tanner* (1917), 224 U. S. 590.) Of anti-trust laws, it has sustained 11 challenged under the Fourteenth Amendment, and 1 under the Commerce Clause, and has held laws invalid in 5 cases. Of gambling laws, it has sustained 7; of legislation relating to liquor and cigarettes, it has sustained 20 challenged under the Fourteenth Amendment, and 12 under the Commerce Clause, and has held 9 invalid. Of game laws, it has sustained 2; of legislation as to cattle quarantine, etc., it has sustained 6 laws challenged under the Fourteenth Amendment, and 7 under the Commerce Clause. Of legislation restricting or regulating the freedom of contract and liberties of individuals, it has sustained 60 laws and held only 3 invalid. Of legislation relative to negroes, it has upheld 13 laws challenged under the Fourteenth Amendment and 2 under the Commerce Clause, and has held invalid 3. Of acts of general legislation, and establishing public improvements, it has upheld 72 and found invalid 7. Of acts of political or municipal legislation, it has upheld 12. Of laws as to navigation, marine liability and liens, pilots, harbor, regulation of immigrants (other than tax cases) challenged under the Fourteenth Amendment, it has upheld 11 and held invalid 2. All the other cases arising under the police power in which State statutes were challenged under the Fourteenth Amendment, or under the Commerce Clause involved regulation of rates of railroad, telegraph, insurance, banking, telephone, grain elevator, or other corporations; they amounted to about 206 in number, of which 32 were held invalid under the Fourteenth Amendment and 24 under the Commerce Clause.

[1] *Social Reform and the Constitution* (1911), by Frank J. Goodnow, 334 *et seq.; Social Legislation and the Courts*, by Walter F. Dodd, *Pol. Sci. Qu.* (1915), XXVII.

As to Judicial Recall, see Theodore Roosevelt in *Outlook*, Jan. 6, 1912; *Majority Rule and the Judiciary* (1912), by William A. Ransom; *Our Judicial Oligarchy* (1912), by Gilbert E. Roe; *The Judicial Recall*, by Rome G. Brown, *Sen. Doc. 892, 62d Cong., 2d Sess.* (1912); *Judicial Recall*, by Rome G. Brown, *Sen. Doc. 617, 63d Cong., 2d Sess.* (1914); *Social Justice and the Courts*, by Theodore Schroeder, *Yale Law Journ.* (1912), XXII; *Report of the Committee on Judicial Recalls, Amer. Bar Ass. Rep.* (1913); *Recall of Judges and Judicial Independence*, by James M. Kerr, *Amer. Law Rev.* (1916), L.

made a wrong decision as to two State statutes — the
New York bakers' ten-hour law and the Kansas labor-
union law — and as to two Federal statutes — the law
forbidding interstate carriers to discriminate against
union-labor, and the child-labor law (both enacted
ostensibly under the Commerce Clause).[1] When serious error can be claimed in only four cases out of 564
involving the police power of the States and out of the
multitude involving the power of Congress acting under
the Commerce Clause, it would seem that the evil
complained of was practically non-existent. Certainly
no other branch of Government, and no other human
institution, ever functioned with a slighter percentage
of error.

The doctrine which the Court has finally worked out
in deciding these constitutional cases may be summed
up briefly as the recognition of "the paramount
right of public necessity." When, in the last decade
of the nineteenth century, it took the radical step of
expanding the old classic phrase defining the objects
of the exercise of the police power — "public health,
safety and morals" — by interpolating the words
"public welfare", it advanced far towards acceptance
of the theory of modern sociological jurists that the law
must recognize the priority of social interests, and that
it must start from the premise that "individual interests are to be secured by law, because and to the

[1] *Adair* v. *United States* (1908), 208 U. S. 161, and *Hammer* v. *Dagenhart* (1918),
247 U. S. 251. It should be noted that the chief other decision which has been the
subject of attack by labor men was not rendered in construing any statute or passing upon the validity of any statute but was merely a decision as to the limits of
the common law rights of laborers to combine — *Hitchman Coal & Coke Co.* v.
Mitchell (1918), 245 U. S. 229, decided in 1918; see *Collective Bargaining before
the Supreme Court*, by Thomas R. Powell, *Pol. Sci. Qu.* (1918), XXXIII; *The Attitude of American Courts towards Restrictive Labor Laws*, by Henry R. Seager, *ibid.*
(1904), XIX. One further decision which has been attacked by labor men very
recently may be noted, *Truax* v. *Corrigan* (1921), 42 Sup. Ct. 124, holding an
Arizona picketing law invalid; see *Yale Law Journ.* (1922), XXXI, 408; *New
Republic*, Jan. 25, 1922.

extent that they are social interests." [1]   Such a theory
is closely approximated in the formula which the Court
has adopted, in testing the validity of legislation purporting to be enacted in the exercise of the State police
power.   This formula appears now to be as follows:
that a law purporting to be enacted for the protection
of the public will not be declared invalid, unless it shall
be made clear to the Court that it was not open to the
State Legislature to find that it had a real or substantial
relation to the protection of the public health, safety,
morals or welfare, or unless it is so clearly arbitrary or
oppressive, or (as Judge Holmes has said) "so unreasonable and so far beyond the necessities of the case as to
be deemed a purely arbitrary interference with lawful
business transactions." [2]

Such being its rule of decision, and the practical
administration of the rule being carried out as disclosed in the summary of cases given above, it is clearly

---

[1] *Judicial Construction of the Fourteenth Amendment*, by Francis J. Swayze, *Harv.
Law Rev.* (1912,) **XXVI**; *The Evolution of Due Process of Law in Decisions of the
United States Supreme Court*, by Francis W. Bird, *Columbia Law Rev.* (1913), XIII;
American Political Ideas (1920), by Charles F. Merriam, ch. v, "The Courts and
Justice", ch. vi, "Responsibility of the Judges to the Democracy", quoting Prof.
Roscoe Pound.

Everett V. Abbott in *Justice and the Modern Law* (1913), says that the doctrine
reached by the Court is "nothing but the formulation in legal phraseology of that
thing which every American so ardently desires, 'a square deal,' and when the Courts
adjudge a statute to be unconstitutional as taking property without due process
of law or as denying the equal protection of the law, all that they really do is to
declare their opinion, in more or less technical phraseology, that somebody is not
receiving that square deal to which he is entitled."

[2] *Muller* v. *Oregon* (1908), 208 U. S. 412; *Broadnax* v. *Missouri* (1911), 219
U. S. 285; *Chicago etc. R. R.* v. *McQuire* (1911), 219 U. S. 549; *German Alliance
Ins. Co.* v. *Kansas* (1914), 233 U. S. 389.   See, however, an attack upon the Court's
formula by Albert M. Kales in *New Methods in Due Process Cases, Amer. Pol. Sci.
Rev.* (1918), XII.

In an interesting article by Learned Hand (now United States District Judge),
on *Due Process of Law and the Eight Hour Day, Harv. Law Rev.* (1908), XXI, it is
said: "Only in those cases which are obvious beyond peradventure that the statute was the result either of passion, or of ignorance or folly, can the Court say
that it was not due process of law.   In this way, the principle may be observed
that with the expediency of the statute the Court has no concern, but only with
the power of the Legislature."

apparent that the Court, so far from being reactionary or obstructive of the development of modern social legislation, has constituted a strong bulwark of the State police power. "A progressive liberalization is manifest as one looks at the decisions from 1890 to 1910," wrote a distinguished law school Dean. "Something very like sociological interpretation has begun in this country." "One of the notable characteristics of our age is that in science, sociology, economics, psychology, philosophy and religion, the movement is from the abstract to the concrete, from speculation to experience, from logic to life. The fact that our Supreme Court has grasped the deeper meaning of this movement, that it looks through technicalities and logical formulas to facts — to reality — has strengthened it in the confidence of the people, and increased its effectiveness for the work properly belonging to it in our coordinate system of government," said a recent legal writer. And an eminent sociologist has also recently said: "On the whole, the American constitutional system has worked well, in spite of the Dred Scott decision and the *Bakers' Case*. And even bad as some decisions have been, progress has been secure and continuous. . . . It is the State Courts which now stand for a belated individualism, and it is only in a few cases that the Federal Supreme Court has erred seriously in this particular." [1]

[1] *The Courts and Legislation*, by Roscoe Pound, *Amer. Pol. Sci. Rev.* (1913), VIII; *Justice Holmes and the Fourteenth Amendment*, by Fletcher Dobyns, *Illinois Law Rev.* (1918), XIII; *Property and Contract* (1914), by Richard T. Ely, II, 691, 698. *Social Reform and the Constitution* (1911), by Frank J. Goodnow, 329 *et seq.*: "So far from the Supreme Court being open to our criticism for giving unduly narrow construction to constitutional provisions in favor of individual rights, as against measures designed for the public welfare, a more candid criticism might suggest that that great tribunal in common with other Courts, had yielded somewhat unduly to public criticism in giving effect to legislation, which, however desirable from the standpoint of social reform, yet involves a measurable encroachment upon some of those individual rights to secure which the 14th Amendment was adopted." *Certainty and Justice* (1914), by Frederic R. Coudert, 57: "Many

Unquestionably, unbiased application of the formula which the Court has worked out for the determination of the validity of a State statute presents a task of high difficulty. As has been well said: "It calls for minds of extraordinary intellectual disinterestedness and penetration, lest limitation in personal experience be interpreted, however consciously or unconsciously, as constitutional limitations. . . . It requires on the part of a Judge the highest degree of analytic acumen and intellectual honesty, to concede to others that latitude of opinion within the bounds of the rational, which is absolutely necessary before he can rightly decide the highly artificial question which he is now compelled to decide." Or as another writer has recently stated: "Working under the powerful pressure of unscrupulous political and economic interests, in a period of active law-making by the community, and more than all, in a period when the economic, social and class origins and implications of law and justice are scrutinized and challenged as never before, the task of legal logic, of penetrating insight, of balanced judgment, of invention of formulas of democratic justice, is more than commonly heavy." [1]

of the State Courts have been over-conservative and are largely responsible for the feeling that has been created against the judiciary as the representative of capitalisitic and conservative power. But the Supreme Court of the United States, with few exceptions has been liberal, recognizing that readjustment is not necessarily revolution." *Social Legislation and the Courts*, by Walter F. Dodd, *Pol. Sci. Qu.* (1913), XXVII: "In recent years a number of Courts have shown a distinct liberalizing tendency. . . . Except for a rather unfortunate lapse in the New York bake-shop case, the Supreme Court of the United States has in the main taken a liberal attitude toward legislation aimed to meet new social and industrial needs." See also *The Police Power, a Product of the Rule of Reason*, by George W. Wickersham, *Harv. Law Rev.* (1914), XXVII; *The Changing Attitude of the Courts Toward Social Legislation*, by Louis M. Greeley, *Illinois Law Rev.* (1910), V.

[1] *The Constitutional Opinion of Justice Holmes*, by Felix Frankfurter, *Harv. Law Rev.* (1916), XXIX; *The Constitution and the Courts*, by John G. Palfrey, *ibid.* (1913), XXVI; *American Political Ideas* (1920), by Charles E. Merriam; "Under the constitutional system as developed in this country, the political philosophy of the Judges is a matter of vital importance;" *Social Legislation and the Courts*, by William F. Dodd, *Pol. Sci. Qu.* (1913), XXVIII. "Settled habits of juristic

But the Court has been and can be valuably aided, in cases involving novel State legislation, through a proper performance by the Bar of its special duty. As the decision of the validity of most statutes now depends upon the application of a well established formula to a constantly changing and growing variety of economic and social facts, that decision, whether the legislation in dispute had any "essential and reasonable relation" to the public welfare designed by the Legislature to be promoted, will depend very largely upon the facts adduced by counsel to establish such relation. Since the presentation of the novel brief in *Muller* v. *Oregon*, 208 U. S. 412, by Louis D. Brandeis, in 1908, the Bar has tended increasingly to be of aid to the Courts. "That was the first case presented on the basis of authoritative data. For the first time, the arguments and briefs breathed the air of reality." [1]

One other duty towards the Court and towards the public is owed by counsel which should be unflinchingly performed, namely, to insist that the doctrine of *stare decisis* can never be properly applied to decisions upon constitutional questions. However the Court may interpret the provisions of the Constitution, it is still the Constitution which is the law and not the decision

thought are characteristic of American legal science. Our legal scholarship is chiefly historical. Our professional thinking upon juristic subjects is almost wholly from the point of view of the 18th Century natural law." *Courts and Legislation*, by Roscoe Pound, *Amer. Pol. Sci. Rev.* (1913), VIII.

[1] *Hours of Labor and Realism in Constitutional Law*, by Felix Frankfurter, *Harv. Law Rev.* (1916), XXIX; *Constitutional Decisions by a Bare Majority of the Court*, by Robert E. Cushman, *Michigan Law Rev.* (1921), XIX; *The Need of Social Statistics as an Aid to the Courts*, by Walter F. Wilcox, *Amer. Law Rev.* (1913), XLVII; *New Methods in Due Process Cases*, by Albert M. Kales, *Amer. Pol. Sci. Rev.* (1918), XII; *Constitutional Limitations and Labor Legislations*, by Ernst Freund, *Illinois Law Rev.* (1910), IV; *Changing Attitude of the Courts towards Social Legislation*, by Louis M. Greeley, *ibid.* (1910), V; *Liberty of Contract*, by Roscoe Pound, *Yale Law Journ.* (1909), XVIII. In the brief of Louis D. Brandeis for defendants in error in *Stettler* v. *O'Hara* on writ of error to the Supreme Court of Oregon, the points of law were stated in three pages, and the evidence to support the contention that the legislative action had a reasonable relation to public health safety or welfare comprised 390 pages.

of the Court.   "To the decision of an underlying question of constitutional law no . . . finality attaches. To endure, it must be right." [1]   Hence, as has been well said recently: "Any citizen whose liberty or property is at stake has an absolute constitutional right to appear before the Court and challenge its interpretation of the Constitution, no matter how often they have been promulgated, upon the ground that they are repugnant to its provisions. . . . When the Bar of the country understands this, and respectfully but inexorably requires of the Supreme Court that it shall continually justify its decisions by the Constitution, and not by its own precedents, we shall gain a new conception of the power of our constitutional guaranties. . . . What we need is constant and unrelenting professional criticism of judicial opinions, and constant unrelenting insistence that judicial errors of reasoning shall be judicially corrected." [2]   Such insistence does not imply that "the Constitution must be bent from its original meaning to suit present exigencies." To attribute such a power to the Judiciary would be intolerable; but it is of the highest importance that the Judiciary should always be pervious to demonstration of judicial error as to the original meaning of the Constitution, and prepared to correct its own mistakes.[3]

Besides the increased importance of the function of counsel in these constitutional cases in modern days,

[1] *Works of George Bancroft* (1852), IV, 549.

[2] *Justice and the Modern Law* (1913), by Everett V. Abbott.

[3] *The Elasticity of the Constitution*, by Arthur W. Machen, Jr., *Harv. Law Rev.* (1901), XIV; *The Doctrine of Stare Decisis as Applied to Constitutional Questions*, by D. H. Chamberlain, *Harv. Law Rev.* (1890), III; *The Doctrine of Stare Decisis*, by Edward B. Whitney, *Michigan Law Rev.* (1904), III; *Judge-Made Constitutional Law*, by Munroe Smith, *Van Norden's Mag.* (1909); *Congress and the Supreme Court*, by H. M. Bowman, *Pol. Sci. Qu.* (1910), XXV; *Stare Decisis and the Fourteenth Amendment*, by Charles W. Collins, *Columbia Law Rev.* (1912), XII; *Some Constitutional Limitations on the Judiciary*, by T. L. Edelen, *Amer. Law Rev.* (1914), XLVIII.

one other factor has tended to keep the Court responsive to the necessity of preserving the police power intact. This factor is the increasing recognition by the Judges themselves of their duty to keep in touch with the progressive economic, social and philosophical ideals of the day. As Roscoe Pound has said: "In periods in which the law is formative or growing . . . it is of great consequence that juristic and judicial thinking be in touch with the best lay thought of the time." [1] Louis D. Brandeis said (shortly before his appointment on the Court): "In the last century, our democracy has deepened. Coincidentally, there has been a shifting of our longing from legal justice to social justice. . . . What we need is not to displace the Courts but to make them efficient instruments of justice; not to displace the lawyer but to fit him for his official or judicial task . . . by broader education, by study undertaken preparatory to practice and continued by lawyer and Judge throughout life: study of economics and sociology and politics which embody the facts and present the problems of today." Whatever may be said of State Court Judges, those of the United States Supreme Court have been thoroughly and increasingly alive to the necessity of intellectual contact with new conditions and theories; and an earlier criticism of the Judiciary that cases are decided "upon the principles of the past . . . and the prejudices which the individualism of common law institutional writers, the dogmas learned in a college course in economics, and habitual association with the business and professional class must inevitably produce" is now by no means justified.[2]

---

[1] Note on *The New Philosophies of the Law*, by Roscoe Pound, *Harv. Law Rev.* (1914), XXVII, 733.

[2] *Common Law and Legislation*, by Roscoe Pound, *Harv. Law Rev.* (1908), XXI; *The Living Law*, by Louis D. Brandeis, *Illinois Law Rev.* (1916), X; see also *The Law and the Facts*, by Woodrow Wilson, *Amer. Pol. Sci. Rev.* (1911), V.

THE PRESENT COURT-ROOM

public opinion as a basis of popular government. We have seen that we cannot have true public opinion unless the minority feel themselves bound to acquiesce in the opinion of the majority. This attitude will never exist in regard to majority action which is tyrannical in nature, and which runs counter to the deeply embedded prejudices and convictions of the minority. In order to safeguard the very existence of popular government, therefore, it has been necessary to erect constitutional safeguards to protect the minority from such action by the majority as would lead the former to resistance or revolt." [1] Moreover, as Burke said, one hundred and thirty years ago: "The restraints on men, as well as their liberties, are to be reckoned among their rights." [2]

That the Court, in its one hundred and thirty years' existence, has fully and worthily fulfilled the purposes for which it was designed by the framers of the Constitution, there can be no doubt; and De Tocqueville's words, written in 1835, are as true today as then: "The Supreme Court is placed at the head of all known tribunals, both by the nature of its rights and the class of justiciable parties which it controls. The peace, the prosperity and the very existence of the Union are placed in the hands of the Judges. Without their active coöperation, the Constitution would be a dead letter; the Executive appeals to them for protection against the encroachment of the Legislative power; the Legislature demands their protection against the

---

[1] *Popular Government* (1921), by Arnold Bennett Hall, 154, 156; see also views of Viscount Bryce in his *Modern Democracies* (1921). See also *Debates in the Federal Convention of 1787* (ed. by Gaillard Hunt and James Brown Scott, 1920), 389, speech of George Mason, stating that the chief of the evils of the republican form of government " were the danger of the majority oppressing the minority, and the mischievous influence of demagogues."

[2] *Reflections on the Revolution in France, Works of Edmund Burke,* III.

designs of the Executive; they defend the Union against
the disobedience of the States; the States, from the
exaggerated claims of the Union; the public interests
against the interests of private citizens; and the conservative spirit of order against the innovations of an
excited democracy." And as Judge Field wrote, on his
resignation in 1897: "As I look back over the more
than a third of a century that I have sat on this Bench,
I am more and more impressed with the immeasurable
importance of this Court. Now and then we hear it
spoken of as an aristocratic feature of a republican
government. But it is the most democratic of all.
Senators represent their States, and Representatives
their constituents; but this Court stands for the whole
country, and as such it is truly 'of the people, by the
people and for the people.' It has, indeed, no power
to legislate. It cannot appropriate a dollar of money.
It carries neither the purse nor the sword. But it possesses the power of declaring the law, and in that is
found the safeguard which keeps the whole mighty
fabric of government from rushing to destruction. This
negative power, the power of resistance, is the only
safety of a popular government."

That the Court is not infallible, that like all other
human institutions it makes its mistakes may be
acknowledged; yet in spite of the few instances in
which it has run counter to the deliberate and better
judgment of the community, the American people will
unquestionably conclude that final judgment as to
their constitutional rights is safer in the hands of the
Judiciary than in those of the Legislature, and that if
either body is to possess uncontrolled omnipotence,
it should be reposed in the Court rather than in Congress, and in independent Judges rather than in Judges
dependent on election by the people in passionate

party campaigns and on partisan political issues. In the words of Attorney-General Wickersham: "Mistakes have been made by the Judiciary. Cases have been wrongly decided and the extension of legal principles to meet new conditions and judicial interpretation of the Constitution has often been slower than impatient reformers desirous of immediate results would wish. Yet no candid critic can say that on the whole the history of the American Judiciary does not furnish as high, if not higher, example of adequate results than that of any other branch of the Government." "They have no patronage with which to reward their followers, and no partisans to sustain them right or wrong; they have no interest except in common with their countrymen, and no ambition except to leave behind them an honored name. Of all men in this world, they have the least temptation to do wrong and the greatest incentive to do right. They are not infallible, and they make their mistakes, but they make fewer mistakes than other men; and so long as they can guard the Constitution of this Republic, it will protect the lives, the liberty and the property of the American people." [1]

This book may well close with the eloquent appeal (quoted in the Introductory Chapter), written in 1856 at a time when American institutions seemed shaken: "Admit that the Federal Judiciary may in its time have been guilty of errors, that it has occasionally sought to wield more power than was safe, that it is as fallible as every other human institution. Yet it has

---

[1] *The Judicial Function*, by George W. Wickersham, *U. of P. Law Rev.* (1912), LX; *The American Judiciary*, by Joseph W. Bailey, *Amer. Bar Ass. Report* (1915); *The Supreme Court and its Constitutional Duty and Power*, by Junius Parker, *Amer. Law Rev.* (1896), XXX; "In times of political upheaval, of sectional animosity, of communistic uprising, the nine quiet men who spend their lives away from the political field, free from the necessity of demagoguery, constitute the very sheet-anchor of the institutions of our land."

been and is, a vast agency for good; it has averted many a storm which threatened our peace, and has lent its powerful aid in uniting us together in the bonds of law and justice. Its very existence has proved a beacon of safety . . . and now let us ask ourselves, with all its imagined faults, what is there that can replace it? Strip it of its power, and what shall we get in exchange? Discord and confusion, statutes without obedience, Courts without authority, an anarchy of principles and a chaos of decision, till all law at last shall be extinguished by an appeal to arms." "If the Judiciary be struck from the system," said William Wirt in 1832, "what is there of any value that will remain? The Government cannot subsist without it. It would be as rational to talk of a solar system without a sun. No, sir, the people of the United States know the value of this institution too well to suffer it to be put down or trammelled in its action by the dictates of others." [1]

[1] *Amer. Law Reg.* (1856), IV, 129; *Wirt*, II, 338–339, argument of Wirt in *Cherokee Nation* v. *Georgia* (1831), 5 Pet. 1. Judge Henry B. Brown, on his retirement, wrote to his Associates on the Court, May 28, 1906: "The antagonisms, sometimes almost fierce, which were developed during the earliest decades of its history and at one time threatened to impair its usefulness, are happily forgotten; and the now universal acquiescence in its decisions, though sometimes reached by a bare majority of its members, is a magnificent tribute to that respect for the law inherent in the Anglo-Saxon race, and contains within itself the strongest assurance of the stability of our institution." 202 U. S.

APPENDIX

[The dates (other than the dates of birth, of declination and death), and the figures as to the votes are taken from the official *Executive Journals of the Senate*, until 1901; after 1901, from the *Congressional Record*. The order is as follows: date of birth; date of appointment or nomination (the date of receipt of nomination by the Senate, when differing from the date of appointment, being inserted in parentheses); date of confirmation by the Senate; date of rejection; date of final postponement of consideration; date of withdrawal of the nomination; date of declination of office after confirmation; date of death.]

John Jay (Chief Justice), born, Dec. 12, 1745; appointed, Sept. 24, 1789; confirmed, Sept. 26, 1789; resigned, June 29, 1795; died, May 17, 1829.

John Rutledge, born, —— 1739; appointed, Sept. 24, 1789; confirmed, Sept. 26, 1789; resigned, March 5, 1791; died, July 23, 1800.

William Cushing, born, March 1, 1732; appointed, Sept. 24, 1789; confirmed, Sept. 26, 1789; died, Sept. 13, 1810.

Robert Hanson Harrison, born, —— 1745; appointed, Sept. 24, 1789; confirmed, Sept. 26, 1789; declined office; died, April 20, 1790.

James Wilson, born, Sept. 14, 1742; appointed, Sept. 24, 1789; confirmed, Sept. 26, 1789; died, Aug. 28, 1798.

John Blair, born, —— 1732; appointed, Sept. 24, 1789; confirmed, Sept. 26, 1789; resigned, Jan. 27, 1796; died, Aug. 31, 1800.

James Iredell, born, Oct. 5, 1751; appointed, Feb. 9, 1790; confirmed, Feb. 10, 1790; died, Oct. 20, 1799.

Thomas Johnson, born, Nov. 4, 1732; appointed, Aug. 5, 1791, Oct. 31, 1791 (Nov. 1, 1791); confirmed, Nov. 7, 1791; resigned, March 4, 1793; died, Oct. 25, 1819.

William Paterson, born, —— 1745; appointed, Feb. 27, 1793; withdrawn, Feb. 28, 1793.

William Paterson, appointed, March 4, 1793; confirmed, March 4, 1793; died, Sept. 9, 1806.

John Rutledge (Chief Justice), born, —— 1739; appointed, July 1, 1795 (Nov. 5, 1795); took his seat Aug. 12, 1795; rejected, Dec. 15, 1795.

William Cushing (Chief Justice), born, March 1, 1732; appointed, Jan. 26, 1796; confirmed, Jan. 27, 1796; declined office, Jan. 1796.

Samuel Chase, born, April 17, 1741; appointed, Jan. 26, 1796; confirmed, Jan. 27, 1796; died, June 19, 1811.

Oliver Ellsworth (Chief Justice), born, April 29, 1745; appointed, March 3, 1796; confirmed, March 4, 1796 (21–1); resigned, Sept. 30, 1800; died, Nov. 26, 1807.

Bushrod Washington, born, June 5, 1762; appointed, Sept. 29, 1798 (Dec. 19, 1798); confirmed, Dec. 20, 1798; died, Nov. 26, 1829.

Alfred Moore, born, May 21, 1755; appointed, Oct. 20, 1799 (Dec. 6, 1799); confirmed, Dec. 10, 1799; resigned, March, 1804; died, Oct. 15, 1810.

John Jay (Chief Justice), born, Dec. 12, 1745; appointed, Dec. 18, 1800; confirmed, Dec. 19, 1800; declined, Jan. 2, 1801.

John Marshall (Chief Justice), born, Sept. 24, 1755; appointed, Jan. 20, 1801; confirmed, Jan. 27, 1801; died, July 6, 1835.

William Johnson, born, Dec. 27, 1771; appointed, March 22, 1804; confirmed, March 24, 1804; died, Aug. 11, 1834.

Henry Brockholst Livingston, born, Nov. 26, 1757; appointed, Nov. 10, 1806, Dec. 13, 1806 (Dec. 15, 1806); confirmed, Dec. 17, 1806; died, March 18, 1823.

Thomas Todd, born, Jan. 23, 1765; appointed, Feb. 28, 1807; confirmed, March 3, 1807; died, Feb. 7, 1826.

Levi Lincoln, born, May 15, 1749; appointed, Jan. 2, 1811; confirmed, Jan. 3, 1811; declined, Jan. 1811; died, April 14, 1820.

Alexander Wolcott, born, Nov. 12, 1775; appointed, Feb. 4, 1811; rejected, Feb. 13, 1811 (9–24).

John Quincy Adams, born, July 11, 1767; appointed, Feb. 21, 1811; confirmed, Feb. 22, 1811; declined, April, 1811; died, Feb. 23, 1848.

Joseph Story, born, Sept. 18, 1779; appointed, Nov. 15, 1811; confirmed, Nov. 18, 1811; died, Sept. 10, 1845.

Gabriel Duval, born, Dec. 6, 1752; appointed, Nov. 15, 1811; confirmed, Nov. 18, 1811; resigned, Jan. 1835; died March 6, 1844.

Smith Thompson, born, Jan. 17, 1768; appointed, Sept. 1, 1823 (Dec. 8, 1823); confirmed, Dec. 19, 1823; died, Dec. 18, 1843.

Robert Trimble, born, —— 1777; appointed, April 11, 1826; confirmed, May 9, 1826 (27–5); died, Aug. 25, 1828.

John Jordan Crittenden, born, Sept. 10, 1787; appointed, Dec. 17, 1828 (Dec. 18, 1828); postponed, Feb. 12, 1829 (27–17); died, July 26, 1863.

John McLean, born, March 11, 1785; appointed, March 6, 1829; confirmed, March 7, 1829; died, April 4, 1861.

Henry Baldwin, born, Jan. 14, 1780; appointed, Jan. 4, 1830 (Jan. 5, 1830); confirmed, Jan. 6, 1830 (41–2); died, April 21, 1844.

James Moore Wayne, born, —— 1790; appointed, Jan. 7, 1835; confirmed, Jan. 9, 1835; died, July 5, 1867.

Roger Brooke Taney, born, March 17, 1777; appointed, Jan. 15, 1835; postponed, March 3, 1835 (24–21).

Roger Brooke Taney (Chief Justice), born, March 17, 1777; appointed, Dec. 28, 1835; confirmed, March 15, 1836 (29–15); died, Oct. 12, 1864.

Philip Pendleton Barbour, born, May 25, 1783; appointed, Dec. 28, 1835; confirmed, March 15, 1836 (30–11); died, Feb. 24, 1841.

William Smith, born, —— 1762; appointed, March 3, 1837; confirmed, March 8, 1837; declined, March, 1837; died, June 10, 1840.

John Catron, born, —— 1786; appointed, March 3, 1837; confirmed, March 8, 1837; died, May 30, 1865.

John McKinley, born, May 1, 1780; appointed, April 22, 1837 (Sept. 18, 1837); confirmed, Sept. 25, 1837; died, July 19, 1852.

Peter Vivian Daniel, born, April 24, 1784; appointed, Feb. 26, 1841 (Feb. 27, 1841); confirmed, March 2, 1841 (22–5); died, June 30, 1860.

John Canfield Spencer, born, Jan. 8, 1788; appointed, Jan. 9, 1844 (Jan. 9, 1844); rejected, Jan. 31, 1844 (21–26); died, May 18, 1855.

Reuben Hyde Walworth, born, Oct. 26, 1788; appointed, March 13, 1844; postponed, Jan. 15, 1844 (27–20); withdrawn, June 17, 1844; died, Nov. 27, 1867.

Edward King, born, Jan. 31, 1794; appointed, June 5, 1844; postponed, June 15, 1844 (29–18); died, May 8, 1873.

Edward King, appointed, Dec. 4, 1844; postponed, Jan. 23, 1845; withdrawn, Feb. 7, 1845.

Samuel Nelson, born, Nov. 10, 1792; appointed, Feb. 4, 1845 (Feb. 6, 1845); confirmed, Feb. 14, 1845; died, Dec. 13, 1873.

John Meredith Read, born, Feb. 21, 1797; appointed, Feb. 7, 1845 (Feb. 8, 1845); not acted upon; died, Nov. 29, 1874.

George Washington Woodward, born, March 26, 1809; appointed,

Dec. 23, 1845; rejected, Jan. 22, 1846 (20–29); died, May 10, 1875.

Levi Woodbury, born, Dec. 22, 1789; appointed, Sept. 20, 1845 (Dec. 23, 1845); confirmed, Jan. 3, 1846; died, Sept. 4, 1851.

Robert Cooper Grier, born, March 5, 1794; appointed, Aug. 3, 1846; confirmed, Aug. 4, 1846; resigned, Jan. 31, 1870; died, Sept. 26, 1870.

Benjamin Robbins Curtis, born, Nov. 4, 1809; appointed, Sept. 22, 1851 (Dec. 11, 1851); Dec. 29, 1851; resigned, Sept. 30, 1857; died, Sept. 15, 1874.

Edward A. Bradford, born, Sept. 27, 1813; appointed, Aug. 16, 1852; not acted upon.

George Edmund Badger, born, April 13, 1795; appointed, Jan. 10, 1853; postponed, Feb. 11, 1853 (26–25); died, May 11, 1866.

William C. Micou, born, —— 1806; appointed, Feb. 24, 1853; not acted upon.

John Archibald Campbell, born, June 24, 1811; appointed, March 21, 1853; confirmed, March 25, 1853; resigned, 1861; died, March 13, 1889.

Nathan Clifford, born, Aug. 18, 1803; appointed, Dec. 9, 1857; confirmed, Jan. 12, 1858 (26–23); died, July 25, 1881.

Jeremiah Sullivan Black, born, Jan. 10, 1810; appointed, Feb. 5, 1861 (Feb. 6, 1861); rejected, Feb. 21, 1861 (25–26); died, Aug. 19, 1883.

Noah Haynes Swayne, born, Dec. 7, 1804; appointed, Jan. 21, 1862 (Jan. 22, 1862); confirmed, Jan. 24, 1862 (38–1); resigned, Jan. 24, 1881; died, June 8, 1884.

Samuel Freeman Miller, born, April 5, 1816; appointed, July 16, 1862; confirmed, July 16, 1862; died, Oct. 13, 1890.

David Davis, born, March 9, 1815; appointed, Oct. 17, 1862 (Dec. 1, 1802); confirmed, Dec. 8, 1862; resigned, March 7, 1877; died, June 26, 1886.

Stephen Johnson Field, born, Nov. 4, 1816; appointed, March 6, 1863 (March 7, 1863); confirmed, March 10, 1863; resigned, Dec. 1, 1897; died, April 9, 1899.

Salmon Portland Chase (Chief Justice), born, Jan. 13, 1808; appointed, Dec. 6, 1864; confirmed, Dec. 6, 1864; died, May 7, 1873.

Henry Stanbery, born, Feb. 20, 1803; appointed, April 16, 1866; not acted upon; died, June 26, 1881.

Ebenezer Rockwood Hoar, born, Feb. 21, 1816; appointed, Dec. 15, 1869; rejected, Feb. 3, 1870 (24–33); died, Jan. 31, 1895.

Edwin McMasters Stanton, born, Dec. 19, 1814; appointed,

Dec. 20, 1869; confirmed, Dec. 20, 1869 (46–11); died, Dec. 24, 1869.

William Strong, born, March 6, 1808; appointed, Feb. 7, 1870 (Feb. 8, 1870); confirmed, Feb. 18, 1870; resigned, Dec. 14, 1880; died, Aug. 19, 1895.

Joseph P. Bradley, born, March 14, 1813; appointed, Feb. 7, 1870 (Feb. 8, 1870); confirmed, March 21, 1870 (46–9); died, Jan. 22, 1892.

Ward Hunt, born, June 14, 1810; appointed, Dec. 3, 1872 (Dec. 6, 1872); confirmed, Dec. 11, 1872; resigned, Jan. 7, 1882; died, March 24, 1886.

George Henry Williams (Chief Justice), born, March 23, 1823; appointed, Dec. 1, 1873 (Dec. 2, 1873); withdrawn, Jan. 8, 1874; died, April 4, 1910.

Caleb Cushing (Chief Justice), born, Jan. 17, 1800; appointed, Jan. 9, 1874; withdrawn, Jan. 13, 1874; died, Jan. 2, 1879.

Morrison Remick Waite (Chief Justice), born, Nov. 29, 1816; appointed, Jan. 19, 1874; confirmed, Jan. 21, 1874 (63–6); died, March 23, 1888.

John Marshall Harlan, born, June 1, 1833; appointed, March 29, 1877 (Oct. 17, 1877); confirmed, Nov. 29, 1877; died, Oct. 14, 1911.

William Burnham Woods, born, Aug. 3, 1824; appointed, Dec. 15, 1880; confirmed, Dec. 21, 1880 (39–8); died, May 14, 1887.

Stanley Matthews, born, July 21, 1824; appointed, Jan. 26, 1881; not acted upon.

Stanley Matthews, appointed, March 14, 1881 (March 18, 1881); confirmed, May 12, 1881 (24–23); died, March 22, 1889.

Horace Gray, born, March 24, 1828; appointed, Dec. 19, 1881; confirmed, Dec. 20, 1881 (51–5); died, Sept. 15, 1902.

Roscoe Conkling, born, Oct. 30, 1829; appointed, Feb. 24, 1882; confirmed, March 2, 1882 (39–12); declined, March, 1882; died, April 18, 1888.

Samuel Blatchford, born, March 9, 1820; appointed, March 13, 1882; confirmed, March 27, 1882; died, July 7, 1893.

Lucius Quintus Cincinnatus Lamar, born, Sept. 17, 1825; appointed, Dec. 6, 1887 (Dec. 12, 1887); confirmed, Jan. 16, 1888 (32–28); died, Jan. 23, 1893.

Melville Weston Fuller (Chief Justice); born, Feb. 11, 1833; appointed, April 30, 1888 (May 2, 1888); confirmed, July 20, 1888 (41–20); died, July 4, 1910.

David Josiah Brewer, born, Jan. 20, 1837; appointed, Dec. 4, 1889; confirmed, Dec. 18, 1889 (53–11); died, March 28, 1910.

Henry Billings Brown, born, March 21, 1836; appointed, Dec. 23, 1890; confirmed, Dec. 29, 1890; resigned, May 28, 1906; died, Sept. 4, 1913.

George Shiras, Jr., born, Jan. 26, 1832; appointed, July 19, 1892; confirmed, July 26, 1892; resigned, Feb. 23, 1903; died, Aug. 21, 1924.

Howell Edmunds Jackson, born, April 8, 1832; appointed, Feb. 2, 1893; confirmed, Feb. 18, 1893; died, Aug. 8, 1895.

William Butler Hornblower, born, May 13, 1851; appointed, Sept. 19, 1893; rejected, Jan. 15, 1894 (24–30); died, June 16, 1914.

Wheeler Hazard Peckham, born, Jan. 1, 1833; appointed, Jan. 22, 1894; rejected, Feb. 16, 1894 (32–41); died, Sept. 27, 1905.

Edward Douglass White, born, Nov. 3, 1845; appointed, Feb. 19, 1894; confirmed, Feb. 19, 1894.

Rufus Wheeler Peckham, born, Nov. 8, 1838; appointed, Dec. 3, 1895; confirmed, Dec. 9, 1895; died, Oct. 24, 1909.

Joseph McKenna, born, Aug. 10, 1843; appointed, Dec. 16, 1897; confirmed, Jan. 21, 1898; resigned, Jan. 5, 1925.

Oliver Wendell Holmes, born, March 8, 1841; appointed, August 11, 1902 (Dec. 2, 1902); confirmed, Dec. 4, 1902.

William Rufus Day, born, April 17, 1849; appointed, Feb. 19, 1903; confirmed, Feb. 23, 1903; resigned, Nov. 13, 1922; died, July 9, 1923.

William Henry Moody, born, Dec. 23, 1853; appointed, Dec. 3, 1906; confirmed, Dec. 12, 1906; resigned, Nov. 20, 1910; died, July 2, 1917.

Horace Harmon Lurton, born, Feb. 26, 1844; appointed, Dec. 13, 1909; confirmed, Dec. 20, 1909; died, July 12, 1914.

Edward Douglass White (Chief Justice), born, Nov. 3, 1845; appointed, Dec. 12, 1910; confirmed, Dec. 12, 1910; died, May 19, 1921.

Charles Evans Hughes, born, April 11, 1862; appointed, April 25, 1910; confirmed, May 2, 1910; resigned, June 10, 1916.

Willis VanDevanter, born, April 17, 1859; appointed, Dec. 12, 1910; confirmed, Dec. 15, 1910.

Joseph Rucker Lamar, born, Oct. 14, 1857; appointed, Dec. 12, 1910; confirmed, Dec. 15, 1910; died, Jan. 2, 1916.

Mahlon Pitney, born, Feb. 5, 1858; appointed, Feb. 19, 1912; confirmed, March 13, 1912; resigned, Dec. 31, 1922; died, Dec. 9, 1924.

James Clark McReynolds, born, Feb. 3, 1862; appointed, Aug. 19, 1914; confirmed, Aug. 29, 1914.

APPENDIX

Louis Dembitz Brandeis, born, Nov. 13, 1856; appointed, Jan. 28, 1916; confirmed, June 1, 1916.

John Hessin Clarke, born, Sept. 18, 1857; appointed, July 14, 1916; confirmed, July 24, 1916; resigned, Sept. 18, 1922.

William Howard Taft (Chief Justice), born, Sept. 15, 1857; appointed, June 30, 1921; confirmed, June 30, 1921.

George Sutherland, born, March 25, 1862; appointed, Sept. 5, 1922; confirmed, Sept. 5, 1922.

Pierce Butler, born, March 17, 1866; appointed, Nov. 23, 1922; confirmed, Dec. 21, 1922 (61–8).

Edward Terry Sanford, born, July 23, 1865; appointed, Jan. 24, 1923; confirmed, Jan. 29, 1923.

Harlan Fiske Stone, born, Oct. 11, 1872; appointed, Jan. 5, 1925; confirmed, Feb. 5, 1925 (71–6).

INDEX

Brewer, David Josiah, appointed Judge, II, 718; opposes *Munn Case*, II, 593; death, II, 726.

Brewster, Benjamin H., urged for Judge, in 1870, II, 507.

Bribery, right of Congress to penalize in Federal election, II, 615.

Bridges, power of Congress and of States over, II, 234–236, 238 n, 631 n.

Brig Struggle, I, 428 n.

Brig Wilson, Marshall's avoidance of slavery issue in, I, 623–624.

Brigantine William, The, I, 343–350.

Briscoe v. *Bank of the Commonwealth of Kentucky*, postponed, I, 790; argument and decision of, II, 27.

Bristow, Benjamin H., considered for Chief Justice, II, 560; urged for Judge, in 1877, II, 566.

British Debts, I, 63, 66 n, 99, 103, 144–146, 190, 444 and note.

Brolan v. *United States*, II, 725.

Bronson, Greene W., argument in *New Jersey* v. *New York*, I, 770–773.

Bronson v. *Kinzie*, decision in, II, 102–105, 133 n.

Bronson v. *La Crosse and Milwaukee R. R.*, II, 639 n.

Bronson v. *Rodes*, II, 501.

Broughton v. *Pensacola*, II, 678.

Brown, Ethan Allan, I, 533, 630.

Brown, Henry B., appointed Judge, II, 718; resigns, II, 720; view of Court, II, 756 n.

Brown, John, view of Judiciary Act, I, 13; view of first Court, I, 45, 65, letter as to Jay's appointment as Ambassador, I, 120.

Brown v. *Maryland*, I, 19; argument and decision in, I, 693–696; II, 368.

Brown v. *United States*, I, 427.

Browning, Orville H., urged as Judge, in 1862, II, 378, 379; argues *Granger Cases*, II, 578.

Brushaber v. *United States*, II, 725.

Buchanan, James, views of Federal power, I, 717; favors Circuit duty, I, 718; drafts minority report, in 1831, against repeal of 25th Section, I, 739; views Taney's opinion in *Holmes* v. *Jennison*, as too centralizing, II, 66; thinks, in 1841, number of Judges too large, II, 79; states limits of doctrine of *McCulloch* v. *Maryland*, II,

92, 95; offered appointment as Judge by Tyler, II, 116; view of John M. Read, II, 120; desired as Judge by Polk, II, 145–146; declines, and indorses John M. Read, II, 146, 147; indorses William B. Reed, II, 147; inaugural address of, and Dred Scott opinion, II, 294–298; views of Dred Scott decision in messages, II, 347 n; appoints Clifford as Judge, II, 322; appoints Black as Judge, II, 364; pessimistic view of the Court, II, 464.

Buckalew, Charles R., attacks *McCardle Case* statute, II, 475–479.

Buckner, B. F., II, 603.

Budd v. *New York*, II, 593 n, 595 n, 697 n.

Buena Ventura, The, II, 707 n.

Burgess v. *Seligman*, II, 698.

Burke, Edmund, as counsel, II, 153.

Burr, Aaron, expedition and trial of, I, 302, 308–312; Jefferson's views of Marshall in *Burr's Case*, I, 401–402.

Bush v. *Kentucky*, II, 610 n.

Butchers Union, etc., Co. v. *Crescent City Co.*, II, 620.

Butler, Andrew P., defends Court, II, 222, 268–269.

Butler, Benjamin F., description of, in 1835, as Attorney-General, I, 791; suggested as Chief Justice, in 1835, II, 8; argues *Kendall* v. *Stokes*, II, 44–48; argues *Hoboken Land Co. Case*, II, 350–351.

Butler, Gen. Benjamin F., argues *Milligan Case*, II, 426; argues *Legal Tender Case*, in 1884, II, 653.

Butler, William Allen, II, 653.

Butler v. *Horwitz*, II, 501.

Buttfield v. *Stranahan*, II, 712.

Cabot, George, I, 146; view of Marshall, I, 179, 180 n; view of Story, I, 418–419.

Caldwell, Elias B., appointed Clerk, I, 158 n; recollection of site of Courtroom, in 1815, I, 459.

Caldwell, John H., candidate for Judge, in 1877, II, 565.

Calhoun, John C., on judicial review, I, 15 n, 18; doctrine of, announced by Chief Justice McKean, I, 368; disappointed by McLean's appointment, I, 706; opposes Baldwin as Judge, I, 712; believes nullification

Calhoun, John C. — *Continued*
and repeal of 25th Section connected,
I, 739; opposes Taney's confirmation, II, 15; views of nomination of
King as Judge, II, 118–119; fears
creation of Interior Department, II,
137; views of, indorsed by anti-
slavery men, II, 340.

California, Judges of, attack Court
jurisdiction, II, 256–258; Federal
Circuit Court for, II, 267; land claims
in, II, 350; anti-Chinese legislation
in, II, 573, 628–629; *Chinese Exclusion Cases* and, II, 695.

California v. *Central Pacific R. R.*, II,
637.

Call, Richard K., as counsel, I, 782.

Callan v. *Wilson*, II, 689 n.

Callender, James, views of Marshall, I,
184 n; Chase's conduct at trial of,
I, 273, 282.

Cameron, Simon, opposes Woodward as
Judge, II, 149.

Campbell, Alexander, I, 145–148; death,
I, 152.

Campbell, George W., and Chase impeachment, I, 289; choice of Congressional caucus for Judge, I, 300.

Campbell, James, as counsel, II, 239.

Campbell, John A., appointed as Judge,
II, 245–247; view of corporations and
tax exemptions, II, 251; description
of, in 1857, II, 318; resigns, II, 375–
376; view of Taney, II, 375; has early
case to test reconstruction law, II,
456 n; argues *Slaughterhouse Cases*,
II, 536; view of decision, II, 546;
argues *Cruikshank Case*, II, 603.

Cannon v. *United States*, II, 697 n.

Capitol, views, in 1800, as to its great
size and expense, I, 169; first Court-
room in, I, 169–171; burning of, by
British, I, 431, 456, 458, 459; fire in
1851–1852 in, II, 241 n; new Senate
Chamber and Court-room, in 1860,
in, II, 362.

Car Service Act, II, 730.

Carlisle, James M., as counsel, II, 382,
491.

Carlisle, John G., considered for Chief
Justice, in 1888, II, 692.

Carmack Amendment, II, 730.

Caroline, Steamer, II, 65, 98–99, 101.

Carpenter, Matt H., argues *Garland*

Case, II, 450; argues *McCardle Case*,
II, 466; his view of his argument,
II, 473; opposes Hoar, II, 504; ar-
gues *Slaughterhouse Cases*, II, 536.

Carriage Tax Case, I, 146–149, 190, 226.

Carrington, Edward, I, 142.

Carrington v. *Merchants Ins. Co.*, I, 788;
Ingersoll's view of, I, 788.

Carver v. *Astor*, I, 714.

Cary, John W., II, 578.

Cass, Lewis, describes Court's jurisdiction over State boundary disputes,
II, 151.

Cassius, The, I, 134.

Catholic, Roman, Taney and Gaston as,
when suggested, in 1835, for Chief
Justice, II, 9 n.

Catlin v. *South Carolina*, I, 104 n.

Catron, John, appointed as Judge, II,
40; description of, in 1854, II, 202,
204 n; writes Buchanan as to Dred
Scott opinion, II, 294–295; description of, in 1857, II, 318; death, II,
408.

Cattle Quarantine, State law as to, held
invalid, II, 629; Acts of Congress as
to, II, 736, 737.

Certiorari, early attempt to remove case
into Federal Court by, I, 63–64.

Cervantes v. *United States*, II, 350.

Chae Chan Ping v. *United States*, II, 695.

Champion v. *Ames*, II, 711, 735.

Champion v. *Casey*, I, 67–68.

Chandler, Zachariah, attacks Dred Scott
decision, II, 328.

Chandler v. *Dix*, II, 715 n.

Charges. See GRAND JURY CHARGES.

Charles River Bridge v. *Warren Bridge*,
I, 19; argument in 1831, I, 746, 773
and note; division of Court, I, 773 n;
in 1834, postponed, I, 790; argument,
in 1837, and decision, II, 21–25;
Story's and Webster's views of decision, II, 25 n, 30; Kent's views of,
II, 28–29; Whig view of, II, 29–32;
Democratic view of, II, 32–33; reasons for decision in, II, 38.

Chase, Salmon P., argues *Jones* v. *Van
Zandt*, II, 155; attacks Court as pro-
slavery, II, 221; attacks removal bill,
II, 265; description of appointment
as Chief Justice, II, 399–408; view of
Evarts, II, 402; first appearance on
Bench, II, 410; admits negro to Fed-

Collamer, Jacob, as counsel, II, 163.

Collector v. Daly, II, 534.

Collet v. Collet, I, 68 n.

Commerce Clause, *Gibbons* v. *Ogden* and views of Marshall and of Monroe, I, 609–610; view of Webster, I, 610–611; views of the country, I, 612–621; effect on slavery issue, I, 621–627; involved in *Brown* v. *Maryland*, I, 693–696; in *New York* v. *Miln*, II, 26; and slavery involved in *Groves* v. *Slaughter*, II, 70; new questions of law after 1845 under, II, 134–139; involved in *Passenger Cases*, II, 168–182; in its connection with free negro laws, II, 158–173, 181–182; in the *Wheeling Bridge Case*, II, 233–236; in the *Pilot Case*, II, 237–238; in the *Sinnot Case*, II, 354; in *Crandall* v. *Nevada*, II, 415; number of cases, from 1860 to 1890, decided under, II, 625; insurance held not commerce under, II, 626; peddlers and drummers under, II, 627–628, 631; immigration under, II, 628–629; cattle quarantine under, II, 629; Jim Crow law under, II, 630; telegraph under, II, 630–631; liquor under, II, 631; tendencies of Court in cases under, II, 694; liquor in interstate transportation, II, 697; and the *Debs Case*, II, 700–701; lotteries under, II, 711; State right to tax corporations doing business under, II, 717; transmission of intelligence by correspondence under, II, 717–718; right to prohibit foreign trade under, II, 724–725; Adamson Law and, II, 725; extensive exercise of power by Congress under, II, 729–731; rise of a National police power under, II, 735–739.

Commercial Bank etc. v. *Buckingham*, II, 159.

Commissioners of Knox County v. *Aspinwall*, II, 352.

Commissions, final disposal of, I, 237 n, 238. See also *Marbury* v. *Madison;* MIDNIGHT JUDGES.

Common Carrier, first case of negligence of, in the Court, II, 62; Angell on, II, 135; early case on, II, 138–139; liability of, II, 640–643. See also EXPRESS BUSINESS; RAILROADS.

Common Law, indictments sustained

by Federal Courts at, I, 112, 159 n, 162–164, 191, 433–434; Chase's decision *contra*, I, 433–434; in Kentucky and Connecticut, in 1807, I, 435–436; decisions of Court against Federal, I, 437, 441; Federal, and *Swift* v. *Tyson*, II, 88–89, 698; no Federal criminal, held in *Wheaton* v. *Peters*, I, 785. See also NATIONAL COMMON LAW.

Congress. See NATIONAL GOVERNMENT; ACTS OF CONGRESS; JUDICIAL REVIEW.

Congressmen, numbers of, admitted to practice before first Court, I, 49–50 n.

Conkling, Roscoe, attacks Court, II, 347–348; opposes Hoar, II, 504; view of, as to 14th Amendment, II, 541; declines Chief Justiceship, II, 553; argues *Corporation Tax Cases*, II, 597; appointed Judge and declines, II, 623–624.

Connecticut, boundary line dispute with New York, I, 155 n.

Conservation, power of United States over, in States, II, 714.

Constitution of the United States, Articles Three and Six of, I, 6, 7; 11th Amendment of, I, 100–102; Amendment to prevent appointment of Judges to other offices, I, 167–168; "necessary and proper" clause, history of, I, 499–503; Amendment to restrict chartering of banks, I, 525; Ohio, in 1820, claims 11th Amendment violated, I, 537; Amendments to make Senate a Court in State Cases, I, 657–661; Amendments proposed, in 1831, for term of years for Judges, I, 743 n; Marshall's service in behalf of, I, 806–807, 812–814; slight difference between Marshall's and Taney's views of, II, 33–38; 5th Amendment, II, 350; 14th Amendment first construed, II, 535–550; 13th and 15th Amendments adopted, II, 600 n; 13th, 14th and 15th Amendments in relation to negro legislation, II, 600–618; 5th Amendment and power to amend corporate charters, II, 642–644; Amendments to limit legal tender powers proposed, II, 659–660; cases, from 1875 to 1885, under 11th Amendment, II,

Constitution — *Continued*
663–671; 16th Amendment, II, 700; 18th Amendment, II, 725 n; 19th Amendment, II, 725 n. See also JUDICIAL REVIEW; ACTS OF CONGRESS.

Constitutionality of Statutes, power to pass upon. See JUDICIAL REVIEW.

Contracts. See IMPAIRMENT OF OBLIGATION OF CONTRACT.

Cook, B. C., II, 578.

Cook, Daniel P., I, 666.

Cook v. *Marshall Co.*, II, 732 n.

Cooley v. *Port Wardens*, II, 155, 237–238.

Cooper, William F., urged for Judge, in 1877, II, 566.

Coppage v. *Kansas*, II, 742, 743 n, 744.

Coppel v. *Hall*, II, 416.

Cornell v. *Coyne*, II, 739 n.

Corporation of Latter Day Saints v. *United States*, II, 697.

Corporations, first cases as to law of, in Supreme Court, I, 285–286; suit by, in Federal Circuit Courts, I, 389–392; changes in charters of, I, 476–492; history of first development of, I, 491 n; decision in *Dandridge Case* as to proof by record, I, 696–699; no grants by implication in charters of, II, 23–25; power of, to do business in outside States, denied by Judge McKinley, II, 50; excitement over decision, II, 50–52; decision as to, in *Bank of Augusta* v. *Earle*, and Whig and Democratic views of, II, 53–62; as Sinbad burdens on country, II, 61 n; influence of, denounced by Tappan, II, 96; right to sue in Federal Circuit Courts upheld, II, 120–124; fear of, by Judge Campbell, II, 122; rights of, and eminent domain, II, 163–165; and 14th Amendment, II, 541; held not a "citizen", II, 567; powers of State to tax, II, 597–598; held a "person", II, 598 n; power of States to prohibit removal of suits by, II, 686; removal of suits in Circuit Courts, II, 705; bill to deny right to sue in Courts other than those of chartering State, II, 705.

Cotting v. *Kansas City Stockyards Co.*, II, 595 n.

County of San Mateo v. *Southern Pacific R. R.* II, 597 n.

Court-room, first in New York, I, 46; first in Philadelphia, I, 53; first in Washington, I, 169–171; description of others in the Capitol from 1808 to 1860, I, 456–463; description of, in *Dartmouth College Case*, I, 483; description by Sumner, in 1835, I, 792; description in 1837 of, II, 22; description in 1854 of, II, 201–202; description in 1859 of, II, 361–362; description in 1860 of new, II, 362.

Covington v. *Kentucky*, II, 677 n.

Covington Drawbridge Co. v. *Shepherd*, II, 352, 639 n.

Covington etc. Turnpike Road Co. v. *Sandford*, II, 595 n.

Coxe, Richard S., as counsel, I, 709, 787; argues *Kendall* v. *Stokes*, II, 44.

Craig v. *Missouri*, I, 19; argument and opinion in, I, 725–726.

Cranch, William, I, 195, 255; issues first volume of reports, I, 288; dissenting opinion in *Swartwout Case*, I, 303; views of Jefferson, I, 304, 307–308; end of series of reports of, I, 454–455.

Crandall v. *Nevada*, II, 415.

Crawford, William H., as counsel, II, 52.

Credit Mobilier, II, 555 n, 646–648.

Creek Indians, Adams' policy as to, I, 730.

Crimes Act of 1825, drafted by Story, I, 442.

Criminal Cases, bill for writs of error to Court in II, 332 n; appeals in, II, 727.

Criminal Indictments, sustained by Federal Courts at common law. See COMMON LAW.

Crittenden, John J., description of argument of *Gibbons* v. *Ogden*, I, 606; recommended for Judge by Clay, and appointed by Adams, I, 701–702; rejected by Senate, I, 702–704; opposes Taney's confirmation, II, 15; description in 1839 of, II, 62; intention of Whigs to appoint, as Judge, II, 82 n; opposes Spencer as Judge, II, 112; candidate for Court in case of Clay's election, II, 116; approves Clayton's bill in 1848, II, 215–216; argues *Fremont Case*, II, 350 n; urged as Judge, in 1861, II, 365.

men, II, 273; writes to Buchanan as to Dred Scott opinion, II, 295–296; description of, in 1857, II, 318–319; view of Dana, II, 383; denounces Court's postponement of *McCardle Case*, II, 482–483; resigns, II, 504; recommends Bradley, II, 516.

Grimball, Ex parte, I, 355 n.

Griswold v. *Hazard*, II, 648 n.

Groesbeck, William B., considered for Chief Justice, in 1873, II, 553.

Groves v. *Slaughter*, argument and decision in, II, 67–73.

Grundy, Felix, opposes Court's power, I, 723.

Guinn v. *United States*, II, 618 n, 724.

HABEAS CORPUS, in case of Bollman and Swartwout, I, 301–308; suspension of, in Senate, I, 302–303; bill by Giles to abolish Court's power to issue, I, 308; Act of 1842 attacked by, Democrats, II, 98–101; suspension of, by President, II, 368–374; repeal of Act of March 3, 1863, urged, II, 444; applications for release of Lincoln assassins by, II, 443–444; Act of Feb. 5, 1867, as to, II, 464–465; Act of 1867 repealed, II, 474–485; *Yerger Case* under original Act of 1789 as to, II, 491; in case under 14th Amendment, denied, II, 610; Act providing for appeal on cases of, II, 687–693; list of statutes as to, II, 687 n. See also *Booth Cases*.

Hagan v. *Forson*, II, 82 n.

Hagan v. *Lucas*, II, 19.

Hagood v. *Southern*, II, 665 n.

Hale, John P., as counsel, praises Court in 1845, II, 153–154; attacks Court as pro-slavery, II, 209, 221, 223, 224, 268; argues *Morris Case*, II, 228; attacks Dred Scott decision, II, 325; defends Personal Liberty law, II, 345.

Hall v. *De Cuir*, II, 630.

Hall, Willis, as counsel, II, 175.

Hallett, Benjamin F., as counsel, II, 188.

Hamilton, Alexander, I, 8, 23; opposes Livingston, I, 34, 35; considered for Chief Justice, I, 35; letter to Harrison, I, 42; asks Jay's view as to Virginia resolutions, I, 52; views as to admiralty jurisdiction, I, 107; objects to asking opinion of Judges, but frames questions, I, 109; drafts indictment in *Henfield's Case*, I, 114; instructions to collectors, I, 115; offered position of Chief Justice, I, 125; views as to Rutledge appointment, I, 132; argues *Carriage Tax Case*, I, 148–149; asked to be counsel in *Fairfax Case*, I, 151–152; drafts Circuit Court bill, I, 186; view of repeal of Circuit Court Act, I, 212, 224 n; opinion as to Yazoo Lands, I, 396–397.

Hamlin, Hannibal, attacks Court as pro-slavery, II, 211; attacks Dred Scott decision, II, 325, 327.

Hammer v. *Dagenhart*, II, 738, 744 n.

Hammond, Charles, report for Ohio Legislature on Bank of the United States, I, 535–536; argues *Osborn Case*, I, 630; Marshall's view of, I, 630 n; offered appointment as Judge, I, 700.

Hampden. See ROANE, SPENCER.

Hancock, John, as to *Chisholm* v. *Georgia*, I, 99; on judicial review, I, 82 n, 99.

Handy, Alexander H., urged as Judge, in 1860, II, 358.

Hanger v. *Abbott*, II, 416.

Hannibal & St. Joseph R. R. v. *Husen*, II, 629.

Hans v. *Louisiana*, II, 715.

Harlan, John M., on influence of lawyers, I, 23; appointed Judge, II, 566; death, II, 726.

Harper, Robert G., as to Circuit Court Act, I, 192–193; view of its repeal, I, 212, 288; counsel for Chase, I, 289; in *Swartwout Case*, I, 305–306; argument in *Deveaux Case*, I, 390; opinion as to Yazoo Lands, I, 394; as counsel, I, 320, 387, 425, 432, 446, 582, 630.

Harper, William, I, 200; defends Court, in Congress, I, 671.

Harrison, Robert H., considered for Chief Justice, I, 35; appointed Judge, I, 42; resigns, I, 43.

Hart v. *Pennsylvania R. R.*, II, 641.

Harter Act, II, 730.

Hartly, Thomas, I, 49.

Hartman v. *Greenhow*, II, 666.

Hawaii v. *Mankichi*, II, 708 n, 710.

Hawes v. *Oakland*, II, 683 n.

Hay, George, I, 311.

Hunter, David, of Rhode Island, I, 151–152, 286, 444–445.

Hunter, William, as counsel, I, 493.

Hunter v. *Fairfax's Devisee,* I, 151–153, 445 n.

Huntington v. *Palmer,* II, 683 n.

Hurtado v. *California,* II, 571.

Hylton v. *United States,* I, 146–149, 262.

IMMIGRATION, legislation of New York in *New York* v. *Miln,* II, 25–26; early increase of, I, 126; State laws as to, held invalid, II, 628–629; right of administration and exclusion of, II, 695–696 and note. See also *Passenger cases.*

Impairment of Obligation of Contract, first case involving, in Circuit Court, I, 67; first case in Supreme Court, I, 285; involved in *Fletcher* v. *Peck,* I, 392–399; first applied to corporate charters by Kent, I, 476 n; involved in *Dartmouth College Case,* I, 476–487; debate in Congress as to application of, to repeal of charter of Bank of United States, I, 509–510; retrospective laws held not, I, 709–710; as to Mississippi bank charters, II, 162; in Ohio Bank cases, II, 250–256; in municipal bond cases, II, 530–531 and note; none, in cases of police power legislation, II, 618–621; in bank tax and bond cases, II, 676–678.

Impeachment, of Judges, I, 73; for decision in *Bas* v. *Tingy,* I, 157; Monroe's view of, for sustaining common law indictment, I, 164 n; talk in 1802 of, I, 227; of Chase, I, 279–294; Jefferson's view of, I, 557–558, 653; of President Johnson, II, 466, 473, 476, 477, 484.

Imprisonment for Debt, abolished first in Kentucky, I, 644, 693.

Inaugural Address, first delivered by Jefferson in writing, I, 206 n.

Income Tax, invalid on Judges' salaries, II, 387; in Wilson Tariff Act held invalid, II, 699–700; amendment of constitution, II, 700; amendment construed, II, 725.

Income Tax Case, II, 699, 702.

Indiana Company v. *Virginia,* I, 92 n.

Ingersoll, Charles J., view of Johnson, I, 287, 389; describes Court-room

in 1810, I, 457; argues *The Antelope,* I, 585; unfavorable view of *Carrington* v. *Merchants Ins. Co.,* and of Webster, I, 788; argument in *Bank of Augusta* v. *Earle,* II, 52–56; view of decision, II, 61 n; urged as Judge in 1845, II, 146.

Ingersoll, Jared, as counsel, I, 55, 94, 106, 114, 123, 133, 148, 152, 317, 318, 320, 369, 384.

Ingersoll, Ralph J., considered for Judge, in 1844, II, 114.

Ingles v. *Sailor's Snug Harbor,* I, 318 n, 713.

Inheritance Tax, upheld, II, 711.

Initiative, State power to adopt, II, 722.

Injunction, government by, II, 704–705; act to regulate, against State officials, II, 717.

Inman Steamship Co. v. *Tinker,* II, 629.

Innes, James, recommended as Judge, I, 141; position at Virginia Bar, I, 181.

Insular Cases, I, 22; II, 218; description of, II, 707–711, 728 n.

Insurance, business of, held not commerce, II, 626; powers of State to regulate rates of, II, 724.

Interior Department, State fears at creation of, II, 137–138.

Intermountain Rate Cases, II, 724.

Internal Improvements, I, 5; debates on, I, 502–503; effect of Marshall's opinion on, I, 544; views of Monroe and of Court on, I, 595–597; power of Congress over, I, 595, 597; II, 633–637.

International Law, part of United States law, I, 112; effect of Court on, I, 565–585; in *Prize Cases,* II, 380–384; continuous voyage cases and, II, 414; duty under, to protect securities of foreign governments, II, 661–662; and the Spanish War and *Insular Cases,* II, 707–711. See also NEUTRALITY; PRIZE COURTS; PRIZE LAW.

International Text Book Co. v. *Pigg,* II, 717–718.

Interstate Commerce. See COMMERCE CLAUSE.

Interstate Commerce Act, II, 729.

Interstate Commerce Commission, established, II, 636.

McCall, Peter, as counsel, II, 218.

McCardle Case, arguments and decisions in, II, 465, 473–474, 480–484, 487–488.

Maclay, William, and Judiciary Act, I, 8, 9.

McClung v. *Silliman*, I, 563.

Macon, Nathaniel, I, 64 n; supports judicial review, I, 254–255; views of Chase's charges to Grand Jury, I, 274; mentioned for Judge in 1823, I, 589; views of extensions of power of Congress, I, 595.

McCray v. *United States*, II, 509 n, 739.

McCready v. *Virginia*, II, 567 n.

McCulloch v. *Maryland*, I, 19, 298; doctrines of, anticipated by *Fisher Case* in 1805, I, 298; decision might have been anticipated in 1810, I, 391–392, 503; description of argument and decision in, I, 506–511; praised by Federalists, I, 511–514; attacked in South and West, I, 514–515; Marshall's view of attacks on, I, 515; attacked by Ohio, I, 525–537; regarded by the Ohio Legislature as a fictitious case, I, 529, 535–537; concurrence of Judges in, I, 654; doctrines of, discussed in 1841 in debate on Fiscal Bank Acts, II, 92–93; principle followed in *Legal Tender Case*, II, 511.

McHenry, James, recommends Chase for appointment, I, 125; appointed Secretary of War, I, 142; letter as to Chase, I, 143.

McIlvaine v. *Coxe's Lessee*, I, 317–318.

McKean, Thomas, candidate for Judge in 1789, I, 40–41, 276; opposes removal of cases to Federal Court, I, 367–368; vetoes resolution in *Holland Land Company Case*, I, 369; views as to *Olmstead Case*, I, 374.

McKee v. *Rains*, II, 684 n.

McKeen, James, II, 653.

McKenna, Joseph, appointed Judge, II, 720.

McKinley, John, as to powers of Congress, I, 716; appointed Judge, II, 41; decision in corporation cases, II, 50; death, II, 241.

McKinley, William, appoints McKenna as Judge, II, 720.

McLane, Louis, views of Court and of Story, I, 719–720; promised appointment as Judge by Jackson in 1829, I, 797, II, 8 n; suggested as Chief Justice in 1835, II, 8.

McLean, John, suggested as Judge, I, 683; appointed Judge, I, 704–707; opinion in *Wheaton* v. *Peters*, I, 785; urged for Chief Justice in 1835, II, 8; views as to State power over slavery, in *Groves* v. *Slaughter*, II, 71–72; opposes decision in Illinois stay-laws, II, 104; defends Court from charge of being pro-slavery, II, 156–157; views of Story, II, 157; description in 1854 of, II, 202, 204 n; action in a fugitive slave law case denounced, II, 262, 273; attacks on, for publication of views on political questions, II, 269–273; views of Judge's right to run for President, II, 269–270; death, II, 374.

McLeod, Alexander, case of, II, 65, 98, 99, 101, 687 n.

McNeill v. *Southern Ry Co.*, II, 715 n.

McPherson, J. D., II, 681.

McReynolds, James C., appointed Judge, II, 726.

Madison, James, I, 8; and Judiciary Act, I, 11, 14; letter as to Jay's appointment as Ambassador, I, 119; view of Hamilton's argument in *Carriage Tax Case*, I, 148–149; as to appointment of Judges as Ambassadors, I, 167; supports judicial review, I, 259–260; refuses to interfere in *Olmstead Case*, and views of, I, 382, 385; Adams' description of inauguration of, I, 394–395; views of Lincoln, Granger, and Adams, I, 407–408; appoints Lincoln as Judge, I, 407; appoints Wolcott, I, 411; appoints Adams, I, 414; appoints Story, I, 415; views as to *McCulloch* v. *Maryland*, I, 517; upholds power of Court in *Cohens Case*, I, 554; opposes repeal of 25th Section in 1831, I, 740.

Madison, Bishop James, I, 189.

Mails, power of Congress to regulate, and to exclude lotteries from, II, 698; power of Congress over newspapers under right to control, II, 723.

Mandamus, will not issue to Federal Judge, I, 121; in *Marbury* v. *Madison*, I, 201, 206, 231, 244; State Court cannot issue to Federal officials, I,

INDEX

constitutional and international law, I, 813 n; J. Q. Adams' view of, II, 2–3; difference between Marshall's and Taney's attitude to Constitution, II, 33–38; John T. Mason's views of, II, 93; opinion of Peters by, II, 106 n; stated by Story to believe *Deveaux Case* a wrong decision, II, 121–122.

Marshall, Samuel S., defends Court, II, 466–467.

Martin and Gilly, Ex parte, II, 484 n.

Martin, Luther, in Federal Convention, I, 6, 8; admitted to practice, I, 56, 286; counsel for Chase, I, 289; in *Bollman Case*, I, 305–306; as counsel, I, 320, 394; argument in *McCulloch v. Maryland*, I, 506–507.

Martin v. Hunter's Lessee, I, 433, 443–450.

Martin v. Waddell's Lessee, II, 89–90.

Martineau, Harriet, describes Court in 1835, I, 790–791.

Maryland Insurance Co. v. Woods, I, 389 n.

Mason, George, as to judicial powers, I, 8.

Mason, Jeremiah, Webster's indebtedness to, in *Dartmouth College Case*, I, 479; as to attacks on Judiciary, I, 659–661; views of Judiciary, I, 672–673; views of Marshall's work, I, 807.

Mason, John Thompson, candidate for Judge, I, 423; view of Marshall's prejudices, II, 93.

Mason, John Y., I, 286.

Mason, Stevens Thomson, as to Circuit Court Act, I, 188; as to Federal Judges, I, 191; as to *Mandamus Case*, I, 204.

Massachusetts, action against decision in *Chisholm Case*, I, 99–100; attitude as to embargo, I, 341–350, 358–365; attitude as to War of 1812, I, 438–440, 451, 453; Marshall's reference to slave laws in, I, 626; asserts State-Rights theories in Rhode Island boundary case, II, 42–43, 148–150; prohibition laws of, in *Thurlow Case*, II, 138, 152–155; immigration laws of, II, 174–182.

Mathews v. Zane, I, 366–367.

Matthews, Stanley, appointed Judge, II, 622–623; death, II, 718.

Maxwell v. Dow, II, 538 n.

Meguire v. Corwine, II, 650 n.

Mercer, Charles F., defends Court in Congress, I, 669–670, 679, 682.

Meriwether v. Garrett, II, 678.

Merryman, Ex parte, II, 368–374.

Metcalfe, Thomas, I, 664.

Mexico, land claims under treaty with, I, 784, II, 350; war with, and cases relating to, II, 207, 218, 219.

Michigan Central R. R. v. Mineral, etc., Co., II, 640.

Micou, William C., offered appointment as Judge, II, 245.

Midnight Judges, I, 188, 201, 224–226, 234. See also *Marbury v. Madison*.

Miles v. United States, II, 697 n.

Military Trial, Lincoln's view of his rights to require, II, 373, 388; held illegal in *Milligan Case*, II, 423–449; involved in *McCardle Case*, II, 465; in Texas, upheld by Hoar, II, 490–491; involved in *Yerger Case*, II, 491; involved in *Ex parte Martin & Gilly*, II, 484 n.

Miller, Samuel F., appointed Judge, II, 379; view of Taney, II, 396; opinion in *Slaughterhouse Cases*, and criticisms of, II, 546–550; considered for Chief Justice in 1873, II, 553; refuses to be candidate for President, II, 563 n; opinion in *United States v. Lee*, II, 672–673; considered for Chief Justice, II, 692; death, II, 718.

Miller v. New York, II, 631 n.

Miller v. Nicholls, I, 370–373, 538–540.

Miller v. United States, II, 417.

Milligan, Ex parte, argument and decision in, II, 374, 388, 423–427; attacks upon, II, 428–442; final outcome of, in lower Courts, II, 427 n; attempts to counteract effect of, II, 443–449; 462 n.

Minge v. Gilmour, I, 262 n.

Minnesota Rate Cases, II, 723.

Minnesota v. Northern Securities Co., II, 712 n.

Minor v. Happerset, II, 567, 691.

Minority, protection to rights of, II, 751–753.

Minority Decisions, alleged, of Court in *Green v. Biddle*, I, 640–641, 685, 790 n; made in *Renner v. Bank of Columbia*, I, 790 n.

Missionaries. See *Worcester v. Georgia*.

power in time of war considered, II, 439–440; power of, as to legal tender, II, 498–527; extension of powers of, under Chase, II, 533; reaction in 1873 against further extension and effect of *Slaughterhouse Cases* on, II, 534–551; increased by decisions in 1890 modifying *Granger Cases*, II, 590–592; increase from 1880 to 1887 of powers of, II, 625–662; control of, over railroads, II, 632–642, and Federal corporations, II, 650–651; and civil service, II, 651–652; and legal tender, II, 652–660; and eminent domain, II, 661 n; and Indian wards, II, 661; and counterfeiting foreign money, II, 661–662; increasing powers of, II, 694–695; over Chinese, II, 695–696; in relation to treaties, II, 696; to protect persons of Judges, II, 696; over Territories, II, 697; over articles in interstate commerce, II, 697; over interstate railroad rates, II, 697, 699; over mails, II, 698; power to sue State to fix boundary lines, II, 698; power of, to protect the public and *Debs Case*, II, 701–702; power to take land for National Cemetery, II, 706; power over insular possessions, II, 707–711; power to tax State liquor selling agents, II, 712; power to tax, II, 711; power over lotteries in interstate commerce, II, 711; power over intrastate rates, II, 723; power over newspapers in mails, II, 723; over railroads in emergency, II, 725; extensions of power of, since 1918, II, 725 n; exercise of power of, over interstate commerce, II, 729–731; exercise of power to aid State liquor laws, II, 731–733; rise of a police power of, under commerce clause, II, 735–739. See also STATES; STATE-RIGHTS.
Neal v. *Delaware*, II, 611.
Neeley v. *Henkel*, II, 708 n.
Negro, laws in South Carolina and other States as to free negroes, I, 623–627, II, 205 n; legislation for protection of, passed on by Court, II, 600–618, 621 n; Jim Crow law as to, invalid, II, 630. See also CIVIL RIGHTS; CIVIL RIGHTS ACTS; RECONSTRUCTION; SLAVERY.

Nelson, Samuel, appointed Judge by Tyler, II, 119; description in 1854 of, II, 203, 204 n; description in 1857 of, II, 319; resigns, II, 536 n.
Nelson v. *Carland*, II, 205 n.
Nereide, The, I, 431–432.
Neutrality, Washington's proclamation of, I, 105; jurisdiction of Court to enforce, I, 106–107, 112–118; cases relating to, I, 123 n, 149–151, 474; Anti-Federalists' view of, I, 190; military expedition in breach of, I, 284 n; rights and obligation of, Johnson's view of, I, 569–570; breaches of, in 1819 and 1822, and cases on, I, 570–580; amendment in 1819 of law of, I, 571; duty of neutrals to act without fraud, I, 788; cases involving, in 1836, violation of, II, 248; violations of, in 1850–1860, II, 249 n; in *Prize Cases*, II, 380–384.
New Hampshire, opposes decision in *Penhallow Case*, I, 122–123; contest between Courts of, and Judge Story, II, 182–185.
New Hampshire v. *Louisiana*, II, 665.
New Jersey, attitude to Court in 1812, I, 443; suit against New York, I, 770–773; laws as to flats and tidewater in *Waddell Case*, II, 89–90.
New Jersey Steam Nav. Co. v. *Merchants Bank*, argument and decision of, II, 160–161.
New Jersey v. *New York*, argument in, I, 770–773.
New Jersey v. *Wilson*, I, 444 n, 476 n.
New Mexico, slavery in, II, 208; boundary line dispute with Texas, II, 217, 220.
New Orleans v. *Houston*, II, 619 n.
Newspapers, power of Congress over, under right to control mails, II, 723.
New World v. *King*, II, 241.
New York, view of politics of, by J. Adams, I, 34; boundary dispute with Connecticut, I, 155 n; insolvent laws of, involved in *Sturges Case* and *Ogden* v. *Saunders*, I, 493–498, 686–692; sued by New Jersey, I, 770–773; jury trial law as to fugitive slaves affected by *Prigg Case*, II, 85–86; law as to commercial instruments of, ignored in *Swift* v. *Tyson*, II, 88–89; and the *McLeod Case*, II, 65,

New York — *Continued*
98, 99, 101; laws of South Carolina
and Virginia directed against vessels
of, II, 169 n, 171; passenger laws of,
invalid, II, 168–180; tonnage and
immigration laws of, held invalid,
II, 628–629.

New York v. *Connecticut*, I, 155.

New York v. *Miln*, postponed, I, 790;
argument and decision in, II, 25–
26.

New York Central R. R. v. *Lockwood*,
II, 640.

Nicholas, George, supports judicial
review, I, 258–259.

Nicholas, Wilson C., as to Circuit Court
Act, I, 188.

Nicholas, The, I, 428 n.

Nicholson, Joseph H., active in Chase's
impeachment, I, 277; proposes Constitutional Amendment for recall of
Senators, I, 295.

Nicol v. *Ames,* II, 711 n.

Non-Partisanship of Supreme Court,
I, 20–23, 30 n, 272, 420; in *Dartmouth
College Case,* I, 487; in *McCulloch
Case,* I, 508–509; in Taney's Court,
II, 33–34; in *Prigg Case,* II, 84–86;
in *Dorr Case* and *Luther* v. *Borden,* II,
186–195; on slavery questions, II,
222–224, 269; in *Prize Cases,* II,
384; in *Slaughterhouse Cases,* II, 549–
550; during Fuller's Chief Justiceship, II, 721–722; in *Insular Cases*
and *Northern Securities Co. Case,* II,
722. See also POLITICS; SUPREME
COURT.

Norris v. *Boston,* argument and decision
of, II, 168–182. See also *Passenger
Cases.*

North Carolina v. *Temple,* II, 715 n.

Northern Securities Co. v. *United States,*
II, 711, 722.

Northwestern Fertilizing Co. v. *Hyde
Park,* II, 619 n.

Nuestra Signora, I, 160 n.

Nullification, I, 368; in Foote Resolution
debate, I, 715–724; Georgia's position in *Cherokee Cases* termed, I, 734,
735, 737, 743; in South Carolina
and Jackson's attitude, I, 774–778;
Calhoun says repeal of 25th Section
and, go together, I, 739; and Wisconsin and Pennsylvania, II, 258–264;

upheld by anti-slavery men, II, 265;
in connection with *Booth Case,* II,
339–344.

OAKLEY, THOMAS J., argument in *Gibbons* v. *Ogden,* I, 599–606.

Oaths, by first Judges, I, 47 n. See also
Test Oath Cases.

Oberlin Rescue Cases, II, 344–345.

O'Conor, Charles, described, II, 457,
461, 462 n.

Ogden, Aaron, supports judicial review,
I, 217; party in *Gibbons* v. *Ogden,*
I, 597–599.

Ogden, David B., as counsel, I, 431, 475,
493, 549, 551, 573; argument in *Gibbons* v. *Ogden,* I, 599–606; argument
in *Ogden* v. *Saunders,* I, 687; argument in *New York* v. *Miln,* II, 26;
argument in *Bank of Augusta* v. *Earle,*
II, 52; argument in *Passenger Cases,*
II, 175.

Ogden v. *Blackledge,* I, 284.

Ogden v. *Saunders,* I, 630, 667; argument and decision of, I, 686–693.

Ogden v. *Witherspoon,* I, 262 n, 285 n.

Ohio, taxes Bank of the United States, I,
506; legislative fight against Bank,
I, 526–537; suits by the Bank against
officials of, I, 529–534; *Oberlin Rescue
Cases,* in 1859 in, II, 344–345.

Ohio Life Ins. Co. v. *Debolt,* I, 298 n;
II, 253.

Ohio-Michigan Boundary Line Dispute,
II, 159 n.

Olcott v. *Supervisors,* II, 528.

Oleomargarine Laws, II, 739.

Olmstead, Gideon, I, 113 n; and Pennsylvania in case of, I, 374–387.

Olmstead Case and Pennsylvania, I,
374–387.

Olney, Richard, view of decision in
Adair Case, II, 715.

Olney v. *Arnold,* I, 444 n.

Opinion, Jay refuses to give, I, 52–53;
Court refuses to give, I, 108–111;
first required to be filed, I, 455 n;
first written and first printed, I, 455 n;
Jefferson's demand for *seriatim*
opinions, I, 653–655.

Oregon, slavery in, II, 208; Federal
Circuit Court for, II, 267.

Original Package, doctrine first applied
in *Brown* v. *Maryland,* I, 695, 696;

doctrine applied to liquor in transport, II, 697, 731.

Osborn v. *Bank of the United States*, description of the origin of the case, I, 529–535; argument and decision, I, 628–632, 667; doctrines of, discussed in debate on Fiscal Bank Acts, II, 92–97; broadening of doctrine of, II, 715–717.

Osborne v. *Mobile*, II, 551.

Oscanyon v. *Winchester Arms Co.*, II, 650 n.

Oswald v. *New York*, I, 57, 104 n.

Otis, Harrison Gray, view of Story, I, 419.

Otto, W. T., II, 681.

Pacific Insurance Company v. *Soule*, II, 416.

Pacific Railroad Removal Cases, II, 685.

Pacific States Telephone and Telegraph Co. v. *Oregon*, II, 722.

Packing the Court, talk of, II, 447, 517–519.

Padelford v. *Savannah*, II, 326 n.

Page, John, on judicial review, I, 83.

Panama, The, II, 707 n.

Paquete Habana, The, II, 707 n.

Parker, Isaac, view as to corporate charters, I, 485.

Parker, Joel, contest with Judge Story, II, 183–185.

Parkersburg, etc., Co. v. *Parkersburg*, II, 631 n.

Parsons, Theophilus, partiality for Great Britain, I, 321 n; as to Embargo Law, I, 341–342; suggestion of appointment to Court, I, 403–404.

Paschal, George W., as counsel, II, 363.

Passenger Cases, I, 19; argument and decision of, II, 174–181; connection of, with slavery issue, II, 168–174, 181–182.

Paterson, William, and Judiciary Act, I, 8, 21 n; opinion in *Van Horne's Lessee* v. *Dorrance*, and its effect on appointment as Chief Justice, I, 69, 176 n; appointed Judge, I, 102; believed the proper appointment for Chief Justice, I, 175–178; views as to Presidential instructions, I, 199–200; view of validity of Circuit Court Act of 1802, I, 271; opposes

Executive power to dispense with the law, I, 284 n.

Paul v. *Virginia*, II, 567, 626.

Pawlet v. *Clark*, I, 476 n.

Peck v. *Jenness*, II, 182–185.

Peckham, Rufus Wheeler, appointed Judge, II, 719; death, II, 720.

Peckham, Wheeler H., appointed Judge but rejected by Senate, II, 719.

Pedro, The, II, 707 n.

Pembina Mining Co. v. *Pennsylvania*, II, 596 n.

Pendleton, Edmund, I, 8, 37, 57, 118.

Pendleton, Nathaniel, recommended as Judge in 1791, I, 57, 118.

Penhallow v. *Doane's Admr's*, I, 122.

Pennoyer, Sylvester, denounces judicial review, II, 703.

Pennoyer v. *McConnaughty*, II, 715.

Pennoyer v. *Neff*, II, 569 n.

Pennsylvania, opposes Federal Government, I, 366–368; resolutions of Legislature in *Holland Land Co. Case*, I, 369; resolutions in *Nicholls Case*, I, 373; actions as to *Olmstead Case*, I, 374–387; resolutions of Legislature, I, 388; fugitive slave law of, held invalid, II, 83–87; treason and other cases under Federal Fugitive Slave Law in, II, 230–231, 263–264.

Pennsylvania Co. v. *Roy*, II, 641.

Pennsylvania v. *Wheeling Bridge*, I, 105 n; argument and decision in, II, 233–236.

Pensacola Telegraph Co. v. *Western Union Telegraph Co.*, II, 630.

Pensioners Act, I, 70–81, 266.

Peonage Law, held invalid, II, 722.

Perry v. *Haines*, II, 711.

Personal Liberty Laws, II, 89; debate on, II, 345–349.

Peterhoff, The, II, 414.

Peters, Judge Richard, in *Hayburn's Case*, I, 71 n; decision on admiralty jurisdiction, I, 107; considered for appointment as Judge of Court, I, 153; as to rumored impeachment, I, 227 n, 289 n; views as to Chase, I, 281; action in *Olmstead Case*, I, 375, 379; favors common law indictment, I, 434, 440–441; Marshall's opinion of admiralty reports of, I, 568–569.

suspected of, II, 565 n; Judges in Fuller's Chief Justiceship free from, II, 721–722. See also NON-PARTISANSHIP OF SUPREME COURT.

Polk, James K., administration of, II, 134 *et seq.*; appoints Woodbury as Judge, II, 145; appoints Woodward as Judge, II, 146; appoints Grier as Judge, II, 147.

Pollock v. *Farmer's Loan and Trust Co.,* II, 699, 702.

Polygamy, laws against, upheld, II, 697 n.

Porto Rico v. *Tapia,* II, 708 n, 711.

Postage Stamps, first use of, II, 136 n.

Potter, Clarkson N., argues *Legal Tender Cases,* II, 498, 524.

Potter, Orlando B., proposes Constitutional Amendment to limit legal tender powers, II, 659–660 and note.

Powell v. *Pennsylvania,* II, 573.

Prescott, William, I, 344, 345.

President, powers of, to enforce neutrality, I, 113; power to appoint Judges to other offices, I, 119–121, 198–199; instructions by, if not in accord with law, disregarded by the Court, I, 199–200, 283–284, 475; first written inaugural address by, I, 206 n; interference with Executive powers of, in *Marbury Case,* I, 232–255; Jefferson's view of right of, to determine constitutionality of an Act of Congress, I, 265–266; interference with Executive powers of, in Mississippi crisis, I, 240; powers of, in connection with *Burr Cases,* I, 302–308; powers of, in connection with Embargo, I, 325; views of Mrs. Adams as to office of, as compared with Chief Justiceship, I, 414 n; fears as to political influence on, in appointing Judges, I, 673, 676, 677, 683; Jackson's view of right of, to determine constitutionality of Acts of Congress, I, 761–764; J. Q. Adams' view of office of, as compared with Chief Justiceship, II, 2–3; right of a Judge to aspire to office of, upheld by McLean, II, 269–270 and note; ambitions for office of, by Chase, II, 400–408; by Davis, II, 565 n; right of Judges to aspire to office of, denied by Waite, II, 563–564; by Miller,

II, 563 n; bill to restrain, from executing reconstruction laws, II, 455–460; power of administrative regulation by, II, 712, 724.

Presidential Instructions, disregarded by Court, I, 199–200, 283–284, 284 n, 328, 475.

Presser v. *Illinois,* II, 567 n.

Prigg v. *Pennsylvania,* argument and decision of, II, 83–87, 212, 221, 223, 225.

Pringle, John J., I, 287.

Prize Cases, argument and decision in, II, 380–384.

Prize Court law, in early Federal Courts, I, 105–109, 115–118, 149, 160 n; conclusiveness of foreign decrees in, I, 319–320, 426; variety of cases, I, 426; developed by Marshall and Story, I, 567–576; in Mexican War, II, 219 n; in *Prize Cases,* II, 380–384; in Spanish War, II, 707–708. See also CIRCUIT COURTS; INTERNATIONAL LAW; NEUTRALITY.

Process Act, I, 648–650.

Prohibition Laws, II, 137, 138 and note, 572; interference of, with interstate commerce, II, 697; wartime, upheld, II, 725 n; national legislative aid to State, II, 731–733.

Prout v. *Starr,* II, 715 n.

Providence Bank v. *Billings,* I, 714.

Public Clearing House v. *Coyne,* II, 698.

Public Lands, Spanish land claims cases and, I, 781–785; power of Congress to lease in the States, II, 64.

Pugh, George E., as counsel, II, 250; defends Court, II, 329.

Pullman Cars, liability of company, II, 641.

Pullman Strike, II, 700.

Pure Food Act, II, 737.

QUARANTINE ACTS, II, 736–737.

Quincy, Josiah, as to Embargo enforcement, I, 361–362; views of Story's appointment, I, 417; advocates secession in 1811, I, 421; J. Adams' letter to, I, 421.

Quincy, etc., R. R. v. *Humphreys,* II, 639 n.

Rahrer, In re, II, 731 n.

Railroad Co. v. *Richmond,* II, 573.

Rush, Richard, opposes common law Federal indictments, I, 439.

Rutledge, Edward, considered for first Court, I, 43–44; offered appointment in 1794, and declines, I, 57.

Rutledge, John, candidate for Chief Justice, I, 34; appointed Judge, I, 43–44; resigns, I, 56–57, 90 n; service on Circuit, I, 90 n; applies for appointment as Chief Justice, I, 127; appointed, I, 128; contest over his confirmation, I, 129–131; rejection by Senate, I, 137; sits as Chief Justice, I, 133–134; death, I, 139.

SAFETY APPLIANCES ACT, II, 730.

Sanford, John F. A., II, 281.

Santa Clara v. *Southern Pacific R. R.*, II, 597 n, 598 n.

Santissima Trinidad, argument and decision of, I, 573–574.

Satterlee v. *Mathewson*, I, 709.

Schenck, Robert C., advocates bill to remove *McCardle Case* from Court, II, 474–475.

Schollenberger v. *Pennsylvania*, II, 732 n.

Schooner Exchange v. *McFadden*, I, 424–425.

Schurz, Carl, views on *Booth Case* and State-Rights, II, 343–344.

Scott v. *Donald*, II, 715 n.

Scott v. *Jones*, II, 159 n.

Seal of Court, first order as to, I, 48.

Searight v. *Stokes*, II, 138–139.

Secession, first announcement in 1810 of doctrine of, I, 420–421; Campbell regarded as upholder of, II, 245–247; Yancey as upholder of, II, 274; effect on Court of War of, II, 368–417. See also CIVIL WAR; RECONSTRUCTION.

Sedgwick, Charles B., II, 382.

Sedgwick, Theodore, and Judiciary Act, I, 11; fears as to new government, I, 64, 146; view of Marshall, I, 179; view of repeal of Circuit Court Act, I, 213.

Sedition Law, I, 5; Anti-Federalist hostility to, I, 164–165, 191, 215; Marshall opposed to, I, 180; general references to, I, 225, 266, 273, 282, 358, 363–365

Selective Draft Cases, II, 725 n.

Semple, James, proposes Constitutional Amendment to prevent judicial review, II, 105.

Sergeant, John, argues *Olmstead Case*, I, 375; argues in *Osborn* v. *Bank*, I, 630, 648; retained as counsel by Cherokees, I, 731; description of his argument in *Cherokee Case*, I, 746–747; argument in *Worcester* v. *Georgia*, I, 754; in *Bank of Augusta* v. *Earle*, II, 52; offered position as Judge by Tyler and declines, II, 113; argument in *Girard Case*, II, 125–127; argues *Planter's Bank Case*, II, 162; last appearance in Court, II, 165; death, II, 241.

Sergeant, Jonathan D., I, 55.

Sergeant, Thomas, I, 114.

Seward, William H., argues *Jones* v. *Van Zandt*, II, 155; favorable view of Taney in 1851, II, 206; attacks Federal power, II, 265; attacks Court as pro-slavery, II, 268; attacks Dred Scott decision, II, 326; proposes reorganization of Court, II, 328; defects of blockade proclamations of, II, 381 and note.

Shankland v. *Washington*, I, 551 n.

Sharkey, William L., files bill in equity for Mississippi, II, 455, 456; described, II, 458; argues *McCardle Case*, II, 466.

Shepley, Ether, urged as Judge in 1845, II, 145.

Sherman, Roger, and Judiciary Act, I, 11.

Sherman Act, sugar case under, II, 699; railroad pools illegal under, II, 707; labor union boycott illegal under, II, 707; holding companies illegal under, II, 711; *Standard Oil Co. and American Tobacco Co. Cases* under, II, 722; decisions under, II, 733–735.

Shippen, Edward, urged as Judge, I, 90 n.

Shipping Board Act, II, 730.

Shiras, George, Jr., appointed Judge, II, 718–719; changes opinion in *Income Tax Case*, II, 700; resigns, II, 720.

Sidney, Algernon, I, 555–556, 559 n, 560–561. See also ROANE, SPENCER.

Siebold, Ex parte, II, 650.

Simmons, James F., upholds doctrines of *McCulloch Case*, II, 94; defends Dred Scott decision, II, 328.

Sinking Fund Cases, II, 595 n, 642–645.

Sinnot v. *Davenport*, II, 354.

Stanton, Edwin M., argues *Wheeling Bridge Case*, II, 234; urged as Chief Justice in 1864, II, 401; fears release of prisoners by habeas corpus, II, 421; appointed Judge, II, 504–506; death, II, 506.

Stare Decisis, inapplicable in constitutional cases, II, 748–749.

Starin v. *New York*, II, 686 n.

State Railroad Tax Cases, II, 683 n.

State-Rights, and *Chisholm Case*, I, 92–102; and judicial review, I, 267; New England and the Embargo and, I, 358, 363–365; and the Eastern States, I, 388; advocates of, denounce *McCulloch* v. *Maryland*, I, 515–525; in connection with Bank of the United States and Ohio, I, 535–536; fears in Congress as to effect of *McCulloch Case*, I, 541–544; advocates of, denounce *Cohens* v. *Virginia*, I, 549–564; advocates oppose *Gibbons* v. *Ogden*, I, 616–619, 620–627; advocates oppose *Osborn* v. *Bank*, I, 631–632; in Georgia in *Cherokee Indian Cases*, I, 729–769; in disputes in 1829–1832 between New York and New Jersey, I, 770–773; in Massachusetts over *Charles River Bridge Case*, I, 773; advocates of, rejoice in 1835 at possibility of a new Chief Justice, I, 807, 812, II, 6, 11–12; upheld by Massachusetts in Rhode Island boundary case, II, 43; effect of *Prigg Case* on, II, 85 n; and the Commerce Clause, II, 136–138; asserted by Massachusetts in *Thurlow Case*, II, 152; considered attacked by *Passenger Cases*, II, 180–182; Whigs uphold, on slavery issue, II, 214; and Wisconsin, I, 259–266; upheld by anti-slavery men, on removal bill, II, 265; Yancey's view of, II, 274; urged by anti-slavery men, II, 333–348.

States, early fears of Federal Government by, I, 62–65; early Circuit Courts hold invalid statutes of, I, 65–69; Anti-Federalists fear Congressional encroachment on, I, 72–75; suits against and debts of, I, 91–102; British debts in, I, 144; judicial review not feared until interfering with statutes of, I, 267; power of, more to be feared in 1815 than Federal Government, I, 421–422; contest between Federal officials and officials of, I, 540; Courts of, have no power to mandamus Federal officials, I, 563; property in hands of officer of, not to be seized by Federal official, II, 19; boundary line involved in *Rhode Island* v. *Massachusetts*, II, 43–44, power to tax Federal officer denied, II, 90–91; encroachments in 1841 on power of, by Bankruptcy, Habeas Corpus and other Acts, II, 91–101; statute regulating Congressional districting of, II, 100–101; boundary lines of, settled by Court, II, 148–152; bankruptcy Court's power over liens created by, denied, II, 182–185; no power to repeal tax exemptions, II, 250–256; no power of, over persons held under fugitive slave law, II, 259–266; no right of Federal Court to sell property attached in Court of, II, 351; conflicts in Admiralty Courts, II, 357 n; no power of, to seize property held by Federal officer, II, 367–368; status of seceding, II, 417, 488–490; attempt of, to challenge reconstruction by suits in Court, II, 455–464; power of, increased by *Slaughterhouse Cases*, II, 539–550; increased by *Granger Cases*, II, 574–589; limited by later decisions, II, 590–592; Judge of, held indictable under 14th Amendment legislation, II, 610; power of, to tax freight tonnage denied, II, 626; power of, over bridges and ferries, II, 631; power of, to tax real estate of United States denied, II, 661; power of United States of eminent domain in, upheld, II, 661 n; debt repudiation of, and 11th Amendment, II, 664, 671, 676; no power to repeal tax exemptions, II, 676–677; right of, to remove suit into Federal Court, II, 685; power of, to prevent removal of suits by corporations, II, 686; no power to fix interstate railroad rates, II, 697; may be sued by United States to fix boundary line, II, 698; power of United States to tax, liquor selling agents, II, 712; sovereignty of, redefined, II, 714; right to sue officials of, extended, II, 715–717; limit of right to tax interstate business corporation, II, 717–718; prohibition laws of, involved, II, 572, 697; power of Congress over intrastate railroad rates of, II, 723; power of, to regulate insurance rates, II, 724; power of Court to enforce decree against, in suit by, II, 724; no right of, to deny removal of cases into Federal Courts, II, 725. See also BOUNDARY LINES; DUE PROCESS; STATE-RIGHTS.

Stay-laws, I, 63, 267 n; in Virginia and Georgia at time of Embargo, I, 353–355; in Tennessee, I, 355 n, 651 n; in Kentucky, I, 644–651; in Illinois and Indiana held invalid, II, 102–104.

Steamboat Monopoly Case. See *Gibbons* v. *Ogden.*

Steele, John, as to judicial review, I, 253–254.

Stephens, Alexander H., views as to *Dred Scott Case,* II, 292, 302.

Stettler v. *O'Hara,* II, 748 n.

Stevens, Thaddeus, attacks *Milligan Case,* II, 448; proposes radical bill against Court's jurisdiction, II, 471, theory of reconstruction, II, 488.

Stevenson, Andrew, proposes repeal of 25th Section, I, 663.

Stewart, William M., defends *McCardle Case* statute, II, 479.

Stockton, Richard, as counsel, I, 317, 431.

Stokes v. *Saltonstall,* II, 62.

Stone v. *Farmers' Loan and Trust Co.,* II, 590.

Stone v. *Mississippi,* II, 618.

Story, Joseph, on non-partisanship of Court, I, 21; view of Hamilton's eloquence, I, 149; view of Chase, I, 281; view of Todd, I, 301; counsel in the *Embargo Case,* I, 344; views as to legality of Embargo, I, 344; as to enforcement of Embargo, I, 357–358; counsel in *Yazoo Lands Case,* I, 396; considered for appointment to Court, I, 401; views of Jefferson of, I, 406–407 n; appointed Judge, I, 415; his qualifications, I, 416–421; his Nationalistic opinions, I, 419–421, 453; views as to his first session, I, 423; views of Pinkney and Dexter, I, 430–431; views as to common law Federal indictments, I, 434 n, 438; seeks new criminal legislation, I, 442; opinion in *Fairfax Case,* I, 446; opinion in *Martin* v. *Hunter's Lessee,* I, 450–453; personal description of, I, 467, 470; opinion in and views of *Dartmouth College Case,* I, 486, 490; view of decision in *McCulloch Case,* I, 511; view of Pinkney, I, 566; development of international and prize law by, I, 565, 567–569; opinion in *Santissima Trinidad,* I, 573–574; attitude as to treaties, I, 580–581; holds slave trade illegal, I, 584–585; letter to Monroe on internal improvements, I, 596; aids Marshall, in writing opinion in *Gibbons* v. *Ogden,* I, 608; broad views of admiralty, I, 635 n; as to attacks on Judiciary, I, 660; views as to Circuit duty and size of Court, I, 675; views of McLean, I, 706; views of Baldwin, I, 712; McLane's fear of, I, 719–720; views of Georgia's action in *Tassel Case,* I, 734, 746; views in 1831 as to necessity of 25th Section and critical condition of Judiciary, I, 740, 743–744; views of decision in *Cherokee Case,* I, 750; views as to *Worcester* v. *Georgia,* I, 755–757; views of Jackson, I, 777–778; publishes Commentary on the Constitution, I, 778–779; views of *Wheaton* v. *Peters,* I, 786; description of, in 1835 by H. Martineau, I, 791; despondency over Marshall's health, I, 803; praise of Marshall, I, 813; anxiety as to Marshall's successor, II, 7–8; views of Taney's appointment, II, 10; presides in 1836 over Court, II, 19; views of *Charles River Bridge Case,* II, 25 n, 28; dissents in 1837 in three cases, II, 27; regrets additional Judges, II, 42; view of McKinley's decision in corporation cases, II, 50–51; view of Taney's decision in *Holmes* v. *Jennison,* II, 66; view of Adams in *Amistad Case,* II, 76; addressed as Chief Justice, II, 83 n; opinion in *Prigg Case,* II, 84–87; opinion in *Swift* v. *Tyson,* 88–89; view of Taney's opinion in *Bronson* v. *Kinzie,* II, 103–104; considers resignation, II, 105; deplores Peters' removal,

Story, Joseph — *Continued*
II, 106–107; views as to qualifications
for a Judge, II, 115; view of corporation's right to sue in Federal Courts,
II, 121; views of *Girard Case*, II,
129, 133; pessimistic views, II, 139–
140; decides to resign, II, 139; Whig
regrets at resignation, II, 140–141;
death, II, 142; Taney's view of, II,
142; Democratic view of, II, 143–
144; McLean's view of, II, 157; con-
test with New Hampshire Court, II,
183–185; requests for Court counsel
to limit length of argument, II, 200 n.
Stoughton, E. W., II, 578.
Strader v. *Graham*, II, 224–225.
Strauder v. *West Virginia*, II, 609.
Strikes, and receivers, II, 700; and
Debs Case, II, 700–704.
Strong, Caleb, and Judiciary Act, I, 8.
Strong, William, I, 25; urged for Chief
Justice in 1864, II, 401; desired by
Grant as Judge, II, 504, 507 and note;
appointed Judge, II, 516–519; resigns,
II, 566.
Stuart v. *Laird*, I, 231, 270–272.
Sturges v. *Crowninshield*, description of
argument and opinion in, I, 492–497.
Sumner, Charles, attacks Court as pro-
slavery, II, 224; attacks Federal
powers, II, 265; view of Court in
1860, II, 359; attacks Taney bust
bill, II, 395–396; advises Lincoln on
Chief Justice, II, 399; favors Chase,
II, 402, 406; witnesses Chase's first
appearance on Bench, II, 410; moves
first admission of negro, II, 411–412;
views of Cushing, II, 559; view of
Waite, II, 691.
Supreme Court, opposition to, I, 4, 5;
and Judiciary Act, I, 11; non-partisanship of, I, 20–23, 30 n, 272, 420;
canon as to holding Acts unconstitutional, I, 23–25; suggested reforms
as to, I, 26–30; dissenting opinions
in, I, 27; appointments on, I, 35–44;
ages and qualifications of first Judges,
I, 44–45; first session in New York,
I, 46–50; first session in Philadelphia, I, 53; refuses to render opinion
to President, I, 110–111; opposition
to appointment of Judges to other
offices, I, 119–120; first Court-room
in Washington, I, 169–171, 191; post-

ponement of Term, by statute, I,
222–224; increasing interest in 1810
in appointments to, I, 400; salaries
of Judges, I, 416 n; omission of 1811
Term of, I, 422; Story's description
of work of, in 1812, I, 423–424; ladies
in Court-room, I, 430, 473; change in
1816 in subjects of litigation in, I,
454; first official reporter of, I, 455;
courtesy to counsel in 1827, I, 470–
471; influence of slavery on, I, 561;
attitude on treaties, I, 565, 580–583,
782–785; assigns counsel in *Piracy
Cases*, I, 579; expresses unofficial
view to Monroe as to internal improvements, I, 596–597; hesitation
to express its views under Commerce
Clause, I, 628; alleged decision of
a minority of, in *Green* v. *Biddle*, I,
640–641; Jefferson's demand for
seriatim opinions of, I, 653–655,
concurrence of five out of seven Judges
of, proposed in Congress, I, 663–669;
changes in Circuit Court system debated in Congress, I, 672–683; Term
of, changed from February to January,
I, 684; wears crape on death of Wirt
and Pinkney, I, 789; description
of, by H. Martineau in 1835, I, 790–
791; description of, by Sumner, I,
791–792; description of, by Bancroft,
I, 792–793; mode of living of Judges,
I, 791–792 and note; two additional
Judges for, in 1837, II, 39–42; declines to attend funeral of man killed
in duel, II, 49; motions made in, to
be in writing, II, 63 n; duty of Judge
of Fourth Circuit to attend in Washington in August abolished, II, 63 n;
Whig confidence in, in 1841, II, 77;
Term of, lengthened in 1844, 147,
148 n; importance of jurisdiction
in settling disputes between States,
II, 143–152; attacked by abolitionists for being pro-slavery, II, 156, 209–
224; defended by Judge McLean from
pro-slavery charge, II, 156–157; action on J. Q. Adams' death by, II,
167 n; length of arguments in,
limited in 1844 by rule, II, 197–200;
suggested by Clayton to decide power
of Congress over slavery, II, 206–209;
described by Curtis in 1851, II, 232–
233; mandate of, disobeyed by Ohio

Court, II, 256–257; loss of confidence in, from Dred Scott decision, II, 316–317; Lincoln's view of decisions of, II, 329–332; desire of South for appointments on, II, 358; attack in 1860 on, II, 359–361; increased to ten in number, II, 380; decreased to seven in number, II, 423; upheld by *Richmond Enquirer* in 1867, II, 439; talk of "packing", by increasing number of Judges on, II, 447; bills for concurrence of Judges proposed, II, 449, 466–471; jurisdiction over *McCardle Case* abolished by Congress, II, 474–480, 485; postpones *McCardle Case* pending action by Congress, II, 480–488; bills to abolish appellate jurisdiction, II, 492–494; number of Judges fixed in 1869 at nine, II, 501; increased confidence in, II, 506; charge that Grant "packed", II, 517–519; attacks on, for municipal bond decisions, II, 531–532; Term begins in October, II, 561 n; increase of 14th Amendment cases in, II, 598–599; refutal of charge of control of, by railroad interests, II, 645; bills for relief of crowded dockets, of, II, 680 n; tendency of decisions under 14th Amendment, II, 693; nationalizing tendency under Commerce Clause, II, 694–695; attacks on, for Income Tax and Debs decisions, II, 699–704; given enlarged power by statute to review cases in State Courts, II, 727; number of cases decided by, at different periods, II, 727 n; development of law as to Nation's powers under the Commerce Clause, II, 729–739; doctrines as to State police power, II, 740–753; supports laws passed under State police power, II, 741–742; not reactionary, II, 745–747, 750–751; must protect rights of minority, II, 751–753; summary of position in history, II, 753–756. See also Acts of Congress; Judges; Judiciary; National Government; Non-Partisanship; States; State-Rights; Terms.

Swann, Thomas, as counsel, I, 787.

Swartwout, Samuel, trial of, I, 302–308.

Swayne, Noah H., appointed Judge,

II, 378; urged as Chief Justice in 1864, II, 401, 417 n; resigns, II, 622; death, II, 622 n.

Swift v. *Tyson*, II, 88–89, 698.

Swift, Zephaniah, opposes judicial review, I, 82, 257.

Taft, William H., defends right of corporations to sue in Federal Courts, II, 123; appoints Lurton as Judge, II, 720; appoints White as Chief Justice, II, 720–721; appoints Hughes, VanDevanter, Lamar, Pitney as Judges, II, 726; appointed Chief Justice, II, 727 n.

Talbot, Isham, attacks Court, I, 663, 667.

Talbot, Thomas H., II, 653.

Talbot v. *Jansen*, I, 133.

Talbot v. *Ship Amelia*, I, 157–158, 185 n, 199.

Taney, Roger B., on judicial review, I, 17, 18; first appearance before Court, I, 693; personal description of, I, 694–695; gives Jackson's views as to enforcement of statutes, I, 762–764; as counsel in *United States* v. *Arredondo*, I, 782; Whig fears in 1834 of appointment of, as Judge, I, 794; appointed Judge in 1835, I, 798; Senate rejects, I, 802; appointed Chief Justice, II, 10; legal qualifications of, II, 12–13; Clay recants his view of, II, 15–16; letter of, to Jackson, II, 18–19; administers oath to Van Buren as President, II, 20–21; opinion in *Charles River Bridge Case*, II, 23–25; economic and social interests of, II, 34–38; fear of the money-power, II, 36–38; views of Clay and Story of, II, 38 n; view of Catron, II, 41 n; opinion in *Holmes* v. *Jennison*, II, 64–66; opinion in *Bronson* v. *Kinzie*, II, 103–104; view of Story's death, II, 142; opinion in *Luther* v. *Borden*, II, 193–195; description in 1854 of, II, 201, 204 n, 205; opinion in *Genesee Chief*, II, 239–240; views of legislative charter methods, II, 253; praised by *N. Y. Tribune* in 1855, II, 273–274; description of, II, 278 n; opinion in *Dred Scott Case*, II, 300–304; view of his opinion by, II, 315; description in

White, Joseph M., as counsel, I, 242, 300, 301.

White Slave Traffic Act, II, 696 n, 737.

White v. *Vermont and Massachusetts R. R. Co.*, II, 353.

White Water Valley Canal Co. v. *Vallette*, II, 639 n.

Wickham, John, I, 145.

Wickliffe, Charles A., proposes repeal of 25th Section, I, 663; advocates Circuit Court bill, I, 682.

Wiggins Ferry Co. v. *East St. Louis*, II, 631 n.

Wigs, wearing of, by the Judges, I, 48 n.

Wilcocks, Alexander, I, 55, 145.

Wilkinson v. *Leland*, I, 710.

Willamette Iron Bridge Co. v. *Hatch*, II, 631 n.

William, The, and The Fanny, I, 106–108.

Williams, George H., appointed Chief Justice and withdrawn, II, 553–556; argues *Reese Case*, II, 603.

Williams, Thomas, proposes bill for concurrence of all Judges, II, 449, 466 n, 497 n.

Williams v. *Armroyd*, I, 426.

Williams v. *Bruffy*, I, 450 n.

Williams v. *Mississippi*, II, 618 n.

Williamson, Case of Passmore, II, 262, 264.

Wilson, Henry, attacks Taney bust bill, II, 395.

Wilson, James, I, 8; applies for Chief Justiceship, I, 33; appointed Judge, I, 42; refuses to certify lawyers for admission to practice before Court, I, 53–55; holds Pensioners Act invalid, I, 70–71, 80 n; suggested as Chief Justice, I, 90 n; opinion in *Chisholm Case*, I, 95 n; Randolph's view of, I, 104; charge in *Henfield's Case*, I, 114; death, 153.

Wilson, James F., proposes bill to remove *McCardle Case* from Court, II, 474.

Wilson, Woodrow, appoints McReynolds, Brandeis, and Clark as Judges, II, 726–727.

Wilson Act, II, 731.

Wilson v. *Blackbird Creek Marsh Co.*, I, 709, II, 27.

Wilson v. *Mason*, I, 200.

Wilson v. *New*, II, 725, 730–731.

Winder, William H., as counsel, I, 573.

Wingate, Paine, and Judiciary Act, I, 8.

Wirt, William, view of Marshall in *British Debts Case*, I, 145; views as to Marshall and Burr trial, I, 310 n; argument in *Dartmouth College Case*, I, 477–482; counsel in *McCulloch* v. *Maryland*, I, 507; desirous of avoiding clash with Pennsylvania and Maryland, I, 539–541; Adams' view of, I, 539; counsel in *Cohens* v. *Virginia*, I, 551; view of Pinkney, I, 566; view of Webster and Tazewell, I, 574–575; argues *Apollon*, I, 582; argument in *The Antelope*, I, 585; recommends Kent for Judge, I, 589–591; argument in *Gibbons* v. *Ogden*, I, 599–606; personal description of, I, 600, 694–695; opinion on South Carolina free negro Law, I, 626–627; as counsel, I, 694, 709; retained as counsel by Cherokees, I, 731; description of his argument in *Cherokee Case*, I, 746–748; argument in *Worcester* v. *Georgia*, I, 754; believes no statutes to allow enforcement of Court's decree, I, 764–765; as counsel in *New Jersey* v. *New York*, I, 770; as counsel in *United States* v. *Arredondo*, I, 782; death, and views of Marshall on, I, 789.

Wisconsin, action of Courts of, in *Booth Cases*, II, 258–266; praised by anti-slavery men, II, 339–344.

Wolcott, Alexander, appointed to Court in 1811, I, 410; opposition to, I, 411–413; rejected by Senate, I, 413.

Wolcott, Oliver, as to Rutledge's appointment, I, 131, 136; as to Ellsworth, I, 140; as to Chase, I, 143; as to Marshall, I, 179.

Wood, George, as counsel, II, 351.

Woodbury, Levi, views as to bankruptcy powers, I, 688; opposes Court's broad construction, I, 722–723; states limits on *McCulloch Case* doctrine, II, 95–96; attacks National Bankruptcy Law, Habeas Corpus Act, and Congressional Restricting Act, in 1841, II, 98–101; appointed Judge, II, 145; upholds early Fugitive Slave Law, II, 155–156; views on Commerce Clause, II, 180–181, 238; description of, in 1854, II, 202; death, II, 226.

Woodruff v. *Parham*, II, 415 n.